Microprocessors
Theory and Applications

Microprocessors
Theory and Applications

Second Edition

Gene A. Streitmatter

Associate Professor
Electronics Technology
Rock Valley College
Rockford, Illinois

Vito Fiore

Director
Microelectronics Center for Innovation
Tri-County Technical College
Pendleton, South Carolina

Reston Publishing Company, Inc.
A Prentice-Hall Company
Reston, Virginia

Library of Congress Cataloging in Publication Data

Streitmatter, Gene A.
Microprocessors : theory and applications.

Bibliography
Includes index.
1. Microprocessors. I. Fiore, Vito,
II. Title.
QA76.5.S783 1982 001.64 81-21155
ISBN 0-8359-4378-X AACR2

10 9 8 7 6 5 4 3 2 1

Printed in the United States of America

To my wife, Mary Ann,
and children, Daneen and Cori,
without whose understanding and encouragement
this book could not exist.

Gene A. Streitmatter

To my family—my wife, Vicki;
our children, Richard, Maria, Robert and Joseph;
and their very special grandmother, Helen Dolezal.
And to my parents, Vito and Della Fiore,
whose efforts and sacrifices made my education
and therefore this book possible.

Vito Fiore

Contents

Illustrations

Figure Number

Figure Number

Figure Number

Figure Number

Tables

Table Number

Preface

Since the first edition of this text came out in 1979, tremendous advances in microprocessor technology have taken place. Hardware and software have become more complex and sophisticated. Chips that were "on the drawing board" in the later 1970s are now widely used and enhanced by new generations. The 16/32-bit microcomputer is a working reality. Microprocessors have become a part of everyday life. Yet basic microprocessor theory remains the same and serves as the foundation for approaching these latest devices and techniques.

This text provides a comprehensive introduction to microprocessors. It is a middle-ground approach combining hardware and software theory and applications. Universal concepts applicable to all models of microprocessors are presented in Chapters 1 through 9. The book is organized in a linear progression from fundamental principles to complete systems covering both the Intel 8080 and Motorola M6800 families in Chapters 10 through 15. The Motorola MC6800 and Intel 8080 have been used throughout the text since their software and hardware serve as typical examples of today's microprocessors.

Starting in Chapter 1 with a general overview of microprocessors which establishes a working language and basic understanding of some of the fundamental concepts, each chapter builds on the previous ones. For example, Chapter 5, "Introduction to Software," presents the basic skills and procedures of programming. In Chapter 9, "Advanced Software," these basic concepts are discussed in more detail since the intervening chapters on bus control, input/output, and memory have provided the necessary background for mastering more specific information.

Chapters 10 through 14 contain specific details and applications of the Intel 8080 and Motorola M6800 family which bring together the fundamental concepts presented in the earlier chapters. Chapter 15 introduces the Motorola MC68000 and Intel 8086 16-bit microprocessors.

Recent developments in microprocessor technology are found throughout the text. New programming techniques include modular programming, top-down approach and partitioning. State-of-the-art hardware such as EEPROMs and high-density semiconductor memories, the MC6829 memory management unit and MC68000 support chips are introduced.

This text contains numerous illustrations of circuits, programs, charts, subsystems, and photographs of micro-dies which directly reinforce the textual information.

A glossary of new terms is provided at the beginning of each chapter. A general glossary containing all these terms as well as the latest state-of-the-art terminology is located at the back of the book.

The appendices have extensive reference information including instruction sets for the Motorola MC6800 and Intel 8080 and supplemental technical data such as numbering systems, conversion tables, integrated circuit listings, standard logic symbols, and an ASCII coding chart.

Upon completing this book, the reader should have gained the fundamental insights necessary for understanding and learning microprocessors that will serve as the framework for continued study in this exciting, state-of-the-art technology.

Acknowledgments

The authors acknowledge with appreciation the permission granted by Motorola Inc. and Intel Corporation to reprint their copyrighted instruction set material, which appears in Appendix 5.

The following people have played an important role of assistance in providing technical information and leads to sources of material: Ron Bishop, Don Jackson, Don Aldridge, Lothar Stern, Fuad Musa, Jim Farrell, Chuck Duncan, Ray ("the common spelling") Begitschke, Burt Schultz and Fred Elkin of Motorola Inc.; Tom Lehmann of Intel Corporation; Ravinder Bhatnager and Ed Morgado of American Microsystems, Inc. A special thanks to Dave Kugler of Hewlett-Packard Company.

A very special thanks is due Fritz Wilson of Motorola Inc., Phoenix, Arizona, for his continuous support and personal encouragement throughout the entire preparation of both editions of this text.

The authors appreciate the guidance and encouragement given to them and the professional polish added to the text by the staff of Reston Publishing Company, Inc., especially Lawrence J. Benincasa, Editor, and Linda Weigle and Ellen Cherry, Production Editors. Thanks also to David Dusthimer and Robert Nash, Editors, for their patience and support throughout the revision of this text.

Of special assistance to the authors during the writing of this book was Helen Dolezal, who spent many hours proofreading the original manuscript and the revisions for the second edition. Also, Vicki Fiore, Associate Technical Publications Specialist, NCR Corporation, E & M Clemson, who served as our manuscript consultant by organizing, editing and typing the text and handling the fine details involved in producing this book.

Special thanks to Sherman Buetsch of the Electronics Department,

Rock Valley College, for his tireless support and assistance with not only his technical expertise but his loyalty and understanding.

Also, Roger Leid, who was Chairman of the Technology Division at Rock Valley College, Rockford, Illinois, when the first edition of this text was written. We are most grateful for his support, constant encouragement and endless patience during the writing time and, most of all, his continued friendship.

Thanks also to Don C. Garrison, John Manly and Jack Hunter of Tri-County Technical College, Pendleton, South Carolina, for their belief in, and support of, state-of-the-art microelectronics education.

Last, but certainly not least, our deepest gratitude to William F. Ridgway for the hundreds of hours spent in designing and manufacturing the microprocessor training equipment that provided us with the applications needed to develop our understanding of the hardware side of the fascinating field of electronics.

Chapter 1

Introduction to the Microprocessor

GLOSSARY

Address A character or group of characters that identifies a register. A particular part of storage or some other data source or destination.

Arithmetic logic unit (ALU) The central processing unit chip logic which actually executes the operations requested by an input command.

Assembly language In microprocessor programs, a series of source statements using mnemonic symbols that assist in the definition of the instruction and are then translated into machine understandable object code such as binary 0s and 1s.

Boolean algebra A mathematical system of logic which deals with classes, proposition, on-off circuit elements; associated by operators AND, OR, NOT, EXCEPT, IF-THEN, which permit computations and demonstrations in any other mathematical system.

Bus One or more conductors used as a path over which information is transmitted.

Central processing unit (CPU) The brain of a computing machine. Performs control, input/output, arithmetic and logical operations by executing instructions obtained from memory sources.

Chip A single substrate on which all the active and passive elements of an electronic circuit have been fabricated by various semiconductor technologies.

Control unit That section which directs the sequence of operations, interrupts coded instructions and sends the proper signals to other circuits to carry out instructions.

Development system A piece of equipment used to design and test prototype operations utilizing both hardware and software techniques.

Execute To perform a specified operation or operational sequence in a program. A command in the program register is performed upon the address indicated.

Fetch The portion of a computer cycle during which the location of the next instruction is determined. The instruction is taken from memory, modified if necessary, and then entered into the register.

Hardware The physical parts or electronic circuitry of a computer system in contrast to the "soft" or programming and firmware components.

Instruction cycle The process of fetching an instruction from memory and executing it.

Instruction set The total structured group of characters to be transferred to the computer as operations are executed.

Machine cycle The basic microprocessor cycle. The shortest complete process or action that is repeated, as well as the minimum length of time in which it can be performed.

Memory A storage device into which information can be inserted and held for use at a later time.

Microprocessor The semiconductor central processing unit (CPU) and one of the principal components of the microcomputer.

Program counter (PC) A register in the CPU that holds addresses necessary to step the machine through the various programs. It specifies the address of the next instruction byte to be fetched from memory and is automatically incremented after each fetch cycle.

Software Programs, languages and procedures of a computer system.

The advance of large-scale integration (LSI) and very-large-scale integration (VLSI) techniques to the point where a **central processing unit (CPU)** and a number of peripheral devices can be contained on a single integrated circuit (IC) chip has created a new set of terminology in the computer field. Questions such as, What is the difference between a computer and a microprocessor? and What is a RAM, a ROM, a PROM, an ALU, a CPU, a bus, a status latch? are frequently asked by persons attempting to become familiar with this new area of technology.

The purpose of this chapter is to help the beginner establish a working language and a basic understanding of some of the fundamental microprocessor concepts which will enable him to progress in his study of microprocessors and their use.

THE MICROPROCESSOR

Definitions

A **microprocessor** is a programmable logic device. That is, the function or logical operation that the device accomplishes may be altered by applying instructional "words" at its input.

The above definition, although correct, is somewhat broad. Technically, the term microprocessor has come to mean the central processing unit (CPU) of a small computer system. By itself, the microprocessor cannot function; but when it is combined with a relatively small number of support circuits, it has most of the characteristics included in the classic definition of a computer. The microprocessor has traded the greater speed and word length of a computer for compact size and low cost.

A microcomputer is a fully operational system based upon a microprocessor **chip** which in itself contains a large percentage of the computer capability. The system possesses all of the minimum requirements of a computer:

- It can input and output data, usually in digital form. This data can be exchanged between the microcomputer and several common input/output devices such as teletype, CRT displays, paper tape reader, floppy disk memories, magnetic tapes, cassette tapes and laboratory instruments.
- It contains an **ALU (arithmetic logic unit)** which performs arithmetic and/or logical operations such as add, subtract, compare, rotate left or right, AND, OR, NEGATE, EXCLUSIVE OR.
- It contains **memory** which is directly addressable and may contain both data and instructional words.
- It is programmable. That is, the data and programmed instructions may be arranged in any desired order, in contrast to a pocket calculator, which is usually fixed in its capabilities and requires a precise keyboard sequence that cannot be altered.

In this text, the terms "microcomputer" and "microprocessor" will be used interchangeably when referring to the whole system. This is consistent with present practice.

Uses and Applications

The uses and applications of microcomputers appear, at present, to fall somewhere between discrete logic, on one hand, and minicomputers on the other. As illustrated in Fig. 1–1, the microprocessor fills the large gap between discrete circuits and the relatively sophisticated minicomputer.

The microprocessor also fills the cost gap between discrete circuits and computers. Refer to Table 1–1.

Because of its relatively low cost and flexibility, the microsystem has an abundance of applications in the home and small business environment. It fills the needs of small manufacturers who cannot afford, or do not need, large computer systems.

Some of the present applications which have already found their way into the market place are:

- Video TV games
- Intelligent computer terminals
- Process controllers

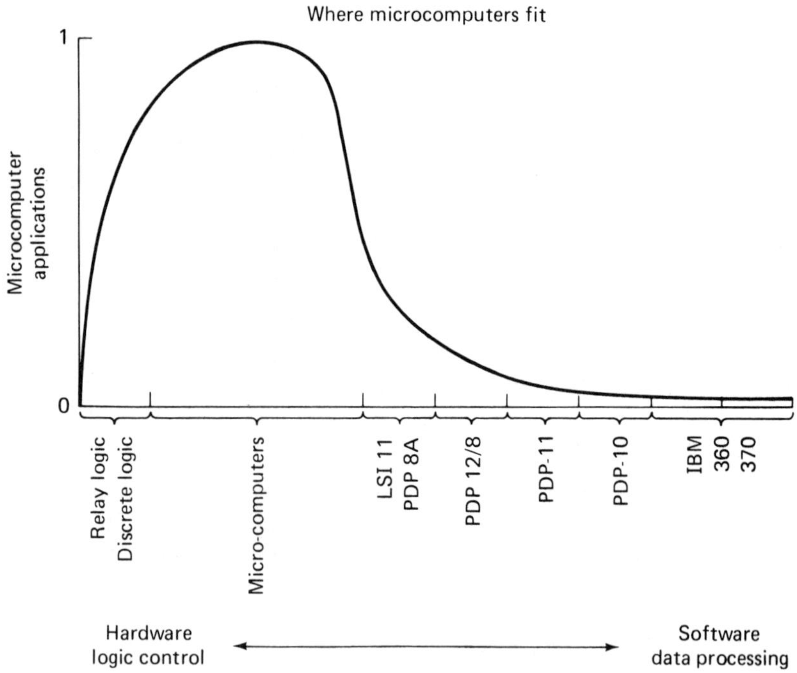

Fig. 1–1. Where microcomputers fit (applications). (*Courtesy of Peter R. Rony, David G. Larsen, and Jonathan A. Titus*)

Table 1–1 Where Microcomputers Fit (Cost)

WORD LENGTH	1	2	4	8	16	32	64
COMPLEXITY	HARD-WIRED LOGIC	PROGRAMED LOGIC ARRAY	CALCULATOR	MICRO-PROCESSOR	MINI-COMPUTER	LARGE COMPUTER	
APPLICATION		CONTROL			DEDICATED COMPUTATION	LOW-COST GENERAL DATA-PROCESSING	HIGH-PERFORMANCE GENERAL DATA-PROCESSING
COST	UNDER $100			$1,000		$10,000	$100,000 AND UP
PROGRAM	READ-ONLY						RELOADABLE
MEMORY SIZE	VERY SMALL 0–4 WORDS	SMALL 2–10 WORDS		MEDIUM 10–1,000 WORDS		LARGE 1,000–1 MILLION	VERY LARGE MORE THAN 1 MILLION
SPEED CONSTRAINTS	REAL TIME	SLOW			MEDIUM		THROUGHPUT-ORIENTED
INPUT-OUTPUT	INTEGRATED	FEW SIMPLE DEVICES			SOME COMPLEX DEVICES		ROOMFUL OF EQUIPMENT
DESIGN	LOGIC	LOGIC + MICROPROGRAM			MICROPROGRAM MACROPROGRAM		MACROPROGRAM HIGH-LEVEL LANGUAGE SOFTWARE SYSTEM
MFG. VOLUME	LARGE						SMALL

(*Reprinted from Electronics, October 17, 1974; Copyright © McGraw-Hill, Inc., 1974.*)

- Telephone switching controls
- Merchandising inventory systems
- Programmable household appliances
- Computerized automotive electronic systems

Microprocessors can also be expanded to serve specialized control functions in the area of industrial tools and machinery. Because they are programmable logic systems, they can be adapted to serve a variety of job functions each of which previously required individually designed circuits. The low cost of production makes them extremely attractive.

It is perhaps this **hardware/software** trade that makes the impact of the microprocessor so great. Entirely different circuit functions can now be accomplished with the same hardware by means of a different set of program instructions. The microprocessor is recognized as the device which finally unites two previously separate areas: that of the hardware designer and the programmer.

Designing with Microprocessors

The introduction of a microprocessor brings about a significant change in the approach to system design that will be used. By extensive use of LSI components, the designer can select large blocks of already fabricated system function, making design of the overall system simpler and easier to complete.

An analogy can be drawn between the microprocessor's use in system design and the present practice of building factory prefabricated homes.

Following the conventional techniques, each home was custom-built, piece by piece. Window and door frames were custom-built on site and each wall was built and set in place according to the architectural plans. Prefabricated homes, on the other hand, are designed around standard production units available. The designer needs only to specify the particular window and door sizes and they arrive on site with the other parts of the house. All that then remains is the assembly of the final product with no loss in quality and a reduction in design and labor costs.

Designing with microprocessors as opposed to discrete logic operates in a similar manner. A discrete logic system is put together piece-by-piece according to the design engineer's specifications. Extensive changes in circuit function require a redesign of the circuit itself. Microprocessor design, on the other hand, becomes a matter of deciding upon the desirable features and purchasing the proper functional blocks to achieve these features. All that remains is the fabrication and assembly of the system. Changes in system function can then be accomplished, for the most part, by changing the program.

The primary advantages of the microprocessor-based system are:

- Low cost
- Ease of system design
- Flexibility
- Easy alteration of function

MAJOR CONCEPTS OF MICROPROCESSORS

Basic Computer Concepts

There are basically four parts to most computers: the memory, the arithmetic logic unit, the control unit and the input/output units (I/O).

The functions of each unit may change slightly from machine to machine, but the general categories will be found in all machines. Their basic operations are explained below.

The **control unit** provides timing instructions and synchronization signals for all the other units. These signals cause the other units to move data, manipulate numbers, output and input information, all of which are dependent upon a user defined program residing in memory.

The memory contains both instructions and data which may be intermixed. Each computer has a basic set of built-in capabilities called the instruction set. The sequence of usage of the instruction set is installed in memory by the programmer. If the program is properly assembled, the programmer can make the computer do very complex tasks. The control unit calls for each instruction contained in the memory, one at a time, and interprets each instruction into control pulses which are then sent out to execute the instruction. When this is completed, the control unit calls for the next word or instruction.

As mentioned previously, the memory may also contain data when the capacity of the arithmetic unit is exceeded. The computer cannot discriminate between data and instructions. It is part of the programmer's responsibility to keep these separated within the memory so that the computer will not attempt to interpret data as instructions or to do arithmetic operations using instructional words.

The arithmetic logic unit (ALU) contains logic circuits that allow it to implement fundamental arithmetic operations such as addition and subtraction and logical functions such as shifting, complementing and **Boolean algebra** operations. The ALU is the focus of activity in most computers. That is, most data flows through the ALU as it is moved from one place to another, all arithmetic and logical operations are accomplished in the ALU, and conditional branching tests take place in the ALU.

All the above operations are useless unless communication with the computer is possible. This process is accomplished through input/output ports and interface circuits tied into the main buses through which the computer sends its signals. The operator communicates with the computer by interfacing an input device like a keyboard and an output device like a video terminal or printer with the system.

Microcomputer Organization

In most microprocessor-based computer systems, the control unit and ALU are usually combined on a single chip which is the microprocessor itself.

Figure 1–2 is a possible intercommunication method typical of a microcomputer.

In Fig. 1–2, the I/O ports have direct access to the memory. From that point, the ALU and control unit may work on the data and instructions. The input and output ports may also be selected and controlled by the control unit.

Another intercommunication configuration that is much more common is shown in Fig. 1–3.

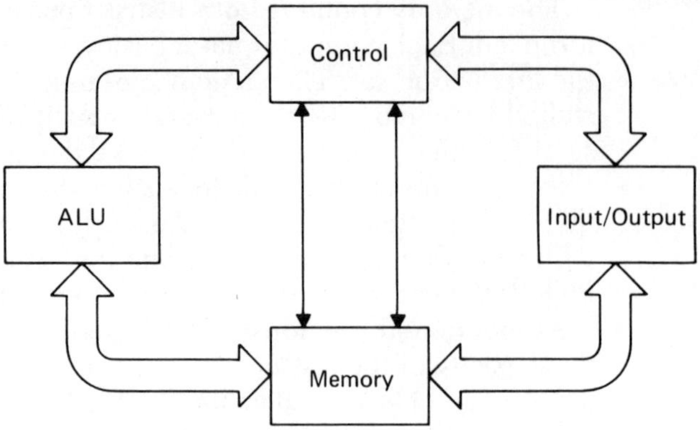

Fig. 1–2. Intercommunication method.

Note that the dotted line in Fig. 1–3 indicates the typical inclusion of a microprocessor chip. A very large percentage of the microcomputer's capability is contained within the CPU. Not shown in Fig. 1–3 are the details of the bus buffering, address decoding and the bidirectional driver circuits that are used quite frequently in microprocessors. However, the main concepts of information flow can be discussed using this diagram.

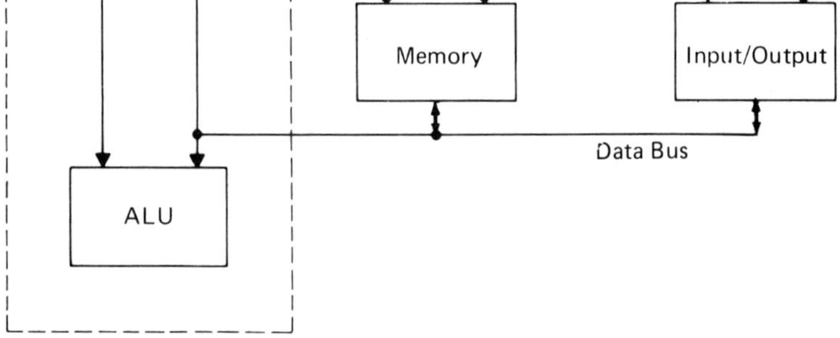

Fig. 1–3. Common intercommunication configuration.

Busing

Figure 1–3 illustrates the three main lines or buses. The terms unidirectional and bidirectional used in relationship to these buses need clarification. Unidirectional means that the data may flow in only one direction, like traffic on a one way street. Bidirectional means that data and information are allowed to flow in either direction. However, the data can only flow in one direction at a time, like traffic on a single lane detour on a highway under construction.

The three main buses of most 8-bit microprocessor systems are:

1. The address bus: usually sixteen unidirectional lines
2. The data bus: usually eight bidirectional lines
3. The control bus: the number of lines varies depending on the system and may have both unidirectional and bidirectional lines.

The diagram in Fig. 1–4 shows how the CPU handles the bus structure. It is essentially the same diagram as Fig. 1–3 but contains more detail to illustrate how the coordination of data flow is accomplished.

If the CPU, in carrying out its instructions, needs to get information from, or give data to, the memory or one of the input/output devices, it puts the address of that device or memory location on the address bus. The presence of the **address** causes the particular device or memory location to place available data at the switches or to open lines from the switches to accept information coming through. This is the only

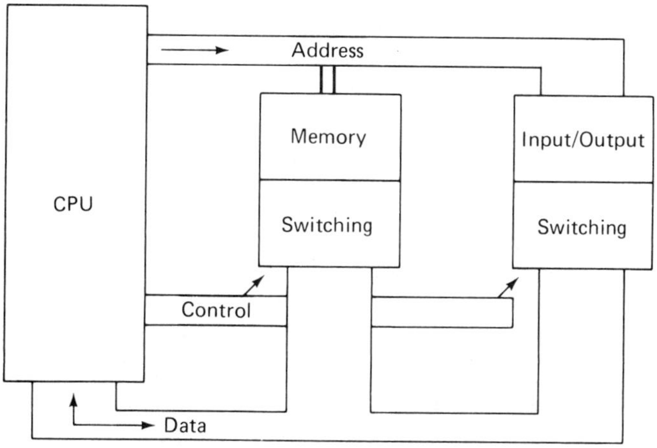

Fig. 1–4. Common bus diagram.

function the address bus serves: to activate devices and memory locations at the proper time for further use by the control and data buses.

The control bus then sends out synchronizing pulses which open and close the switching systems to allow them to pass data through, to or from the data bus.

The actual information transfer between units takes place on the data bus, usually in the form of eight parallel lines carrying simultaneous pulses which constitute data words. Data can flow in both directions depending upon timing and switching control signals placed on the control bus by the CPU through the controller circuits. The address bus is usually a 16-line bus upon which the destination of the data is coded from the CPU through the buffer decoder circuits.

This short explanation serves to demonstrate the basic operation between buses. A more complete understanding may be achieved by means of a brief discussion of the basic operations performed by the CPU.

The Instruction Cycle

One of the most basic operations of the CPU is the fetch and execute operation which constitutes the **instruction cycle.**

A **program counter** inside the CPU automatically keeps track of where the next instruction is located in memory. When the system is first turned on or has been reset, the program counter is automatically set where the first instruction is stored. This address from the program counter is placed on the address bus causing the instruction to be brought in from memory or fetched. It is then put in the control section where it is decoded determining how the CPU will accomplish that instruction. The program counter is automatically incremented by one count and, after the instruction has been executed, the cycle starts all over again with another **fetch.**

This process of fetch, decode, increment (PC), **execute,** fetch, decode, increment . . . repeats continuously as long as the clock is driving the CPU.

The frequency of the clock determines the time necessary to accomplish the instruction cycle. What takes place during the execution portion of the cycle depends upon the instruction fetched. It is necessary to understand that each instruction cycle may consist of several **machine cycles** accomplished within the CPU and predetermined by the manufacturer's construction of the logic and architecture of the chip. Each machine cycle may also consist of several transition states which occur at a rate of one per clock cycle.

During the execution phase of the cycle, the CPU may be required to use both memory and I/O devices to accomplish its function. If this is necessary, it again uses the three buses previously described.

The ability to carry out a specific set of instructions and the sophistication and speed with which they are accomplished will vary from chip to chip. However, there are some basic categories that appear regularly.

1. Fetch
2. Memory read
3. Memory write
4. Stack read
5. Stack write
6. Input
7. Output
8. Halt
9. Interrupt

Remember that the first machine cycle of any instruction cycle is fetch. The precise transitions and machine cycles that take place for various instructions will be discussed later in the software sections.

Instruction Sets

Each manufacturer has spent a considerable amount of time and effort to provide a versatile and complete **instruction set** with his device. When a microprocessor is purchased, it is capable of accomplishing a unique set of operations that have been built in by the manufacturer. These operations fall into several basic categories including:

1. Data transfer
2. Arithmetic functions
3. Control functions
4. Logical manipulations

The method by which these operations are accomplished and the amount and complexity of the instructions will vary from device to device and must therefore be taken into consideration when deciding which microprocessor to buy.

At the time of purchase, the manufacturer will provide a complete and detailed listing of the instruction set and frequently user's manuals which are essential to understanding the limits and capabilities of the device.

Having purchased a particular device, the user is "on his own" from then on to become proficient in effectively using the device. The sophistication and efficiency of his system depends, to a great extent, upon how well he learns and understands the instruction set of his device.

The complete instruction sets of various microprocessors now available and the use of these instructions in programming will be discussed in later chapters. For now, it is sufficient to recognize the importance of understanding the particular instruction set for the device purchased.

SOFTWARE CONCEPTS

Levels of Language

The term software has come to mean the program contained in the computer. Early computers used machine language. That is, they had stored within their memories a sequential set of binary numbers in the form of 0s and 1s. As programs became more complex, it was apparent that the construction of a machine level program for each machine to do a specific job function was too time consuming. Consequently, the field of software began to develop.

Machine language (0s and 1s) is at the most basic level. The next step up in sophistication is the mnemonic language which is more human in character since it consists of numerals and letters that can be interpreted into instructions. In order that the programmer need not think at the machine level, assemblers and/or interpreters have been developed to translate this mnemonic set of instructions into machine language. The use of mnemonics and the interpretive languages as programming techniques is known as **assembly language.**

Because some programming routines are used over and over again and tend to show up in many programs, executive and monitor programs, sometimes called utility packages, were developed. As the sophistication of utility program usage increased, the higher level languages began to appear. The higher level languages such as BASIC, FORTRAN, COBOL, and Pascal are really very sophisticated executive utility packages that contain all the interpreters and assemblers necessary for the operator to communicate with the machine in somewhat conversational terms.

The higher level program package then interprets and assembles these terms down to machine level commands. A single command in higher level terminology may generate several hundred machine level steps to accomplish the necessary manipulation.

Microprocessor Level

Today's microprocessors accept machine language only. The microprocessor industry is constantly developing software to upgrade the language capabilities of the devices. With the proper amount of memory and user library support from the manufacturers, many systems have already been developed which allow the programmer to work at the high language level with larger machines simulating the microprocessor for the purpose of developing software packages. These packages can then be loaded into the memory of the microprocessor system thus eliminating much time-consuming effort on the part of the programmer.

However, these **development systems,** as they are called, are expensive; and the individual developing his own system usually cannot afford the investment. He will, therefore, probably find himself working at the assembly language level and doing the assembly by hand. For this reason, software in this text will be approached at the assembly level.

QUESTIONS

1. What are the minimum requirements of a computer?
2. Make a list of some of the microprocessor applications you have seen yourself.
3. What are the main advantages of microprocessors over conventional computer systems?
4. What is a bus?
5. Explain the difference between unidirectional and bidirectional.
6. What purpose does an address serve?
7. Explain the differences among instruction cycle, machine cycle and transition states.
8. List the general categories of instruction operations.
9. List the general categories of machine cycle operations.
10. In your own words, explain the relationship of various language levels.

Chapter 2

Binary Introduction

GLOSSARY

Base (base number) The radix of a number system; 10 is the radix for the decimal system, 2 is the radix for the binary system (base 2).

Base complement A number derived from the finite positional notation of another by one of the following rules: true complement—subtract each digit from 1 less than the base, then add 1 to the least significant digit and execute all required carries; base minus 1's complement—subtract each digit from 1 less than the base.

BCD (binary coded decimal) A positional value code in which each decimal digit is binary coded into 4-bit "words."

Bit A single binary digit consisting of either a 0 or a 1 symbol.

Byte A group of adjacent binary digits processed as a unit. Usually an 8-bit parallel grouping.

Carry A digit or equivalent signal resulting from an arithmetic operation that causes a positional digit to equal or exceed the base of the numbering system. A binary bit or flag indicating that a previous computer operation has resulted in an overflow of register capacity.

Decimal system Base-ten number system.

Hexadecimal Base-sixteen number system.

Numbering system A system of abstract symbols used to express quantity.

Octal Base-eight numbering system.

Symbol complement (base minus 1's complement) Complementing procedure of subtracting a digit from the highest symbolic value in the number system.

The study of microprocessors, or, for that matter, of any area of digital electronics involving data handling or calculation, requires a basic understanding of the binary number system. The purpose of this chapter is to provide that basic introduction.

NUMBERING SYSTEMS

Counting

All **numbering systems** originate in how counts of things are symbolized. They are characterized by the number of symbols used to represent the count. Since the **decimal system** is the most familiar to the reader, it provides a good starting point for discussion of numbering systems.

Decimal system. The decimal system is comprised of ten (10) symbols: 0,1,2,3,4,5,6,7,8,9. Any value of count may be represented by a combination of these symbols. Any count (0) to (9) may be represented using a single symbol. Any count beyond that, however, must use a combination of two or more symbols to represent its value. This is accomplished by providing a system of place value by column position. The columns have increasing value moving from right to left.

In the farthest right column each symbol represents the number of units count in sequence 0,1,2,3,4,5,6,7,8,9. One complete count of the system of symbols in a given column is considered a cycle for that column. The value of each count in this column then increases the previous count by (10^0) or unity. The exponent, in this case 0, represents the number of times the symbol system has been counted through in the next lower column. In this case, there is no next lower column so the exponent 0 indicates a unit count occurring in that column.

In the second column, the symbols represent how many times the first column cycle of counts has been completed. The exponent statement of column value of the second column is (10^1) showing that the symbols in this column are representing how many times the first column cycle count has been completely used.

The number 33 would represent three complete 10 counts and three units counts into the next cycle in the first column.

10^1	10^0
3	3

Likewise, the number 4529_{10} would indicate

$4-10^3$ Four complete cycles in the third column
$5-10^2$ Five complete cycles in the second column

$2-10^1$ Two complete cycles in the first column
$9-10^0$ Nine counts completed in the first column

Every time a complete cycle of counts is accomplished in a column, the next column to the left is increased by one symbol count and the present column is reset to "0" and started again.

This system of counting is not unique. The only thing unique is the number of symbols used or the **base** upon which it is constructed. The decimal system uses ten symbols, the **octal** system uses eight symbols, the trinary system uses three symbols, the **hexadecimal** system uses sixteen symbols. The method of keeping place value is the same for all systems.

Octal system. The octal system has only eight symbols: 0,1,2,3,4,5, 6,7. The (8^0) or unity column completes its cycle in eight counts and the (8^1) column indicates the number of times the first column cycle of counts has been completed.

The number 5232_8 would indicate:

$5-8^3$ Five complete cycles in the third column
$2-8^2$ Two complete cycles in the second column
$3-8^1$ Three complete cycles in the first column
$2-8^0$ Two counts completed in the first column

Binary system. The binary system is no different than the other systems. Only two symbols are used: 0,1.

The number 1011_2 indicates

$1-2^3$ One complete cycle in the third column
$0-2^2$ Zero complete cycles in the second column
$1-2^1$ One complete cycle in the first column
$1-2^0$ One count completed in the first column

Because of familiarity and habit, the attempt is always made to relate other base systems to the decimal system and state their value in decimal symbols. In actual fact, this accommodation for the human interpretation of value requires extra hardware and software (programming).

The number 1011_2 means that eleven total counts have occurred just as clearly as the number 11_{10} means that eleven counts have occurred in the decimal system. The only reason that 1011_2 in binary looks "funny" is because it is not familiar.

Working with digital systems requires familiarity with several number systems:

Decimal
Binary
Octal
Hexadecimal
Binary coded decimal (a special system)

Other systems are also used but those listed above are the most common. Arithmetic and data processing may be accomplished using all of these systems.

Basic arithmetic procedures must be understood in order to progress. The decimal system will be used as the model system in the explanation of basic arithmetic procedures since the reader is most familiar with it.

Machine system. *The binary system is the primary machine system.* All basic operations are done by the machine in binary. The data is then processed for display into some other base system for the user's convenience.

When writing and using different number systems, it is standard practice to note the number base by using a subscript. For example:

$$1101_2 \quad 375_8 \quad 375_{10} \quad 375_{16}$$

If this is not done, the value of the number is undefined.

A series of tables and comparisons of value are in Appendix 1 for reference.

Conversion Between Systems

The translation from one numbering system to another can become confusing if approached from a mathematical standpoint. The conversion becomes much simpler if handled consistently at the machine language level or binary format.

Column grouping. In the conversion between simple binary and binary representation of any other system, the primary difference between the systems is the way in which the columns are grouped. Many of today's microprocessors operate on an 8-column system. This grouping of eight binary digits or **bits** is called a **byte.**

The decimal number 74_{10}, when stated in binary, is an 8 bit byte 01001010_2. In order to find the octal equivalent of decimal 74_{10}, group the binary form in groups of three digits.

001	001	010
1	1	2

The decimal number 74_{10} is equivalent to the octal number 112_8.

Note that any time the grouping of digits has not come out even, all leading digits are assumed to be zero. Eight-bit microprocessors and, in fact, most computer systems, are designed to handle numbers in basic binary format. A number result is most commonly displayed in decimal format for evaluation.

BCD (binary coded decimal). There is no binary grouping that completely represents the decimal numbers up to ten. A grouping of three digits handles up to seven and a grouping of four digits goes beyond ten to sixteen. For this reason, machines using a decimal format of entry and display include in their programming structure a **BCD** to binary and a binary to BCD conversion program that is used for entry and display. If these programs are not included in the basic program structure, the operator must become proficient in the recognition and handling of the display format being used by the machine.

Table 2–1 of equivalent values illustrates the conversion from system to system working through the binary system.

However, understanding the basic relationship between the systems is not sufficient. Proficiency with value recognition and arithmetic ability should be developed.

Table 2-1 Equivalent Values

DECIMAL X_{10}	BINARY X_2	GROUPED by 3's X_8	GROUPED by 4's X_{16}
0	0000	00	0
1	0001	01	1
2	0010	02	2
3	0011	03	3
4	0100	04	4
5	0101	05	5
6	0110	06	6
7	0111	07	7
8	1000	10	8
9	1001	11	9
10	1010	12	A
11	1011	13	B
12	1100	14	C
13	1101	15	D
14	1110	16	E
15	1111	17	F
16	10000	20	10

ARITHMETIC

Addition

Addition is the summation of two or more previously complete counts. The addition of two numbers is accomplished by tallying the total number of counts in any given column and providing a **carry** into the next column if the tally exceeds the symbol system.

Example 2–1

Decimal: Add 295_{10} and 386_{10}.

First align column value positions.

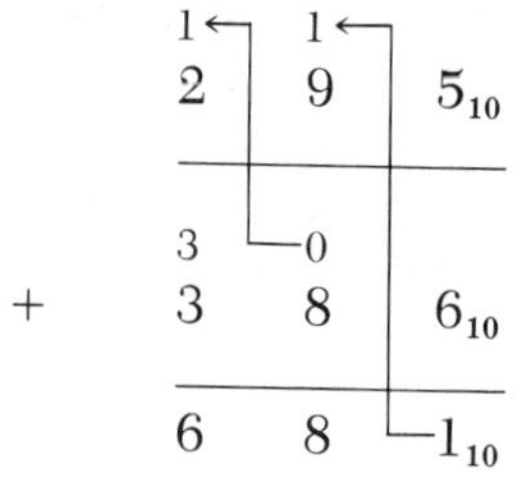

Add first column.

This exceeds the symbol system and so a carry into the second column must be provided.

Add second column.

Again, the sum exceeds the symbol system and a carry is provided in the third column.

Add third column.

No carry.

In any numbering system, the sum of any two numbers in a column will not result in a carry of more than unity into the next column and the carry has a value equal to the base count times the column value.

Example 2–2 in decimal illustrates the basic addition procedure applicable in all base systems.

Example 2–2

Base 10: Add 279_{10} and 365_{10}.

Align column values	1 ←	1 ←	
	2	7	9_{10}
	+ 3	6	5_{10}
Add first column			14
Result is larger than 9 (9 is the greatest symbol value)			− (10)
Subtract the base value and carry 10			4
Add second column		14	
Result exceeds 9		− (10)	
Subtract the base value and carry 10		4	
Add third column	6		
Result less than 9			
SUM	6	4	4_{10}

All addition is done in this way for any base used. A step by step procedure follows.

1. Numbers are added in pairs.
2. Add the column sum.
3. If the column sum exceeds the largest symbol value, carry one base value to the next column and reduce the present column sum by one base value.
4. Note the remainder after the reduction.

Using this set of rules, addition can be done in any base chosen.

In the following examples, decimal equivalents have been used for the summation and reduction of columns for the convenience of the reader.

Example 2–3

Base 16: Add $3A5_{16}$ and $87C_{16}$.

				Decimal Equivalent
Align column values	1 ←	1 ←		
	3	A	5_{16}	933_{10}
	+ 8	7	C_{16}	+ 2172_{10}
Add first column			17	
Exceeds 15; subtract base			− (16)	
Carry 16			1	
Add second column		18		
Exceeds 15; subtract base		− (16)		
Carry 16		2		
Add third column	C			
SUM	C	2	1_{16}	= 3105_{10}

The addition of binary numbers follows the same set of rules.

Example 2–4

Binary: Add 1011_2 and 1101_2

					Decimal Equivalent
	1 ←	1 ←	1 ←		
Align column values	1	0	1	1_2	11_{10}
	+ 1	1	0	1_2	+ 13_{10}
First column sum exceeds 1				2	
Reduce and carry one base value				− (2)	
				0	
Second column sum exceeds 1			2		
Reduce and carry one base value			− (2)		
			0		
Third column sum exceeds 1		2			
Reduce and carry one base value		− (2)			
		0			

Fourth column sum exceeds 1		3				
Reduce and carry one base value	↓	− (2)				
	1	1				
SUM	1	1	0	0	0_2 =	24_{10}

As long as numbers are added in pairs, this system will not fail. No column addition can result in a carry greater than one base value (1) into the next column.

Subtraction

In order to illustrate subtraction, it is again convenient to start with the base 10 numbers. The procedure is:

1. Subtract numbers in pairs.
2. Align column values.
3. Subtract the least significant column first.
4. If the subtrahend exceeds the minuend, borrow one base unit from the next most significant column and carry out the subtraction.
5. Note the final differences.

Example 2–5

Decimal: $24_{10} - 8_{10}$

			Borrow
Align column values		1	→ (10)
	Minuend	2	4_{10}
First column subtrahend exceeds minuend	Subtrahend	− 0	8_{10}
Borrow from second column and find new difference			6
Subtract second column		1	
DIFFERENCE		1	6_{10}

This set of rules will work for any base.

Example 2–6

Base 8: $342_8 - 176_8$

				Decimal Equivalent
		(8)		
Align columns	2	3	(8)	
	3	4	2_8	226_{10}
	− 1	7	6_8	$-\ 126_{10}$
First column: subtrahend exceeds minuend				
Borrow from second column and find new difference			4	
Second column: subtrahend exceeds minuend				
Borrow from third column and find new difference		4		
Third column: subtract	1			
	1	4	4_8 =	100_{10}

Example 2–7

Binary: $1110_2 - 1001_2$

					Decimal Equivalent
Align columns			0	2	
Minuend	1	1	1	0_2	14_{10}
Subtrahend	− 1	0	0	1_2	$-\ 9_{10}$
First column: subtrahend exceeds minuend					
Borrow from second column and find new difference				1	
Second column: subtract			0		
Third column: subtract		1			
Fourth column: subtract	0				
DIFFERENCE	0	1	0	1_2	5_{10}

COMPLEMENT METHODS

Complements

While the previous method of subtraction is relatively easy for humans, the decision to borrow is a point of difficulty for a machine. Therefore, a more machine-oriented method of subtraction is required. Because the procedure is somewhat removed from the conventional way in which subtraction is accomplished, a short explanation of the term complement follows.

The term **base complement** means the number which, when added to the existing number, will result in the next full power of the base. For example:

Example 2–8

The 10's complement of 4 is 6.

$$4 + 6 = 10^1 = 10_{10}$$

The 10's complement of 45 is 55.

$$45 + 55 = 10^2 = 100_{10}$$

The 10's complement of 7864 is 2136.

$$7864 + 2136 = 10^4 = 10000_{10}$$

The 8's complement of 3_8 is 5_8.

$$3 + 5 = 8^1 = 10_8$$

The 8's complement of 264_8 is 514_8.

$$264_8 + 514_8 = 8^3 = 1000_8$$

The 16's complement of 3A4 is C5C.

$$3A4 + C5C = 16^3 = 1000_{16}$$

The 16's complement of 2C is D4.

$$2C + D4 = 16^2 = 100_{16}$$

The 2's complement of 1011 is 0101.

$$1011_2 + 0101_2 = 2^4 = 10000_2$$

The 2's complement of 101 is 011.

$$101_2 + 011_2 = 2^3 = 1000_2$$

The method for finding the complement numbers is quite straightforward. Find the symbol complement and add one.

The **symbol complement** is found by subtracting the original number from the highest symbol in the system.

The highest symbol for the base 10 (decimal) system is 9.
The highest symbol for the base 16 (hexadecimal) system is F.
The highest symbol for the base 8 (octal) system is 7.
The highest symbol for the base 2 (binary) system is 1.

Repeating the procedure for finding the base complement: *To find the base complement, find the symbol complement and add one.*

For the 10's examples, the highest symbol in the 10's system is 9. Therefore the 9's complement of 4 is 5. Then add one for the base complement, 6.

Example 2–9

The 9's complement of 45_{10} is

99	
−45	
54	9's complement
+ 1	Add 1
55	10's complement

Example 2–10

The 9's complement of 7864_{10}

9999	
−7864	
2135	9's complement
+ 1	Add 1
2136	10's complement

For the 8's examples, the highest symbol in the 8's system is the 7. The 8's complement may be found by first finding the 7's complement and adding 1.

Example 2–11

The 7's complement of 3_8 is 4_8 and

$$\begin{array}{rl} 7 & \\ -3 & \\ \hline 4 & \text{7's complement} \\ +1 & \text{Add 1} \\ \hline 5 & \text{8's complement} \end{array}$$

Example 2–12

The 7's complement of 264_8 is

$$\begin{array}{rl} 777 & \\ -264 & \\ \hline 513 & \text{7's complement} \\ +\quad 1 & \text{Add 1} \\ \hline 514 & \text{8's complement} \end{array}$$

For the base 16 examples, the highest symbol in the system is F. The 16's complement is found by finding the F's complement and adding 1.

Example 2–13

The F's complement of $3A4_{16}$ is

$$\begin{array}{rl} FFF & \\ -3A4 & \\ \hline C5B & \text{F's complement} \\ +\quad 1 & \text{Add 1} \\ \hline C5C & \text{16's complement} \end{array}$$

The F's complement of $2C_{16}$ is

$$\begin{array}{rl} FF & \\ -2C & \\ \hline D3 & \text{F's complement} \\ +\quad 1 & \text{Add 1} \\ \hline D4 & \text{16's complement} \end{array}$$

For the base 2 examples, the highest symbol in the system is 1. The 2's complement is found by adding 1 to the 1's complement.

Example 2–14

The 2's complement of 1011_2 is

$$\begin{array}{rl} 1111 & \\ -\,1011 & \\ \hline 0100 & \text{1's complement} \\ +\quad 1 & \text{Add 1} \\ \hline 0101 & \text{2's complement} \end{array}$$

The 2's complement of 101_2 is

$$\begin{array}{rl} 111 & \\ -\,101 & \\ \hline 010 & \text{1's complement} \\ +\quad 1 & \text{Add 1} \\ \hline 011 & \text{2's complement} \end{array}$$

Subtraction

This little trick of complementing allows subtraction by adding the base complement utilizing the symbol complement.

1. Find the symbol complement of the subtrahend.
2. Add this complement to the minuend.
3. Add one and ignore any carry.

The carry that may occur in the process of doing subtraction by this method becomes meaningless and is dropped. If included in the answer, the carry results in an answer that is always ($\text{Base}^{\text{number of columns}}$) too high. This fact does become useful later in the discussion of signed numbers.

Example 2–15

$$\begin{array}{llcl} \text{Base 10 example:} & \text{Minuend} & & \text{Subtrahend} \\ & 374_{10} & - & 275_{10} \\ \text{9's complement of} & 275_{10} & = & 724_{10} \end{array}$$

$$\begin{array}{rl} 374 & \\ +\ 724 & \\ \hline \cancel{1}098 & \\ +\qquad 1 & \text{Add 1} \\ \hline \cancel{1}099_{10} & \text{Drop carry 1} \end{array}$$

Example 2–16

	Minuend		Subtrahend
Base 16:	$4AC_{16}$	−	$24B_{16}$

Subtrahend complement

F's complement

$$\begin{array}{r} FFF \\ -\ 24B \\ \hline DB4_{16} \end{array}$$

$$\begin{array}{rl} 4AC & \\ +\ DB4 & \\ \hline 1260 & \\ +\quad 1 & \text{Add 1} \\ \hline 1261_{16} & \text{Drop carry 1} \end{array}$$

Decimal Equivalent

$$\begin{array}{rcr} 4AC_{16} & = & 1196_{10} \\ -\,24B_{16} & = & -587_{10} \\ \hline 261_{16} & = & 609_{10} \end{array}$$

Example 2–17

	Minuend		Subtrahend
Base 2:	11010_2	−	10111_2

Subtrahend complement: 1's complement 01000

$$\begin{array}{rl} 11010 & \\ +\ 01000 & \text{1's complement} \\ \hline 100010 & \\ -\qquad 1 & \text{Add 1} \\ \hline 100011 & \text{Drop carry 1} \end{array}$$

Decimal Equivalent

$$\begin{array}{rcr} 11010_2 & = & 26_{10} \\ -\,10111_2 & = & +23_{10} \\ \hline 00011_2 & = & 3_{10} \end{array}$$

Signed Numbers

The base complement in binary is called the 2's complement. It has some distinct advantages when used with computers in the handling of signed numbers since the most significant bit (MSB) is the sign bit.

A 0 in the MSB position indicates a positive number and a 1 indicates a negative number. The number 5 is represented as 00000101 and −5 is 10000101 in true binary form. By adopting the procedure of representing all negative numbers in 2's complement form, the sign is handled automatically. The number −5 then becomes 11111011. If this convention is adopted, all addition and subtraction operations will result in positive numbers being in true binary form and negative numbers will be in 2's complement form with the MSB being automatically in proper sign form.

Example 2–18

Using the values 5_{10} and 7_{10}

Add $+5_{10}$ and $+7_{10}$

5	00000101	true form
7	00000111	true form
12	00001100	true form

Add -5_{10} and -7_{10}

−5	11111011	2's complement
−7	11111001	2's complement
−12	11110100	2's complement

Add -5_{10} and $+7_{10}$

−5	11111011	2's complement
+7	00000111	true form
+2	00000010	true form

Add $+5_{10}$ and -7_{10}

5	00000101	true form
+(−7)	11111001	2's complement
−2	11111110	2's complement

Subtract $+5_{10}$ from $+7_{10}$

7	00000111	true form
−(+5)	11111011	2's complement
+2	00000010	true form

Subtract $+7_{10}$ from $+5_{10}$

+5	00000101	true form
−(+7)	11111000	2's complement
−2	11111110	2's complement

Subtract -7_{10} from -5_{10}

−5	11111011	2's complement
−(−7)	00000111	true form
+2	00000010	true form

Note that the subtraction of a negative number causes a 2's complement to be generated for a 2's complement resulting in a true form positive number. Thus subtracting a negative is equivalent to adding a positive.

Example 2–19

Subtract -5_{10} from -7_{10}

−7	11111001	2's complement
−(−5)	00000101	true form
−2	11111110	2's complement

Most microprocessor instruction sets provide subtraction via the 2's complement method and adjust a carry bit indicator to indicate whether or not a borrow operation is required. The instruction sets also normally include the ability to complement a number present in the accumulator. This allows the operator to provide 2's complement operations independent of a subtract routine.

FRACTIONS

Place Value

This chapter, having already explained the place value (column value) of whole numbers in the binary system, in the previous section, would be incomplete without a discussion of fractional values and their binary representation.

As with the decimal system, the whole number and fractional values are separated by a dot or binary point. Also, as in the decimal system, the value of the numbers gets progressively less, moving from left to right as demonstrated in Table 2–2.

Table 2-2 Binary and Decimal Fractional Numbers

Decimal	10^3	10^2	10^1	10^0	.	10^{-1}	10^{-2}	10^{-3}	10^{-4}
Value	1000	100	10	1	.	1/10	1/100	1/1000	1/10000
Binary	2^3	2^2	2^1	2^0	.	2^{-1}	2^{-2}	2^{-3}	2^{-4}
Value	8	4	2	1	.	1/2	1/4	1/8	1/16

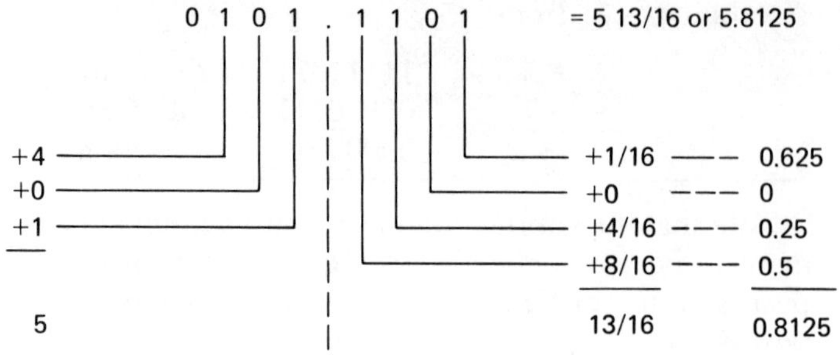

Fig. 2–1. Evaluation of a binary statement.

As with any system, the amount of accuracy possible depends on the number of digits involved. If the smallest value available is 1/16, no number will be inaccurate by more than 1/16 error. A binary statement is evaluated in the manner shown in Fig. 2–1.

Procedures

The addition and subtraction of binary fractions follow the same procedures used for whole numbers.

Example 2–20

	Base 2	Base 10			
Add	0010.0101	2.3125	or	2	5/16
	+ 0100.1011	4.6875	or	4	11/16
	01111.0000	7.0		7	

The handling of arithmetic processes beyond add, subtract and complement is normally accomplished by programming.

SUMMARY

In an effort to place the material in this chapter in perspective, a quick review of the principles is included here.

1. All numbering systems are based on the number of symbolic counts in the system.

2. The programmer should be familiar with the following numbering systems.

a. Decimal
b. Binary
c. Octal
d. Hexadecimal
e. BCD (Binary coded decimal)

3. A carry or a borrow from a column is valued at one full base count.

4. Conversion of values from one system to another is most easily accomplished at the machine level (binary).

5. The rules for addition and subtraction are the same in all systems.

6. The handling of signed numbers is most directly accomplished by the base complement method.
   a. Negative numbers are stored in base complement.
   b. Subtraction is accomplished by complementing the subtrahend and adding. (Notation of sign is automatic in the MSB position.)
   c. A 1 in the MSB indicates (−).
      A 0 in the MSB indicates (+).

7. Binary fractions are handled by the same procedures as whole numbers.

8. Most arithmetic operations beyond addition and subtraction are handled by programming.

QUESTIONS

1. Name the primary numbering systems that need to be understood in working with digital systems.
2. Explain the significance of the exponent value in any counting system.
3. What is meant by the term base?
4. What is the basic numbering system used by computers? Why is it used?
5. What is BCD and why is it used in many machines?
6. All basic arithmetic operations are carried out in the same way in all systems. State the procedures for addition and subtraction (both methods).
7. Given the following pairs of numbers:

   39_{10} and 21_{10} 1_{10} and 6_{10} 1257_{10} and 325_{10}

   a. Convert the pairs to hexadecimal.
   b. Convert the pairs to octal.

c. Convert the pairs to 8-bit binary.

Is it possible to do all of the above conversions as specified? Why or why not?

d. Add the numbers in base 10, base 2, base 8 and base 16.

e. Check your answers by converting the answers to base 10. Are they all correct?

f. Write the numbers' 2's complement, 7's complement, and F's complement.

g. Subtract the numbers using 2's complement. How did you handle the negative number?

8. Write the following base ten numbers in binary fractions:

1/16 .275 .625 1/2 1/256 1/83 .125

Chapter 3

Digital Concepts for Microprocessors

GLOSSARY

Active high/low A statement referring to the signal requirement to cause the device to become active. "Active" refers to the state or condition of operation. Computer components are active when they are directed or excited by a control signal.

Clock A pulse generator that controls the timing of the switching circuits and memory states thus determining the speed at which the major portion of the computer or timing circuits operate.

Debouncing Eliminating unwanted pulse variations caused by mechanically generated pulses when contacts repeatedly make and break in a bouncing manner.

Edge triggered Circuit action is initiated at the rising or falling edge of the control pulse.

Flip-flop A type of circuit having two stable states and usually two input terminals (or signals) corresponding to each of the two states. The circuit remains in either state until the corresponding signal is applied. Also, a similar bistable device with an input that allows it to act as a single-stage binary counter.

D flip-flop A delay flip-flop whose output is a function of the input which appeared one pulse earlier.

RS flip-flop A flip-flop consisting of two cross-coupled NAND gates having two inputs designated R and S. A 1 on the S input and a 0 on the R input resets (clears) the flip-flop to the 0 state. A 1 on the R input and 0 on the S input sets it to the 1 state.

RST flip-flop A flip-flop having three inputs: R, S and T. This unit works like the RS flip-flop except that the T input is used to cause the flip-flop to change states.

Gate A circuit having two or more inputs and one output. The output depends on the combination of logic signals at the inputs. The five basic gates are: AND, OR, NAND, NOR, EXCLUSIVE OR.

Latch A circuit that can be locked into a particular condition and remains stable until changed. Also, to hold a particular condition of output.

Level triggered Circuit action is initiated by the presence of the control signal voltage.

Multiplexing A process of transmitting more than one signal at a time over a single link, route or channel in a communications system.

Triggered A pulse starts an action which then functions for a certain length of time under its own control.

Truth table A mathematical table showing the Boolean algebra relationships of variables.

The study of microprocessors requires a degree of experience and background in digital circuits and integrated devices. In approaching this text, a mastery of the basic concepts of digital circuitry and combinational logic is assumed.

This chapter focuses on some of these basic concepts as they are applied to microprocessor circuits and systems. In most courses and texts, digital logic and circuits are presented from a passive or simple truth table approach to function. The more desirable perspective for microprocessor application is that of active signal control devices. This chapter, therefore, will contain various active **gate** applications.

ACTIVE GATES

Consider for a moment a simple two input AND gate. If the designer wishes to pass an input signal at certain times and not pass it at others, he may think of the other input as a pass or enabling signal. If input A is the intelligence input and signal B is the pass or enabling line, when B input is at 0, the A input cannot pass through the gate and when B is at 1, the output signal will follow input A. In this way, signal B may be considered the gate control signal. An AND gate could then be viewed as a signal gate with an **active high** control line. That is, when the control line is high (1), the gate is active (activated).

In this same manner, an OR gate could be considered an active low gate, a NAND gate as an active high inverter and a NOR gate as an

active low inverter. This concept can be reinforced by thinking of input A as a constantly changing square wave input signal and, with this in mind, considering the effect on the output of the gate as the B input is changed periodically from 0s to 1s.

The results of this exercise would look something like Fig. 3–1 which shows the four types of gates.

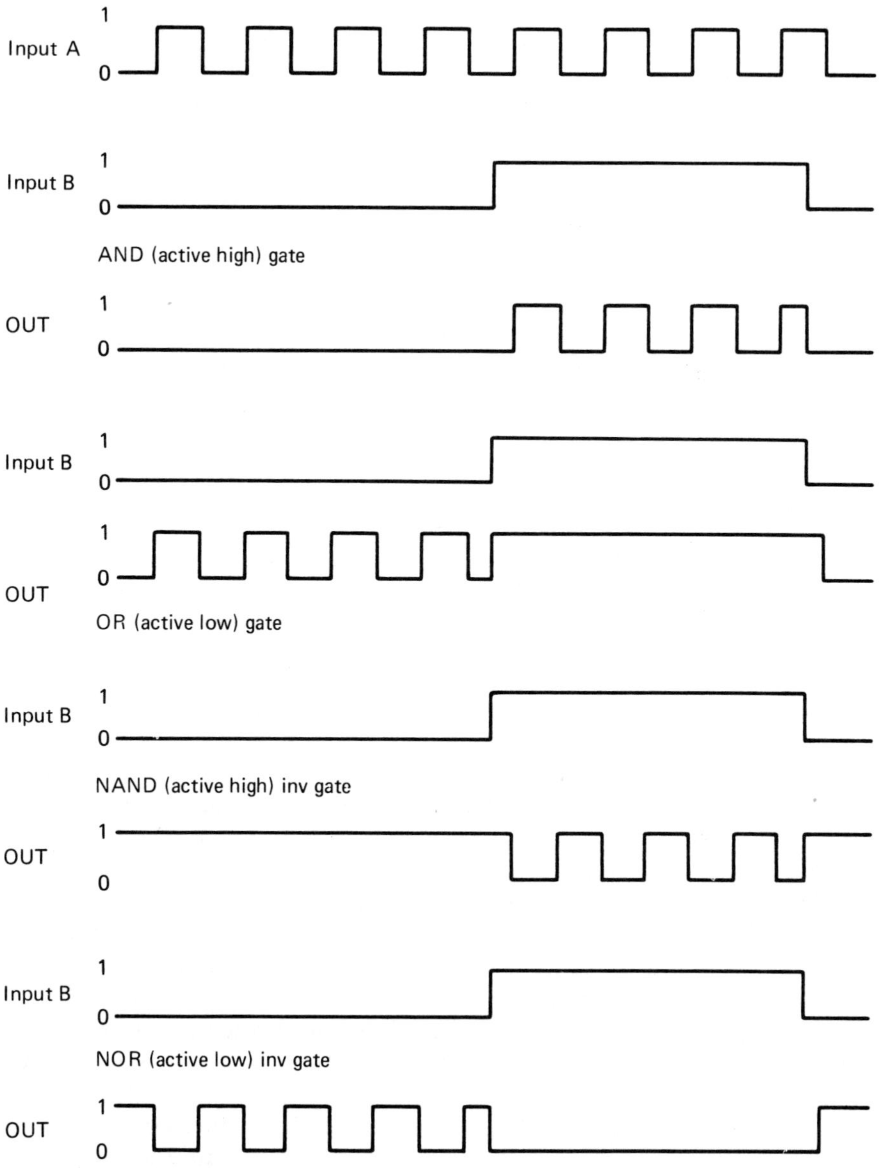

Fig. 3–1. Active gate signal diagrams.

The inverter may also be thought of in two ways: as a device which changes 0s and 1s and vice versa or as an input converter from active high to active low and vice versa. This can be confirmed by installing an inverter on the B input of the gate in question. The results would then conform to the following conditions:

AND—active low
OR—active high
NAND—active low invert
NOR—active high invert

The installation of an input inverter or converter can be shown schematically by putting an invert circle at the input to the gate.

This train of thought can be further pursued through experimentation with various configurations of gates and inverters to achieve the desired input and output conditions. Do not narrowly apply the circuits available. The manufacturers of logic circuits have provided a wide variety of circuit functions for the designer and, with a little imagination, a broad minded approach and a minimum amount of circuit manipulation, a great degree of flexibility in applications can be achieved.

Debouncer Circuits

One of the problems often encountered in a microprocessor circuit is the generation of multiple bits when a mechanical switch is closed. This problem is accurately described by the term "bounce." The phenomenon of the switch contacts bouncing can continue from a few microseconds to a few milliseconds. The microprocessor operating at microsecond speeds for bit processing will process this bounce train as randomly applied numbers of bits.

The desired result of **debouncing** a switch is to have one transition occur for each deliberate switch change. This can be accomplished by hardware methods or under program control called software debounce. This discussion will concern itself with hardware methods of debouncing.

The basic procedure for accomplishing a hardware debounce is to feed the switch data to a latching circuit or a simple solid state memory. When the switch makes contact for the first time, the circuit stabilizes or latches in that condition so that repeated pulses from the switch due to bounce have no further effect on the circuit condition.

Figure 3–2 shows two circuits which may be utilized for debouncing purposes.

The NAND gate debouncer is **triggered** or toggled from one state to the other by the application of a 0 or ground by an SPDT switch to the

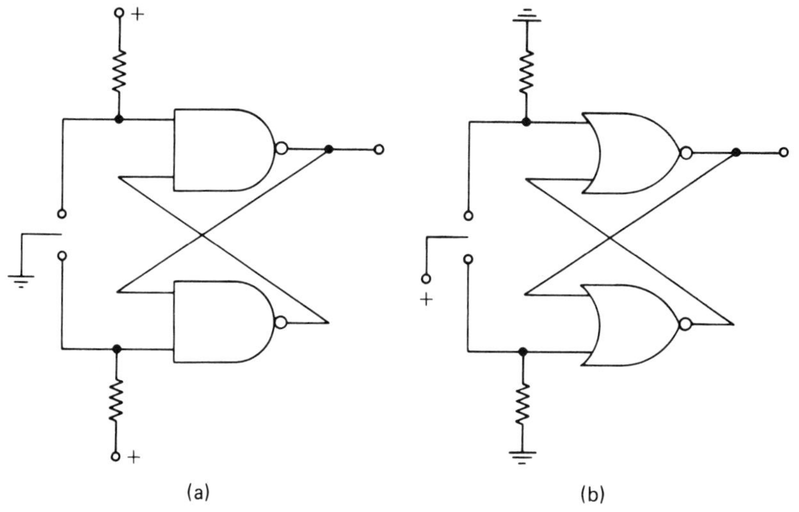

Fig. 3–2. Debouncing circuits.

appropriate input. Once the ground input is applied, the output of that side goes to a 1 condition and is coupled to the input of the other NAND gate causing its output to fall to 0. This 0 being coupled back to the input of the first gate causes it to stabilize or **latch** into the 0 input, 1 output condition.

The NOR gate debouncer operates in a similar manner except that it is toggled by the application of a $+V_{CC}$ or 1 condition. Choosing which of these two circuits to use depends upon whether the type of switching or triggering desired is positive or negative pulses.

The circuits shown in Fig. 3–2 are used for debouncing SPDT switches. Figure 3–3 is a cross coupled inverter circuit for debouncing SPST switches. In this circuit, the capacitor assists in accomplishing the debounce by absorbing short duration bounces and only charges or discharges beyond the triggering thresholds when the switch remains open or closed for a relatively long time.

These circuits have the ability to react once and only once to a repeatedly applied signal to any one lead that is of interest. This ability provides the "debounce" characteristic. When mechanical contacts are closed or opened, they make and break from a few times to several hundred times during their settling period. These simple logic circuit arrangements cause the output to transition only once no matter how many bounces occur.

As with most logic circuits, there is more than one way to think about this logic block. Its ability to maintain a given condition without

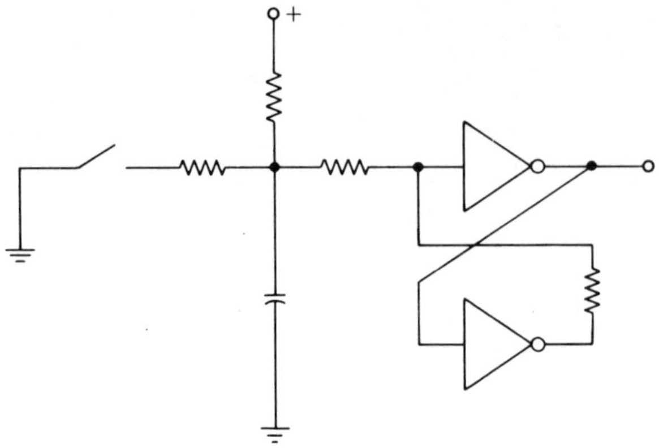

Fig. 3–3. Cross coupled inverter circuit for debouncing SPST switches.

further application of a signal permits it to be used as a simple solid-state memory or latch as the application requires. Its ability to set to one condition and reset or change to the alternate condition results in a **flip-flop** which will be described in the next section. This basic arrangement of logical gates will be encountered again and again while investigating various digital circuits.

RS Flip-Flop

The cross coupled NAND gate and NOR gate configurations used in the previous section for mechanical debouncing may also be used as an **RS flip-flop** (set-reset flip-flop—Yes, the reversal of terms is a standard practice!) The resistors used for input condition maintenance are removed and it is understood that the input lines are maintained at their normal levels by preceding logical circuitry.

The circuits, symbols and **truth tables** for both RS flip-flops are given in Fig. 3–4.

These units are also sometimes called master-slave flops because they are not **edge triggered.** If a device is **level triggered** or clocked it is normally called a master-slave device. If it is edge triggered or clocked, it is normally called a D-type or data type. The difference between level clocking and edge clocking may seem trivial at first thought. However, it will be a point of continuous frustration to the novice in digital circuits unless the confusion is cleared away.

In level clocking, it is the *state* or required level being *present* that allows the action to be completed. In edge clocking, it is the *change* of state or required *transition occurrence* that causes the action to take

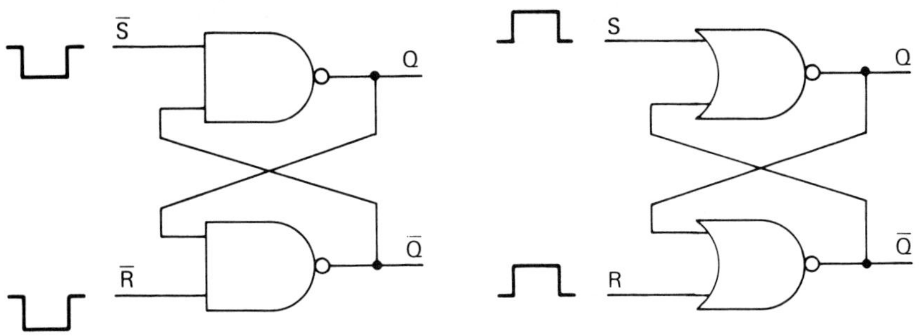

(a) Circuits

(b) Symbols

$\overline{S}$	$\overline{R}$	Q	$\overline{Q}$	
0	0	1	1	(not allowed)
0	1	1	0	
1	0	0	1	
1	1	–	–	(no change)

S	R	Q	$\overline{Q}$	
0	0	–	–	(no change)
0	1	0	1	
1	0	1	0	
1	1	0	0	(not allowed)

(c) Truth Tables

Fig. 3–4. RS flip-flops.

place. *If there is any doubt as to the type of device being used, consult the data sheets for the device.*

There are several disadvantages to the simple RS flip-flop. First, it is not clocked. The outputs change immediately upon application of the input signals and do not wait for a clocking command. The only delay is the characteristic propagation time of the elements. This can lead to unchecked transition races occurring throughout complete circuits. In a synchronized system, this can be disastrous.

The second problem involves the disallowed input conditions causing contradictory output conditions. Third, connecting a series of simple RS flip-flops in cascade does not result in a sequential or *controlled* occurrence of events which is required for clocked systems. Finally, simple RS flip-flops are lacking the very desirable feature of easy conversion to a binary divider and/or shift register configuration.

RST Flip-Flop

The first problem encountered with the simple flip-flop—absence of clocking—can be overcome by the addition of input clock gating similar to that discussed in the section on active gates. The **clock pulse** is now going to act as the control and the set and reset lines as the signals to be passed. Circuit arrangements are shown in Fig. 3–5.

Connecting the set and reset lines through the AND gates prevents the signals from passing unless the active level of the clock exists. This input gating arrangement does not solve the problems of the disallowed state, the cascade race and the difficult conversion. Also, any transitions that might occur on the set and reset lines would propagate through the system while the clock is valid because it is level triggered and not edge triggered.

This clocking system is referred to as a single phase clock system because a single clock level accomplishes both the input and output operations at the same time. That is, they occur simultaneously and are caused by the presence of the clock pulse. Any logic system with this single phase characteristic is susceptible to racing.

The race problem can be eliminated by creating a 2-phase or 2-stage logic system. Such a system takes two clock phases or states to accomplish a complete propagation from input to output.

Consider the circuit in Fig. 3–6.

Notice that the clock input is inverted in the slave section causing it to clock or pass data during clock low condition; the master unit has a noninverted clock input causing it to pass data during clock high condition. Since the clock is a single pulse common to both inputs, these pass conditions are mutually exclusive and cause input operation to occur during clock high and output operation to occur during clock low. This 2-phase arrangement allows controlled data passage with the occurrence of one clock pulse. This arrangement also prevents race conditions because the transition or edge of the clock has become the cause of the changes that occur. The positive edge enables the input or master and disables the output or slave. The negative edge disables the input or master and enables the output or slave.

When the circuit in Fig. 3–6 is considered as a block unit, it can truly be called an edge-triggered (set-reset) **RST flip-flop.** It is negative edge-triggered because the output duplicates the input at the in-

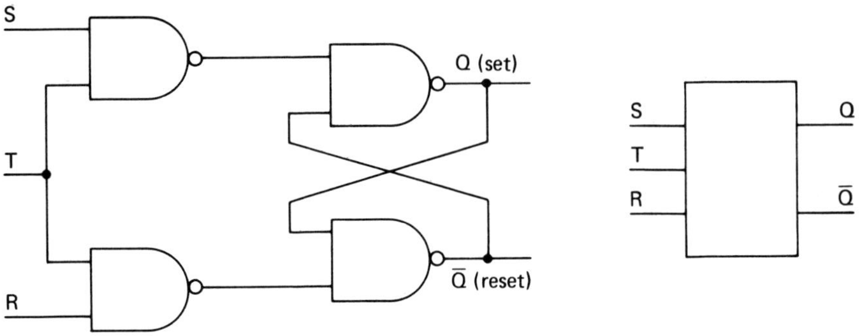

S	R	T	Q	$\overline{Q}$	
0	0	1	—	—	(no change)
0	1	1	0	1	(reset)
1	0	1	1	0	(set)
1	1	1	1	1	(not allowed)
X	X	0	—	—	(no change)

X = don't care

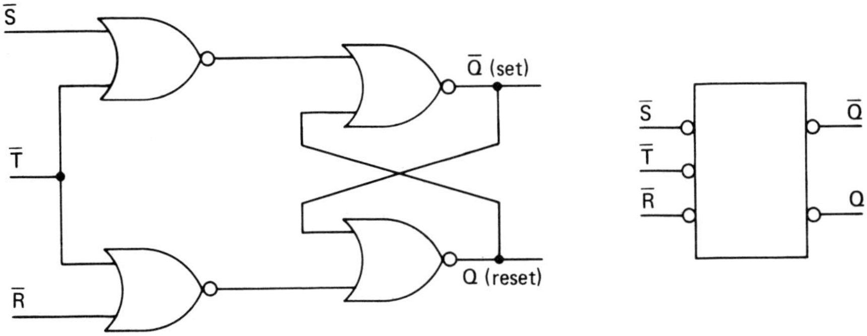

$\overline{S}$	$\overline{R}$	$\overline{T}$	Q	$\overline{Q}$	
0	0	0	0	0	(not allowed)
0	1	0	1	0	(set)
1	0	0	0	1	(reset)
1	1	0	—	—	(no change)
X	X	1	—	—	(no change)

X = don't care

Fig. 3–5. (a) Gated RS flip-flop (RST) active high clock. (b) Gated RS flip-flop (RST) active low clock.

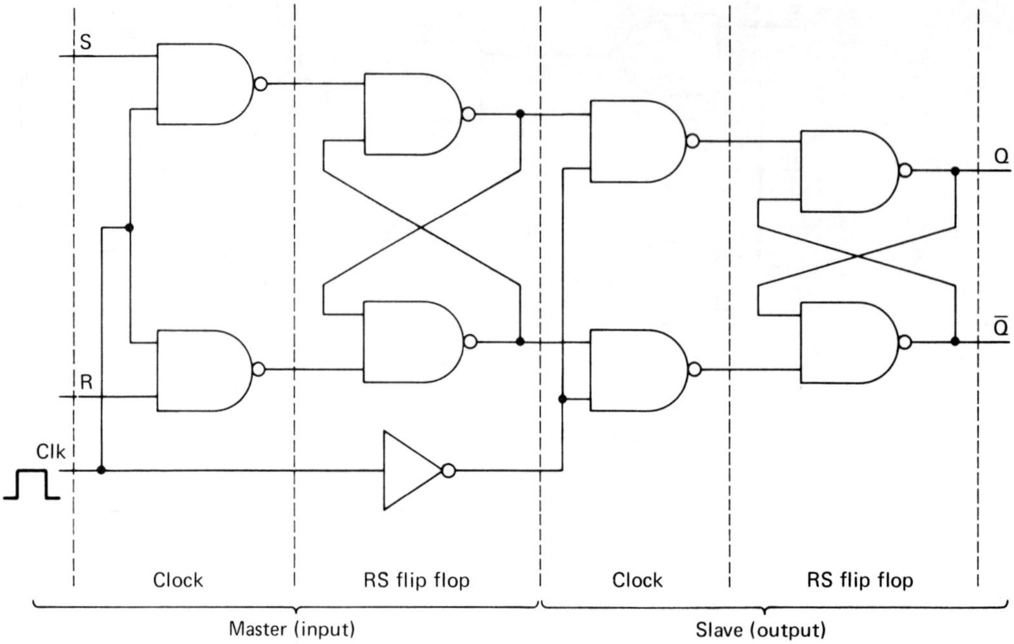

(a) Circuit

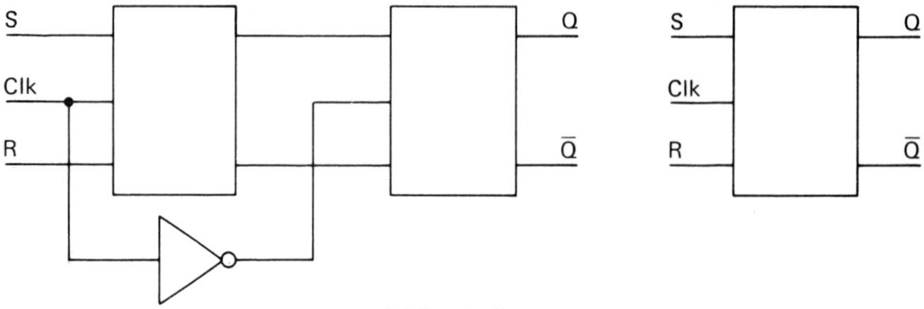

(b) Symbolic

S	R	clk	Q	$\bar{Q}$	
0	0	↓	—	—	(no change)
0	1	↓	0	1	
1	0	↓	1	0	
1	1	↓	1	1	(not allowed)

(c) Truth Table

Fig. 3–6. Master-slave (2-phase clocking, negative edge).

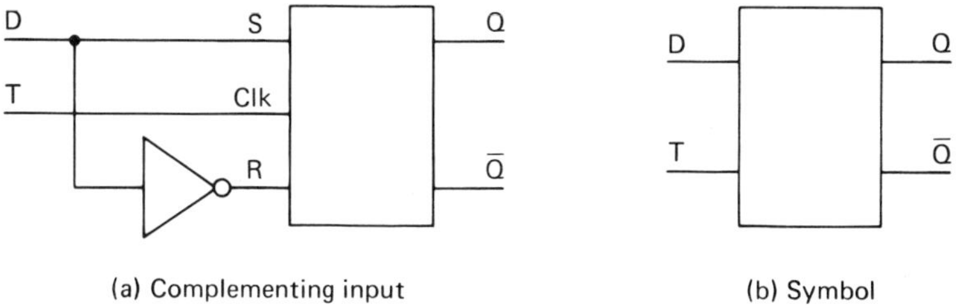

Fig. 3–7. (a) D-type flip-flop; (b) logic symbol.

stant the negative occurs. A positive edge arrangement can be made by inverting the clock on the master section rather than on the slave section.

D Flip-Flop

All of the problems except one have now been overcome. The device is clocked, 2-phase in character (no race) and edge triggered. The final problem of invalid output condition can be rectified by connecting an inverter from the S to R inputs as shown in Fig. 3–7 (a).

This variation of the RST flip-flop is known as the **D flip-flop.** The D flip-flop has only one input or data line which will be duplicated at the Q output when a proper edge occurs. (Both positive and negative edge types are available.) The logical symbol is shown in Fig. 3–7 (b).

In a 7474 TTL D flip-flop, the equivalent gate circuit arrangement is different than that which has been discussed here. Three input gate devices are used to reduce the number of gates required to implement the master and slave section. A direct set and reset input capability is included for the convenience of the user. These direct input capabilities are independent of the clock input.

FLIP-FLOP APPLICATIONS

As with most basic logic block functions, the uses of flip-flops are many and varied depending primarily upon the imagination of the designer and his ability to apply the basic characteristics of the device in question to his needs. Some of the very common uses of the D flop are explored in the following circuit discussion. Experiment with circuits provided here to gain experience in the handling of digital circuitry and integrated circuits.

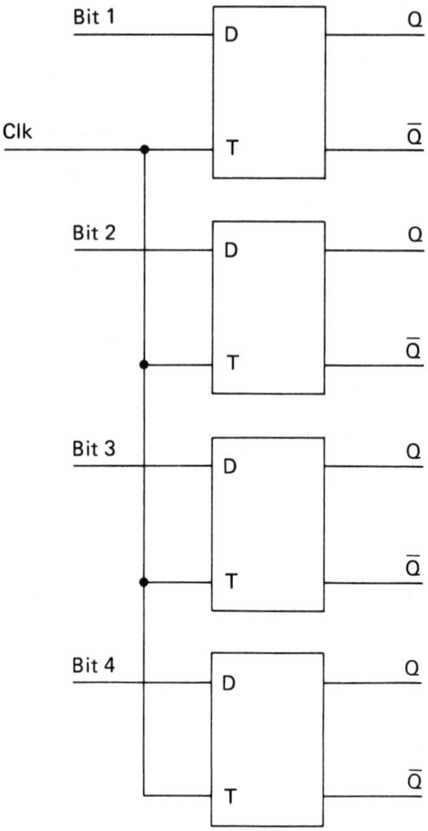

Fig. 3–8. Multiple-bit latch.

Flip-Flops as Latches

One of the most obvious applications for a D flop is as a latch or 1-bit memory. Its predominant characteristic is its ability to catch and hold a data line condition at the time of the clock edge. If several 7474 D flops are connected in parallel as shown in Fig. 3–8, a multibit latch can be simulated. The desired output level may also be selected. The original data or its 1's complement may be used.

Flip-Flops as Frequency Dividers

If the D flip-flop is connected so that its complementary output is fed back to the input, its output line will change at every valid edge condition of the clock. Since only one clock edge is valid, it will require two clock pulses to return the output lines to their original condition creating a very simple divide-by-2 frequency divider.

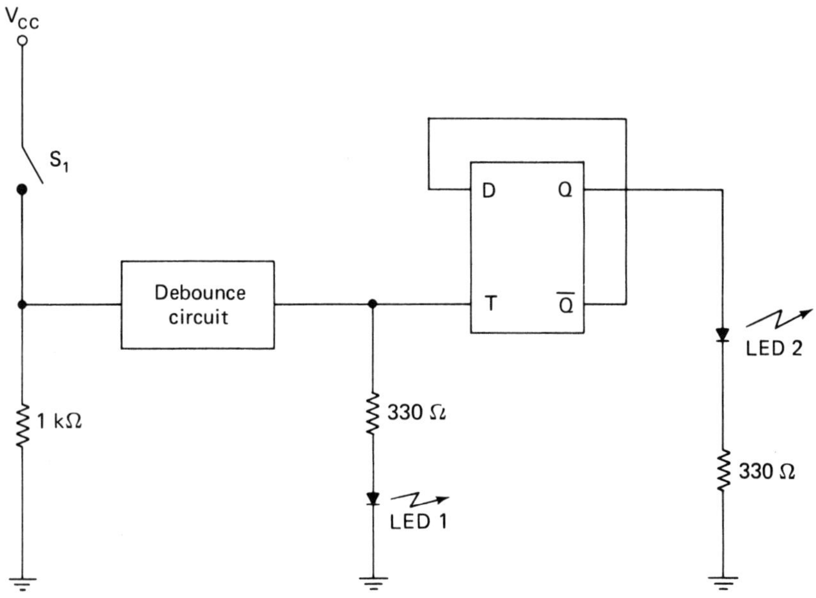

Fig. 3–9. Frequency divider (divide-by-2).

For experimental purposes, the circuit in Fig. 3–9 could be connected.

When the clock switch is repeatedly opened and closed, LED 1 changes condition twice for each change of LED 2. Note: if the debounce circuit were not provided, the output/input comparison would not be observable because the number of pulses generated by the switch is not dependable.

Flip-Flops as Counters

If a series of D flip-flops are connected in sequence and connected as frequency dividers, a binary counter will result as shown in Fig. 3–10.

Flip-Flops as Shift Registers

Cascading a series of D flip-flops results in a serial input-parallel output shift register as shown in Fig. 3–11.

Many other variations and circuit arrangements of these basic applications can be found in semiconductor manufacturers' application manuals.

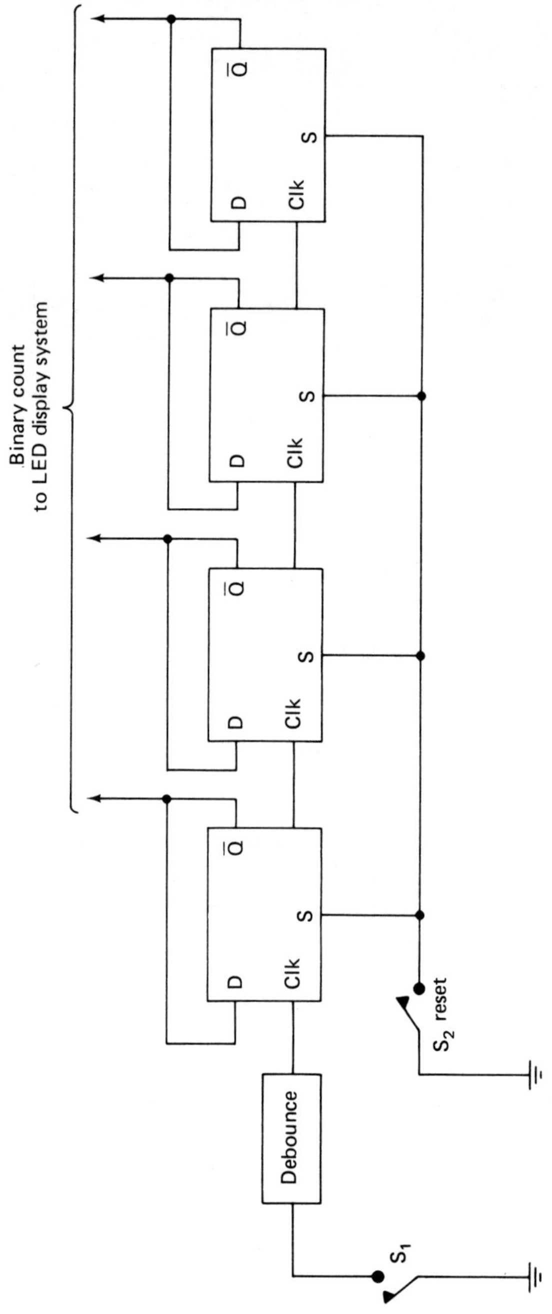

Fig. 3–10. Binary counter.

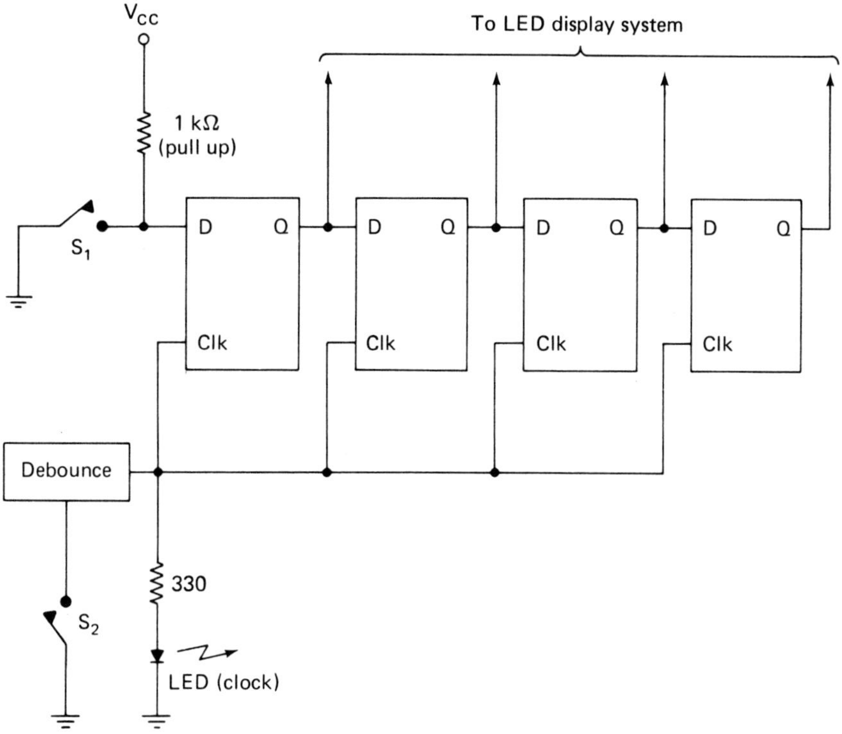

Fig. 3–11. Serial input—parallel output shift register.

DECODERS

The Principle

The process of decoding data by logic can be very complex if the data that is output is intricately related to the input. The purpose of decoding is to provide unique single or multiple-bit outputs for a given unique input.

One of the simplest forms of decoding is causing a particular data-line to be activated depending upon the binary input. As an example, consider the problem of decoding a single bit into two possible condition indicators. That is: when the bit is high, turn on output 1; when the bit is low, turn on output 2.

The circuit in Fig. 3–12 (a) exemplifies this simple problem.

When the input line is at a 0 condition, the output 1 is off and output 2 is on. Conversely, when the input is a 1 condition, output 1 is on and

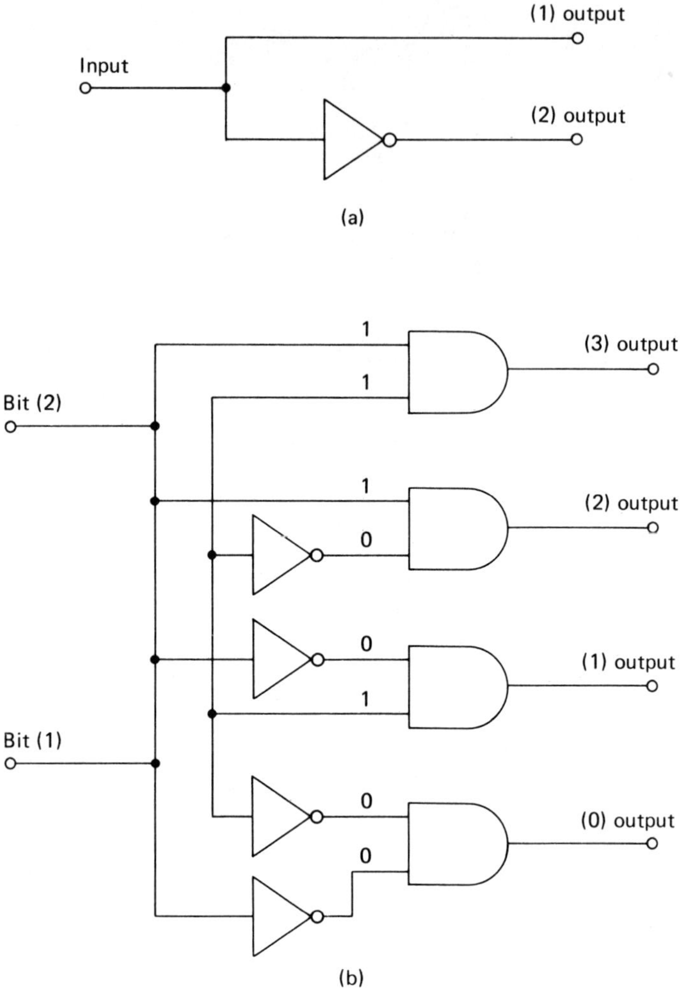

Fig. 3–12. (a) Single line decoder; (b) two line decoder.

output 2 is off. This approach can be expanded to two, three or any number of bits of input.

Decoding a 2-bit input set into one of four signal single line selections is still relatively simple as shown in Fig. 3–12 (b).

By extending this idea of combinational gating of input lines, a variety of decoders can be constructed. A commercial example of the system in use today is the 7442 4-line to-10-line or (1-of-10) decoder. The logic diagram is given in Fig. 3–13.

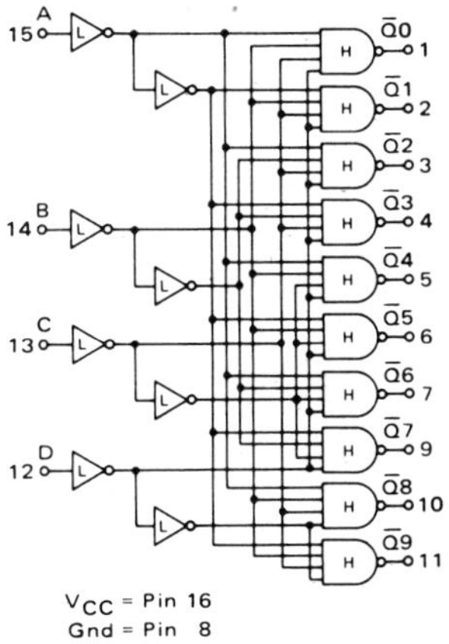

Fig. 3–13. Logic diagram 7442. (*Courtesy Motorola Inc.*)

At first glance, the ability to decode large binary numbers may seem to require a prohibitive number of gates and packages. To an extent this is true when accomplishing the task directly in one circuit. There is another approach, however, which allows cascading decoder circuits to reduce the complexity of design.

Distributed Decoding

The use of one line of input to a gate to allow a signal to pass on the other line has already been discussed in this chapter in the section on gating and again used in providing clocking for the RS flip-flop. This concept will be applied again in this decoder section as the circuit enable input function.

By applying this cascade decoding concept to the 2-bit decoder just discussed, a 4-to-16 decoder can be easily constructed. Keeping in mind that the two least significant bits (LSB) pattern is repeated for each unique set of bits for the two most significant bits (MSB), a circuit can be constructed that uses the two MSBs to enable decoder circuits for the two LSBs as shown in Fig. 3–14.

This cascade system can be expanded to accomplish the decoding of almost any arrangement of memory or circuit enabling system and is, in fact, a widely employed method of memory address decoding in use today. Some of the commercial decoders available today are the 7442 (4-to-10), 74154 (4-to-16) and 74144 (1-of-4). The enabling of these circuits is done internally in most cases and most use an active low enabling scheme.

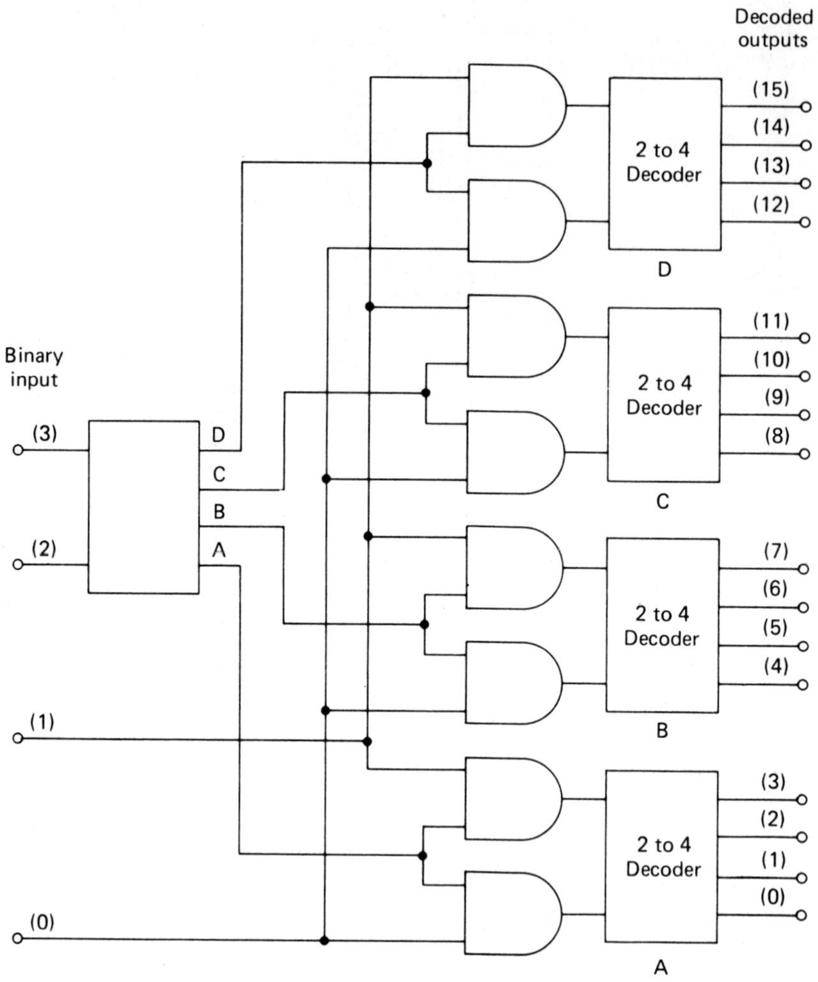

Fig. 3–14. 4-to-16 cascade decoder.

Demultiplexing

As with other decoders, this particular decoding scheme can be used in more than one way. For example, the 7442 4-to-10 line decoder can also be applied as a 1-of-8 line demultiplexing unit. Demultiplexing is the process of distributing data to selected output lines. It is for this reason that demultiplexing chips are sometimes called data distribution chips. The 7442 decode chip has as inputs three address lines and one data line. If a constantly varying data input is applied to the data line, it will appear at the output line specified by the 3 address lines.

An experimental circuit, Fig. 3–15, is easy to construct for verification.

With all address switches at 0, repeatedly activating the data switch will cause the data to be present on the 0 output line. In turn, applying other address inputs via the switches and applying data (0s and 1s) to the data lines will cause the data to appear at the output line selected by the address switches.

Multiplexing

The idea of demultiplexing can be reversed. That is, one of a group of data input lines selected by address will appear at a single output line. This procedure is called **multiplexing** or data selecting. It can be illustrated in the following way. Assume that the required function is to select, at different times, one of eight different data lines to appear

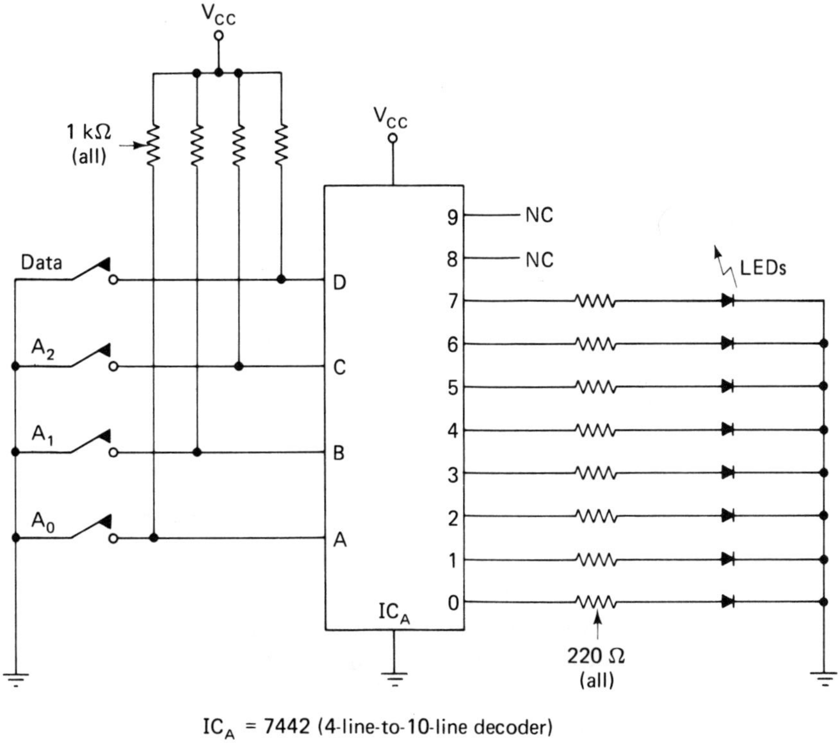

Fig. 3–15. Data distribution (demultiplex).

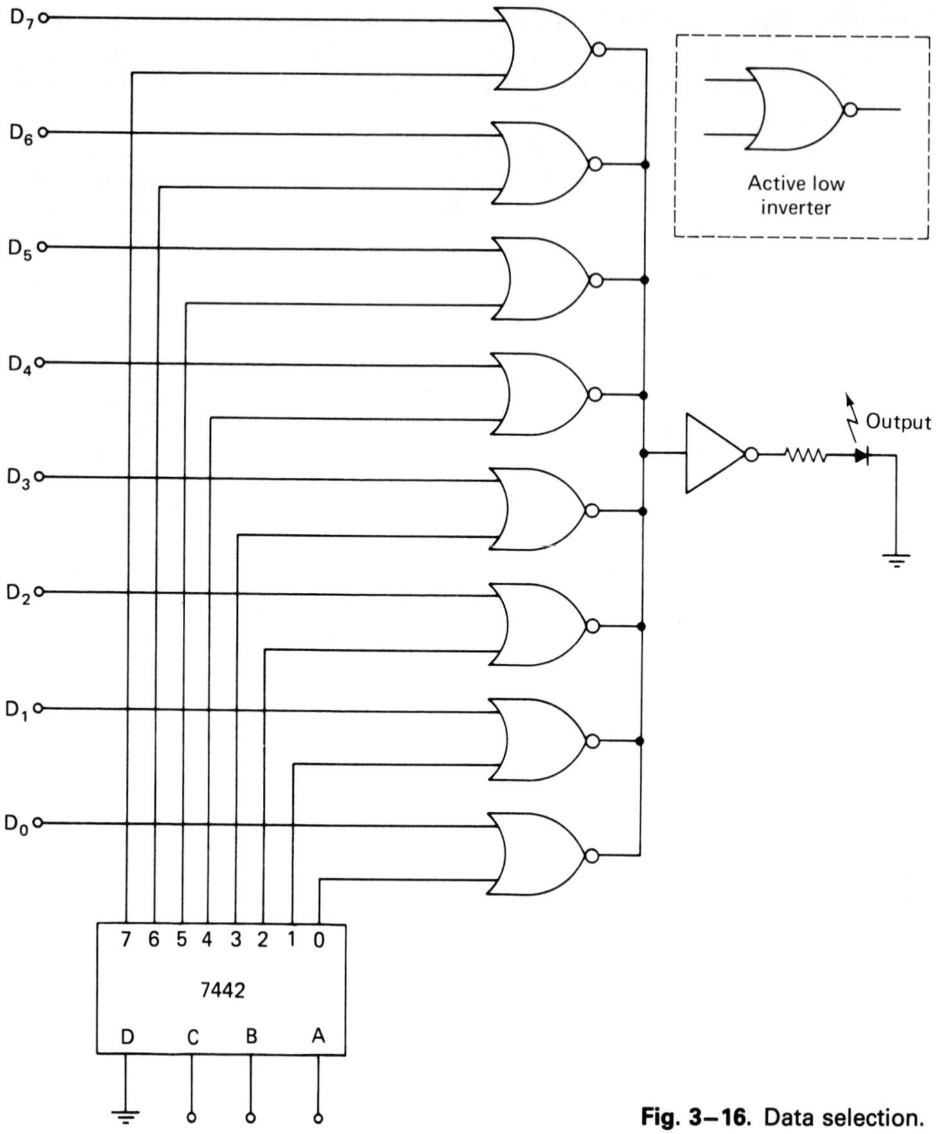

Fig. 3–16. Data selection.

at the output line of a system. Again, the 7442 decoder chip could be used to select the proper data line as shown in Fig. 3–16.

With this circuit arrangement, the address line selected goes low causing the proper NOR gate to become active and pass data to the output. Because the NOR gate output is inverted, it is reinverted on the output line to duplicate the input data. This multiplexing concept is commercially available in several combinations such as the 74150 (1-of-16), 74151 (1-of-8) and 74153 (1-of-4).

CODE CONVERTERS

The use of multiplex and demultiplex chips can be further applied as code converters as well as simple decoders.

Generating Logic Functions

In some cases of design it may become necessary to provide a custom package or circuit that obeys particular truth table requirements as illustrated in Table 3–1.

Rather than resorting to digital design application of Karnaugh mapping, deMorgan's theorem and minimization techniques, the solution can be easily handled using a simple 1-of-16 multiplex chip such as the 74150.

By connecting the properly selected input lines to either a 0 or 1 as required by the truth table, the proper 0 or 1 response can be selected by applying the truth table input requirements as data line addresses. The circuit is shown in Fig. 3–17.

This method is significant because the truth table requirements may be changed at will by making the 0s and 1s for the input lines switch selectable. The choice of employing this method is determined by several considerations such as complexity and time spent for "gates

Table 3-1 Truth Table

INPUTS	OUTPUT REQUIRED
0000	0
0001	0
0010	1
0011	1
0100	1
0101	0
0110	0
0111	1
1000	0
1001	1
1010	0
1011	1
1100	1
1101	0
1110	1
1111	1

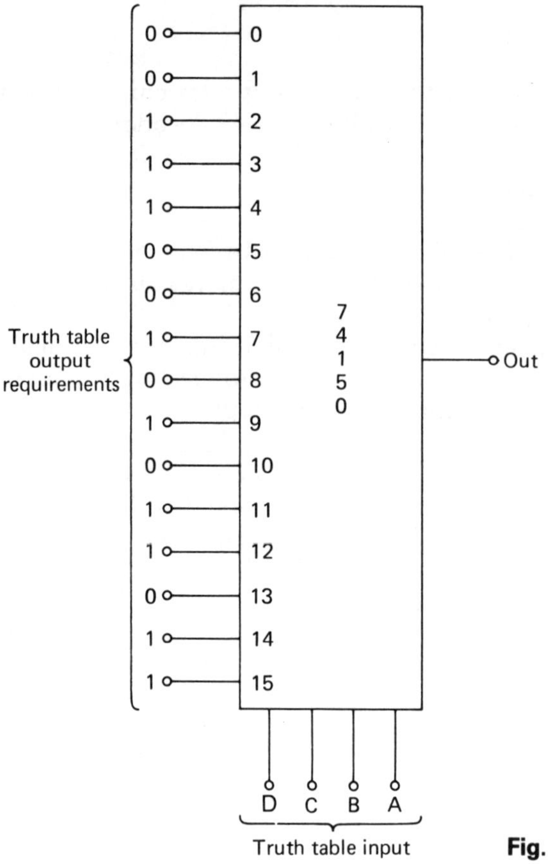

Fig. 3–17. 16-bit data selector.

only" design, cost of the whole system and whether or not the circuit will require frequent changes as a finished product.

Read Only Memories (ROMs)

The use of multiplex devices lends itself nicely to the construction and fabrication of customized ROMs. A ROM is a universal "look up table." That is, for each unique *set* of inputs there is a unique *set* of outputs. They are available from manufacturers in either blank or preprogrammed form. The preprogrammed devices are expensive because they are manufactured with the table mask installed and the design cost of the mask is a significant portion of the overall cost. Preprogrammed ROMs find their primary market in the manufacturing production runs where the design cost can be distributed over several thousand pieces.

Another type of ROM is the PROM or field programmable read only memory. The user may purchase "blank" PROMs from the semiconductor manufacturer and program them himself using special equipment that will burn in these units at his facility. This gives the ROM user much greater flexibility since he can "burn in" a PROM on site and hence reduce turn around time significantly.

The problem of program changes still remains. During the prototyping period, a number of changes are likely to be needed in both software and hardware. With a PROM, once a program is burned in, the process is irreversible and no changes can be made to the program.

Fortunately, another member of the ROM family provides the nonvolatility that is required yet permits the system designer to alter the program even after it is entered into the ROM. This type of memory is called an EPROM or erasable programmable read only memory which makes use of the capacitive charge phenomenon introduced during the programming cycle. When necessary, the EPROM may be reprogrammed periodically by erasing the current program with the application of a specialized ultraviolet light source focused on the transparent lid which is on the top of the package. The EPROM requires special programming and erasing equipment. However, the cost of this equipment is justified by the flexibility and fast turn around time these units provide.

A more recent development is the EEPROM, electrically erasable programmable read only memory. The EEPROM has program/erase capability onboard. Such in-system program alteration does not require the specialized equipment needed for programming and erasing the EPROM. So the EEPROM is cost-effective and ideally suited for systems requiring information updates.

SUMMARY

As was stated in the introduction to this chapter, the material presented here provides a basic introduction to the digital concepts necessary for microprocessor applications. In summation, the concepts presented are:

- Basic gates used as active devices
- Using basic gates for flip-flop circuits, debouncing, latches, counters and shift registers
- Decoding concepts
- Multiplexing and demultiplexing
- Read only memories

The manufacturers of microprocessors are keenly aware of the profuse availability of various digital solutions to the unique problems that arise with microprocessors. In an attempt to simplify the user's dilemma of how best to accomplish particular interface operations, the manufacturers have spent considerable time, money and effort to produce families of chips specifically designed to be compatible with their microprocessors.

QUESTIONS

1. Name the basic gates.
2. There are two ways to think of functions served by gates. Which is preferred by microprocessors? Why?
3. Define the terms active high and active low.
4. What does the inverter accomplish in the active gate concept?
5. What is contact bounce?
6. What should debouncing accomplish?
7. An SPDT switch debouncer is basically what type of circuit?
8. Explain the meaning of the term flip-flop.
9. Explain the difference between a master-slave and a D-type flip-flop.
10. Explain the difference between edge clocking and level clocking.
11. What does the term race mean?
12. How do single phase clocked systems differ from 2-phase clocked systems?
13. State some of the basic flip-flop applications.
14. What does a decoder do?
15. Explain the difference between multiplex and demultiplex.
16. What is a ROM?
17. What are the advantages of EPROMs and EEPROMs in terms of flexibility and cost-effectiveness?

Chapter 4

The Instruction Sets

GLOSSARY

Addressing mode The method that selected registers use when locating the source or the destination operands.

Data Facts, numbers or other information that can be processed or produced by a computer.

Machine language The basic binary code used by all computers. It can be written in either hexadecimal or octal.

Macroinstruction An instruction consisting of a sequence of microinstructions which are inserted into an object routine for performing a specific operation.

Microinstruction A bit pattern stored in a microprogram memory word that specifies the operation of the individual LSI computing elements and related subunits such as main memory and input/output interfaces.

Mnemonics A programming shorthand using letters, numbers and symbols adopted by each manufacturer to represent the instructions in his instruction set.

Operand The fundamental quantity which specifies where the mathematical or logical operation is to be performed.

Operating code (op code) The specific code containing source statements that generates machine codes after assembly.

Programming model Pictorial representation of the functional elements and architectural features that can be manipulated by the instruction set.

The instruction set of a microprocessor is like the letters of the alphabet. When considered individually, for their own ability, they may not seem too significant. When put together in proper sequence with adequate planning their possibilities become almost endless. Like an effective writer, a skilled programmer knows the abilities and nuances of the instructions well enough to make dramatically efficient and subtly programmed operations. As with writing, there is the flavor of art and creativity in program construction. A good program, like a good book, reads smoothly and ties together well.

This chapter describes the basic instruction capabilities of most microprocessors in much the same way that the first studies of a language deal with rules and phonics and progress to sentence structure and parts of speech. Later chapters deal with programming as an area of study much like the study of literature and composition.

Programs can be written in as many varied individual styles as literature. Each person must develop the technique that best suits his own style. As with authors, some programmers are great, most are adequate and others will never master the fundamentals beyond the basic needs of survival.

The study of programming must begin with the basic rules and their restrictions. The rules the programmer must follow depend upon the **machine language** involved and *must* be obeyed. The instruction sets provided with each machine are the rules and restrictions placed on the programmer. They must be understood before any programs are written for that machine.

In this chapter, the general categories of instructions and their capabilities will be explored and then expanded to two particular machine sets: the Intel 8080/8085 and the Motorola MC6800/6802.

CPU PROGRAMMING MODEL

Internal Organization

By keeping a **programming model** of the microprocessor clearly in mind, a reasonably organized understanding of microprocessor instruction sets can be achieved. Each instruction represents a manipulation the device can accomplish. The way in which that manipulation is carried out depends on the design elements or architecture provided by the manufacturer. Each manufacturer has developed his own system, which, of course, he feels is the best architectural arrangement for carrying out the instructions he had included in his set. Some manufacturers provide two accumulators, others provide only one. A wide variety of memory address registers and pointer register arrangements are available and varying numbers of data registers are promoted.

For the purposes of general discussion, a typical arrangement is shown in Fig. 4–1. The internal flow control and buffering systems typical in all microprocessors are not shown in this diagram.

Figure 4–1 provides a road map of the internal workings of the CPU. Note that there are two instruction registers inside: one labeled **macroinstruction** and the other labeled **microinstruction.** In the course of executing a string of instructions that have been installed in external memory, the sequence of events typically follows this pattern.

Operational Sequence

Fetch 1. An address is established in the program counter (sometimes called the memory address register) as the result

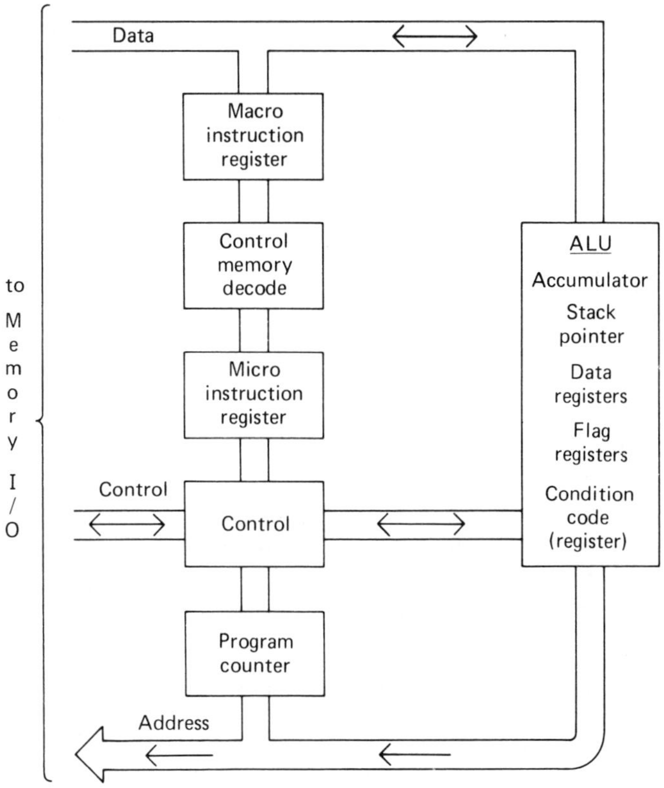

Fig. 4–1. Internal structure (general).

of a previous instruction cycle or as a result of the application of power to the system. This address specifies the location, in memory, of the next instruction to be executed.

2. Through a sequence of control signals this address becomes an output to the system on the address bus. The data at the location specified is brought in on the data bus and installed in the macroinstruction register.

Decode 3. This macroinstruction*, in essence, is an address for the control memory that specifies where in its coded memory it is to start executing the internal sequence of events to accomplish the operations. This preprogrammed sequence of events in the control memory constitutes the microinstructions, which control the internal operations of the CPU.

Execute 4. The sequence of events specified by the microinstructions are carried out. A new address is established in the program counter and the process either begins again or more data is brought in from memory. In fact, this preprogrammed sequence of events provided by the manufacturer when the control memory was produced constitutes the instruction set of the microprocessor.

PROGRAMS IN MEMORY

The programmer or operator does not have access to this set of microinstructions. The program residing in main memory is a microinstruction shopping list specifying the order in which the microinstruction groups are to be used.

Memory Arrangement

Externally, a repetitive fetch, execute, fetch, execute, fetch, execute operation is occurring. Every time a fetch occurs, the CPU brings in from memory a new instruction to be executed or data to continue the operation of some previous instruction. Each set of bits brought in

* Note: The term "macro" here refers to the ALU frame of reference. As far as the ALU is concerned this instruction is macro in form. Moving outside the microprocessor, these macroinstructions will become the smallest machine instructions usable and will thus be referred to as microinstructions. The terms micro and macro are relative terms which will be further explained in point 5 in the summary of points.

constitutes one byte. Some instructions may require no additional data to accomplish their operation while other instructions may require one and sometimes two additional data bytes to complete the operation. A sequence of instruction and data bytes resides in the memory external to the CPU put there by the program writer and arranged in proper order to accomplish some overall task. The arrangement of instruction and data bytes in memory might look something like Fig. 4–2.

In studying Fig. 4–2, it is important to observe and become accustomed to the intermixing of the instructions and **data.** Instructions that require only a single byte and no additional data for execution are followed immediately by another instruction. Instructions requiring one additional byte of data are followed immediately by that data byte. The same is true for instructions requiring two additional bytes.

Microprocessors may use either a fixed length (1-byte) or a variable length (one, two or three bytes) of instruction format depending on the architecture and instruction requirements provided by the manufac-

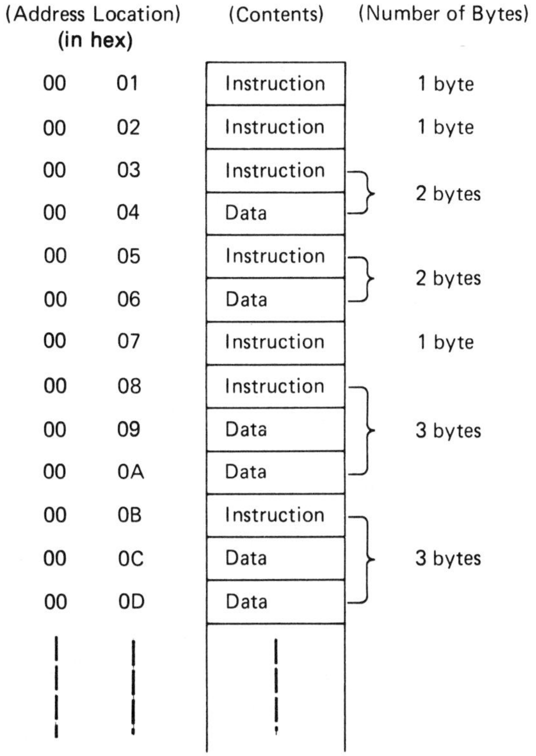

Fig. 4–2. Instruction/data memory arrangement.

turer. Most microprocessors sold are the variable length type because of the complexity of their instruction sets.

Summary of Points

To summarize the points thus far:

1. Microprocessors have either a fixed or a variable length format.
2. The instruction set is installed by the manufacturer during production of the control memory portion of the CPU and is made up of the preprogrammed microinstructions (internal).
3. The sequence of usage of these microinstructions is controlled by the program memory external to the CPU. The programmer sets up this sequence when he writes the program into memory.
4. The microprocessor steps through the program in a fetch and execute cycle repeated continuously.
5. The terms micro and macro have various meanings. Fixed operations which may be carried out by the issuing of a single machine instruction are normally classed as *micro*instructions. Fixed operations requiring two or more machine instructions are generally classed as *macro*instructions. For example, a microcomputer system that has preprogrammed functions such as sin, cos, factorial, square root and examine memory installed in permanent memory may be said to be macroprogrammed. By the same guideline, the machine instructions brought in from memory are considered to be macro to the internal operation of the processor.

INSTRUCTION SET TERMINOLOGY

Operation Versus Operand

Most instructions can be broken into two parts: the operation code or **op code** and the **operand** or **addressing mode.** The op code specifies what is to happen and the operand specifies where the action is to take place. Instructions may be classed in two very broad categories:

Data-based
Non-data-based

Data-based instructions must be long enough to specify the location of the data in question. This type of instruction normally requires more than one byte to be completed.

Non-data-based instructions normally contain only an op code and can be manipulated inside the CPU. While this is not a hard and fast rule, it is generally true. These types of instructions are usually only one byte long.

Classification

The types of categories of op code can be reduced to four:

1. Transfer or data movement
2. Logical and arithmetic operation
3. Program control
4. Special operations

Transfer instructions control the flow of information through the system. Movement of data may take place internally within the CPU or externally from the CPU to memory or from memory to the CPU or between I/O devices and the CPU.

Arithmetic and logic instructions are manipulative in character and perform basic arithmetic (add, subtract, carry) and logical (AND, OR, exclusive OR) operations. These operations use the accumulator as the primary focus of operation. Other elements of the system such as the memory, input and output registers and internal CPU registers may become involved, but the results of the operation are usually left in the accumulator when complete. This group of instructions also sets up the conditions that are tested during program control instructions. These test conditions, called flags, are usually installed in a special register for later reference.

Program control instructions alter the contents of special registers inside the CPU itself. Altering the program counter allows the implementation of discontinuous program flow. By changing the address of the next instruction location, the flow of operation can be branched or altered. These instructions can be conditionally or unconditionally executed by testing the condition code or flag register bits such as zero, sign, carry and overflow.

Special instructions do not fit any of the other three categories. Instructions such as enabling and disabling interrupts, altering the stack pointer and setting mask registers are common in this category. Manufacturers usually provide their "attractive" features and special characteristics for promotion in this group.

Addressing Modes

The microprocessor user should not consider this set of four categories as final. The classification of instructions is sometimes very foggy and does not depend strictly on the op code class. Many times an operand classification system is brought in as part of the overall classification system by the manufacturers. Classification terms have come into existence to describe more completely the functions of some instructions. This is why most manufacturers provide two and sometimes three sets of classifications for the user.

1. Instruction type (op code class)
2. Data format (number of bytes)
3. Address mode (operand class)

The least clearly defined and most often abused terminology exists in the area of addressing modes. Part of the confusion and nonstandard terminology stems from the fact that address information may be generated by arithmetic or logical operations, prestored in pointer registers by other instructions, contained within the instruction word itself or implied within the execution phase of operation.

Debates arise among advocates of different microprocessors because the number of addressing modes is treated as an indicator of the sophistication and flexibility of the processor. In many cases, what one manufacturer calls immediate addressing, another will class as direct addressing and vice versa. What one calls direct another will call extended. The *only* sure way of discussing a particular device's addressing modes is by accepting the manufacturer's definition for that device. Final authority for the classification of instructions rests with the manufacturers.

Following are the addressing mode definitions for the Intel and Motorola systems.

1. When no discrete operand address is present, the mode is *immediate* (the operand is contained in the instruction.) Both Motorola and Intel use additional terminology to describe this classification. Motorola uses the term implied while Intel classes this type of addressing as register. Both manufacturers provide a classification called immediate which requires one additional byte of data. Motorola provides one other addressing classification called accumulator.

2. When the operand portion of an instruction contains the operand address the mode is *direct*. Both Motorola and Intel have a direct classification. Motorola's direct addressing implies an 8-bit (256 bytes) range operand. Intel's direct addressing mode implies a 16-bit (64K-byte range). Motorola also provides a mode called extended which is similar to Intel's direct mode.

3. When the operand portion of the instruction contains the address of a register or pointer which will contain the actual operand, the

mode is *indirect.* Motorola classifies this type of addressing as indexed.

4. When an address is developed by calculation or manipulation the mode is *relative.*

It is quite common to find manufacturers adhering to the first three definitions and yet ignoring the fourth in favor of their own terminology which describes more directly how the relative address is generated. Specific addressing modes and classification systems for both the Motorola MC6800/6802 and Intel 8080/8085 may be found in Appendix 5, Instruction Sets.

Do not make the mistake of assuming that all instructions of the immediate type are 1-byte instructions containing both the op code and operand. A variable length instruction format allows the operand field to be contained in additional bytes containing either data or address information. The only final recourse to resolving classifications and addressing mode confusion is to consult the manufacturer's definitions and adhere to them in reading his literature.

Mnemonics

The term **mnemonics** means the system of letters, numbers and symbols adopted by each manufacturer as abbreviated forms of the instructions in his instruction set. In most cases, the mnemonic is constructed from partial words or the first letters of the verbal statement of the instruction. For example, the instructions for

Add immediate may be ADI
Load accumulator may be LDA
Subtract may be SUB
Increment may be INR
Software interrupt may be SWI.

The mnemonic abbreviation is usually limited to three letters. Another customary practice is to follow the mnemonic form with an abbreviated operand field. For example, ANA r means "And Accumulator with Register." Register is the operand and the designated register would be included in the instruction code or STA A which stands for "Store Accumulator A." If the CPU programming model contained six or eight separate registers this one mnemonic could represent six or eight separate instructions each having a common op code but different operands.

THE INSTRUCTIONS

As previously mentioned, each producer of microprocessors has constructed an instruction set for his device. The Intel and Motorola mnemonic codes are presented in a tabularized format in Tables 4–1 and 4–2.

The diversity of practice in writing mnemonics and the wide variety of instructions provided by the producers can be appreciated by studying the two tables. Detailed descriptions of each instruction and how it functions are found in the instruction sets in Appendix 5.

Intel Table Description

All the Intel mnemonic and operand designations are contained in Table 4–1. In the columns and rows bordering the table both the octal and hexadecimal codes are arranged for easy association with a particular instruction.

For example, in order to find the hexadecimal code for the load H and L (direct) look up the LHLD box. The most significant digit is to the left (2) and the least significant digit is directly above (A). So, the code for LHLD is (2A) hex. The procedure, of course, may be reversed. The octal codes are handled in the same manner with a slight difference. When working on the right side of the chart the (two) MSDs are found in the right hand column labeled OCT. When working on the left half the MSDs are found on the left. The LSD for octal is handled the same as for hexadecimal code.

A * in a box indicates an additional byte required; 2 * indicate two additional bytes. Around the chart where consistent row or column groupings can be observed are the op code mnemonics and operand designations.

For example, in the MOV H,B instruction the op-code mnemonic is MOV and the operand is H (destination) and B (source). Notice that the mnemonic MOV and the H operand may be found in the left and right columns. Directly above the [H ← B] box is the B operand. The arrow in the box shows the direction of the move from B to H.

Many of the characteristics of the instructions and their relationship to one another can be analyzed by studying the chart and border classifications and codes. A study of these relationships makes remembering the instructions and their associated codes much easier. Some of these relationships are listed here.

1. All conditional control instructions are even-numbered codes (even-numbered columns).

2. 0 flag conditions are all on the left.
   1 flag conditions are all on the right.
3. All conditional commands associated with a zero bit check are in the (C) hex code row.

Similar relationships and natural grouping may be found on the chart and are worth studying.

Motorola MC6800/6802 Instruction Map Table Description

In Table 4–2 Motorola has organized the MC6800/6802 instruction set in a neat and convenient instruction map. In the vertical column farthest to the left is the MSB (most significant bit) of the two hexadecimal character op code. In the uppermost row is the LSB (least significant bit) of the two hexadecimal character op code.

For example, assume that the op code 86 is given. The MC6800/6802 instruction map table may be used to easily discover what the hexadecimal op code 86 indicates. Begin by locating the MSB of the op code—in the example 8—in the MSB column which is the column farthest to the left. Now locate the LSB of the op code, which is 6 in this example, in the LSB row that is found as the uppermost row. The instruction in mnemonic form is found at the intersection of the MSB column location 8 and the LSB row location 6. Note at this intersection the following:

LDA
(A)
(IMM)

The instruction mnemonic LDA (load accumulator) is found at the upper left, the (A) at the middle right indicates that accumulator A is to be used and the (IMM) in the lower left states that the addressing mode is immediate.

For the sake of practice, determine what the op code 97 stands for. By using Table 4–2, the instruction 97 is found to be:

STA
(A)
(DIR)

This means store accumulator A using the direct addressing mode.

Note that Motorola uses some of the unimplemented op codes during the final phases of the manufacturing cycle.

Table 4-1 Intel Instruction Set

MNEU	REG	OCT	HEX	← Pair Manipulation	LXI	STORE	INX →	INR ← Single Manipulation	DCR	MVI →	SPECIAL
			REG	B	C	D	E	H	L	M	A
			OCT	0	1	2	3	4	5	6	7
			HEX	0 0000	1 0001	2 0010	3 0011	4 0100	5 0101	6 0110	7 0111
MNEU	REG	OCT	HEX								
	B	00	0 0000	NOP	LXI B **	Indirect STAX B	INX B	INR B	DCR B	MVI B *	RLC
	D	02	1 0001		LXI D **	Indirect STAX D	INX D	INR D	DCR D	MVI D *	RAL
	H	04	2 0010	RIM	LXI H **	Direct** SHLD	INX H	INR H	DCR H	MVI H *	DAA
	SP M	06	3 0011	SIM	LXI SP **	Direct** STA	INX SP	INR M	DCR M	MVI M *	STC
MOV	B	10	4 0100	B←B	B←C	B←D	B←E	B←H	B←L	B←M	B←A
MOV	D	12	5 0101	D←B	D←C	D←D	D←E	D←H	D←L	D←M	D←A
MOV	H	14	6 0110	H←B	H←C	H←D	H←E	H←H	H←L	H←M	H←A
MOV	M	16	7 0111	M←B	M←C	M←D	M←E	M←H	M←L	HLT	M←A
ADD	A	20	8 1000	B	C	D	E	H	L	M	A
SUB	A	22	9 1001	B	C	D	E	H	L	M	A
ANA	A	24	A 1010	B	C	D	E	H	L	M	A
ORA	A	26	B 1011	B	C	D	E	H	L	M	A
Z	6	30	C 1100	RNZ	POP B BC	JNZ **	JMP **	CNZ **	PUSH B BC	ADI *	RST 0
Cy	0	31	D 1101	RNC	POP D DE	JNC **	OUT *	CNC **	PUSH D DE	SUI *	RST 2
P	2	34	E 1110	RPO	POP H HL	JPO **	XTHL	CPO **	PUSH H HL	ANI *	RST 4
S	7	36	F 1111	RP	POP PSW AF	JP **	DI	CP **	PUSH PSW AF	ORI *	RST 6
Flag Bit				Return	POP	JUMP		CALL	PUSH	ARITH	RESTART
				Cond	UNC	Cond	UNC	Cond	UNC	Immediate	UNC

(Flag Bit) "Reset" Cond ←

	DAD	LOAD	DCX	INR	DCR	MVI	SPECIAL					
← Pair Manipulation →				← Single Manipulation →								
B	C	D	E	H	L	M	A	REG				
0	1	2	3	4	5	6	7	OCT				
8 1000	9 1001	A 1010	B 1011	C 1100	D 1101	E 1110	F 1111	HEX				
								HEX	OCT	REG		
	DAD B	Indirect LDAX B	DCX B	INR C	DCR C	MVI C *	RRC	0 0000	01	C	Register Manipulation	TRANSFER OF DATA
	DAD D	Indirect LDAX D	DCX D	INR E	DCR E	MVI E *	RAR	1 0001	03	E		
	DAD H	Direct** LHLD	DCX H	INR L	DCR L	MVI L *	CMA	2 0010	05	L		
	DAD SP	Direct** LDA	DCX SP	INR A	DCR A	MVI A *	CMC	3 0011	07	SP A		
C←B	C←C	C←D	C←E	C←H	C←L	C←M	C←A	4 0100	11	C	MOV	
E←B	E←C	E←D	E←E	E←H	E←L	E←M	E←A	5 0101	13	E	MOV	
L←B	L←C	L←D	L←E	L←H	L←L	L←M	L←A	6 0110	15	L	MOV	
A←B	A←C	A←D	A←E	A←H	A←L	A←M	A←A	7 0111	17	A	MOV	
B	C	D	E	H	L	M	A	8 1000	21	A	ADC	ARITH / ACCUMULATOR
B	C	D	E	H	L	M	A	9 1001	23	A	SBB	
B	C	D	E	H	L	M	A	A 1010	25	A	XRA	LOGIC
B	C	D	E	H	L	M	A	B 1011	27	A	CMP	
RZ	RET	JZ **		CZ **	CALL **	ACI *	RST 1	C 1100	31	6	Z	CONTROL
RC		JC **	IN *	CC **		SBI *	RST 3	D 1101	33	0	Cy	
RPE	PCHL	JPE **	XCHG	CPE **		XRI *	RST 5	E 1110	35	2	P	
RM	SPHL	JM **	EI	CM **		CPI *	RST 7	F 1111	37	7	S	
Return		JUMP		CALL		ARITH	RESTART			*Flag* bit		
Cond	UNC	Cond	UNC	Cond	UNC	Immediate	UNC					

→ "Set" Condition (Flag Bit)

Table 4-2 Motorola Instruction Set

MSB \ LSB	0	1	2	3	4	5	6	7	8	9	A	B	C	D	E	F
0	*	NOP (INH)	*	*	*	*	TAP (INH)	TPA (INH)	INX (INH)	DEX (INH)	CLV (INH)	SEV (INH)	CLC (INH)	SEC (INH)	CLI (INH)	SEI (INH)
1	SBA	CBA	*	*	*	*	TAB (INH)	TBA (INH)	*	DAA (INH)	*	ABA (INH)	*	*	*	*
2	BRA (REL)	*	BHI (REL)	BLS (REL)	BCC (REL)	BCS (REL)	BNE (REL)	BEQ (REL)	BVC (REL)	BVS (REL)	BPL (REL)	BMI (REL)	BGE (REL)	BLT (REL)	BGT (REL)	BLE (REL)
3	TSX (INH)	INS (INH)	PUL (A)	PUL (B)	DES (INH)	TXS (INH)	PSH (A)	PSH (B)	*	RTS (INH)	*	RTI (INH)	*	*	WAI (INH)	SWI (INH)
4	NEG (A)	*	*	COM (A)	LSR (A)	*	ROR (A)	ASR (A)	ASL (A)	ROL (A)	DEC (A)	*	INC (A)	TST (A)	*	CLR (A)
5	NEG (B)	*	*	COM (B)	LSR (B)	*	ROR (B)	ASR (B)	ASL (B)	ROL (B)	DEC (B)	*	INC (B)	TST (B)	*	CLR (B)
6	NEG (IND)	*	*	COM (IND)	LSR (IND)	*	ROR (IND)	ASR (IND)	ASL (IND)	ROL (IND)	DEC (IND)	*	INC (IND)	TST (IND)	JMP (IND)	CLR (IND)
7	NEG (EXT)	*	*	COM (EXT)	LSR (EXT)	*	ROR (EXT)	ASR (EXT)	ASL (EXT)	ROL (EXT)	DEC (EXT)	*	INC (EXT)	TST (EXT)	JMP (EXT)	CLR (EXT)
8	SUB (A) (IMM)	CMP (A) (IMM)	SBC (A) (IMM)	*	AND (A) (IMM)	BIT (A) (IMM)	LDA (A) (IMM)	*	EOR (A) (IMM)	ADC (A) (IMM)	ORA (A) (IMM)	ADD (A) (IMM)	CPX (A) (IMM)	BSR (REL)	LDS (IMM)	*
9	SUB (A) (DIR)	CMP (A) (DIR)	SBC (A) (DIR)	*	AND (A) (DIR)	BIT (A) (DIR)	LDA (A) (DIR)	STA (A) (DIR)	EOR (A) (DIR)	ADC (A) (DIR)	ORA (A) (DIR)	ADD (A) (DIR)	CPX (A) (DIR)	*	LDS (DIR)	STS (DIR)
A	SUB (A) (IND)	CMP (A) (IND)	SBC (A) (IND)	*	AND (A) (IND)	BIT (A) (IND)	LDA (A) (IND)	STA (A) (IND)	EOR (A) (IND)	ADC (A) (IND)	ORA (A) (IND)	ADD (A) (IND)	CPX (A) (IND)	JSR (IND)	LDS (IND)	STS (IND)
B	SUB (A) (EXT)	CMP (A) (EXT)	SBC (A) (EXT)	*	AND (A) (EXT)	BIT (A) (EXT)	LDA (A) (EXT)	STA (A) (EXT)	EOR (A) (EXT)	ADC (A) (EXT)	ORA (A) (EXT)	ADD (A) (EXT)	CPX (A) (EXT)	JSR (EXT)	LDS (EXT)	STS (EXT)
C	SUB (B) (IMM)	CMP (B) (IMM)	SBC (B) (IMM)	*	AND (B) (IMM)	BIT (B) (IMM)	LDA (B) (IMM)	*	EOR (B) (IMM)	ADC (B) (IMM)	ORA (B) (IMM)	ADD (B) (IMM)	*	*	LDX (IMM)	*
D	SUB (B) (DIR)	CMP (B) (DIR)	SBC (B) (DIR)	*	AND (B) (DIR)	BIT (B) (DIR)	LDA (B) (DIR)	STA (B) (DIR)	EOR (B) (DIR)	ADC (B) (DIR)	ORA (B) (DIR)	ADD (B) (DIR)	*	*	LDX (B) (DIR)	STX (B) (DIR)
E	SUB (B) (IND)	CMP (B) (IND)	SBC (B) (IND)	*	AND (B) (IND)	BIT (B) (IND)	LDA (B) (IND)	STA (B) (IND)	EOR (B) (IND)	ADC (B) (IND)	ORA (B) (IND)	ADD (B) (IND)	*	*	LDX (IND)	STX (IND)
F	SUB (B) (EXT)	CMP (B) (EXT)	SBC (B) (EXT)	*	AND (B) (EXT)	BIT (B) (EXT)	LDA (B) (EXT)	STA (B) (EXT)	EOR (B) (EXT)	ADC (B) (EXT)	ORA (B) (EXT)	ADD (B) (EXT)	*	*	LDX (EXT)	STX (EXT)

DIR = Direct Addressing Mode
EXT = Extended Addressing Mode
IMM = Immediate Addressing Mode

IND = Index Addressing Mode
INH = Inherent Addressing Mode
REL = Relative Addressing Mode

A = Accumulator A
B = Accumulator B

*Unimplemented Op Code

The Programming Models

Throughout the rest of the text, sample programs and instruction sequences will be presented. Always try to analyze the instructions presented in light of the programming models for the system being used. The programming models for the Motorola MC6800/6802 and Intel 8080/8085 appear in Fig. 4–3 and Fig. 4–4. Diligent, step-by-step analysis of the instructional sequences provided will make the content of the material much more meaningful.

A programming model contains all the elements and architectural features that are used or manipulated by the instruction set.

SUMMARY

1. Most instructions have two parts:
   a. Op code—specifies operation
   b. Operand—where or upon what data the operation is to occur.
2. There are two broad categories of instructions:
   a. Data-based—require data
   b. Non-data-based—manipulation
3. All instructions can be classed in one of four types:
   a. Transfer
   b. Arithmetic and logic
   c. Program control
   d. Special
4. Classification of instructions varies from company to company.
5. Mode of addressing is probably the least standard of any of the categorizing systems.
6. Final responsibility for definitions and classifications of instructions rests with the producer of the device.
7. Many manufacturers have developed other terms to describe their addressing modes which are more descriptive of the functional procedure.
8. Mnemonics are a shorthand method of writing instructions. There are very few rules for the construction of these abbreviations other than they are usually three letters long and may or may not have operand abbreviations appended to them.

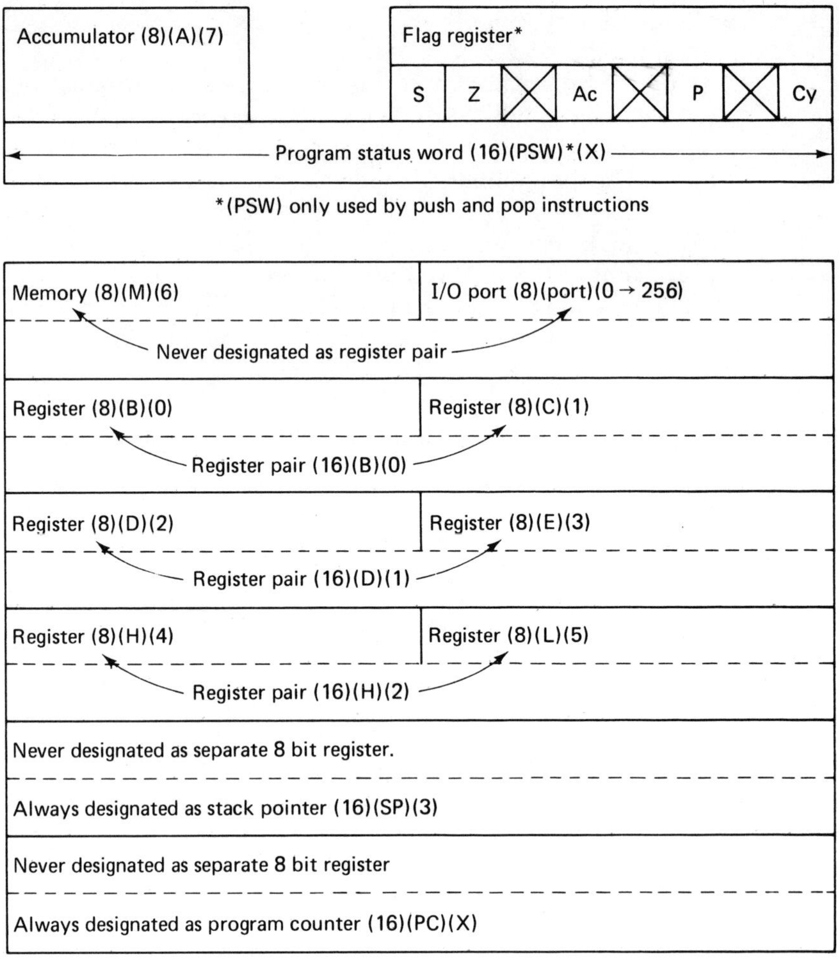

S = sign   Z = zero   Ac = auxiliary carry   p = parity   cy = carry

Key to programming model code designation

Name (number of bits) (mneumonic letter designation) (octal number   DDD or SSS designation)

*Bits are considered separately by branching instructions.

Fig. 4–3. Intel programming model.

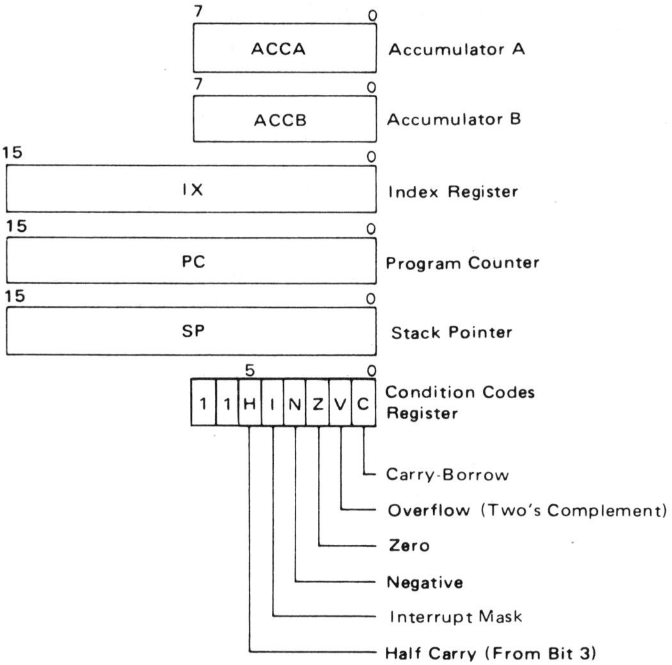

Fig. 4–4. Motorola MC6800/6802 programming model. (*Courtesy Motorola Inc.*)

9. When analyzing an instructional sequence, a programming model of the device should be kept clearly in mind.

QUESTIONS

1. What is a programming model?
2. What is the difference between macroinstructions and micro-instructions?
3. Define variable length format.
4. There are two parts to an instruction. Name and define them.
5. Name the four general categories of op codes.
6. Give the addressing modes and explain how they function for the Intel 8080/8085.
7. Give the addressing modes and explain how they function for the Motorola MC6800/6802.
8. What are mnemonics?

9. Look up the mnemonic symbol for the following instruction codes given in hexadecimal for the Intel 8080/8085.

00	3C	6B
B2	C3	22
D2	CF	0B
76	FF	1F
4A	8D	

10. Look up the mnemonic symbols for the following instruction codes given in hexadecimal for the Motorola MC6800/6802.

1B	43	7E
27	19	86
2A	4A	01
20	88	97
4F	4C	

Chapter 5

Introduction to Software

GLOSSARY

Algorithm A prescribed set of well-defined rules or processes for the solution of a problem in a finite number of steps.

Branch Conditional A point at which alternate paths of accomplishment can be caused to occur dependent on conditions.

Branch Unconditional To always continue operation at some other point.

Branching A method of selecting, on the basis of the computer results, the next operation to execute while a program is in progress.

Control To exert influence or cause change. Devices that carry out instructions in proper sequence and apply signals to other devices.

Data Information not of an instructional type. A general term used to denote information that can be processed or produced by a computer.

Diagnostic A program that utilizes specific functions and capabilities of a system to test or exercise those functions, giving indications of their correctness.

Flag A bit or bits stored for later use, indicating the existence of a previous or a present condition.

Flow chart A programmer's tool for determining a sequence of operations as charted using sets of symbols, directional marks and other representations to indicate stepped procedures of computer operation; a chart containing all the logical steps in a particular computer program; also referred to as a flow diagram.

Iterating To repeat an operation or program loop several times in a progressive manner, each repetition or iteration accomplishing a fractional portion of the final result.

Logic Applying reasoning or sound sense. As applied to programming, the reasonable development of a proper sequence of events.

Machine Level In binary form when used to indicate language sophistication or capability as contrasted with a high-level language.

Nesting The use of routines and looping subroutines within large routines in such a way that execution occurs in a recursive manner.

Partitioning The isolation, identification, or separation of functions or job blocks. The defining of submodules or routines necessary to a program solution.

Precision Exact, careful, strict. Pertaining to clarity and care in procedural accomplishment.

Programming Model A pictorial representation of the functional elements and architectural features that can be manipulated by an instruction set.

Syntax Rules of structure applied to the instructions in a computer language.

Programming is the art of giving precise instructions. In everyday life, most humans are not very precise in the instructions and requests given to others simply because they make the assumption that the receiver of those instructions will interpret them correctly. Most disagreements and conflicts are caused because one party has communicated incompletely with the other. The fastest way to irritate someone is to follow his directions literally and do only those things which are possible under the given circumstances.

COMPLETE PROBLEM APPROACH

An example of an incomplete request is the common dinner phrase, "Pass the salt, please." If there were a group of computers sitting at the table, the salt would never be passed. Why? There is, in this simple request, much missing information such as:

1. What is salt?
2. Where is the salt?
3. Who is to pass the salt?
4. To whom is the salt to be passed?
5. What is the procedure?

For the salt to be passed properly and arrive at its desired destination, the person giving the instructions has to make sure that all the necessary information inherent in the request is available. That is, prior to making the request, the positions to which the salt could be passed, those people who may pass the salt and the proper sequence of actions to accomplish the passing of the salt must be specified. The term salt must be defined. The person to receive the salt must identify himself. His position at the table must be a valid one for the reception of the salt. Finally, the person who is nearest to the salt at the time of the request must be able to react to the request.

In much the same way, the job of the programmer is not a simple one. Like the person requesting the salt, he must necessarily "think of everything." If he does not, the program being designed will not work.

As one reads texts on programming methods, a pattern of approach to problem solving begins to emerge. It is just good common sense—if you are confronted with a problem, it makes sense to know as much about the problem as you possibly can before attempting a solution. You need to understand the limits of the requirements, the definitions of the terms involved, and the desired results if a solution is to be found. One cannot hope to solve a problem if the problem is not completely understood first. This phase of problem solving is referred to as generating program requirements, defining the parameters, or partitioning the solution.

Defining the Problem

During the search for the problem definition, a lot of the decision making concerning the method of solution is done. The definition of the problem must be as complete as possible. An analogy here seems appropriate. Let us assume that the problem is to get to Peoria, Illinois by the 15th of January at 9:00 in the morning. Some basic questions must be answered before the method of solution becomes apparent:

1. Where exactly is Peoria?
2. Where exactly am I?
3. What is the date today, and what time is it? (If it is 6:00 P.M. on January 14 and you are in San Francisco, you must make some quick decisions about modes of transportation and the solution to the problem.)

Next, some questions that could affect the details of the solution must be answered:

1. How much money can be spent?
2. Why am I going to Peoria? Recreation? Business?
3. Will a return trip be necessary?

The point is this. Although the original statement of the problem was clear and precise, there was not enough information in the statement to start generating a solution. This process of defining the problem obviously affects the choice of solution. The more thoroughly it is done, the easier the final solution decisions become.

Once the initial questions have been answered as completely as possible, it is time to restate the problem in more concise terms, calling out the details that affect the solution. For example, the problem is to fly to Peoria, Illinois on the 10:00 P.M. flight leaving San Francisco. The flight is Ace Airlines #109. The purpose of the trip: business meeting at 9:00 A.M. tomorrow morning (take one suit); return flight is at 3:00 P.M. tomorrow on flight #247. The temperature in Peoria tomorrow is predicted to be − 15°F with blizzard conditions prevailing throughout the day (pack weather gear). At this stage of solution, one can safely assume that the trip is on and that a solution is at least possible. Therefore, it is time to take action to accomplish the solution. The necessary arrangements must be accomplished one at a time, and priorities must be assigned. This process of deciding what to do first, second, third, and so on is called *ordering* or *sequencing* the problem. Next, break the problem down into individual job functions to be accomplished. Once the major jobs have been broken out, one begins asking pertinent questions about each of the job blocks to break them down further. This process of breaking the problem down into its component parts is called *partitioning*. It is primarily an intellectual activity involving asking the right questions and making the right decisions based on the answers to those questions. One can attach many terms and fancy titles to this process, but what it boils down to is a clear, methodical, and logical thinking through of a possible solution.

To put the definition phase of program design into perspective, it must be understood that one cannot answer *all* the questions that are inherent in the solution before the design begins. Some of the proper questions will only become apparent as the solution begins to emerge. However, one thing is clear: the clearer the problem statements are at the beginning, the easier the questions are to ask and answer as one approaches the end product.

The computer programmer has a unique problem in that he or she has available a machine that will do anything it is asked to do as long as the programmer can figure out how to tell it exactly *what* to do. The task is made somewhat more difficult by the fact that computers are exquisitely stupid. No assumptions can be made. The machine must be told everything *exactly* and *precisely*. This exactitude and precision is the frustrating part to us human beings. Humans do not typically think in precise and detailed ways. Generalization is the rule and exactness is the exception when humans get involved.

The amount of frustration one experiences in writing programs is inversely proportionate to the discipline one has achieved in making precise and logical decisions.

Approaching the Problem

In most cases, programming is accomplished in a sequence that starts with general concepts and progresses, by necessity, to the details of machine level object codes. Each of the phases of the sequence must be well documented so that the programmer's train of thought is easily understood by others who may be required to use the program. For the purpose of documentation and clarity, a system of symbols and statements has been created for use by the programmer and program user. This system is implemented by a hierarchy of flowchart diagrams. The levels of detail included in the flow chart diagrams are defined as follows.

1. Conceptual level: sequential set of general statements concerned with what is to be accomplished at each block of the program.
2. Algorithm level: sequential set of detailed statements concerned primarily with how each conceptual statement is to be accomplished.
3. Instruction level: sequential set of instructions that will accomplish the objective of each algorithm block. Usually in mnemonic format and tailored to the capabilities of a particular machine instruction set.
4. Machine level: the set of binary coded instructions in the format that the machine is capable of accepting.

The conceptual and algorithm levels are not normally developed with a particular microprocessor in mind. The instruction and machine levels, however, are always generated using a particular microprocessor's instruction set as the guide to the ultimate sequence required.

Designing the Program

Look at the flowchart in Figure 5–1 carefully. The first operation of any programmer is to define the problem and determine if a solution is possible. Once the commitment to go for a solution has been made, the next job is to begin the design. As shown in Figure 5–2, the primary task is to arrive at a sequence of tasks that will result in proper operation. In the definition phase, the major functions to be accomplished have already been laid out. These can then be broken down

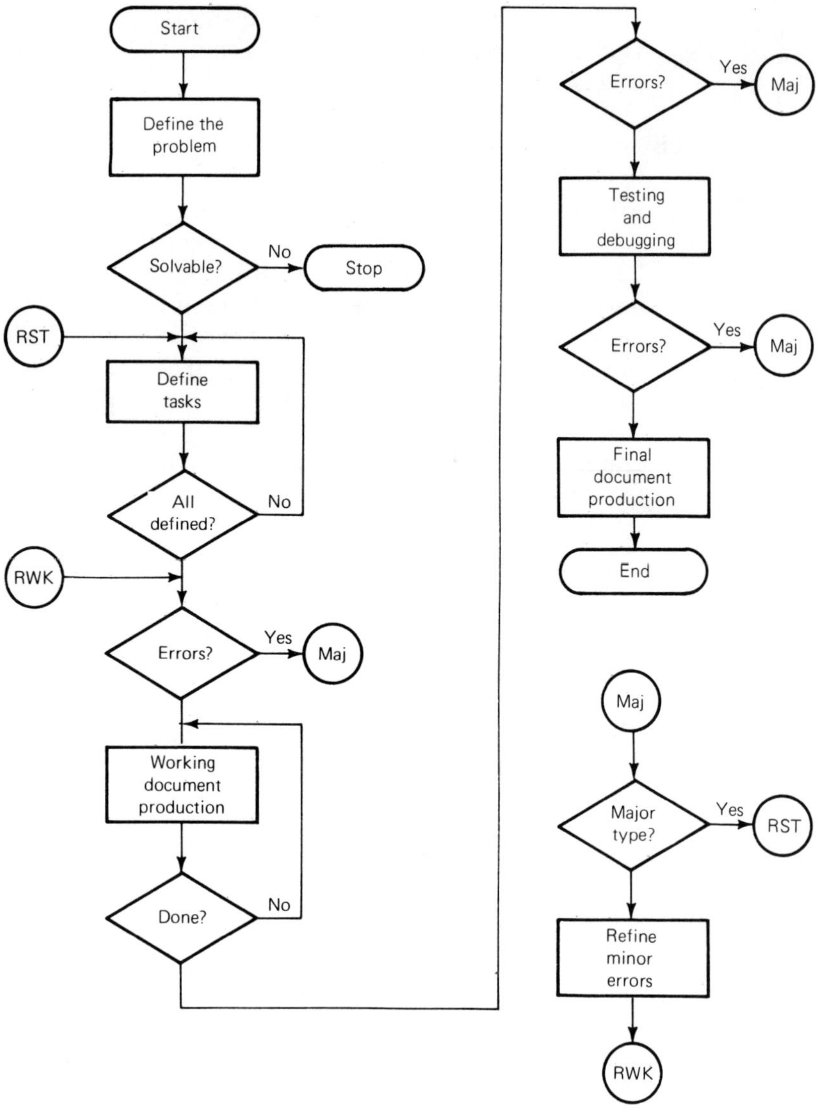

Fig. 5–1. Flowchart for sequence of solution.

into subordinate tasks and routines that are related through either data flow or control flow aspects of the major blocks. The term *data flow* refers to where the data resides at what time in the program operation. For example, the general flow of data is to first acquire the data from a source outside the computer system, process it, and then display it. In diagram form, this might look as shown in Figure 5–3. In the early

Sequence of Solution

Steps	Stage
Find the parameters and restrictions State the desired results Determine the forms of input and output Partition or modularize the tasks as much as possible	Define the problem
Sequence the tasks in logical order Determine the hierarchy of dependency Define the data and control flow linkages	Design the program
Determine the language Write the modules or subtasks Check for syntax and terminology Produce flowcharts, source listings, and object files	Produce a working document
Run the program Isolate the problems The final operation document	Test and check the program

Fig. 5–2. Sequence of solution.

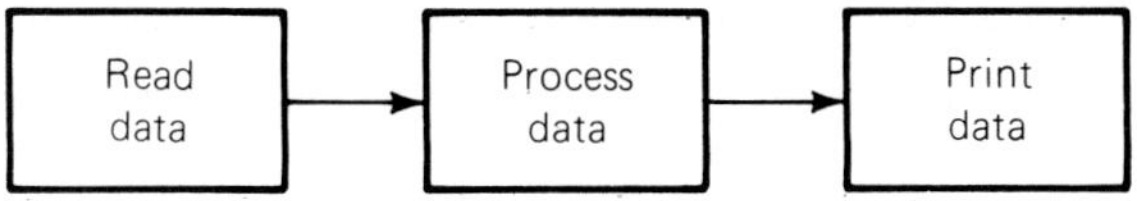

Fig. 5–3. Data flow routine.

stages of refinement and design, the generalized blocks may seem trivial; however, they form the basis for later expansion.

Control flow may be more familiar to the reader as what are classically called *flowcharts*. Flowcharts are an early definition of how material is to be processed and when. In general terms, data flow defines *what* is to be done, and control flow defines the *how* and *when* aspect of the process. These early "thinking" diagrams will become the major documentation that keeps the programmer in touch with the system he or she is creating. As the successive refinements of detail proceed further and further, the interrelationship and dependency become more pronounced. This is precisely why the early stages of design are so important. If the early definitions are not clear, the later design can become a nightmare of revising, rethinking, and patching up a bad program.

The overall design task should not be considered complete until no errors are apparent. Also, the task statements should, as much as possible, be in a common language such as English. The use of a particular computer language or terminology will only complicate things at this stage of development. The result of this effort should be workable algorithms that deal with the problem solution and that are not machine or language oriented beyond the general considerations for computer systems. Particular machine capabilities and languages fall into the realm of the working documents.

The production of working documents involves transforming the algorithms into a particular language format or machine program. The difficulty of this phase of the programming problem depends to a great extent on the language level capabilities of the machine involved.

Programming Steps

In summary, the general procedure used in programming is as follows.

1. **Define the task** Collect all the pertinent data concerning input, outputs and requirements of the program to be written.

2. **Conceptual flow** Define the sequence of major operational blocks. Thoroughness here is essential. The blocks should primarily define what is to occur and not how it is to be accomplished.

3. **Algorithm flow** Each conceptual block is broken down into steps of accomplishment. These steps are primarily devoted to the how consideration of the program. Algorithms should not be biased to a particular machine. A mental trace of the program should be done here to catch any errors of operations that might occur.

4. **Instruction level flow** The algorithm steps are expanded upon and adapted to a particular machine characteristic. No major program-

ming changes should be attempted at this level. Primary considerations here are the machine instructions, microprocessor architecture, bit manipulations and address handling.

5. **Machine level coding** The instructional steps are converted into binary bit trains and numbers. This conversion is normally handled by a resident program within the machine system being used. Manual coding is very error-prone.

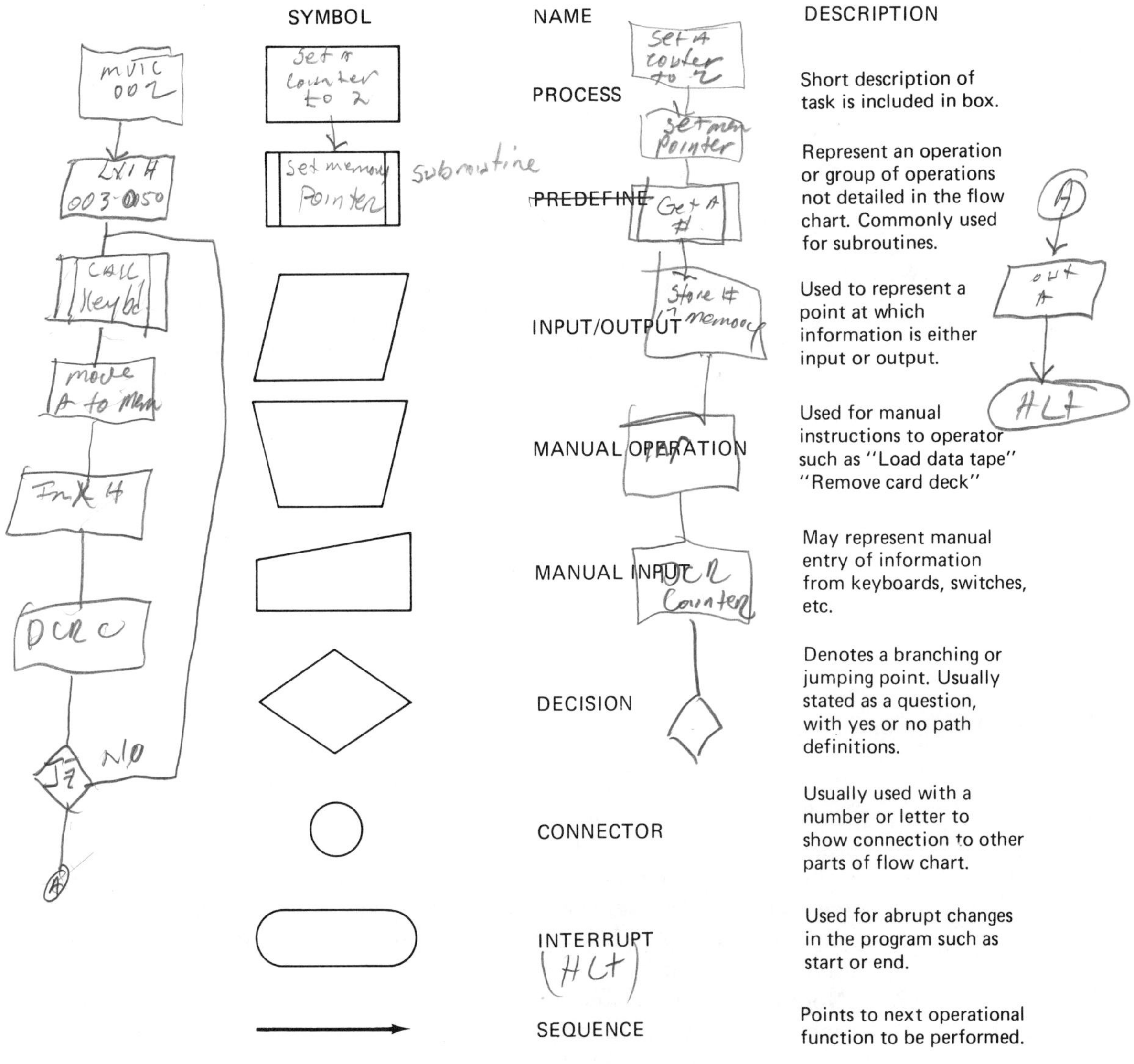

Fig. 5–4. Common flow chart symbols.

Flow Chart Symbols

Included in Fig. 5–4 are a few of the most common flow chart symbols used in programming.

THE PROGRAMMING MODEL

Microprocessors manufactured today only accept machine-level instructions. However, many manufacturers have developed microcomputer systems that accept a limited number of high-level language packages. The average household consumer is likely to purchase one of these home personal computers and use the specialized programs that have been developed for them. Most personal computer packages have been developed using BASIC, and most of the home users will not be intimately involved with the host machine language. The industrial technician, however, will very likely not be using a high-level language. A person dealing with the microprocessor itself will most likely be operating at the machine code or assembly level. When working at this level of program design or analysis, it is necessary that a clear image or model be available to the programmer, either on paper or in his or her mind.

A programming model consists of a diagram that includes all the registers and functional blocks that the instruction set or language commands can manipulate. When the program design effort finally gets to the working document stage where specific machine-level instructions are being utilized, it is a great assistance to the programmer to be able to visualize the bit manipulations, transfers, and flag structures. The two programming models that will be used throughout this text are shown in Figures 5–5 and 5–6.

Testing and Documentation

The testing phase of the design function is clearly that point at which the developed program is actually run, monitored for errors, and redesigned. If all of the prior design operations have been done properly, any errors found should be minor rather than major. Major design errors at this stage of development can be disastrous, causing a complete redesign. They can be very costly from both a time and a money standpoint.

Note that in the flowchart shown in Figure 5–1 there are decision points after each operation where the preceding work is checked for logic, precision, and accuracy. Any errors found should be immedi-

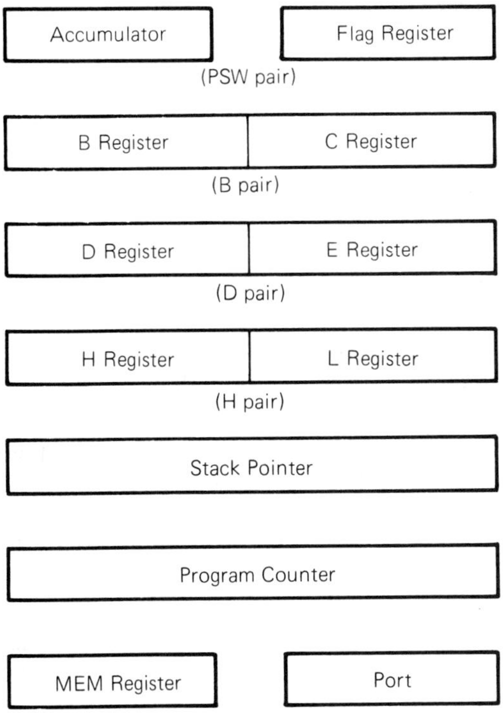

Number of Bits Per Register		Mnemonic Designation
Accumulator	(8)	(A)
Flag	(8)	—
ProgStatus Word	(16)	(PSW)
B Register	(8)	(B)
C Register	(8)	(C)
B Pair	(16)	(B)
D Register	(8)	(D)
E Register	(8)	(E)
D Pair	(16)	(D)
H Register	(8)	(H)
L Register	(8)	(L)
H Pair	(16)	(H)
Stack Pointer	(16)	(SP)
Program Counter	(16)	(PC)
Memory Register	(8)	(M)
Port variable		(Hex #)

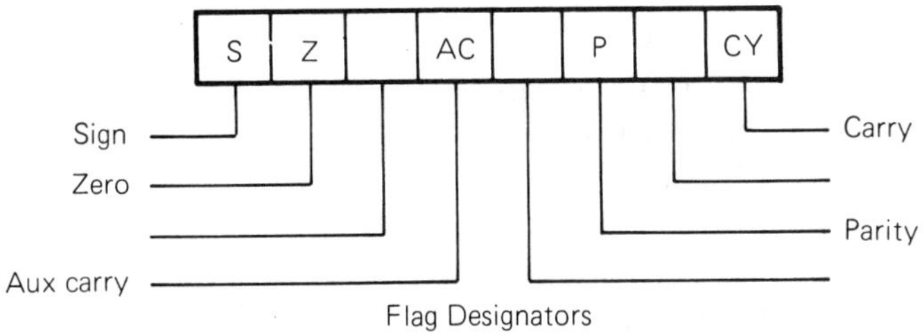

Fig. 5–5. 8080/8085 programming model.

ately rectified and should not be put off until later because it is difficult to change a program late in the design stage.

The final operation in any design is the documentation of the working program and the generation of operator instructions. The final document will be used not only by program operators but also by people who will maintain and update the program in the future. Therefore, it must be very thorough and complete, including any maintenance

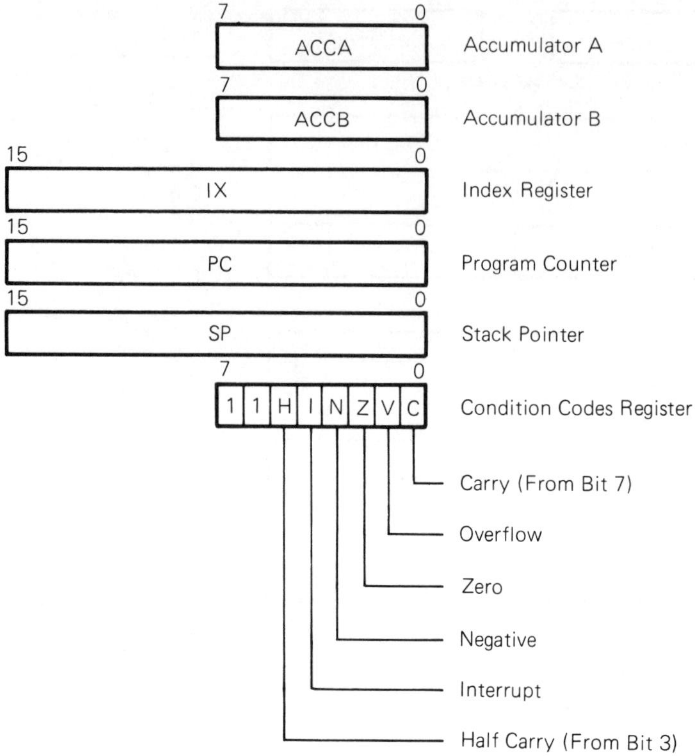

Fig. 5–6. MC6800/6802 programming model. (*Courtesy Motorola Inc.*)

diagnostics, operator instructions, flowcharts, or program listings that enhance the understanding of the program and its operation.

The next section of this chapter deals with more specific methods of design. The reader will observe that the sequence of approach to programming advocated in this section is mirrored in the specific methods discussed. This repetition should impress on the reader the importance of a methodical and well-structured approach to programming. This important concept is often not appreciated or even accepted by programmers until late in their development. Some programmers are never able to accept a highly structured and sequential approach as "the better way." These people, however, are in the minority among their programming colleagues.

APPROACHES TO PROGRAMMING

A good synonym for programming is planning; that is, planning what operations are to be accomplished and in what order. As in planning, programming can be approached in many different ways. The way in which a person organizes his or her thoughts to write a program is as unique and individualized as the person involved. There is no one best way to write programs. Every person must develop the method and approach that best suits his or her own personality or work technique.

Programming by its nature is an organizational task that requires time, effort, and discipline to learn and to maintain. Some of the more accepted methods and techniques are discussed in this section in hopes that the reader will find a combination of methods that will serve his or her future programming efforts.

Flowcharts

Flowcharting is probably the best known and the most widely recognized programming technique. It is also the technique that is the most universal in its application and versatile in its use. Flowcharting techniques are used in many areas other than computer programming. It is the visual aspect of flowcharts that makes them universally applicable and recognizable to people other than programmers.

Most programming texts promote the idea that flowcharting is one of the primary methods used in the design phase of writing programs and that it is normal for a program to have been completely flowcharted prior to the actual writing of individual machine instructions and codes. In the real world this is not the case. Most programmers tend to discount charts and consider them a nuisance. Flowcharts are usually produced after the fact and are relegated to the documentation phase of the programming effort. This approach to writing programs causes a lot of lost time and misdirected effort. Flowcharts and good planning *should* be done prior to machine coding and the assembly process. The average person is not capable of holding within his or her mind all of the details and information necessary to the whole structure of a complex program. The reason most programmers either ignore or misuse flowcharts is subtly hidden in the way most people are introduced to programming. Obviously one cannot begin to learn programming by writing complex programs, and simple programs can be developed without a visual aid. Consequently, flowcharts are usually an afterthought at this stage. Likewise, most teachers require flowcharts for programs submitted for grading. The student, therefore, usually draws the flowcharts *after* completing the program. This habit develops early and dies hard. It is only later in a programmer's career, when perhaps he or she becomes a supervisor in a programming group, that an appreciation for flowcharts develops.

Flowcharts are visual aids to the mental planning process. Their advantages are usually not appreciated until one is confronted with a complex program that is difficult to grasp. Likewise, some of the disadvantages do not become apparent until one is involved with extremely complex programs. For flowcharts to take their proper perspective, it must be remembered that they are used as planning aids and are not an end in themselves.

Advantages of Flowcharts

1. Flowcharts clearly show the sequence of operation and, therefore, aid in locating errors in the debugging process.
2. Flowcharts are of great assistance in breaking down a project into small manageable tasks.
3. Flowcharts can be easily read, understood, and used in areas other than programming.
4. Flowcharts use standard diagrams, symbols, and techniques that are widely known.

Disadvantages of Flowcharts

1. Flowcharts tend to be "rats nest" drawings and are difficult to design clearly. As program complexity increases, readability decreases; consequently, designers have a difficult time in trading off the inclusion of details of operation against the clarity of presentation.
2. Flowcharts are not hardware oriented. That is, they are little help in locating problems related to timing, shorts, disconnected wires, input/output data structures, and the like.
3. Flowcharts are not testable. The only way to verify a flowchart is to check it against the final program. Debugging a flowchart is a mental process that cannot be connected like a circuit for testing. Therefore, the correctness of a flowchart is difficult to either prove or disprove except through logic.

The advantages of flowcharts outweigh their disadvantages. If used properly in the design stages of development, they are a tremendous thinking aid. But when they are produced as a documentation afterthought, their disadvantages seem to loom large in the mind. After all, why put oneself through all that detailed work when the program is already working?

In summary, the advantages of flowcharts are best utilized in the design function. If used in this way, the final documentation of the program will be of a better quality and more easily produced. However, an attempt to include too much detail in a flowchart can make the flowchart design almost as difficult as the program solution itself.

Figure 5–4 shows the basic flowchart symbols, their names, and their fundamental uses. These symbols are standard and have been made into templates for easy drawing. The following paragraphs briefly discuss each symbol.

Flowchart Symbols

Input/Output. An easy way to keep the input/output symbol function clear in your mind is to remember its shape. It is not a nice, square-cornered rectangle like the process symbol. This indicates that it is not a strictly defined function. That is, any operation or function related to input or output is coded using this symbol. Even lighting indicator lamps or rewinding tape would be included. There are other symbols that have been used to indicate the I/O method more graphically, but they are not universally acceptable.

Connector. The connector symbol can be used for two functional indications and has four symbol variations. It can be used to indicate a branch instruction or an entry point. A branch instruction changes the normal flow of operation and allows execution to continue at a point other than the next sequential step. The connector symbol indicating a branch instruction always has the flow line entering from the top or the left (see Figure 5–7(a)).

The symbol in Figure 5–7(a) with the flow line entering from the top is an unconditional branch. This is because exits from a page drawing are always made at the bottom or to the right. A conditional branch is always used with a decision symbol, and the exit is always to the right; therefore, the flow line enters from the left as shown in Figure 5–7(b).

A conditional or unconditional branch connector represents an instruction. An entry connector, however, does not represent an instruction; it serves as a label for an instruction. The label is contained in-

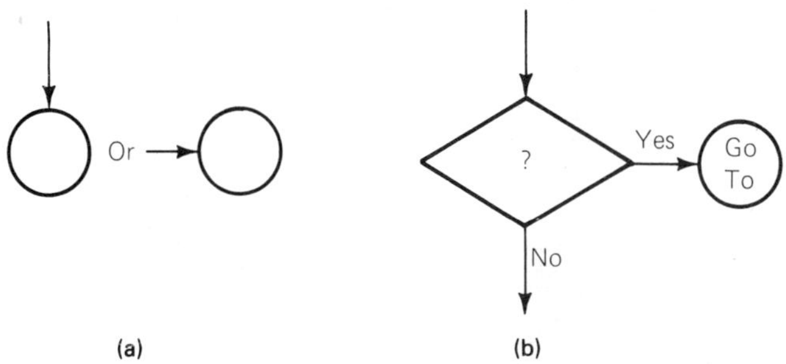

Fig. 5–7. (a) Unconditional branch; (b) conditional branch.

side the connector. For every branch connector, there must be a corresponding entry connector. They are paired symbols, and the labels inside must correspond exactly.

Entry symbols are drawn with the flow line exiting from the bottom or the right (see Figure 5–8(a)). Here again, entry will always be from the top of the page or from the left when entering the middle of a se-

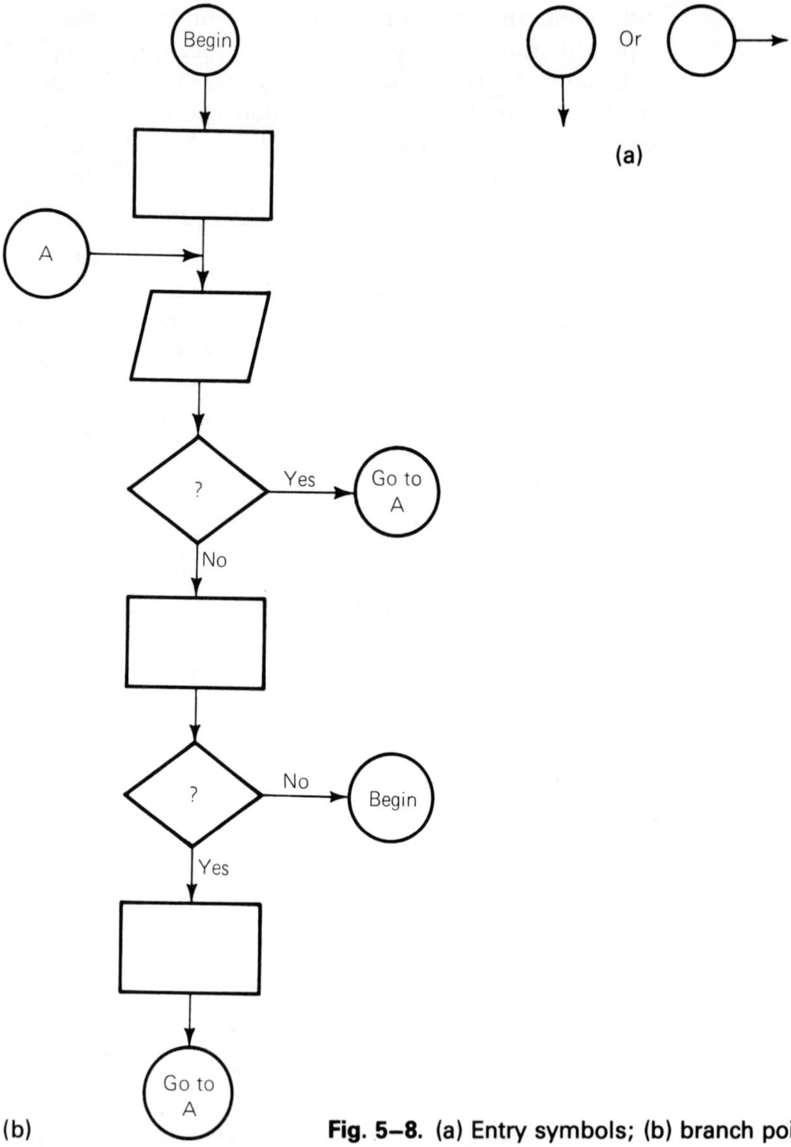

Fig. 5–8. (a) Entry symbols; (b) branch points.

quence. Each entry point must have a unique label and can only occur once. Branch points, however, are not unique. That is, more than one branch can refer to a single entry point, but each entry point is unique. A symbolic example is shown in Figure 5–8(b).

A summary of connector rules is as follows:

1. A connector may be used for branch instructions or entry point labels.
2. Branches have flow lines entering, and entry points have flow lines exiting.
3. An unconditional branch must be the last symbol in a sequence.
4. Branches and entries are paired.
5. Entry into the middle of a sequence must be from the left.

Decision. A computer is more than a calculator because of its ability to alter its operation based upon conditions that arise during processing. This ability is provided by decision- or condition-oriented instructions. Decisions are made in a computer by testing or comparing operational conditions with prestored or specified conditions. These conditional comparisons fall into two categories:

1. Specific content (value or literal content).
2. Relationship of equality ($<$, $>$, $=$, or $\neq$).

When a comparison is made, it is considered to be a test. The computer may then choose only one of two paths of operation dependent on the results of the test. When representing this testing and decision-making process symbolically, only one test per symbol is allowed, and only two alternatives are allowed per test result. In other words, a decision may have only one entry, test one condition, and have only two possible exits, one for a yes (the condition exists) answer and one for a no (the condition does not exist) answer. The symbol is diamond shaped with a flow line at the top, right, and bottom points. The flow is into the top and out the right or bottom. Inside the diamond is a question in either letter or numerical form stating the test condition being compared. (For example, 0?, not 0?; <5?, >7?; 'M'?, 'O'?.) As stated before, only one condition at a time can be checked. Note that nonnumeric literals are contained in quotes, and numerics are simply stated with the required digits. Note that a yes response usually causes a conditional branch to a minor or alternate sequence (see Figure 5–9). This is not a requirement, but it is a common practice. A no answer to a test usually results in a continuation of the normal or major sequence. The normal unaltered path is usually considered to be the *major* or main sequence; the conditional branch or altered path is considered to be the abnormal or *minor* sequence. The minor sequences are also sometimes called *subroutines.*

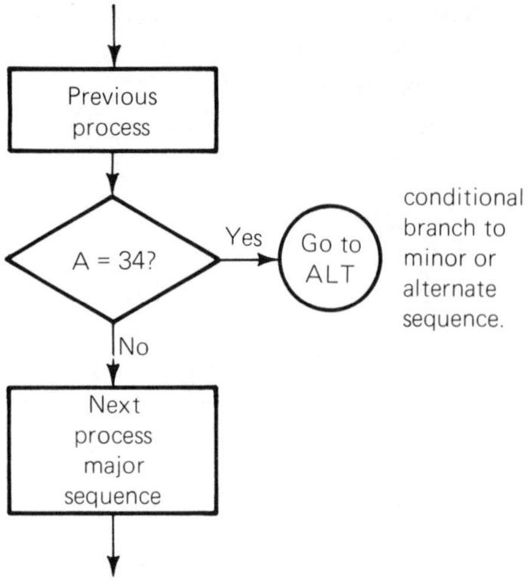

Fig. 5–9. Conditional branch to minor or alternate sequence.

In flowchart diagrams, minor sequences may be drawn anywhere on the page that is convenient. There are no established rules for placement of minor sequence drawings. A point of clarity is necessary here. All subroutines are considered to be minor sequences. However, all minor sequences are not necessarily subroutines. A minor sequence is any sequence that occurs because of a conditional branch operation. A subroutine, however, is any sequence that is branched to for efficiency, and it may be utilized either conditionally or unconditionally.

Process. The process symbol states (inside a rectangular symbol) in either algebraic form or verbal form the manipulation or process accomplished at that point in the program.

Terminator. The terminator is the last instruction in a program or sequence. It usually consists of either a stop or a halt instruction. It is also usually associated with an end of job routine that finishes up or finalizes any "loose ends" when a particular job function has been completed, such as reading a deck of cards or accepting a block of data from a tape. The terminator symbol is also sometimes found at the beginning of a routine labeled initialization and represents instructions that set the initial parameters or conditions under which an operation begins.

The Top-Down Approach

The top-down approach to programming is actually more of a philosophy than a method. It is the approach expounded in the first half of this chapter. The fundamental points merit repeating for clarity and reinforcement. The sequence is as follows:

1. Defining
2. Designing
3. Coding
4. Testing and debugging
5. Documenting

The top-down approach requires strict adherence to precise design definitions and functional statements. The design phase is marked by the partitioning and breaking down of subtasks into increasingly detailed, yet simpler subfunctions. An outstanding feature of the top-down approach is its faithfulness to quality assurance and checking of errors at every stage of development.

A true disciple of the top-down approach to programming will say with very little hesitation that if the method is adhered to religiously, every program written will operate correctly the first time. Although real world experience discounts this 100 percent success rate, a large success rate with little debugging time has been accomplished using this approach.

Programmers that use other approach methods spend more time debugging and recoding than they do designing. Top-down programming forces a programmer to think first and program after. And that is a good philosophy of approach to any problem. The use of the top-down approach also naturally leads to the incorporation of modular and structured programming techniques.

One psychological advantage of the top-down method is that it provides an early feeling of up and running programs. This is accomplished by the use of dummy stubs that act as breakpoints for checking program operations up to a given point. Simulation modules that provide specified responses to the program prior to the actual completion of the subordinate task module are often employed. Perhaps the main advantage of using the top-down approach is that it reduces the possibility that a given block or subfunction will be designed, coded, and tested before one is sure that it will "fit" the overall system. With the top-down system, the entire program emerges in levels or stages of development that can be checked for correctness before the design process moves on.

The disadvantages of the top-down method are not immediately obvious:

1. Although the top-down philosophy assumes a modular approach, it does not usually result in general modules that can be adapted to other programs or adopted into a library system. This is because the

design philosophy is solution oriented to solve specified requirements that are not universal.

2. Some modules can be extremely difficult to write, especially if they have to satisfy the requirements of several different portions of the major program.

3. Because of its specific solution nature, the top-down approach does not take good advantage of existing programs or lend itself well to the use of libraries.

4. Errors in the top-down approach are usually caught early in the design. If a major error slips through the checks and balances system, the effect is catastrophic, and the problem ripples through the whole system rather than being confined to a single module.

If a general statement had to be made concerning the disadvantages of the top-down method, it would have to be that the approach is too specific and that it does not allow for the production of general function programs. The program results can be so "tight" and interrelated that, like a finely tuned engine, sometimes the balance is too delicate for the real world, and minor adjustment can cause it to simply fall apart.

Modular Programming

The process of dividing a program into subtasks and those tasks into subtasks is called *modular programming*. The advantages and disadvantages of modular programming are as follows:

Advantages of modular programming

1. If they are written with independent characteristics, modules can be used in many other programs and lend themselves nicely to the building of program libraries. Likewise, previously written modules can usually be adapted to present needs.

2. Errors are usually confined to a single module, and changes can be made without much rippling effect throughout the whole system.

Perhaps the major advantage of modular programming is the effort to produce universal modules, which are, as much as possible, standalone types and self contained. This containment of function definitely enhances the debugging and testing phases of program design. If a little of this universal philosophy is incorporated into the strict top-down approach in the partitioning function, the result tends to eliminate some of the disadvantages of both methods. The disadvantages of the modular system are as follows:

Disadvantages of modular programming

1. Since they are written in an independent manner (in many cases by different people), modules have a tendency to be difficult to fit together in an overall system.

2. Modules are written separately, thereby repeating functional operations and causing accusations of inefficiency in both time and memory. This separate production also leads to increased documentation costs and difficulty in testing and debugging the modules.

Whereas the top-down method tends to be too strict and specialized, the modular approach tends to be too lax in overall design criteria and too universally oriented to solve specific tasks easily. This author believes that the proper approach is somewhere between the two methods. Adhering to the top-down philosophy early in the definition and design phases while the breaking out of the modules is being accomplished overcomes the major problem with the modular method, which is relating the modules to each other at the end and tying them all together.

Structured Programming

Structured programming consists of three flow structures that satisfy all program requirements. These three structures can be nested and iterated repeatedly to obtain a desired result. The three structures are shown in Figure 5–10.

The advantages and disadvantages of structured programming are as follows:

Advantages of structured programming

1. The flowcharts become easier to construct and read in a top-to-bottom fashion. (Note that all structures have only one entry and one exit.)

2. The program becomes more standardized in its form and terminology, and structures break down into modules with less effort.

3. The structures tend to be self-documenting in that each expansion can be directly traced back to the previous level of design.

Disadvantages of structured programming

1. Many programmers feel awkward in their attempts at solutions and "closed in" in their creativity.

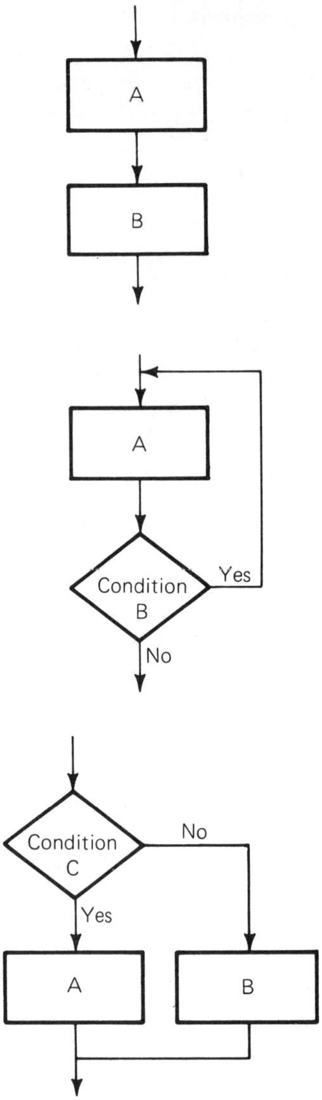

Definition and Expansion Rules

Do A Then B
(simple sequential accomplishment)
Do A Then B. A can replace any other functional block C that breaks down into the form C = B(A). That is, the results of function A are operated on by B.

Do A While B

(an iterating loop) A Do While loop can replace function A as long as the iteration operation results in condition B.

If C Then A Else B

(alternate processes)
An If Then Else operation can replace a functional block where condition C exists within the function being replaced. In that case, A and B are fully defined.

Fig. 5–10. Three structured programming structures.

2. Structured programming is not high-level oriented. (This actually tends to be an advantage to the microprocessor programmer, who usually is working at a low level of approach.)

What structuring accomplishes, in essence, is discipline. It forces the modular programmer to "fit" the program he or she is writing into a systematic, organized format. Today structured programming is unfamiliar to most programmers, and as a result, they experience frustration and restrictions to what they consider to be their style. Structured programming methods are best used in large, low-level language programs where software development costs for testing and debugging are important.

Structured programming brings a measure of discipline and restriction to the freewheeling methods of modular programming. Modular programming helps generalize the specificity of the top-down approach. In summary, the following approach is recommended. Use the top-down philosophy to define the program and maintain a constant check on its correctness. Construct the resulting modules using the structured forms, and finally, whenever reasonable, generalize the modules for later application and use.

COMMONLY USED CONCEPTS

Branching

There are some procedures used in programming so often that they deserve mention in this introductory chapter. The first is **branching.** Branching is the process of providing the program with the possibility of following separate lines of progress through the sequence, creating a branch or decision point.

There are basically two types of branches that can be constructed: the conditional jump and the conditional subroutine. The microprocessor can be made to recognize certain numerical and logical conditions which can occur in the course of processing data. Primarily, they are the existence of zero, the sign of a number (positive or negative), the occurrence of a carry from a particular bit position and the existence of parity (odd and even). Most microprocessors are configured with a special storage register inside the microprocessor where indicators or flags can be left, if and when any of the conditions come into existence. This register is called the flag or condition codes register. When a conditional instruction is encountered in a program, it will be acted upon or not acted upon depending on the status of one of the bits in this register.

An example of how this might appear on the conceptual level is shown in Fig. 5–11. Suppose, after accomplishing the simple addition previously discussed, the requirement that no negative answers be accepted were to be installed. This could be accomplished quite easily by placing a jump if (−) instruction in the sequence immediately following the addition. Conceptually, it would look like Fig. 5–11.

The program would now operate in the following way. When the addition instruction is used, in most microprocessors the condition of

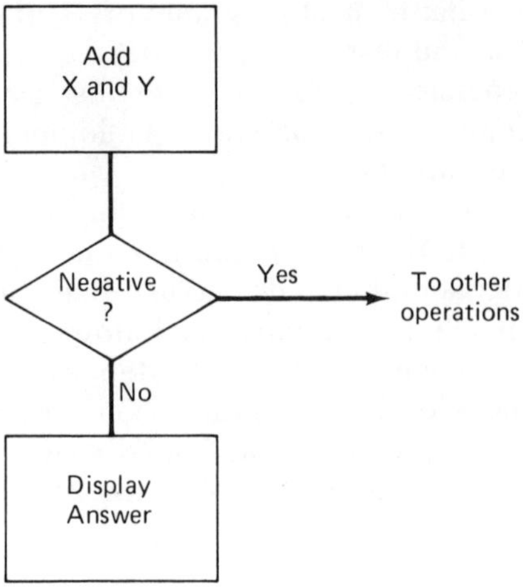

Fig. 5–11. Jump or branch if negative conceptual level.

the accumulator is checked and, if the operation has caused the accumulator to generate a carry, become zero or become negative, a flag bit is placed appropriately in the flag or condition codes (CCR) register. When adding two numbers any of these conditions can occur if signed numbers are being used.

The instruction jump or branch if (−) causes the microprocessor to check the sign bit in the flag or condition codes register. If the sign bit is in a positive condition, the instruction sequence continues as though the jump instruction had never occurred. If the flag bit indication is negative, the microprocessor acts on the jump instruction setting its program counter to the address associated with the instruction. This same procedure would be followed for any of the conditional instructions. The method of specifying the new memory address varies from one microprocessor to another but the basic concept is the same.

Subroutines

As mentioned in the previous section, a branch may be either in the form of a jump or a subroutine call. The **subroutine** is basically a series of instructions that are used repeatedly in the course of running the major program. Its main reason for existence is to save program steps and to shorten the program execution time.

The step saving character of a subroutine requires some explanation. Suppose a routine is to be written to multiply a sequence of several numbers. Multiplication can be accomplished by a method called repeated addition. This method requires repeatedly adding a number to itself the number of times specified by a second number. A routine to accomplish the multiplication of two numbers can be written and, depending on the numbers, may be twenty or thirty steps long. The problem here, however, is to multiply not just two numbers, but a sequence of numbers. If there were ten numbers to be multiplied, the program could be two or three hundred steps long. By using the subroutine idea, a program could be written to get the sequence of numbers located properly for multiplication and then call for the subroutine. In this way, the multiply routine needs to be written only *once* and then called on ten times resulting in a saving of two hundred to two-hundred-fifty steps.

Conceptually, the program appears as in Fig. 5–12.

Notice that this arrangement has several features:

1. An unconditional call for the subroutine
2. A conditional branch which determines if the operation is completed or not
3. A loop condition that restarts the routine again if the operation is not finished.

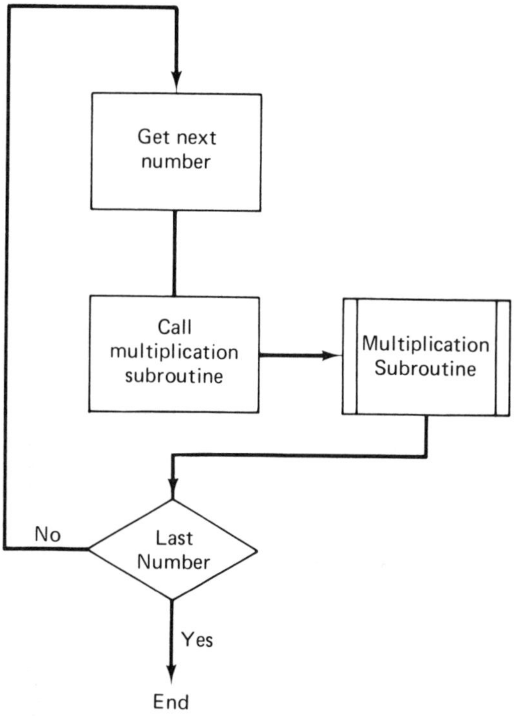

Fig. 5–12. Program for multiplication subroutine.

While it may not be clear at this point how each of these conceptual blocks might be accomplished, it should be noted that the jump and subroutine call instructions provide a tremendous decision making power. The implementation of the individual concept blocks depends on the decisions required and the ability of the programmer to create the branch conditions.

The use of subroutines also offers the programmer certain design freedoms not available in straight line programming. That is, he can design subroutines as separate modules or utility routines and call on them as they are needed in the main program operation. This approach does require that the subroutines be relatively independent and adhere to the "think of everything" philosophy. The modular programming approach is a sophisticated method and requires background experience beyond the beginner level as well as a thorough understanding of the capabilities of the particular machine involved.

QUESTIONS

1. Before attempting a solution to a problem, what should be done?
2. What is partitioning?
3. Define the term "software."
4. What is the sequence of program design?
5. Why is documentation so important?
6. What does the phrase "top-down programming" mean?
7. What is an algorithm?
8. Name the flow chart symbols shown below.

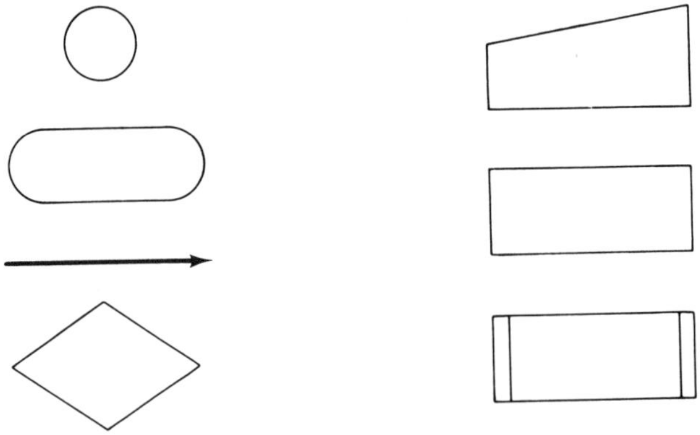

9. What is branching?

10. How does the condition or flag register become invalid in some branch instructions?
11. What is a subroutine?
12. Why are subroutines used?
13. What is the difference between accuracy and precision?
14. What is the mental attitude one should have when writing programs?
15. What is the overall sequence of solution for program development?
16. What is the value of the early "thinking" diagrams?
17. What is meant by language level?
18. How does assembly language differ from machine language?
19. What language level is the technician most likely to be using?
20. Why are programming models useful?
21. Why is constant documentation so important?
22. What fundamental skill is common to all programming methods?
23. What is the primary advantage of flowcharting?
24. When is flowcharting the most useful?
25. What is the primary disadvantage of flowcharting?
26. List and name the common flowchart symbols.
27. What is it that sets a computer apart from a calculator?
28. Explain the difference between a major and a minor sequence.
29. What is the most pronounced characteristic of the top-down method?
30. What is the primary disadvantage of the top-down approach?
31. How does the modular programming concept of modules differ from the top-down approach?
32. Name the three structures of structured programming.
33. How does structuring help the documentation process?
34. What is the major disadvantage of the structured method?
35. Why do you think the author recommends "blending" the three programming methods? Do you think he is right?

PROPOSED EXPERIENCE EXERCISES

1. Flowchart the physical process of a pedestrian crossing a busy intersection. The conditions are as follows:
   a. There are stoplights with "Walk" and "Don't Walk" indicators.
   b. Start with the pedestrian at the intersection with traffic moving.

c. Be sure to include the following:
   1. A good definition of the problem.
   2. A list of functional modules.

d. Do the following:
   1. Do not assume that the "walking" process is predefined.
   2. Be complete and mentally "trace" the operation to see if the pedestrian lived through the process. (Did he watch for someone running the light or turning?)

2. Use proper symbols and procedures to flowchart the following routine:

   a. Input data from a teletype.
   b. Check for valid data.
   c. If data are valid, move data to output location.
   d. Send data to printer.
   e. If data are not valid, input more data.
   f. After data are printed, repeat the entire process. This process is continuous and nonterminating.

3. Flowchart the following conditional statements: If condition A exists, do function G, then H; if not, check for condition B. If B exists, do function F, then H; if not B, do function H.
4. Consider the following flowchart. Write the numbers that would be printed.

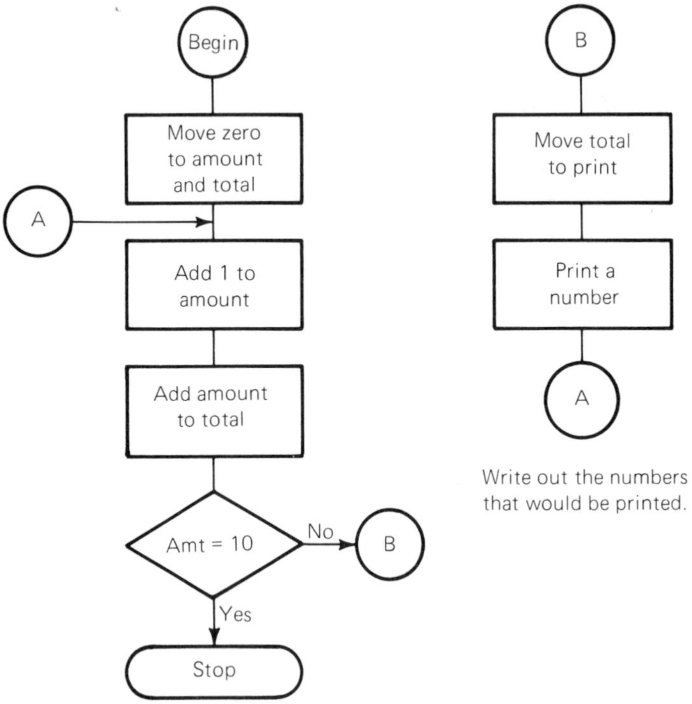

5. Redraw the flowchart below to make the operation more efficient.

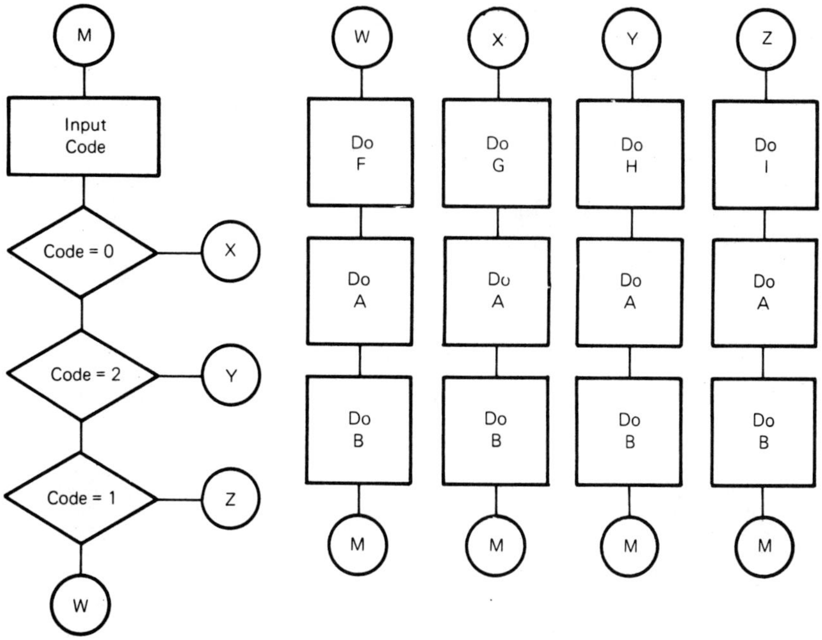

Chapter 6

Bus Control

GLOSSARY

Control bus A group of bidirectional lines originating either at the CPU or the peripheral equipment used to control transfer or reception of signals to or from the CPU.

CS Abbreviation for chip select.

Data bus Eight bidirectional lines capable of transferring data to and from CPU, storage and peripheral devices.

Decoding assignment The use of hardware circuit configurations to determine the function that a particular line performs when used for addressing.

Direction control The process of diverting or altering the flow of data between various devices and systems. Usually accomplished by enabling buffers with decoded control signals.

Enable A signal condition that permits some specific event to proceed whenever it is ready.

High Z A condition of high-impedance characteristics causing a low current load effect.

Interfacing The process of developing an electrical circuit that enables a device to yield or acquire information from another device.

Interrupt A signal that halts the operation of a running program to perform a special, high-priority routine.

Leading edge The rising or falling edge of a pulse that occurs first in time.

Memory-mapped I/O The process of connecting memory address lines to I/O decoding systems so that I/O devices are handled and treated as memory locations.

Programmable interface A general purpose I/O device; a typical TTL compatible interface.

Read The process of accessing data from an external device or system. The transfer of information between devices.

3-state device Any integrated circuit device in which two of the states are conventional binary (0, 1) and the third state is high impedance. The high-impedance state on the device's output reduces power drain and allows other devices access to the common bus.

Timing diagram A pictorial diagram showing the various time relationships among a variety of interdependent pulses or signals.

Trailing edge The rising or falling edge of a pulse that occurs last in a related pair of edges.

Write The process of sending data to an external storage device or system.

The complex nature of the timing within a microprocessor can cause the beginner to become confused about how all the movements of information are kept orderly within the system. To a great degree, this anxiety over timing and control is unfounded. Most of the timing and sequence of operations of the system are predetermined by the manufacturer of the device.

The user, for example, has no control over when the address for the instruction to be fetched occurs. Instead, the user should study the timing diagrams and specifications provided with the device to determine what combination of synchronization pulses on the control bus may be utilized to accomplish the desired timing of particular hardware configuration.

The purpose of this chapter is to discuss some of the more common considerations the user must deal with in the timing and control of bus structures.

SYSTEM REVIEW

The overall sequence of operations has been previously discussed in Chapters 1, "Introduction to the Microprocessor," and 4, "Instruction Sets." In those chapters, the emphasis was on the cyclic and very repetitive nature of the fetch-execute cycle of the microprocessor itself. In the instruction set chapter, it was noted that, within this overall fetch-execute sequence, a more detailed study would reveal a sequence of bus usage. This sequence generally follows the pattern:

Fetch
1. Address (instruction fetch)
2. Control (memory read timing)
3. Data (transfer of instruction)

Execute
4. Address (I/O or memory, depending on instruction)
5. Control (synchronize execution)
6. Data (transfer of data)
7. Additional sequence (address, control, data) may be repeated depending on the requirements of the instruction being executed.

This overall picture of the operation is accurate as far as it goes. However, it is too general for understanding the timing, decoding and latching circuitry which abound in most microprocessor systems. When discussing the control of the busing systems and the external devices associated with a microprocessor, the interpretation of **timing diagrams** and coincident bit timing considerations must be covered in detail.

TIMING AND CONTROL

Multiple-Bit Timing

Study Fig. 6–1. Note that all three bus structures, address, data and control, are represented in this generalized system. The device requirement statements indicate that the coincidence of the **CS** (chip select) and R (read) signals, when associated with a particular address, will cause data which has been stored at the location to be brought out of the device and placed on the data bus. The same address coincident with CS and W (write) will cause data present on the data bus to be taken in by the device and stored at the location specified by the address.

Keep in mind that the internal structure of the device itself places these requirements on the bus system and not the other way around. Through programming, the microprocessor is capable of the timing flexibility needed to meet the device requirements. This is why it is so important that the system designer and the programmer know the device timing and signal requirement specifications.

Normally, the devices that are attached to the bus are somewhat universal in their design but have very rigid signal requirements. An

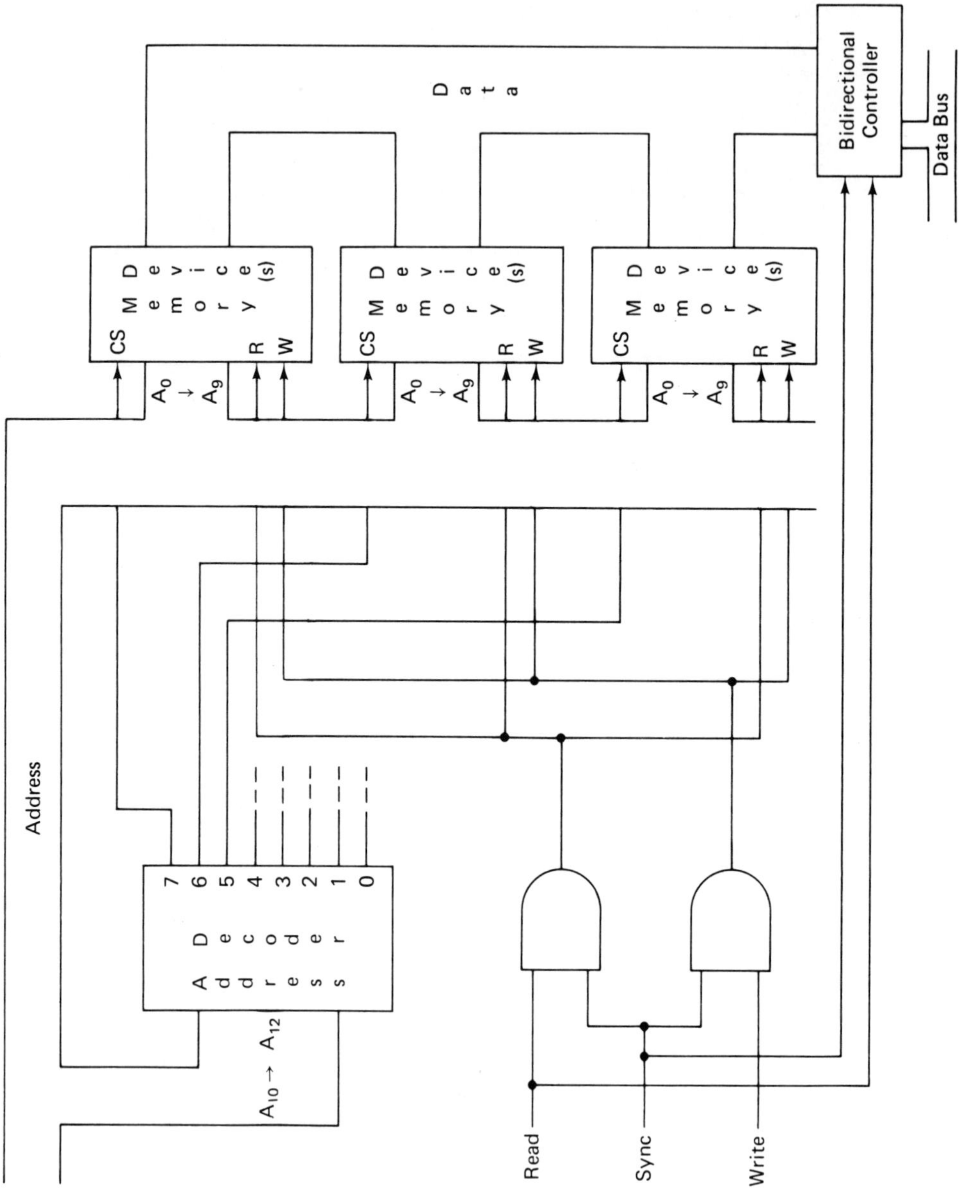

Fig. 6–1. Device selection timing and control.

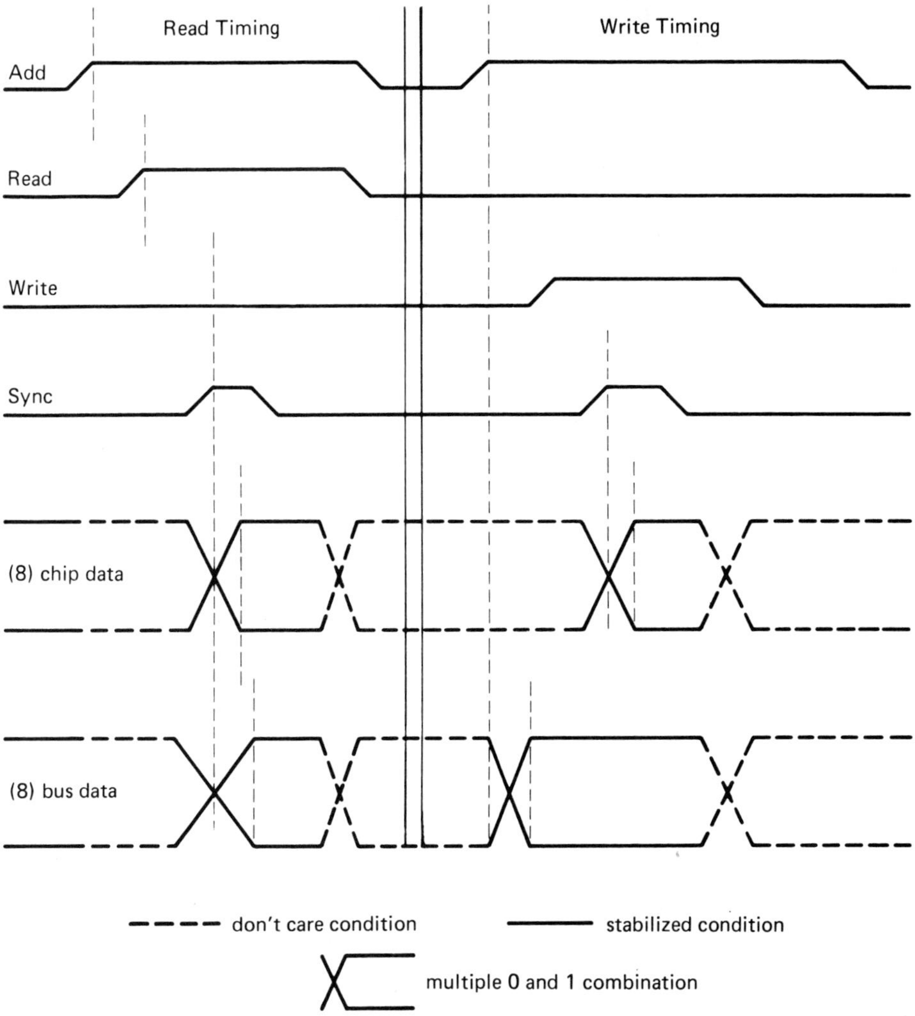

Fig. 6–1. continued.

example of this is the commonly used memory chip 2102A. It requires a specific sequence of timed signals to do its job of storing and retrieving data and yet it is commonly used throughout the whole spectrum of microprocessor systems. The 2102A functions just as well when driven by an MC6800/6802 as when used by an 8080/8085. Again, the microprocessor and its associate busing systems must be adapted to the device requirements; the device is *not* adapted to the microprocessor.

This procedure of adapting the signals to the devices to be used by the system is called **interfacing.** In order to intelligently interface devices to microprocessor systems, the concept of bus control must be understood.

Again, consider Fig. 6–1 and observe what happens to the memory devices as the bus structures go through the following sequence of timing from the microprocessor.

First, the address is placed on the address bus. The first ten lines ($A_0 - A_9$) are directly connected to each memory device. The next three lines ($A_{10} - A_{12}$) are connected to the input of the decoder circuit. The ten lines arriving at the memory device cause the internal structure of *all* of the memory devices to locate and get ready to act on a particular memory location. At this point, the internal operation of the device is not of primary concern. It is sufficient to understand that any one of the devices receiving the address is now capable of responding when called to operate.

The three lines attached to the decoder cause a unique single line output from the decoder. As is illustrated in Fig. 6–1, each unique chip select (CS) line controls one of the devices in question. The net result of all of this decoding and addressing is that all the devices are readied to be activated by the first ten address bits and the one to be used is selected by the next three address lines being decoded. The device selected is then ready to either input or output data depending on which line is activated—the R (read/output) or W (write/input).

The next activity of the microprocessor is concerned with the control bus specifically and, to a certain extent, involves the data bus. If the operation being performed is a read function, the data bus lines are released to float, that is, caused to go into a high-impedance state, and the control lines are activated. If the operation is a write function, the data to be transferred is placed on the data bus and the control lines are activated.

In Fig. 6–1, the activation of the read line in coincidence with a sync or clock pulse accomplishes two things.

1. It applies a read pulse to all chips for a period equal to the length of the sync pulse.
2. It sets the direction of flow through the directional controller.

When the read pulse arrives at the chip selected by the previous operation, the data is transferred from the device through the directional controller to the data bus. This data is then accepted by the microprocessor into its internal register.

Activating the write line sets the controller for input flow direction, which allows data previously placed on the bus to be felt at the data inputs for the memory chips. The coincidence of the write and sync pulse causes a write pulse to be applied to the write line of all chips. The coincidence of this write pulse and the CS previously applied causes the selected chip to accept the data at the data input lines during the time the W (write) pulse is in existence.

The timing and flow control in a microprocessor system is accomplished by this type of multiple-bit coincidence gating. While this example is generalized to illustrate sequence, it does show the need for the consideration of both the microprocessor timing and device requirements. Some peripheral circuitry may be set up to accept or send data due to level of pulses while others will operate due to edge clocking and will require additional consideration for rising and falling edge development. This can require the further addition of inverters to change the timing from **leading edge** to **trailing edge.**

Latching and 3-State

In the process of designing the interface and timing circuitry, the appropriate signals sometimes do not arrive at the proper time to accomplish the operation and must be either blocked off from arriving at the devices in question or temporarily "remembered" for short periods of time until they can be used. The temporary storage of signals is most commonly done by latching circuits.

The isolation of external devices and circuits is usually done with **3-state** devices inserted in the access lines to or from the circuit in question. The term 3-state indicates the number of conditions which the output of the device may assume: a 0 (low-state), a 1 (high-state) or **high Z** (high-impedance). The 0 and 1 conditions are similar to the 0s and 1s discussed in previous chapters.

The high-impedance state, however, causes the output line of the device to act like an open circuit with leakage currents approaching 0 amps. Using the high-Z (high-impedance) state offers the advantage that a great number of devices can be attached to a single signal line without the leakage current load causing detrimental loading effects. Without this ability to "unload" the bus systems in a microprocessor, the number of functional units that could be attached would be so limited as to make the system commercially unattractive. By using the 3-state technology, the bus system can be made to operate as though only one device at a time were attached to the bus.

One other primary advantage of using 3-state devices is that the effective bus configuration at any given time may be altered by the proper application of address decoding and control signals.

As an example of this, consider the circuit in Fig. 6–2(a). When control lines $\bar{A}$ and $\bar{B}$ are in the 1 state, signal flow through the system in either direction is completely blocked. By causing $\bar{B}$ to go to the 0

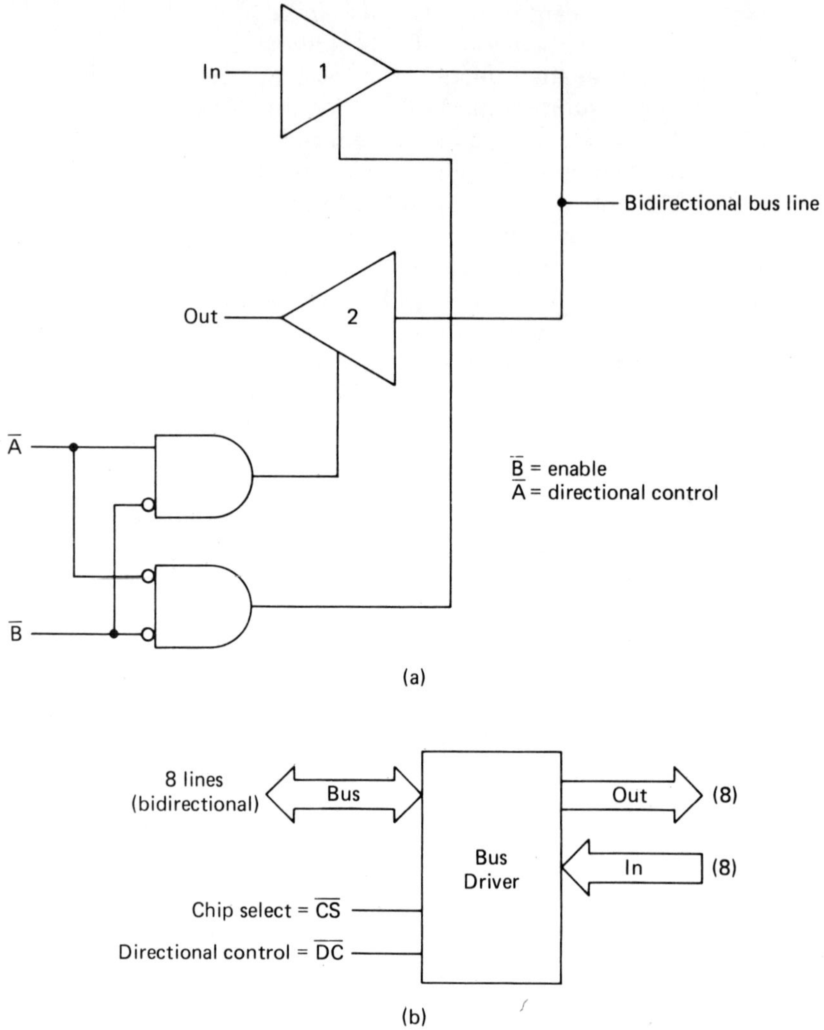

Fig. 6–2. Bidirectional control.

state, signals may flow in either direction depending on the condition of the $\bar{A}$ line. If $\bar{A}$ is true (0) the signal flow path is from the IN line to the bus line. If $\bar{A}$ is false (1), the flow path is from the bus line to the OUT line. Because the $\bar{A}$ signal is common for both conditions, the directions of flow are mutually exclusive. This arrangement then controls the direction of signal flow to and from the bus structure. In appropriate microprocessor terminology, $\bar{B}$ **enables** the circuit and $\bar{A}$ is directional control.

If several more pairs of 3-states were connected in parallel with the control lines, an entire eight bits could be controlled. Also, since the inverters provide added drive in both directions, this circuit could be called a bidirectional bus driver. The control function of this block is represented in Fig. 6–2(b) and finds many applications throughout microprocessor systems.

Again, the principle illustrated here is only representative of a general concept and exact circuits and signal requirements must be determined by the specification sheets provided by the device manufacturers. The designation of terms and signal names will vary from device to device and from manufacturer to manufacturer.

Programmed Control

The control of signal flow by application of other signals is not a new concept to the computer designer. More recent developments resulting from this idea combined with the latching or memory function have led several producers to develop devices known as **programmable interfaces** or ports.

The basic idea is a simple one. Consider the bidirectional control device just discussed. If, instead of being applied only at the time they are needed, the control signals are latched into a particular condition any time prior to their use, the synchronizing signals are only required to allow the signals to pass.

For example, suppose the **direction control** line in Fig. 6–2(a) were latched in a 1 condition early in a program sequence. The device would always act as an output device whenever the enable line was set to 0. The latching of the 1 condition could be considered to have programmed the device as an output port. While this is an oversimplification of a programmable interface, the concept of applying a prior "control word" to set up a particular port configuration is an important one and will be brought up again in the chip studies later in the text. Although the devices themselves can become quite complex, the idea behind the circuitry is relatively simple.

The concepts of multiple-bit coincidence, latching, 3-state control and programmed control are all very fundamental concepts that find application throughout the microprocessor bus structures. They provide the necessary synchronization, selection and programmed configurations for management of the complex signals and operations of which a microprocessor is capable. The understanding of the three bus systems and their functional relationship to each other is fundamental to handling microprocessor systems and interfacing. Because of the importance of these fundamental relationships, a summary of the functional uses and their basic handling is included here.

ADDRESS BUS

Primary Function

Normally, the address bus consists of sixteen unidirectional lines used primarily for the selection of different devices and systems to be used at various times during operation of the instructions. The lines are used for both memory and I/O operations. Many microprocessor systems consider one page of memory to be 256 bytes long. In that case, the addresses within the page would be selected by the lower eight lines ($A_0 - A_7$) and the selection of which page is to be addressed would be accomplished by the upper eight bits. In all cases, the physical arrangement or board grouping will determine the line assignments for decoding.

Decoding Assignments

Figure 6–3 illustrates how **decoding assignments** can be accomplished.

Assume that the memory boards in this system are 4 K boards and each board is subdivided in 1 K groupings on board (Groups 1,2,3 and 4). The address line assignments would appear as in Fig. 6–3 (a). The first ten lines, $A_0 - A_9$, would provide the address for each location within the 1 K byte groups. Lines A_{10} and A_{11} would be decoded for selecting which group is to be activated to respond. The remaining lines, $A_{12} - A_{15}$, would be decoded to enable the proper board. This arrangement is a very common one for the 2102A 4K RAM board arrangment.

Two other popular board arrangements are shown in Fig. 6–3 (b) and (c) for the 2708 (1 K byte) EPROM chip and the 1702 (256-byte) EPROM.

These three assignment diagrams visually explain the assignment systems.

1. As many lines as are required for the chip being used are taken for byte addressing starting with A_0. For a 256-byte chip $A_0 - A_7$; for a 1 K byte chip $A_0 - A_9$ and so on.
2. Next the onboard arrangement is decoded. If the board contains four chips, the next two lines are used. If the board contains eight chips, three lines are used. If the board contains sixteen chips, four lines are used and so on.
3. Any remaining lines are used for activating the desired board.

In most cases, the board selection decoding is done onboard and is

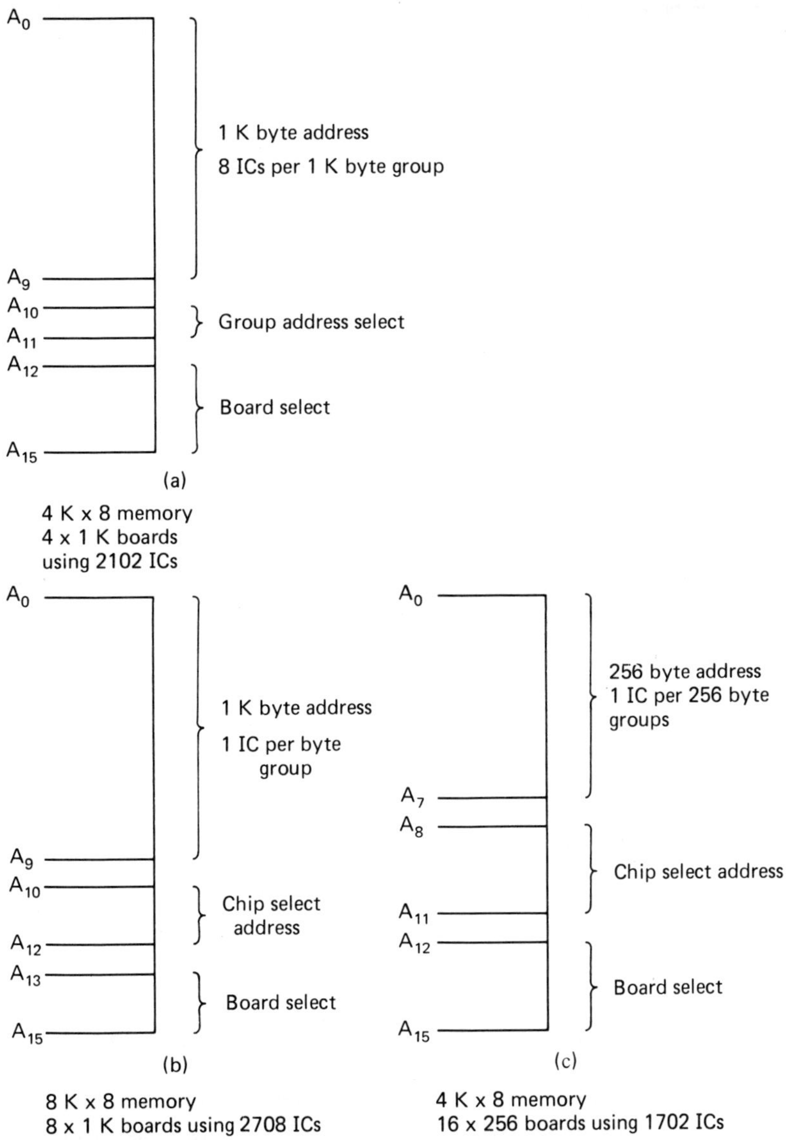

Fig. 6–3. Address assignments.

made either switch or jumper selectable for user definition. An example of this is shown in Fig. 6–4.

When the user installs the jumper, the board address is determined. Because the board decoding determines whether or not the chip and byte addresses are allowed to pass the 3-state buffers, the chips on-board receive the address only if the proper board address is present.

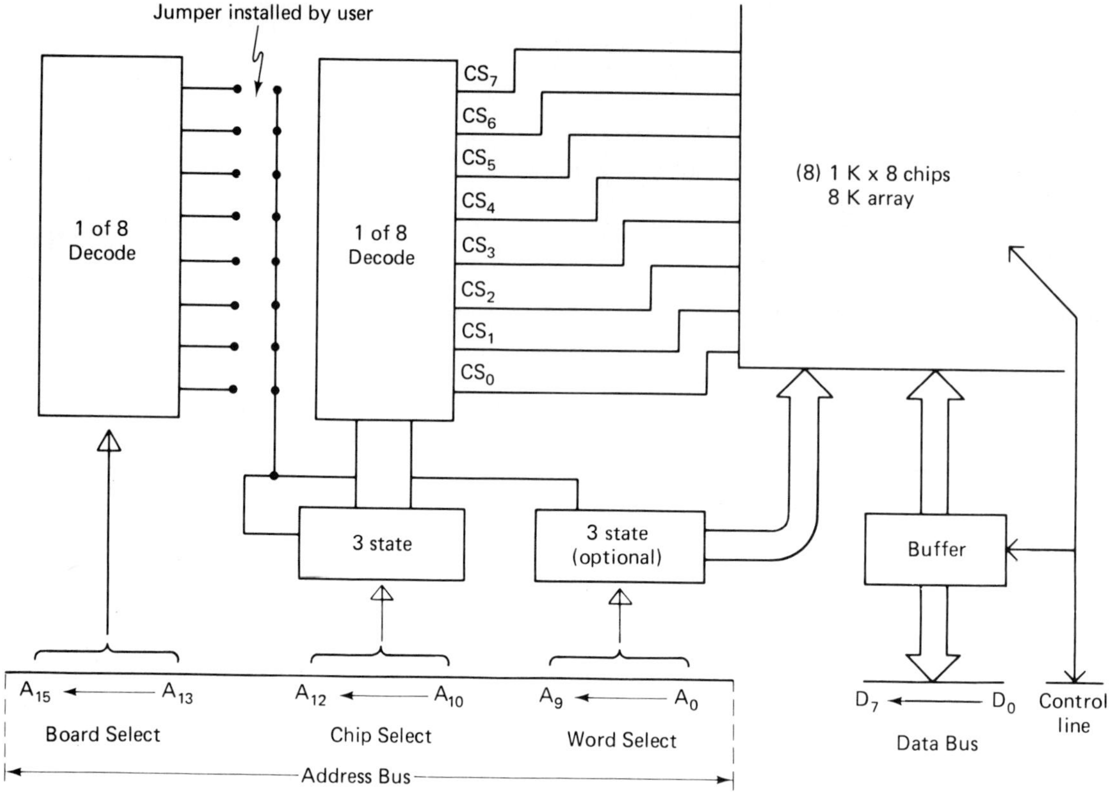

Fig. 6–4. Typical onboard decoding.

I/O Addressing and Memory-Mapped I/O

I/O address selection and assignment are carried out in a manner similar to that described in the decoding assignments section.

Another technique for using the address lines associated with I/O operation is called **memory-mapped I/O.** Memory-mapped I/O is accomplished using individual address lines as device enable lines for the input-output devices. If, for example, the system being used does not contain an entire complement of memory devices (64K), there will be unused address lines which can be used for activation of I/O devices. Since most users build their memory starting from the lowest addresses, the lines used for memory mapping normally are the most significant one or two address lines. Figure 6–5 shows a typical arrangement of I/O and memory.

When this method of mapping is used, the usable memory is limited

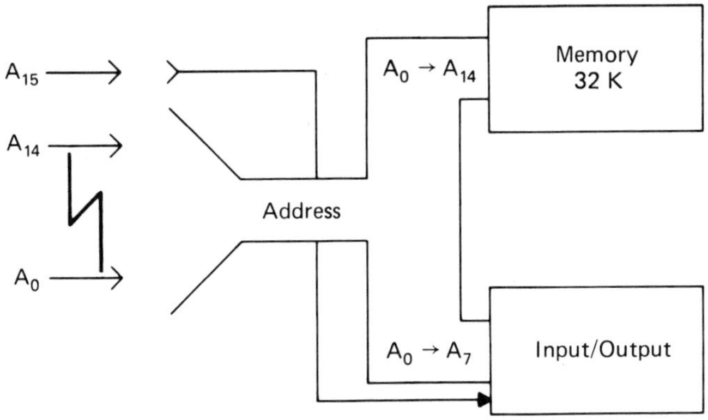

Fig. 6–5. Input/output memory mapping.

to 32 K because only the first fifteen lines of address are devoted to memory. It does provide the use of all memory instructions in connection with the I/O system simply by addressing I/O devices as memory locations in the upper 32 K of memory. This provides the user with a much wider variety of instructions for dealing with I/O devices. The disadvantage of losing the upper 32 K of memory can be overcome by providing external circuitry to discriminate between memory operations and I/O operations. This, in turn, allows for the use of the sixteenth address bit in connection with memory functions.

The Motorola system has provided for this differentiation between memory and I/O operation internally in its CPU which treats all I/O devices as memory locations without limiting the usable memory. This is accomplished by providing a more complete scheme of addressing modes within the instruction set.

The Intel system has not provided for automatic memory mapping and therefore has a simpler addressing mode structure with the requirement that the memory mapping must be provided by external circuitry.

DATA BUS

Primary Function

The **data bus** usually consists of eight bidirectional lines used to transfer various types of data throughout the system. Because it is carrying this information into and out of the system, it has very closely controlled timing and configuration circuitry. This circuitry normally consists of latches, 3-state devices and discrete gating arrangements that vary widely depending on the desired results for the system being utilized.

Types of Data

The types of information which are carried by the data bus fall into the following categories.

1. Numerical data
2. Instruction codes
3. Address information
4. Device identification
5. Control words.

The last three categories require a short explanation. Address information is the operand address information required by many direct and indirect addressing mode instructions. The term device identification refers to the codes that accompany most interrupt operations. When the microprocessor receives an interrupt request on its interrupt lines, it scans the data bus for an identifying code from the device requesting the interrupt. The control word category refers to those codes sent to programmable peripheral devices to set up their mode of operation as previously discussed in the programmed control section.

CONTROL BUS—LINE DEFINITIONS

The **control bus** is probably the least standardized of all the bus structures. The number of lines, their directional character and purpose vary widely from system to system. Almost all control lines are involved with the synchronization of the systems. There are also some very common control terms which apply to most systems.

Read Active during input to the data bus. May be dedicated to either memory or I/O. May also be found common to both. If dedicated, it will normally carry an identifying letter or abbreviation memory read (MR) or I/O read (IR).

Write Activated during output to the data bus. May be found dedicated or common as with the read line.

Interrupt Activated by peripheral devices to cause programming branches for handling of the data provided by the peripheral device.

Interrupt acknowledge Activated by the microprocessor to indicate to the peripheral devices that it is ready to accept data.

Hold, ready, wait A variety of special lines activated by either the microprocessor itself or the peripheral devices to suspend, temporarily, operation of the microprocessor while other operations occur within the system.

Sync (*often called* **strobe** *or* **clock**) A line carrying a synchronization signal that is either the clock pulse itself or a closely related signal.

In studying various microprocessors, the user will encounter a variety of special control lines and nomenclature unique to the device or the system. There is no option but to accept the manufacturer's definition of these lines.

QUESTIONS

1. For any instruction, what is the overall sequence of operation?
2. For any instruction, what is the sequence of bus usage?
3. Why is timing so important?
4. Explain why multiple-bit coincidence timing is so important to the concept of bus control.
5. How is a CS pulse generated by an address?
6. What part does the control bus play in selecting data?
7. What is the difference between read and write operations?
8. What services do 3-state devices provide in bus control?
9. What kinds of information can the data bus carry?
10. Explain what the words "programmed control" mean as they apply to port applications.
11. In your own words, explain what a port is and what function it serves.
12. How are decoding assignments made?
13. How does memory-mapped I/O differ from I/O decoding and usage?

Chapter 7

Input/Output

GLOSSARY

ACIA Asynchronous Communications Interface Adapter. The MC6850 provides the data formatting and control to interface serial asynchronous data communications information to parallel bus-organized systems. It functions either as a serial-to-parallel converter or as a parallel-to-serial converter.

ASCII American Standard Code for Information Interchange. A widely used code in which alphanumerics, punctuation marks and certain special machine characters are represented by unique 7-bit binary numbers.

Asynchronous Operation of a switching network by a free running signal which triggers successive instructions; the completion of one instruction triggers the next.

Baud A unit of data transmission speed, sometimes variable, but usually bits per second.

Bidirectional bus driver Circuitry that provides for both electrical isolation and increased current load capability in both signal flow directions. When an arrangement provides for multiple line handling, it becomes a *bus* driver.

Control word (data) One or more items of data whose 0 and 1 arrangement determines the mode of operation, direction or selection of a particular device, port or program flow.

DMA A mechanism for the high-speed direct transfer of information between memory and peripherals without CPU intervention.

Handshaking Electrical provision for verification that a proper data transfer has occurred. A data-ready/data-received signal scheme that assures orderly data transfer.

Loading An indication that current is being drawn. Connecting a device that draws current from the line creates loading.

Modem A MOdulator/DEModulator device that converts signals in one form to another kind of equipment. In particular, the device that changes digital data into a form suitable for computers and terminals to communicate over telephone lines.

Parity A binary digit appended to an array of bits to make the sum of all bits always odd or always even. A method for checking the accuracy of transmitted or transferred binary data.

Port An electrical logic circuit configuration that is a signal input or output access point in the microprocessor bus system.

Programmed I/O The control of data flow in and out of the microprocessor completely under software direction. It implies a lack of independent port activity.

Synchronous A switching network that operates at the same frequency and phase. A constant time interval between successive bits, characters and events.

Input and output have been discussed previously, in general terms, as those devices through which the CPU has access to the outside world. This chapter contains a more detailed description of how this access is achieved. All three bus structures are involved in effecting this access. The electrical system through which the access is achieved, in both directions, is called a **port.**

The extensive variety of ports breaks down into two types: interrupting and noninterrupting. Each of these categories can be further divided into programmable and nonprogrammable.

This section will deal primarily with the noninterrupting type of ports. These noninterrupting systems are sometimes called **programmed I/O** ports. This terminology, however, can become quickly confused with the term programmable port. The difference is that programmed I/O describes the mode of operation and the term programmable port describes the type of hardware. Programmed I/O means that the microprocessor is in control of the operation by executing the program. In other words, the port is not functionally capable of independent action. Without explicit control by the microprocessor, the port is inactive. Programmable ports, on the other hand, are capable of operating independently of the microprocessor once they have been programmed (told what to do) by the microprocessor.

The nonprogrammable port is usually simpler and less expensive to incorporate into a system, but requires a greater software overhead. That is, more programming is required to deal directly with the port because it is incapable of uncontrolled operation. As the sophistication of microprocessor systems increases, the nonprogrammable port is losing its popularity and may eventually fade from the field. It is still worthy of discussion here because the basic principles of input/output ports are more easily understood if uncomplicated by the programmable aspects of the more sophisticated hardware.

There is another type of input/output operation which will be covered in Chapter 10. It is called **DMA** (direct memory access). In this operation, the CPU function is temporarily suspended and data is transferred directly from the external system to the microprocessor memory.

In either one of the two major categories, interrupting and noninterrupting programmed I/O, there are some conditions which must be met.

1. The microprocessor may communicate via the bus system with only one device at a time. This does not apply to DMA operations because the microprocessor is shut down during the transfer.
2. All devices must be synchronized.
3. The flow of data must be controlled and routed to the proper location in either direction.

PORTS AND PORTING

A port is a set of logical circuits that allow controlled access to the bus structure. A complete port capability consists of the following three features consistent with the above conditions.

1. An address decoding capacity
2. A synchronization section
3. Data transfer buffers and lines.

When using the noninterrupting method of I/O, the CPU, while progressing through the program, will encounter program instructions causing it to activate a port address. The Motorola MC6800/6802 microprocessor treats port address in the same manner as memory location. The Intel 8080/8085 microprocessor handles the port addressing separately from memory addresses. In either case, the address will appear as a standard presentation on the address bus. This is then decoded by the standard methods of address decoding provided by the hardware of the system. (Address schemes were just discussed in Chapter 6, "Bus Control.")

Once the address has been properly decoded a single line, called a chip select (CS), is activated which enables one particular port. (Refer to Fig. 7–1.) This process meets the requirement that the microprocessor communicate with only one port at a time. During the same machine cycle, the microprocessor will activate the R/W (read/write) pulse line which synchronizes the timing of the data exchange between the CPU and the port. This meets the second requirement that the transfer be synchronized.

Most port data lines, including the data lines of the CPU itself, are either latched or buffered or both. That is, a temporary holding point is provided for data flowing in both directions. For example, when data is being sent from the microprocessor to a particular port, the synchronizing pulse causes the output buffer of the processor to release the data onto the data bus at the same time as the port buffer is opened to receive the data. Since only one port is selected at a time, the data flow is controlled and directed to the proper location, meeting the third criteria for data transfer.

The same is true in the reverse direction. Figure 7–1 is a simplified diagram showing only those lines involved with a single data port. The direction of the data flow is primarily a function of timing of the R/W line. However, there are other lines available to assist in this function. In the Intel 8080/8085 CPU, these additional lines are the STSTB (status strobe) and DB_{IN} (data bus in). In the Motorola

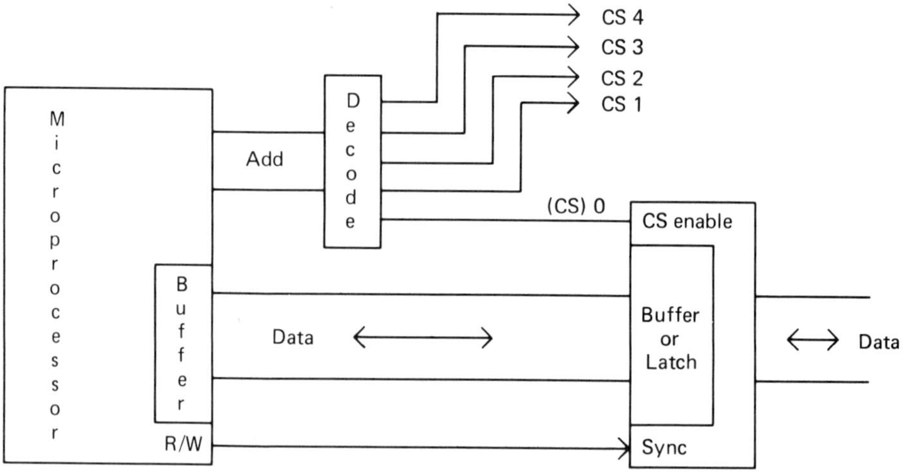

Fig. 7–1. Simplified data port.

MC6800/6802, they are VMA (valid memory address) and DBE (data bus enable). Because the control of direction is important to the operation of the system, some time will be spent here showing the difference between an input port and an output port.

NONPROGRAMMABLE PORTS

Output Ports

Several special 8-bit port chips available from various manufacturers are designed specifically for microprocessor applications. Directional control is better illustrated by constructing a port from standard TTL logic chips. Consider the circuit in Fig. 7–2.

Figure 7–2 is a simple latch arrangement that satisfies all the requirements of an 8-bit output port. Remember, the characteristic of a 7475 is that as long as the enabling pulse is high, the Q output follows the D input. As soon as the enabling pulse goes low, the transfer of data ceases and the last condition is latched or held. Further inputs at D have no effect on Q output. Two conditions must occur in coincidence for the enabling pulse to go high. Both the $\overline{CS}$ and $\overline{W}$ signals must be present for data to pass through the latch circuit. The data present when either $\overline{CS}$ or $\overline{W}$ disappear is the data which is held for output.

In Fig. 7–2, the proper address generates the $\overline{CS}$ through the decoding system. In most systems this proper address is generated one or two clock cycles prior to the placing of the data in the data bus relieving any concern about the availability of the port selection signal. The data output is typically stable for a considerable amount of time prior to the R/W pulses being activated.

So, the actual synchronization of the pulses is already taken care of by the microprocessor manufacturers. The user's only real concern is that he provide for the decoding and coincidence of the signals. If the logical circuit is provided, the timing is also provided.

An output port of this type can be easily constructed without too much concern for data bus loading because of the high input impedance of the latch circuitry. Additionally, the microprocessor can, in effect, "throw" data at this port and then go away and forget about it. Once latched, the data is held until changed. This means no **handshaking** is required.

Handshake Ports

The handshake concept as it applies to ports means that some provision is made for verification that data has been passed properly. It is

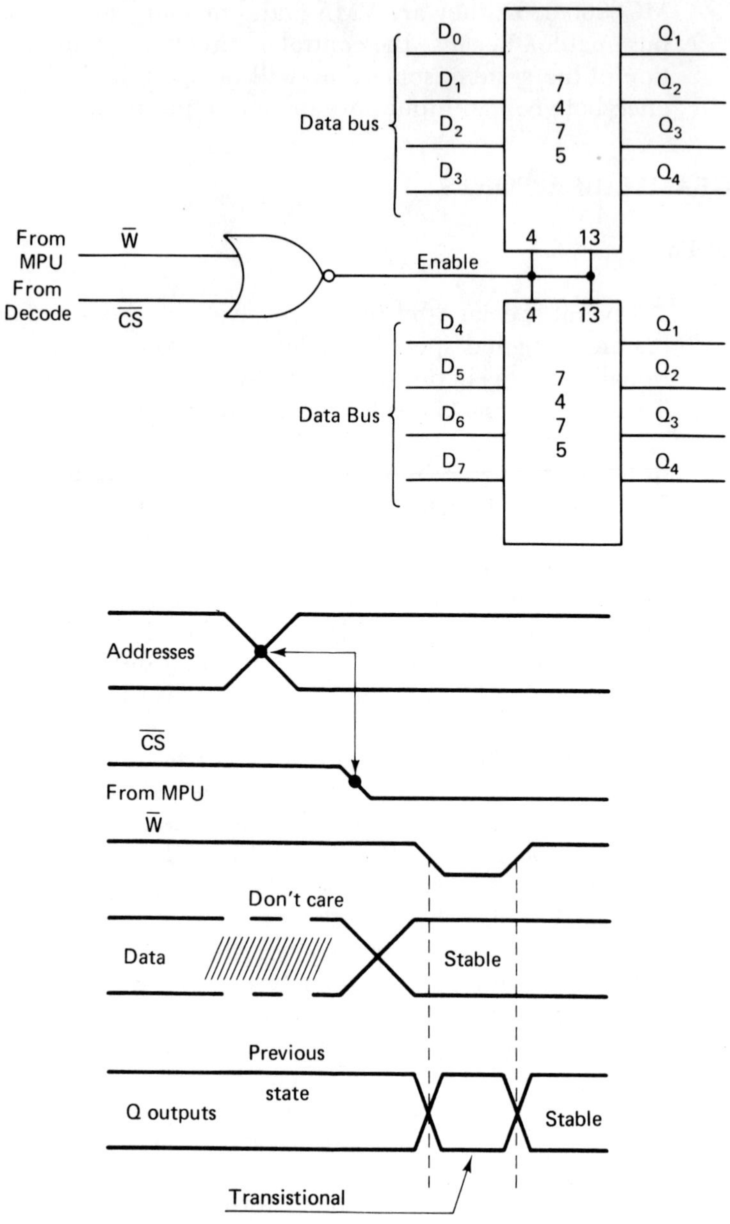

Fig. 7–2. Output port with timing.

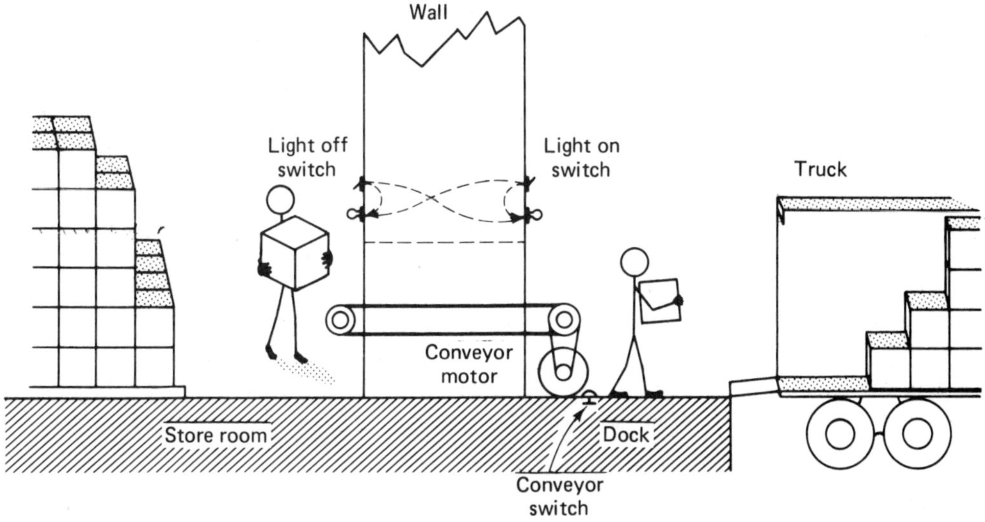

Fig. 7–3. Handshake analogy.

usually only necessary in high speed systems where blocks of data are being transferred. An analogy for a handshake system is presented in Fig. 7–3.

In Fig. 7–3, two men are at a warehouse: one inside the storeroom, the other outside on the dock. They cannot talk to each other because of the wall between. The man outside has control of the conveyor. The inside man's job is: *when the light goes on, put a box on the belt and turn the light off.* The outside man controls the operation in the following way. *When he returns from stacking a box in the truck and is ready for another box, he turns the light on; when the light goes off, he activates the conveyor until he receives the box which he takes to the truck and stores. Then he returns to the conveyor and turns the light on again.*

Figure 7–4 is the circuit for which this analogy holds.

The program flow diagram to operate this system might look like Fig. 7–5.

Notice in the flow diagram, Fig. 7–5, that the program first sends a signal to port 2 enabling the peripheral device. The peripheral device loads port 0 with data and then loads port 1 with a 0 on line 7. The microprocessor meanwhile idles in the loop waiting for the 0 to appear. When the 0 does appear, the microprocessor turns off the handshake request, brings the data in from port 0, checks to see if it has transferred the correct number of bytes of data and, if not, it loops back

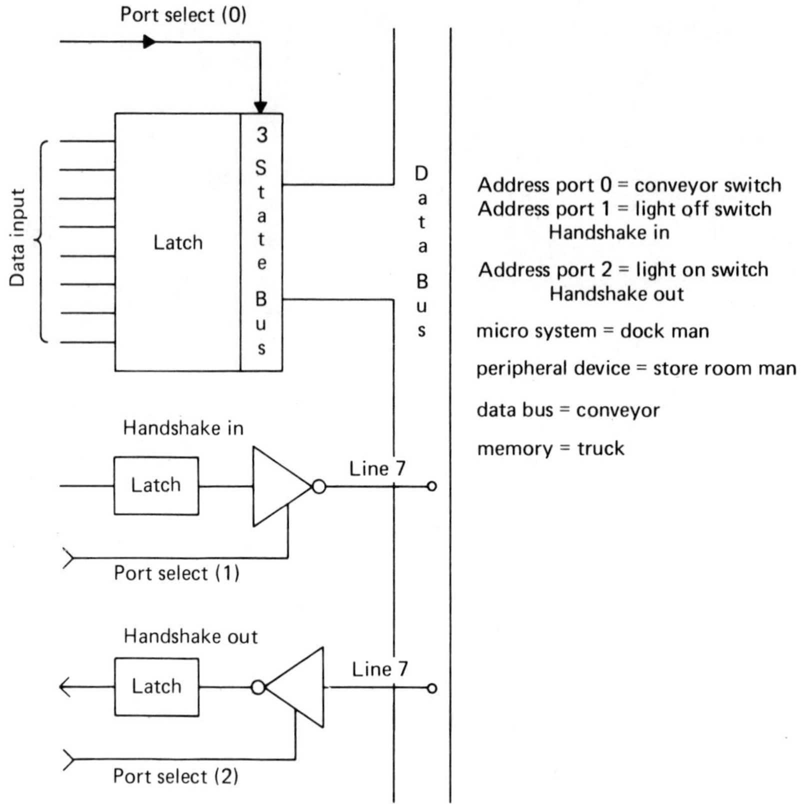

Fig. 7–4. Handshake circuit.

again to activate the port enable signal and goes through the whole process again.

This example and its associated analogy were illustrated using an input port direction for two reasons.

1. Handshaking occurs more often in an input port system because it is more common for the peripheral to be slower than the microprocessor. The handshake operation allows the microprocessor to control the port as to when it is allowed to input data and still assure that all data is being transferred.

2. The arrangement of the buffering system on a data input port usually differs from that of an output port.

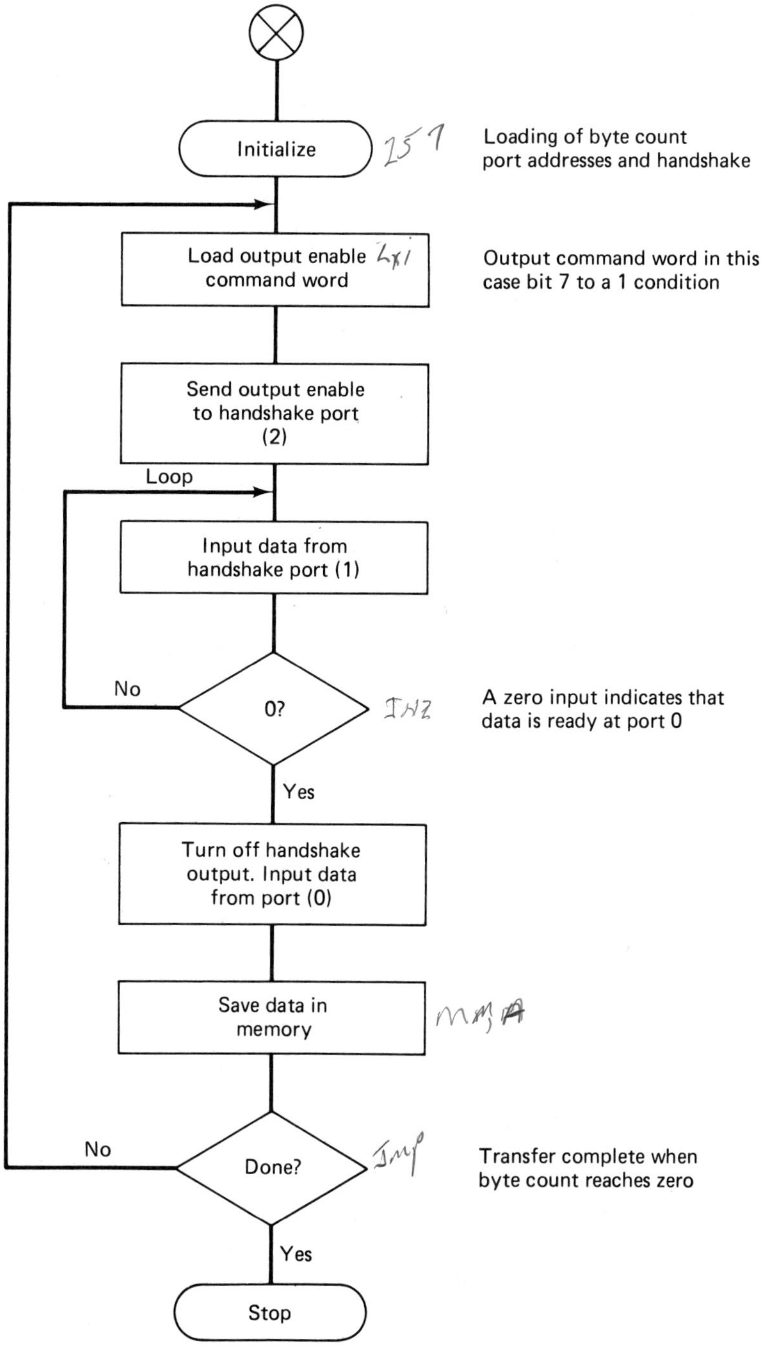

Fig. 7–5. Flow diagram for handshake operation.

Input Ports

Input ports differ from output ports in two ways. One is obvious: the flow of data is *into* the system rather than *out*. The other difference, which is not as apparent, has to do with the buffering arrangement. Most microprocessors in production today are MOS devices which are TTL compatible. That is, their voltage level specifications are similar to those of TTL technology. Their current delivery capability, however, is usually limited to a very few peripheral devices per line if not buffered or boosted in some way. The input impedance of TTL devices is normally very high and the output impedance is very low.

As the TTL devices are connected as output systems for the microprocessor, there is a very low current load created except when the signal is passed. This is desirable since it means that a large number (usually ten) of output systems of this type will not create an undue amount of current sink from the microprocessor when they are inactive. On the other hand, when these same devices are connected as input devices they present a low-impedance (high-current level) when inactive and unless they are somehow isolated or buffered, the number of devices that can be connected is quite limited (usually one).

The 3-state technology devices provide the solution to this problem. On a TTL input port, the 3-state device will be connected between the data bus and the output of the input device as shown in Fig. 7–6.

As discussed in Chapter 6, "Bus Control," these devices provide for a high impedance when inactive. Hundreds or even thousands of input systems can be connected concurrently and only those systems selected by the microprocessor will create a **loading** situation at any given time. Not only does this eliminate the current loading problem, it also provides an alternate avenue for timing control.

For example, the microprocessor can cause the data to be brought to the port location at one time and latched and come back to clock the data through the 3-state devices. For a heavily loaded system, this 2-stage input control is a great advantage. Most preconstructed ports provided by microprocessor manufacturers include this system arrangement.

Typical Device

There are several very attractive ports available which are reasonably priced and easily adapted to specific systems. The option to develop customized ports from discrete components is always available. However, the person just becoming familiar with microprocessor systems is much more likely to be successful with a commercial device.

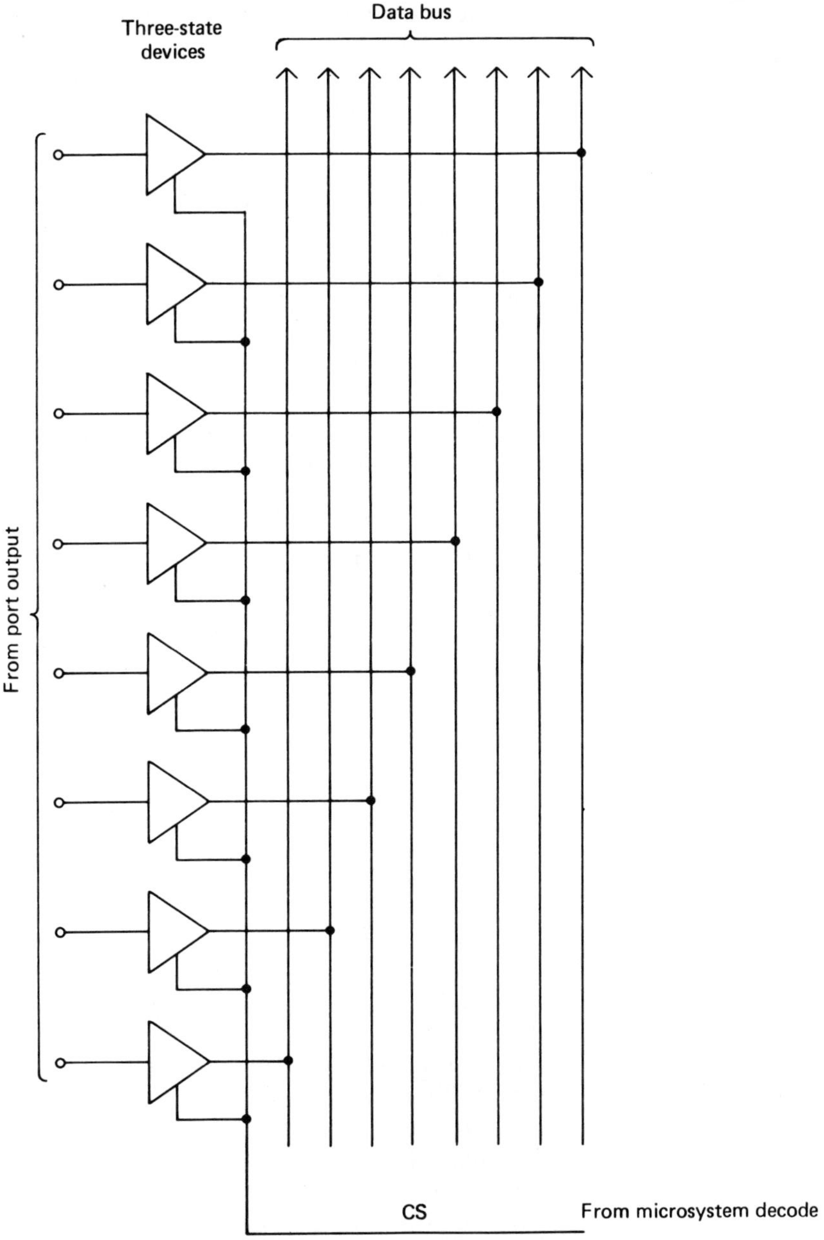

Fig. 7–6. Input 3-state buffering.

One such device which is easily applied as either an input or output port is the 8212 8-bit input/output port. It is produced by Intel but is just as compatible with the Motorola MC6800/6802 as it is with the Intel 8080/8085. It is selected for discussion here, because of its simplicity and universal applicability, as a very typical nonprogrammable port device.

The system in Fig. 7–7 is a set of D flip-flops feeding a set of 3-state buffers. The eight sets are all connected so that the control and selection signals activate the devices simultaneously. A short discussion concentrating on the circuitry inside the dotted lines of Fig. 7–7 should suffice to illustrate the basic operation of the device.

Other than the data in and data out lines, there are only three lines entering the area: enable, clock and clear. Until the enable line activates the 3-state devices, they remain in the high-impedance state and no signal may pass. This fact provides for all kinds of signal activity to occur on the input sides of the port with no detrimental effects to the output.

Note that the data latches are level clocked. That is, as long as the clock is high, Q follows D; when the clock goes low, the data present at the time of the negative going edge is latched. The $\overline{\text{CLR}}$ input causes the data at all Qs to go to 0. This clear command may be overridden by the clock signal. That is, if the clock and $\overline{\text{CLR}}$ pulses are coincident, the clock will dominate the action and cause present data to be latched.

With these few facts in mind, it is easy to see how data can be properly passed to or from the microprocessor data bus.

Assuming that the microprocessor has control of the clock and the enable line through the control logic, data may be passed in the following manner. Whatever data is present at the input will be latched when the clock is brought low.

There is a 15 nanosecond set up time which means that the clock line should not be activated until at least 15 nanoseconds after the data pulses have arrived to assure that no data is in transition state.

The enable line is then activated and the latched data is presented to the output. There is a 40 nanosecond delay possible after the enable pulse before the output can be considered valid. This 40 nanoseconds plus the 15 nanoseconds means that the output control signals should remain stable for a minimum of 55 nanoseconds to assure proper data transfer. Even at a 5 MHz clock rate for the microprocessor, the machine cycles are 200 nanoseconds in duration so the concern over pulse duration becomes negligible. In other words, the port is at least four times as fast as the microprocessor at the present time. A microprocessor would have to be operating at 20 MHz to begin causing timing problems with this port device.

PIN CONFIGURATION

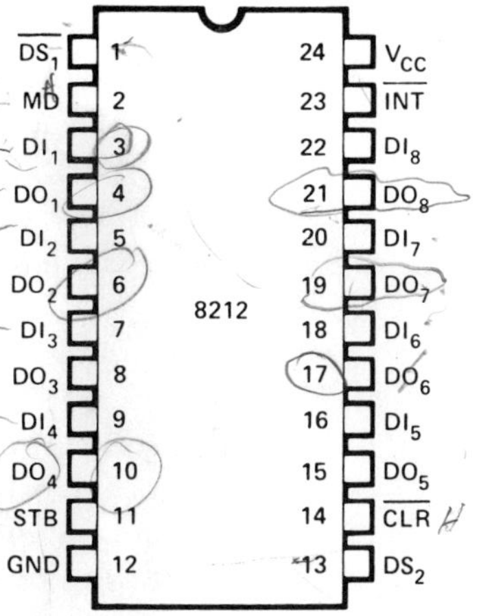

LOGIC DIAGRAM

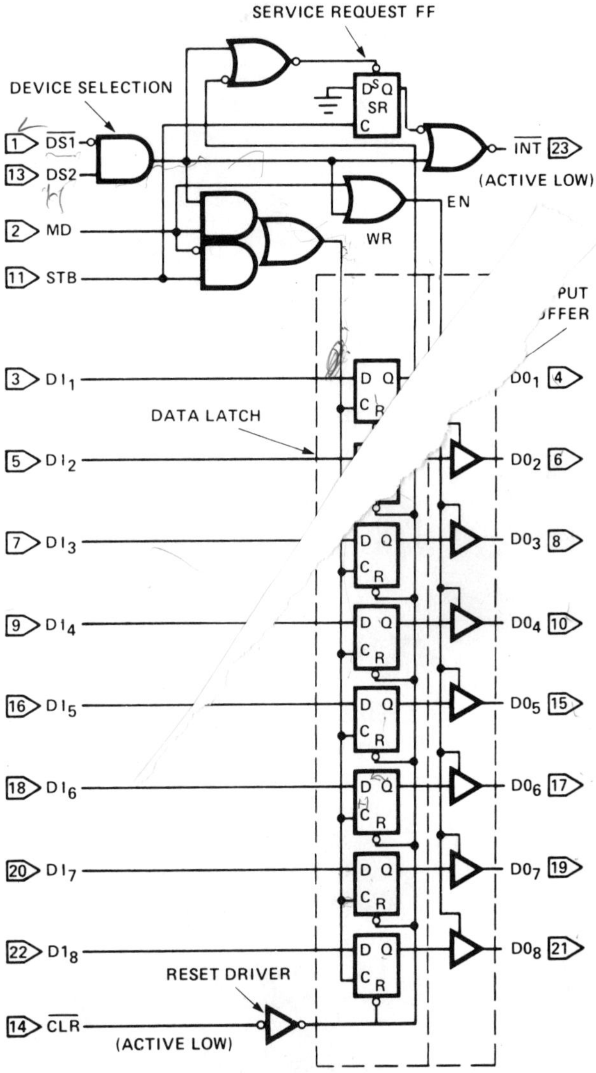

PIN NAMES

DI_1-DI_8	DATA IN
DO_1-DO_8	DATA OUT
$\overline{DS_1}$-DS_2	DEVICE SELECT
MD	MODE
STB	STROBE
$\overline{INT}$	INTERRUPT (ACTIVE LOW)
$\overline{CLR}$	CLEAR (ACTIVE LOW)

Fig. 7–7. 8212 logic diagram and pin out. (*Reprinted by permission of Intel Corporation © 1975*)

Looking now at the control logic shows how this device can be made to serve various port configuration functions. The mode line (pin 2) serves two functions: (1) it determines the source of the clock pulse and (2) it either enables the output (MD high) or it turns control of the line over to the data selection logic (MD low). When the device is connected in input configuration, it is normally tied low giving control of the buffers to the microsystem through the device selection address decoding. The strobe line acts as the clock line when MD equals 0 and as an interrupt request when appropriate.

This universal port can be configured in a variety of ways. For the detailed connections of various applications, consult the *Intel Data Catalog.*

A few of these applications are listed here.

1. Gated buffer
2. **Bidirectional bus driver**
3. Handshaking port
4. Latch
5. Interrupting ports

The next section also shows how a pair of 8212s can be made into a programmable input/output port.

PROGRAMMABLE PORTS

As mentioned earlier, the theory inherent in the programmable ports is quite straightforward. However, the actual hardware needed to accomplish the programmable characteristics is quite complex. Thankfully, the only necessary involvement with the actual internal hardware aspects of the devices at this point is addressing them through program commands and understanding in general what is occurring within the device.

The basic concept of how directional flow of data could be controlled on a one line basis was already discussed in the "Bus Control" chapter. The 8212 port chip introduced in the previous section will be used here to illustrate the principal technique of programmable ports. Two devices specifically designed as programmable ports will then be illustrated and explained in some detail.

General Procedure

Almost all programmable devices are set up to be operated in essentially the same way. They have an internal control register which is loaded from the data bus when a particular address accompanies the data. The data loaded into the control register constitutes the **control word.** This control word is used by the device to set up a particular internal hardware configuration of input and output directions for individual lines or groups of lines. That hardware may then be used in the mode until changed by another control word. A single programmable input/output port can be controlled using a pair of 8212 chips.

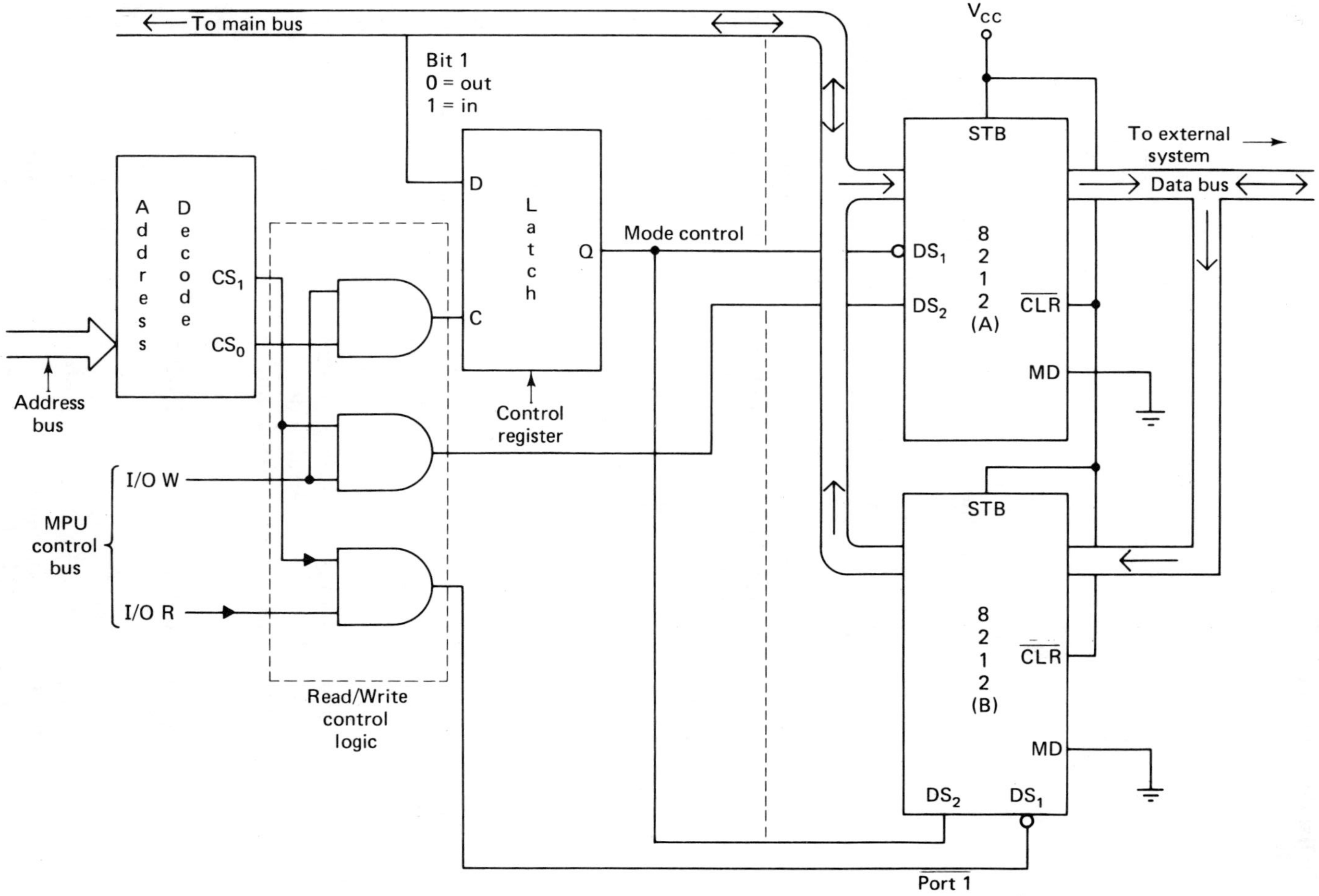

Fig. 7–8. Discrete hardware programmable port using 8212 devices.

Discrete System

The connections to the 8212 are shown in Fig. 7–8. By tying the STB and CLR to V_{CC} and the mode to ground, each of the 8212s is ready to operate as a simple gated buffer when selected. The device is activated by the selection logic of $\overline{DS1}$ and DS2. These selection lines are connected through external circuitry which accomplishes the program control capability.

The address decoder will generate a CS_0 any time address 00 is used and a CS_1 any time address 01 is used. Consider what happens when 00 data is sent to port 00. First, CS_0 becomes valid. Data bit 1 becomes 0 and, at the proper time (MPU control timing), the I/O W signal clocks the 0 data bit into the latch. The coincidence of CS_0 and I/O W accomplishes clocking the signal through the AND gate. The Q output of the latch is now at 0. The 0 is felt at the selection lines of both A and B 8212s causing A to be enabled for further selection and B to be disabled for further selection. Note the active low input requirement of DS_1 chip A and the active high input requirement of DS_2 chip B. The hardware has been effectively configured as an output port and will remain so until the latch status is changed. This latch is acting as the control register and the data sent to port 00 is the control word.

The use of this (NOW) output port 1 is similar to that of any standard, programmed I/O output port. Data written to I/O address 01 will be passed through the A chip out to the external system.

If a data byte 01 is sent to port 00, the hardware will be configured in an input mode by a 1 being placed at the Q output of the latch enabling chip B and disabling chip A. Data would then pass through chip B from the external system when I/O address 01 is read. Since the MPU logic assures that the read and write lines are mutually exclusive, no directional transfer problems can occur.

Note again that the design of this port hardware is not timing-oriented. That is, the design relies on the timing of the MPU. The hardware is only required to provide signal coincidence. This system is also relatively universal in design. It can be effectively connected to an 8080/8085, MC6800/6802, and so on.

THE INTEL 8255 PROGRAMMABLE PERIPHERAL INTERFACE (PPI)

The Intel 8255 Programmable Peripheral Interface is a preconstructed programmable port. This device will also be discussed in Chapter 10, "The Intel 8080: Architecture and Support Chips."

Compare Fig. 7–8 with the block diagram of the 8255 in Fig. 7–9.

PIN CONFIGURATION

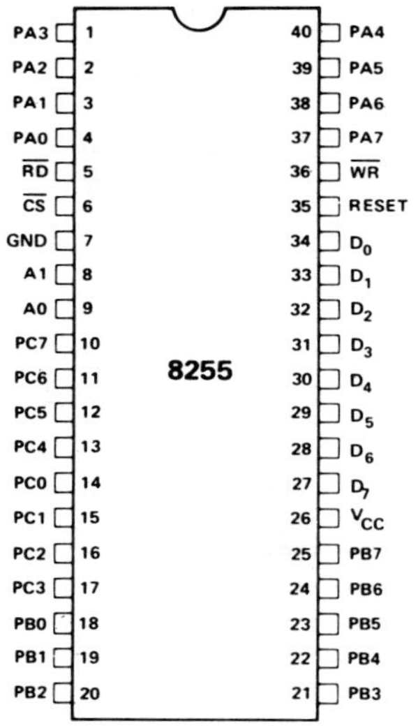

PIN NAMES

D_7–D_0	DATA BUS (BI-DIRECTIONAL)
RESET	RESET INPUT
$\overline{CS}$	CHIP SELECT
$\overline{RD}$	READ INPUT
$\overline{WR}$	WRITE INPUT
A0, A1	PORT ADDRESS
PA7-PA0	PORT A (BIT)
PB7-PB0	PORT B (BIT)
PC7-PC0	PORT C (BIT)
V_{CC}	+5 VOLTS
GND	ø VOLTS

8255 BLOCK DIAGRAM

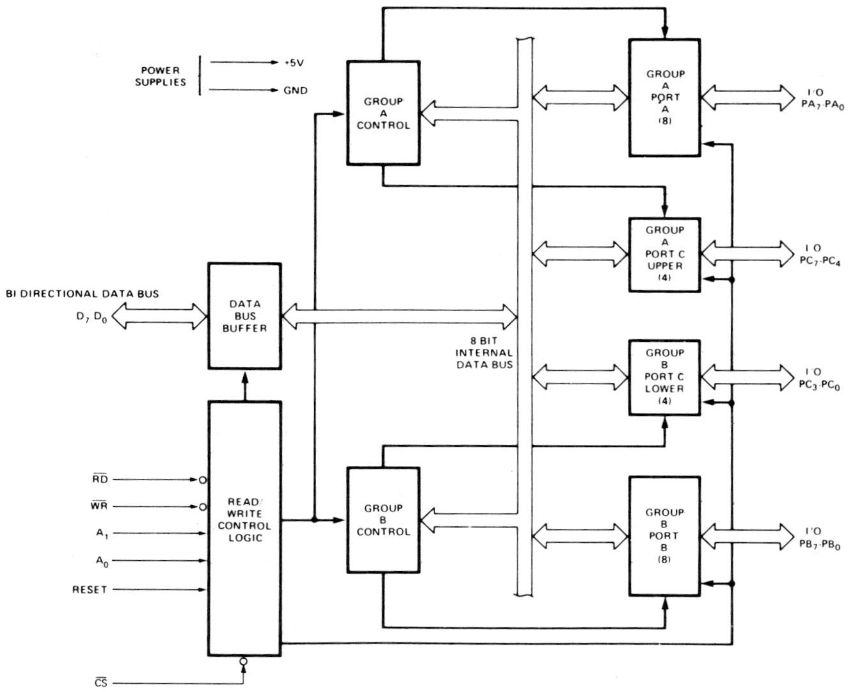

Fig. 7–9. 8255 block diagram and pin out. (*Reprinted by permission of Intel Corporation © 1975*)

Do not become overly concerned with the interal operation of the device but concentrate on the sequence of events (address, data and control) that must occur to (1) program the device for mode of operation and (2) access the port configurations set up.

The following items should be noted before discussion.

1. $\overline{CS}$, $\overline{WR}$, $\overline{RD}$ input pins to the device are all active low. (0 constitutes the valid or true state for enabling.)

2. $\overline{CS}$ is the primary enable line (unless $\overline{CS}$ is low the device is inactive).

3. $\overline{RD}$ low enables the microprocessor to input data through the device. $\overline{WR}$ low enables the microprocessor to output data through the device.

4. The control register and port addressing is done using A_0 and A_1 inputs. The two inputs are normally tied to the main address bus lines A_0 and A_1 but do not necessarily have to obey that convention. Connecting them to other address lines changes the absolute addresses of the three ports and the control register.

Addressing

In using the device, the control word is first sent to select both mode and port configuration. When the control word is sent, a particular addressing format must be followed.

Table 7–1 8255 Basic Operation

A_1	A_0	$\overline{RD}$	$\overline{WR}$	$\overline{CS}$	INPUT OPERATION (READ)
0	0	0	1	0	Port A → data bus
0	1	0	1	0	Port B → data bus
1	0	0	1	0	Port C → data bus
					OUTPUT OPERATION (WRITE)
0	0	1	0	0	Data bus → port A
0	1	1	0	0	Data bus → port B
1	0	1	0	0	Data bus → port C
1	1	1	0	0	Data bus → control
					DISABLE FUNCTION
X	X	X	X	1	Data bus → 3-state
1	1	0	1	0	Illegal condition

The 8255 is constructed with twenty-four data lines divided into two subgroups, group A and group B. Each subgroup is made up of a simple 8-bit port (A or B) and, depending upon the mode of operation, three, four or five lines form a third port (port C). The basic operations of the device are defined according to Table 7–1.

The device is addressed by the microprocessor as either four consecutive port locations or as four consecutive memory locations. If the device address decoding is being handled in I/O port method, A_2 through A_7 should generate the chip select $\overline{CS}$. If the device address decoding is being handled as memory, the $\overline{CS}$ should be generated by A_2 through A_{15}. The address assignments then would look like Fig. 7–10.

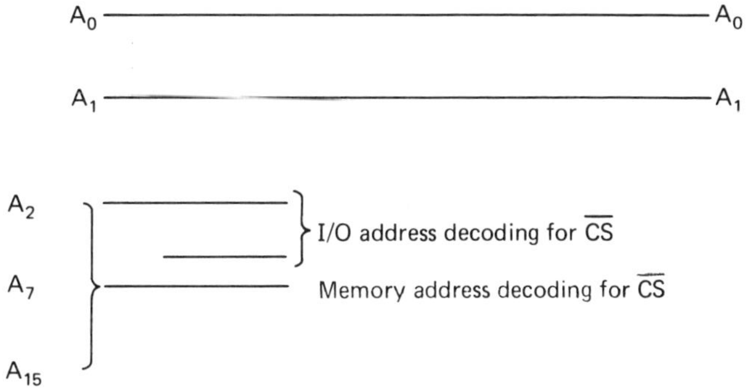

Fig. 7–10. 8255 address assignments.

Selection Table

A_1	A_0	$\overline{CS}$	I/O		Memory
0	0	0	Port A	or	first register location
0	1	0	Port B	or	second register location
1	0	0	Port C	or	third register location
1	1	0	Control	or	fourth register location
x	x	1		not selected	

Control Word Format

In the control word format for mode selection and port configuration, three modes of operation may be selected.

Mode 0—simple input/output

Mode 1—strobed I/O
Two 8-bit data ports with 4-bit control and handshaking ability

Mode 2—strobed bidirectional I/O
One 8-bit port (A only), 5-bit control and handshaking ability.

In order to select one of these modes, data bit 7 of the control word must be high (1). When this criteria is met, all of the port assignments and mode selection options are defined by the 0 and 1 combinations in bits 1 through 6 of the control word. The format of assignment for the rest of the control word is shown in Table 7–2.

Table 7–2 illustrates that a great variety of possible port configurations has been packed into the chip. For example, if both group A and B are selected to operate in mode 0, there are fifteen possible combinations of port configurations that may be selected by various combinations of bits D_4, D_3, D_1 and D_0. Further, there are three modes for group A and two modes for group B giving six possible combinations of mode selection.

In all, ninety possible combinations of port configuration, not counting the ability to control individual bits of port C, can be set up. Obviously, all of them cannot be discussed. Detailed coverage of these and a variety of applications are provided by Intel in the data catalogs and user's manuals.

The address decoding previously discussed is external to the chip and may be handled by standard 8080 I/O decoding or as decoded memory register locations. Therefore, it is just as easily applied to a Motorola MC6800/6802 microprocessor as the Intel 8080/8085 since the Motorola chip handles its I/O devices as memory locations anyway. Motorola also has developed a variety of programmable devices for use in peripheral applications. Two of the more common devices are discussed here.

MOTOROLA I/O DEVICES

Although the microprocessor is a powerful, sophisticated and versatile device, a very real problem exists in virtually all microprocessor systems. It is input/output—getting electrical signals into and out from the microprocessors. The solution to the I/O problem must be efficient and, at the same time, cost effective.

When Motorola Semiconductors Inc. had the MC6800 in its embryo stage, several major prerequisites became apparent.

1. Eliminating the requirement of multiple voltage sources.
2. Supplying complete documentation for the microproducts
3. Offering a complete family of integrated circuits to support the MC6800 microprocessor

Table 7–2 Control Word Format

	MODE/BIT ENABLE					
D_7	1 = enable mode set for rest of control word 0 = enable bit set operations for rest of control word					
	MODE SELECTION (A)					
D_6 D_5	Mode selection for group A (made up of port A and upper 5 bits of port C) 00 = mode 0 01 = mode 1 1X = mode 2					
D_4	sets port A I/O configuration 1 = input 0 = output					
D_3	defines the upper 5 bit functions of port C					
	Pc7	Pc6	Pc5	Pc4	Pc3	*
	1 = I/O	I/O	I3F (A)	$\overline{\text{STB}}$ (A)	INTR (A)	
	0 = OBF (A)	$\overline{\text{AcKA}}$	I/O	I/O	INTR (A)	
	MODE SELECTION (B)					
D_2	mode selection for group B (made up of port B and lower 3 bits of port C) 0 = mode 0 1 = mode 1					
D_1	sets port B I/O configuration 1 = input 0 = output					
D_0	defines low 3 bit function of port C					
	Pc2	Pc1	Pc0			†
	1 = $\overline{\text{STB}}$ (B)	IBF (B)	INTR (B)			
	0 = $\overline{\text{ACK}}$ (B)	$\overline{\text{OBF}}$ (B)	INTR (B)			

†* In mode 0 port C is grouped in 4 bits upper and lower and may be set for input or output by a 1 or a 0 respectively. The specialized pin assignments apply only when used in concurrence with mode 1.

* If used in concurrence with mode 2 it makes no difference whether port C bits are set as input or output. All are assigned functions shown

$\overline{\text{OBF}}$ = output buffer full IBF = input buffer full INTR = interrupt to processor $\overline{\text{ACK}}$ = port acknowledgment reception of data $\overline{\text{STB}}$ = strobes data into latch from port

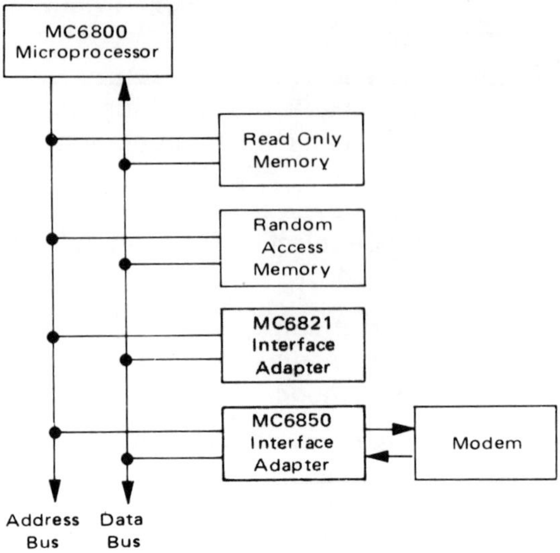

Fig. 7–11. MC6800 microcomputer system block diagram. (*Courtesy Motorola Inc.*)

The MC6800 fulfilled the first requirement with a single TTL 5 V level source. Second, Motorola's technical literature is some of the most complete in the industry. And regarding support integrated circuits, Motorola saw the problem of I/O and solved it by designing the MC6821 Peripheral Interface Adapter or PIA and MC6850 Asynchronous Communications Interface Adapter or ACIA.

Figure 7–11 is a block diagram of the main sections of a basic microprocessor system using the MC6821 for parallel I/O and the MC6850 for serial I/O.

The I/O interface requirements met by the PIA and ACIA are:

1. General purpose: to handle the many different types of peripherals and their specific electrical signal requirements
2. Programmable: to insure the needed versatility
3. Byte-organized data lines: flexibility and/or standardization
4. Control lines: enhance efficiency with MPU

The MC6821 Peripheral Interface Adapter (PIA)

The MC6821 PIA is used for parallel interfacing. Figure 7–12 is a block diagram of this microprocessor support device.

Note that the interconnection points on the left, which include the data bus group and the memory address and control/interrupt group,

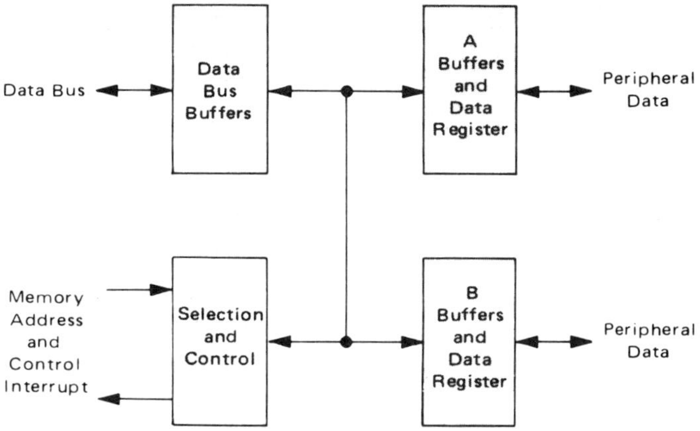

Fig. 7–12. MC6821 Peripheral Interface Adapter block diagram. (*Courtesy Motorola Inc.*)

are connected to the microprocessor bus system. On the right side of the diagram, the peripheral data A and peripheral data B groups are the parallel I/O lines connected to peripheral devices in the world outside the microprocessor system.

These programmable I/O lines create a great degree of flexibility. The expanded block diagram in Fig. 7–13 illustrates that the function of the sixteen peripheral data lines as either input lines or as output lines is simply programmed as needed for a particular application.

Example of configuring I/O lines. A brief example of configuring these I/O lines will demonstrate how easily this task can be implemented. For example, the application may require eight input lines and eight output lines. During the initialization of the system, the microprocessor program will establish the I/O configuration the PIA will take. The MC6821 is designed to react to the following I/O coding.

The output registers, sections A and B, are each eight bits wide. For this particular example calling for eight input lines and eight output lines, the A section will function as the set of eight input lines and the B section will function as the eight output lines. During initialization, the binary coding that is placed in the data direction register A and likewise the binary coding that is sent to the data direction register B will cause these sixteen lines (eight lines per register section) to behave as input or output lines.

The specific coding is: a binary 0 will cause that particular line to take on input characteristics and a binary 1 will cause a line to function as an output line. Hence the binary code 0000 0000 sent to data

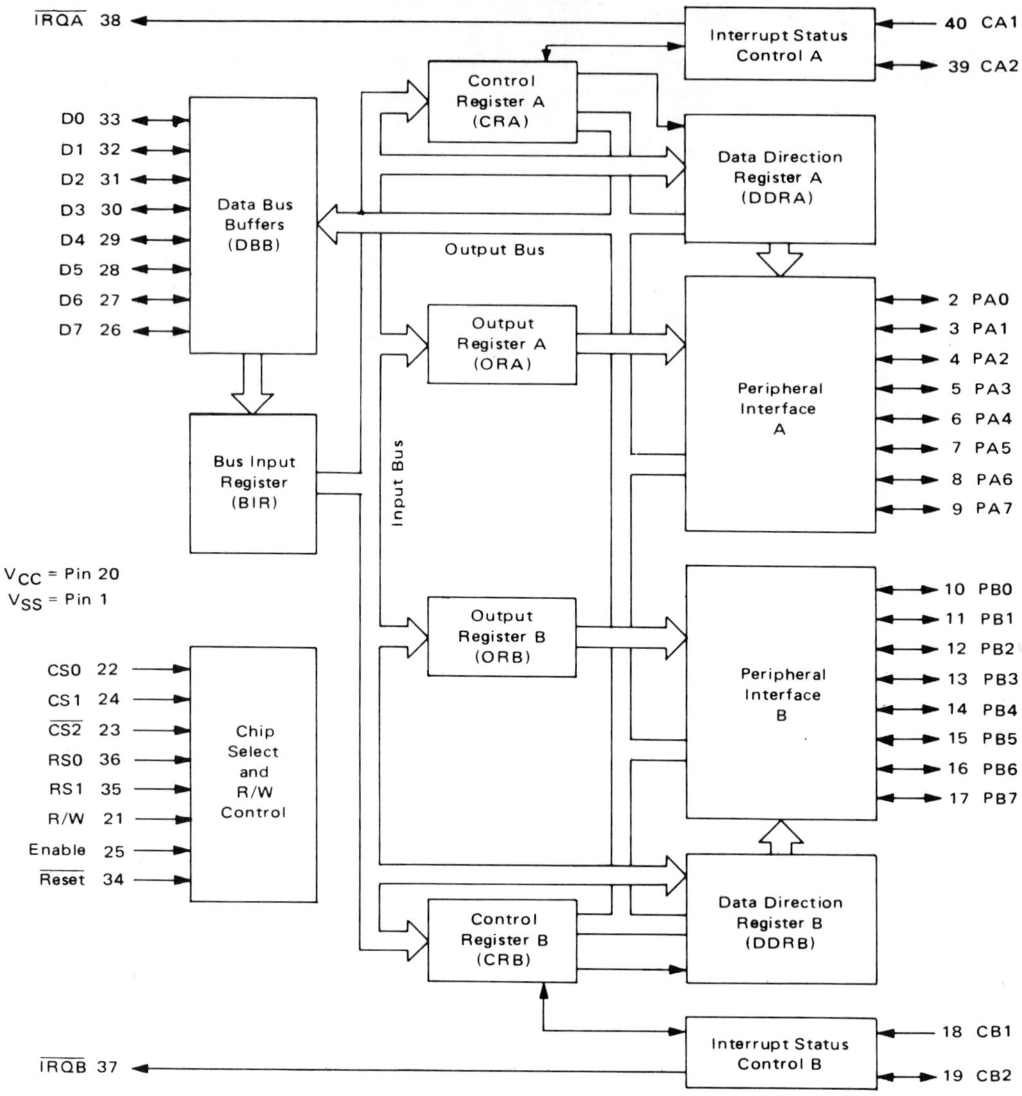

Fig. 7–13. PIA expanded block diagram. (*Courtesy Motorola Inc.*)

direction register A will accomplish the eight input lines required and the binary code 1111 1111 will cause data direction register B to set up section B as the needed eight output lines.

Altering the I/O configuration. This 8-input and 8-output configuration can be altered by altering the program. In the next application, for example, every other line must be output, input, output, input and so on. During initialization, the binary coding 1010 1010 sent to the data direction register will establish the output, input, output, input . . . pattern that is being called for. The I/O configuration of the microprocessor interface is extremely flexible because of its truly programmable nature.

The four control lines can be used to increase efficient operation with the MPU by permitting the necessary handshake control logic for input and output peripheral operation.

Summary of the MC6821 PIA. The MC6821 Peripheral Interface Adapter provides the universal means of interfacing peripheral equipment to the MC6800 microprocessing unit. The device is capable of interfacing the MPU to various peripherals via two 8-bit bidirectional peripheral data buses and four control lines.

The functional configuration of the PIA is programmed by the MPU during system initialization. Each of the peripheral data lines can be programmed to act as input or output, and each of the four control-interrupt lines may be programmed for one of several control modes. The above features allow a high degree of flexibility in the overall operation of the interface.

The key features of the MC6821 PIA can be stated as follows:

- 8-bit directional data bus for communication with MPU
- Two bidirectional 8-bit buses for interface to peripherals
- Two programmable control registers
- Two programmable data direction registers
- Four individually-controlled interrupt input lines; two usable as peripheral control outputs
- Handshake control logic for input and output peripheral operation
- High-impedance, 3-state and direct transistor drive peripheral lines
- Program controlled interrupt and interrupt disable capability
- CMOS drive capability on side A peripheral lines
- Two TTL drive capability on all A and B side buffers
- TTL compatible
- Static operation*

The MC6850 Asynchronous Communications Interface Adapter (ACIA)

The MC6850 is a companion part to the parallel interface adapter, MC6821 PIA. Figure 7–14 is a simplified block diagram of the ACIA.

* *MC6821 Data Sheet* (Austin, Texas: Motorola Inc., 1977), p. 1.

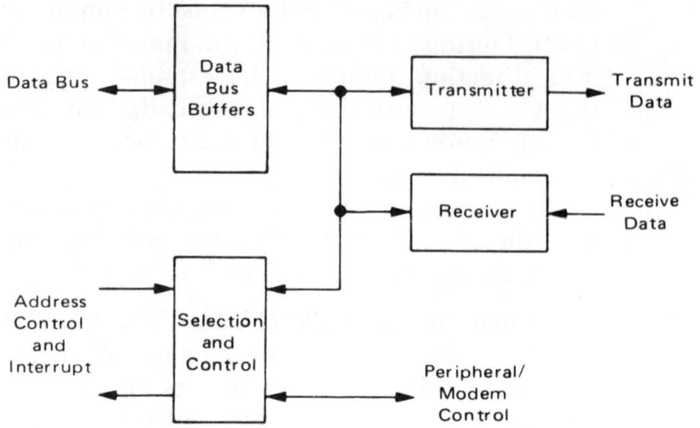

Fig. 7–14. MC6850 Asynchronous Communications Interface Adapter block diagram. (*Courtesy Motorola Inc.*)

A microprocessor manipulates data in parallel form. However, there are many occasions when data interfacing to and from the microprocessor system must be in serial format. The ACIA handles the task of serial interfacing very effectively.

Interface example. The concept of serial-to-parallel/parallel-to-serial conversion is crucial to understanding microprocessor interfacing. A typical communication application using this conversion is shown in Fig. 7–15 (a,b,c).

The teletypewriter (TTY) is usually a serial data receiving and sending machine. The MPU is a parallel data receiving and sending machine. In order for the two machines to communicate, a parallel-to-serial/serial-to-parallel format conversion process must take place.

This conversion is done through a serial communication loop because it requires only one series circuit to send or receive binary data. If this same communication example were to implement a parallel data sending and receiving loop, eight circuits in a parallel arrangement would be required instead of the less complicated serial data loop. Hence, a serial communication loop reduces the overall cost and circuit complexity. The drawback is a considerable increase in the time required to send a group of 8-bit words—one bit after another—in a series fashion versus faster transmission in parallel. This exemplifies a typical performance-cost tradeoff.

The timing for a typical transmitter **asynchronous** operation is illustrated in Fig. 7–16.

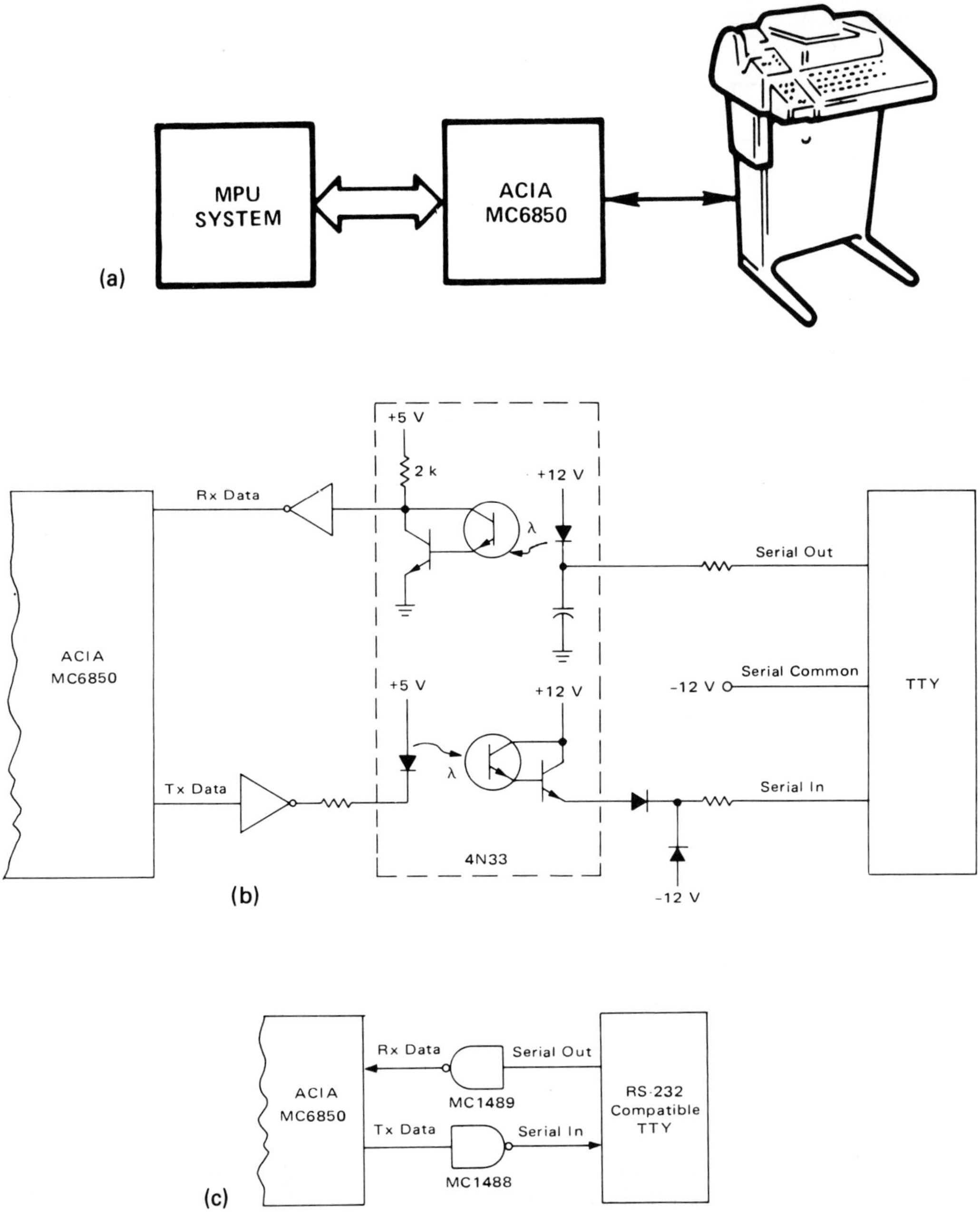

Fig. 7–15. (a) MPU to TTY interface. (b) Teletype interface. (c) RS-232 interface. (*Courtesy Motorola Inc.*)

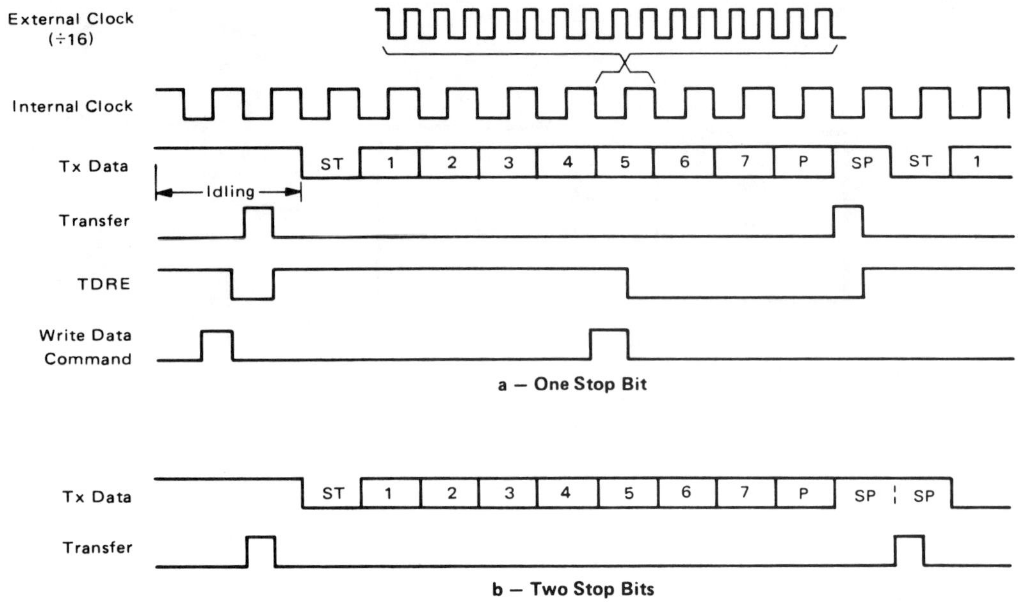

Fig. 7–16. Transmitter asynchronous operation. (*Courtesy Motorola Inc.*)

Figure 7–17 is an expanded block diagram of the MC6850 ACIA. Notice the parallel connection to the MPU in data lines D0-D7 and the standard control bus and timing lines on the left of the ACIA block diagram. The serial loop consists of the transmit data line (pin 6) and the receive line (pin 2) on the right of the diagram.

This microprocessor support device is, like most support interfacing devices mentioned in this text, machine independent. That is, these devices can be used with virtually any 8-bit microprocessor regardless of the manufacturer.

Summary of the MC6850 ACIA. The MC6850 Asynchronous Communications Interface Adapter provides the data formatting and control to interface serial asynchronous data communications information to bus-organized systems such as the MC6800 microprocessing unit.

The bus interface of the MC6850 includes select, enable, read/write, interrupt, and bus interface logic to allow data transfer over an 8-bit bidirectional data bus. The parallel data of the bus system is serially transmitted and received by the asynchronous data interface, with proper formatting and error checking. The functional configuration of the ACIA is programmed via the data bus during system initialization. A programmable control register provides variable

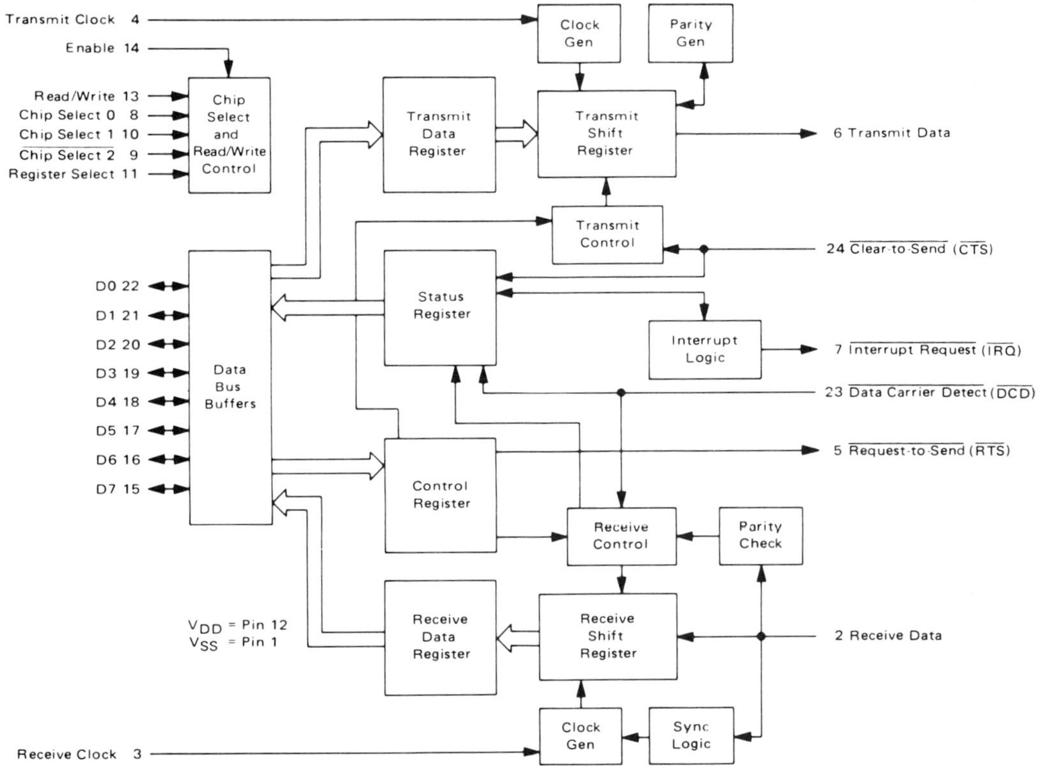

Fig. 7–17. ACIA expanded block diagram. (*Courtesy Motorola Inc.*)

word lengths, clock division ratios, transmit control, receive control and interrupt control. For peripheral or **modem** operation, three control lines are provided. These lines allow the ACIA to interface directly with the MC6860 0-600 bps digital modem.

The most important features of the ACIA are:

- Eight and 9-bit transmission
- Optional even and odd parity
- **Parity**, overrun, and framing error checking
- Programmable control register
- Optional ÷ 1, ÷ 16, and ÷ 64 clock modes
- Up to 500 Kbps transmission
- False start bit deletion
- Peripheral/modem control functions
- Double buffered
- One or two stop-bit operation

SUMMARY

Study of this chapter should result in an appreciation of the wide variety of specialized devices available as I/O devices. Only a few specific devices have been introduced here because they present a very generalized approach to porting. In the final chapters of this text, a variety of other devices available to the user for more specialized applications will be discussed.

QUESTIONS

1. What are the two basic categories of ports?
2. Explain the difference between programmed I/O and programmable I/O ports.
3. What is DMA?
4. What is a port?
5. What three conditions must a port satisfy?
6. How does the Motorola MC6800 differ from the Intel 8080 in port addressing?
7. In your own words, briefly describe the sequence of events that allows transfer of data through a port.
8. What is handshaking?
9. When is handshaking usually necessary or desirable?
10. How do input ports differ from output ports?
11. What two things do the 3-state devices accomplish in most ports?
12. What does the MD (mode) line do on the 8212 I/O port?
13. What does a control word do for a programmable port?
14. Why are most programmable ports set up to respond to more than one address?
15. What is meant by control word format?
16. Explain the difference between I/O address decoding and memory address decoding.
17. Describe the procedure to establish eight input lines and eight output lines using the Motorola MC6821.
18. How many total input lines are possible with the MC6821?
19. How many total output lines are possible with the MC6821?
20. Can the Motorola MC6850 ACIA be used to convert serial data to parallel data as well as to convert parallel data to serial data? How?
21. What is the maximum transmission rate in bit/seconds for the MC6850?

22. Can the MC6850 ACIA be used with either 8-bit or 9-bit word length transmissions?
23. The Motorola MC6850 can function with either even or odd parity. True or false? Why?
24. What ACIA divide-by option would be used to interface a 300 baud (bit time = 3.33 milliseconds) printer if the data reference frequency is 5800 Hz? Note that baud rate $= \frac{\text{sec}}{\text{bit time}}$.
25. At what baud rate does a system implementing an MC6850 ACIA using the divide-by-64 option and having a data reference frequency of 7040 Hz operate?

Chapter 8

Memory

GLOSSARY

Dynamic random access memory A memory device that stores data as charge on a capacitive component and therefore needs refreshing regularly in order to retain its contents.

EEPROM Electricity erasable programmable read only memory.

EPROM Erasable programmable read only memory; ideally suited for uses where fast turn around and pattern experimentation are important.

Mask A device made of a thin sheet of metal that contains an open pattern used to shield selected portions of a base during a deposition process.

Nonvolatile A memory type that holds data even if power has been disconnected.

PROM Programmable read only memory. A semiconductor diode array that is manufactured with a pattern of either all 1s or all 0s and is user programmed by fusing or burning out diode junctions.

RAM Random access memory. Provides immediate access to any storage location point in memory by means of vertical and horizontal coordinates. Information may be written in or read out in the same very fast procedure.

Read To access information from external storage and transmit this information to an internal storage.

ROM Read only memory. A nonvolatile memory device programmed by a mask pattern as part of the final manufacturing stage.

Information is stored permanently or semi-permanently and is read out but not altered in operation.

Scratchpad A nickname for CPU memory pertaining to information that the CPU holds temporarily. RAM or registers used to store temporary intermediate results (data) or memory addresses (pointers).

Static operation Data stored in a conventional bistable flip-flop that need not be refreshed.

Volatile Storage medium requiring continuous power dissipation in order to retain information.

Write To record information in a register, location or other storage device or medium.

In earlier sections of this text, the concept of memory was introduced. Now a more complete discussion of this important area of a microcomputer system is in order. Before the specific types of memory can be understood, some general terms should be defined.

In all types of computer systems, from a small dedicated microprocessor system to the largest full size computer, memory plays a very essential part. The memory section of the microcomputer system serves the purpose of holding either information that the computer will need or information that the computer has already generated which will be utilized in the future.

RELATIONSHIP CPU AND MEMORY

An interdependency exists between the CPU and memory. In the instruction sets chapter, the idea of a continuous fetch and execute cycle was emphasized. The CPU is continuously fetching instructions and/or data *from memory.* This important concept of the CPU relying on memory cannot be over-emphasized. The CPU is a very important and powerful part of a complete microprocessor system but it cannot function effectively without memory.

The CPU needs to be told what to do and when to do it. This, of course, is the role of instructions. The orderly arrangement of these instructions and data is the purpose of a computer program (software). The instructions and data are entered into memory—not the CPU—by the computer programmer. The CPU has the capability to interpret and carry out these instructions and to act on the data information that is fetched from memory.

Instruction and Data Interpretation

A problem that most beginners have with understanding the interrelationship between the CPU and memory can be solved if it is clearly understood that the CPU *does not* contain the instructions and/or data of a microprocessor system. The CPU has the ability to interpret these instructions and/or act upon the data that is transferred from memory to the central processing unit.

Read/Write

Before discussing the first and most versatile type of memory, the **RAM,** which stands for random access memory, two terms used in reference to memory should be defined. The term **write** means that information (instructions or data) is put into memory. The term **read** means that information (instructions or data) is taken from memory. Recall that all information is in the binary format (1s or 0s). This group of 1s and 0s is put into memory (written) or taken out of memory (read).

RAM

As previously mentioned, the term RAM stands for random access memory. Random means that any one of the different memory locations can be written into or read from with equal ease and that it takes the same amount of time to address any one of the different memory locations within the same device.

Volatility

There are several other terms used in studying memories. One is the term **volatile.** Volatility, when used in reference to memories, means the inability to retain the information placed in memory after power has been removed. The term **nonvolatile** means that all information placed into memory is retained even when power is removed. The semiconductor RAM memory is of the volatile type. That is, when power is removed, all information previously written in memory is lost.

Requirements for a typical system are:

1. The ability to read and write into memory.
2. The need to retain information such as an executive monitor even in the event of power loss.

Read/Write

A problem develops because memory needs to have both nonvolatility and read/write capability. At the time of this writing, there is not one RAM chip that has both of these desirable functions. The memory chips are either of the RAM family and have the read/write capability but are volatile or of the ROM family and have only the read capability but are nonvolatile.

Scratchpad

The section of the microcomputer memory which uses random access memory chips is often referred to as **scratchpad** meaning that the stored information is useful only for a short period of time and will very likely be changed frequently. An example of this would occur where variables and answers are stored during a mathematical operation.

The Motorola MCM6810 RAM

A closer look at a typical random access memory type of integrated circuit such as the Motorola MCM6810 RAM, shown in Fig. 8–1, would be helpful for a more complete understanding of the finer details of a microprocessor RAM IC memory chip.

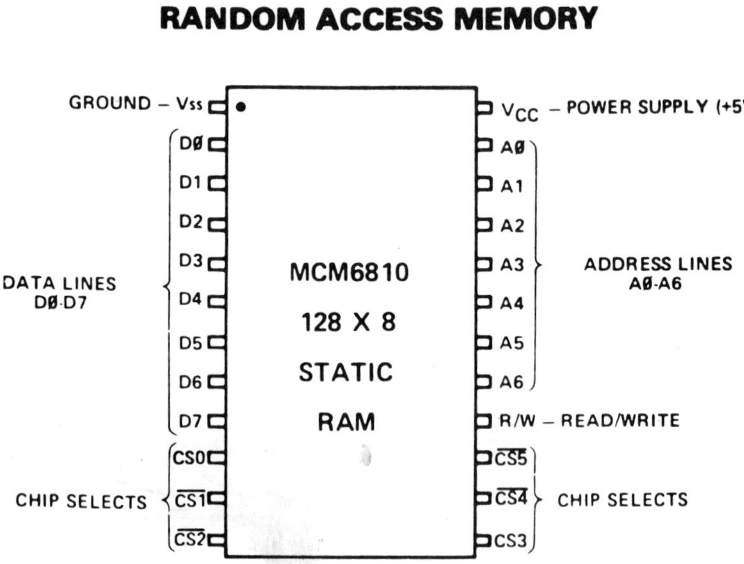

Fig. 8–1. Random access memory (RAM). (*Courtesy Motorola Inc.*)

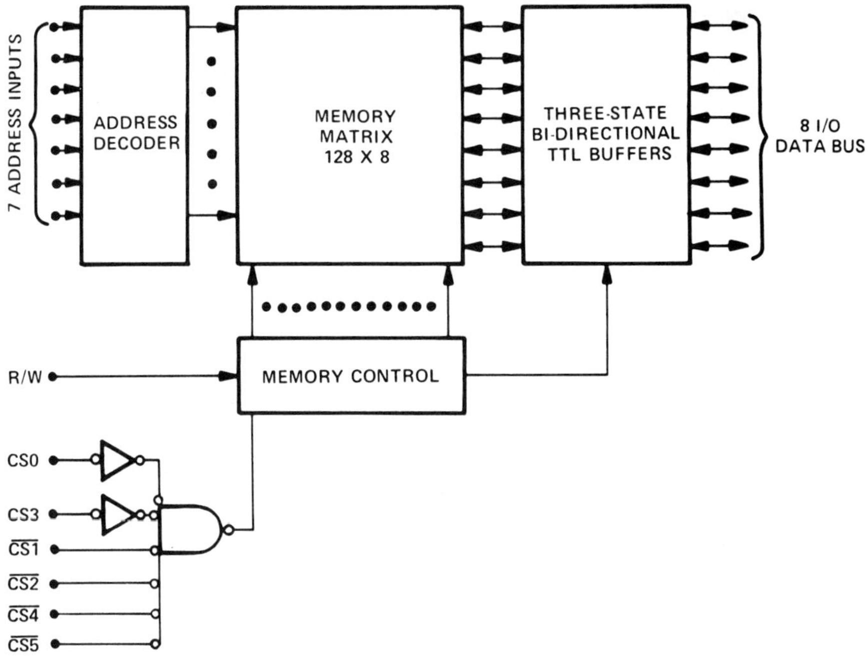

Fig. 8–2. MCM6810 functional block diagram. (*Courtesy Motorola Inc.*)

The identifying characteristic of the MCM6810 is a byte-organized memory designed for use in bus-organized systems. It is fabricated with N-channel silicon gate technology. For ease of use, the device operates from a single power supply, has compatibility with TTL and DTL and needs no clocks or refreshing because of **static operation.** This memory provides random storage in byte increments and memory expansion is provided through multiple chip select inputs.[1]

Study the functional block diagram appearing in Fig. 8–2 which indicates the intrastructure of this RAM: the address decoder, memory matrix 128-by-8, three bidirectional TTL buffers and memory control. In short, the MCM6810 is organized as 128 bytes of 8 bits, has static operation, features bidirectional 3-state data input/output, offers six chip select inputs (four active low, two active high), is TTL compatible and requires a single 5 V supply.[2]

The read/write feature of the RAM makes it a very versatile memory device. However, its volatility presents a special problem.

[1] *M6800 Microcomputer System Design Data* (Phoenix, Arizona: Motorola Inc., 1976), p. 111.
[2] *M6800 Design Data,* p. 111.

The Next Generation

The next generation of semiconductor RAM memories has advanced to higher density (more memory cells/chip) and higher operating frequencies.

As illustrated in Fig. 8–3, Motorola purposely designed the pin assignments of its standard 16-pin dual-in-line packages to allow the hardware designer to upgrade his memory systems readily and cost effectively as the need arises.

These chips exemplify recent RAM developments. They are fabricated using HMOS high performance N-channel silicon gate technology. Complete address decoding is done on chip with address latches incorporated. Data out is controlled by $\overline{CAS}$ allowing for greater system flexibility. All inputs and outputs, including clocks, are fully TTL compatible. These devices incorporate one-transistor cell design and dynamic storage techniques.

Three upward compatible RAM using this high density technology are the MCM4517, MCM6632, and MCM6664.

The Motorola MCM4517 16K × 1 RAM. The MCM4517 is a 16,384-bit, high-speed, **dynamic random access memory.** It is organized as 16,384 1-bit words. This new breed of 5-volt only dynamic RAM combines high performance and improved reliability. By multiplexing row and column address imputs, the MCM4517 requires only seven address lines.

Figure 8–4 is a block diagram of the MCM4517. Refer to Fig. 8–3 for its pin assignments and designations.

Among the key features of the MCM4517 16K × 1 dynamic RAM are:

- Organized as 16,384 words of one bit
- Single 5 volt operation
- Fast 100 ns operation
- Low power dissipation: 150 mW maximum (active); 14 mW maximum (standby)
- 3-state data output
- Internal latches for address and data input
- Early-write common I/O output capability
- 64K compatible 128-cycle, 2 ms refresh
- $\overline{RAS}$ only refresh mode
- $\overline{CAS}$ controlled output
- Upward pin compatibility from the 16K RAM (MCM4116) to the 64K RAM (MCM6664)
- Allows negative overshoot $V_{IL} = -2$ V

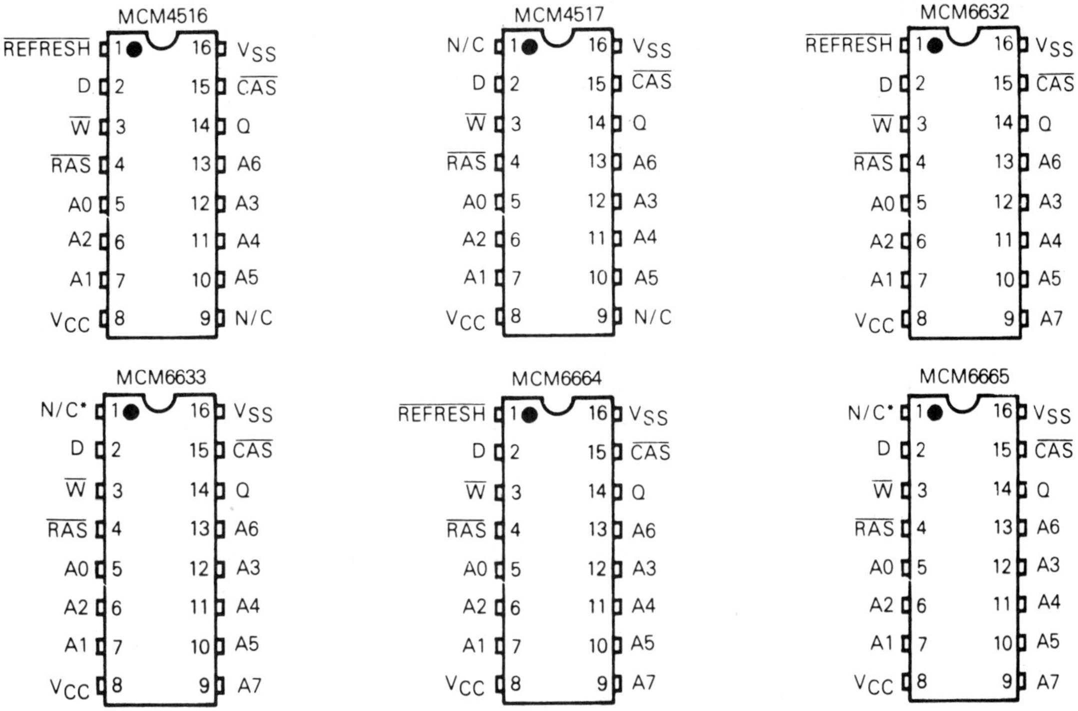

PIN NAMES	
$\overline{\text{REFRESH}}$	Refresh
A0-A7	Address Input
D	Data In
Q	Data Out
$\overline{\text{W}}$	Read/Write Input
$\overline{\text{RAS}}$	Row Address Strobe
$\overline{\text{CAS}}$	Column Address Strobe
V_{CC}	Power (+5 V)
V_{SS}	Ground

Fig. 8–3. High density RAM pin assignment comparison. (*Courtesy Motorola Inc.*)

- Hidden $\overline{\text{RAS}}$ only refresh capability[3]

The Motorola MCM6632 32K × 1 RAM. The MCM6632 represents the next level of memory cell density. It is organized as 32,768 1-bit words. In addition to the $\overline{\text{RAS}}$ only refresh mode, refresh control

[3] *MCM4517 Advance Information* (Austin, Texas: Motorola Inc., 1980), p. 1.

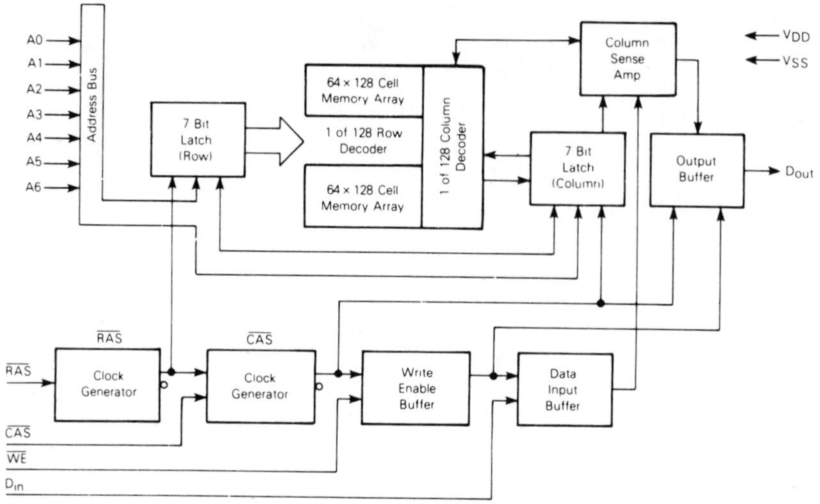

Fig. 8–4. MCM4517 block diagram. (*Courtesy Motorola Inc.*)

available on pin 1 provides automatic and self-refresh modes. The MCM6632's architecture is illustrated in Fig. 8–5.

A comparison of the MCM6632 dynamic random access memory pin assignments to those of the MCM4517 as shown in Fig. 8–3 demonstrates its upward pin compatibility with the 16K RAM.

The MCM6632 32K × 1 RAM features include:

- Organized as 32,768 words of one bit
- Single +5 V operation
- Fast 150 ns operation
- Low power dissipation: 275 mW maximum (active); 30 mW maximum (standby)
- 3-state data output
- Internal latches for address and data input
- Early-write common I/O capability
- 16K compatible 128-cycle, 2 ms refresh
- Control on pin 1 for automatic and self refresh
- $\overline{\text{RAS}}$ only refresh mode
- $\overline{\text{CAS}}$ controlled output
- Upward pin compatible from the 16K RAM series[4]

The Motorola MCM6664 64K × 1 RAM. The Motorola MCM6664 is the most complex semiconductor RAM memory device covered in

[4] *MCM6632* (Austin, Texas: Motorola Inc., 1980), p. 1.

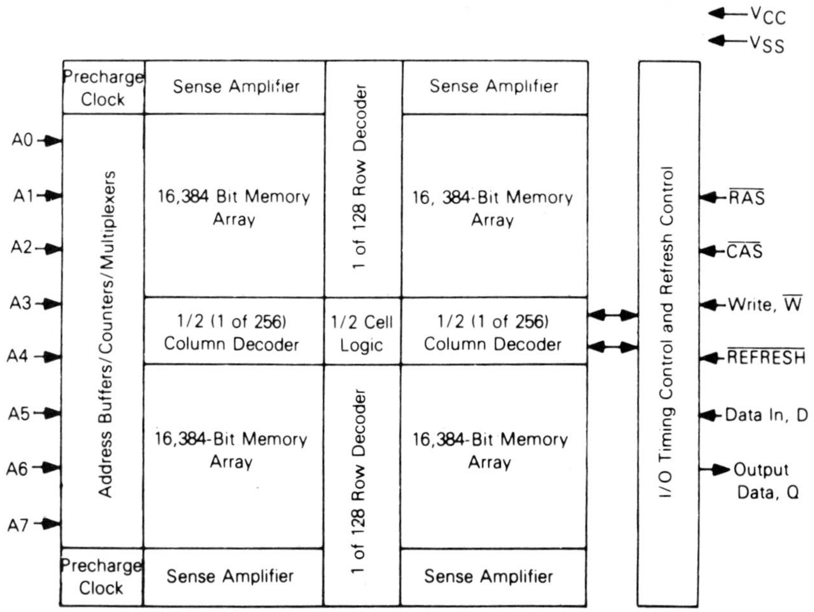

Fig. 8–5. MCM6632 architecture. (*Courtesy Motorola Inc.*)

this section. It is a good example of the extensive advances that have been made since the first edition of this text appeared in 1979.

The MCM6664 is a 65,536-bit, high-speed, dynamic random access memory that is organized as 65,536 1-bit words. It has the same architecture and key features as the MCM6632 but a greater number of memory cells. Refer to Fig. 8–4.

Refer once again to Fig. 8–3 and note the ease of upgrading from the 16K × 1 to the 32K × 1 and even the 64K × 1 types of dynamic random access memory. As the demand increases for greater and more powerful microprocessor-based systems, this upward pin compatibility feature becomes more and more desirable.

ROM

Nonvolatility

The next type of microprocessor memory to be discussed will overcome the volatility drawback of the RAM. This type of memory is referred to as **ROM** or read only memory. As the term implies, this type of memory can only be *read from* and *not written into* by the user.

Since the ROM has the feature of nonvolatility, it lends itself to applications such as dedicated subroutines including mathematical packages, monitor programs, debug programs and any program that has a fixed structure where there is no need to make changes to the program that resides in the ROM.

Monitor Programs

Motorola has several such debug and monitor programs in its microcomputers such as the MIKbug, JBUG, MINIbug II, and MINIbug III. Intel has similar monitor and debug programs, for example the SDK-85 Monitor Version 2.1 and Interp 80.

Program Mask

The programming of the read only memories is usually done during the final phases of the integrated circuit manufacturing cycle. A specially designed **mask** which sets the required bit pattern that was specifically designed for this dedicated ROM is made to meet the program criteria supplied by the user. This dedicated masking is rather expensive and can usually be justified only when a large volume of chips is needed.

The Motorola MCM6830 ROM

A specific example of this type of memory is shown in Fig. 8–6.

The MCM6830 is a mask-programmable byte-organized memory designed for use in bus-organized systems. It is fabricated with N-channel silicon gate technology. The device operates from a single power supply, is TTL compatible and is static in operation. Memory expansion is provided through multiple chip select inputs. The active level of the chip select inputs and the memory content are defined by the microprocessor user. The data output lines are 3-state in nature.[5]

A more detailed "inside" view of this ROM is shown in Fig. 8–7, which indicates the sub blocks of the entire IC: memory control, address decoder, memory matrix and 3-state buffers.

High Density ROM: The Motorola MCM68365 Read Only Memory

A previous section indicated the enhancements that have taken place in higher density RAM semiconductor memory. Parallel to these improvements, the ROM family has upward compatible members such as the MCM68A316 2K × 8, the MCM68A332 4K × 8 and

[5] *M6800 Design Data*, p. 115.

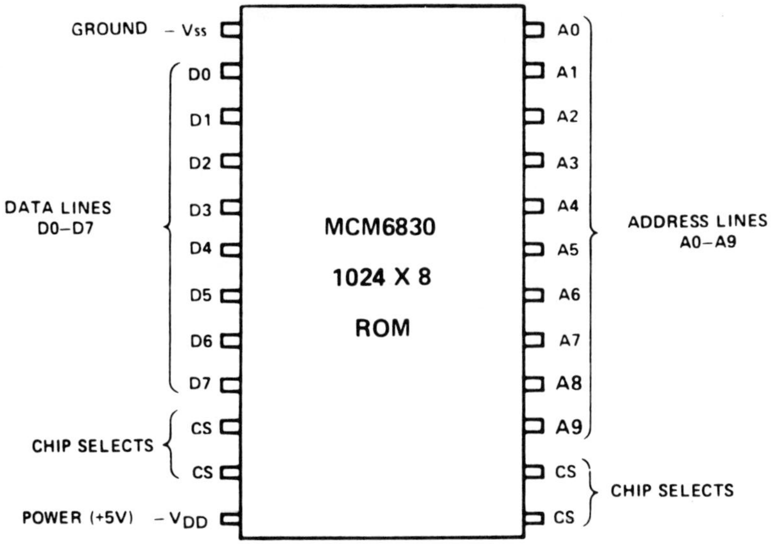

Fig. 8–6. Read only memory (ROM). (*Courtesy Motorola Inc.*)

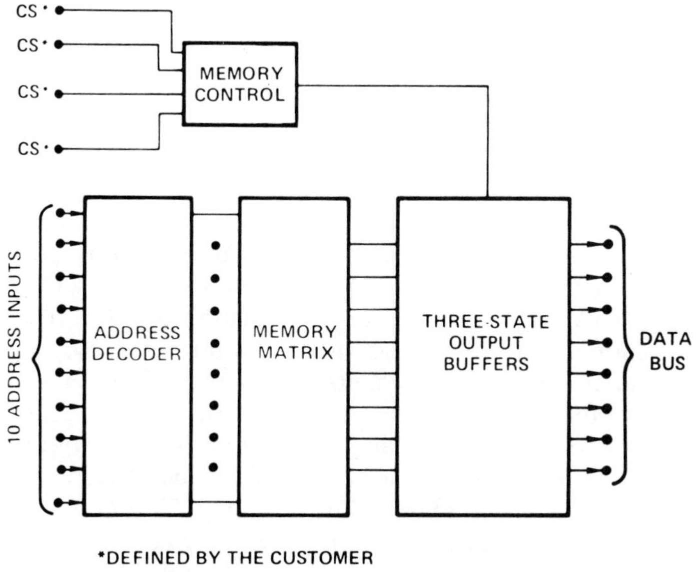

Fig. 8–7. MCM6830 ROM functional block diagram. (*Courtesy Motorola Inc.*)

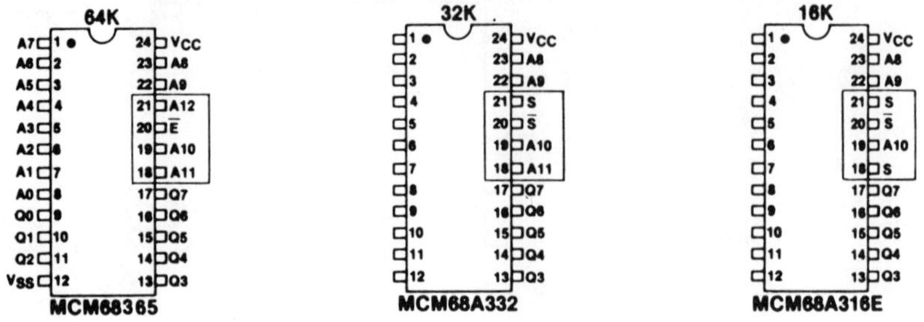

Fig. 8–8. Industry standard pinouts, Motorola ROM family. (*Courtesy Motorola Inc.*)

PIN NAMES	
A0-A12	Address
$\overline{E}$	Chip Enable
Q0-Q7	Data Output
V_{CC}	+5 V Power Supply
V_{SS}	Ground

Fig. 8–9. MCM68365 ROM pin names. (*Courtesy Motorola Inc.*)

MCM68365 8K × 8 mask-programmable read only memories. Figure 8–8 shows the industry standard pinouts for Motorola's pin-compatible ROM family.

Besides the trend to design the pin assignments for upward compatible parts within the family, a companion pin-compatible EPROM is readily available. This compatibility is ideal for the transition from prototype design to final production.

The pin names for the MCM68365 64K ROM are listed in Fig. 8–9.

The MCM68365 is a mask-programmable byte-organized memory designed for use in bus-organized systems. It is fabricated with N-channel silicon gate technology. For ease of use, the device operates from a single power supply, has compatibility with TTL and needs no clocks or refreshing because of static operation. The memory is compatible with the M6800 microcomputer family, providing read only storage in byte increments. The active level of the chip enable input and the memory content is defined by the user. The chip enable input deselects the output and puts the chip in a power-down mode.

Figure 8–10 provides a look inside the MCM68365 64K ROM. Note the number of address lines (A_0-A_{12}). Thirteen lines are required to completely decode this 8192-byte device.

One technique of determining the number of memory locations addressable is to use the following design equation:

$$2^x = N$$

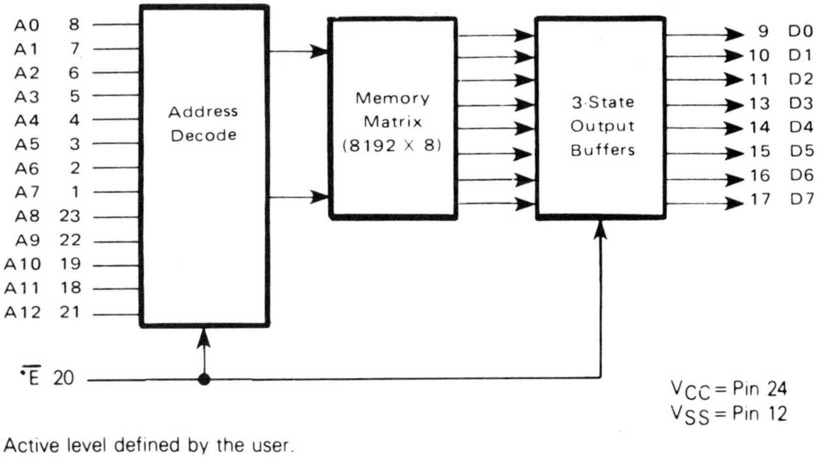

Fig. 8–10. MCM68365 ROM block diagram. (*Courtesy Motorola Inc.*)

where x = number of address lines
N = number of memory locations.

Using the MCM68365 as an example, the following would result.

$$2^x = N$$

where x = 13 (Note: A_0-A_{12} represents 13 lines)
$2^{13} = N$
therefore N = 8192

The result is the structure of this ROM.

A typical microcomputer block diagram for the MCM68365 is illustrated in Fig. 8–11.

The highlights of the MCM68365 64K-bit read only memory are:

- Fully static operation
- Automatic power down
- Low power dissipation: 225 mW active (typical); 30 mW standby (typical)
- Single ± 10% 5 volt power supply
- High output drive capability (2 TTL loads)
- 3-state data output for OR ties
- Mask programmable chip enable
- TTL compatible
- Pin compatible with 8K MCM68A308, 16K MCM68A316E, and 32K MCM68A332 mask programmable ROMs.[6]

[6] *MCM68365 Advance Information* (Austin, Texas: Motorola Inc., 1980), p. 1.

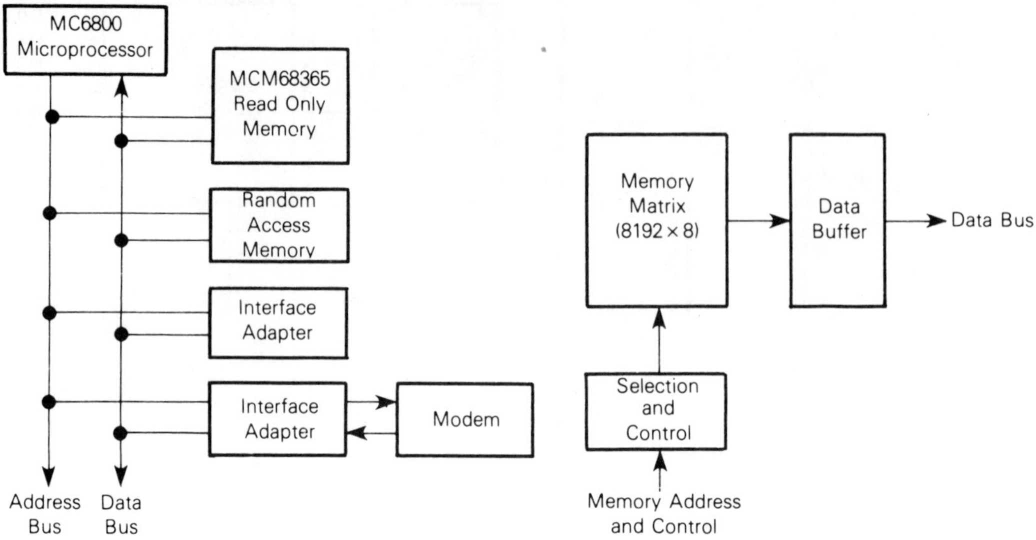

Fig. 8–11. Typical microcomputer block diagram. (*Courtesy Motorola Inc.*)

The ROM integrated circuit has solved the problem of volatility. However, the high fee for specialized masking is justified only for large volume users. What about the small quantity runs between 10 to 500 devices? Or, what about the research and development and prototyping projects that, because of their very nature, would require software changes? The integrated circuit manufacturers have an answer to these questions—the **EPROM.**

EPROM

Nonvolatility

The EPROM has the favorable characteristic of nonvolatility similar to the mask programmable ROM as well as the desirable feature of alterable bit patterns which allow fast turn around when software changes are required. This is virtually inevitable during a project development cycle.

Theory of Operation

The fundamental operation for an EPROM is based on the capacitive change phenomenon that takes place during the programming stage. An electrical charge is placed on the MOS transistor during the

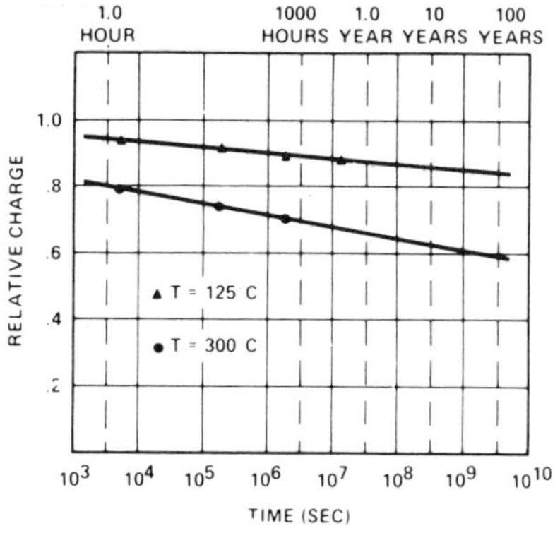

Fig. 8–12. Charge decay versus time. *(Reprinted by permission of Intel Corporation, © 1977)*

programming stage and the erasing cycle occurs when an ultraviolet light source is focused on the transparent lid, which is located on the top of the integrated circuit package. This allows the user to expose the chip to the ultraviolet light to erase the present bit pattern. After this exposure cycle is completed, a new bit pattern can then be written into this memory device.

Because the individual MOS devices behave in much the same manner as capacitors, there is a leakage effect that occurs over a period of time. A typical charge decay versus time is indicated in Fig. 8–12.

The graph indicates that, even after a 10-year time period at T = 125°C, better than eighty percent of the initial charge is still present. This is more than sufficient to preserve the correct bit pattern.

The Intel 2708 EPROM

The specific example which will be discussed in this section is the Intel 2708 EPROM. The pin configuration for this memory integrated circuit is shown in Fig. 8–13.

The Intel 2708 is fabricated with the N-channel silicon gate technology and is organized in a 1024-by-8 structure. This EPROM memory integrated circuit is, therefore, often referred to as an 8192-bit erasable and electrically reprogrammable read only memory.

A detailed block diagram of the 2708 appears in Fig. 8–14.

The address inputs and data I/Os are TTL compatible during read and programming. The data outputs are 3-state to facilitate memory expansion by OR-tying. Initially, and after each erasure, the device contains all "1s." Programming, or introducing "Os," is accomplished

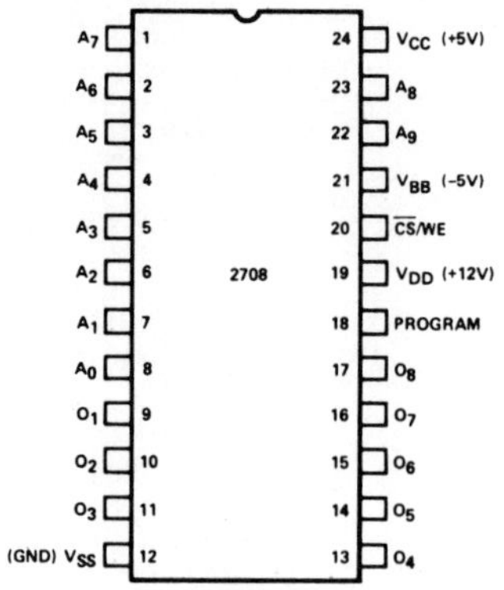

PIN NAMES

A_1-A_9	ADDRESS INPUTS
O_1-O_8	DATA OUTPUTS
CS/WE	CHIP SELECT/WRITE ENABLE INPUT

Fig. 8–13. 2708 pin configuration. (*Reprinted by permission of Intel Corporation, © 1977*)

by: applying TTL level addresses and TTL level data; a + 12 V Write Enable signal; then sequencing through all addresses consecutively a minimum of 100 times, applying a 26-V program pulse at each address. All addresses must be programmed during each programming session; programming single words or small blocks of words is not al-

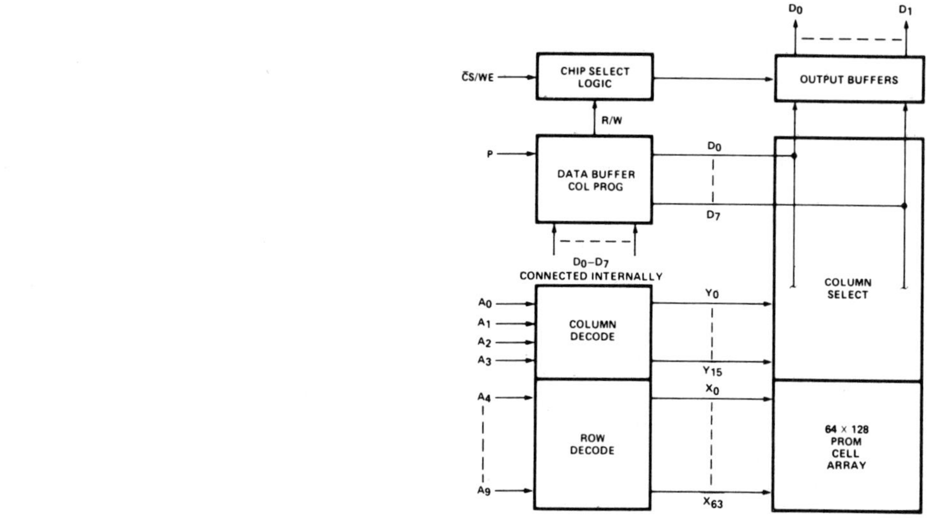

Fig. 8–14. 2708 block diagram. (*Reprinted by permission of Intel Corporation, © 1977*)

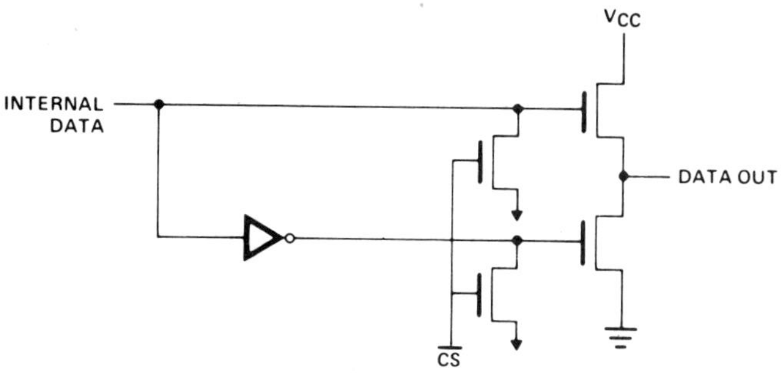

Fig. 8–15. 2708 output buffer. (*Reprinted by permission of Intel Corporation, © 1977*)

lowed. Approximately 100 seconds are required to program the entire device.[7]

A typical output buffer section is found in Fig. 8–15 which illustrates the 2708 output buffer circuit.

The equivalent schematic of the output buffer shown in Fig. 8–15 indicates the output buffer consists of a pair of MOS transistors connected in a push-pull configuration. $\overline{CS}$ enables both transistors when true; when $\overline{CS}$ is false, both output devices are turned off providing 3-state output operation. The output buffer will provide a V_{OL} of 0.45 V at an I_{OL} of 1.6 ma and a V_{OH} of 2.4 V at an I_{OH} of -1.0 ma.[8]

Note that specialized equipment is required to program and erase the 2708 EPROM.

Motorola High Density EPROMs

The following sections present a brief look at the high density members of the Motorola EPROM family. As noted in Fig. 8–16, the EPROM family has the same upward pin compatibility as the RAM and ROM families.

The MCM2716 2048 × 8-bit EPROM

The MCM2716/27L16 is a 16,384-bit erasable and electrically reprogrammable PROM designed for system debug usage and similar applications requiring nonvolatile memory that can be reprogrammed periodically. The transparent lid on the package allows the memory

[7] *Intel Memory Design Handbook* (Santa Clara, California: Intel Corporation, 1977), p. 8–1.

[8] *Intel Memory Design Handbook*, p. 8–3.

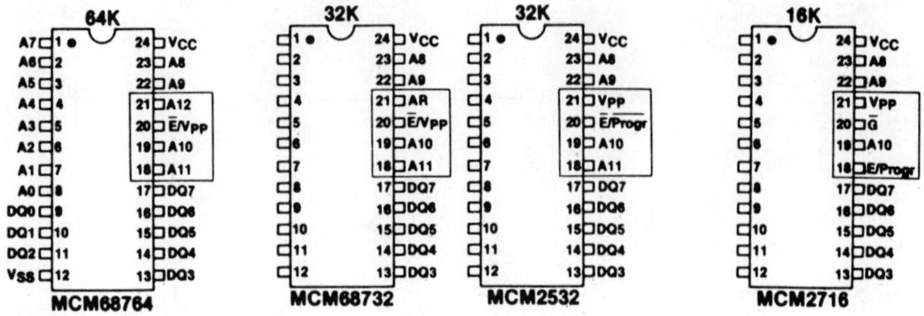

Fig. 8–16. Industry standard pinouts, Motorola EPROM family. (*Courtesy Motorola Inc.*)

content to be erased with ultraviolet light. For ease of use, the device operates from a single power supply and has a static power-down mode. Pin-for-pin mask programmable ROMs are available for large volume production runs of systems initially using the MCM2716/27L16.

New industry standard nomenclature has been developed and incorporated on the MCM2716 pin names which are listed in Fig. 8–17. The pin assignment was illustrated in Fig. 8–16.

The main features of the MCM2716 include:

- Single 5 V power supply
- Automatic power-down mode (standby)
- Organized as 2048 bytes of eight bits
- Low power version 27L16
  - 27L16-35 Active 50 mA max
    Standby 10 mA max
  - 27L16-25 Active 70 mA max
    Standby 15 mA max
- TTL compatible during read and program
- Pin compatible to MCM68A316E
- Output enable active level is user selectable[9]

[9] *MCM2716/MCM27L16* (Austin, Texas: Motorola Inc., 1980), p. 1.

*Pin Names	
A	Address
DQ	Data Input/Output
$\overline{E}$/Progr	Chip Enable/Program
$\overline{G}$	Output Enable

*New industry standard nomenclature

Fig. 8–17. MCM2716 pin names. (*Courtesy Motorola Inc.*)

The MCM68732 4096 × 8-bit EPROM

The MCM68732/68L732 is a 32,769-bit erasable and electrically reprogrammable PROM designed for applications requiring nonvolatile memory that could be reprogrammed periodically, or for replacing 32K ROMs. For ease of use, the device operates from a single power supply and has a static power-down mode. Pin-for-pin compatible mask programmable ROMs are available for large volume production runs of systems initially using the MCM68732.

Key features of this device include:

- Single +5 V power supply
- Automatic power-down mode
- Organized as 4096 bytes of eight bits
- Low power dissipation
- Fully TTL compatible
- Standard 24-pin DIP for EPROM upgradability
- Pin compatible to MCM68332 mask programmable ROM
- Pin compatible with the MCM2532 32K EPROM in the read mode
- Low power version

MCM68L732	Active 60 mA maximum
	Standby 15 mA maximum
MCM68L32-35	Active 100 mA maximum
	Standby 25 mA maximum

The footprint of the MCM68732 is found in Fig. 8–16. Its special industry standard pin names appear in Fig. 8–18.

Theory of operation. The following paragraphs provide an overview of the theory of operation of the MCM68732 including programming instructions, read operation description, and erasing instructions. The other high density EPROMs operate in a similar fashion.

Programming instructions. After the completion of an erase operation, every bit in the device is in the 1 state (represented by output high). Data are entered by programming zeros (output low) into the

*Pin Names	
A	Address
AR	Address Reference
DQ	Data Input/Output
$\overline{E}/V_{PP}$	Chip Enable/Program

*New industry standard nomenclature

Fig. 8–18. MCM68732 pin assignment. (*Courtesy Motorola Inc.*)

required bits. The words are addressed the same way as in the read operation. A programmed 0 can be changed to a 1 only by ultraviolet light erasure.

To set the memory up for program mode, the $\overline{E}/V_{PP}$ input (pin 20) should be between +2.0 and +6.0 V, which will 3-state the outputs and allow data to be set up on the DQ terminals. The V_{CC} voltage is the same as for the read operation. Only 0s will be programmed when 0s and 1s are entered in the 8-bit data word.

After address and data setup, 25 V programming pulse (V_{IH} to V_{IHP}) is applied to the $\overline{E}/V_{PP}$ input. A program pulse is applied to each address location to be programmed. To minimize programming, a 2 ms pulse width is recommended. The maximum program pulse width is 55 ms and the maximum program pulse amplitude is 26 V.

Multiple MCM68732s can be programmed in parallel by connecting like inputs and applying the program pulse to the $\overline{E}/V_{PP}$ inputs. Different data may be programmed into multiple MCM68732s connected in parallel by selectively applying the programming pulse only to the MCM68732s to be programmed.

Read operation. After access time, data is valid at the outputs in the read mode. A single input ($\overline{E}/V_{PP}$) enables the outputs and puts the chip in active or standby mode. With $\overline{E}/V_{PP} = 0$, the outputs are enabled and the chip is in active mode; with $\overline{E}/V_{PP} = 1$, the outputs are 3-stated and the chip is in standby mode. During standby mode, the power dissipation is reduced.

Multiple MCM68732s may share a common data bus with like outputs OR-tied together. In this configuration, the $\overline{E}/V_{PP}$ input should be high on all unselected MCM68732s to prevent data contention.

Erasing instructions. The MCM68732 can be erased by exposure to high intensity shortwave ultraviolet light with a wavelength of 2537 angstroms. The recommended integrated dose (i.e., UV intensity, X exposure time) is 15 Ws/cm^2; the erase time is 36 minutes. The lamps should be used without shortwave filters and the MCM68732 should be positioned about one inch away from the UV tubes.[10]

The MCM68764 8192 × 8-bit EPROM

The MCM68764 is a 65,536-bit erasable and electrically reprogrammable PROM. This device is supplied in a standard 24-pin package as shown in Fig. 8–19.

The internal structure of the 64K-bit or 8K-byte EPROM consists of the control logic section, the X and Y decoders, the Y gating section

[10] *MCM68732/MCM68L732* (Austin, Texas: Motorola Inc., 1980), pp. 1–3.

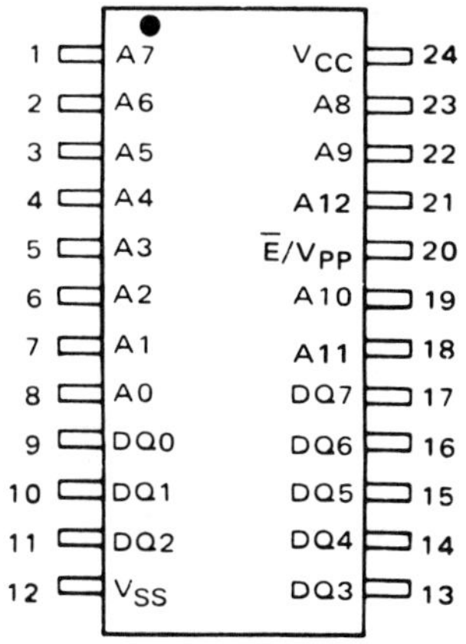

*PIN NAMES	
A	. . . . Address
DQ	. . . . Data Input/Output
$\overline{E}/V_{PP}$	. . . . Chip Enable/Program
$\overline{G}$	. . . . Output Enable

*New industry standard nomenclature

Fig. 8–19. MCM68764 pin assignment. (*Courtesy Motorola Inc.*)

and the MOS N-channel silicon gate semiconductor memory matrix section. Refer to the block diagram in Fig. 8–20.

The block diagram in Fig. 8–20 also represents the basic structure of the other Motorola high density EPROMs.

PROM

To make the coverage of integrated circuit memory devices complete, the **PROM** or programmable read only memory must be mentioned.

The PROM is a member of the read only memory family. Its significant characteristics are: it is nonvolatile and user programmable. The major difference between the PROM and EPROM is that the PROM, unlike the EPROM, cannot be reprogrammed. The capability to be reprogrammed is, of course, one of the very favorable features of the EPROM.

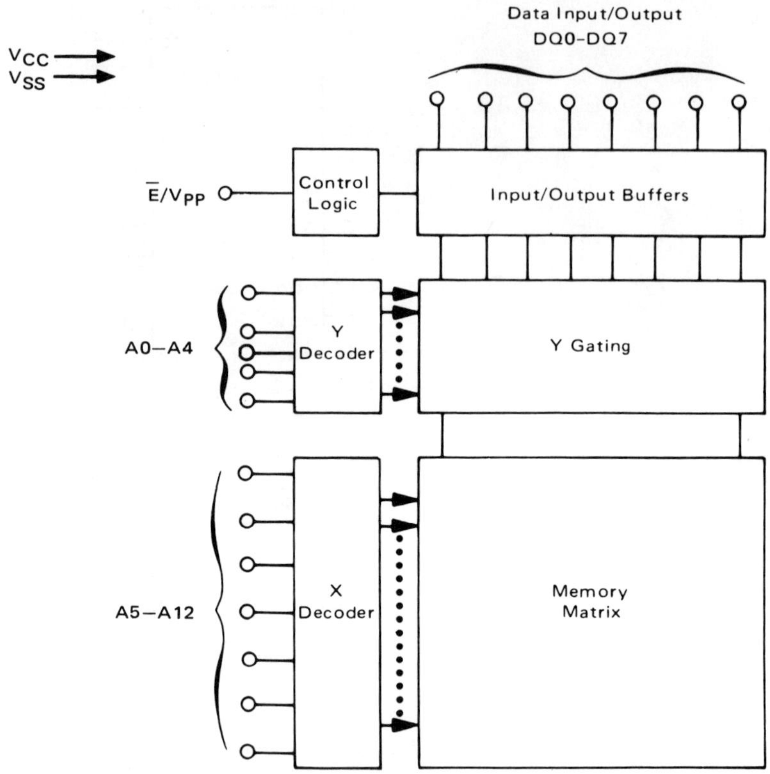

Fig. 8–20. MCM68764 block diagram. (*Courtesy Motorola Inc.*)

Theory of Operation

The PROM is programmed by causing an electrical current to exceed the current carrying capability of a "fuse link" thereby opening the appropriate link, which results in this particular memory cell taking a logic 0 state. The PROM is supplied by the integrated circuit manufacturer with all cells assuming the logic 1 state. Keep in mind that once the PROM is programmed by a fuse link being "blown out," the process, unlike the EPROM, is irreversible.

Typical Fuse Cell

Each cell consists of a single transistor in an emitter-follower configuration with the silicon fuse connected to the column line. The thickness of the silicon fuse is nominally 3000 angstroms. Resistivity of the fuse is controlled by doping as in standard integrated circuits. The fuse if blown with a pulse train of successively wider pulses with

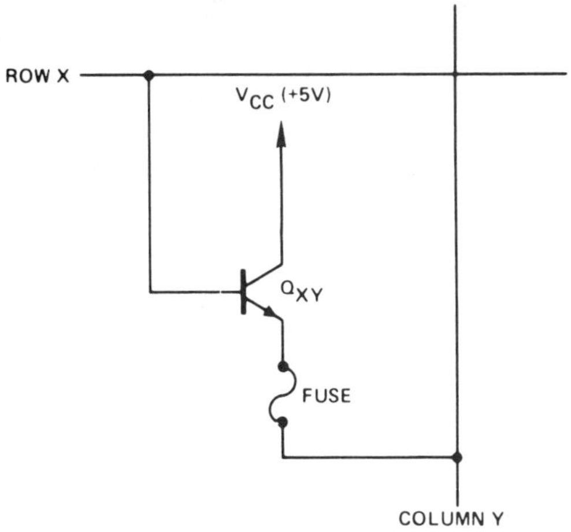

Fig. 8–21. Typical fuse cell. (*Reprinted by permission of Intel Corporation, © 1977*)

a current of 20 to 30 ma typically needed to blow the fuse. During this "blowing" operation, temperatures estimated at 1400° C are reached in the notch of the polysilicon fuse. At these temperatures, the silicon oxidizes and forms an insulating material.

Fig. 8–22 shows blown and unblown fuses.

The use of silicon eliminates conductive dendrites and the existence of conductive materials in the fused gap. Since silicon is a standard integrated circuit material, no new contact problems or problems with dissimilar materials are encountered. Growback does not exist with the silicon fuse.[11]

[11] *Intel Memory Design Handbook*, pp. 7–4, 7–5.

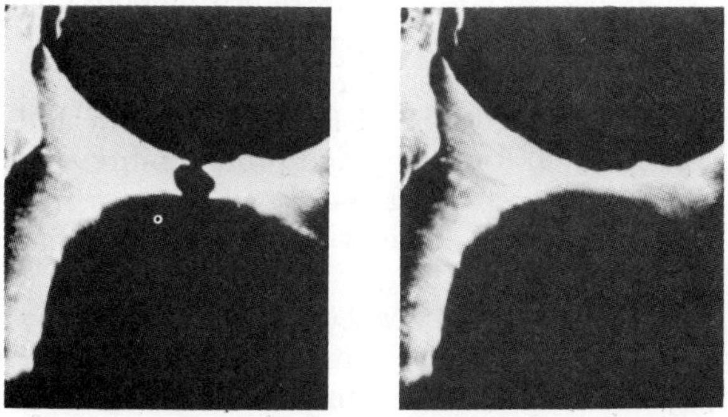

Fig. 8–22. Blown and unblown fuses. (*Reprinted by permission of Intel Corporation, © 1977*)

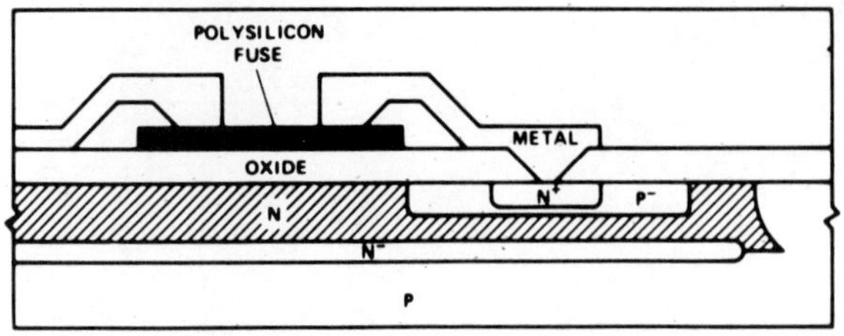

Fig. 8–23. Polysilicon fuse cross section. *(Reprinted by permission of Intel Corporation, © 1977)*

Consider that up to a thousand or more of these fuse cells exist in some of the larger semiconductor integrated circuit memory devices.

To further illustrate the manufacturing intricacies involved in constructing one of these devices, a cross-sectional view of a typical fuse cell is shown in Fig. 8–23.

EEPROM

The newest member of the nonvolatile semiconductor memory family is the **EEPROM** or electrically erasable PROM. The EEPROM saves time and money because of its in-system erase versus ultraviolet light erase, and its reprogram capability.

MCM2801

The MCM2801, whose pinout is shown in Fig. 8–24, is a 256-bit serial electrically erasable PROM designed for handling small amounts of data in applications requiring both nonvolatile memory and in-system information updates. It has external control of timing functions and serial format for data and address.

The MCM2801 EEPROM is fabricated in floating gate technology for high reliability and producibility. The floating gate technology is illustrated in Fig. 8–25.

Figure 8–26 is a complete block diagram of the MCM2801 EEPROM.

A typical MCM2801 V_{PP} circuit is shown in Fig. 8–27.

As is the case with all semiconductor devices, both the manufacturer and the designer are concerned about product reliability. The device data retention in terms of years and endurance over thousands of program/erase cycles is shown graphically in Fig. 8–28.

PIN ASSIGNMENT

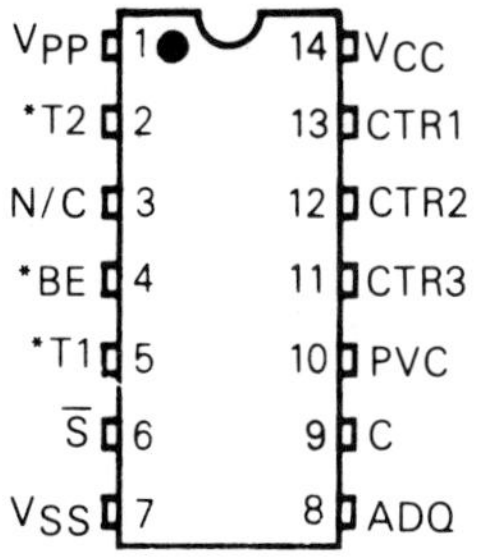

*For normal operation, these inputs should be hardwired to V_{SS}.

PIN NAMES

ADQ........................Multiplexed Address/ Data-In/Data-Out
C.......................................Clock
PVC....................Program Voltage Control
CTR1, 2, 3.................................Control
BE......................................Block Erase
S̄..Chip Select
T1, T2.....................................Test Pins

Fig. 8–24. MCM2801 EEPROM pin assignment. (*Courtesy Motorola Inc.*)

- PROCESS: TWO-LEVEL POLYSILICON NMOS
- MEMORY OPERATION: FOWLER NORDHEIM EMISSION OF ELECTRONS TO AND FROM FLOATING GATE THROUGH THIN OXIDE (< 200Å) TO EFFECT V_T SHIFTS
- CROSS SECTION VIEW:

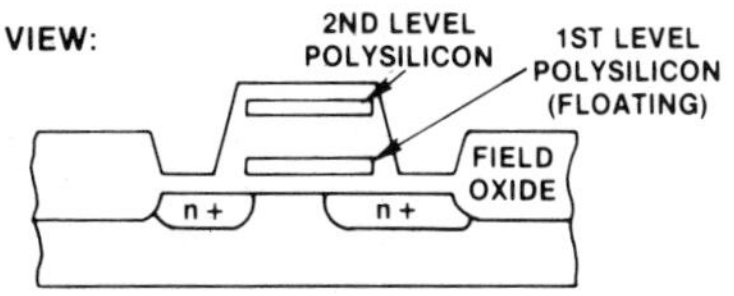

- CELL OPERATION

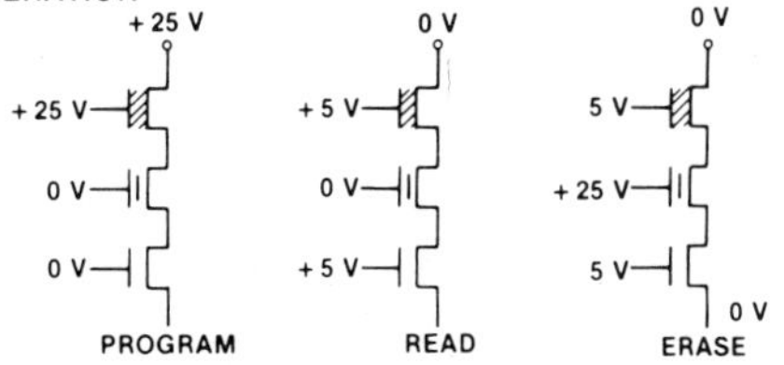

Fig. 8–25. MCM2801 EEPROM cell. (*Courtesy Motorola Inc.*)

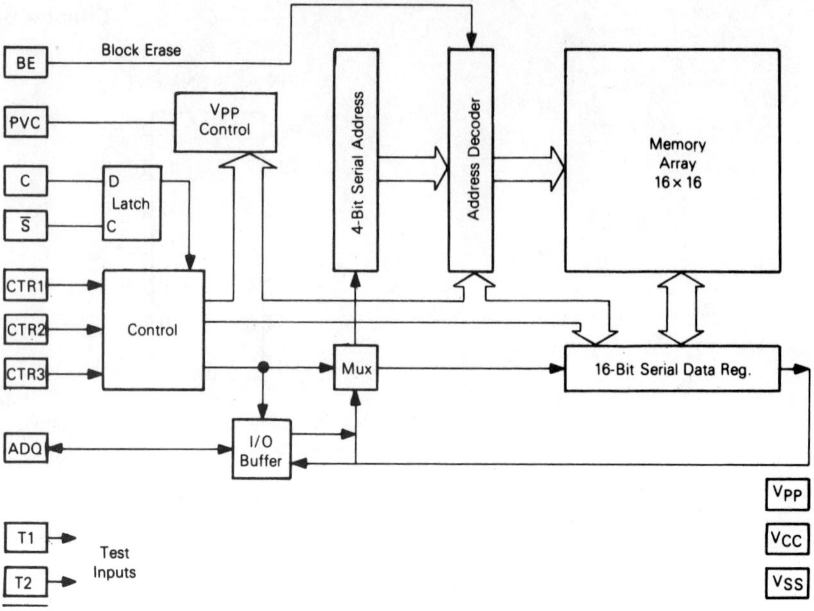

Fig. 8–26. MCM2801 block diagram. (*Courtesy Motorola Inc.*)

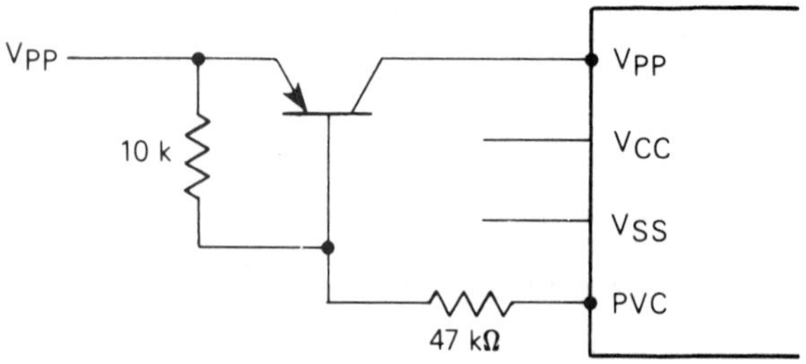

Fig. 8–27. V_{PP} control. (*Courtesy Motorola Inc.*)

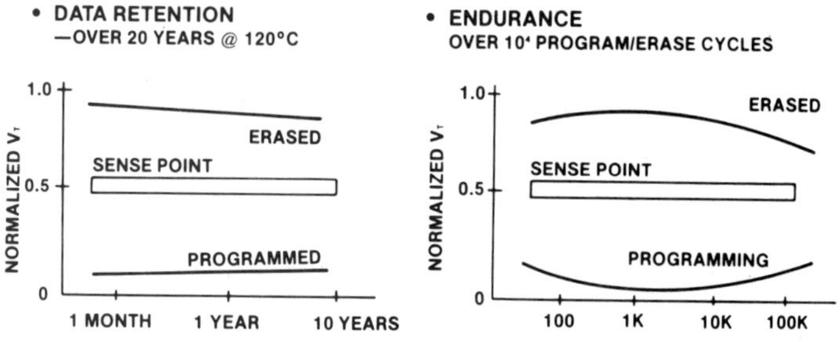

Fig. 8–28. EEPROM realiability. (*Courtesy Motorola Inc.*)

The MCM2816

The big brother to the MCM2801 EEPROM is the MCM2816. It has a capacity of 2K × 8 bytes of storage.

A few of the MCM2816's most notable characteristics are:

- Single +5 volt power supply
- Fully static design
- Pin compatibility with MCM2716
- Standard +25 volt write/erase supply voltage level

Functional Description

The following description of the MCM2801 typifies the EEPROM family functions.

This memory stores sixteen words of sixteen bits each. All functions are controlled by a 3-bit parallel instruction bus and an applied clock.

Read-out. By referring to Fig. 8–29, note that the (3-bit parallel) serial address instruction code is presented while the 4-bit serial address is shifted in on the I/O bus through the ADQ pin.

The read instruction is presented for one clock time. This reads the words from the new address in the memory array and parallel loads it into the shift register. Refer to Fig. 8–30.

The serial data-out instruction is presented for sixteen clock pulses, causing the data to be shifted out on the I/O bus through the ADQ pin. During the serial data-out instruction, data is recirculated to allow further readout of the original data without access to the memory array.

Writing. (Note the following in Fig. 8–31.)

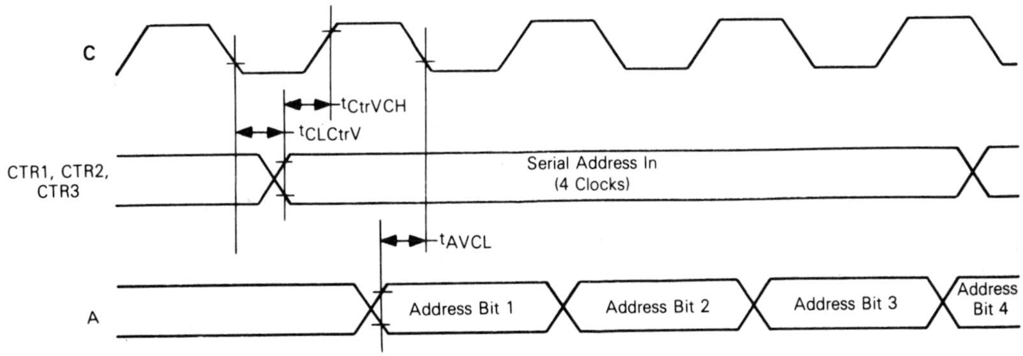

Fig. 8–29. Serial address in. (*Courtesy Motorola Inc.*)

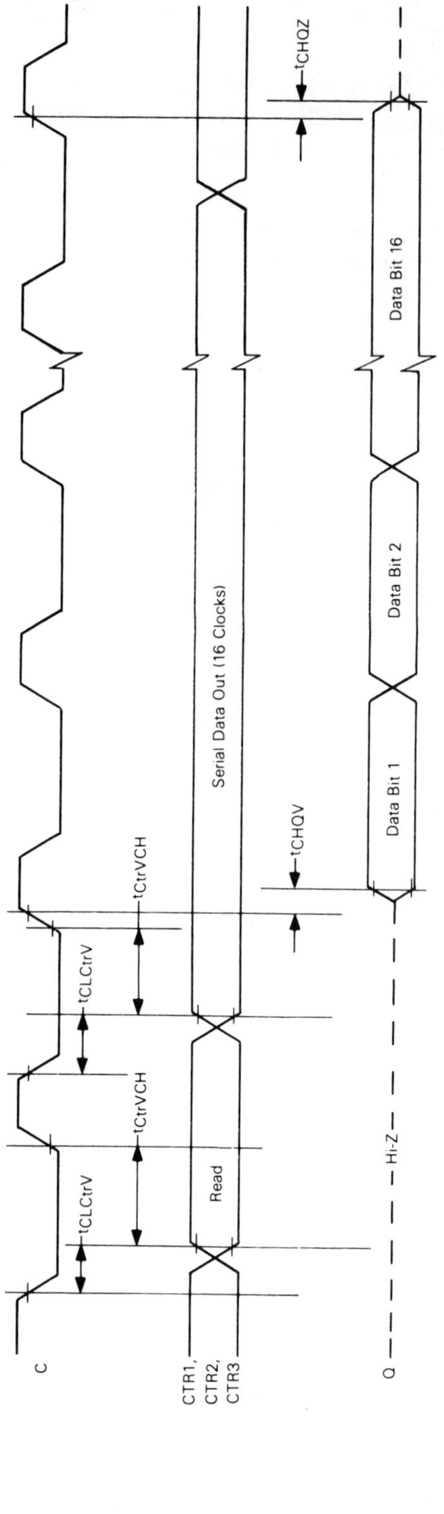

Fig. 8–30. Read and serial data out. *(Courtesy Motorola Inc.)*

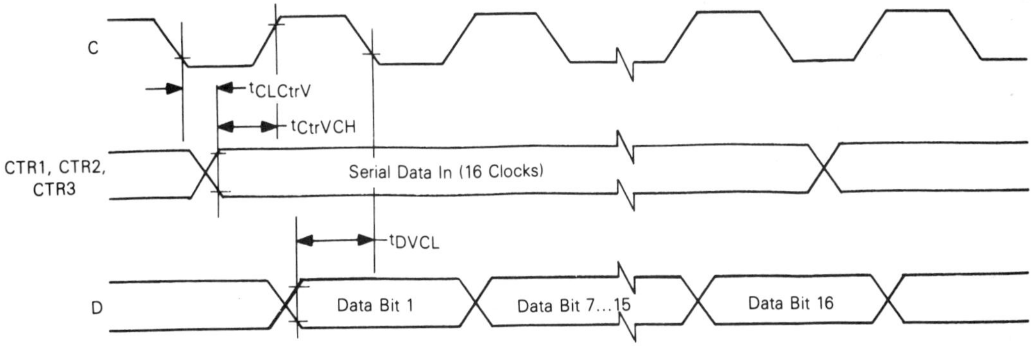

Fig. 8–31. Serial data in. (*Courtesy Motorola Inc.*)

1. The address is changed, if necessary, in the same manner as the readout.

2. Data is serially loaded onto the chip by presenting the serial data-in instruction for sixteen clock pulses.

3. The word erase instruction is presented for the specified erase time. This erases only the addressed word.

4. The write instruction is presented for the specified write time. This transfers the data to the selected address in the EEPROM.

Standby. The standby instruction, when strobed by the clock, puts the memory in a quiescent state where the output is in the high-impedance state and the clock presence or absence will not affect the chip.

Clock. The active high clock signal is used for loading instruction codes, for introducing serial addresses and data, and for shifting serial data out. The clock has no influence on any other function. The clock cycle is detailed in Fig. 8–32.

Data protection. The timing diagram for the erase-write cycle is shown in Fig. 8–33.

When V_{PP} is turned off, data stored in the array is always protected. A V_{PP} control output is provided for switching the V_{PP} supply. It consists of a pull-down device to V_{SS}. This device is turned on only when: V_{CC} is present and a write or word erase code has been loaded with a clock pulse.

A schematic for this external V_{PP} control was proposed in Fig. 8–27.

When this feature is not used for data protection, V_{PP} must not be present if V_{CC} is not supplied. The test 1, test 2, and block erase pins

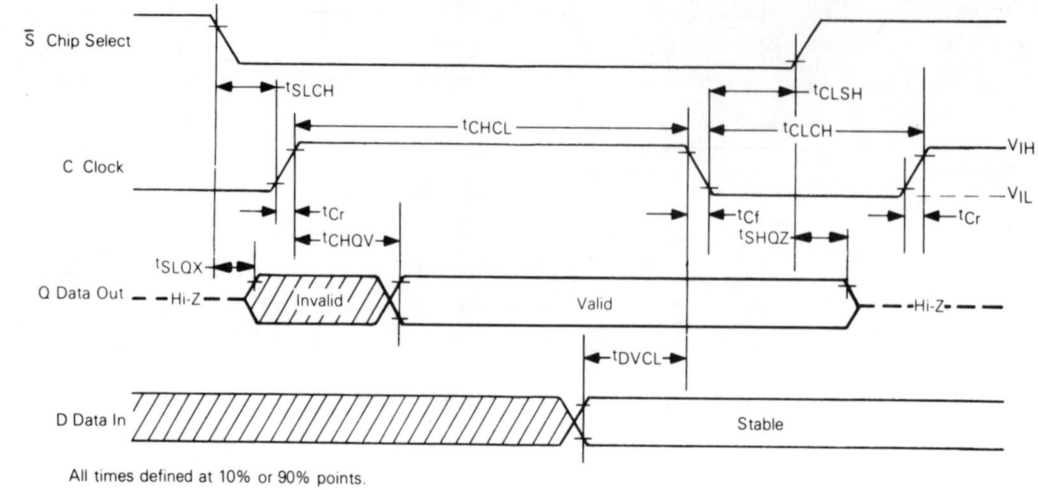

Fig. 8–32. Clock cycle detail. (*Courtesy Motorola Inc.*)

are provided for testing purpose only and should be hard-wired to V_{SS} in any application.

Power-up/power-down sequence. Using an external V_{PP} control as given in Fig. 8–27, V_{PP} and V_{CC} may be turned on or off in any sequence without disturbing data in the nonvolatile memory array, providing that neither a word erase nor a write is present on the control inputs, or that $\bar{S}$ = low, or that C = high.

Instruction sequences. The clock signal has no effect during write or erase.

Read should be presented for one clock cycle only since frequent unnecessary use may disturb data.

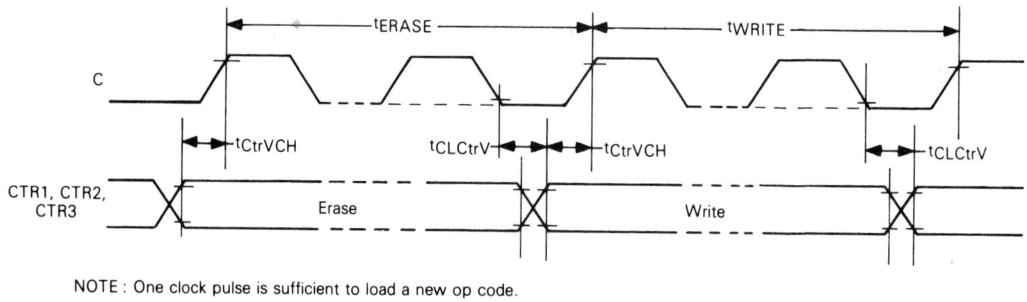

Fig. 8–33. Erase-write sequence. (*Courtesy Motorola Inc.*)

Write (for any address) must be preceded by the word erase instruction at the same address.

All instructions except serial data-out cause the data output drive to be high-impedance.

V_{PP} is necessary for write, word erase, and in conjunction with the block erase pin. In all other cases, it can be switched to high-impedance, V_{CC} or V_{SS}.

Block erase can be used for testing purposes. For clearing the whole array, V_{PP} should be applied and the BE pin kept at V_{CC} for the normal erase time.

When the chip is deselected ($\overline{S} = 1$), the output buffer is in the off state.

The test 1 and test 2 pins are for manufacturing use only and are not available to the user.[12]

SUMMARY

It is appropriate to begin the summary of this chapter on integrated circuit semiconductor memory by referring to a ROM-PROM family tree as shown in Fig. 8–34.

An important point regarding this family tree is that PROMs are manufactured using bipolar technology as well as MOS technology whereas EPROMs are manufactured using MOS technology and are not available in the bipolar technology group. Generally, bipolar devices are a factor of 10 faster than MOS devices.

[12] *MCM2801 Advance Information* (Austin, Texas: Motorola Inc., 1980), pp. 1–3.

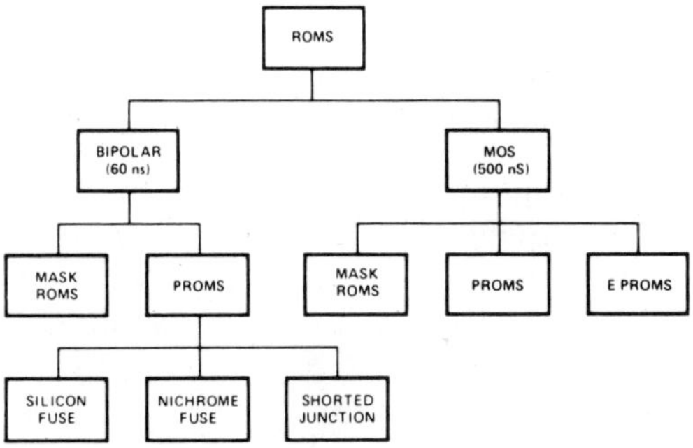

Fig. 8–34. PROM/ROM technology family tree. (*Reprinted by permission of Intel Corporation, © 1977*)

RAM

The term RAM stands for random access memory. Its major characteristics are:

1. Read from or write into capability
2. Content of memory is volatile.

Its primary applications are in the area of temporary storage of instructions and data information which is sometimes referred to as the scratchpad area of memory.

ROM

The ROM or read only memory has two identifying characteristics:

1. Nonvolatility
2. Information can only be read from this device

The ROM device is usually mask-programmed during the final stages of the manufacturing cycle. It is well suited for applications where a large volume of the same device is needed.

Examples of usages for the masked programmed ROM would be in fixed subroutines, mathematical packages and monitor programs such as the Motorola MIKbug program.

The ROM program is permanent. That is, once entered during the masking cycle, the program cannot be altered.

EPROM

The EPROM or erasable programmable read only memory has as its major characteristics:

1. Nonvolatility
2. Read only capability
3. Programmable as well as erasable

This program-erase cycle can be run literally hundreds of times. These devices find their major applications in microprocessor systems where nonvolatility is essential and, at the same time, where the need to change or modify the software program is likely to arise from time to time.

PROM

The PROM or programmable read only memory has the characteristics of:

1. Nonvolatility
2. Read only capability
3. Can be programmed

Once the PROM is programmed (burned in), the program bit pattern is permanent and may not be altered. The "burning in" of these devices requires specialized equipment which is available from most microprocessor manufacturers.

EEPROM

The EEPROM or electrically erasable PROM is the newest of the nonvolatile semiconductor memory devices. It is ideally suited for applications requiring both nonvolatile memory and in-system information updates.

QUESTIONS

1. What are the major characteristics of the RAM?
2. What features does the RAM have that do not exist in the ROM, EPROM and PROM devices?
3. Give several examples of situations where ROMs would be ideally suited.
4. What unique feature does the EPROM exhibit that is not found in the ROM and PROM semiconductor memory devices?
5. Discuss the similarities and differences between the EPROM and PROM devices.
6. Explain in your own words what takes place during the programming and erasing stages of the EPROM IC.
7. What is the main difference between the ROM and PROM devices?
8. Would you recommend using a ROM or an EPROM for a dedicated one-time run of one hundred memory devices? Why?
9. Explain why the user cannot reprogram a PROM device.
10. List the specific semiconductor memory devices and their characteristics as discussed in this chapter.
11. What does the term EEPROM stand for?
12. How does the EEPROM compare with the PROM? With the EPROM?
13. Give an example where it is advantageous to have pin assignment compatibility between EPROMs-PROMs and ROMs.
14. Why would it be desirable to have a RAM pin compatible with an EPROM or ROM?
15. What is the major difference between a static RAM and a dynamic RAM?

Chapter 9

Advanced Software

GLOSSARY

Assembler A software program that translates symbolically represented instructions into their binary equivalents.

Assembly A process by which instructions written in symbolic form by the programmer are changed to machine language.

Breakpoint An operator installed branch point that causes a break in the processor activity, allowing for analysis of existing conditions.

Label A set of symbols used to identify or describe an item, record, message, or file. Used in place of an absolute memory address in microcomputer programming.

Loop A sequence of instructions that is written only once but executed many times (iterated) until some predefined condition is met.

Macro code A coding system that assembles groups of computer instructions into single code words and therefore requires interpretation or translation so that an automatic computer can follow it.

Nest A subroutine or block of data embedded into a larger routine or block of data.

Pseudo op (pseudo code) A code that expresses programs in source language. An arbitrary code independent of the hardware of a computer and designed for convenience in programming.

Stack A block of successive memory locations that are accessible from one end on a Last-in-First-Out (LIFO) basis.

Stack pointer Coordinated with the storing and retrieval of information in the stack.

Subroutine A subordinate program that can be used repeatedly throughout a major program. A minor series of program operations.

Top-down approach A method or technique of programming which advocates proceeding from the general to the specific with constant quality assurance checks within the structure.

INTRODUCTION AND REVIEW

The purpose of this chapter is to explain the more common techniques of simple programs and some of the terminology and practices connected with assembly level language. First, a quick review of the concepts presented thus far in this text is appropriate.

In Chapter 4, "The Instruction Sets," and Chapter 5, "Introduction to Software," the basic concepts of programming and the significance of the instruction sets were discussed. The importance of the **top-down approach** to programming and the absolute necessity for good documentation should be re-emphasized here. The neatest and most efficient program ever devised is useless if it is not well documented in a clear and easily understood format. Remember, the procedure is to start with the problem clearly defined, develop the conceptual solution, proceed to the algorithms for each concept, convert the algorithms into mnemonic or assembly language, and finally, translate this into machine code.

At each level of program design, complete documentation and constant checking of errors are required. The sooner any problem is detected, the easier it is to correct.

ASSEMBLY LEVEL PROGRAMMING

It is unlikely that the beginner will have access to an **assembler** or higher level machine that will allow him to work in conversational languages. Instead, the object code will most likely be entered from either a standard hexadecimal or octal keypad or from an ASCII keyboard. This does not mean that assembly level programming need not be learned. In fact, the **assembly** and generation of the object code must be done manually. Knowing how to do manual assembly proves to be a distinct advantage when using an assembler. The discipline and skills required for manual assembly are the same as those required when using an assembler but are more rigorous in practice.

To clearly understand the requirements of writing assembly level programs, it is necessary to become familiar with the different types of headings and arrangements of listings that appear on a fully assembled program.

Assembly Listings

In reading an assembled program listing, keep in mind that ninety per cent of the material is there only for the benefit of analysis by the programmer or program user. The only item on the list that actually resides in the memory of the machine is the object code. Although the exact arrangement of the assembly listing may vary slightly, the following items are almost always included.

Sequence: every line written, including comments and notes about the program, is numbered. The numbering practiced will vary depending on the editor program being used. Motorola, for example, numbers the line sequence by tens, that is, 10, 20, 30, etc. The sequence column of an assembly listing is a convenient method of locating particular items within the listing because it is the only column list that is consistent throughout the program. All other columns and lists will have numbering gaps whenever comments and notes are made.

Location: the location column is a list of the actual memory addresses where the object code resides. It is normally in 4-digit hexadecimal format and is immediately followed by the object code. The location address always specifies the address of the first object code in that line.

Object codes: the object code list contains the actual hexadecimal codes which constitute the program. Each line contains one complete instruction including the op code and the operand (also sometimes called the instruction and the argument).

Label: in most cases, while writing a program, the programmer will not know until the very end what the exact address or location of a programmed instruction or subroutine will be. A technique of using labels has been developed for the purpose of specifying locations until the actual location is known.

For example, a group of instructions which accomplish an addition routine might be labeled ADD. Any time the programmer wishes to refer to this group, the **label** ADD would then be used. When the final assembly of the program is accomplished, these labels are equated to addresses. If, in the final assembly, the ADD routine starts at location 02A5, the instructions

BEQ→ ←ADD or JMP ADD

would become BEQ→ ←02A5 or JMP 02A5

Somewhere within the listing the programmer must then provide an index of labels for that program showing the label and its associated address.

Source listing: a listing of the mnemonics for the instruction contained in the line. The listing will include the op code and operand in standard mnemonic format with proper labels and codes appended.

Table 9–1 Motorola Partial Assembly Listing

```
E035 8D 4D             BSR    DISNMI    DISABLE NMI INTERRUPTS
E037 30                TSX              DECR PC BY 1
E038 6D 06             TST    6,X       BACKUP PC ON STACK
E03A 26 02             BNE    *+4
E03C 6A 05             DEC    5,X
E03E 6A 06             DEC    6,X
E040 8D 21             BSR    GETXB     GET TAB ADDR AND VFLAG
E042 27 14             BEQ    TDISP     NO BRKPTS, GO DISPLAY REGS
                 *
                 * REMOVE BRKPTS WHILE WE ARE IN JBUG. THEY
                 * WILL BE RESTORED ON A GO OR PROCEED
                 *
                 ******HERE TO REMOVE BREAKPOINTS******
E044 FF A01E TZONK     STX    BPADR     SAVE IN TEMP
E047 A6 02             LDA A  2,X       GET OP CODE TO RESTORE
                 * SAFEGUARD AGAINST MULTI DEFINED BRKPTS
                 *
E049 81 3F             CMP A  #$3F
E04B 27 07             BEQ    GENA      BRANCH IF MULTI-DEF
E04D EE 00             LDX    0,X       GET ADDR OF BKPT
E04F A7 00             STA A  0,X       RESTORE OP CODE
E051 FE A01E           LDX    BPADR     GET TABLE POSITION
E054 8D 08   GENA      BSR    ADD3X     GET NEXT POSITION AND DECB
E056 26 EC             BNE    TZONK     GO AGAIN
E058 BF A008 TDISP     STS    SP        SAVE USER'S STACK POINTER
E05B 7E E206           JMP    KEYDCE    GO DISPLAY REGS
                 *
                 ****SUBROUTINE TO GET NEXT TABLE ENTRY
                 *
E05E 08      ADD3X     INX
E05F 08                INX
E060 08                INX
E061 5A                DEC B            DECR CTR
E062 39                RTS              LET CALLER DO CTR CHECK
                 *
                 ****SUB TO GET TABLE ADDR IN X VFLAG IN B
                 *
E063 CE A022 GETXB     LDX    #BPTAB    GET TABLE BASE ADDR
E066 F6 A01D           LDA B  VFLAG
E069 39                RTS
```

(*Courtesy Motorola Inc.*)

Comments: the area used for line comments and program notes for clarity. The documentation quality of a program is greatly enhanced by comments.

Finally, to put all of these in perspective, two partial assembly listings, Tables 9–1 and 9–2, are included here for study.

Table 9–2 Intel Partial Assembly Listing

```
LOC   OBJ        SEQ      SOURCE STATEMENT

                     ;              THE BUFFER CONTAINS A CHARACTER, THE FUNCTION FLAGS
                     ;              THE BUFFER AS EMPTY AND RETURNS THE CHARACTER
                     ;              AS OUTPUT.
                     ;
                     RDKBD:
02E7  21FE20                  LXI      H,IBUFF ; GET INPUT BUFFER ADDRESS
02EA  7E                      MOV      A,M     ; GET BUFFER CONTENTS
                                       ; HIGH ORDER BIT = 1 MEANS BUFFER IS EMPTY
02EB  B7                      ORA      A       ; IS A CHARACTER AVAILABLE ?
02EC  F2F302                  JP       RDK10   ; YES - EXIT FROM LOOP
02EF  FB                      EI       ; NO - READY FOR CHARACTER FROM KEYBOARD
02F0  C3E702                  JMP      RDKED
                     RDK10:
02F3  3680                    MVI      M,EMPTY ; SET BUFFER EMPTY FLAG
02F5  F3                      DI               ; RETURN WITH INTERRUPTS DISABLED
02F6  C9                      RET
                     ;
                     ;**********************************************************************
                     ;
                     ; FUNCTION: RETF - RETURN FALSE
                     ; INPUTS: NONE
                     ; OUTPUTS: CARRY = 0 (FALSE)
                     ; CALLS: NOTHING
                     ; DESTROYS: CARRY
                     ; DESCRIPTION: RETF IS JUMPED TO BY FUNCTIONS WISHING TO RETURN FALSE.
                     ;              RETF RESETS CARRY TO 0 AND RETURNS TO THE CALLER OF
                     ;              THE ROUTINE INVOKING RETF.
                     ;
                     RETF:
02F7  37                      STC              ; SET CARRY TRUE
02F8  3F                      CMC              ; COMPLEMENT CARRY TO MAKE IT FALSE
02F9  C9                      RET
                     ;
                     ;**********************************************************************
                     ;
                     ; FUNCTION: RETT - RETURN TRUE
                     ; INPUTS: NONE
                     ; OUTPUTS: CARRY = 1 (TRUE)
                     ; CALLS: NOTHING
                     ; DESTROYS: CARRY
                     ; DESCRIPTION: RETT IS JUMPED TO BY ROUTINES WISHING TO RETURN TRUE.
                     ;              RETT SETS CARRY TO 1 AND RETURNS TO THE CALLER OF
                     ;              THE ROUTINE INVOKING RETT.
                     ;
                     RETT:
02FA  37                      STC              ; SET CARRY TRUE
02FB  C9                      RET
                     ;
                     ;**********************************************************************
                     ;
                     ; FUNCTION: RGLOC - GET REGISTER SAVE LOCATION
                     ; INPUTS: NONE
                     ; OUTPUTS: HL - REGISTER SAVE LOCATION
                     ; CALLS: NOTHING
                     ; DESTROYS: B,C,H,L,F/F'S
```

In most microprocessor literature the full assembly format will not be used. A shortened format which contains only the source list with labels and comments will probably be found. In most cases, locations information will become useless when the program is installed in the user system because it will reside at a different beginning location.

Manual Assembly

Once the program is written and checked for correctness of operation it is ready to be assembled. The process of assembling a program can be somewhat tedious and lengthy, but it is not difficult. In long programs, it is quite easy to make errors and the primary problem is carelessness.

1. *Assign an address to each instruction.* Start with the first instruction in the program and assign it the beginning address in the memory where it will reside. Go to the next instruction and determine its address. For example, if the first instruction were a 3-byte instruction at location 1000_{16}, the second instruction would be at 1003_{16}. Go through all instructions assigning an address for each. When finished, check all addresses again for correctness. (This is where most errors are made.)

2. *Construct a symbol table (label address).* Write down the list of labels and, next to that, the address location of each label. For example:

Example 9–1

Name	*Location*
Start	1000_{16}
Loop 1	$100A_{16}$
Add	1013_{16}
Dpy 6	$103C_{16}$

The convention of writing address locations in assembly listings varies from manfacturer to manufacturer. Motorola provides the four hexadecimal digits and, because it is an assembly list, it is understood that they are hexadecimal numbers. Intel has adopted the convention that all hexadecimal numbers are followed by an H and must start with a digit. If the starting number is a letter rather than a digit a 0 is inserted. Therefore, the number $AB5C_{16}$ would appear in a Motorola list as AB5C and Intel would list it as 0AB5CH. These added digits in the Intel listing can cause confusion to those unfamiliar with this convention.

3. *Final instruction construction:* start at the beginning of the program. Write down the location and instruction code for each instruction. Any time a symbolic name or label is encountered, the symbol table is referred to for the address code or numeric value. When this operation has been completed, there should be no undefined or unused labels left over. If there are leftover symbols, a mistake has occurred either in the logic of the program or in the assembly process itself.

An example of manual assembly is given in Table 9–3.

After the final construction is finished, it should be checked again for corrections regarding:

1. The logic of the program
2. The correctness of all labels and branch addresses
3. The correct codes for each instruction
4. Clarity

Once these checks have been made, the programmer should add comments and explanations as necessary to clarify the operations and functions of the program.

Symbolic Labels

For the novice programmer the most confusing items at the assembly level are probably the use and handling of symbols and labels when constructing programs. Their final impact has just been demonstrated in the previous section on manual assembly which covered the purpose and function of labels and symbols as they apply to assembly language programming.

As was pointed out in Chapter 5, "Introduction to Software," the writing of a program does not begin at the instruction level. It begins at the concept level and works down through algorithms to the instruction or source listing level. At the concept and algorithm levels, the final addresses and code number cannot possibly be known or, as a matter of fact, even the type of machine that is going to be used. Therefore, it is convenient to assign names or labels to points in a program or routine that are to be used.

The names and labels adopted at the algorithm level are finally carried through to the symbol list developed in the last section. One might argue that letters of the alphabet or numbers would do just as well. However, experience shows that names and meaningful labels assist in writing complex programs, in that they provide a functional association for clarity and ease of design.

Some precautions are warranted when using labels. Every symbol

Table 9-3 Manual Assembly Example

Start	LXIH		Buff
	MVI	C	#
	MVI	A	Dcont
	STA		Contrl
Loop	MOV	A,M	
	STA		Dspy
	INX	H	
	DCR	C	
	JNZ		Loop
	HLT		

#1 assign address

Buffer uses 6 bytes at location 2000
First instruction is at 2006

2006	Start	LXIH		Buff
2009		MVI	C	#
200B		MVI	A	Dcont
200D		STA		Contrl
2010	Loop	MOV	A,M	
2011		STA		Dspy
2014		INX	H	
2015		DCR	C	
2016		JNZ		Loop
2019		HLT		

#2 symbol table

Start	2006
Buff	2000
#	06
Dcont	90
Cntrl	1900
Dspy	1800
Loop	2010

#3 final construction

LOCATION	OBJ	LABEL	MNEMONIC	
2006	21 0020	Start	LXI H	Buff
2009	0E 06		MVI C	#
200B	3E 90		MVI A	Dcont
200D	32 0019		STA	Cntrl
2010	7E	Loop	MOV	A,M
2011	32 0018		STA	Dspy
2014	23		INX	H
2015	0D		DCR	C
2016	C2 1020		JNZ	Loop
2019	76		HLT	

or label is unique and must have a location or definition. It may appear more than once in the assembly but it must always consistently have the same definition or refer to the same location. In other words, no two labels can refer to the same location and each label must have only one definition. Finally, use labels and symbols sparingly. A label for every step in the program is worse than no labels at all.

Assemblers

A programmer fortunate enough to have access to an editor-assembler or development system produced by many of the manufacturers for their devices will encounter the **macro codes** and **pseudo ops.** While these are labor saving devices from a programming standpoint, they do add considerably to the list of things to remember in learning programming.

An assembler provided by the manufacturer performs the operations discussed in the section on manual assembly in a very similar manner. In accomplishing the assembly, the assembler program will require the same type of information used for the manual assembly. That is, it must be told where the program is to originate, the definition of each operand label other than address operands and it must be told when it is finished.

When the assembler program is obtained from the manufacturer, an instruction manual detailing the format and procedures for using the program is provided. The procedures and formats provide the pseudo op instructions which are those instructions dealing with the assembler program directly and providing information similar to that used in manual assembly. Pseudo op instructions do not generate machine language code and are therefore classed as nongenerative.

Some of the more common pseudo op instructions encountered are ORG, END, EQU.

ORG The ORG instruction provides the assembler with the location of the first instruction.

END Tells the assembler it is at the end of the program.

EQU The equate instruction allows definition of names and values.

In Table 9–3, the label Dcont would have been equated to 90.

```
Dcont    EQU    90
```

The assembler then uses this in constructing the symbol table.

Other pseudo ops commonly encountered would fall into DS (define storage) for the Intel assembler or, for the Motorola assembler,

RMB (reserve memory bytes). This instruction allows the programmer to set aside memory to be used or defined later. In Table 9–3, the buffer area would require definition as to its location and length in terms of bytes.

8080				6800		
Buff	EQU	2000H		Buff	EQU	2000
Buff	DS	6		Buff	RMB	6

These two assembly pseudo ops would cause the assembler to set aside six bytes of memory starting at location 2000 for use by the program.

Macro Programming

The programmer will also encounter macros which generate multiple lines of operations code by the use of one assembly instruction. These macros must be separately defined since each manufacturer has his own unique way of formulating the macroinstructions. The use of assemblers and macro assemblers requires specific study with the system being used. In general, the procedure is as follows.

The programmer indicates that a macro is being defined and gives it a name. He then proceeds to define the op codes that instruction should cause to be inserted into the program. At any later time in the programming procedure, this macro name may be used to generate that code string in machine language.

As has already been indicated, very little uniformity exists in the use of assemblers and macros among manufacturers or even for the same microprocessors. Therefore, no more time will be spent here on exact discussion. The user will learn these skills by studying the manufacturer's literature in the area of programming.

SOME COMMON TECHNIQUES

Following familiarization with the instruction set of the system to be used, the next step is learning some of the more common procedures and techniques for accomplishing a variety of routine operations. The objective of this section is to provide a basic complement of programming sequences that accomplish the most commonly encountered operations.

The general categories covered are:

1. Loops, nests and branch operations
2. Basic arithmetic
3. Bit control

Loops, Nests and Branching

The branching or condition oriented instructions available in the Motorola MC6800/6802 and the Intel 8080/8085 microprocessors are one of their most attractive features. The conditional branching instructions allow the programmer to test the results of operations with many less steps than would be required to make the tests without these conditional instructions.

One of the most common uses of the conditional instructions is the creation of **loops** within a program sequence. Creating a loop effects repeated operation of a given sequence. A simple example of an unconditional and unterminated loop is given in Example 9–2.

Example 9–2

8080/8085			MC6800/6802		
LOC	Label		LOC	Label	
2000H	Loop:	INR B	2000	Loop:	INC B
2000H		JMP Loop	2000		BRA Loop

This set of instructions creates an extremely tight loop that will continue to function indefinitely causing register B to increment through from 0 to maximum repeatedly. This loop contains certain problems since the starting value of B is not defined and once this loop is started it cannot be exited under any conditions.

Example 9–2 illustrates that every loop should contain three parts: an initialization, a main body and a termination or exit possibility. Example 9–2 contains only the main body. The initialization portion of a loop sets the beginning conditions which, when modified by the main body, will eventually allow exit from the loop.

Example 9–3 is a proper counting loop.

Example 9–3

8080/8085				MC6800/6802		
	MVI	B	20		LDX	20
Loop	DCR	B		Loop	DEX	
	JNZ		Loop		BNE	Loop

Notice that the initialization causes a countdown starting at 20. The conditional main body does the countdown and the conditional branch allows exit at a 0 count.

The main body of the loop may contain any effective operation that does not destroy the termination possibility. For example, in checking for a particular key entry from a keyboard, if the proper key has not been pressed in three tries, the loop is to terminate. This could be set up as shown in Fig. 9–1.

A series of such loops could be put together to provide command key recognition procedures. Not only may loops be strung together in séries (one after another), they can also be set up so that there are loops within loops. This arrangement is called nesting.

A typical **nest** of two loops might look like Table 9–4.

The use of conditional branch instructions is not limited to the use and creation of loops. They are also used to provide alternate path direction within a program. The almost infinite variety of program decisions originate within this framework of the ability to test the conditional flags and branches, depending upon the found condition. The creation and execution of complex decisions and routines is limited only by the programmer's ability to create conditions that can be checked within the context of the routine.

The programmer must know which instructions will and will not affect the flag or conditional register and keep track of the conditions of those registers.

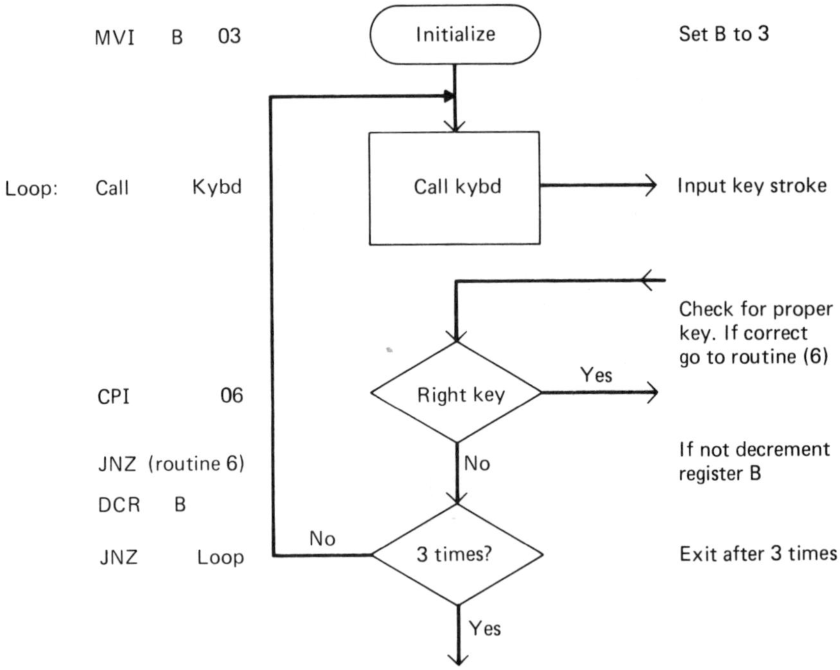

Fig. 9–1. 3-try keyboard entry loop.

Table 9–4 Typical Nest of Two Loops

	LDA	COUNT (1–FF)	Initialize A
Loop 1	DEC A		Count down outer loop
	BEQ	DONE	Done at zero
	LDX	Value	Initialize inner loop
Loop	CPX		Check for 0
	BEQ	Loop 1	Go to outer loop
	DEX		Count down inner loop
	JMP	Loop	Go inner loop
Done:			

Flags

How are conditions checked? Primarily they are checked by a comparison process. In an arithmetic or logical operation, both the 8080/8085 and the MC6800/6802 provide conditional binary bit(s) installed in a special register within the CPU indicating what condition occurred in the arithmetic or logical operation. This binary bit is called a *flag* because it leaves an indication or message that a particular condition exists. In the MC6800/6802, this register is called a conditional code register. In the 8080/8085, the conditional code register is called a flag register.

If an arithmetic or logical operation causes the accumulator contents or some register contents within the CPU to become zero, the zero bit within the flag register is set. The decision to go to a different sequence of operation is then initiated by a conditional jump or conditional branch instruction. Instructions such as jump if not zero, jump if zero, branch if zero, and branch if not zero check the bit in the conditional code register or flag register. The new instructional address contained within a 3-byte branch instruction or 3-byte jump instruction is installed in the program counter. Therefore, the operation continues at a location in memory different from the memory location that would have occurred if the bit had not existed. Consequently, the branching process consists of two elements:

1. A condition that is to be checked
2. A branching operation when the condition occurs

Intel 8080/8085 Flags

In the 8080/8085, the conditional flag register can contain an indication of zero or nonzero, carry or not carry, positive or negative data, parity (even or odd), and auxiliary carry or overflow from bit three to bit four. In the MC6800/6802, the conditions that can be checked are: the carry or borrow bit, which indicates that an overflow from bit seven has occurred, or an underflow was required in a subtraction; the B or overflow bit, which occurs when a 2's complement operation causes an overflow or excess of either plus or minus 127 in the counter; the zero flag, which is similar to the 8080/8085 in that a zero causes it to be set and a nonzero causes it to be reset; the negative, which indicates positive or negative; and the half carry, which corresponds to the auxiliary carry in the 8080/8085. This range of decision-making capability constituted by five and six bits respectively provides for very intricate decision-making processes to occur.

Both microprocessors have instructions that can manipulate these bits in the condition registers. In the 8080/8085, it is the set carry bit and the complement carry operation. In the MC6800/6802, it is the set carry and clear carry operation. The MC6800/6802 also has a set overflow and clear overflow, a set interrupt mask, and a clear interrupt mask. The interrupt mask is a special condition in the MC6800/6802 that is included in the conditional register; whereas in the 8080/8085, the interrupt mask register is a 4-bit register allowing for four vectored interrupts. The decision-making instructions in the 8080/8085 instruction set are as follows: jump if carry, jump if noncarry, jump if minus, jump if plus, jump if zero, jump if nonzero, jump if parity even, and jump if parity odd. There are also branch instructions (CALL and RETURN) that branch on all of these conditions. There is one special instruction in the 8080/8085 set that accomplishes a branching operation by a nonconditional arrangement where the program counter and the H and L register pair are exchanged.

Motorola MC6800/6802 Flags

The MC6800/6802 branch or conditional branching groups also check the register contents as follows: branch if carry clear, branch if carry set, branch if equal, branch if greater than or equal to, branch if greater than, branch if higher, branch if less than or equal to, branch if lower or the same, branch if less than zero, branch if minus, branch if not equal to zero, branch if overflow clear, branch if overflow set, and branch if plus. (The MC6800/6802 also has the branch to subroutine and jump to subroutine instructions and the return from subroutine group as in the 8080/8085 system.)

Branch conditions can be created in several ways. One method uses a count-down or count-up register. For example, in order to cause ten iterations of a loop to occur, a count register can be made by installing a ten in a special register in the CPU or memory. Each time a loop is accomplished, the register is decremented by one and a check is made. In other words, a conditional branch instruction is initiated by a branch if zero or jump if zero. Consequently, the loop continues until the count-down register has reached zero (the last time around the loop).

Another way for checking a condition is by a direct comparison instruction. The microprocessor makes a comparison of the accumulator contents by a subtraction process. The subtraction occurs in an auxiliary accumulator condition register and the accumulator value itself remains unchanged. However, as the comparison is done, the flags resulting from the subtraction are set. A branch or jump instruction may then be used to check the conditions set by the effective subtraction operation.

Another method of creating conditions is by logical manipulation or masking of bits in the system. This is done by logical ANDs, logical ORs and exclusive ORs.

Basic Arithmetic

When dealing with arithmetic operations in microprocessors, the primary separation is between single precision and multiple precision operations. The Motorola MC6800/6802 and Intel 8080/8085 provide for both types of operation in that they have instructions included in their basic sets to carry out arithmetic operations, some of which include carry conditions and others which do not include carry conditions. The basic difference between single precision and multiple precision is that in single precision operations the prior state of the carry bit is not included in the operation. In multiple precision, the same operations may be done repetitively but with each repetition the possible overflow from the previous operation is transferred to the current operation through the carry bit. This requires that prior to starting multiple precision operations, the carry bit must be cleared since there can be no previous carry in to the least significant byte of a multiple byte number.

There is a slight difference in meaning between multiple precision and double precision. Both are, in fact, multiple precision. However, the term double precision usually is used in connection with inherent capabilities provided in the instruction set. Some microprocessors provide for 16-bit (double-byte) addition to be accomplished by one instructional command. Precision beyond two bytes is accomplished by programming and would be classified as multiple precison operations beyond double precision.

Single precision addition and subtraction. There are three modes of arithmetic available in the 8080/8085 instruction set: memory, register and immediate for both addition and subtraction.

To accomplish an Add or Sub memory operation, the location in memory must be previously specified by the contents of the HL register pair. In this case, the H and L pair is acting as a memory pointer to retrieve data. The addition occurs and the results reside in the accumulator register. The instruction is a 1-byte instruction. The ADI instruction is a 2-byte string by which the second byte is added to the accumulator and the result resides in the accumulator.

The Motorola MC6800/6802 equivalents of the Intel Add M, Sub M, ADI (data) and SBI (data) are Add A, Add B, Sub A and Sub B, any one of which may be accomplished by immediate, direct, indexed or extended modes. The MC6800/6802 ABA and SBA instructions cause the two registers in the MC6800/6802 CPU to be added or subtracted and the results reside in the A accumulator. The 8080/8085 equivalent instructions are the Sub (reg) and ADD (reg). The results reside in the accumulator and any one of the six scratch registers may be used.

A comparison of these equivalents is given in Table 9–5.

Multiple precision addition and subtraction. The 8080/8085 instruction set contains a double precision Add capability. This is the DAD or double add which allows one of the four register pairs available in the CPU to be added to the contents of register pair H and L. The result resides in H and L.

The 8080/8085 carries out multiple precision adds and subtracts using ACI, ADC, SBI and SBB in any one of three modes (immediate, memory or register). The MC6800/6802 provides two instructions for multiple precision. The ADC and SBC may use any one of the addressing modes.

Table 9–6 of basic arithmetic operations illustrates how the preceding instructions may be used.

All the add routines in Table 9–6 have been made into subtraction

Table 9–5 Intel-Motorola Single Precision Equivalents

8080/8085	MC6800/6802
Add M	Add A or Add B
Sub M	Sub A or Sub B
Add reg	ABA
Sub reg	SBA
ADI (data)	Add or sub (immediate mode)

Table 9–6 Intel 8080/8085 Basic Arithmetic Operations Example

Memory			
TOM	DS	1	
	LXI H	TOM	Point at TOM
	XRA	A	Clear A
Get TOM	ADD	M	Add TOM
Register			
DICK	DS	1	
	LXI H	DICK	Point to DICK
Get DICK	MOV B	M	Get DICK
	XRA	A	Clear A
	ADD	B	Add DICK
Immediate			
HARRY	EQA	5	
Get HARRY	XRA	A	Clear A
	ADI	(HARRY)	Add HARRY

simply by changing the instruction to Sub M, Sub r or SBI (data). Also, the accumulator has been cleared because it contained a number from which the subtraction would have been done.

Multiple precision is shown in Table 9–7.

Bit Manipulation

The ability to control and manipulate bits within an 8-bit word structure is necessary because all data cannot be arranged in 8-bit fields. The ability to convert codes is a prime example. In converting from binary to BCD or from binary to ASCII, there is not a one to one relationship between bit structures so bit testing and configuration recognition are required. In general, there are three types of bit manipulations which can be accomplished: retrieval, insertion and recognition.

Retrieval is the isolation and/or removal of from one to seven bits from an 8-bit field.

Recognition is the isolation and testing of from one to seven bits of an 8-bit field.

Insertion is the changing or altering of the bit pattern of from one to seven bits of an 8-bit field.

Table 9-7 Multiple Precision

	Count	EQ	20H
	Word 1	DS	4
	Word 2	DS	4
	Num 1	EQ	31H
	Num 2	EQ	41H
	LDA	Count	Get count
	MOV	B,A	Save count
	LXI H	Num 1	Point to first
	LXI D	Num 2	Point to second
	ANA	A	Clear carry
Add	LDAX	D	Get number 2
	ADC	M	Add number 1
	MOV	M,A	Save
	INX	D	Move pointer
	INX	H	to next byte's
	DCR	B	Done?
	JNZ	ADD	No-add next byte
End	JMP	End	Yes-end

Retrieval is most commonly accomplished by a process called masking. Masking is usually carried out by the logical AND instruction. For example, in order to isolate the fourth, fifth and sixth bits of an 8-bit field, the word would be logically ANDed with a 70_{16}.

Example 9–4

	0AAA1011
AND	01110000
Result	0AAA0000

The 0s in the ANDed field serve as the elimination mask causing the original data at those bit positions to be eliminated.

The masking procedure can also be used to assure a 0 field within a given bit pattern. This technique is employed to create a skeleton word into which a new field of data is to be inserted. For example, in order to change the pattern of 01 [0110] 10 into 01 [1001] 10 without a complex routine of addition and calculation, the procedure in Example 9–5 could be followed.

Example 9–5

Original pattern	01011010
AND mask	11000011
Mask result	01000010
OR pattern to be inserted	00100100
Result of merge	01100110

The process of inserting bits is called merging of patterns or words. Merging is most commonly done using the OR instruction.

The testing or recognition of a particular value or pattern can be done in several ways. Two of the most common methods are first isolating the field and then shifting the pattern right until the least significant bit aligns with bit 0 of the 8-bit field. The register would then contain the value of the bit pattern which can be recognized by either arithmetic or logical operations. The second method involves isolating the field and making a direct comparison for the value. The compare or equal branching instructions are used quite commonly for testing bits.

For Example 9–6, suppose bits 2, 3 and 4 were to be evaluated for a value less than 4_2.

Example 9–6

Original	xxxAAAxx
Mask	00011100
	000AAA00
Compare	00010000
Result	Positive or negative flag condition

If the result of this operation in Example 9–6 was positive, the AAA field would have been greater than, or equal to, 4; if negative, it would have been less than 4. The positive or negative condition indicator could then be used to act upon the result.

A quick method of clearing the accumulator is to exclusively OR it with itself. This causes all bits to become 0.

The circumstances and desired results of bit manipulation are as varied as the programs in which they are used. The underlying principle is to first isolate the bits involved and then to act upon them through logical, arithmetic or conditional checks.

STACK METHODS

A **stack** is a special location in memory where temporary data are saved for future use. Both the 8080/8085 and the MC6800/6802 have a CPU register called a **stack pointer** that always points to the last data put into the stack. At the beginning of any program, an initialization process loads the stack pointer at a memory location decided upon by the programmer. The memory location can be anywhere that does not interfere with other programming.

The initialization process is accomplished in the 8080/8085 primarily by the instruction LXI SP, which is a load immediate of two address bytes into the stack pointer. The initialization of the stack pointer in the MC6800/6802 is accomplished by the LDS instruction that loads two address bytes into the stack. The two bytes, in both cases, represent the top of the stack.

The 8080/8085 and the MC6800/6802 operate their stacks almost identically. Both use a PUSH instruction that moves the specified registers to the stack memory area. But when the 8080/8085 pushes a register pair, the stack pointer is first decremented, the most significant byte of eight bits is moved to the stack location (minus one) address, and then the least significant byte of eight bits is moved to the stack location (minus two) address. The MC6800/6802 PUSH instruction first moves the most significant 8-bit byte to the stack location, the stack pointer is decremented causing the most significant byte to be moved to the stack location, and then the least significant byte is moved to the stack location (minus one).

To retrieve data from the stack, the POP instruction is used in the 8080/8085, and the PULL instruction is used in the MC6800/6802. Both POP and PULL instructions exactly reverse the process of the PUSH instruction. That is, the least significant byte comes back first, and the most significant byte comes back last.

There are some important concepts that must be clear to the user of the stack. The meaning of the terms top and bottom as they refer to memory and the stack must be understood. As shown in Figure 9–2, memory is set up like a series of rectangular boxes laid one on top of the other and is numbered from bottom to top increasing from 0000 to FFFF hexadecimal. When one initializes the stack to the top of stack location, it is pointing to the highest memory location it will be using. As data are stored in the stack, the stack decrements, or counts down, to lower numbered addresses.

Another important concept is that more than one location in memory can be designated as a stack. It is not unusual for a programmer to set aside a number of areas in memory for subroutines or independent modules to prevent interplay between modules. This requires the

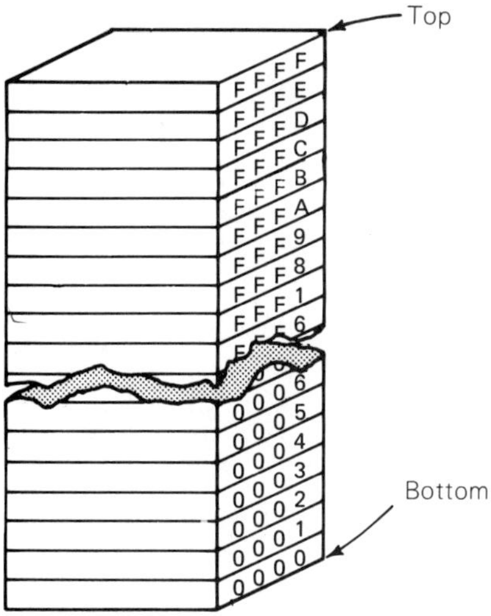

Fig. 9–2. Memory organization.

stack pointer to be reinitialized with a new address each time a subroutine is entered.

The programmer must have some concept of the size that the stack will grow to as it is being utilized. If a large amount of subroutines and temporary data is to be saved in the stack, a large block of memory must be set aside to prevent the stack from interfering with the main program.

Figure 9–3 is a control flow diagram of a series of subroutines. When a new subroutine is called upon to operate, a call or jump to subroutine causes the stack to be loaded with two to eight bytes of data. This loading of the stack saves the environment of the present program, so that when a return from a subroutine is acted upon, the environment is restored to its original condition, and the original program continues.

In an 8080/8085 program using three subroutine levels (assuming that one or two PUSH instructions exist within each subroutine), the stack should consist of approximately twenty to twenty-five bytes because for each subroutine call, two bytes will be loaded into the stack, and the stack will decrement by two. If each subroutine contained two PUSH instructions, each PUSH instruction would result in an additional two bytes being pushed into the stack. This could result in eighteen bytes of stack being utilized. Therefore, setting aside twenty-five bytes would provide a good safety margin.

During interrupt subroutine calls (if the subroutines are accomplished by interrupting processes), the stack storage utilizes six bytes as it branches to the subroutine. Therefore, with three subroutine

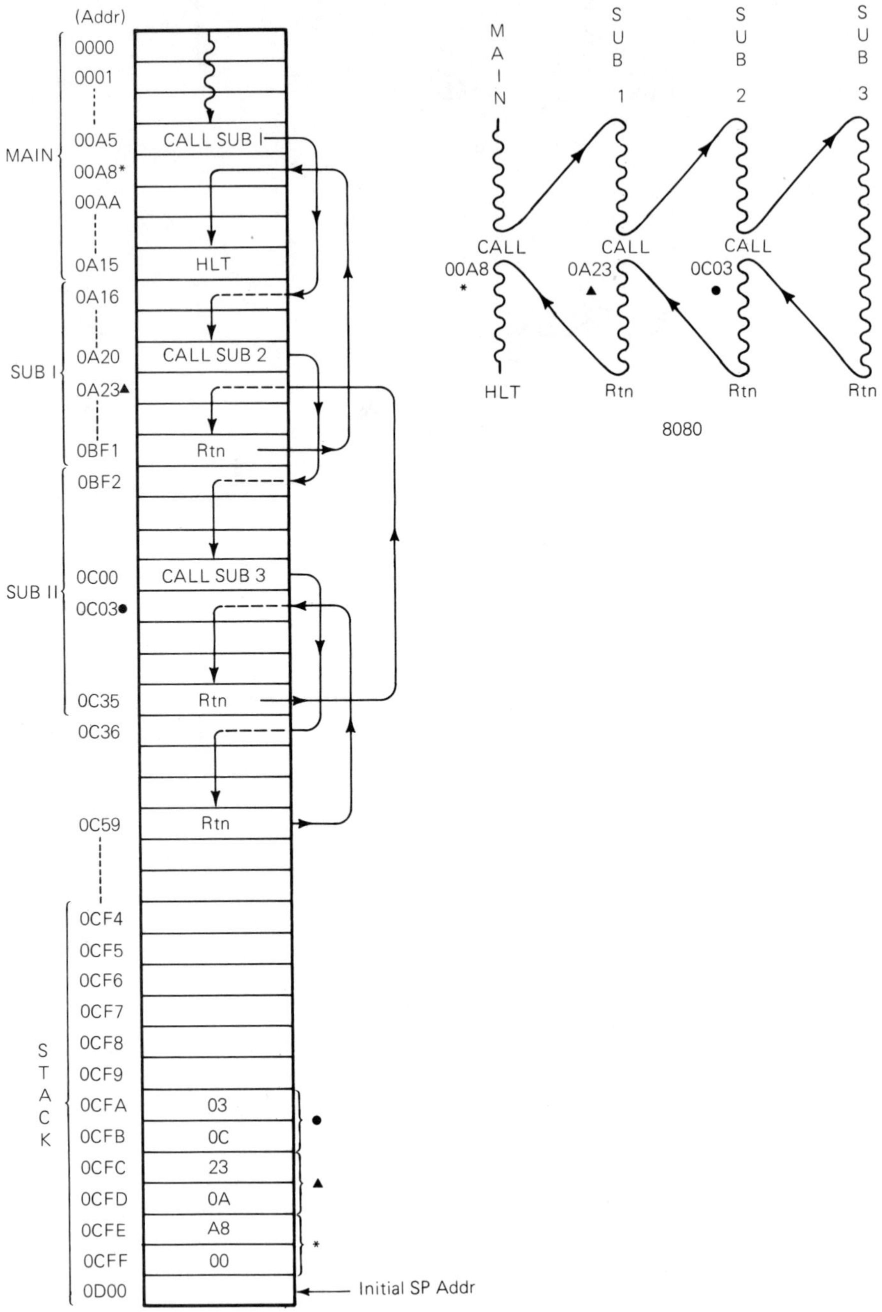

Fig. 9–3. 8080/8085 stack operation.

levels done by interrupt, and a couple of pushes in each program, thirty bytes of stack could be used up. The normal subroutine branches, however, work in the same manner as the 8080/8085 branches, storing only two bytes into the stack.

8080/8085 and MC6800/6802 Stack Methods

The PUSH-PULL, PUSH-POP, RETURN, and return from subroutine (RTS) instructions of the MC6800/6802 and the 8080/8085 are similar. Both microprocessors can adjust the stack pointer by either incrementing or decrementing; that is, causing it to change value by one. In the MC6800/6802, this is provided by the INS and DES instructions. The 8080/8085 uses INX and DCX.

Two instructions allow an index register to adjust the stack. An address can be put into the index register and then transferred to the stack, or the stack pair can be transferred to the index register. For this, the MC6800/6802 uses the transfer to index register or TSX instruction and the reverse TXS instruction. In the 8080/8085, the exchange of the stack pointer and the index register is accomplished by the SPHL instruction, in which the contents of the H and L register pair are transferred to the stack pointer, and in this case, the H and L registers serve as the index register.

To summarize, the stack is used to save temporary data or environmental data when desirable or when interrupts occur and to save return addresses when subroutines or interrupts are activated. The primary instructions are PUSH-POP, PUSH-PULL, CALL (8080/8085), and JUMP or BRANCH (MC6800/6802). The MC6800/6802 interrupts also cause additional storage of data.

Subroutines

Subroutines are intimately tied into stack operations. A **subroutine** is a minor program that exists within a large program. The minor routine used repeatedly by major routines is a subordinate routine.

Subroutines are used for efficiency. That is, when a group of instructions is utilized repeatedly within a program, memory usage is more efficient if the group of instructions is written only once as a subroutine and then called upon at appropriate times by the program. This can result in a considerable saving of memory if done properly.

The use of subroutines also leads to clearer documentation in the top-down method. The breaking down of modules in the top-down method lends itself well to calling upon subroutines rather than using the standard GO TO statement or unconditional jump statement.

After a subroutine is called upon, it must return to the same location from which it was called. This is where the stack gets involved. Figures 9–3 and 9–4 show that the main line of the program can operate with branches to subroutines in several different locations. Branching to a subroutine causes the next instructional location in the main program to be automatically saved in the stack. The program counter is then loaded with the beginning address of the subroutine, which causes the operation of the subroutine to begin at the new address location. If there were only one subroutine operation occurring at this branching point, there would be one subroutine level. However, if within the subroutine there were a branch or a jump to another subroutine instruction, a second return address would be saved in the stack, and a second subroutine would exist. Consequently, there would be two subroutine levels.

Obviously, this process could continue to many levels. The levels utilized in either of the MC6800/6802 or the 8080/8085 are limited only by the available memory or stack size. When the return instruction is encountered, the return address that was saved by the stack is automatically pulled from the stack and reinstated in the program counter, causing the program operation to continue immediately at the instruction following the branch to subroutine instruction.

The subroutine instructions in the MC6800/6802 are the branch to subroutine and the jump to subroutine. They can be conditional or unconditional. In the 8080/8085, the CALL instruction is the primary subroutine instruction. There is no jump subroutine. However, there are conditional jumps which do not save the return address. The

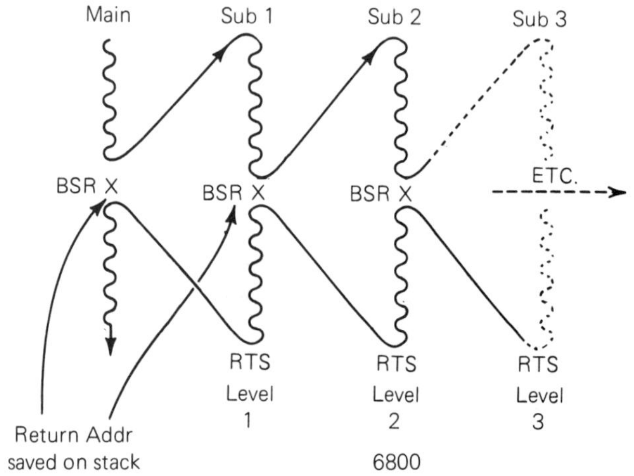

Fig. 9–4. MC6800/6802 stack operation.

MC6800/6802 has additional subroutine capabilities: software interrupt, wait for interrupt, and nonmaskable interrupt. This interrupting process occurs at unplanned times because interrupt is usually initiated by external hardware. In the MC6800/6802, the stack saves the register conditions and the environment of the CPU automatically. The 8080/8085 microprocessor does not automatically save the environment. The programmer must write the environment saving PUSH instructions into the subroutine.

The 8080/8085 equivalent of the MC6800/6802 software interrupt and wait for interrupt operations is the restart instruction. In the 8080/8085 restart instruction, the call to subroutine is automatic, and the return address is automatically saved on the stack and at the restart memory location, where the vector to the beginning of the subroutine is located. The only true difference between an interrupt and a normal subroutine is that an interrupt is an unplanned event and a subroutine is a planned event written into the program. Because of the unplanned character of an interrupt, some special saving operations and considerations for the program in operation at the time of the interrupt are necessary.

DEBUGGING

Debugging is the process of removing or rectifying problems within a program structure. Because the problems that may arise in a program are so diverse and unpredictable, the discussion of debugging must be reduced to general guidelines of how to isolate the problem. It is assumed here that the problem is related to software and does not originate in hardware malfunction.

The worst situation that can occur, of course, is to have only one output indication at the conclusion of operations in an extremely long program and not to be getting that output. Another undesirable situation is one where the problem appears only in very unique and seldom occurring circumstances.

Finding Errors

The process of isolating the problem is, in the final analysis, much like that of any standard trouble shooting technique. The tools used are somewhat different but the procedure is similar. First, eliminate the obvious possibilities. Make sure that all parts of the program are properly in place in memory. (A program cannot operate without all of its functions.) Rethink the flow of the program operations. (Good documentation is important here.) While rethinking the overall flow of the process, try not to get so involved with the details that the major logical errors are missed. In other words, avoid the can't-see-the-forest-for-the-trees situation.

The basic approach to finding errors is tracing the progress of the program as it operates. Without specialized equipment, the tracing of the operation can become a very difficult and time consuming mental exercise of rethinking. The likelihood of making the same errors over and over mentally also exists.

If a logic analyzer is available, the problem can be located more easily. These instruments are designed to facilitate tracing of the actual program progress as it is being executed. This, in turn, allows the operator to determine where the program is failing. Once the problem is understood, it can usually be corrected quite easily. (Most errors are made in subtle logic.) The greatest advantage of the analyzer is that the operator gains access to each instructional step that occurs in a "snapshot" situation, which allows adequate time to consider what is happening in the microprocessor at each step.

Any other method requires the troubleshooter to make an analysis from either real output or artificial output indications after the mistake has occurred and then attempt to deduce or guess where the program went wrong. This narrowing down of the location of the error can, in many cases, be accomplished by a technique of **breakpoints.**

Breakpoint analysis. The concept of using breakpoints is quite simple. When a program is not functioning properly, the operator must determine where the error or errors are occurring. The creation of artificial halt or action breaks in the flow of the operation allows examination of the progress of the program up to that point.

If everything is proper at that point in the operation, the action can be restarted and stopped later. When an error is finally found by this method, the assumption can be made that the error has occurred somewhere between the present breakpoint and the previous valid set of indications. To further clarify this procedure, think of a program as a linear progression of occurrences. See Fig. 9–5.

There may or may not be loops and repetitive operations within the operation. In an attempt to isolate the problem, artificial branching instructions are installed which cause the program flow to break away. Checks are made in this manner at points 1 and 2. At point 1, the program is functioning properly. At point 2, however, the program has failed. New breaks are installed at points 3 and 4. Three is good; 4 is bad. Breakpoint 5 is installed and found to be bad. The problem must then be occurring between points 3 and 5. This procedure would continue until the exact problem is found.

In most cases, a breakpoint will consist of an unconditional branching instruction to service routine which allows access to the internal

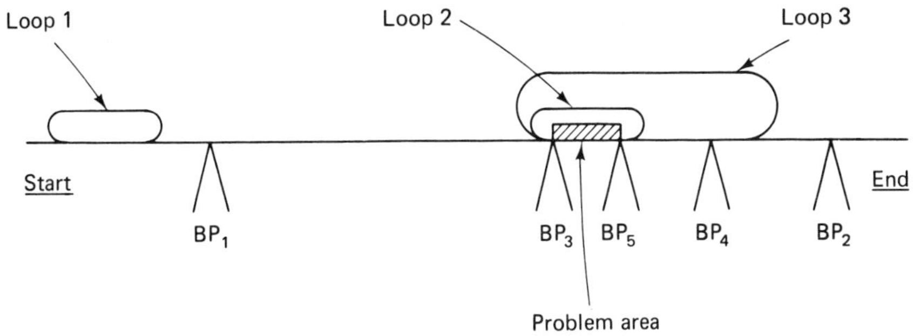

Fig. 9–5. Use of breakpoints.

registers and memory. The use of breakpoints is most powerful when used to check the actual processing. However, the activity of installing and removing breakpoints eventually reaches a point of diminishing returns. That is, the problem has been narrowed down to within a few steps and the breakpoint procedure becomes one of installing a breakpoint at every step along the way and then removing it after it has served its purpose. When the problem analysis reaches the point where each step leading up to the problem point is critical, the use of a single step routine is more efficient.

Single step. Single step monitor operations allow the operator to examine the progress of the program at the completion of every instructional step. The single stepping operation is normally accomplished by a monitor routine which is designed to keep track of the user program count and accomplish each instruction one at a time. At the completion of each cycle, the user program status is stored in a special memory location and the operation is halted temporarily until the next step is called for. During the temporary halt, the operator may examine and modify register and memory data to check process operations.

The two techniques just discussed are probably the two most powerful of the many debugging techniques used. By efficient use of breakpoints, the operator can isolate the general area of the problem and then use single step operation techniques to specifically locate the error. Once the error is found, the same techniques used to first install the program are used to alter the program.

Installing Changes

If programming is being done using an assembler-editor, the insertion and removal of program operations is greatly simplified since most of these monitor programs provide editing commands for this purpose. When the program changes are being done in less sophisticated systems, the insertion of a single additional instruction can involve the re-keying of the rest of the following steps involved after the change is inserted.

One way to avoid this problem of having to re-key long strings of instructions is to periodically install nonfunctional instructions in the instructional string when the program is being written originally. A few no-op instructions every twenty-five or thirty steps can save a lot of time during the debug and revise operations.

Another technique to avoid confusion is to install changes starting at the end of the program first. The true importance of this technique may not be immediately clear to the novice programmer, so consider for a moment the following situation.

The programmer has written a short 256-step program starting at location 00_{16} and ending at location FF_{16}. He has determined that five changes requiring four additional instructions are required. See Example 9–7.

Example 9–7

At location	*Changes required*
30	add 2 steps
8C	delete 3 steps
A5	add 3 steps
AA	add 4 steps
D7	delete 2 steps

If the additional steps are inserted at location 30, the locations of all the other changes after location 30 will have increased by two steps. When the changes at location 8C (now 8E) are finished, all following steps are now one less. Just keeping track of the locations of errors can cause change errors thereby compounding the original problem.

If the changes are made beginning with location D7, no other locations preceding that change are affected. And no confusion is generated about the location of the original errors. Again, the presence of periodic no ops will save time in re-keying the program. A little experience in the use of these suggested techniques will give the user a great appreciation for their validity and value.

SUMMARY

The intent of this chapter was not to provide indepth instruction in all programming techniques but rather to point the reader in the right direction in his approach to developing his own skills. Many specialized books are available which deal in much greater detail with specific software programs and techniques for specific microprocessors. One of the fastest ways to learn programming methods is to analyze programs already in existence and make note of those techniques which are compatible with the programmer's own logic and style. The term style here means that each programmer should attempt to develop his own "bag of tricks" and not attempt to copy exactly the methods and techniques that some other programmer finds comfortable.

Learning to be a good and efficient programmer takes time and lots of experience (mistakes). Do not try to sit down tomorrow and develop a 2K-byte monitor executive program. Begin rather with a really neat 5-step decision loop.

GOOD LUCK!!!

QUESTIONS

1. Write down the types of programming systems available to you for use. Be sure to note the hardware and software capabilities.
2. List and define the items that will be found in most assembly listings.
3. What is a symbol table?
4. Explain the procedure for doing manual assembly.
5. Explain the meaning of the terms pseudo op and macro as they apply to editor assembler systems.
6. Explain the difference among loops, nests and branches.
7. What is a flag?
8. What is multiple precision?
9. Why is bit manipulation capability an important feature of a microprocessor?
10. What is masking?
11. What is a bit field?
12. What is the basic procedure for bit manipulations?
13. What is a stack? How does it operate?
14. What is a stack pointer?
15. What is the basic approach for finding errors?
16. Explain how breakpoints are used in program debugging.
17. Explain when single step operations would be used rather than breakpoint procedure.

Chapter 10

The Intel 8080: Architecture and Support Chips

GLOSSARY

Architecture The functional capabilities provided by the manufacturer in the design of the device including such specifications as word length, voltage levels and other logical and electrical requirements.

Interrupt A signal that causes the microprocessor to discontinue its present operation and branch to an alternative program routine. The physical pin connection line input to the main processor unit.

Masking A technique for sensing specific binary conditions and ignoring others typically accomplished by placing 0s in bit positions of no interest and 1s in bit positions to be sensed.

Multilevel interrupt The possibility of more than one direct interrupt connection to the device provided by the manufacturer; may be vectored or nonvectored.

Priority The relative weight of importance assigned.

Scanning The process of polling the interrupting devices to determine the origin of the interrupt signal. Differentiation between polled I/O and polled interrupts.

Single-line interrupt An indication that the manufacturer has provided only one direct interrupt connection to the device; may be vectored or, more commonly, nonvectored.

Status word A binary arrangement providing indication of present condition.

Vector A location finder (address) usually indicating the starting point of a particular operation or routine. An automatic prestored address used in the interrupt process.

Vectored interrupt An automatic branch operation to a predetermined start point when an interrupt occurs.

ARCHITECTURE OF A CPU

The **architecture** of a CPU refers to the physical and functional arrangement of a particular device provided by the manufacturer. The functional aspects of architecture are normally incorporated into the program models as discussed in Chapter 4, "The Instruction Sets" and Chapter 5, "Introduction to Software." The programming model does not incorporate the electrical and timing considerations of the functional model shown in Fig. 10–1.

Note that this functional diagram is much more complete as well as more complex than the programming model. The internal interconnection, the available lines or pinouts and the functional electrical characteristics must all be considered when constructing microprocessor systems.

The *Intel 8080 Microcomputer Systems User's Manual* provides a brief discussion of the architecture, parts of which are included here.

A typical central processor unit (CPU) consists of the following interconnected functional units:

Registers
Arithmetic/Logic Unit (ALU)
Control Circuitry

Registers

Registers are temporary storage units within the CPU. Some registers, such as the program counter and instruction register, have dedicated uses. Other registers, such as the accumulator, are for more general purpose use.

Accumulator. The accumulator usually stores one of the operands to be manipulated by the ALU. A typical instruction might direct the ALU to add the contents of some other register to the contents of the accumulator and store the result in the accumulator itself. In general, the accumulator is both a source (operand) and a destination (result) register.

Often a CPU will include a number of additional general-purpose registers that can be used to store operands or intermediate data. The availability of general-purpose registers eliminates the need to "shuffle" intermediate results back and forth between memory and the accumulator, thus improving processing speed and efficiency.

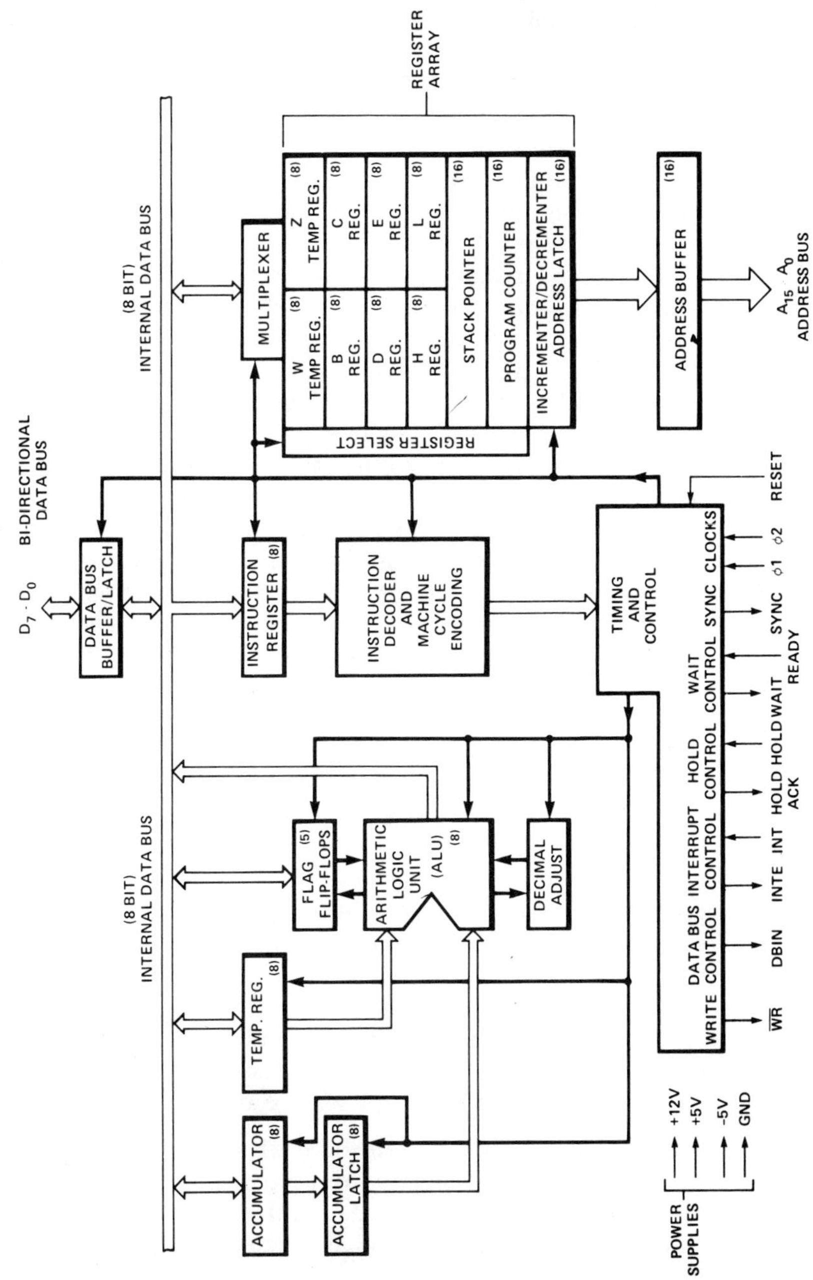

Fig. 10–1. 8080 CPU functional block diagram. *(Reprinted by permission of Intel Corporation, © 1975)*

Program counter and stack pointer. The instructions that make up a program are stored in the system's memory. The central processor references the contents of memory in order to determine what action is appropriate. This means that the processor must know which location contains the next instruction.

Each of the locations in memory is numbered to distinguish it from all other locations in memory. The number which identifies a memory location is called its address.

The processor maintains a counter which contains the address of the next program instruction. This register is called the program counter. The processor updates the program counter by adding "1" to the counter each time it fetches an instruction, so that the program counter is always current (pointing to the next instruction).

The processor has a special way of handling subroutines in order to insure an orderly return to the main program. When the processor receives a call instruction, it increments the program counter and stores the counter's contents in a reserved memory area known as the stack. The stack thus saves the address of the instruction to be executed after the subroutine is completed. Then the processor loads the address specified in the call into its program counter. The next instruction fetched will, therefore, be the first step of the subroutine.

Processors have different ways of maintaining stacks. Some have facilities for the storage of return addresses built into the processor itself. Other processors use a reserved area of external memory as the stack and simply maintain a pointer register which contains the address of the most recent stack entry. The external stack allows virtually unlimited subroutine nesting. In addition, if the processor provides instructions that cause the contents of the accumulator and other general purpose registers to be "pushed" onto the stack or "popped" off the stack via the address stored in the stack pointer, multilevel interrupt processing is possible. The status of the processor (i.e., the contents of all the registers) can be saved in the stack when an interrupt is accepted and then restored after the interrupt has been serviced. This ability to save the processor's status at any given time is possible even if an interrupt service routine itself is interrupted.

Instruction register and decoder. Each operation that the processor can perform is identified by a unique byte of data known as an instruction code or operation code. An 8-bit word used as an instruction code can distinguish between 256 alternative actions, more than adequate for most processors.

The processor fetches an instruction in two distinct operations. First, the processor transmits the address in its program counter to the memory. Then the memory returns the addressed byte to the processor. The CPU stores this instruction byte in the register known as the instruction register and uses it to direct activities during the remainder of the instruction execution.

The mechanism by which the processor translates an instruction code into specific processing actions requires more elaboration than can be afforded here. The concept, however, should be intuitively clear to any logic designer. The eight bits stored in the instruction register can be decoded and used to selectively activate one of a number of output lines, in this case up to 256 lines. Each line represents a set of activities associated with execution of a particular instruction code. The enabled line can be combined with selected timing pulses to develop electrical signals that can then be used to initiate specific actions. This translation of code into action is performed by the instruction decoder and by the associated control circuitry.

Arithmetic/Logic Unit (ALU)

All processors contain an arithmetic/logic unit which is often referred to simply as the ALU. The ALU, as its name implies, is that portion of the CPU hardware which performs the arithmetic and logical operations on the binary data.

The ALU must contain an adder which is capable of combining the contents of two registers in accordance with the logic of binary arithmetic. This provision permits the processor to perform arithmetic manipulations on the data it obtains from memory and from its other inputs.

Most ALUs provide other built-in functions including hardware subtraction, Boolean logic operations and shift capabilities.

The ALU contains flag bits which specify certain conditions that arise in the course of arithmetic and logical manipulations. Flags typically include carry, zero, sign and parity. It is possible to program jumps which are conditionally dependent on the status of one or more flags. Thus, for example, the program may be designed to jump to a special routine if the carry bit is set following an addition instruction.

Control Circuitry

The control circuitry is the primary functional unit within a CPU. Using clock inputs, the control circuitry maintains the proper sequence of events required for any processing task. After an instruction is fetched and decoded, the control circuitry issues the appropriate signals (to units both internal and external to the CPU) for initiating the proper processing action. Often the control circuitry will be capable of responding to external signals, such as an interrupt or wait request. An interrupt request will cause the control circuitry to interrupt main program execution temporarily, jump to a special routine to service the interrupting device, then automatically return to the main program. A wait request is often issued by a memory or an I/O element that operates slower than the CPU. The control circuitry will idle the CPU until the memory or I/O port is ready with data.[1]

ARCHITECTURE OF THE 8080 CPU

The 8080 CPU consists of the following functional units:

- Register array and address logic
- Arithmetic and logic unit (ALU)
- Instruction register and control section
- Bidirectional, 3-state data bus buffer

Registers

The register section consists of a static RAM array organized into six 16-bit registers:

- Program counter (PC)
- Stack pointer (SP)
- Six 8-bit general purpose registers arranged in pairs, referred to as B,C; D,E; and H,L
- A temporary register pair called W,Z

The program counter maintains the memory address of the current program instruction and is incremented automatically during every instruction fetch. The stack pointer maintains the address of the next available stack location in memory. The stack pointer can be initialized to use any portion of read-write memory as a stack. The stack pointer is decremented when data is "pushed" onto the stack and incremented when data is "popped" off the stack (the stack grows downward).

The six general-purpose registers can be used either as single registers (8-bit) or as register pairs (16-bit). The temporary register pair, W,Z, is not program addressable and is only used for the internal execution of instructions.

Eight-bit data bytes can be transferred between the internal bus and

[1] *Intel 8080 Microcomputer Systems User's Manual* (Santa Clara, California: Intel Corporation, 1975), pp. 1–1 – 1–3.

the register array via the register-select multiplexer. Sixteen-bit transfers can proceed between the register array and the address latch or the incrementer/decrementer circuit. The address latch receives data from any of the three register pairs and drives the 16 address output buffers (A_0–A_{15}) as well as the incrementer/decrementer circuit. The incrementer/decrementer circuit receives data from the address latch and sends it to the register array. The 16-bit data can be incremented or decremented or simply transferred between registers.

ALU

The ALU contains the following registers:

- An 8-bit accumulator
- An 8-bit temporary accumulator (ACT)
- A 5-bit flag register: zero, carry, sign, parity and auxiliary carry
- An 8-bit temporary register (TMP)

Arithmetic, logical and rotate operations are performed in the ALU. The ALU is fed by the temporary register (TMP), the temporary accumulator (ACT) and the carry flip-flop. The result of the operation can be transferred to the internal bus or to the accumulator; the ALU also feeds the flag register.

The temporary register (TMP) receives information from the internal bus and can send all or portions of it to the ALU, the flag register and the internal bus.

The accumulator (ACC) can be loaded from the ALU and the internal bus and can transfer data to the temporary accumulator (ACT) and the internal bus. The contents of the accumulator (ACC) and the auxiliary carry flip-flop can be tested for decimal correction during the execution of the DAA instruction.

Instruction Register and Control

During an instruction fetch, the first byte of an instruction (containing the op code) is transferred from the internal bus to the 8-bit instruction register.

The contents of the instruction register are, in turn, available to the instruction decoder. The output of the decoder, combined with various timing signals, provides the control signals for the register array, ALU and data buffer blocks. In addition, the outputs from the instruction decoder and external control signals feed the timing and state control section which generates the state and cycle timing signals.

Data Bus Buffer

This 8-bit bidirectional 3-state buffer is used to isolate the CPU's internal bus from the external data bus (D_0 through D_7). In the output mode, the internal bus content is loaded into an 8-bit latch that, in turn, drives the data bus output buffers. The output buffers are switched off during input or nontransfer operations.

During the input mode, data from the external bus is transferred to the internal bus. The internal bus is precharged at the beginning of each internal state, except for the transfer state.[2]

Notice that the discussion of the architecture is concerned with how the internal operations of the microprocessor are accomplished and, in many cases, whether or not the external lines are buffered. When the system designer begins to attach circuitry to this device he is, in effect, extending the architecture outside the chip and must, therefore, consistently observe the proper timing and electrical capabilities of the CPU. These details can be found in the *Intel 8080 Microcomputer User's Manual* and will not be incorporated here.

A completely discrete component system compatible with the chip could be designed following the data provided by the manufacturer. Because this procedure would be extremely time-consuming and costly for the system designer, all microprocessor manufacturers, including Intel, provide families of support chips which adhere to the electrical and functional requirements of the CPU. A typical connection diagram and application information for the support chip under consideration are usually included in the data and specifications. Many of these support chips have been designed for a specific operation while others are designed for general use.

Several of these supporting devices will be discussed here briefly to demonstrate the simplicity of design these devices provide. For more detailed discussion, refer to the manufacturer's data catalogs.

SUPPORT CHIPS

8228 System Controller and Bus Driver

One of the primary differences between the 8080 CPU operation and that of other microprocessors is the short duration of a data byte called the **status word.** At the beginning of each machine cycle the CPU, for a period of approximately one clock cycle, puts a coded data

[2] *8080 User's Manual*, pp. 2–2, 2–3.

byte on the data bus which forewarns or preconditions the external logic of the system. While this data is on the bus, the 8224 puts out a strobe pulse called status strobe which is used as a clocking signal for an 8-bit latch called a status latch. The status latch then holds that preconditioning information for later use in completing the machine cycle.

There are three other control pulses which are critical to the timing of the external system. They are DB_{IN} or data bus input, $\overline{WR}$ or write/read not, and HLDA or hold acknowledge. The 8228 chip incorporates in its circuitry the necessary logic to accommodate the status word and the three control signals and process them into discrete synchronization signals for memory and I/O usage. Additionally, it provides for bidirectional data bus buffering and control. This is all provided by a single 28-pin package designed specifically for the 8080A CPU and can be easily connected as shown in the interfacing diagram in Fig. 10–2 and Fig. 10–3. The precise timing and electrical characteristics can be found in the *Intel Data Catalog.*

8255 Programmable Peripheral Interface (PPI)

The 8255 shown in Fig. 10–4 provides, on one chip, three directionally controlled ports which may be changed by sending the proper control word to the device prior to using it in a particular configuration. The control word is installed by sending a port address which results in A_0 and A_1, both being the 1 condition. Refer to Fig. 10–5, the basic operation table. When addressed in this manner, the chip accepts the information on the data bus and installs it in the control register. By proper use of control words, the ports can be operated in basically three modes. Refer to Fig. 10–4.

0 = I/O

1 = strobed I/O

2 = bidirectional bus

Within these three general modes there are a variety of port configurations which can be specified as both input and output or combination types.

An added feature is the ability to set and reset individual bits or data lines and to source 1 ma of current at 1.5 V allowing direct connection to a variety of peripheral devices.

The sequence of operation is essentially as follows. The control word is sent to the proper address which is any unused address that

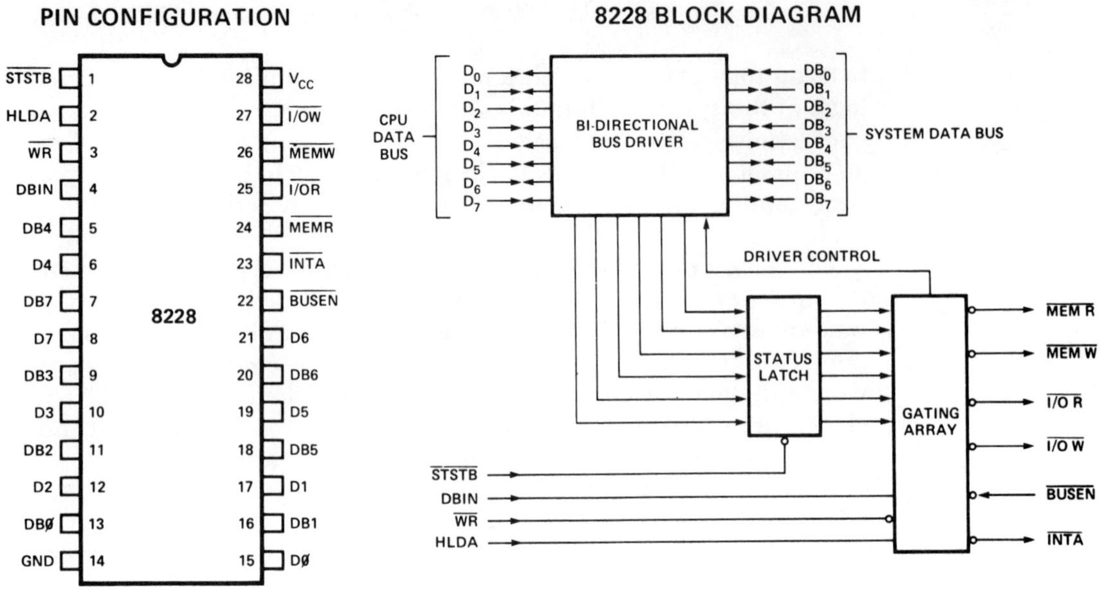

PIN NAMES

D7-D0	DATA BUS (8080 SIDE)	INTA	INTERRUPT ACKNOWLEDGE
DB7-DB0	DATA BUS (SYSTEM SIDE)	HLDA	HLDA (FROM 8080)
I/OR	I/O READ	WR	WR (FROM 8080)
I/OW	I/O WRITE	BUSEN	BUS ENABLE INPUT
MEMR	MEMORY READ	STSTB	STATUS STROBE (FROM 8224)
MEMW	MEMORY WRITE	Vcc	+5V
DBIN	DBIN (FROM 8080)	GND	0 VOLTS

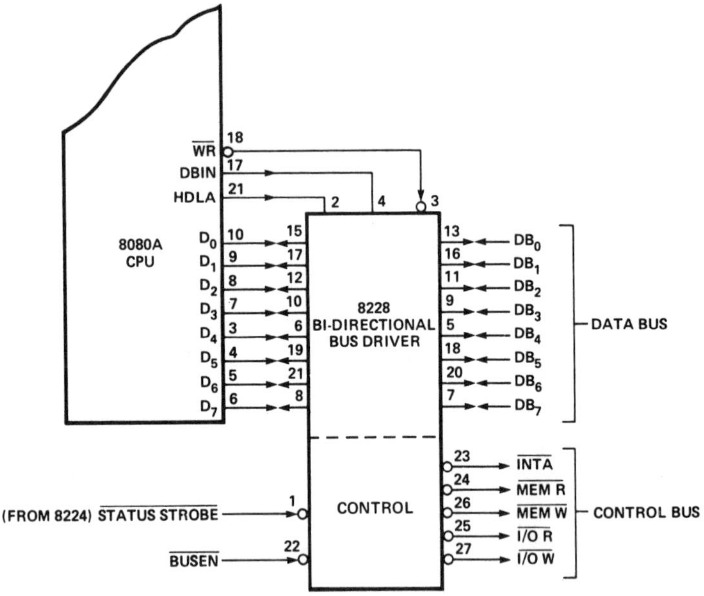

Fig. 10–2. 8228 pin configuration, block diagram, application connection. (*Reprinted by permission of Intel Corporation, © 1975*)

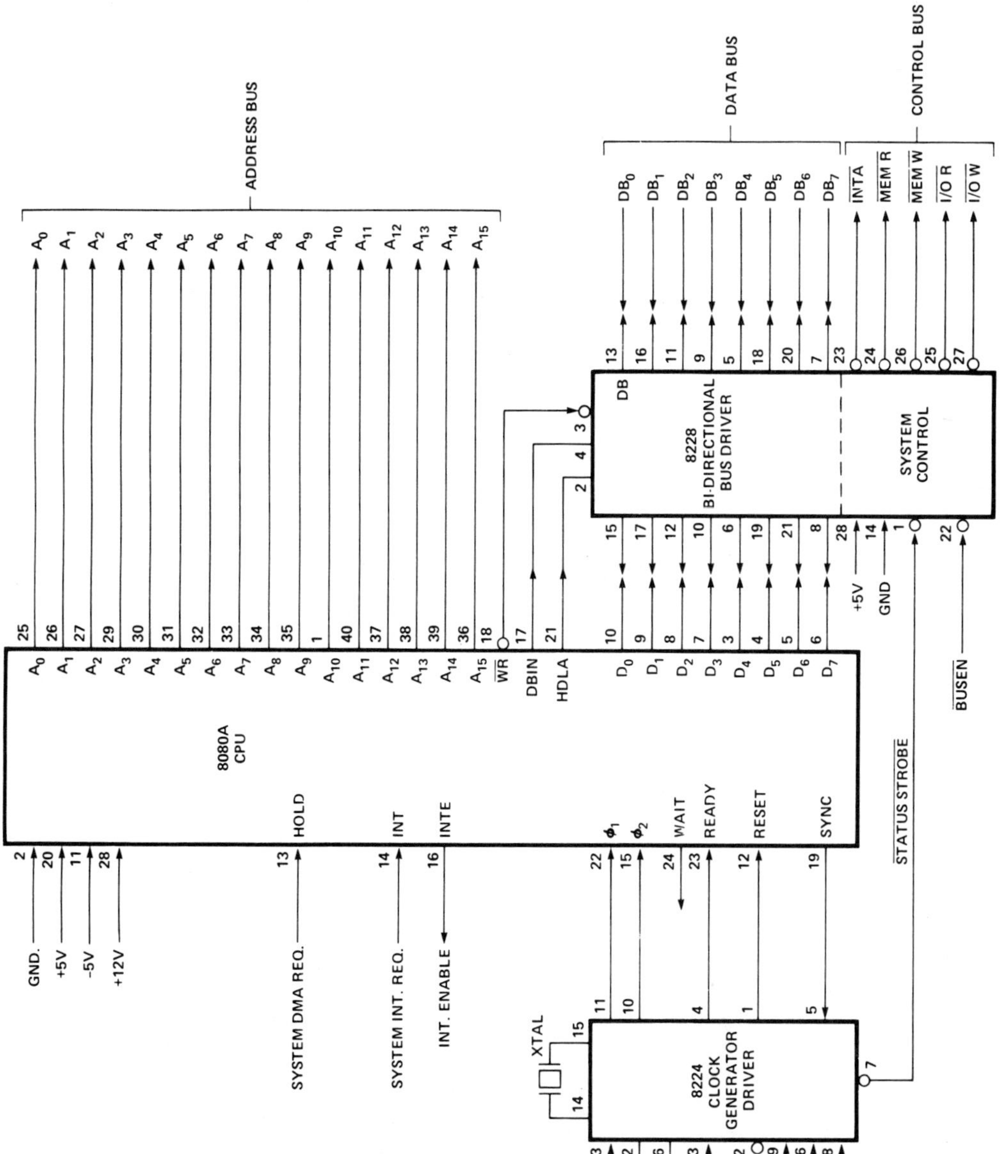

Fig. 10–3. **8080A CPU standard interface for 8228 controller.** ***(Reprinted by permission of Intel Corporation, © 1975)***

8255 BLOCK DIAGRAM

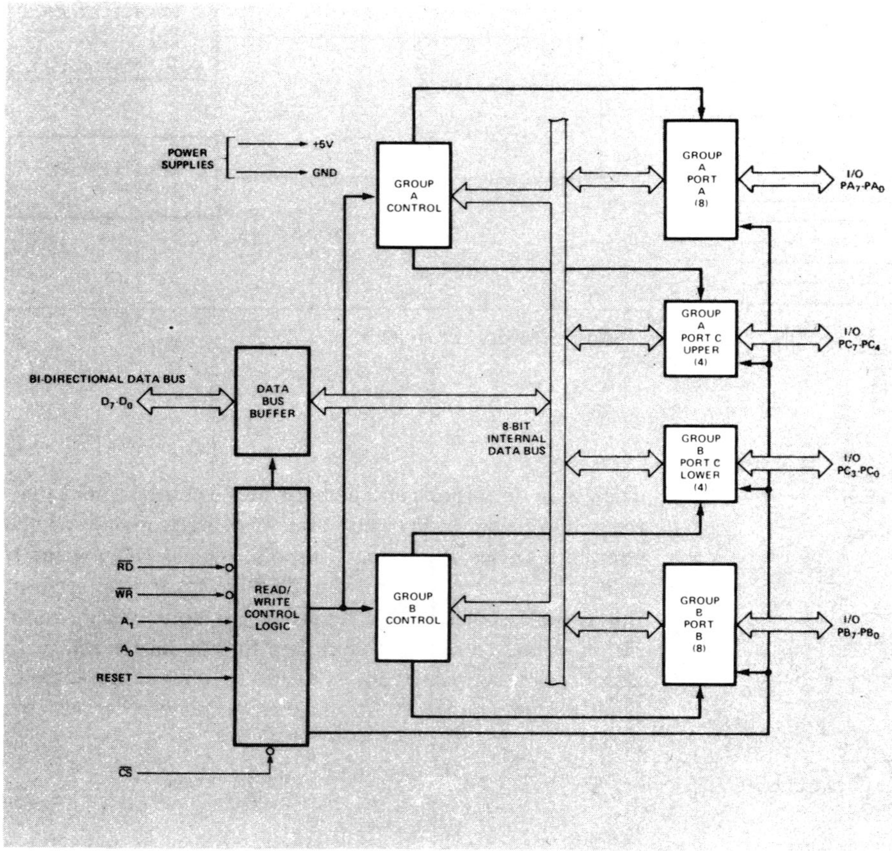

PIN CONFIGURATION

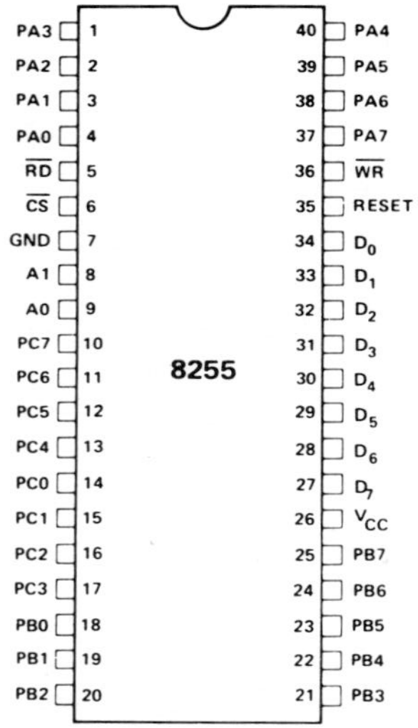

PIN NAMES

D_7–D_0	DATA BUS (BI-DIRECTIONAL)
RESET	RESET INPUT
$\overline{CS}$	CHIP SELECT
$\overline{RD}$	READ INPUT
$\overline{WR}$	WRITE INPUT
A0, A1	PORT ADDRESS
PA7-PA0	PORT A (BIT)
PB7-PB0	PORT B (BIT)
PC7-PC0	PORT C (BIT)
V_{CC}	+5 VOLTS
GND	Ø VOLTS

Fig. 10–4. 8255 pin configuration, block diagram, basic mode definitions and bus interface. (*Reprinted by permission of Intel Corporation, © 1975*)

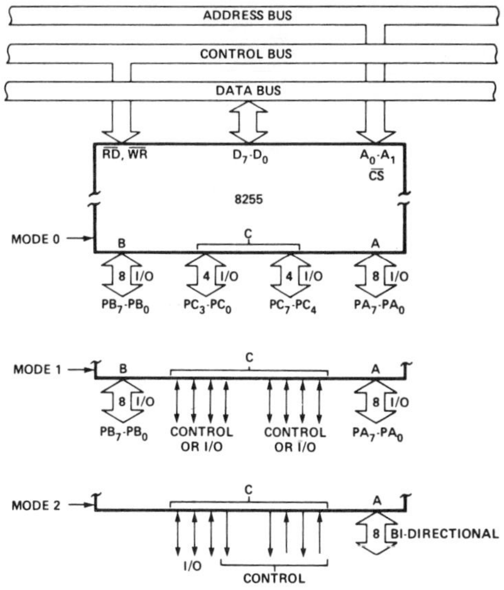

Fig. 10–4. *(Continued)*

has the two LSBs (least significant bits) in a high state. For example, 03_{10} binary equivalent 00000011; 07_{10} binary equivalent 00000111; $0B_{16}$ binary equivalent 00001011.

The control word sets the mode and port configuration. This mode and configuration remain intact until changed by another control word. The control word format and bit definitions are shown in Fig. 10–5. The various ports may then be read or written into according to the basic operation table in Fig. 10–5. Again, for more detailed electrical information and exact interface data, refer to the *Intel Data Catalog.*

Many of the systems which are connected to a microprocessor as peripheral equipment require **interrupt** servicing. That is, they are not subordinate to the microsystem all the time but rather operate more or less independently of the microprocessor and only need microprocessor aid occasionally. Microprocessor manufacturers provide a variety of specialized support chips for handling these peripheral systems.

Most of these systems are handled more efficiently by either interrupting or DMA procedures. For this reason, the discussion of interrupting ports and DMA procedures are included here along with the support chips.

8255 BASIC OPERATION

A_1	A_0	$\overline{RD}$	$\overline{WR}$	$\overline{CS}$	INPUT OPERATION (READ)
0	0	0	1	0	PORT A ⇒ DATA BUS
0	1	0	1	0	PORT B ⇒ DATA BUS
1	0	0	1	0	PORT C ⇒ DATA BUS
					OUTPUT OPERATION (WRITE)
0	0	1	0	0	DATA BUS ⇒ PORT A
0	1	1	0	0	DATA BUS ⇒ PORT B
1	0	1	0	0	DATA BUS ⇒ PORT C
1	1	1	0	0	DATA BUS ⇒ CONTROL
					DISABLE FUNCTION
X	X	X	X	1	DATA BUS ⇒ 3-STATE
1	1	0	1	0	ILLEGAL CONDITION

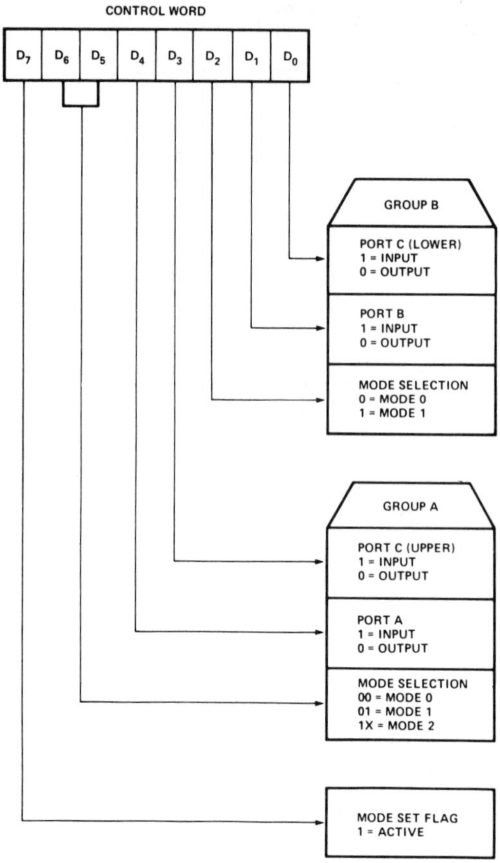

Fig. 10–5. Control word format bit definitions, 8255 basic operation. (*Reprinted by permission of Intel Corporation, © 1975*)

INTERRUPTING PORTS

Introduction to Interrupts

The discussion of handling interrupts is quite appropriate in this support chip chapter because the primary difference between an interrupt service routine and a standard subroutine is the hardware initiation of the routine. Because the entry into an interrupt service routine is so similar to a subroutine operation, a short review of the CPU response to a subroutine branching instruction is in order.

When a subroutine instruction is encountered, the microprocessor responds by saving the present program count in the stack and installing the new beginning address in the PC register. When a return instruction within the subroutine is encountered, the processor retrieves the saved address from the stack and installs it in the program counter, effectively transferring control first to the subroutine and then back to the main program.

In interrupt processing, this same sequence occurs with one difference: the action is not initiated by a preplanned instruction but rather by external hardware setting the interrupt flip-flops or interrupt flags inside the microprocessor. During the completion of each instruction cycle, the microprocessor checks this internal interrupt flag and, if it is set, it temporarily suspends the present operation in favor of the service routine being called for by the interrupting device. The difference between types of interrupts is determined by the methods used to present the starting address of the service routine to the program counter.

There are basically two ways in which interrupts can be recognized by a microprocessor: by polled methods or by vectored methods. The term polled here should not be confused with the programmed control polling methods of handling input/output. The polled I/O method usually means that the whole set of I/Os being operated are interrogated one at a time to determine if servicing is required or not. This same polling procedure may be initiated as the result of an interrupt signal. When used in this way, polling is usually called **scanning** to differentiate it from the standard polled I/O system.

The scanned or polled method of interrupt handling is a software approach for generating the address vector for the PC register whereas the vectored method means that the address vector or the address vector memory location is automatically installed in the PC register. The term vector in this context is, in many cases, misused. A **vector** is a pointer address. That is, it is the entry address of a software routine.

A rather elaborate analogy is probably the easiest way to illustrate first, what an interrupt port is and second, the difference between polled and **vectored interrupts.**

Interrupt Analogy

Imagine a classroom situation where the instructor is lecturing on a particular subject and a class of students is listening to the lecture. Periodically during the course of the lecture, students wish to ask questions, contribute ideas or generally participate in response to a question. What goes on in the classroom is quite similar to what goes on in the microprocessor interrupt system. If a student wishes to interrupt the lecture for any reason, he raises his hand indicating to the instructor that he either wants, or is ready to give, information. The instructor may take two courses of action: he may temporarily ignore the hand or he can acknowledge it. This is analogous to having an interrupt mask either set or reset. If the interrupt mask is set, the microprocessor will acknowledge the interrupt; if it is not set, the interrupt will go unanswered.

If the instructor chooses to acknowledge the interruption, he may nod his head toward the student, point at him or call his name. This acknowledgement by the instructor causes the student to go into action by asking a question or by making a proper response of some type. When the student has ceased his activity, the instructor responds appropriately to the question or dialogue and then returns to his main function which is to continue the lecture or demonstration.

The analogy is fairly simple to make. The instructor corresponds to the central processor, the students are the I/O devices and the medium of transfer is verbal. The sequence of events for a microprocessor system would be as follows.

The main microprocessor is going about its assigned task of executing a particular program operation. It has the internal flip-flop set so it is capable of recognizing interrupting signals. That is, the interrupt is not masked. One of several peripheral devices sends an interrupt signal into the processor. As soon as it is able, the processor sends back an interrupt acknowledge signal to the device. This IACK or INTA signal then causes the device to begin functioning in communication with the microprocessor in a predefined manner. As soon as the device and the processor complete their operation, the processor returns to its original task. Although this analogy should make clear exactly what an interrupt is and how it is handled, there are still several problems which can only be answered by making the analogy more complicated.

Now the classroom situation has been set up where the student does not raise his hand but rather pushes a button on his desk, which turns on a light on the instructor's desk. The instructor now knows that one of the students wishes to interrupt. His problem is discovering which one is calling. All methods of searching for the right student would come under the heading of polling or scanning. The instructor could go through the entire class asking each student if he had turned on the light until he found the right student and then the associated dialogue could begin.

This system of response to interrupts works well as long as only one student at a time wishes to interrupt. Consider the problem of the student at the back of the class who wishes to interrupt but happens to push his button at the same time as two or three other students in the front. In effect, his interrupt will not be recognized. This is also the main drawback of a software polling system.

In a better system, the student who presses his button would have his seat number flash on a display in front of the instructor. The instructor would then respond by acknowledging that seat number directly and immediately. This system would be similar to a vectored interrupt system in which the main processor knows, by virtue of the identity accompanying the interrupt, which device is asking to be recognized. The method of providing the device identity also varies from system to system and depends mainly on the basic interrupt architecture provided by the manufacturer.

As with all analogies, these will fail if carried too far, but they do convey an explanation of the operation of interrupts. With that understanding fresh in mind, it is time to look at specific interrupt methods.

Interrupt Methods

Masking. All microprocessor systems provided with an interrupting capability are also provided with an ability to ignore interrupts. This is normally accomplished internally by the use of a flip-flop controlled gate. When the flip-flop or flag is properly set, the interrupting signals will be allowed to pass; if the flag is not set, the interrupting signals will be blocked or masked. **Masking** used in connection with interrupts means that the interrupt device is prevented from bothering the central processor. Nonmaskable interrupts are those interrupt pins which cannot be blocked.

Most microprocessor systems also provide for remembering if an interrupt has occurred while masked. This is usually done with another flip-flop called either an interrupt status flag or a pending interrupt flag. If a device attempts to interrupt while it is masked, the status or pending flag is set to "remember" that an interrupt was attempted. When the interrupt is later unmasked, the remembered interrupt will normally cause an immediate interrupt operation to occur.

Priority. There is another method by which interrupts may be controlled. The interrupting devices are given weight of importance or **priority** over other devices. Most manufacturers provide, either internally or externally within their chip family, a priority method of handling interrupts.

Depending upon which microprocessor is purchased, the user may be confronted with several arrangements. He may have only one interrupt line (single line) to which he may "OR tie" all interrupting systems. He must then develop a software polling routine to determine which I/O device generated this interrupt. He may also encounter interrupt lines available to him which may be of either the multilevel or vectored type. Any of these systems can be prioritized by external circuitry if priority is not internally established within the microprocessor itself.

A **single line interrupt** system requires a software scanning routine to determine which interrupting device is calling. The sequence of polling in the software routine establishes the priority of the devices. The first device polled receives highest priority; the last device polled receives lowest priority.

In a **multilevel interrupt** system, the priority is established by the manufacturer during the development of the microprocessor. Multilevel inputs may also be vectored so that they cause an automatic branching operation to a predefined memory location. Priority in a multilevel system can also be established by having nonmaskable interrupt lines. In most microprocessors, the differentiation between multilevel systems and vectored systems is not easily distinguished. For most beginners, sorting out the differences and methods of handling interrupts are problems because the definitions are loosely used by the manufacturers.

The best approach to understanding interrupts is establishing the hardware differences and then attempting to sort out the software drive methods, with the understanding that different manufacturers use dissimilar terms to describe similar operations.

Types of interrupts. Interrupts may be single line or multilevel. Within these two very general categories are maskable and nonmaskable types. These can be further subdivided into internal or external (software of hardware) initiation. The term vectored implies that branching is automatic upon the initialization of the interrupt operation. In fact, all interrupts are finally vectored to the service routines. The difference between vectored and nonvectored interrupts breaks between the address being pre-established and the address being developed or calculated.

SUPPORT CHIPS FOR INTERRUPT

8214 Priority Interrupt Control Unit (PICU)

Many commercial systems will have more than one port of input and output. They may be handled by programmed I/O operations but this is memory expensive. A more efficient method is by priority interrupt methods. The 8214 provides a single chip priority capability.

As noted in the *Intel User's Manual,* the 8214 is an 8-level priority interrupt control unit designed to simplify interrupt driven microcomputer systems.

The PICU can accept eight requesting levels, determine the highest priority, compare this priority to a software controlled current status register and issue an interrupt to the system along with vector information to identify the service routine.

The 8214 is fully expandable by the use of open collector interrupt output and vector information. Control signals are also provided to simplify this function.

The PICU is designed to support a wide variety of vectored interrupt structures and reduce package count in interrupt driven microcomputer systems.[3]

8-Level controller (8080) application. The most common application of the 8214 is that of an 8-level priority structure for the 8080 or 8008 microcomputer systems.

Shown in Fig. 10–7 is a detailed logic schematic of a simple circuit that will accept eight input requests, maintain current status, issue the interrupt signal to the 8080 and encode the proper RST instruction to gate onto the data bus.

The eight requests are connected to the 8214 by the designer in whatever order or priority is to be preassigned. For example, eight keyboards could be monitored and each assigned a degree of importance (level of priority) so that faster processor attention or access can be assigned to the critical or time dependent tasks.

The inputs to the current status register are connected to the data bus so that data can be written out into this "port."

An 8212 is used to encode the RST instruction and also to act as a 3-state gate to place the proper RST instruction when the 8080 data bus is in the input mode. Note that the $\overline{\text{INT}}$ signal from the 8214 is latched in the SR flip-flop of the 8212 so that proper timing is maintained. The 8212 is selected (enabled) when the INTA signal from the

[3] *8080 User's Manual,* p. 5–153.

PIN CONFIGURATION

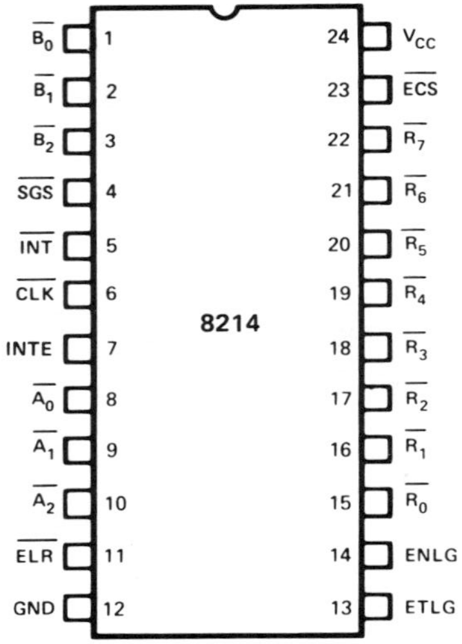

LOGIC DIAGRAM

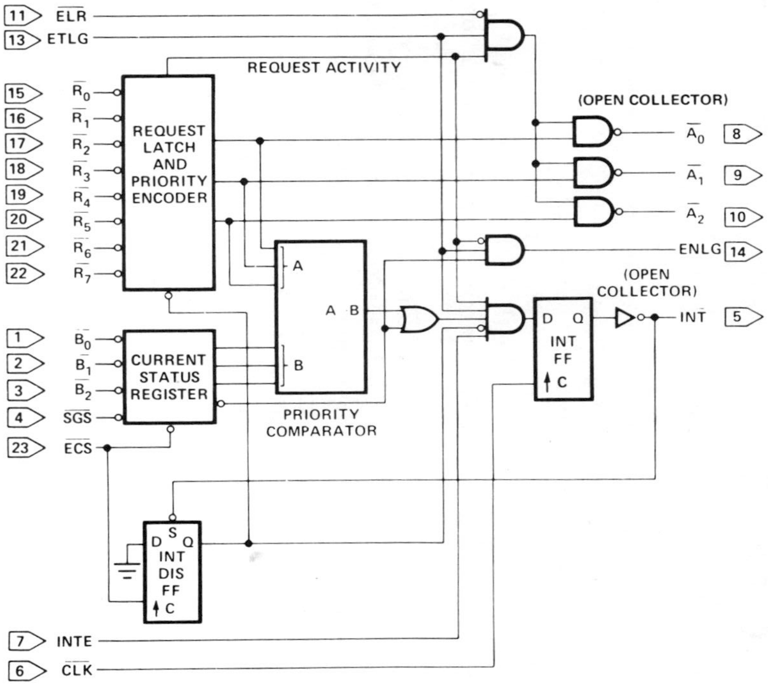

PIN NAMES

INPUTS	
$\overline{R_0\text{-}R_7}$	REQUEST LEVELS (R_7 HIGHEST PRIORITY)
$\overline{B_0\text{-}B_2}$	CURRENT STATUS
$\overline{SGS}$	STATUS GROUP SELECT
$\overline{ECS}$	ENABLE CURRENT STATUS
INTE	INTERRUPT ENABLE
$\overline{CLK}$	CLOCK (INT F-F)
$\overline{ELR}$	ENABLE LEVEL READ
ETLG	ENABLE THIS LEVEL GROUP
OUTPUTS:	
$\overline{A_0\text{-}A_2}$	REQUEST LEVELS — OPEN COLLECTOR
$\overline{INT}$	INTERRUPT (ACT. LOW) — OPEN COLLECTOR
ENLG	ENABLE NEXT LEVEL GROUP

Fig. 10–6. 8214 pin configuration, logic diagram. (*Reprinted by permission of Intel Corporation, © 1975*)

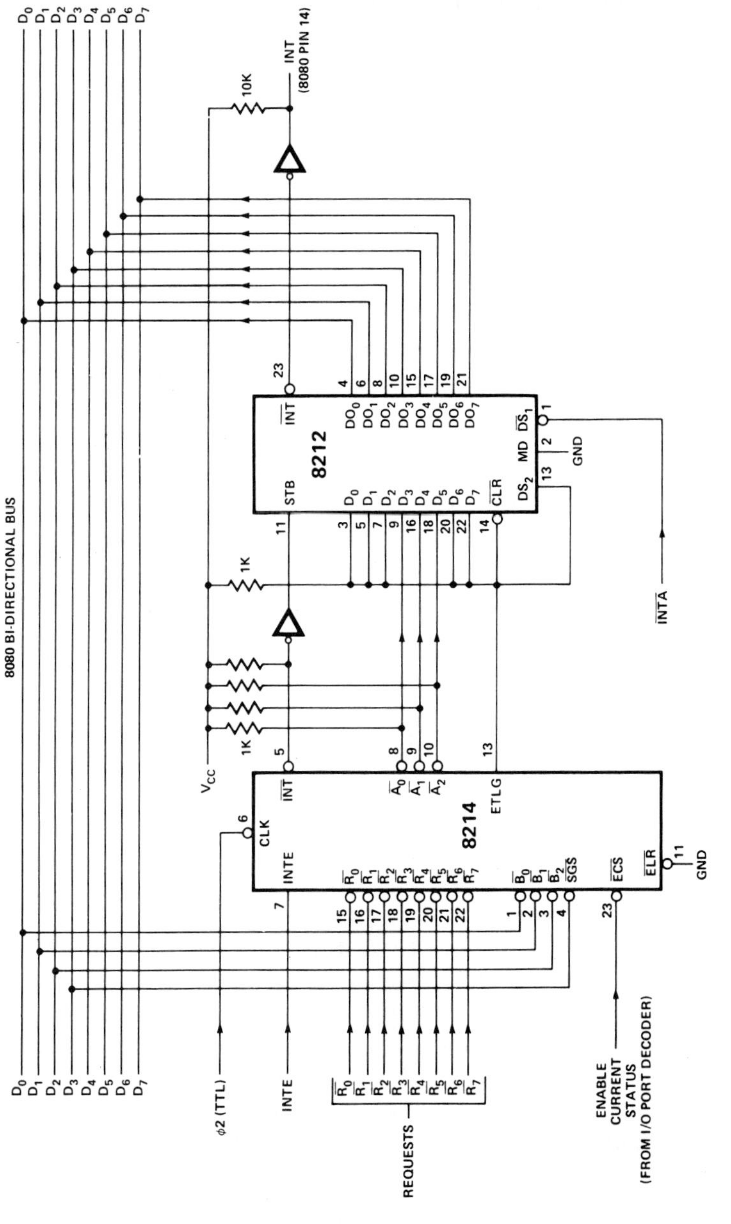

Fig. 10–7. 8214 interface connection. *(Reprinted by permission of Intel Corporation, © 1975)*

8080 status latch and the DBIN from the 8080 are active. This assures that the RST instruction will be placed on the data bus at the proper time. Note that the $\overline{INT}$ output from the 8212 is inverted and pulled up before it is connected to the 8080. This is to generate an $\overline{INT}$ signal to the 8080 that has the correct polarity and meets the input voltage requirements (3.3 V).

Basic operation. When the initial interrupt request is presented to the 8214 it will issue an interrupt to the 8080 if the structure is enabled. The 8214 will encode the request into 3 bits (modulo 8) and output them to the 8212. After the acknowledgement of the interrupt has been issued by the 8080 the enclosed RST instruction is gated onto the data bus by the 8212. The processor executes the instruction and points the program counter to the desired service routine. In this routine the programmer will probably save the status of the register array and flags within a series of push instructions. Then, a copy of the current interrupt level (modulo 8) can be "built" in the accumulator and output to the current status register of the 8214 for use as a comparison reference for all further incoming requests to the system.

This vectored 8-level priority interrupt structure for 8080 microcomputer systems is a powerful yet flexible circuit that is high-performance and has a minimal component count.[4]

Figure 10–8 illustrates two things: first, the relative interface connection of the PICU with respect to the interrupting ports themselves and second, a variety of application connections for the 8212 support chip discussed in Chapter 7, "Input/Output."

8259 Programmable Interrupt Controller (PIC)

The 8080 system of interrupt handling has a single maskable interrupt line which initiates the following procedure. When the interrupt occurs, the CPU finishes its present instruction and sends back an interrupt acknowledge (INTA) signal and accepts a single instruction from the data bus. This is the only case where an I/O device is provided access to the instruction decode register inside the CPU. When the I/O system receives the INTA signal, it presents a restart instruction code to the data bus. This RST (restart) instruction has a vector field of three bits (bits 3, 4, and 5) which causes the CPU to automatically branch to one of eight vector memory locations. The 8080 can therefore handle up to eight vectored I/O devices. Priorities are established externally through hardware.

The vector locations in the 8080 are shown in Table 10–1.

The 8080 does not automatically save its register data. Software pro-

[4] *8080 User's Manual*, p. 5–157.

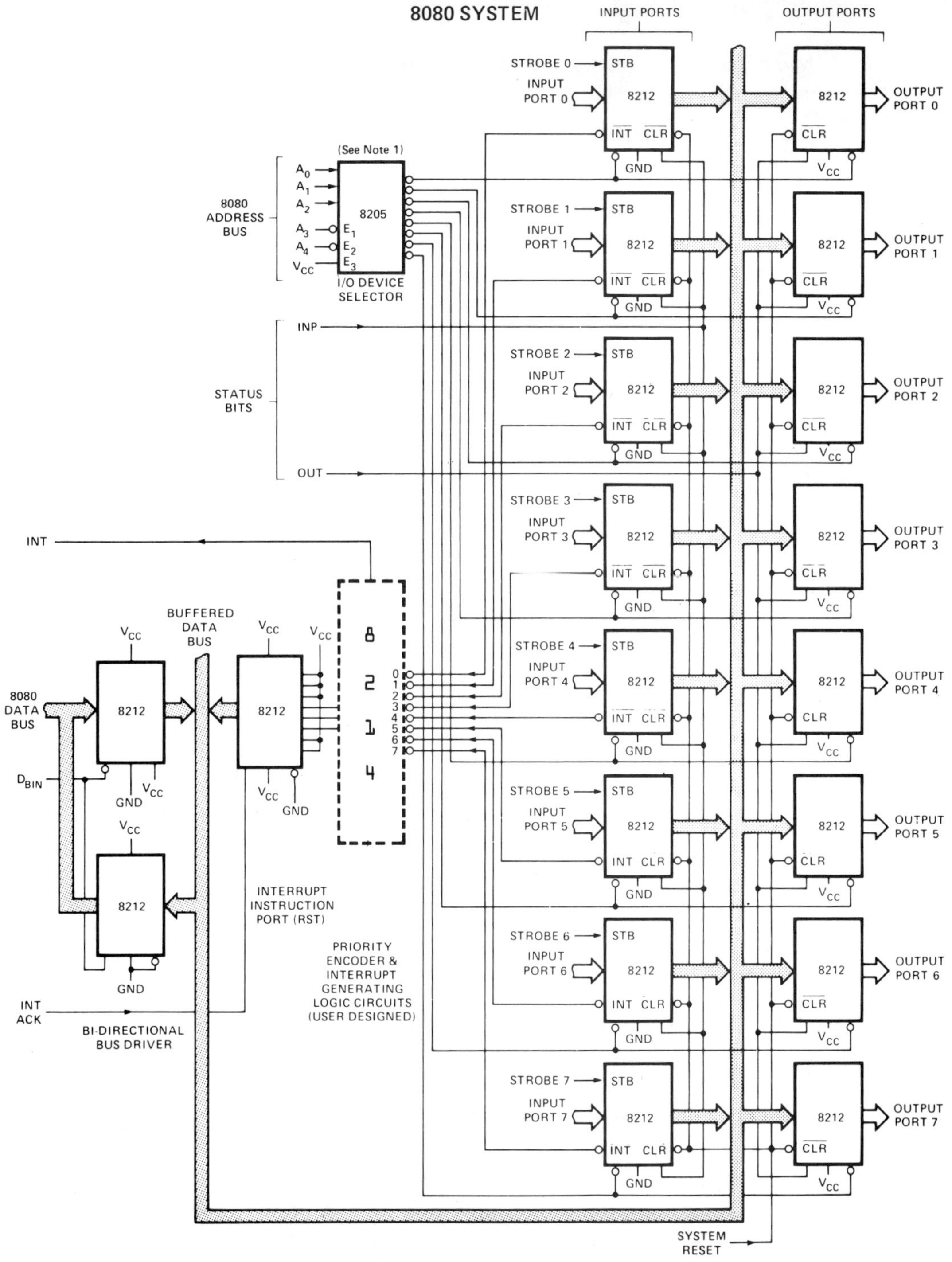

Note 1. This basic I/O configuration for the 8080 can be expanded to 256 input devices and 256 output devices all using 8212 and the appropriate decoding.

Fig. 10–8. 8214 system relationship for priority interrupt. (*Reprinted by permission of Intel Corporation, © 1975*)

Table 10-1 8080 Restart Vector Locations

	INTERRUPT	VECTOR LOCATION
RST 0	000	000
RST 1	001	010
RST 2	010	020
RST 3	011	030
RST 4	100	040
RST 5	101	050
RST 6	110	060
RST 7	111	070

visions should be established to save the main program data at the start of the I/O servicing task.

The 8214 PICU is provided by Intel for small system priority control. It is not programmable nor is it expandable to more than 8-level priority.

Intel provides another chip which is designed to work with the 8080 system in handling multiple priority interrupts. If the 8259 is used, the peripheral device is required to be capable of generating an interrupt signal and of following those standard I/O communications of any peripheral port.

The 8259 can handle up to eight vectored priority interrupts for the CPU. It is cascadable up to sixty-four interrupts without additional circuitry. It is specifically designed for use in real time, interrupt driven microcomputer systems. It responds to systems software like a peripheral I/O device and is programmed.

The main feature of the 8259 is its use of the call instruction for vectoring rather than the standard RST (restart). The manual sequence of events during interaction of the 8259 as described in the *Intel Data Catalog* follows.

1. One or more of the interrupt request lines (IR7-0) are raised high, setting the corresponding IRR-bit(s).

2. The 8259 accepts these requests, resolves the priorities and sends an INT to the CPU.

3. The CPU acknowledges the INT and responds with an $\overline{\text{INTA}}$ pulse.

4. Upon receiving an $\overline{\text{INTA}}$ from the CPU group, the highest priority ISR-bit is set, and the corresponding IRR-bit is reset. The 8259 will also release a CALL instruction code (11001101) onto the 8-bit data bus through its D7-0 pins.

5. This CALL instruction will initiate two more $\overline{\text{INTA}}$ pulses to be sent to the 8259 from the CPU group.

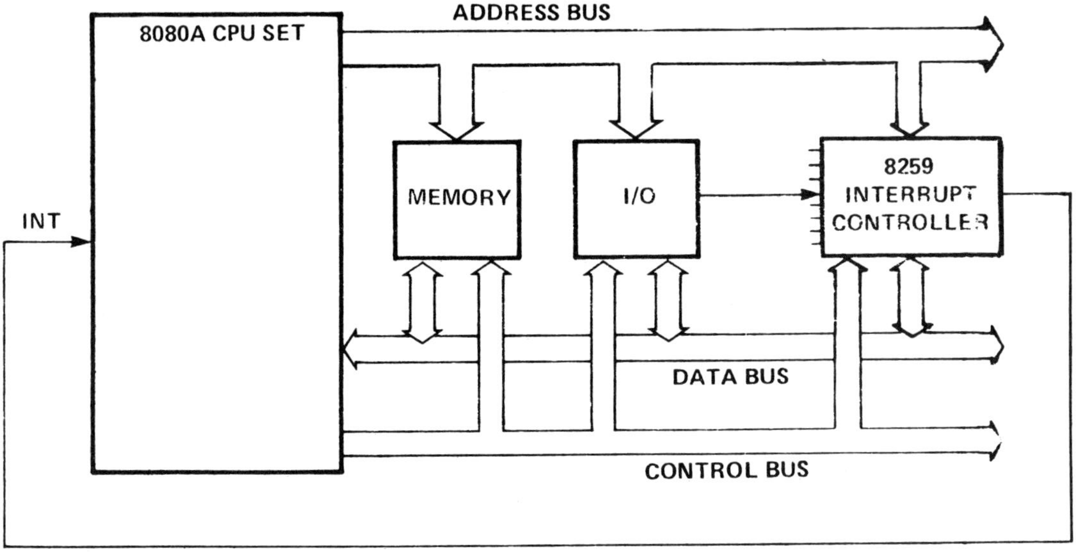

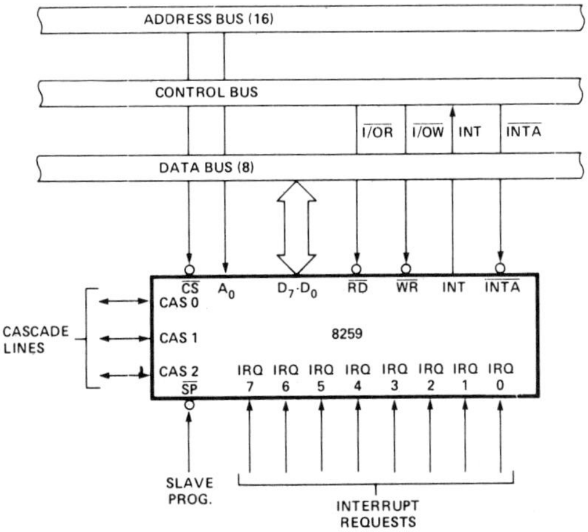

Fig. 10–9. 8259 interface circuitry. (*Reprinted by permission of Intel Corporation, © 1977, 1978*)

6. These two $\overline{\text{INTA}}$ pulses allow the 8259 to release its preprogrammed subroutine address onto the data bus. The lower 8-bit address is released at the first $\overline{\text{INTA}}$ pulse and the higher 8-bit address is released at the second $\overline{\text{INTA}}$ pulse.

7. This completes the 3-byte CALL instruction released by the 8259. The ISR bit is not reset until the end of the subroutine when an EOI (end of interrupt) command is issued to the 8259.[5]

[5] *Intel Data Catalog* (Santa Clara, California: Intel Corporation, 1978), p. 12–115.

Interfacing the 8259 to the 8080 bus configuration is very simple as shown in Fig. 10–9.

The main advantages of the 8259 are: it is a simple connection system, it is programmable and it is expandable to sixty-four vectored interrupts. It uses a "call" vector which allows it to vector any one of the 64 K locations for service routines rather than only eight as with the use of the standard restart instruction. The standard interrupt restart system can also be utilized concurrently with the 8259 operation.

DMA

There is another type of interrupting which is quite different from the usual interrupt methods just discussed. It is called DMA (direct memory access).

Purpose

The purpose of DMA is to save data transfer time. For example, if the microprocessor is operating at a 4 MHz clock rate, an average instruction process period might be from 1 to 4 microseconds. Picking an average of 3 microseconds per instruction, a fifteen instruction transfer loop might take 45 microseconds to accomplish one data byte transfer to or from a particular I/O device. This results in a transfer rate of approximately 22 K bytes/second.

Additionally, while the transfer of a block of data is being accomplished, the CPU is completely devoted to this one job and not free to do anything else. Assuming 500 bytes are to be transferred, 20 to 25 milliseconds could be spent in accomplishing the transfer. If, on the other hand, DMA is used and a 500 nanosecond access time memory is used, the same transfer can be accomplished in approximately 25 microseconds—a time saving of almost 99%. The transfer takes about only .01% of the "normal" time.

In order to provide a better feeling for the relationship between transfer rate and method of handling, a short discussion example is included here.

To accomplish programmed I/O operations, the CPU sends the start command for the device. Then it goes into a wait loop until the device responds creating a 100% software overhead and a maximum transfer rate dependent upon two things: the device response time and the wait loop execution time. Assuming the external device is capable of 100 bytes per second transfer rate and the wait loop is shorter than 1/100 second, the external device's transfer rate becomes the transfer rate for the CPU with 100% dedication to the function.

If an interrupting procedure is used, it starts the device and then goes about doing other job functions until interrupted by the device. When the interrupt occurs, the CPU branches to the service routine, makes the transfer and then returns to its main function. Again assuming a 100 byte per second transfer rate for the interrupting device and a 100 microsecond service routine, the software overhead becomes 1% and the total time spent in transfer is about 10 milliseconds.

Using DMA techniques for the same device, the total time dedicated to the transfer would be 100 memory cycles. With a 450 nanosecond memory that works out to about 10 microseconds with little or no software overhead. These points are summarized in Fig. 10–10.

Procedure

DMA can be accomplished in two ways: by complete suspension of CPU activity until the transfer is completed or by a "cycle stealing" process. In either case, the peripheral device must have the digital logic capability to take control of the address and data bus structures.

The procedure is basically as follows. The peripheral device sends a signal that it is ready to conduct a DMA transfer operation. This signal is applied to the hold pin of the 8080 CPU. This may be done directly or through a controller device such as the 8257 programmable DMA controller to be discussed shortly. The micro responds by sending back an acknowledgement that its operation has been suspended and that the address and data bus are free to be used. When the peripheral receives the acknowledgement signal it then proceeds to use memory directly rather than operating through the microprocessor. When it has completed its operation, it then drops the hold request line and the micro returns to its operation.

As far as the microprocessor is concerned, the peripheral device operations are transparent. That is, its own processing operation is in no way altered except that occasionally the process is temporarily suspended.

Considerations

The only difference between complete block transfer DMA and cycle stealing is the way in which the peripheral handles the DMA request operation. In the complete transfer operation, the peripheral would activate the request line on a continuous basis until the transfer is complete. In doing a cycle stealing operation, it would make the request once for each byte to be transferred and then allow the microprocessor to continue operation until the peripheral is ready for the

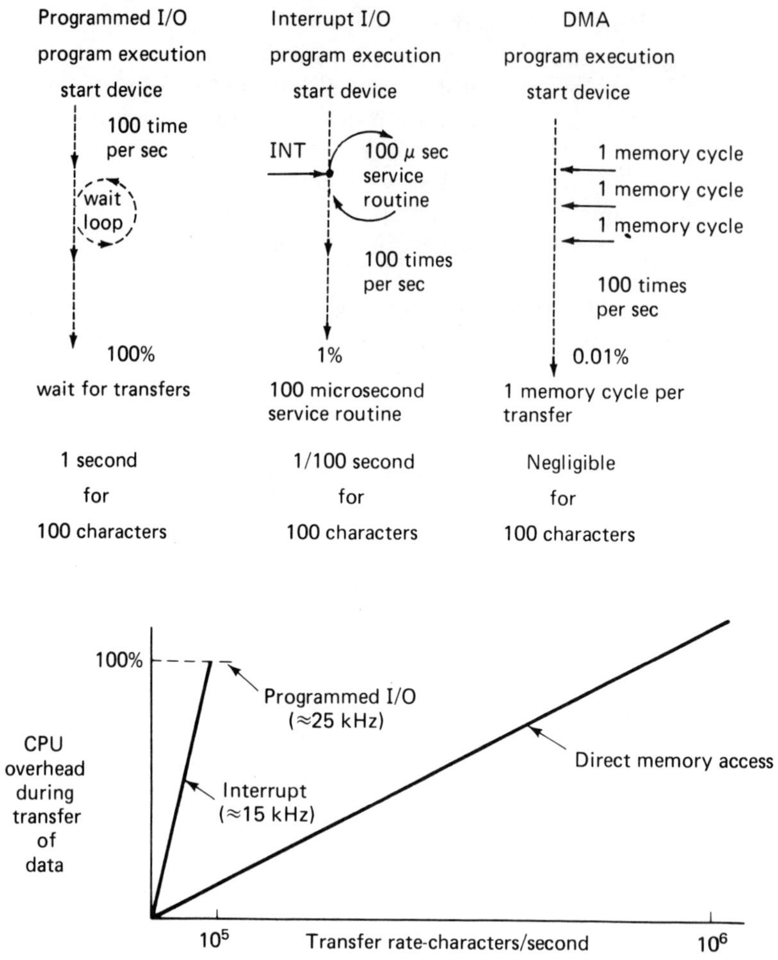

Fig. 10–10. Summary of transfer rate comparison. (*Reprinted by permission of Intel Corporation, © 1977*)

next byte. The choice of method depends on the speed of the peripheral, the access time of the memory involved and the size of the data block to be transferred. If the data block is small, the cycle stealing technique is usually quite satisfactory. However, if the block to be transferred is large, the more efficient complete transfer method is more desirable. One other factor involved in the method decision is whether the microprocessor can afford to be out of touch with the systems it is running for the period required for complete block transfer. If not, then the cycle stealing method is a must.

8257 Programmable DMA Controller

Intel provides a programmable DMA controller in a 40-pin package. The 8257 is a 4-channel DMA controller with priority request logic. Upon peripheral request it generates a sequential memory address which allows peripherals to read and write directly to or from memory. It is capable of operating from 20 to 30 nanoseconds access time per byte and therefore constitutes an extremely fast transfer device. It accomplishes its acquisition of the bus system by sending a hold request pulse to the CPU. It is capable of peripheral cycle count and can provide "DMA complete" signals for the peripheral.

The general interconnection scheme is shown in Fig. 10–11. Detailed instructions for programming and system applications can be found in Intel data catalogs.

Included here is a pictorial diagram, Fig. 10–12, showing the family of devices that Intel provides to support its 80 series microprocessor in interfacing to peripheral devices.

Although this has been a limited presentation of specialized support chips, it should give an indication of the flexibility and sophistication that can be achieved with relative ease by staying with the "family" of chips provided by the manufacturers.

A list of the Intel family chips and their applications is included in Appendix 3.

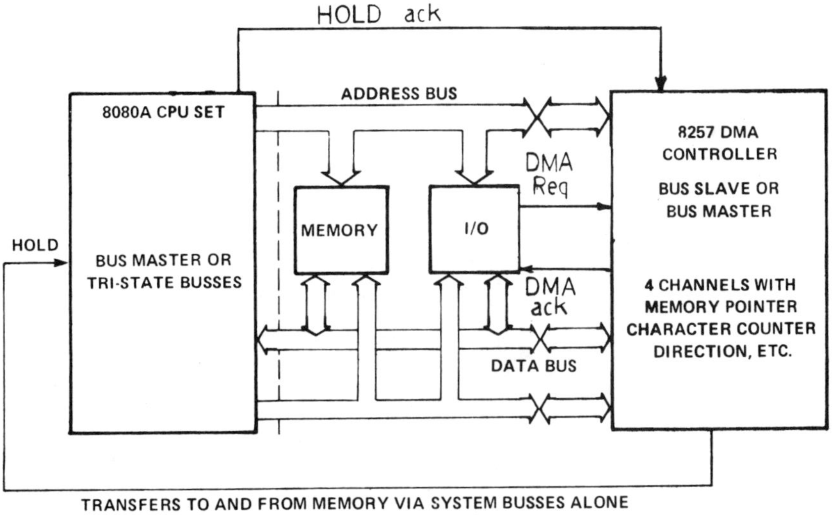

Fig. 10–11. Direct memory access input/output. (*Reprinted by permission of Intel Corporation, © 1977*)

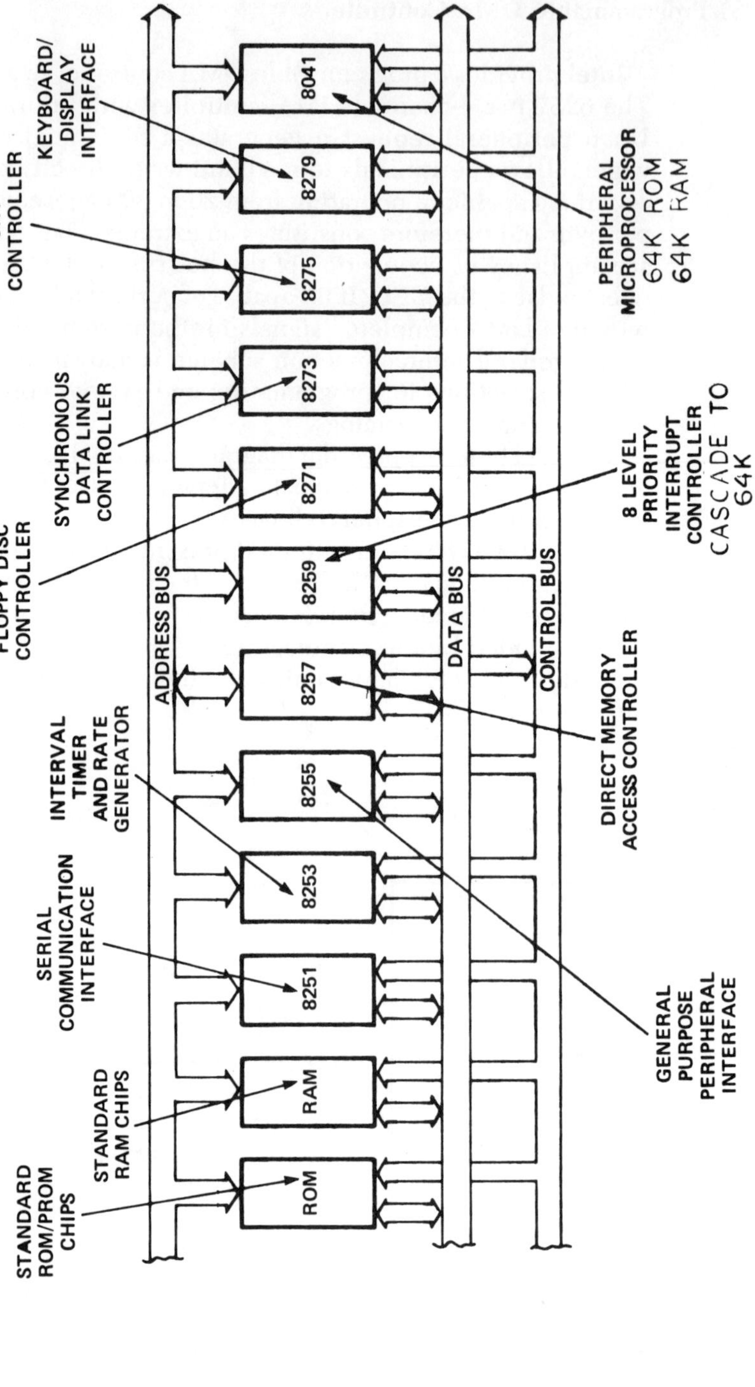

Fig. 10–12. 8080A/8085 peripheral family. *(Reprinted by permission of Intel Corporation, © 1977)*

QUESTIONS

1. What does the term architecture mean as applied to microprocessors?
2. Explain the use of the status word in system control.
3. Give the names and abbreviations for the following devices and include a brief statement of each one's function.

8228	8224	8214	8257
8080	8212	8259	8255

4. In your own words, explain the difference between an interrupt service routine and a subroutine.
5. What is a vector?
6. What does it mean when a system is said to have prioritized interrupts?
7. What is a nonmaskable interrupt?
8. What is the difference between a hardware interrupt and a software interrupt?
9. What is a pending interrupt?
10. Multilevel interrupts are normally vectored. What does this mean?
11. Explain in your own words the interrupt system provided in the 8080.
12. What is the basic reason for using DMA techniques?
13. What are the factors involved in deciding upon the request method for DMA?

Chapter 11

Intel 8080 Applications

In this chapter, an actual system that has many of the features typical of microprocessor systems will be discussed in some detail. This system is not presented here to illustrate sophisticated techniques and methods, but rather to demonstrate a relatively simple, complete system that illustrates some fundamental applications.

CIRCUIT DISCUSSION

General Layout

Figure 11–1 is a block diagram of a clock monitor system that will activate one of four individual output lines at preselected times. This block diagram contains the CPU, memory, status latch, I/O decode, input ports and output ports which are the basic blocks of any system, as discussed in Chapter 1, "Introduction to the Microprocessor."

Porting System

In the I/O port circuit, Fig. 11–2, each input port consists of a single 8212 (8-bit bus port). Each port is connected to the 7-segment display so that each segment (unmultiplexed) constitutes one line of input. The eighth line (pin 22) is grounded to assure a zero input.

Each port is connected to the I/O decode section through the inverting (DS1) line (pin 1) and the $\overline{\text{IN}}$ line is connected through the other (DS2) line (pin 13). The internal logic of the 8212 is such that both pulses ($\overline{\text{DS1}}$ and DS2) must be present in coincidence for information

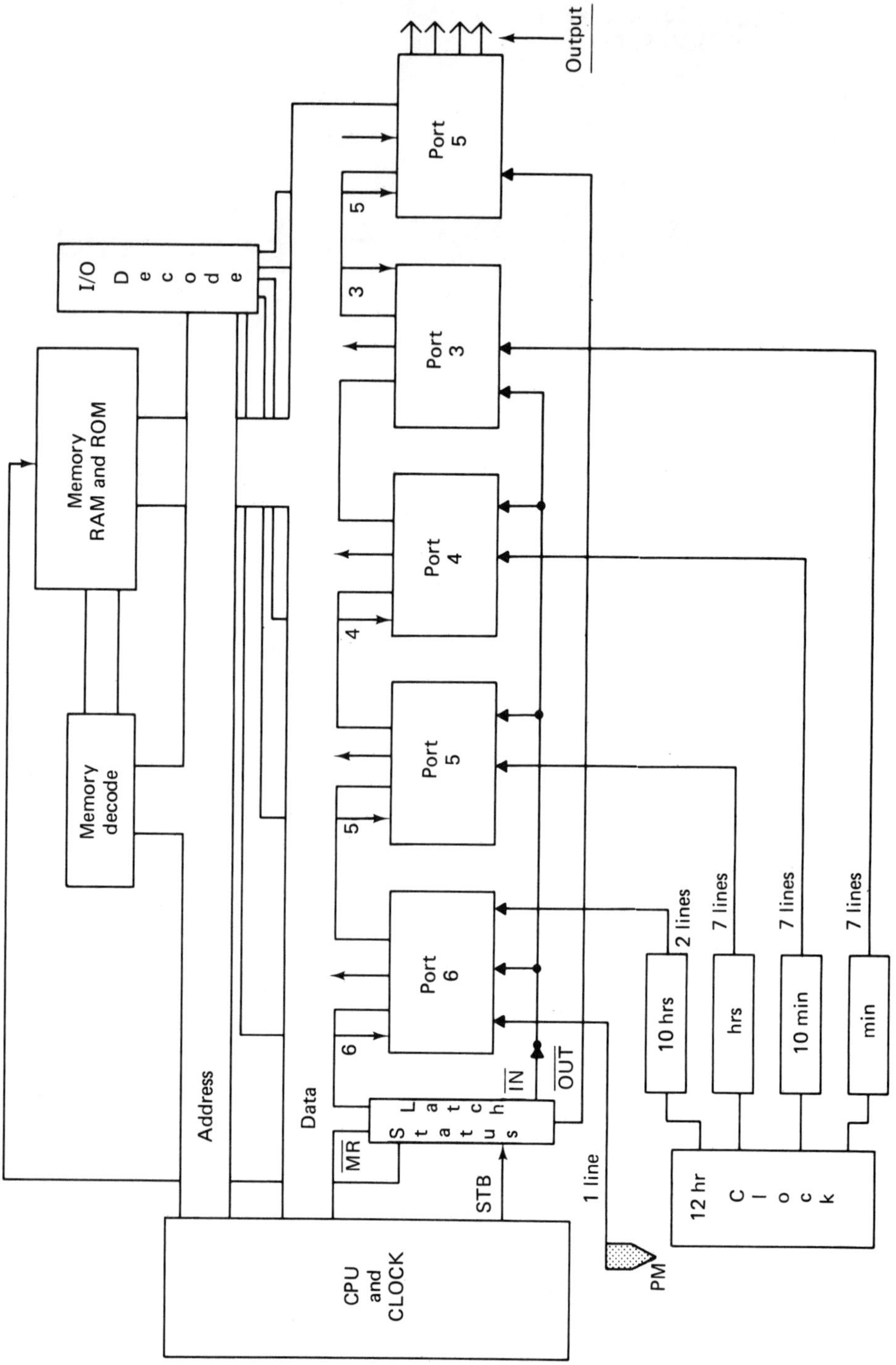

Fig. 11–1. General circuit arrangement.

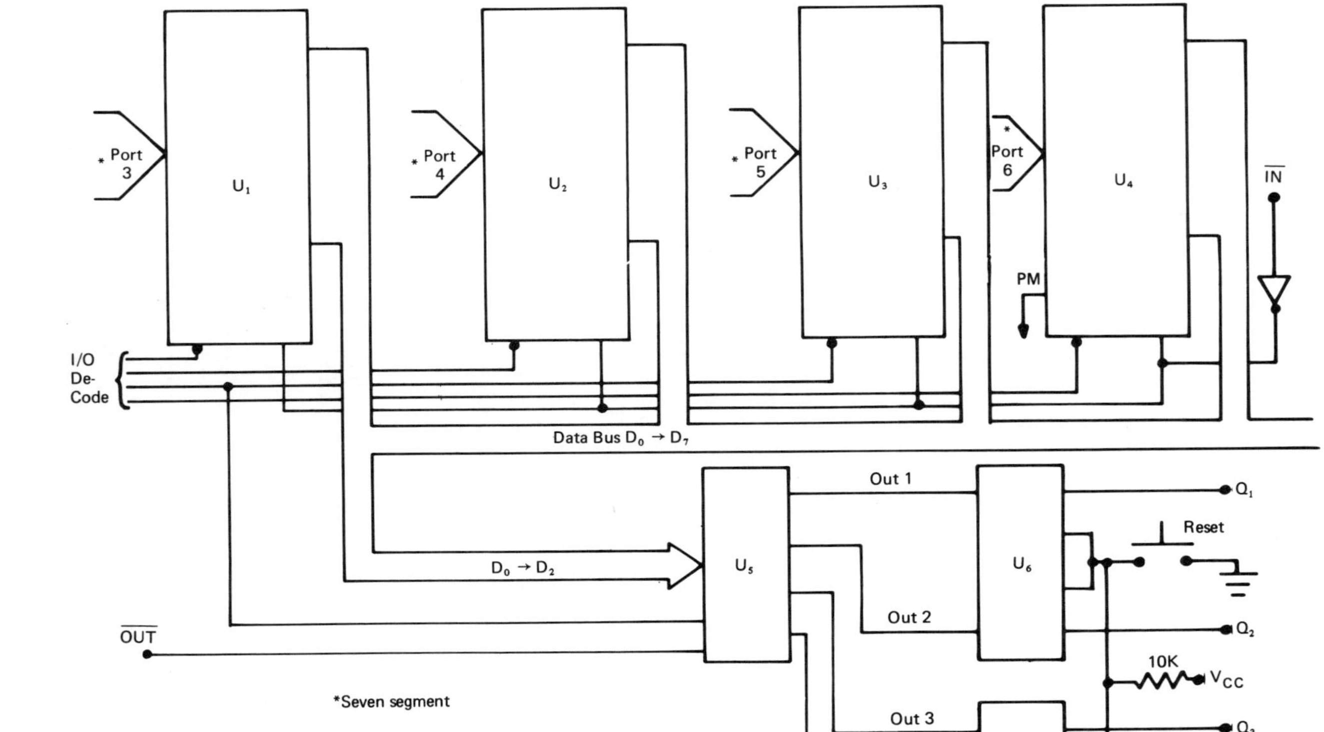

INTEGRATED CIRCUIT POWER PIN CONNECTIONS

U₁ 8212		U₂ 8212		U₃ 8212		U₄ 8212		U₅ 8205		U₆ 7474		U₇ 7474	
V_{CC}	GND	V_{CC}	GND	V_{CC}	GND	V_{CC}	GND	V_{CC}	GND	V_{CC}	GND	V_{CC}	GND
11	6	11	2	11	2	11	2	6	8	2	7	2	7
14	12	14	12	14	12	14	3	16		4		4	
24	22	24	22	24	22	24	9			10		10	
							12			12		12	
							16			14		14	
							18						
							20						

Fig. 11–2. I/O port system.

to pass through the port. Refer to the discussion of the 8212 chip in the programmable port section of Chapter 7, "Input/Output," concerning the tying of the clear and strobe lines to V_{CC}. It is sufficient here to note their presence.

Detailed Port Sequence

On each port, there is a constant input from the 7-segment displays that only changes periodically. When an input instruction occurs in the instruction sequence, it is followed by a port designation.

For example:

COMMAND	CODE	
input	DB_{16}	byte 1
port 3	03_{16}	byte 2

The 8080A CPU reacts to this sequence in the following manner. (Refer to Fig. 11–3.) After the first byte has been fetched and loaded into the instruction register, the CPU puts out a status command which constitutes an input read command. This accomplishes two things. First, it causes the status latch to contain an input command latched and ready to go. Second, it triggers a second fetch cycle for the next byte or instruction which is then loaded into the Z and W internal registers. These registers are then unloaded onto the address lines for decoding through the I/O decoder. This action causes the proper I/O device select line to go to 0. The DBIN line now causes the latched input command line to trigger the port and whatever comes through goes into the accumulator for further processing.

In an attempt to achieve a precise understanding of the sequence of an input instruction, it is worthwhile to study, in some detail, the input instruction timing diagram, Fig. 11–4 and Fig. 11–5. This study will also provide an experience in putting together, visually and mentally, several diagrams that are interrelated. A large part of learning about microprocessors is developing the skill to do just that.

The diagrams in Figs. 11–4, 11–5 and 11–6 will form the basis for the following discussion.

Figures 11–4 and 11–5 are input and output timing diagrams constructed from the timing diagrams provided by Intel in the *8080 Microcomputer Systems User's Manual.* Figure 11–6 is the status word chart showing the data word presented for status information latching at the indicated times.

Notice the bracketed numbers appearing throughout Figs. 11–4 and 11–5. Taken from the Intel *User's Manual,* they are explained in a list of twenty notes. Only those notes which are pertinent to these diagrams are excerpted here according to the numbering system established in the original list.

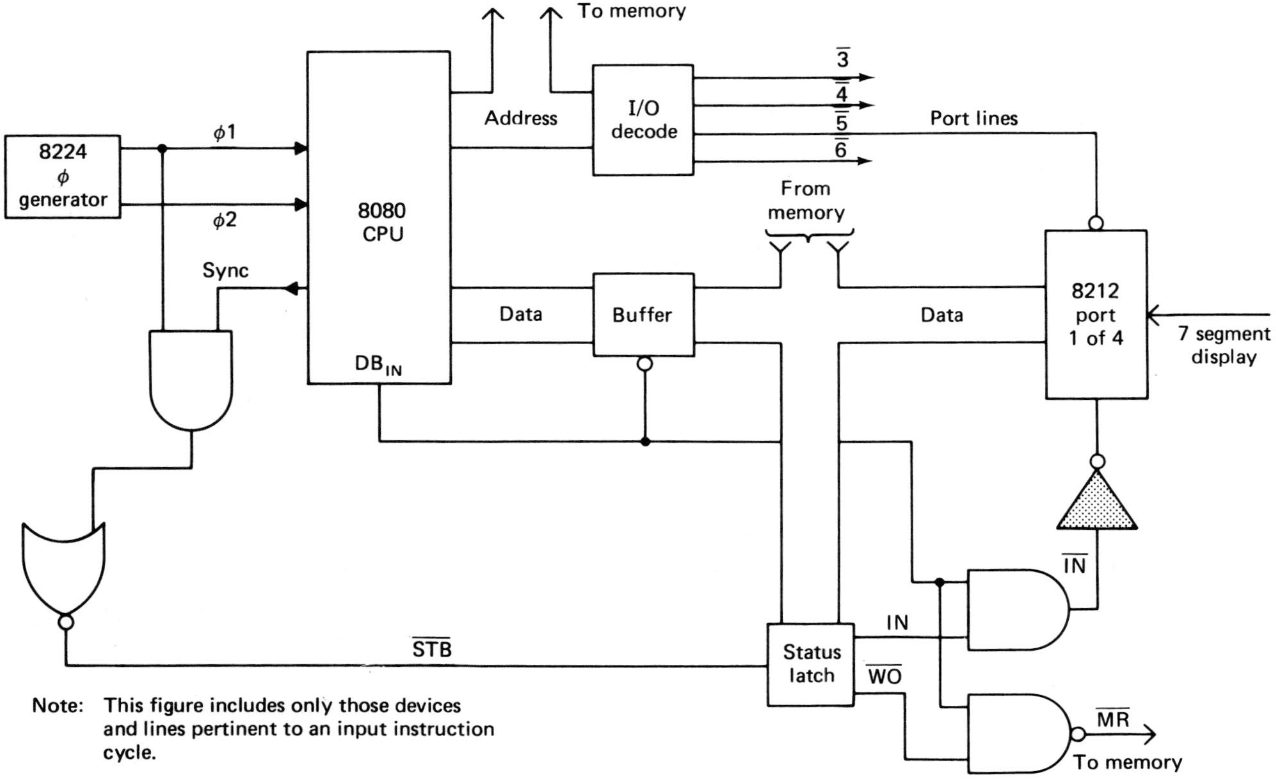

Note: This figure includes only those devices and lines pertinent to an input instruction cycle.

Fig. 11–3. Port control block diagram.

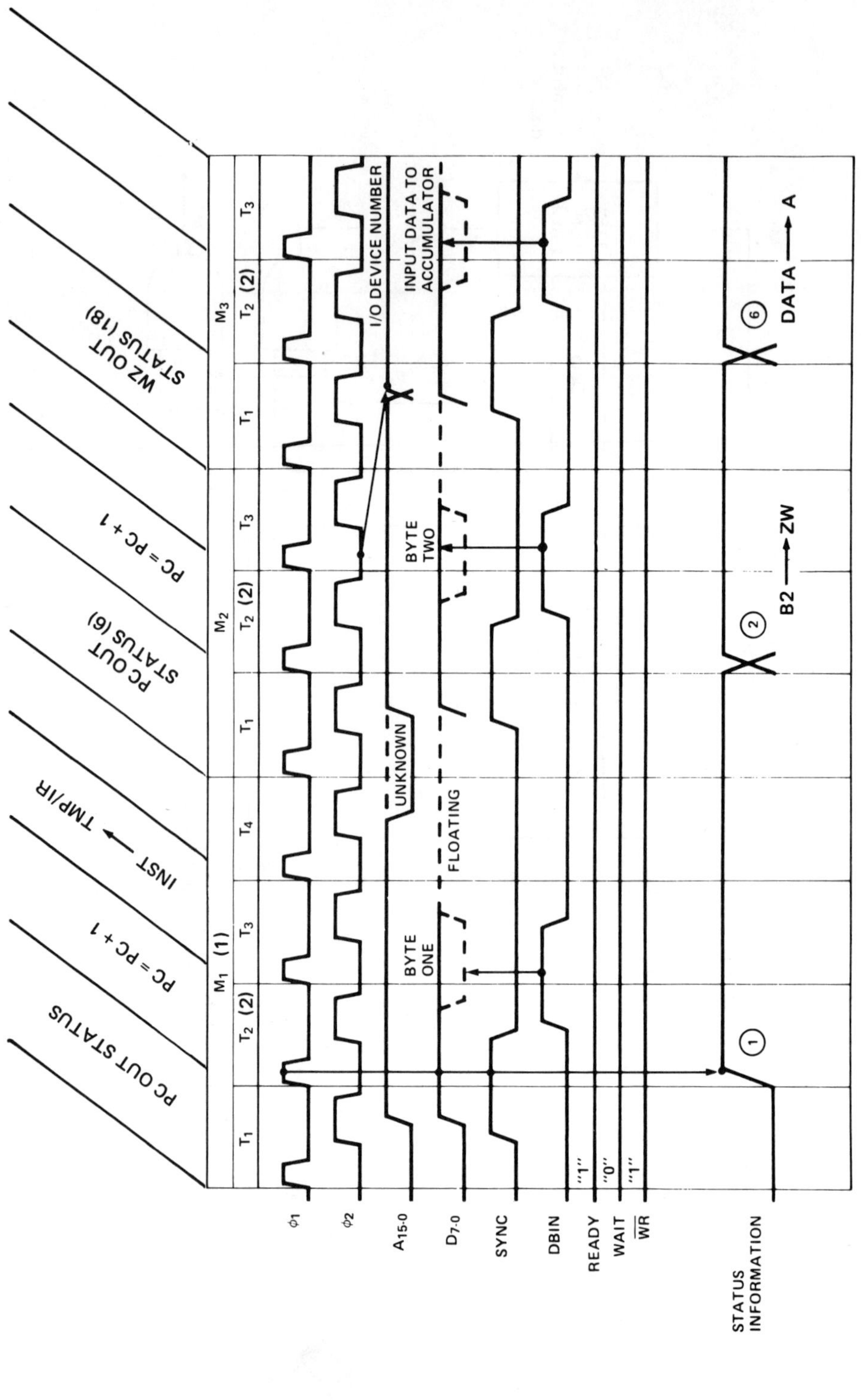

Fig. 11–4. Input timing. *(Reprinted by permission of Intel Corporation, © 1975)*

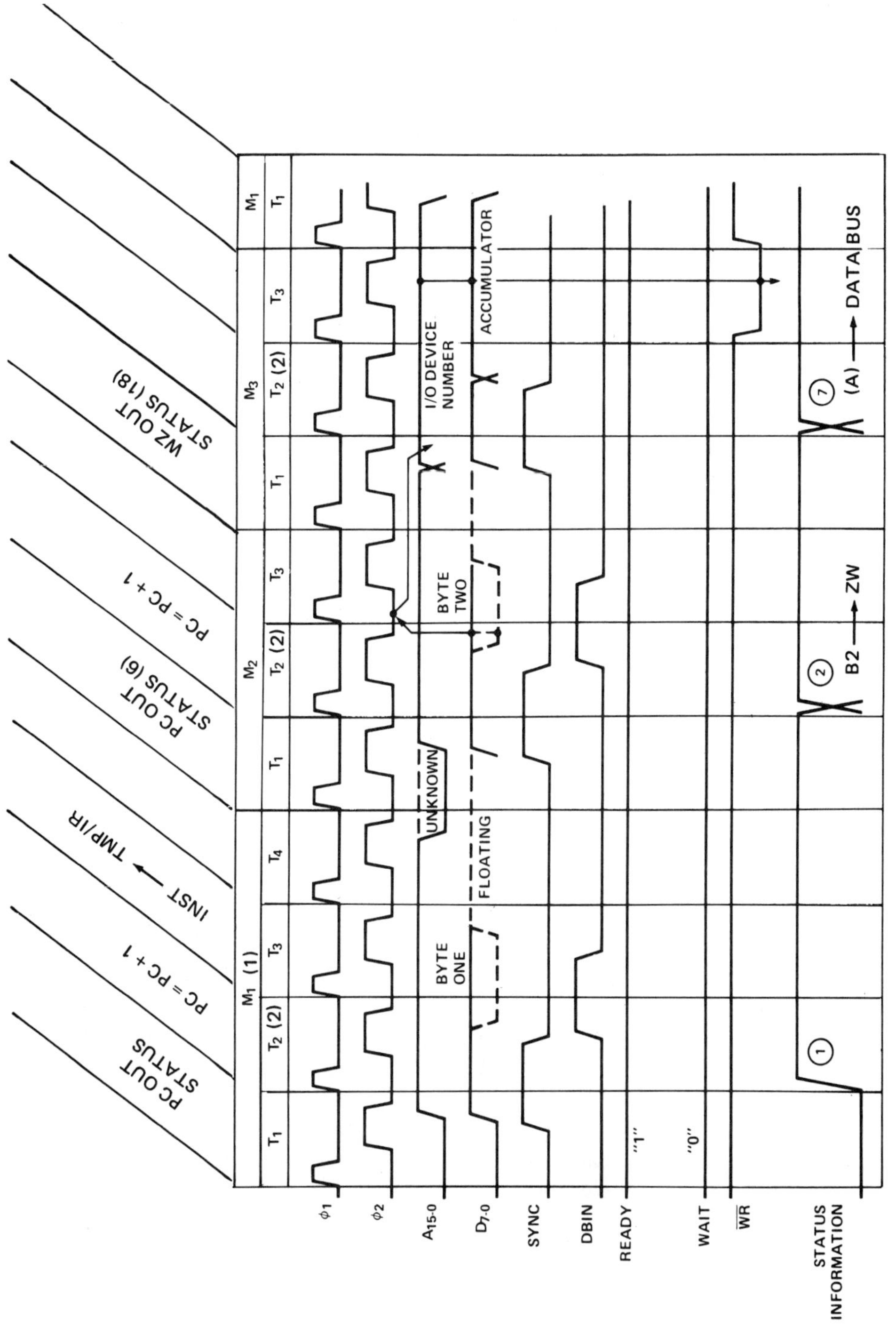

Fig. 11–5. Output timing. *(Reprinted by permission of Intel Corporation, © 1975)*

STATUS WORD CHART

DATA BUS BIT	STATUS INFORMATION	TYPE OF MACHINE CYCLE									
		INSTRUCTION FETCH	MEMORY READ	MEMORY WRITE	STACK READ	STACK WRITE	INPUT READ	OUTPUT WRITE	INTERRUPT ACKNOWLEDGE	HALT ACKNOWLEDGE	INTERRUPT ACKNOWLEDGE WHILE HALT
		(1)	(2)	(3)	(4)	(5)	(6)	(7)	(8)	(9)	(10) ← (N) STATUS WORD
D_0	INTA	0	0	0	0	0	0	0	1	0	1
D_1	$\overline{WO}$	1	1	0	1	0	1	0	1	1	1
D_2	STACK	0	0	0	1	1	0	0	0	0	0
D_3	HLTA	0	0	0	0	0	0	0	0	1	1
D_4	OUT	0	0	0	0	0	0	1	0	0	0
D_5	M_1	1	0	0	0	0	0	0	1	0	1
D_6	INP	0	0	0	0	0	1	0	0	0	0
D_7	MEMR	1	1	0	1	0	0	0	0	1	0

Fig. 11–6. Status word chart. (*Reprinted by permission of Intel Corporation, © 1975*)

1. The first memory cycle (M1) is always an instruction fetch; the first (or only) byte, containing the op code, is fetched during this cycle.

2. If the READY input from memory is not high during T2 of each memory cycle, the processor will enter a wait state (TW) until READY is sampled as high.

6. Memory read subcycles; an instruction or data word will be read.

18. I/O subcycle: the I/O port's 8-bit select code is duplicated on the address lines 0–7 (A_{0-7}) and 8–15 (A_{8-15})[1]

The M_1 cycle of any instruction is always a fetch operation which brings the command from memory and loads it into the instruction register. A brief summary of the three states of the fetch cycle follows.

[1] *Intel 8080 Microcomputer Systems User's Manual* (Santa Clara, California: Intel Corporation, 1975), p. 2–20.

M_1 T_1—Address stabilizes (PC)
Data stabilizes (status word) 1
Sync rises

T_2—Sync and $\phi 1$ generate $\overline{STB}$
Status info latched
DBIN rises

T_3—DBIN and $\phi 1$ generate $\overline{MR}$
Byte appears on data bus and is stored in temporary instruction register

T_4—(Optional)
Varies depending on instruction fetched
May not be used

T_5—(Optional)
Depends on instruction
May not be used

The execution phase of the operation starts at the beginning of the M_2 cycle.

M_2T_1 Machine Cycle 2, Transition State 1

During the T_1 state of the M_2 cycle, the sequence diagram shows that the information in the program counter stabilizes on the data line. On the timing diagram, the (A_{0-15}) lines become solid, the (D_{0-7}) also becomes solid. The sync line rises and is fed to the clock. (The address in the program counter is the address of byte 2 of the input command.)

M_2T_2 Machine Cycle 2, Transition State 2

During the T_2 state of M_2, the sync and $\phi 1$ combine in the clock logic to create a $\overline{STB}$ pulse (Fig. 11–3). This causes the status word to be latched in the status latch. (Note status information line on timing diagram, Figs. 11–4 and 11–5.) The status word is a 2-memory read (Fig. 11–6). DBIN combines with $\overline{WO}$ bringing byte 2 (port address) in from memory.

M_2T_3 Machine Cycle 2, Transition State 3

Byte 2 is absorbed by CPU and internally stored in the W,Z register pair (Figs. 11–4 and 11–5).

M_3T_1 Machine Cycle 3, Transition State 1

During this state, the address and data lines stabilize (Fig. 11–4 and 11–5). The address is the content of W,Z register pair (port address) and the data is status word 6 input read. The synchronization pulse now rises and stabilizes.

M_3T_2 Machine Cycle 3, Transition State 2

Sync and $\phi 1$ combine in clock (Fig. 11–3) to latch status word by creating a $\overline{STB}$. (Note status information line.) DBIN rises combining with IN to bring in the port data.

M_3T_3 Machine Cycle 3, Transition State 3

Data lines input to the accumulator. Final condition: data from port now in accumulator.

Study this sequence thoroughly. The only difference between an input command DB and an output command D3 is that during the last state, data travels from the accumulator, and during the M_3T_2 state, the status word is a 7 output write status word.

PROGRAM DISCUSSION

Command Considerations

In the following program, the input and output commands are the only two used that interact with the world outside the microprocessor and the only two that must be understood thoroughly.

An analysis of the program will demonstrate how it runs the circuits. However, several facts must first be understood thoroughly. Reference to Chapter 4, "The Instruction Sets," at this point would be helpful.

1. Any time an instruction deals with the use of memory (other than a standard fetch), it will use the data in register pair HL (internal registers) as the address for memory location. **THIS IS VERY IMPORTANT!!**
2. A compare (M) command sets the zero flag to 1 if, and only if, the data in the accumulator and the data in memory (at location designated by HL register) are an exact match.
3. An immediate command will interpret the next one or two bytes (depending on the instructions) as data to be entered.
4. Jump commands will interpret the next two bytes as the address to jump to. This is done by putting the two bytes in the program counter.
5. Add, subtract, increment and decrement commands are all internal operations.

The following analysis of the program will be presented in a manner similar to that used in the design of the program and will therefore serve as an example of program design.

Program Considerations

First, the general problem to be solved should be stated as precisely as possible and the other requirements and criteria to be used should be defined.

State problem.

To monitor a 4-digit (seven segments each) 12-hour clock with PM indicator for the purpose of activating one of four output lines at one of four separate and programmable times.

Determine hardware requirements.

Four input ports
- *Three to input seven segments*
- *One to input B and C segments of digit 4 and PM indicator*

One output port to output a data word to be hardware decoded into output pulses.

Decide basic program procedure.

Check each digit separately against prestored time values, progressing from the most often changed to the least often changed. If any digit does not match, start over with the next time value until all four times have been checked. If no match is found, reset and start over.

If this portion of the plan is done carefully and thoroughly, the later designing becomes much easier.

Timetable System

Look-up table. The timetable memory in Table 11–1 has been constructed for visual convenience. Each row constitutes one complete set of four (4) clock digits. Each column position represents the port that brings in the digit. The numbers in the rows are the octal and hexadecimal addresses of the memory location containing the prestored digits to be compared.

The code system in Table 11–2 is not a matter of choice, but rather a matter of necessity because 7-segment displays are being monitored.

Table 11-1 Timetable Memory Map (Octal/Hexadecimal)

	DIGIT 4 PORT 6	DIGIT 3 PORT 5	DIGIT 2 PORT 4	DIGIT 1 PORT 3
Time 1	135/5D	131/59	125/55	121/51
Time 2	136/5E	132/5A	126/56	122/52
Time 3	137/5F	133/5B	137/57	123/53
Time 4	140/60	134/5C	130/58	124/54

The segment designations of a 7-segment display are illustrated in Fig. 11–7.

Segment A is connected to the least significant data line and segment G is connected to the most significant data line. As was previously mentioned, line 8 is grounded to assure a zero input for ports 3,4, and 5. Port 6 has the PM indicator tied to line 8.

Table 11–2 Port 6 Code (Fourth Digit and AM/PM). Ports 3, 4 and 5 Codes (Digits 1, 2 and 3)

Code Key for Port 6

	Symbol	Octal	Hexadecimal
AM	no digit	000	00
PM	no digit	200	80
AM	1	006	06
PM	1	206	86

Code Key for Ports 3, 4, 5

Segment Code G FED CBA	Symbol	Octal	Hexadecimal
00 111 111	0	077	2F
00 000 110	1	006	06
01 011 011	2	133	5B
01 001 111	3	117	4F
01 100 110	4	146	66
01 101 101	5	155	6D
01 111 101	6	175	7D
00 000 111	7	007	07
01 111 111	8	177	7F
01 101 111	9	147	67

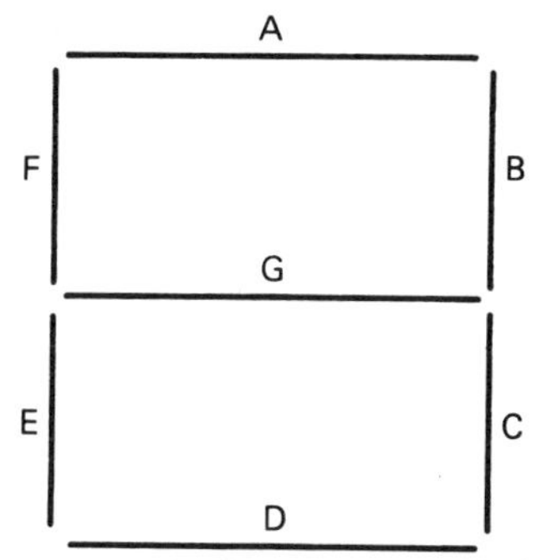

Fig. 11–7. 7-segment designations.

This physical arrangement leads to the following code system shown in Table 11–2.

Table 11–3 is an example of a typical set of prestored times.

Program Criteria

Procedure chosen: basic criteria decisions

1. Use the HL register to maintain the timetable address of the digit being checked. (Choosing HL for this purpose eliminates many steps in addressing the table. Any time an instruction deals with use of memory, other than a standard fetch, it will use the data in register pair HL as the address for memory location.)

2. The DE register is chosen to maintain the number of the time being checked (Time 1, Time 2, etc.)

3. The first digit of each time is checked. If no match is found, there is no reason to check the other digits.

4. If agreement (match) is encountered on any first digit, then the second digit is to be checked. If this agrees, then digit 3 is to be checked, and so on.

Table 11-3 Prestored Memory Table (Octal/Hexadecimal)

		P6	P5	P4	P3
T_1	1200 PM	206/86	133/5B	077/2F	077/2F
T_2	-200 AM	000/00	133/5B	077/2F	077/2F
T_3	1145 AM	006/06	006/06	146/66	155/6D
T_4	-915 PM	200/80	157/6F	006/06	155/6D

5. Any time a nonmatch (miss) is encountered, the first digits must be checked again.

6. Even if one time group meets agreement to complete output, that should not negate checking all other numbers under the same procedure.

NOTE: Only four times are being checked. Therefore, a full time cycle count would be four.

The flow diagram in Fig. 11–8 results from the preceding criteria.

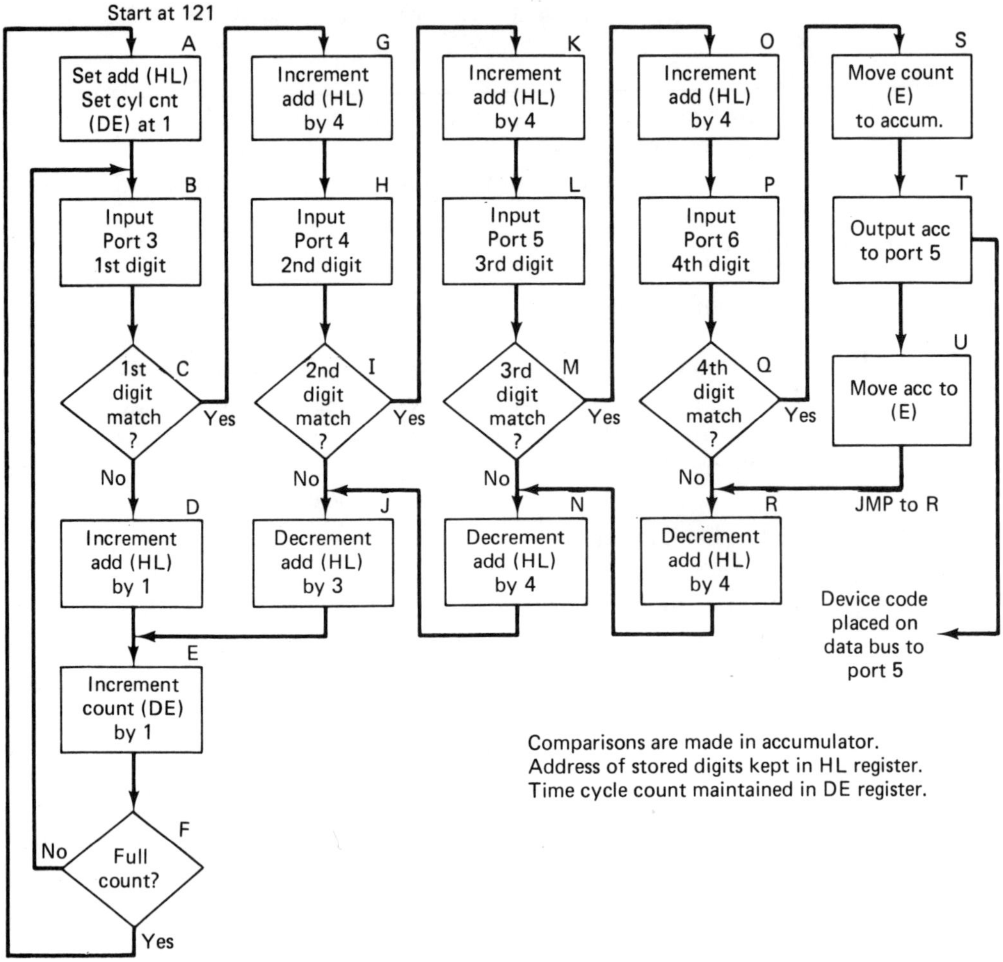

Fig. 11–8. Program flow diagram.

Flow Chart Explanation

Study the diagram of the flow chart in Fig. 11–8. The diamond shaped boxes indicate where comparisons of the stored number and the input digits are made, determining the direction the program will take at that point.

The program starts at point A with the initial address (121_8) being loaded into the HL pair and a time cycle count of (1) being loaded into the DE pair.

Point (B) inputs the first digit.

Point (C) checks for a match.

Point (D) If no match is found, increment the address

Point (E) and increment the time cycle count.

Point (F) Check if count is 4. If not, go back to point (B); if yes, start again at point (A).

At point (C), if a match is encountered, the address is immediately advanced by (4), moving it horizontally across the timetable and the next port is input and checked for match in blocks G, H and I. If no match is found, the address is decreased by only 3, causing it to return to the first digit checking at the next time slot.

Address Handling

For the purpose of clarity, a record of the address will be set up, keeping track as matches are found and missed. This should be used in conjunction with the flow diagram, Fig. 11–8. Remember that all addresses are in hexadecimal form and refer to locations in the memory, Table 11–1.

If problems are encountered in understanding Table 11–4 and how it relates to the flow diagram and memory table, try again using Table 11–5 which shows time on the clock and time stored in the memory table. Remember, when a comparison is done, it is the address in the (HL) register at that time which is used to designate the necessary location being compared.

Now construct a chart using the format in Table 11–6.

Full Program

Now study the program itself with fully assembled machine code for the 8080 and comments in Table 11–7. Study it one block at a time to see how each block accomplishes its operations. It will help to compare the flow program and fully assembled program.

Table 11–4 Timetable Addressing Record

	INC/DEC	ADDRESS (HL) (HEXADECIMAL)	CYCLE COUNT (DE) INC
Start A		51	001
First digit (match)	(+4) →	55	001
Second digit (miss)	(−3) →	52	(+1) → 002
First digit (match)	(+4) →	56	002
Second digit (match)	(+4) →	5A	002
Third digit (miss)	(−4−3) →	53	(+1) → 003
First digit (match)	(+4) →	57	003
Second digit (match)	(+4) →	5B	003
Third digit (match)	(+4) →	5F	003
Fourth digit (miss)	(−4−4−3)	54	(+1) → 004
First digit (match)	(+4) →	58	004
Second digit (match)	(+4) →	5C	004
Third digit (match)	(+4) →	60	004
Fourth digit (match)			004
Output cycle count	(−4−4−4−3)		004
Full cycle count		Start at A	

Table 11–5 Memory Table of Prestored Times and Time on Clock (Octal/Hexadecimal)

Time on Clock pm 12:34

AM 135/50 1	139/59 0	125/55 3	121/51 4
AM 136/5E 0	132/5A 2	126/56 0	122/52 4
AM 137/5F 1	133/5B 2	127/57 3	123/53 4
PM 140/60 1	134/5C 2	130/58 3	124/54 4

Table 11–6 Chart Construction

	Inc/Dec	Address	Cycle Count (DE) INC
Start A		51	001
		____	____
		____	____
		____	____
		↓	↓

Note that instead of labels, block letters have been used to facilitate cross referencing the flow diagram and the assembled program.

OUTPUT PORT

The final consideration is the method of output when a match is complete for all four digits. By studying the program, it becomes obvious that the contents of the DE register pairs are always made to reflect the time group number being checked—Time 1, Time 2, and so on. When a fourth digit match occurs, the contents of the DE pair (time group number) is moved to the accumulator and then output to port 5. In this way, the contents of DE appear on the data bus to be decoded by the port.

For example, if the third group of numbers had resulted in a complete match, the number 003_8 would appear on the data bus. In block U, the number is put back into DE for further use and further checking of other digit groups.

The following discussion refers to Figs. 11–1 and 11–2. The 8205 is one of eight binary decoders which put out a pulse to the 7474 latch as a clock pulse input. Which line activates depends upon the number on the data bus at the time of the output command. (The output command sequence was already discussed in the detailed port sequence of this chapter and may be reviewed at this time.)

When the output command in block T occurs, it causes the contents of DE to appear on the data bus. As previously explained, it causes the I/O decode to put out a $\overline{5}$ pulse and it causes an $\overline{\text{OUT}}$ from the status latch. The coincidence of the $\overline{\text{OUT}}$ and $\overline{5}$ enables the 8205 decoder. The 8205 then decodes so that when a clock pulse appears at one of the clock terminals, a one is latched at the output until it is manually reset. This output pulse may then be used in any manner the designer wishes. For example, it may turn things on or off, start motors or create an alarm.

Table 11–7 Complete Program

LOC	OBJ			SEQ	Block	Source Statement		/	Comment
0300	21	51	03	001	A	LXI	H		; Locate timetable top
0303	11	01	00	002		LXI	D		; Set cycle count
0306	DB	03		003	B	IN	3		; Input port 3
0308	BE			004	C	CMP	M		; 1st digit match?
0309	CA	17	03	005		JZ		G	; Yes: go to block G
030C	23			006	D	INX	H		; No: increment table
030D	13			007	E	INX	D		; Inc cycle count
030E	3E	04		008	F	MVI	A	04H	; Check cycle count
0310	BB			009		CMP	E		; Full cycle?
0311	CA	00	03	010		JZ		A	; Yes: go to block A
0314	C3	06	03	011		JMP		B	; No: go to block B
0317	3E	04		012	G	MVI	A	04H	; Increment table
0319	85			013		ADD	L		; address by
031A	6F			014		MOV	L, A		; 4
031B	DB	04		015	H	IN	4		; Input port 4
031D	BE			016	I	CMP	M		; 2nd digit match?
031E	CA	28	03	017		JZ		K	; Yes: go to block K
0321	7D			018	J	MOV	A, L		; No: decrement table
0322	D6	03		019		SUI		03	; address by 3
0324	6F			020		MOV	L, A		;
0325	C3	00	03	021		JMP		E	; Go back to block E
0328	3E	04		022	K	MVI	A	04H	; Increment table
032A	85			023		ADD	L		; address by
032B	6F			024		MOV	L, A		; 4
032C	DB05			025	L	IN	5		; Input port 5
032E	BE			026	M	CMP	M		; 3rd digit match?
032F	CA	39	03	027		JZ		0	; Yes: go to block 0
0332	7D			028	N	MOV	A, L		; No: decrement
0333	D6	04		029		SUI		04H	; table address by 4
0335	6F			030		MOV	L, A		;
0336	C3	21	03	031		JMP		J	; Go back to block J
0339	3E	04		032	O	MVI	A	04H	; Increment table
033B	85			033		ADD	L		; address by
033C	6F			034		MOV	L, A		; 4
033D	DB	06		035	P	IN	6		; Input port 6
033F	BE			036	Q	CMP	M		; 4th digit match?
0340	CA	4A	03	037		JZ		S	; Yes: go to block S
0343	7D			038	R	MOV	A, L		; No: decrement
0344	D6	04		039		SUI		04H	; table address
0346	6F			040		MOV	L, A		; by 4
0347	C3	32	03	041		JMP		N	; Go back to block N
034A	7B			042	S	MOV	A, E		; Get present count
034B	D3	05		043	T	OUT	5		; Output port 5
034D	5F			044		MOV	E, A		; Save count
034E	C3	43	03	045	U	JMP		R	; Go back to block R
0351				046					; Top of timetable

SUMMARY

Remember that the system illustrated here is not a sophisticated system. It does function with the hardware and software presented. The authors have operated the system in its exact form as presented. If the reader wishes to set up his own example, the following considerations should be observed.

1. The 7-segment display inputs are nonmultiplexed (constant level output).
2. Any 8080 CPU system that incorporates a method of program entry and at least ninety-six bytes of RAM may be used provided the bus structure is available to the user.
3. The user may change the port designation (if so desired) by altering the appropriate instructions. To reduce the number of software changes, however, the port designations should be maintained in sequential order: 5, 6, 7, 8–10, 11, 12, 13 and so on. This is necessary because the cycle count and output decoding is sequential in nature.

This simple system can form the basis of some very interesting timing control variations and is a lot of fun to play with for the experience it provides.

Chapter 12

The Motorola 6800: Architecture and System Interfacing

The material in this chapter will be focused entirely on the Motorola MC6800 microprocessor, specifically its architecture and the major support integrated circuits that are used in an MC6800 microcomputer system. The architecture of a microprocessor establishes its essential differences from other microprocessors.

For the microprocessor system designer to achieve the maximum benefit from the features the manufacturer has built into his products, it is extremely important that he have a solid understanding of the architecture. He must also be familiar with the integrated circuits that belong to the processor family and the instructions and different addressing modes for the particular system that is being utilized.

Because much of this information involves very specific technical details, the authors feel that selected portions of the information presented here should be taken directly from the *Motorola M6800 Microcomputer System Design Data Manual.*

The MC6800 family of parts has been designed to minimize the number of required components and support packages. This was accomplished by designing the MC6800 microprocessor with the total system problem in mind. All microprocessor systems require some form of static or dynamic memory. This requirement was fulfilled by the 1024 × 8 bit ROM (MCM6830AL) and the 128 × 8 bit RAM (MCM6810AL). The need for specialized data transfer functions was realized early, which led to the Peripheral Interface Adapter (MC6821). This MC6800 system is attractive to the system user because these peripheral parts appear to the microprocessor as simply memory locations on the address and data bus.

This architecture accomplished several things at the system level.

First, it simplified the interface between memory and peripheral ports and, second, it eliminated the use of I/O instructions. Both of these features increase system throughput.

Other features of the MC6800 family are that the output buffers are capable of driving standard TTL and only one power supply is required (+5 volts). This means the MC6800 family can directly interface with standard TTL logic without the need for additional power supplies.

The intent of this section is to define in detail the MC6800 system architecture. This includes defining a minimum system and discussing requirements of complex systems. It also includes a discussion of the static and dynamic interaction between the microprocessor, memories and peripherals. This leads to static and dynamic specifications on the MC6800 data bus and address bus. Further, it includes a discussion and specification of the microprocessor clocks and how they interact with the system and a definition of the microprocessor control lines such as 3-state control, halt, normal interrupt, nonmaskable interrupt and how they are implemented in a system environment. And finally, it includes a description of what occurs on the circuit interfaces during instruction execution.

SYSTEM COMPONENT DESCRIPTIONS

Before discussing the MC6800 system, a general description of the MC6800 microprocessor, the 1024 × 8 bit ROM, the 128 × 8 bit RAM, the PIA and the ACIA is needed, as well as a detailed description of the microprocessor and peripheral input/output lines.

MC6800 Microprocessor

A symbolic diagram of the microprocessor and its input/output is shown in Fig. 12–1. The processor is a bidirectional, bus-oriented, 8-bit parallel machine with sixteen bits of address. For most systems, depending on interconnection capacitance, the processor is capable of directly interfacing with eight peripheral parts and one TTL load on the same bus at a 1 MHz minor cycle clock rate. For systems requiring additional peripheral parts, a Data Bus Extender (BEX) is available.

The processor has two 8-bit accumulators which are used to hold operands and the results from the arithmetic logic unit (ALU). The 16-bit index register stores sixteen bits of memory address for the index mode of memory addressing. The stack pointer is a 2-byte (8 bits per byte) register that contains the address of the next available location in an external push-down/pull-up stack. This stack is normally a random

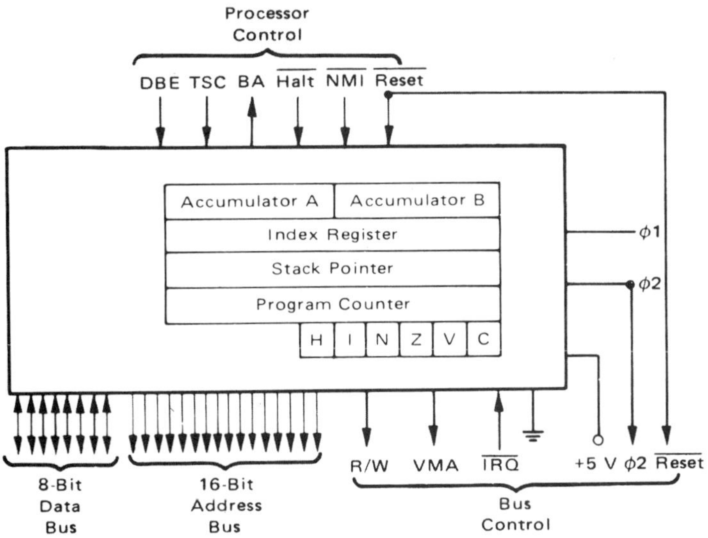

Fig. 12–1. MC6800 microprocessor and input/output lines. (*Courtesy Motorola Inc.*)

access read/write memory that may have any location (address) that is convenient. In those applications that require storage of information in the stack when power is lost, the stack must be nonvolatile. The program counter is a 16-bit register that contains the program address. And finally, a condition code register (flag register) contains six bits of condition codes. The condition codes indicate the results of an ALU operation: negative (N) zero (Z), overflow (V), carry from bit 7 (C) and half carry from bit 3 (H). These bits of the condition code register are used as testable conditions for the conditional branch instructions. Bit 4 is the interrupt mask bit (I). The unused bits of the condition code register (B6, B7) are always 1s.

The minimum instruction execution time is 2 microseconds when f_0 = 1 MHz. Processor control lines include reset, which automatically restarts the processor, as well as interrupt request and nonmaskable interrupt to monitor peripheral status. Finally, there is a 3-state control, data bus enable and a half control line which can be used for direct memory access (DMA) or multiprocessing.

MCM6810A 128 × 8-Bit RAM

The RAM is a static memory which interfaces directly to the MC6800 microprocessor. The RAM is organized in a 8-bit byte fashion.

The RAM has six chip select inputs, four active low and two active high, which interface directly to the address bus.

The RAM bus interface shown in Fig. 12–2 demonstrates the simplicity of interface in the MC6800 system. Since all MC6800 components operate at the same TTL levels and with the same drive capability, the data, address and control lines can be interconnected without adding external TTL buffers. Memory timing specifications have been set to permit simple operation at full speed with the microprocessor.

Four of the chip selects of the MCM6810A are used to decode the system address lines. In small and medium sized systems, this address decoding will be sufficient to distinguish all packages in the system without using any additional address decoding packages.

MCM6830A 1024 × 8-Bit ROM

The 8 K ROM is a static memory which also interfaces directly to the MC6800 microprocessor. The output drivers are level compatible with the MC6800 family. The ROM is organized in an 8-bit byte fashion similar to the RAM. It has ten address lines and four chip selects.

The ROM bus interface in Fig. 12–3 is as straightforward as that of the RAM. All outputs may be connected directly to the data bus without drivers.

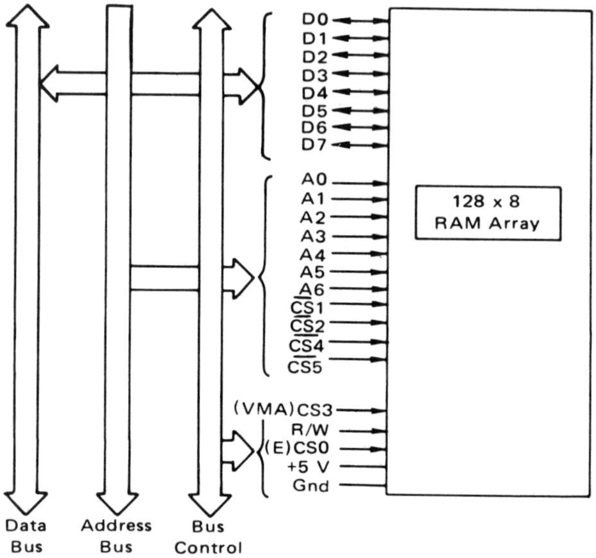

Fig. 12–2. MCM6810A RAM bus interface. (*Courtesy Motorola Inc.*)

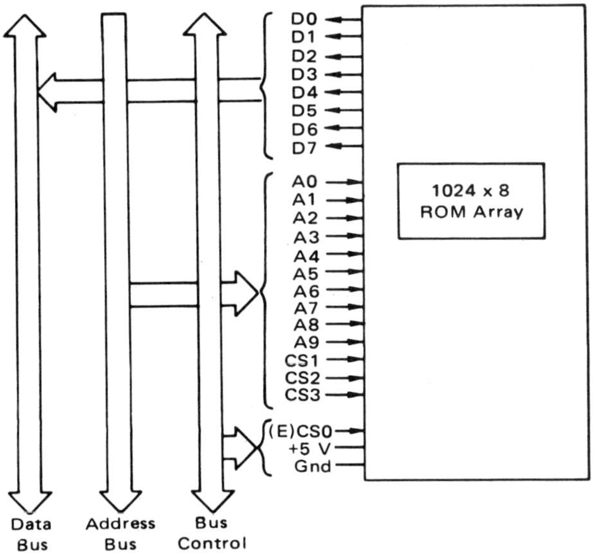

Fig. 12–3. MCM6830A ROM bus interface. (*Courtesy Motorola Inc.*)

Three chip selects (mask programmable) on the MCM6830A are used to provide address decoding in the system. In many systems, the decoding possible with these lines will be sufficient to distinguish the ROM.

MC6821 Peripheral Interface Adapter (PIA)

The MC6821 Peripheral Interface Adapter provides a universal means of interfacing peripheral equipment to the MC6800 microprocessor through two 8-bit bidirectional peripheral data buses and four control lines. No external logic is required for interfacing to many peripheral devices.

The functional configuration of the PIA is programmed by the microprocessor during system initialization. Each of the peripheral data lines can be programmed to act as an input or output, and each of the four control/interrupt lines may be programmed for one of several control modes. This allows a high degree of flexibility in the overall production of the interface.

Figure 12–4 shows the PIA system interface lines—the data bus lines D0–D7, chip selects CSO, CS1 and CS2, R/W, enable E, the register selects RS0 and RS1, reset and interrupt request lines $\overline{\text{IRQA}}$ and $\overline{\text{IRQB}}$. The data bus lines, chip selects, read/write and enable have the

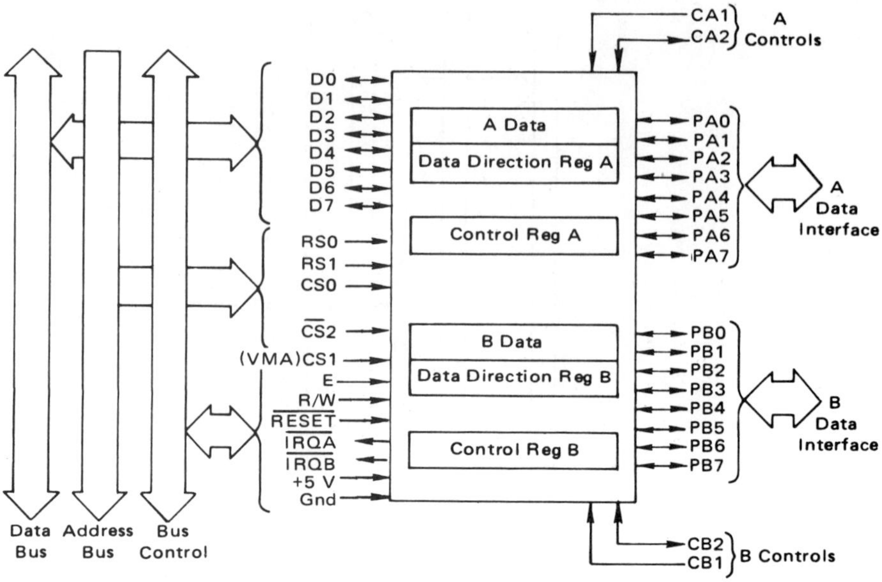

Fig. 12–4. MC6821 PIA bus interface. (*Courtesy Motorola Inc.*)

same static and dynamic characteristics as the other peripherals in the MC6800 system.

The reset line is used to initialize the PIA. The register select lines RS0 and RS1 serve the same purpose in the PIA as address lines do in memory. They address the control and status registers, thereby making the PIA look like memory to the microprocessor.

MC6850 Asynchronous Communications Interface Adapter (ACIA)

The MC6850 Asynchronous Communications Interface Adapter provides the data formatting and control to interface serial asynchronous data communications information to the MC6800 microprocessor.

The parallel data of the bus system is serially transmitted and received (full-duplex) by the asynchronous data interface with proper formatting and error checking. The functional configuration of the ACIA is programmed via the data bus during system initialization. A programmable control register provides variable word lengths, clock division ratios, transmit control, receive control and interrupt control. Three I/O lines are provided to control external peripherals or modems. A status register is available to the processor, and reflects the current status of the transmitter and receiver.

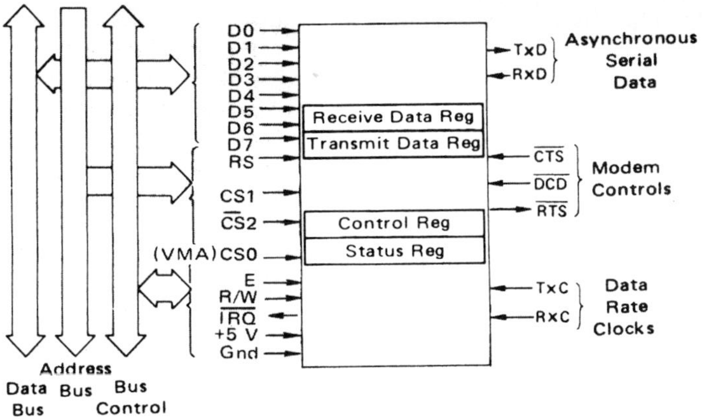

Fig. 12–5. MC6850 ACIA bus interface. (*Courtesy Motorola Inc.*)

Figure 12–5 shows the ACIA system interface lines—the data bus lines D0–D7, chip selects CS0, CS1 and $\overline{CS2}$, read/write, the enable E, the register select RS and the interrupt request output $\overline{IRQ}$.

MICROPROCESSOR INTERFACE LINES

The microprocessor input/output is broken into three groups: the bus interface lines, the bus control lines and the processor control lines. Description of bus interface and bus control lines are covered here. A description of the MPU control lines such as halt and data bus enable are covered later.

Address Bus Lines (A0–A15)

Sixteen pins are used for the address bus. The outputs are 3-state bus drivers. When the output is turned off, it is essentially an open circuit. This permits the MPU to be used in DMA applications. Putting TSC in its high state forces the address bus and R/W lines to go into 3-state mode.

Data Bus Lines (D0–D7)

Eight pins are used for the data bus. It is bidirectional, transferring data to and from the memory and peripheral devices. The 3-state drivers can be put into the 3-state mode by forcing DBE low.

Clock Inputs Phase One and Phase Two

Two pins are used for the 2-phase nonoverlapping clock.

Read/Write Line (R/W)

The read/write line is an output which signals to the peripheral and memory devices whether the MPU is in a read (high) or write (low) state. The normal standby state of this signal is read (high). Three-state control going high will turn read/write to the high-impedance state. Also, when the processor is halted, it will be in the high-impedance state.

Valid Memory Address Line (VMA)

This output indicates to peripheral devices that there is a valid address on the address bus. In normal operation, this signal should be utilized for enabling the RAM and peripheral interfaces such as the PIA and ACIA. This signal is active high. The output buffer is not 3-state.

Interrupt Request Line ($\overline{IRQ}$)

This level sensitive input requests that an interrupt sequence be generated within the machine when $\overline{IRQ}$ is low (Fig. 12–13). The processor will wait until it completes the current instruction that is being executed before it recognizes the request. At that time, if the interrupt mask bit in the condition codes register is not set, the machine will begin an interrupt sequence. The contents of the index register, program counter, accumulators and condition codes register are stored away on the stack and the interrupt mask bit is set so no further interrupts may occur. At the end of the cycle, a 16-bit address will be placed on the address bus that points to a vectoring address which is located in memory locations FFF8 and FFF9. An address loaded at these locations causes the MPU to jump to an interrupt routine in memory.

The $\overline{halt}$ line must be in the high state for interrupts to be serviced; interrupts will be latched internally while $\overline{halt}$ is low. The wire-OR capability of the $\overline{IRQ}$ input requires a 3 K ohm minimum external resistor to V_{CC}.

PERIPHERAL AND MEMORY INTERFACE LINES

The peripheral and memory interface lines are the data bus D0–D7, the address inputs, the register selects RS0–RS1, chip selects, R/W, the enable E and interrupt request ($\overline{IRQ}$). A description of these follows.

Data Bus (D0–D7)

The peripheral data bus lines are bidirectional and capable of transferring data to and from the processor and peripheral devices. The drivers are 3-state input-output buffers.

Address Inputs (A0–A15)

Sixteen address lines are available for addressing peripherals and memories. Seven are used for addressing the internal locations of the RAM and ten are used for addressing internal locations of the ROM. The address inputs are high-impedance.

Register Selects (RS0–RS1)

The register select inputs on the peripherals such as PIA and the ACIA are analogous to the address inputs of the RAM and ROM. Bus address lines are tied directly to the register select inputs, in a minimum system configuration.

There are six locations within the PIA accessible to the microprocessor data bus: two peripheral registers, two data direction registers, and two control registers. Selection of these locations is controlled by the RS0 and RS1 inputs togethers with CRA–2/CRB–2 in the control register as shown in Table 12–1.

The register select input (RS) performs a somewhat different function in the ACIA than in the PIA. The state of RS in the ACIA in conjunction with R/W determines which of four registers will be read by the microprocessor or written into by the microprocessor, as shown in Table 12–2.

Chip Selects (CS0–CS5)

Chip selects on the peripheral and memory devices are used to distinguish one device from another. The number of chip selects avail-

Table 12-1 PIA Internal Addressing

RS1	RS0	CONTROL REGISTER BIT CRA-2	CONTROL REGISTER BIT CRB-2	LOCATION SELECTED
0	0	1	X	Peripheral Register A
0	0	0	X	Data Direction Register A
0	1	X	X	Control Register A
1	0	X	1	Peripheral Register B
1	0	X	0	Data Direction Register B
1	1	X	X	Control Register B

Courtesy Motorola Inc.
X = Don't Care

able varies from three on the PIA to six on the RAM. The chip selects may tie directly to the microprocessor address bus and VMA line in a minimum system configuration. They are high-impedance inputs. The peripheral devices are enabled by various combinations of "true" and "not true" chip selects.

Read/Write (R/W)

The read/write is a high-impedance input which is used to control the direction of data flow through the processor data bus interface. When R/W is high (MPU read cycle) the peripheral data bus drivers are turned on and the selected location is read. When R/W is low, the data bus drivers are turned off and the MPU writes into the selected location.

Enable (E)

The enable input E is the peripheral enable signal. The E input is a high-impedance input which enables the peripheral output data buff-

Table 12-2 ACIA Internal Addressing

RS	R/W	REGISTER
0	0	Control Register
0	1	Status Register
1	1	Receive Data Register
1	0	Transmit Data Register

Courtesy Motorola Inc.

ers. One of the chip selects is used for the E enable on the RAM and the ROM.

Peripheral Interrupt Request ($\overline{\text{IRQA}}$ and $\overline{\text{IRQB}}$)

The only difference between the special function peripherals (the ACIA and PIA) and memories from a system input/output pin consideration is that the peripheral parts have interrupt outputs which are used as a request for servicing.

$\overline{\text{IRQA}}$ and $\overline{\text{IRQB}}$ from the PIA are OR tied to the system $\overline{\text{IRQ}}$ line. Since the PIA may be used to detect incoming interrupt signals on any of its control lines, this connection must be made in order to initiate the interrupt sequence at the processor. The $\overline{\text{IRQ}}$ will be pulled down by the PIA following detection of an active transition on any control line which has been enabled as a system interrupt. $\overline{\text{IRQ}}$ will be held low until the interrupt is serviced. Thus no interrupts will be lost to the system even if the interrupt mask is set at the processor.

The ACIA interrupts the microprocessor under conditions that differ from those described for the PIA. Assuming the ACIA transmitter and receiver interrupts are enabled by bits in the control register, the ACIA will interrupt the MPU if the transmitter data register is empty, the receiver data register is full or if the $\overline{\text{data carrier detect}}$ input goes high indicating a loss of the modem carrier.

STATIC AND DYNAMIC CHARACTERISTICS

Now that the microprocessor family interface has been defined, it is necessary to define the static and dynamic characteristics. Also, the microprocessor clocks, maximum ratings, power supply tolerances, temperature ranges and test conditions will be defined. After these definitions are complete one will be able to put together a system and discuss interaction.

Static Specifications

Table 12–3 shows the static specifications covering the microprocessor and peripherals. The table specifies clock levels, output levels, leakages and capacitance in one table, making all the static information available for easy use.

Table 12-3 Static Characteristics

Characteristic		Symbol	Min	Typ	Max	Unit
Input High Voltage — All Inputs except MPU $\phi 1$ and $\phi 2$		V_{IH}	V_{SS} + 2.0	—	V_{CC}	Vdc
MPU $\phi 1$ and $\phi 2$		V_{IHC}	V_{CC} - 0.3	—	V_{CC} + 0.1	
Input Low Voltage — All Inputs except MPU $\phi 1$ and $\phi 2$		V_{IL}	V_{SS} - 0.3	—	V_{SS} + 0.8	Vdc
MPU $\phi 1$ and $\phi 2$		V_{ILC}	V_{SS} - 0.1	—	V_{SS} + 0.3	
Input Leakage Current (V_{in} = 0 to 5.25 Vdc)		I_{in}				μAdc
(V_{CC} = 5.25 Vdc) All Inputs except MPU $\phi 1$ and $\phi 2$			—	1.0	2.5	
(V_{CC} = 0) MPU $\phi 1$ and $\phi 2$			—	—	100	
Three-State (Off State) Input Current		I_{TSI}				μAdc
(V_{in} = 0.4 to 2.4 V, V_{CC} = 5.25 Vdc) D0-D7			—	2.0	10	
A0-A15, R/W			—	—	100	
Output High Voltage (Load A of Figure 8, V_{CC} = 4.75 Vdc)		V_{OH}	V_{SS} + 2.4	—	—	Vdc
Output Low Voltage (Load A of Figure 8, V_{CC} = 4.75 Vdc)		V_{OL}	—	—	V_{SS} + 0.4	Vdc
Output Leakage Current, IRQ of Peripherals (V_{in} = 2.4 Vdc)		I_{LOH}	—	1.0	10	μAdc
Capacitance*	MPU $\phi 1$ and $\phi 2$	C	80	120	160	pF
(V_{in} = 0, T_A = 25°C,	MPU TSC		—	—	15	
f = 1.0 MHz)	MPU DBE		—	7.0	10	
	MPU Logic Inputs		—	6.5	8.5	
	All Other Inputs		—	6.0	7.5	
	D0-D7, A0-A15, R/W, VMA		—	10	12.5	
	IRQ Output		—	3.0	5.0	
	All Other Outputs		—	6.0	10	
$\phi 1$ and $\phi 2$ Overshoot/Undershoot — Input High Level		V_{OS}	V_{CC} - 0.5	—	V_{CC} + 0.5	Vdc
— Input Low Level			V_{SS} - 0.5	—	V_{SS} + 0.5	
Clock Overlap Voltage (Figure 7)		V_{OV}	—	—	0.5	Vdc

*Capacitances are periodically sampled rather than 100% tested.

(*Courtesy Motorola Inc.*)

Dynamic Properties of the Data and Address Bus

Figure 12–6 and Table 12–4 show the dynamic characteristics of the data and address bus interface. Address, chip selects R/W and VMA are all valid at t_{AS} (address setup time). The microprocessor then puts the address out at t_{AD} (address delay time).

The read access time $t_{ACC} = t_{AS} + t_{DDR}$, with t_{DDR} being the read data delay time. The peripheral data setup time is specified by t_{DSW}. The processor then puts data out at t_{DDW} (write data delay time). Hold time for data bus transfers is specified by t_H.

Table 12-4 Dynamic Characteristics

Characteristic	Symbol	Min	Typ	Max	Unit
Address Setup Time	t_{AS}	190	–	–	ns
Allowable Data Delay Time (Read)	t_{DDR}	–	200	350	ns
Memory Read Access Time	t_{acc}	–	–	540	ns
Data Setup Time (Read)	t_{DSR}	100	–	–	ns
Available Data Setup Time (Write)	t_{DSW}	225	–	–	ns
Input Data Hold Time	t_H	10	–	–	ns
Output Data Hold Time	t_H	10	30	–	ns
Address Hold Time	t_{AH}	50	75	–	ns
Address Delay	t_{AD}	–	220	300	ns
Data Delay (Write)	t_{DDW}	–	165	225	ns
Interrupt Request Release Time	t_{IR}	–	0.7	1.2	μs
Frequency of Operation	f	0.1	–	1.0	MHz
Clock Timing ($\phi 1$ and $\phi 2$)					
Cycle Time	t_{cyc}	1.0	–	10	μs
Clock Pulse Width (Measured at V_{CC} 0.3 V) $\phi 1$	$PW_{\phi H}$	430	–	4500	ns
$\phi 2$		450		4500	ns
Clock Up Time	t_{ut}	940	–	–	ns
Rise and Fall Times $\phi 1$, $\phi 2$ (Measured between V_{SS} + 0.3 V and V_{CC} · 0.3 V)	$t_{\phi r}$, $t_{\phi f}$	5.0		50	ns
Delay Time or Clock Separation (Measured at V_{SS} + 0.5 V)	t_d	0	–	9100	ns
Overshoot Duration	t_{OS}	0	–	40	ns
E Enable Pulse Width	PW_E	0.45	–	25	μs
E Enable Rise and Fall Time	t_{Er}, t_{Ef}		–	25	ns
Processor Controls					
Processor Control Setup Time (Figure 12, 13, 14, 15)	t_{PCS}	200	–	–	ns
Processor Control Rise and Fall Time (Figures 12, 13, 14, 15)	t_{PCr}, t_{PCf}		–	100	ns
Bus Available Delay (Figure 15)	t_{BA}	–	–	300	ns
Three State Enable (Figure 16)	t_{TSE}	–	–	40	ns
Three State Delay (Figure 16)	t_{TSD}	–	–	700	ns
Data Bus Enable Down Time During $\phi 1$ Up Time (Figure 6)	$t_{\overline{DBE}}$	150	–	–	ns
Data Bus Enable Delay (Figure 6)	t_{DBED}	300	–	–	ns
Data Bus Enable Rise and Fall Times (Figure 6)	t_{DBEr}, t_{DBEf}	–	–	25	ns

Note: Dynamic properties of most of the M6800 peripheral and memory parts exceed the requirements specified above, allowing for system flexibility.

(Courtesy Motorola Inc.)

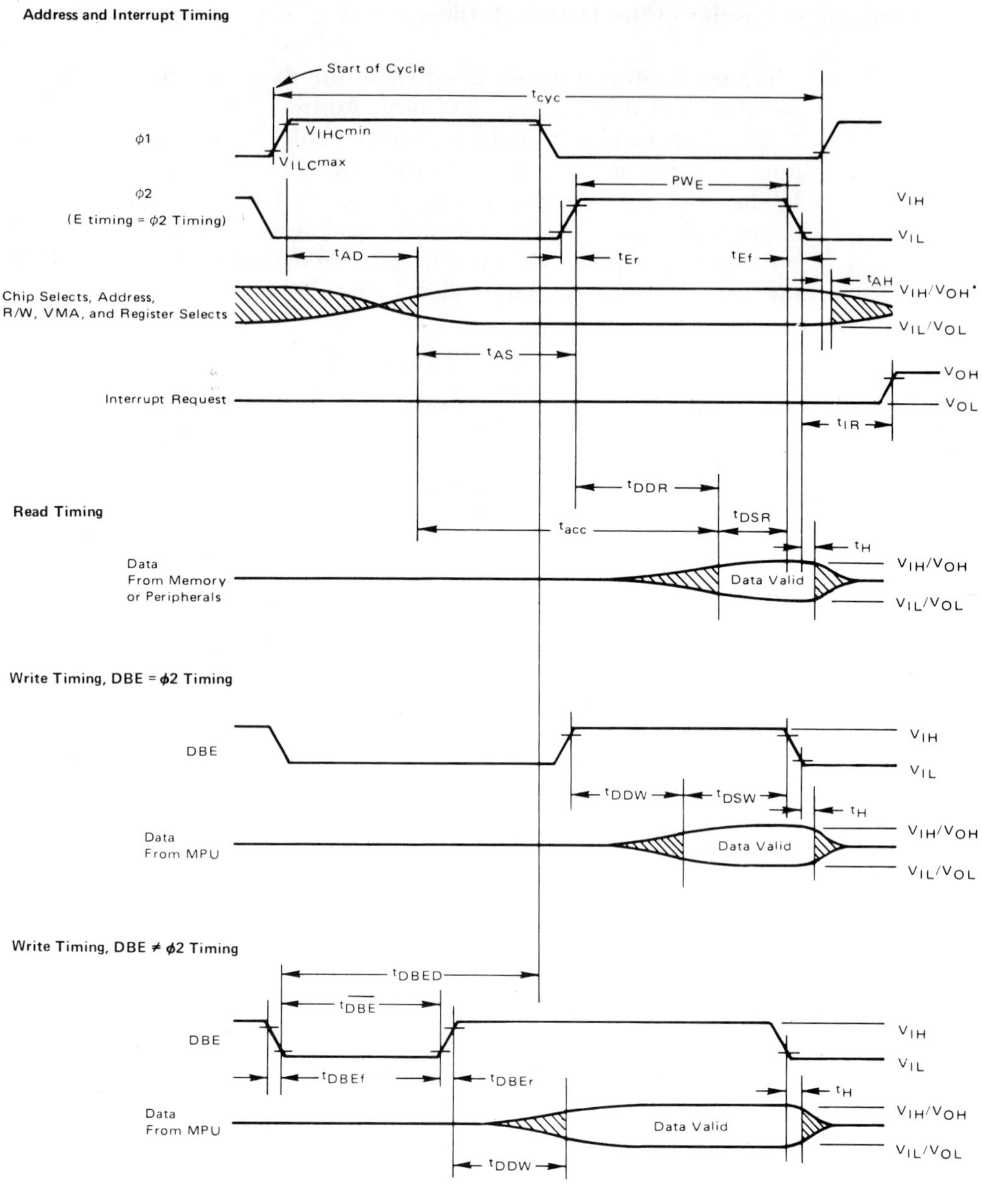

*Output levels of 0.4 V and 2.4 V with input levels of 0.8 V and 2.0 V guarantee a minimum 0.4 V dynamic noise immunity at "1" and "0" levels.

Data Not Valid

Fig. 12–6. Bus interfacing. (*Courtesy Motorola Inc.*)

The interrupt request release time is t_{IR}. The $\overline{\text{interrupt request}}$ output driver in the peripheral parts is an open-drain device. A 3 KΩ pull-up resistor is required on the $\overline{IRQ}$ line. In a minimum system, the open-drain devices are all tied together and then tied to the $\overline{IRQ}$ input of the microprocessor. An interrupt is sensed by the microprocessor when $\overline{IRQ}$ is low.

Notice the logic levels specified in Fig. 12–6. All parts are tested to output levels of 0.4 and 2.4 V with input levels of 0.8 and 2.0 V at the specified times. This will guarantee a minimum of 0.4 V dynamic noise immunity on the "1" and "0" levels.

Microprocessor Clocks $\phi 1$ and $\phi 2$

Figure 12–7 shows the microprocessor clocks, and Tables 12–3 and 12–4 show the static and dynamic clock specifications. The high level is specified at V_{IHC} and the low level is specified at V_{ILC}. The allowable clock frequency is specified by f (frequency). The clock overshoot is specified by V_{OS} (overshoot voltage) for a maximum duration of t_{OS} (overshoot time). The minimum $\phi 1$ and $\phi 2$ high level pulse widths are specified by $PW_{\phi H}$ (pulse width high time). To guarantee the required access time for the peripherals, the clock up time, t_{ut}, is specified. Clock separation, t_d, is measured at a maximum voltage of V_{OV} (overlap voltage). This allows for a multitude of clock variations at the system frequency rate.

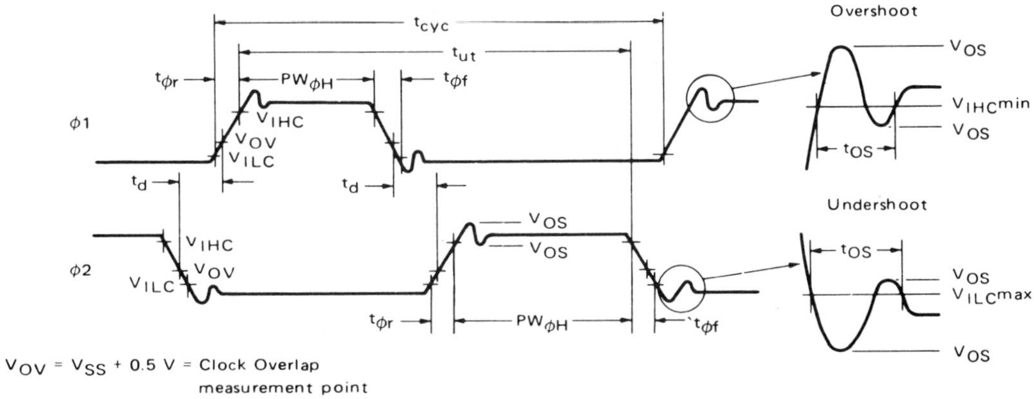

Fig. 12–7. Microprocessor $\phi 1$ and $\phi 2$ clocks. (*Courtesy Motorola Inc.*)

Table 12-5 Maximum Ratings

RATINGS	SYMBOL	VALUE	UNIT
Supply Voltage	V_{CC}	-0.3 to +7.0	Vdc
Input voltage	V_{IN}	-0.3 to +7.0	Vdc
Operating temperature range	T_A	0 to +70	°C
Storage temperature range	T_{stg}	-55 to +150	°C

Courtesy Motorola Inc.

Maximum Ratings

Table 12–5 shows the maximum ratings. The most important specifications in the table from a user's standpoint are the operating power supply range of +4.75 V to +5.25 V and the operating temperature range of 0° C to 70° C ambient.

Test Conditions

The dynamic test load for the data bus, as shown in Fig. 12–8, is 130 pF and one standard TTL load. The 11.7 KΩ resistor accounts for 205 μA of 2.4 V level leakage current. The $\overline{\text{interrupt request}}$ test load is also shown in Fig. 12–8. The load consists of a 3 KΩ resistor to V_{CC} and 100 pF of capacitance. Notice that the data bus lines, the address lines, the $\overline{\text{interrupt request}}$ line and the E enable line are all specified and tested to guarantee 0.4 V of dynamic noise immunity on the "1" and "0" logic levels.

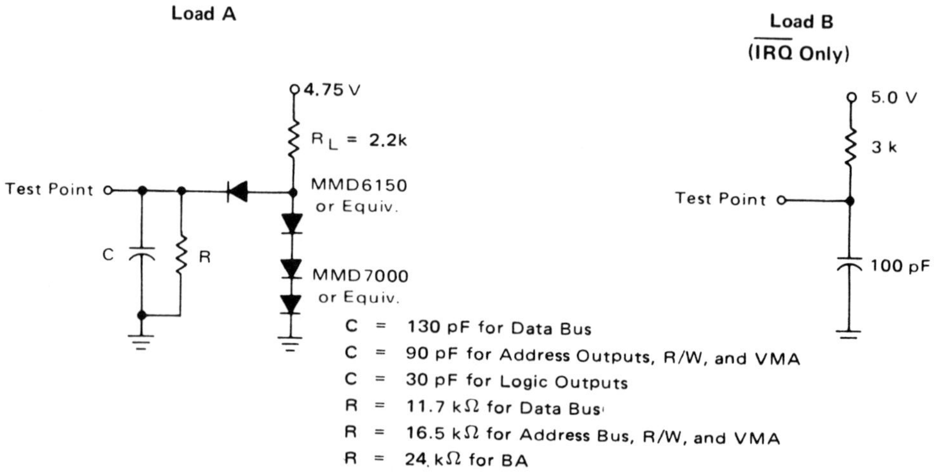

Fig. 12–8. Test loads. (*Courtesy Motorola Inc.*)

A MINIMUM SYSTEM

A minimum MC6800 system is defined as any size system within the basic load limitation of the MPU. Fig. 12–9 shows a minimum system consisting of the microprocessor, three RAMs, two ROMs, two PIAs and one ACIA. A maximum of eight peripherals are allowed on the bus in this configuration. This limitation is due to the capacitive loading specification of 130 pF on the microprocessor and peripheral data bus buffers—that is, 30 pF of interconnect capacitance and 100 pF of data bus buffer capacitance.

Systems having more than eight peripherals can be implemented by using the bus extender (BEX), additional TTL gates and the microprocessor control lines. A useful curve showing the data bus and address bus drive capability with respect to bus loading for typical conditions is shown in Fig. 12–10. Data bus buffer and address bus buffer delays typically increase at a rate of 0.5 ns/pF for pure capacitive loading.

System Clock

This microprocessor requires two clocks, $\phi 1$ and $\phi 2$, as shown in Fig. 12–9. A third clock, the E enable, which is in phase with $\phi 2$, is needed to transfer data to peripherals. Data transfers to the processor are made during the $\phi 2$ time. The $\phi 2$ clock is also tied to the microprocessor data enable (DBE) which enables the data bus output buffers.

The write timing for this condition is shown in Fig. 12–6 (DBE = $\phi 2$) and Table 12–4. If additional data setup or hold time is required on an MPU write, the DBE down-time can be decreased as shown in Fig. 12–6 (DBE $\neq \phi 2$). The minimum down time for DBE is $t_{\overline{DBE}}$ as shown in Table 12–4, and must occur within a $\phi 1$ up-time. The minimum delay from the trailing edge of DBE to the trailing edge of $\phi 1$ is t_{DBED}. By skewing DBE with respect to E in this manner, data setup or hold time can be increased.

The capacitive drive requirement for the E enable line for this system is 60 pF–90 pF for peripheral E input capacitance and 30 pF for interconnections. The MC6871A clock circuit provides $\phi 1$ and $\phi 2$ signals which meet the MPU requirements. It also provides a TTL compatible E enable output ($\phi 2$, TTL) which leads $\phi 2$ by approximately one TTL drive circuit stage delay. In the system shown, the data bus buffers go to their 3-state mode with the trailing edge of $\phi 2$ and E allowing for sufficient hold time ($\approx$300 ns). In systems having TTL loads on the data bus, E can be tied to DBE. Variations between E and $\phi 2$ do not affect the processor or peripheral data bus hold time requirements providing the trailing edge of E occurs after the trailing edge of $\phi 2$.

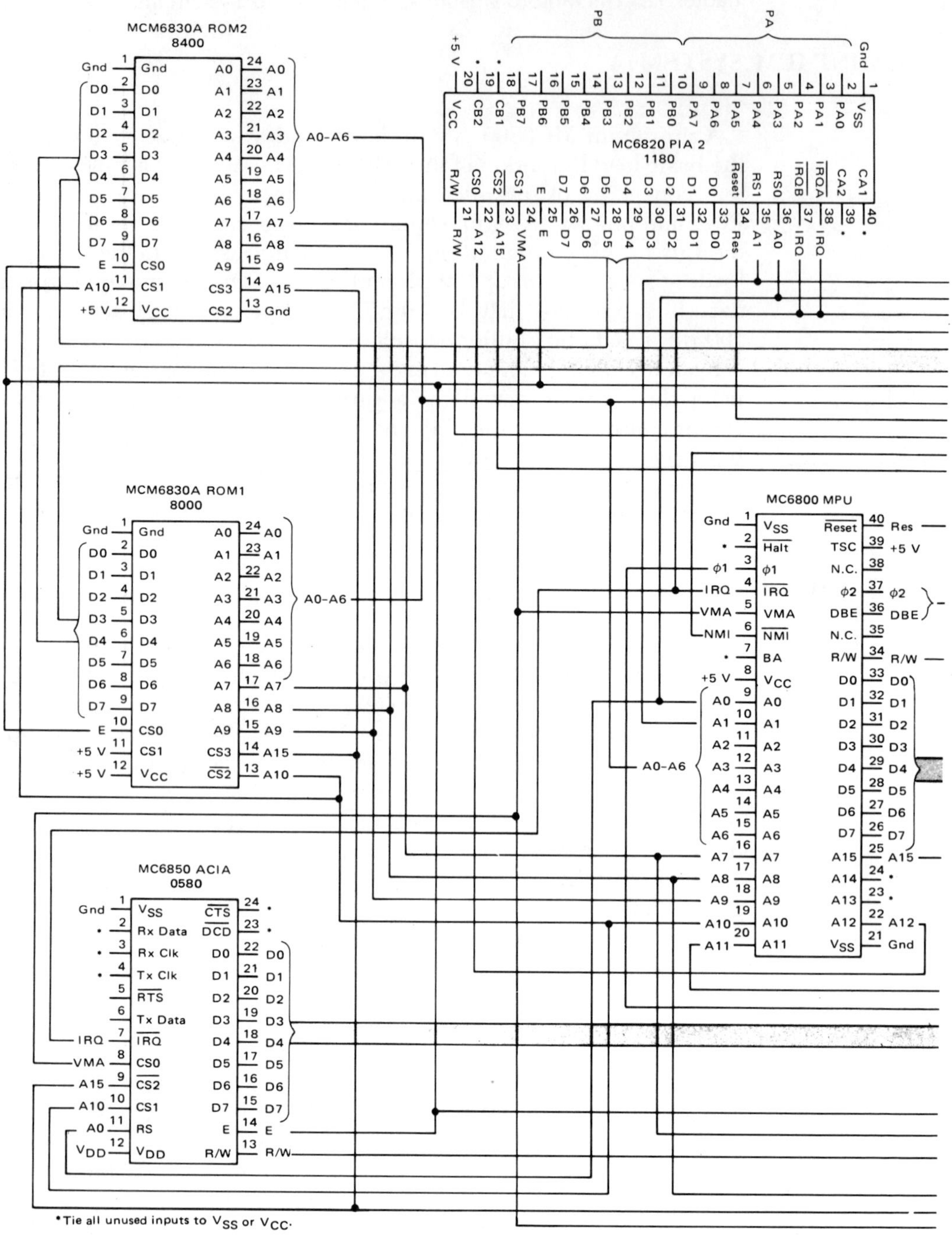

Fig. 12–9. Typical system interconnections. (*Courtesy Motorola Inc.*)

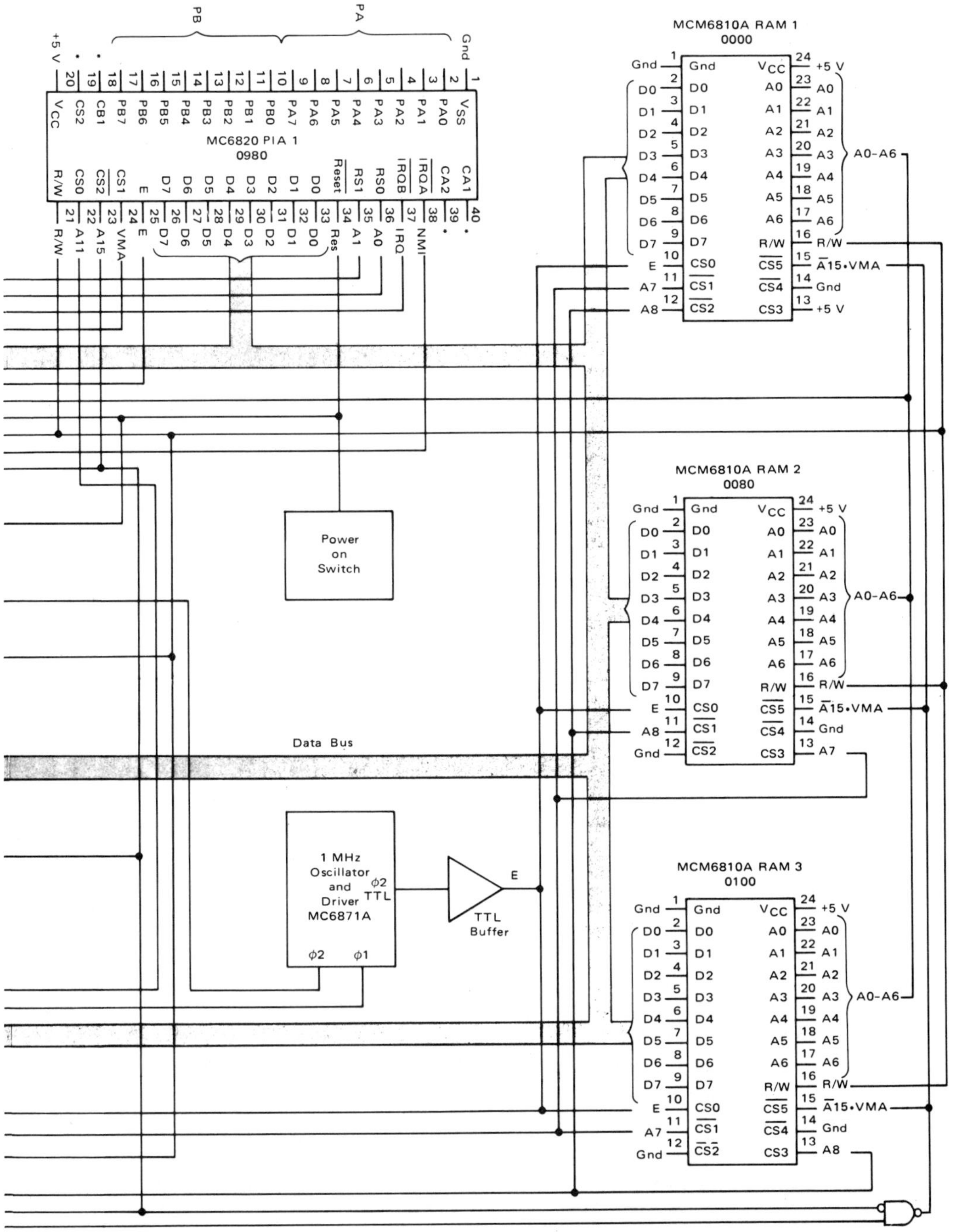

Fig. 12–9. continued.

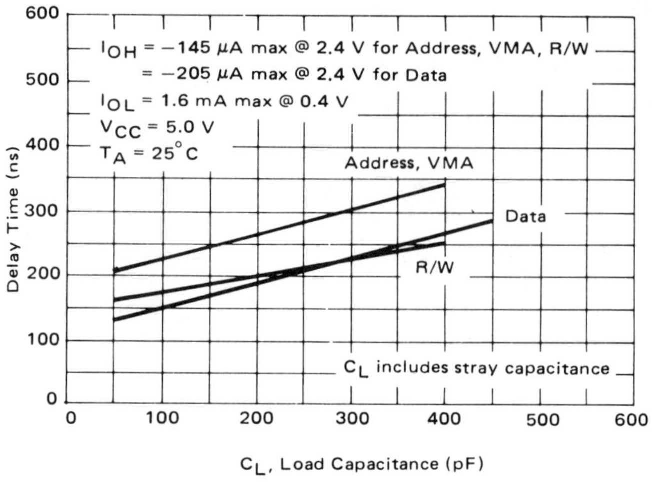

Fig. 12–10. Typical bus delay times versus capacitive loading. (*Courtesy Motorola Inc.*)

Addressing Peripherals and Memory

As shown in Fig. 12–6, all address lines are valid by address setup time t_{AS}. The address lines, chip selects and the E enable are tied to the ROM as shown in Fig. 12–9. The address lines required for addressing the ROMs are shown in Table 12–6. A true address bit selects a true chip select and an $\overline{\text{address}}$ bit selects a $\overline{\text{chip select}}$. Figure 12–9 also shows the address, chip select, E enable and R/W interconnection for the RAMs, the PIAs, and the ACIA, with Table 12–6 showing the address lines required.

Notice the VMA is used as a chip select to the peripherals. VMA is needed because interrupts on these parts are cleared on a read of data from the peripherals. The microprocessor requires from two to twelve cycles to do an instruction. During these portions of an instruction in which the data bus is not active, the R/W line is held high, the address lines are in an indeterminate state and the data bus buffers are in an indeterminate state. Thus a false read of a peripheral could occur, and if that peripheral was interrupting the microprocessor, the interrupt would be cleared. Tying VMA into one of the chip selects solves this problem since VMA is high only when there is a valid memory address on the address bus. If the $\overline{\text{halt}}$ control line, the wait for interrupt instruction, or the TSC control line is used, address and R/W lines float, which could result in a false write into memory. If $\overline{\text{halt}}$,

Table 12-6 Address Lines for System of Fig. 12-9

DEVICE	ADDRESS	CHIP SELECTS	SELECT CODE
ROM 1	A0–A9	$\overline{A}$10 A15	8000
ROM 2	A0–A9	A10 A15	8400
RAM 1	A0–A6	$\overline{A}$7 $\overline{A}$8 $\overline{A}$15 VMA	0000
RAM 2	A0–A6	A7 $\overline{A}$8 $\overline{A}$15 VMA	0080
RAM 3	A0–A6	$\overline{A}$7 A8 $\overline{A}$15 VMA	0100
ACIA 1	A0	A10 VMA $\overline{A}$15*	0580
PIA 1	A0 A1	A11 VMA $\overline{A}$15*	0980
PIA 2	A0 A1	A12 VMA $\overline{A}$15*	1180

Courtesy Motorola Inc.

*When addressing the ACIA and PIAs, A7 and A8 must be high to disable the RAMs. When addressing the RAMs, A10, A11 and A12 are held low.

TSC and WAI are required in a minimum system, a TTL AND gate is used to AND one of the chips selects with VMA as shown.

Address space was chosen as shown in Table 12–6 for the following reasons. When the microprocessor power comes up, the address FFFE goes out on the address lines, followed by FFFF (the address of the start up program is stored at FFFE and FFFF). Thus, A15 was chosen to select the ROMs. The ROM address bits are A0 through A9. A10 was chosen as the other chip select so that ROM addressing would be contiguous. The ROM chip selects are programmable; for this example CS1 and CS3 are defined as true and CS2 as not true (chip select).

$\overline{A}$15 can be used to select all peripherals except the ROMS. The RAM address bits are A0 through A6. A7 and A8 make the address space for the RAMs contiguous.

When using direct addressing, the address bus high bits (A8 through A15) are all zeros. Then RAM 1 and RAM 2 in Table 12–6 form 256 contiguous locations for direct addressing. When selecting the ACIA and PIAs, the RAMs are deselected by keeping A7 and A8 high.

The ACIA is selected with $\overline{A}$15, VMA and A10. A10 can be reused since the state of A15 determines whether A10 is used as a ROM address line or the ACIA address line. The PIAs are selected with $\overline{A}$15, VMA and two of the remaining unused address lines—A11 and A12.

MPU ADDRESS MODES

The MC6800 has a set of 72 different instructions. Included are binary and decimal arithmetic, logical, shift, rotate, load, store, condi-

Table 12–7 Microprocessor Instruction Set—Alphabetic Sequence

ABA	Add Accumulators
ADC	Add with Carry
ADD	Add
AND	Logical And
ASL	Arithmetic Shift Left
ASR	Arithmetic Shift Right
BCC	Branch if Carry Clear
BCS	Branch if Carry Set
BEQ	Branch if Equal to Zero
BGE	Branch if Greater or Equal Zero
BGT	Branch if Greater than Zero
BHI	Branch if Higher
BIT	Bit Test
BLE	Branch if Less or Equal
BLS	Branch if Lower or Same
BLT	Branch if Less than Zero
BMI	Branch if Minus
BNE	Branch if Not Equal to Zero
BPL	Branch if Plus
BRA	Branch Always
BSR	Branch to Subroutine
BVC	Branch if Overflow Clear
BVS	Branch if Overflow Set
CBA	Compare Accumulators
CLC	Clear Carry
CLI	Clear Interrupt Mask
CLR	Clear
CLV	Clear Overflow
CMP	Compare
COM	Complement
CPX	Compare Index Register
DAA	Decimal Adjust
DEC	Decrement
DES	Decrement Stack Pointer
DEX	Decrement Index Register
EOR	Exclusive OR
INC	Increment
INS	Increment Stack Pointer
INX	Increment Index Register
JMP	Jump
JSR	Jump to Subroutine
LDA	Load Accumulator
LDS	Load Stack Pointer
LDX	Load Index Register
LSR	Logical Shift Right
NEG	Negate
NOP	No Operation
ORA	Inclusive OR Accumulator
PSH	Push Data
PUL	Pull Data
ROL	Rotate Left
ROR	Rotate Right
RTI	Return from Interrupt
RTS	Return from Subroutine
SBA	Subtract Accumulators
SBC	Subtract with Carry
SEC	Set Carry
SEI	Set Interrupt Mask
SEV	Set Overflow
STA	Store Accumulator
STS	Store Stack Register
STX	Store Index Register
SUB	Subtract
SWI	Software Interrupt
TAB	Transfer Accumulators
TAP	Transfer Accumulators to Condition Code Reg.
TBA	Transfer Accumulators
TPA	Transfer Condition Code Reg. to Accumulator
TST	Test
TSX	Transfer Stack Pointer to Index Register
TXS	Transfer Index Register to Stack Pointer
WAI	Wait for Interrupt

(Courtesy Motorola Inc.)

tional or unconditional branch, interrupt and stack manipulation instructions.

Table 12–7 shows the microprocessor instruction set. Table 12–8 shows the instruction addressing modes and associated execution times.

Table 12–8 Instruction Addressing Modes and Associated Execution Times

	(Dual Operand)	ACCX	Immediate	Direct	Extended	Indexed	Inherent	Relative
ABA		•	•	•	•	•	2	•
ADC	x	•	2	3	4	5	•	•
ADD	x	•	2	3	4	5	•	•
AND	x	•	2	3	4	5	•	•
ASL		2	•	•	6	7	•	•
ASR		2	•	•	6	7	•	•
BCC		•	•	•	•	•	•	4
BCS		•	•	•	•	•	•	4
BEA		•	•	•	•	•	•	4
BGE		•	•	•	•	•	•	4
BGT		•	•	•	•	•	•	4
BHI		•	•	•	•	•	•	4
BIT	x	•	2	3	4	5	•	•
BLE		•	•	•	•	•	•	4
BLS		•	•	•	•	•	•	4
BLT		•	•	•	•	•	•	4
BMI		•	•	•	•	•	•	4
BNE		•	•	•	•	•	•	4
BPL		•	•	•	•	•	•	4
BRA		•	•	•	•	•	•	4
BSR		•	•	•	•	•	•	8
BVC		•	•	•	•	•	•	4
BVS		•	•	•	•	•	•	4
CBA		•	•	•	•	•	2	•
CLC		•	•	•	•	•	2	•
CLI		•	•	•	•	•	2	•
CLR		2	•	•	6	7	•	•
CLV		•	•	•	•	•	2	•
CMP	x	•	2	3	4	5	•	•
COM		2	•	•	6	7	•	•
CPX		•	3	4	5	6	•	•
DAA		•	•	•	•	•	2	•
DEC		2	•	•	6	7	•	•
DES		•	•	•	•	•	4	•
DEX		•	•	•	•	•	4	•
EOR	x	•	2	3	4	5	•	•

	(Dual Operand)	ACCX	Immediate	Direct	Extended	Indexed	Inherent
INC		2	•	•	6	7	•
INS		•	•	•	•	•	4
INX		•	•	•	•	•	4
JMP		•	•	•	3	4	•
JSR		•	•	•	9	8	•
LDA	x	•	2	3	4	5	•
LDS		•	3	4	5	6	•
LDX		•	3	4	5	6	•
LSR		2	•	•	6	7	•
NEG		2	•	•	6	7	•
NOP		•	•	•	•	•	2
ORA	x	•	2	3	4	5	•
PSH		4	•	•	•	•	•
PUL		4	•	•	•	•	•
ROL		2	•	•	6	7	•
ROR		2	•	•	6	7	•
RTI		•	•	•	•	•	10
RTS		•	•	•	•	•	5
SBA		•	•	•	•	•	2
SBC	x	•	2	3	4	5	•
SEC		•	•	•	•	•	2
SEI		•	•	•	•	•	2
SEV		•	•	•	•	•	2
STA	x	•	•	4	5	6	•
STS		•	•	5	6	7	•
STX		•	•	5	6	7	•
SUB	x	•	2	3	4	5	•
SWI		•	•	•	•	•	12
TAB		•	•	•	•	•	2
TAP		•	•	•	•	•	2
TBA		•	•	•	•	•	2
TPA		•	•	•	•	•	2
TST		2	•	•	6	7	•
TSX		•	•	•	•	•	4
TXS		•	•	•	•	•	4
WAI		•	•	•	•	•	9

NOTE: Interrupt time is 12 cycles from the end of the instruction being executed, except following a WAI instruction. Then it is 4 cycles.

(Courtesy Motorola Inc.)

The MPU address modes are:

1. Immediate
2. Direct
3. Indexed
4. Extended
5. Implied
6. Relative
7. Accumulator (ACCX)

A description of these address modes follows, with emphasis on what is occurring in each machine cycle on the address bus, data bus, R/W line and the VMA line. A cycle-by-cycle representation is shown in Fig. 12–11. When VMA is low the data bus and address bus are in an indeterminate state.

Immediate Addressing

Immediate addressing is an addressing technique in which the first byte of the instruction contains the operator and the second byte contains the operand. Exceptions to this are the LDS and LDX instructions which have the operand in the second instruction.

Referring to Fig. 12–11, during the first half of cycle 1, the program counter (PC) current address is put on the line, R/W goes high designating a read operation and VMA goes high designating the current address is a valid memory address. During the second half of cycle 1, the LDA operator code is put on the data bus from memory and loaded into the MPU. The MPU program counter is incremented and the operand, which is usually data, is loaded into the MPU on cycle 2. The operator of the next instruction follows on the next cycle.

Direct Addressing

In direct addressing, the address of the operand is contained in the second byte of the instruction. Direct addressing allows the user to directly address the lowest 256 bytes in the machine—locations zero through 255. Enhanced execution times are achieved by storing data in these locations. In most configurations, it should be a random access memory.

Referring to Fig. 12–11, the address in the program counter is put on the address bus and the LDA operator code is loaded into the MPU during cycle 1. The program counter is incremented and during cycle 2, eight bits of address are loaded into the address bus low (ABL) register which contains the lower eight bits of the 16-bit address register of the MPU. The upper 8 bits, which are contained in the address bus

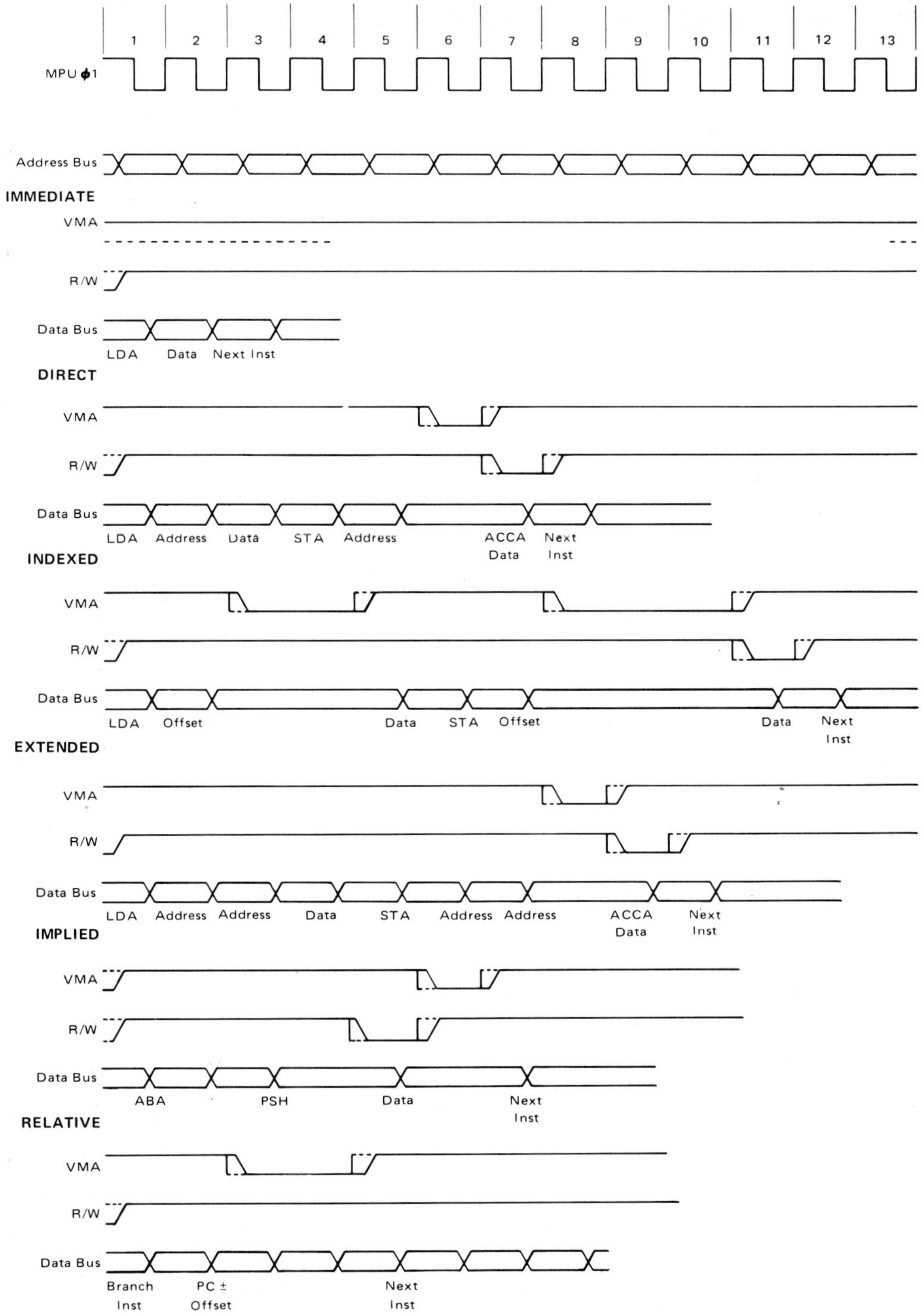

Fig. 12–11. Address modes. (*Courtesy Motorola Inc.*)

high (ABH) register, are forced to all zeros. In the third cycle the new address is put on the address bus and the operand is loaded into the MPU.

An STA instruction is handled in the same manner as an LDA instruction except there is an additional cycle required, which is cycle 6 in the diagram. Due to the MPU architecture this additional cycle is required to move the accumulator internally in the machine. During this cycle the data bus is in an indeterminate state and VMA goes low. The actual storing of data then occurs on cycle 7. The next instruction follows as shown.

Indexed Addressing

In indexed addressing, the address contained in the second byte of the instruction is added to the index register's lowest eight bits in the MPU. The carry is then added to the higher order 8 bits of the index register. This result is then used to address memory. The modified address is held in a temporary address register so there is no change to the index register. These are 2-byte instructions.

In the first two cycles of an indexed address instruction, the LDA operator code is loaded into the MPU followed by the index offset. In the third cycle the low order byte of the index register is loaded into the adder and added to the offset; the carry propagates during cycle 4. The VMA goes low during these two cycles while the MPU is preparing the indexed address. The new address then goes on the line during cycle 5.

The STA indexed instruction is handled in the same manner as the LDA instruction, again with the exception that an additional cycle is required due to the MPU architecture. VMA is held low then for three cycles for the STA instruction instead of two for the LDA instruction.

Extended Addressing

In extended addressing, the address contained in the second byte of the instruction is the eight higher order address bits of the operand. The third byte of the instruction contains the lower eight bits of the address. This is an absolute address in memory and these are 3-byte instructions. Extended addressing is the same as direct addressing except the address field is a full sixteen bits. This means the LDA and STA instructions require an additional cycle (cycles 2 and 6) to fetch the high order eight bits of the address. Notice that in cycle 8 VMA is low signifying the data bus is in an indeterminate state. This is again due to the internal architecture of the MPU.

Implied Addressing

There are two types of implied addressing instructions: those which do not require an address and those which do require an address. These are 1-byte instructions. An example of an instruction which does not require an address is ABA. Here the contents of accumulator A are added to accumulator B and the result put in accumulator A. The data bus and address bus are valid only on the first cycle of the instruction as shown in Fig. 12–11.

For those instructions which do require an address, the address is held by an internal MPU register such as the stack pointer. Thus no data is required to develop an address. An example of this type of instruction is PSH.

Looking again at Fig. 12–11, the data bus and address bus are valid on cycle 3 to fetch the PSH operator. In cycle 4, the MPU is moving data internally and VMA does not go low. During this time the address bus contains the address of the next instruction in ROM and the MPU is doing an invalid read. In cycle 5, the stack pointer is loaded into address bus buffers and data is written into the stack. On the next cycle, VMA goes low and the stack pointer is decremented. The next instruction then follows.

Relative Addressing

In relative addressing, the address contained in the second byte of the instruction is added to the program counter's lowest eight bits plus two. The carry or borrow is then added to the high eight bits. This allows the user to address data within a range of − 126 to + 129 bytes of the present instruction. These are 2-byte instructions which perform branch functions.

Referring again to Fig. 12–11, the operator code is fetched from the memory location stored in the instruction register during cycle 1. The program counter offset is loaded into the MPU during cycle 2. The offset is added to the low order bits of the program counter in cycle 3 and the carry is propagated during cycle 4. During these two cycles, VMA goes low while the MPU is operating on the offset data. The next instruction is loaded during cycle 5.

Accumulator (ACCX) Addressing

In accumulator only addressing, either accumulator A or accumulator B is specified.

An example is ASLA (arithmetic shift left, on the A accumulator).

These are 1-byte, 2-cycle instructions and the address bus and data bus are active only during the first cycle of the instruction when the operator is being loaded from memory. During the second cycle the machine performs the operation and VMA is high.

PROCESSOR CONTROLS

The microprocessor has six processor control lines (Fig. 12–1) which are:

$\overline{\text{Reset}}$
$\overline{\text{NMI Non-Maskable Interrupt}}$
$\overline{\text{Halt}}$
BA (Bus Available)
TSC (Three-State Control)
DBE (Data Bus Enable)

Two of the control lines, $\overline{\text{Reset}}$ and DBE are required for all systems. The remaining control lines can be utilized to enhance throughput and flexibility depending on the system application.

Along with the discussion on $\overline{\text{NMI}}$ will be a discussion of the wait for interrupt (WAI) instruction and the $\overline{\text{interrupt request}}$ ($\overline{\text{IRQ}}$) line since the three interrupt types are closely aligned.

$\overline{\text{Reset}}$

The $\overline{\text{reset}}$ input is used to reset and start the MPU from a power-down condition resulting from a power failure or initial start-up of the processor. This input can also be used to reinitialize the machine at any time after start up.

If a high level is detected in this input, this will signal the MPU to begin the reset sequence. During the reset sequence, the contents of the last two locations (FFFE, FFFF) in memory will be loaded into the program counter to point to the beginning of the reset routine. During the reset routine, the interrupt mask bit is set and must be cleared under program control before the MPU can be interrupted by $\overline{\text{IRQ}}$. While reset is low (assuming a minimum of eight clock cycles have occurred) the MPU output signals will be in the following states: VMA = low, BA = low, data bus = high impedance, R/W = high (read state) and the address bus will contain the reset address FFFE. Fig. 12–12 illustrates a power-up sequence using the $\overline{\text{reset}}$ control line. After the power supply reaches 4.75 V, a minimum of eight clock cycles are required for the processor to stabilize in preparation for restarting. During these eight cycles, VMA will be in an indeterminate state so any devices that are enabled by VMA which could accept a false write during this time (such as a battery-backed RAM) must be disabled until VMA is forced low after eight clock cycles. $\overline{\text{Reset}}$ can go high asynchronously with the system clock any time after the eighth cycle.

$\overline{\text{Reset}}$ timing is shown in Fig. 12–12 and Table 12–4. The maximum rise and fall transition times are specified by t_{PCr} and t_{PCf}. If reset is high at t_{PCS} (processor control setup time), as shown in Fig. 12–12, in any given cycle, then the restart sequence will begin on the next cycle as shown. The $\overline{\text{reset}}$ control line may also be used to reinitialize the MPU system at any time during its operation. This is accomplished by pulsing $\overline{\text{reset}}$ low for the duration of a minimum of three complete $\phi 2$ cycles. The reset pulse can be completely asynchronous with the MPU system clock and will be recognized during the $\phi 2$ if setup time t_{PCS} is met.

Non-Maskable Interrupt ($\overline{\text{NMI}}$) and Wait for Interrupt (WAI)

The MC6800 is capable of handling two types of interrupts: maskable ($\overline{\text{IRQ}}$) as described earlier and non-maskable ($\overline{\text{NMI}}$). $\overline{\text{IRQ}}$ is maskable by the interrupt mask in the condition code register while $\overline{\text{NMI}}$ is not maskable. The handling of these interrupts by the MPU is the same except that each has its own vector address. The behavior of the MPU when interrupted is shown in Fig. 12–13, which details the MPU response to an interrupt while the MPU is executing the control program.

The interrupt shown could be either $\overline{\text{IRQ}}$ or $\overline{\text{NMI}}$ and can be asynchronous with respect to $\phi 2$. The interrupt is shown going low at time t_{PCS} in cycle 1 which precedes the first cycle of an instruction (op code fetch). This instruction is not executed; instead the program counter (PC), index register (IX), accumulators (ACCX), and the condition codes register (CCR) are pushed into the stack.

The interrupt mask bit is set to prevent further interrupts. The address of the interrupt service routine is then fetched from FFFC, FFFD for an $\overline{\text{NMI}}$ interrupt and from FFF8, FFF9 for an $\overline{\text{IRQ}}$ interrupt. Upon completion of the interrupt service routine, the execution of RTI will pull the PC, IX, ACCX and CCR off of the stack; the interrupt mask bit is restored to its condition prior to interrupts.

Figure 12–14 is a similar interrupt sequence, except in this case, a WAIT instruction has been executed in preparation for the interrupt. This technique speeds up the MPU's response to the interrupt because the stacking of the PC, IX, ACCX and the CCR is already done. While the MPU is waiting for the interrupt, bus available will go high

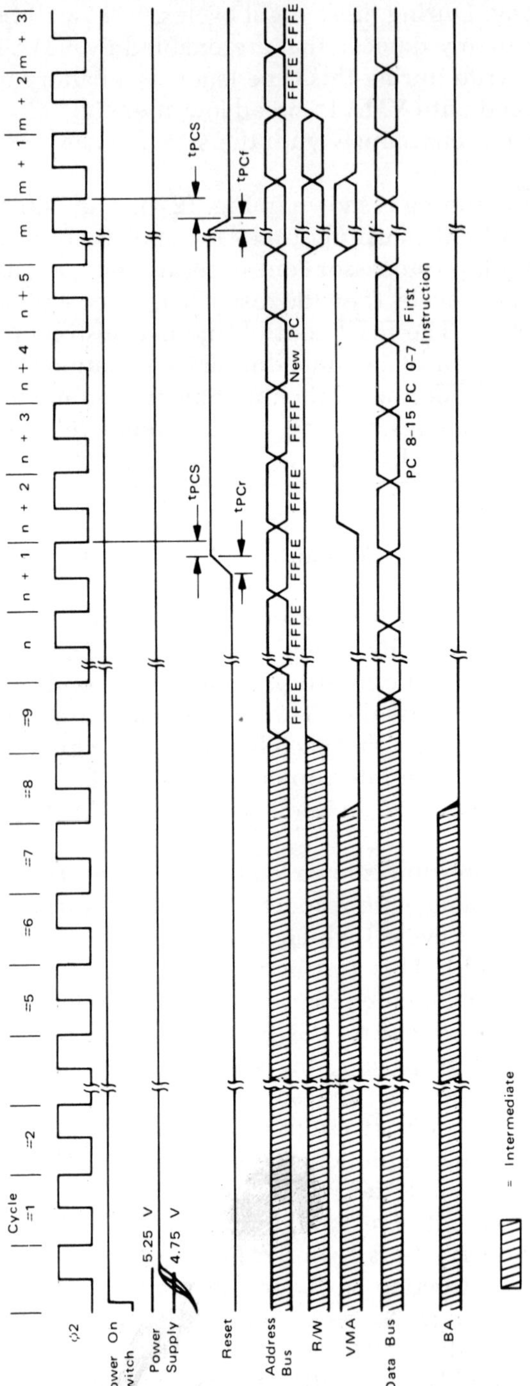

Fig. 12–12. $\overline{\text{Reset}}$ **timing.** ***(Courtesy Motorola Inc.)***

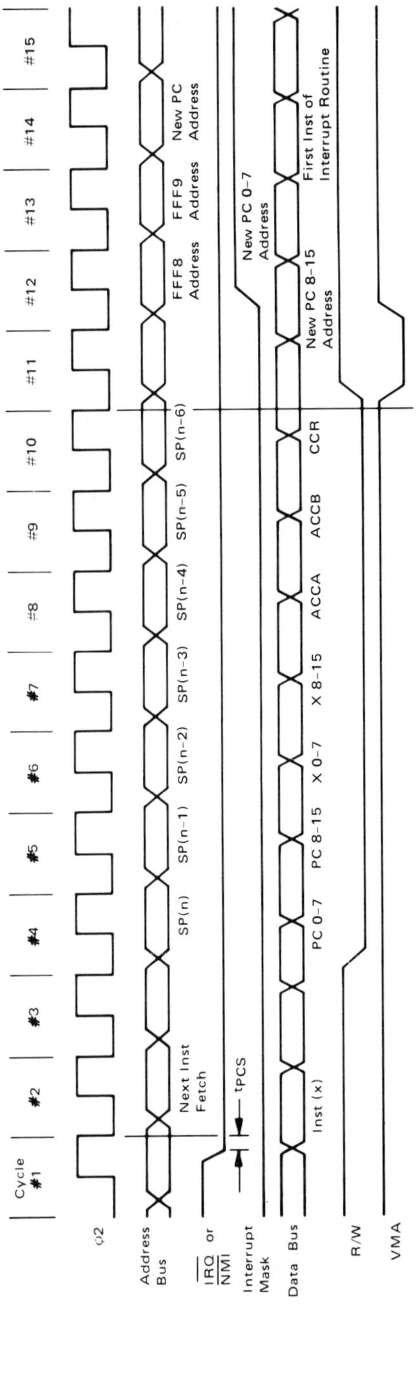

Fig. 12–13. Interrupt timing. *(Courtesy Motorola Inc.)*

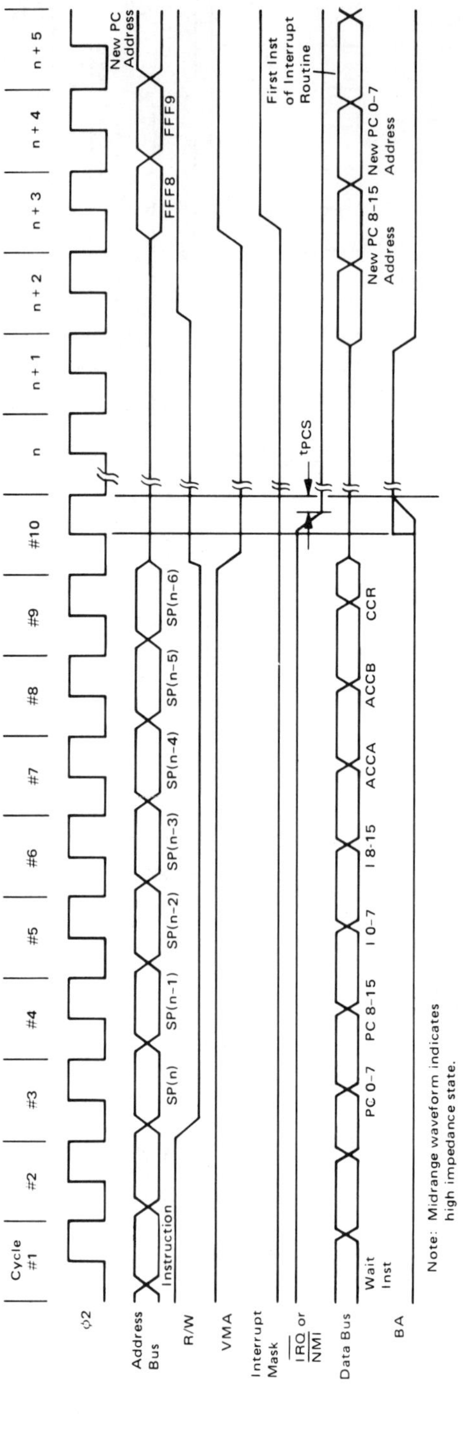

Fig. 12–14. Wait instruction timing. (*Courtesy Motorola Inc.*)

indicating the following states of the control lines: VMA is low, and the address bus, R/W and data bus are all in the high-impedance state. After the interrupt occurs, it is serviced as previously described.

$\overline{\text{Halt}}$ and Single Instruction Execution

The $\overline{\text{Halt}}$ line provides an input to the MPU to allow control of program execution by an outside source. If $\overline{\text{halt}}$ is high, the MPU will execute the instructions; if it is low, the MPU will go to a halted or idle mode. A response signal, but available (BA), provides an indication of the current MPU status. When BA is low, the MPU is in the process of executing the control program; if BA is high, the MPU has halted and all internal activity has stopped.

When BA is high, the address bus, data bus and R/W line will be in a high-impedance state, effectively removing the MPU from the system bus. VMA is forced low so that the floating system bus will not activate any device on the bus that is enabled by VMA.

While the MPU is halted, all program activity is stopped, and if either $\overline{\text{NMI}}$ or $\overline{\text{IRQ}}$ interrupt occurs, it will be latched into the MPU and acted on as soon as the MPU is taken out of the halted mode. If a $\overline{\text{reset}}$ command occurs while the MPU is halted, the following states occur: VMA = low, BA = low, data bus = high impedance, R/W = high (read state) and the address bus will contain address FFFE as long as $\overline{\text{reset}}$ is low. As soon as the $\overline{\text{halt}}$ line goes high, the MPU will go to locations FFFE and FFFF for the address of the reset routine.

Fig. 12–15 shows the timing relationships involved when halting the MPU. The instruction illustrated is a 1-byte, 2-cycle instruction such as CLRA. When $\overline{\text{halt}}$ goes low, the MPU will halt after completing execution of the current instruction. The transition of $\overline{\text{halt}}$ must occur t_{PCS} before the trailing edge of $\phi 1$ of the last cycle of an instruction (point A of Fig. 12–15). Halt must not go low any time later than the minimum t_{PCS} specified.

The fetch of the op code by the MPU is the first cycle of the instruction. If $\overline{\text{halt}}$ had not been low at point A but went low during $\phi 2$ of that cycle, the MPU would have halted after completion of the following instruction. BA will go high by time t_{BA} (bus available delay time) after the last instruction cycle. At this point in time, VMA is low and R/W, address bus and the data bus are in the high-impedance state.

To debug programs it is advantageous to step through programs instruction by instruction. To do this, $\overline{\text{halt}}$ must be brought high for one MPU cycle and then returned low as shown at point B of Fig. 12–15. Again, the transitions of $\overline{\text{halt}}$ must occur t_{PCS} before the trailing edge of $\phi 1$. BA will go low at t_{BA} after the leading edge of the next $\phi 1$, indicating that the address bus, data bus, VMA and R/W lines are back on the bus. A 1-byte, 2-cycle instruction such as LSR is used for this example also. During the first cycle, the instruction Y is fetched from address M + 1. BA returns high at t_{BA} on the last cycle of the instruction indicating the MPU is off the bus. If instruction Y had been three cycles, the width of the BA low time would have been increased by one cycle.

Three-State Control (TSC)

When the 3-state control (TSC) line is a logic "1," the address bus and the R/W line are placed in a high-impedance state. VMA and BA are forced low whenever TSC = "1" to prevent false reads or writes on any device enabled by VMA. While TSC is held high, the $\phi 1$ and $\phi 2$ clocks must be held high and low respectively, in order to delay program execution (this is required because of the bus lines being in an indeterminate state). Since the MPU is a dynamic device, the $\phi 1$ clock can be stopped for a maximum time $PW_{\phi H}$ without destroying data within the MPU. TSC then can be used in a short direct memory access (DMA) application.

Fig. 12–16 shows the effect of TSC on the MPU. TSC must have its transitions at t_{TSE} (3-state enable) while holding $\phi 1$ high and $\phi 2$ low as shown. The address bus and R/W line will reach the high-impedance state at t_{TSD} (3-state delay), with VMA being forced low. In this example, the data bus is also in the high-impedance state while $\phi 2$ is being held low since DBE = $\phi 2$. At this point in time, a DMA transfer could occur on cycles 3 and 4. When TSC is returned low, the MPU address and R/W lines return to the bus. Because it is too late in cycle 5 to access memory, this cycle is dead and used for synchronization. Program execution resumes in cycle 6.

Bus Available (BA)

The bus available signal will normally be in the low state; when activated, it will go to the high state indicating that the microprocessor has stopped and that the address bus is available. This will occur if the halt line is in the low state (Fig. 12–15), or if the processor is in the WAIT state (Fig. 12–14) as a result of the execution of a WAIT instruction. At such time, all 3-state output drivers will go to their off state and other outputs to their normally inactive level. The processor is removed from the WAIT state by the occurrence of a maskable (mask bit 1 = 0) or nonmaskable interrupt. Note that if TSC is in the high state, bus available will be low.

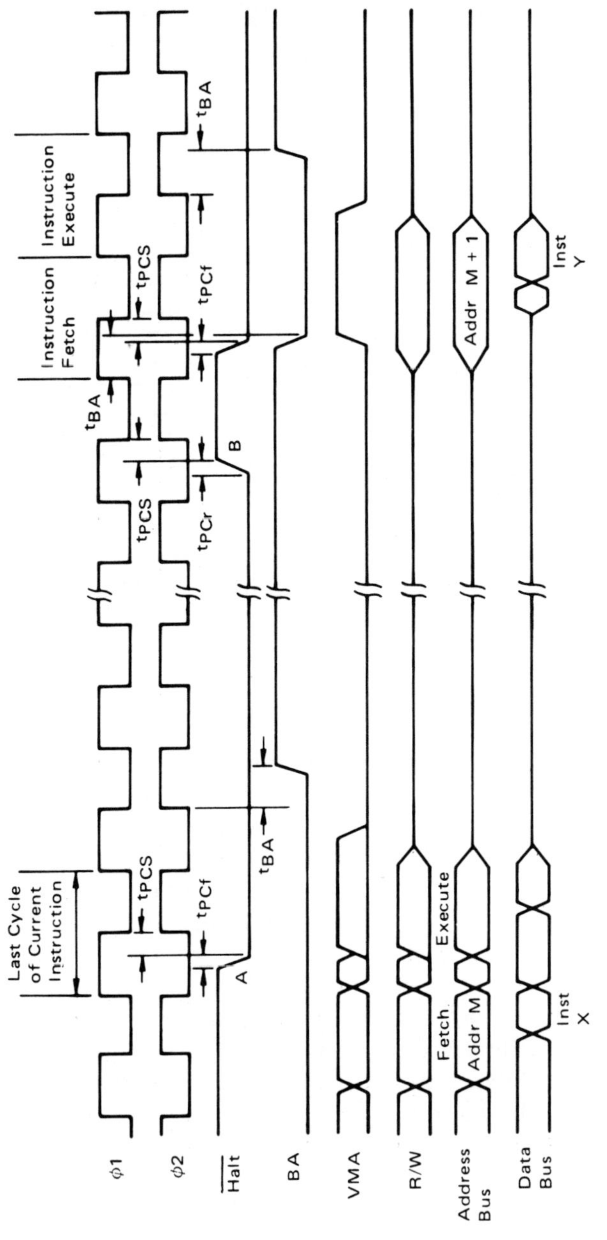

Note: Midrange waveform indicates high impedance state.

Fig. 12–15. $\overline{\text{Halt}}$ **and single instruction execution for system debug.** *(Courtesy Motorola Inc.)*

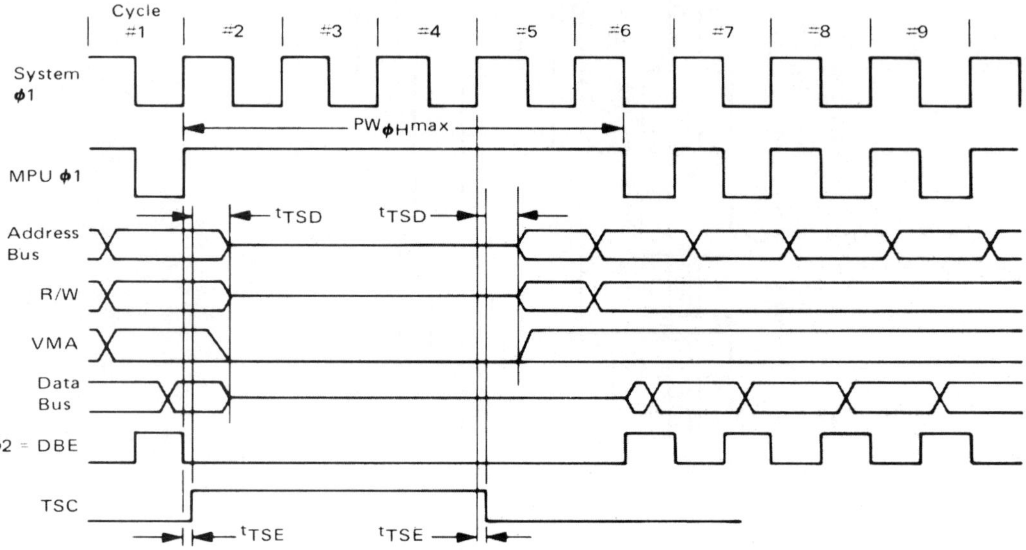

Fig. 12–16. 3-state control timing. (*Courtesy Motorola Inc.*)

Data Bus Enable (DBE)

DBE is the 3-state control signal for the MPU data bus and will enable the bus drivers when in the high state. This input is TTL compatible; however, in normal operation it would be driven by the $\phi 2$ clock. During an MPU read cycle, the data bus drivers will be disabled internally. When it is desired that another device control the data bus, such as in DMA applications, DBE should be held low.

If additional data setup or hold time is required on an MPU write, the DBE down time can be decreased as shown in Fig. 12–6 (DBE $\neq \phi 2$). The minimum down time for DBE is $t_{\overline{DBE}}$ as shown in Table 12–4, and must occur within $\phi 1$ up time. The minimum delay from the trailing edge of DBE to the trailing edge of $\phi 1$ is t_{DBED}. By skewing DBE with respect to E in this manner, data setup or hold time can be increased.[1]

SUMMARY

The purpose of presenting the detailed material describing the MC6800 MPU and support integrated circuits in this chapter is twofold. First, it illustrates all of the fine details that are essential in con-

[1] *Motorola MC6800 Microcomputer System Design Data Manual* (Phoenix, Arizona: Motorola Inc., 1976), pp. 2–20.

sidering a complete microprocessor system. Second, in the authors' opinion, reading and studying a typical technical literature section, with which all people involved with this exploding field of microelectronics must become familiar, is a learning experience in itself.

Because of the fast rate of change in solid-state electronics as evidenced by the devices covered in the next chapter, a great deal of technical information is disseminated by means of this type of literature. Product previews, specification sheets, data books and application notes are a very real and vital part of this exciting field of microprocessor technology.

QUESTIONS

1. Explain the functions of the following processor control lines:

DBE	$\overline{\text{HALT}}$
TSC	$\overline{\text{NMI}}$
BA	$\overline{\text{RESET}}$

2. What does VMA mean?
3. Explain the meaning of the phrase 2-phase nonoverlapping clock.
4. How many address lines are available on the MC6800 MPU? Why?
5. Which of the following lines are unidirectional and which are bidirectional?

Data lines	VMA line
Address lines	TSC line
Read/write line	$\overline{\text{IRQ}}$ line

6. How many "standard I/O" lines are available on the MC6821 PIA?
7. How many control I/O lines are available on the MC6821 PIA?
8. Is the frequency the same for the MPU and the ACIA Tx and Rx data? Explain.
9. Discuss the following. The MC6800 system design approach is attractive to the system designer and user because the interface peripheral devices appear as memory locations on the address and data buses.
10. Construct a block diagram of a minimum MC6800-based microsystem with the following characteristics:

    RAM 256 bytes
    ROM 1024 bytes
    Serial I/O
    Parallel I/O

Chapter 13

Motorola's Next Generation: 6801, 6802, 6805, 6809

GLOSSARY

AVMA Advanced valid memory address. An output signal indicating that the MC6809E will use the bus in the following bus cycle.

CMOS A technology using both P and N channel devices in a complementary MOS arrangement.

Concatenated Linked together in a series or chain. For example, two 8-bit bytes can be concatenated to form one 16-bit word.

$\overline{\text{FIRQ}}$ Fast interrupt request. An interrupt request that stacks only the contents of the condition code register and the program counter.

HMOS High density NMOS.

MCU Microcomputer unit.

MMU Memory management unit.

Multiprocessor Various computer configurations consisting of more than one independently initiable processor, each having access to a common, jointly-addressable memory.

NMOS N-channel metal oxide on silicon technology.

Position independent A program that will run correctly when the same machine code is positioned arbitrarily in memory.

Quadrature clock The Q (quadrature) clock leads the E clock by approximately one-half of the E clock time. Address information from the processor is valid with the leading edge of the Q clock.

Recursion A routine that calls itself.

Reentrant A routine that allocates different local variable storage upon each entry. Thus, a later entry does not destroy the processing associated with an earlier entry.

UART Universal asynchronous receiver/transmitter; in a UART, the transmitter converts parallel data bits into serial form for transmission, the receiver section does the reverse operation.

The purpose of this chapter is to familiarize the reader with the state-of-the-art of the M6800 microprocessor/microcomputer family. The trend in integrated circuit technology of putting more and more electronic components in a smaller and smaller area of silicon is exemplified by the development and production of the next generation of the M6800 microprocessor/microcomputer family.

Since the inception of microprocessor technology in the early 1970s, a vast number of improvements have inevitably been made, especially in the areas of circuit complexity and overall processor performance.

The decade from 1970 to 1980 witnessed an evolution in LSI MOS microprocessor density. The device count per square mils went from 2500 devices/44,000 sq. mils in 1970 to 68,000+ devices/63,000 sq. mils in 1980. This increase in circuit complexity has been accompanied by an increase in operating frequency from 500 KHz to 10 MHz and beyond.

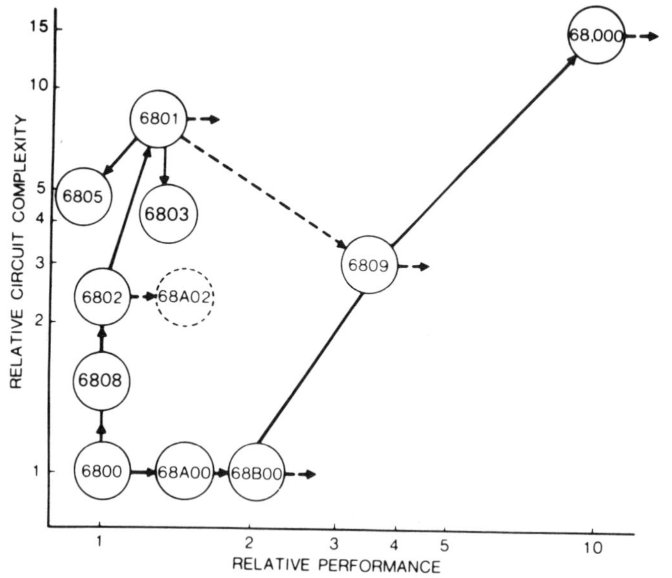

Fig. 13–1. Motorola's microprocessor evolution. (*Courtesy Motorola Inc.*)

The microprocessor evolution in the Motorola family can be traced from the basic 8-bit, 1 MHz MC6800 to the most advanced 16-bit, 10 MHz MC68000 as shown in Fig. 13–1.

MICROPROCESSOR VS. MICROCOMPUTER

A major distinction between a microprocessor and a microcomputer regards support functions such as RAM, ROM, and I/0. These functions are onboard the microcomputer but some or all must be added as peripheral chips to a microprocessor to make it truly functional.

In most cases, the MC6800 MPU required the original M6800 family of support chips before it would satisfy most applications. The support chips included RAM (MC6810), ROM (MC6830), serial I/0 (MC6850 or MC6852), parallel I/0 (MC6820), and a system clock (MC6870). Refer to Fig. 13–2.

One of the definite enhancements brought about by a significant increase of chip devices per area of silicon is the stand alone or single chip microcomputer. By definition, this device has RAM, ROM, clock and serial and/or parallel I/0 onboard.

The two single chip microcomputers presented in this chapter are the MC6801, including the closely related MC6803, and the MC6805xx family. The specific members of the MC6850xx family are the MC6805P2, the MC6805R2, the MC6805U2, the MC6805P3 (EPROM version), and the MC146805E2 (CMOS).

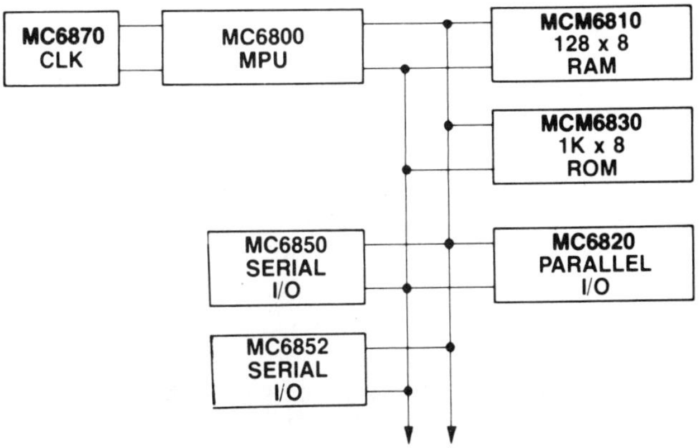

Fig. 13–2. The original M6800 family. (*Courtesy Motorola Inc.*)

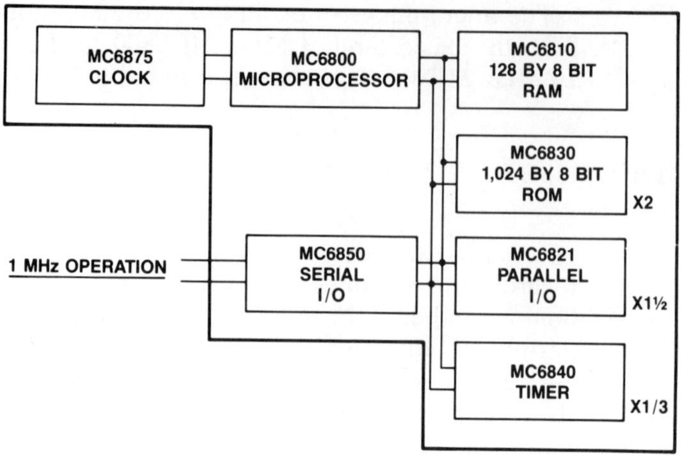

Fig. 13–3. MC6801 chip functionality block diagram. (*Courtesy Motorola Inc.*)

THE MC6801

The MC6801 is an excellent example of increased complexity and enhanced performance. It is recognized as one of the most powerful single chip microcomputers available today. The major support chips most often required in a micro-based system have been put directly onboard as illustrated in Fig. 13–3.

The notations x2, x1½, and x⅓ indicate the basic make-up of the support functions. The MC6830 1K-by-8 ROM is multiplied by two (x2). Therefore, the MC6801 has 2K-by-8 of ROM onboard. Likewise, it features one-and-one-half (x1½) an MC6821 PIA and one-third (x⅓) a basic MC6840 timer. All of these features are on a single piece of silicon about 50,000 square mils in size with a total of approximately 40,000 equivalent devices.

Description

The MC6801 **MCU** is an 8-bit microcomputer system which is expandable using the MC6800 microprocessor family. The MC6801 MCU is object code compatible with the MC6800 instruction set with improved execution times of key instructions plus several new 16-bit and 8-bit instructions. These new instructions are given in Table 13–1.

The MC6801 MCU can operate as a single chip or be expanded to 65 K words. It also has 2K bytes of ROM, 128 bytes of RAM on-board, a UART, parallel I/0 and three 16-bit timer functions.[1]

[1] *Product Preview MC6801 NP-93* (Phoenix, Arizona: Motorola Inc., 1978), p. 1.

Table 13–1 MC6801 New Instructions

ABX	Adds the 8-bit unsigned accumulator B to the 16-bit X-Register taking into account the possible carry out of the low order byte of the X-Register.	IX ← IX + ACCB
ADDD	Adds the double precision ACCAB to the double precision value M:M+1 and places the results in ACCAB.	ACCAB ← (ACCAB) + (M:M+1)
ASLD	Shifts all bits of ACCAB one place to the left. Bit 0 is loaded with a zero. The C bit is loaded from the most significant bit of ACCAB.	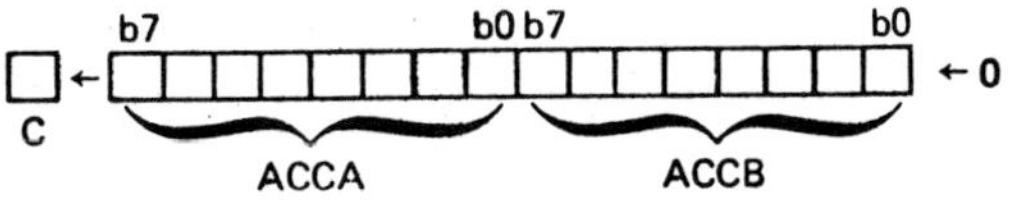
LDD	Loads the contents of double precision memory location into the double accumulator A:B. The condition codes are set according to the data.	ACCAB ← (M:M+1)
LSRD	Shifts all bits of ACCAB one place to the right. Bit 15 is loaded with zero. The C bit is loaded from the least significant bit of ACCAB.	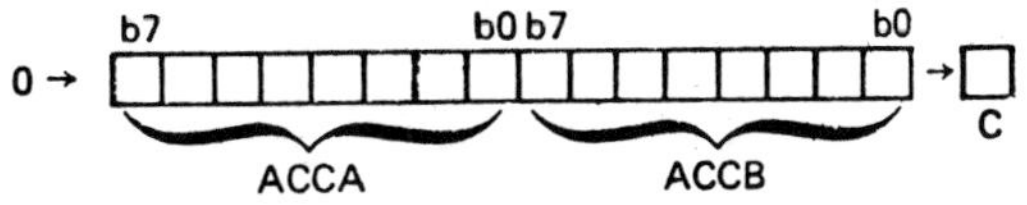
MUL	Multiplies the 8 bits in accumulator A with the 8 bits in accumulator B to obtain a 16-bit unsigned number in A:B.ACCA contains MSB of result.	ACCAB ← ACCA * ACCB
PSHX	The contents of the index register is pushed onto the stack at the address contained in the stack pointer. The stack pointer is decremented by 2.	↓ (IXL), SP ← (SP) − 0001 ↓ (IXH), SP ← (SP) − 0001
PULX	The index register is pulled from the stack beginning at the current address contained in the current address contained in the stack pointer +1. The stack pointer is incremented by 2 in total.	SP ← (SP) + 1; ↑ IXH SP ← (SP) + 1; ↑ IXL
STD	Stores the contents of double accumulator A:B in memory. The contents of ACCAB remain unchanged.	M:M+1 ← (ACCAB)
SUBD	Subtracts the contents of M:M+1 from the contents of double accumulator AB and places the result in ACCAB.	ACCAB ← (ACCAB) − (M:M+1)

(Courtesy Motorola Inc.)

The MC6801 MCU appears in block diagram form in Fig. 13–4. Note the thirty-one programmable parallel I/0 lines that could be used to manage external peripherals and the serial I/0 (UART) port for controlling communications equipment.

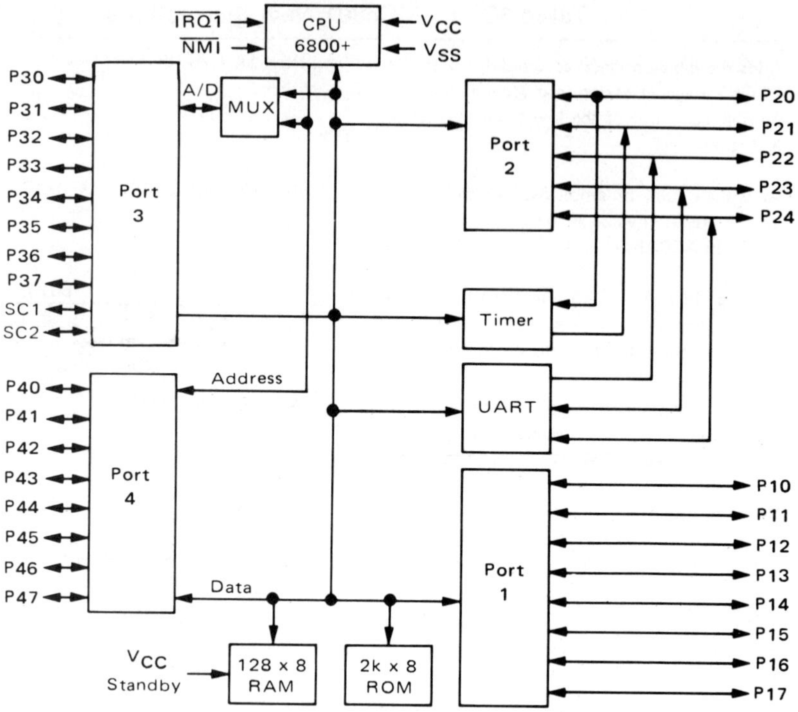

Fig. 13–4. MC6801 single chip microprocessor block diagram. (*Courtesy Motorola Inc.*)

Typical Applications

Some very brief examples are presented here as typical applications that could use the MC6801 MCU.

1. *Low cost data communications.* In Fig. 13–5 is an application of the MC6801 MCU being used in a low cost data communications system with simple serial I/0 peripherals such as shift register, facilitated by an on-chip serial I/0 port.

2. *Expanding parallel I/0 capacity.* Expanding parallel I/0 capacity is simplified by use of I/0 ports to expand the chip's data bus and address bus to external MC6800-oriented peripherals. This is shown in Fig. 13–6.

3. *Multiple MC6801 MCUs.* The third and final example is given in Fig. 13–7.

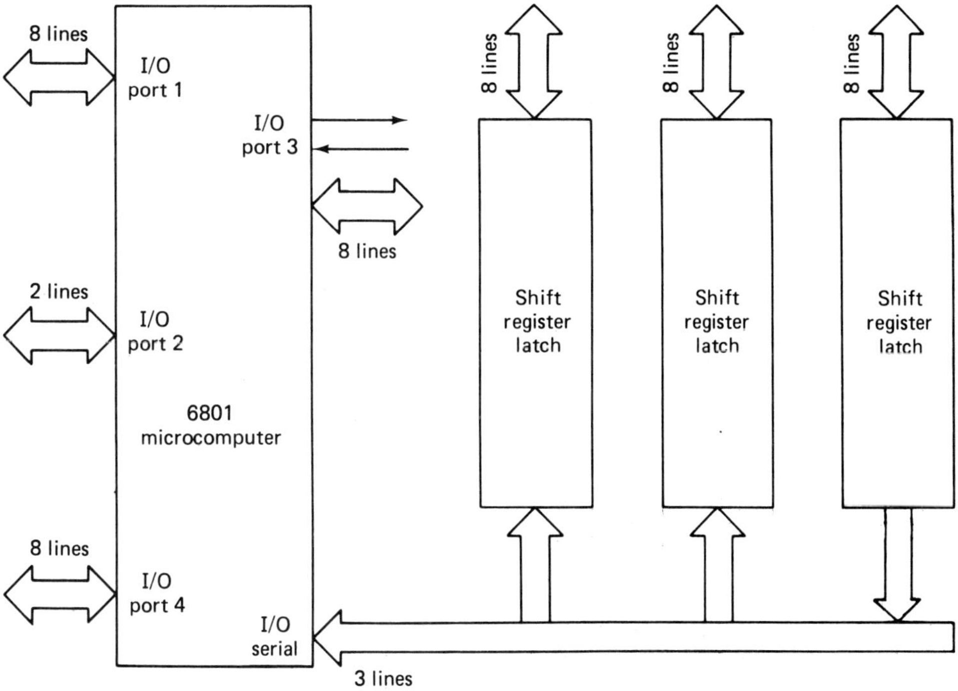

Low-cost Data Communications with simple serial I/O peripherals, such as shift registers, is facilitated by an on-chip Serial I/O port.

Fig. 13–5. Data communication configuration. (*Courtesy Motorola Inc.*)

Fig. 13–7 shows the concept of multiple MCUs. Using the serial I/0 port, a number of MC6801s can be arranged in a masterslave **multiprocessor** setup.[2]

Features

Summarizing the MC6801:

- Expanded MC6800 instruction set
- Onboard **UART**
- Object code compatible with MC6800
- 16-bit timer
- Single chip or expandable to 65 K words
- 2K bytes of ROM

[2] *Motorola Microcomputer Components—System on Silicon* (Phoenix, Arizona: Motorola Inc., 1978), p. 18.

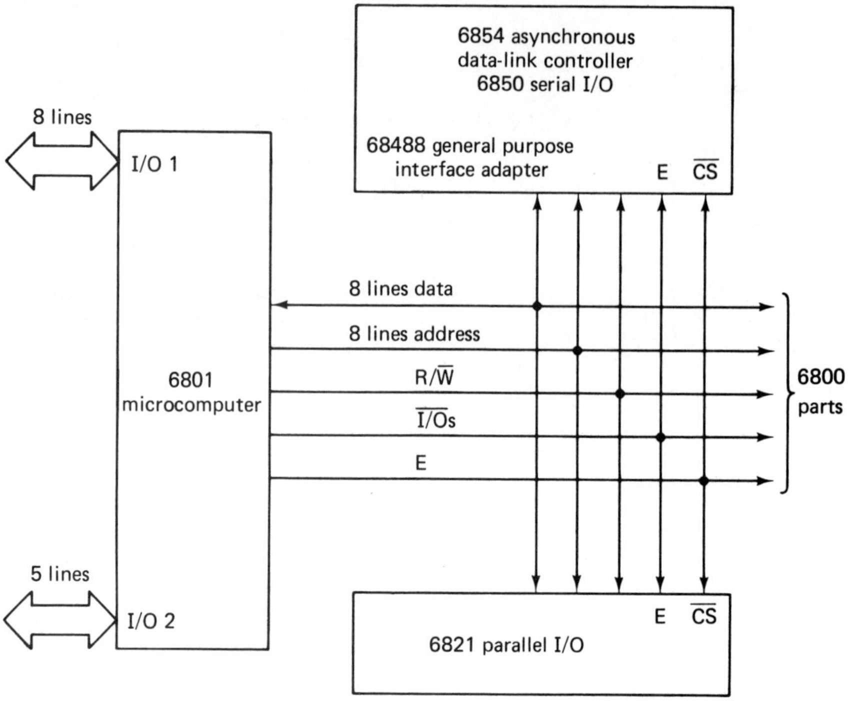

Expanding parallel I/O capacity is simplified by use of I/O ports to expand the chips data bus and address bus to external M6800-oriented peripherals.

Fig. 13–6. Example of expanded parallel I/O capacity. (*Courtesy Motorola Inc.*)

- 128 bytes of RAM (64 retainable)
- 31 parallel I/0 lines
- Internal clock/divided-by-four mask option
- TTL compatible inputs and outputs
- Interrupt capability[3]

The MC6803

It has become rather common practice for semiconductor manufacturers to design and fabricate closely related members of a microprocessor/microcomputer family that differ only slightly from one another. For example, both chips are the same except one is minus ROM.

[3] *MC6801*, p. 18.

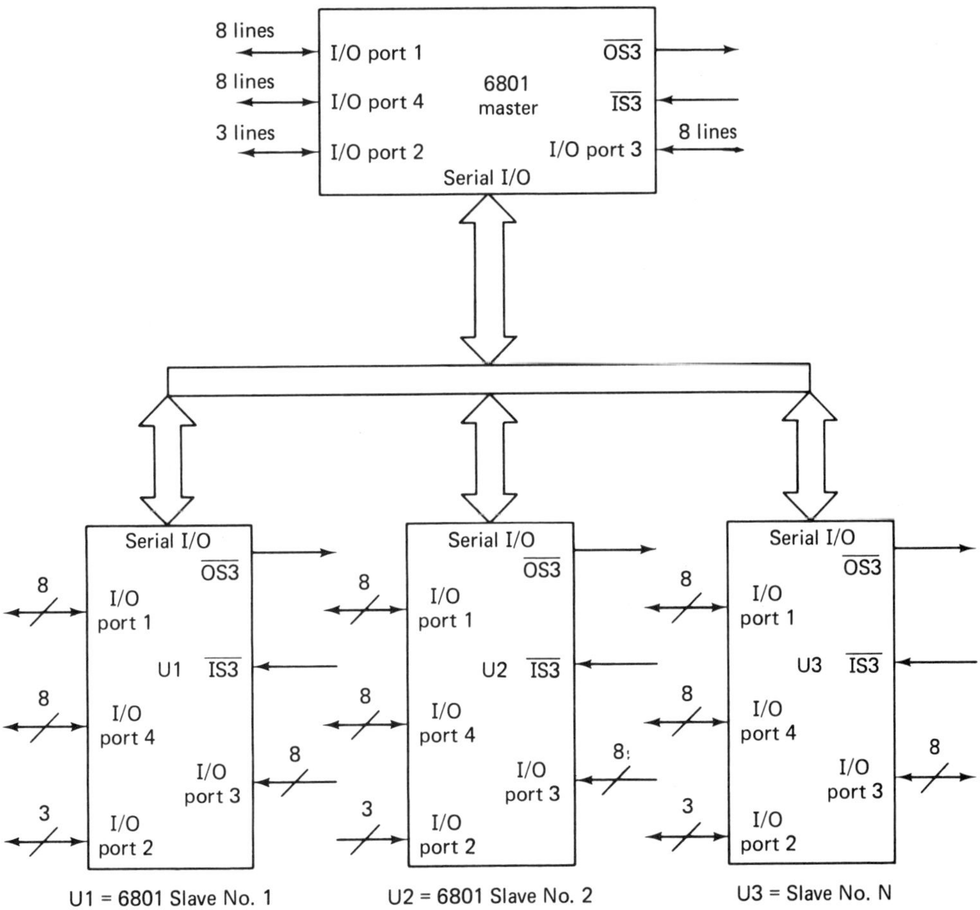

Using the serial I/O port, a number of MC6801s can be arranged in a master-slave multiprocessor setup.

Fig. 13–7. Multiple MC6801 MCUs. (*Courtesy Motorola Inc.*)

The MC6803 single chip microcomputer is a prime example of this. A close look at Fig. 13–8 indicates that the only difference between the MC6803 and the MC6801 is that the MC6803 is ROMless. It still has all the powerful features of the MC6801 but is ideal for applications that do not require the onboard read only memory.

The MC6803 is an 8-bit microcomputer which employs a multiplexed address and data system allowing expandability to 65K words. The MC6803 is object code compatible with the MC6800 instruction set and includes improved execution times of key instructions. There are several new 16-bit and 8-bit instructions, including an 8-by-8 mul-

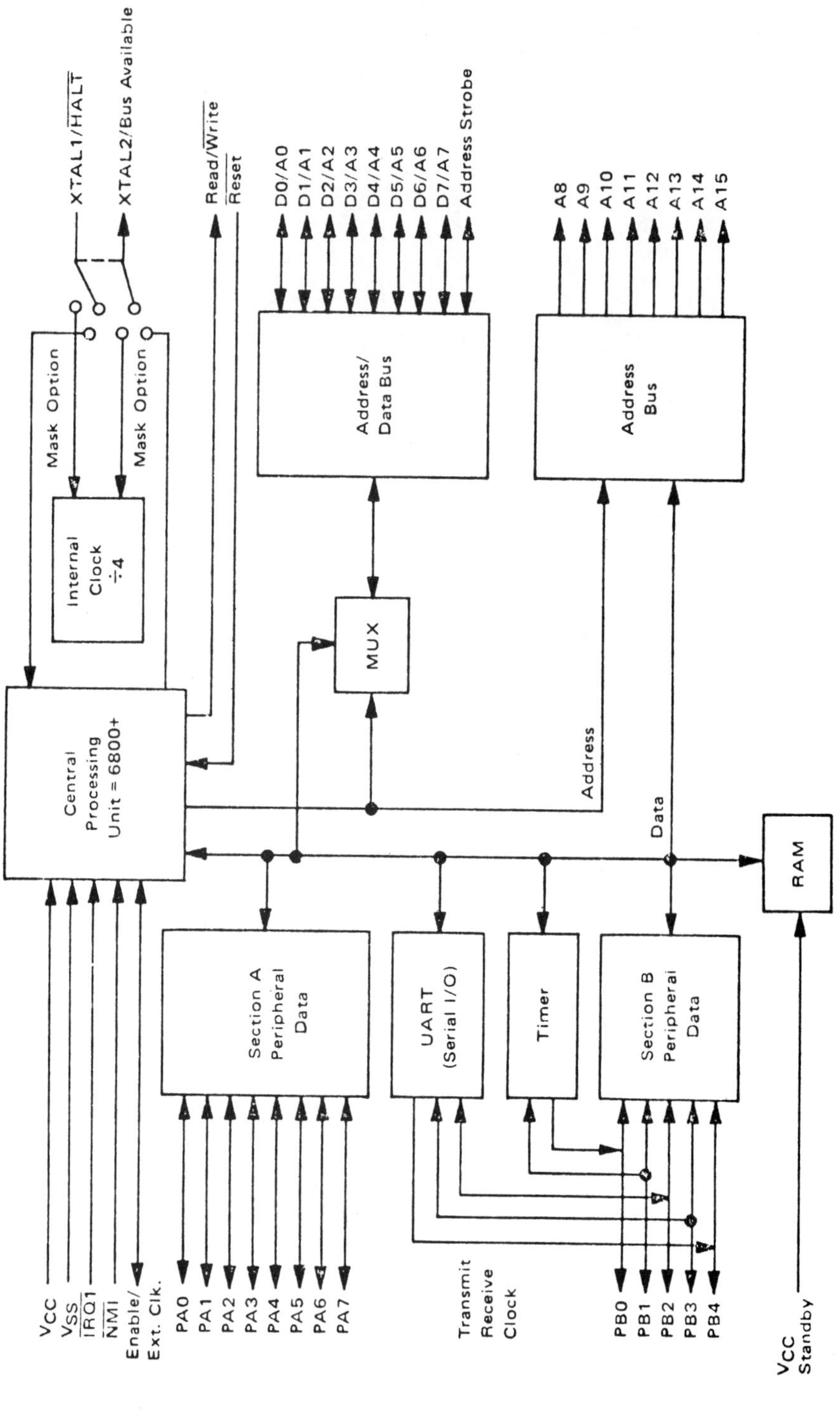

Fig. 13–8. MC6803 block diagram. *(Courtesy Motorola Inc.)*

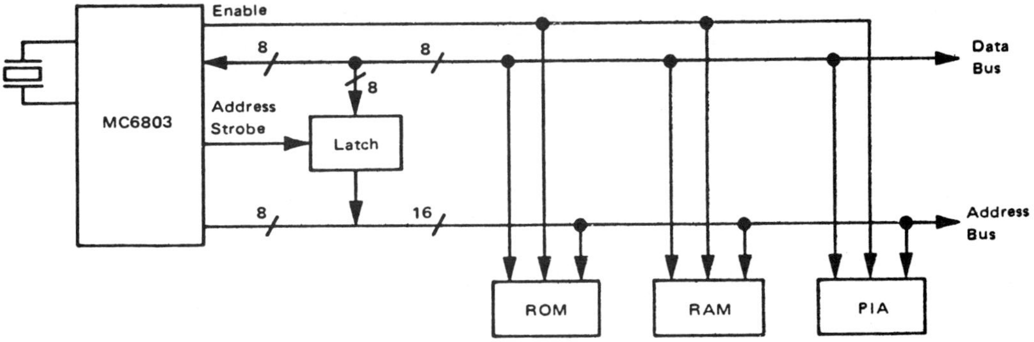

Fig. 13–9. MC6803 system configuration. (*Courtesy Motorola Inc.*)

tiply with 16-bit word result. (These new instructions shown in Table 13–1.)

Pay particular attention to the 8-by-8 multiply feature which is of tremendous value and very helpful to the software design by making multiplication simpler and faster.

Notice the following internal features in Fig. 13–8. First, the MC6803 internal clock requires only the addition of an external crystal for MCU (microcomputer unit) operation. The MC6803 internal clock's divide-by-four circuitry allows for use of the inexpensive 3.58 MHz color burst crystal. The 128 bytes of RAM, UART, parallel I/0 and 3-function 16-bit timer are on-board. Furthermore, the MC6803 is fully TTL compatible and requires only one +5.0 volt power supply.

The MC6803 MCU is fully expandable to 65K words allowing for a system containing several peripherals plus memory. A typical MC6803 system configuration is shown in Fig. 13–9.[4]

When studying Fig. 13–9, note that the ROM, RAM and PIA are the same types used with the MC6800. This component compatibility becomes very important when it becomes necessary to either expand or modify the present microsystem in use.

Summarizing the key features of the MC6803 MCU:

- Expanded MC6800 instruction set
- Full object code compatibility with the MC6800 MPU
- Multiplexed address and data
- Compatible with existing MC6800 peripherals
- 8-by-8 multiply with 16-bit result

[4] *Product Preview MC6803 NP-94* (Phoenix, Arizona: Motorola Inc., 1978), p. 1.

Fig. 13-10. Microphoto of MC6802 chip. (*Courtesy Motorola Inc.*)

- Up to 13 parallel I/0 lines
- 128 bytes onboard RAM
- Onboard RAM retainable with V_{CC}/standby
- UART (serial I/0) onboard
- 16-bit timer onboard
- Internal clock-divide-by-four circuitry
- Full TTL compatibility
- Full interrupt capability[5]

[5] *MC6803*, p. 1.

THE MC6802

Description

The MC6802 shown in Fig. 13–10 is a monolithic 8-bit microprocessor that contains all the registers and accumulators of the MC6800 plus an internal clock oscillator and driver on the same chip. In addition, the MC6802 has 128 bytes of RAM on board located at hexadecimal addresses 0000 to 007F. The first thirty-two bytes of RAM, at hexadecimal addresses 0000 to 001F, may be retained in a low power mode by utilizing V_{CC} standby, thus facilitating memory retention during a power-down situation.

The MC6802 is completely software compatible with the MC6800 as well as the entire family of MC6800 parts. Hence, the MC6802 is expandable to 65K words. Furthermore, it is fully compatible with all the peripherals and features the same MPU architecture and capabilities as the MC6800. It works with the same instruction set as the MC6800, but reduces the component count of a minimum microcomputer system to only two compared with a minimum of four with the earlier MPU (MC6800). A typical example of a 2-component microcomputer system is shown in Fig. 13–11.

The built-in clock operates at a maximum frequency of 2 MHz but the chip designers have added an on-chip divide-by-four circuit to

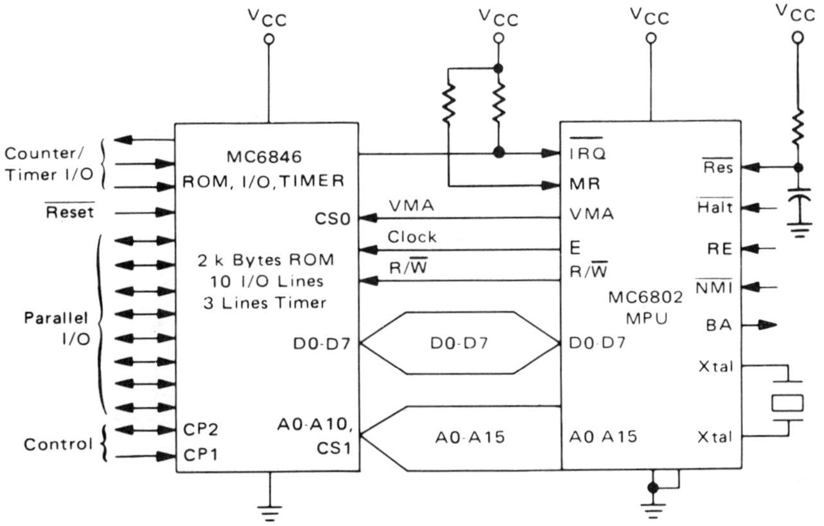

Fig. 13–11. Typical 2-component microcomputer. (*Courtesy Motorola Inc.*)

permit the use of an external 8 MHz crystal in lieu of a far more expensive 2 MHz crystal.

An expanded block diagram of the MC6802 is given in Fig. 13–12. In Fig. 13–12, note the thirty-two bytes in RAM and the RAM control. As mentioned earlier, the first thirty-two bytes of the built-in RAM may be operated in low power mode from an external power source, for example V_{CC} standby, to prevent the loss of information during a power down. Recall from the memory chapter that RAM is

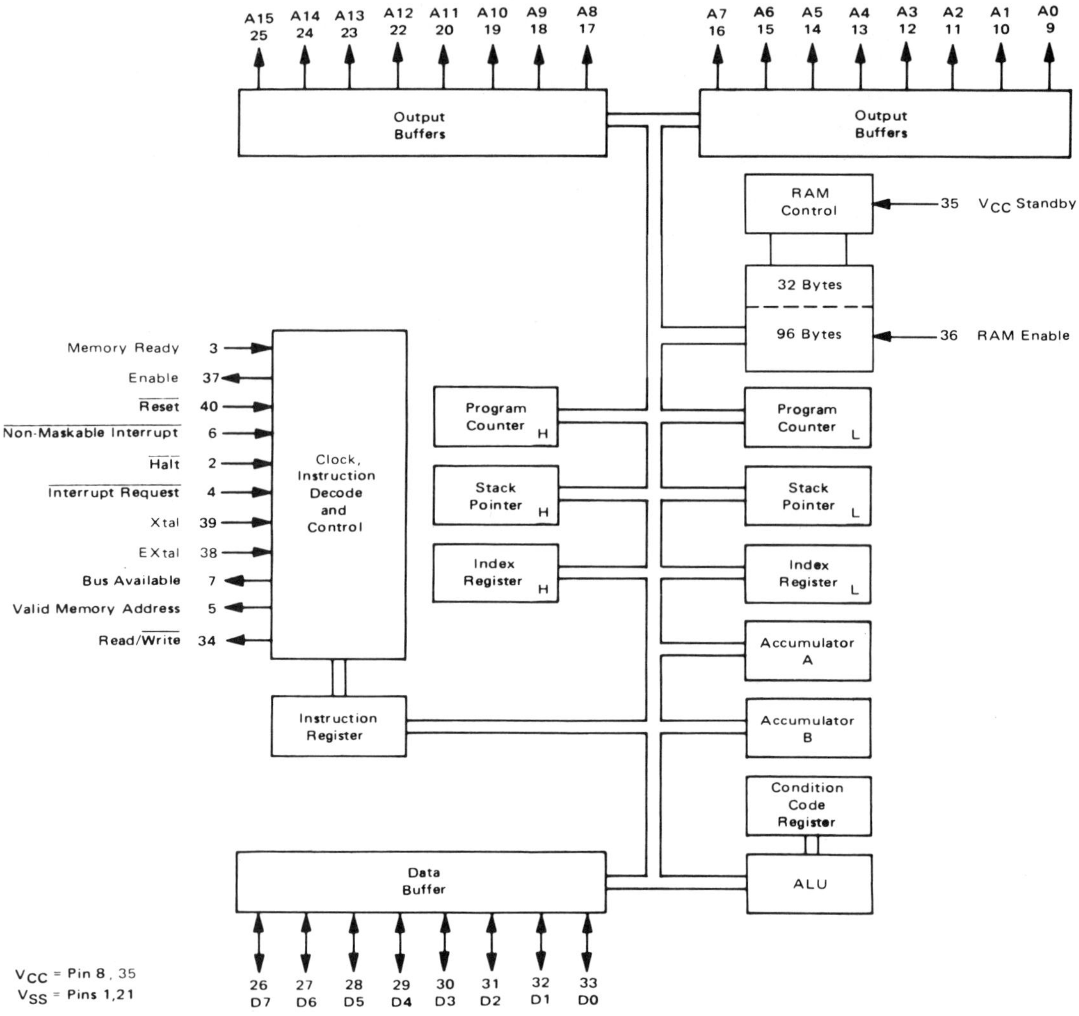

Fig. 13–12. Expanded block diagram of MC6802. (*Courtesy Motorola Inc.*)

volatile and all information is lost once power is removed. This RAM safeguard is an important feature that the microcomputer designer should take into consideration.

Summarizing the major features of the MC6802:

- On-chip clock circuit
- 128-by-8-bit on-chip RAM
- 32 bytes of RAM are retainable
- Software compatible with the MC6800
- Expandable to 65 K words
- Standard TTL compatible input and outputs
- 8-bit word size
- 16-bit memory addressing
- Interrupt capabilities[6]

The MC6808

The MC6808 is a very close relative to the MC6802 microprocessor. It is a monolithic 8-bit microprocessor that contains all the registers and accumulators found in the MC6802 as well as the internal clock oscillator and driver. But, unlike the MC6802, it does not have RAM onboard.

The MC6808 is a cost effective MPU that allows the designer to use it in consumer as well as industrial applications without sacrificing industrial specifications. One of the more popular consumer products implementing the MC6808 is Motorola's single board color computer called the Microchroma 68. This computer provides alphanumerics and graphics that can be displayed directly on a standard unmodified color or black and white television.

Fig. 13–13 is an expanded block diagram of the MC6808 MPU. A careful comparison between Figs. 13–12 and 13–13 indicates that the only difference in MPU architecture between the MC6802 and MC6808 is that the MC6802 is equipped with 128 bytes of on-chip RAM whereas the MC6808 offers no on-chip RAM. Other than this difference, the two MPUs are identical.

The MC6808 is supplied in a 40-pin package as shown in Fig. 13–14. The MPU user should be aware that pin number 36 must be tied to ground (V_{SS}). This applies only to the MC6808 and not to the MC6802.

A typical microprocessor interface basic building block for the MC6808 is illustrated in Fig. 13–15.

[6] *MC6802 Data Sheet DS9818-R1* (Austin, Texas: Motorola Inc., 1981), pp. 1–5.

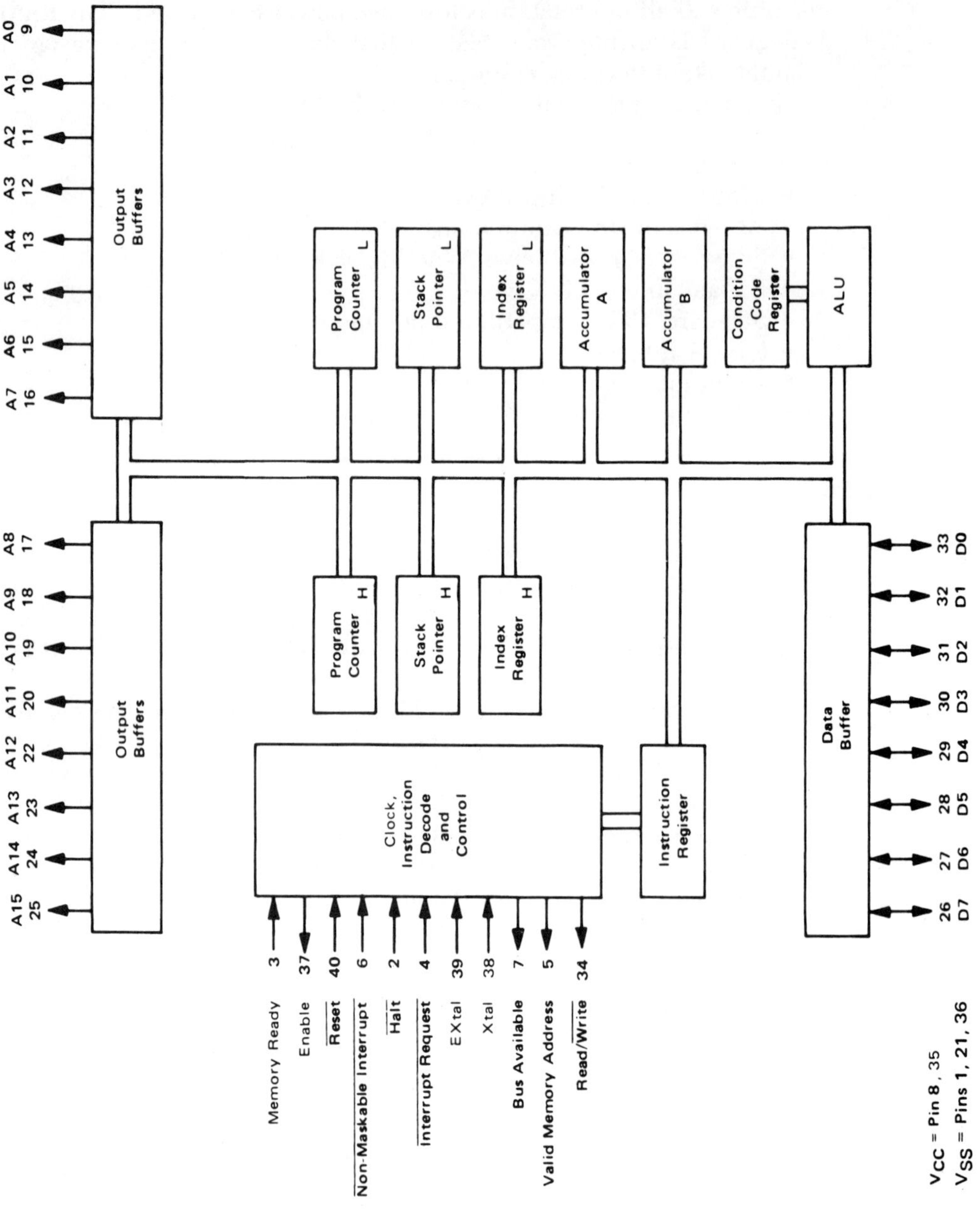

Fig. 13–13. MC6808 expanded block diagram. *(Courtesy Motorola Inc.)*

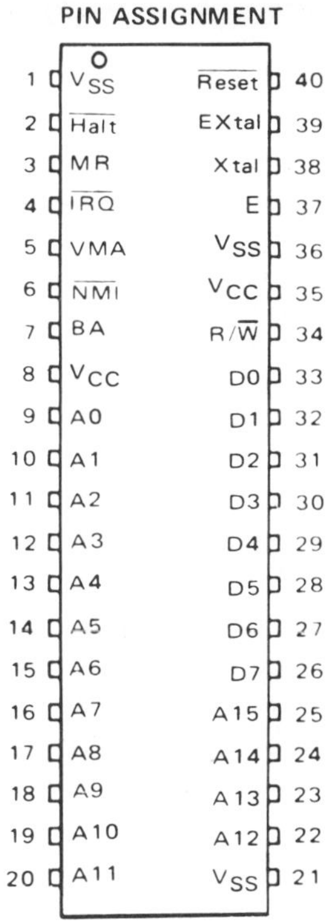

Fig. 13–14. MC6808 40-pin package. (*Courtesy Motorola Inc.*)

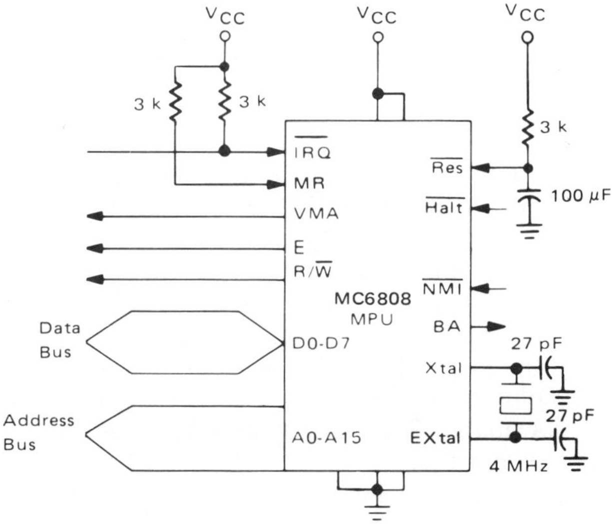

Fig. 13–15. MC6808 typical interface block diagram. (*Courtesy Motorola Inc.*)

The key features of the Motorola MC6808 MPU are:

- On-chip clock circuit
- Software compatible with the MC6800
- Expandable to 65K words
- Standard TTL compatible inputs and outputs
- 8-bit word size
- 16-bit memory addressing
- Interrupt capability

THE M6805 FAMILY

The microcomputers and microprocessors in the Motorola M6805 family are designed to provide an 8-bit processor using familiar architecture plus optimization for controller applications. The architecture includes features not usually found on machines of this class such as on-chip timer/counter with interrupt, complete external interrupt, multiple subroutine nesting, true bit manipulation, and index register and numerous configurations.

Place in the Microspectrum

The M6805 family architecture and instruction set are very similar to the MC6800. Any programmer who has worked with the MC6800 can attain equivalent proficiency with the MC6805 family in a relatively short time. In some respects, the M6805 family is more powerful than the MC6800 (depending on the application) as a result of architecture optimization.

Controller applications. The M6805 family architecture has been optimized for controller applications rather than general purpose data processing operations. Several features contribute to this optimization.

The instruction set is specifically designed for byte-efficient program storage. Byte efficiency permits a maximum amount of program function to be implemented within a finite amount of on-chip ROM. Improved ROM efficiency allows the use of the M6805 family in applications where other processors might not perform the task in the available ROM space. More features can be included in applications where ROM space is more adequate. In some cases where the user wishes to include programs for more than one application, the appropriate program can be selected by the power-up initialization program. The ability to nest subroutines, the addition of true bit test and manipulation instructions, the multi-function instructions and the versatile addressing modes all contribute to the byte efficiency.

Superficial comparisons of the number of bytes per instruction for the M6805 family, when compared to other machines in this class, can be very misleading. A single M6805 family instruction occupying two or three bytes accomplishes as much real programming work as several single byte instructions, or a subroutine, would accomplish in many other processors.

The bit test and bit manipulation instructions permit the program to:

branch on bit set
branch on bit clear
set bit
clear bit

These instructions operate on any individual bit in the first 256 address spaces. As such, the bit manipulations access I/0 pins, RAM bits and ROM bits.

One of the chief measures of the effectiveness of a computer architecture is its ability to access data. The M6805 family has several major memory addressing modes. They include immediate, direct and extended, plus three distinct indexed modes. The programmer is thus given the opportunity to optimize the code to the task. The indexed addressing modes permit conversion tables, jump tables and data tables to be located anywhere in the address space. The use of look-up tables is an important tool in controller type applications.

Efficient addressing methods are coupled with instructions that manipulate memory without disturbing the program registers. Consequently, RAM can be used for the same functions that other processors use general purpose registers (increment, decrement, clear, complement, test).

M6805 family members have a very versatile, efficient and easy to use I/0 structure. All microcomputer I/0 function registers are memory mapped into the first sixteen address spaces, thereby taking advantage of the efficient addressing modes, the many memory reference instructions and the use of RAM (or I/0 registers) as general purpose registers. For example, there are sixty-four unique instructions that permit the programmer to modify an I/0 port. The programmer's problem is not so much how to accomplish a given I/0 task, but rather choosing the most effective method from the many methods available. In addition, as with other M6800 family I/0 devices, most M6805 family I/0 pins are individually programmed as inputs or outputs under software control.

Family options. A fundamental purpose of the M6805 family is to offer a common architecture around which various on-chip I/0 and memory options are configured. Different microcomputer versions are configured by selecting from among the available options.

The family includes both HMOS (MC6805xx) and CMOS (MC146805xx) devices which provide a choice of end product technology. Architectural choices include RAM and ROM size, the number of I/0 pins, output drive capability and other kinds of hardware I/0 options.

Choice of Technologies

The first option to be selected by the system designer is the use of **HMOS** or **CMOS** processor technology. The following sections describe HMOS and CMOS technologies.

HMOS. The **NMOS** (N-channel Metal Oxide on Silicon) technology has been the mainstay of the M6800 family. The current state of the continual shrinking of NMOS is called HMOS (High-density NMOS).

The HMOS inverter circuit shown in Fig. 13–16, illustrates the operating principles of HMOS logic. Two transistors are series connected between ground (V_{SS}) and V_{DD}. One is an active N-channel transistor and the other is a turned-on pull-up transistor. When a logic low is applied to the circuit input, the N-channel transistor is reverse biased and represents a high impedance compared to the pull-up transistor. The pull-up transistor provides the same function as a resistor. A load connected to the circuit output can be driven to a logic high by the supply current through the pull-up transistor.

When a logic high is applied to the circuit input, the N-channel transistor is turned on and becomes a very low resistance to V_{SS} causing the output to go low and a current, equal to V_{DD}-V_{SS}/R, to flow through the pull-up transistor.

Other logic circuits constructed in HMOS technology use series and parallel combinations of the N-channel transistors. However, they all operate on the same principle: the active N-channel transistor is used to sink current from the output and a passive load transistor, behaving like a resistor, is used to source current to the output.

The current flowing through the pull-up load transistor when the N-channel transistor is turned on accounts for most of the power consumed in an HMOS integrated circuit.

The prime consideration in choosing an HMOS M6805 family microcomputer is its lower price. Motorola's highly efficient fabrication process results in a greater yield than other processes. The decreased

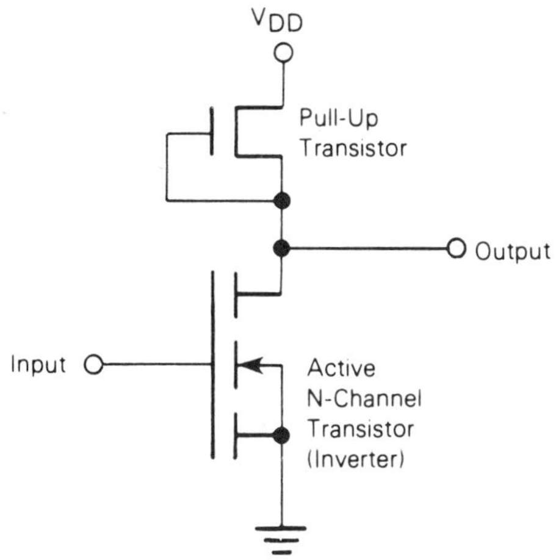

Fig. 13–16. HMOS inverter circuit. (*Courtesy Motorola Inc.*)

production costs ultimately result in lower selling prices. The economics of large scale production also contribute to a low selling price.

The high speed of HMOS, when compared to PMOS or other NMOS processors, produces a very high performance/price ratio.

A low voltage inhibit (LVI) feature may be selected on HMOS versions. The LVI option forces a RESET when the supply voltage drops below a threshold which guarantees correct operation. The CMOS family members offer wide operating voltage and clock speed ranges which preclude establishing an LVI threshold.

CMOS. An emerging microcomputer technology is CMOS which stands for complementary MOS, both P-and N-channel devices.

The CMOS inverter circuit shown in Fig. 13–17 illustrates the operating principles of CMOS logic. In CMOS, the pull-up transistor is replaced with an active P-channel transistor. In this type of circuit, one transistor complements the other: when one is turned on the other is turned off. The characteristics of the P-channel transistor are such that a high signal input turns it off; conversely, a low signal input turns it on.

The active P-channel transistor sources current when the output is high (input low) and presents a high impedance when the output is low (input high). So there is essentially no current flow within the inverter whenever the output is low. The overall result is extremely low power consumption because there is no power loss through the active pull-up transistor.

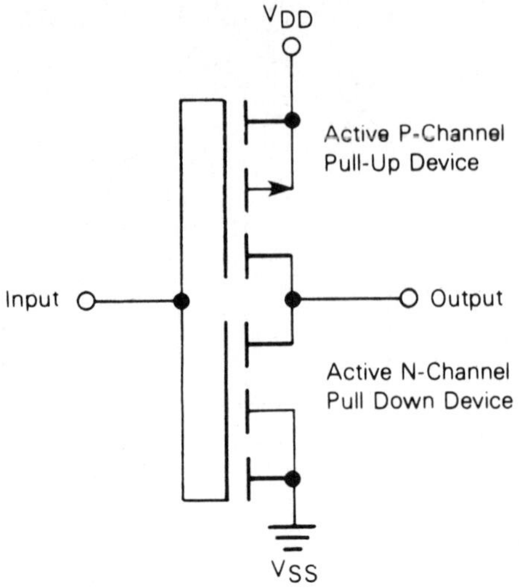

Fig. 13–17. CMOS inverter circuit. (*Courtesy Motorola Inc.*)

The switch point of the CMOS inverter is at approximately 50% of the supply voltage (V_{DD}) instead of being determined by the threshold of the N-channel transistor. Because of this, the operating voltage range of a CMOS device is much wider than that of an HMOS device. This permits a greater choice of supply voltages or allows the use of a less regulated power supply.

The unique properties of CMOS are increasingly attractive. Some applications are simply not feasible with PMOS, NMOS or HMOS microcomputers. Maximum power consumption of CMOS parts ranges from 1/15 to 1/200 of that of an equivalent HMOS part. Low power consumption is important in several classes of applications.

1. *Portable equipment:* Hand-held and other portable units operate from self-contained batteries. Battery drain is frequently important in such applications, making CMOS microcomputers desirable.

2. *Battery back-up:* CMOS is appropriate in ac powered applications when some or all system functions must continue during a power outage. A small, rechargeable battery keeps a CMOS MCU operable.

3. *Storage batteries:* Automotive and telephone equipment operate from large batteries. Automobile battery drain must be low when the engine is not running. Telephones must operate independent of ac power.

4. *Heat dissipation:* Packaging constraints sometimes preclude dissipating electronics generated heat; or, the heat is costly to dissipate.

5. *Power costs:* The cost of electricity to power the equipment becomes a significant factor in calculating the total life cycle cost of equipment which operates continuously.

The CMOS technology inherently operates over a wide range of supply voltages making it appropriate where the supply voltage fluctuates such as in battery powered equipment; or, if line power is available, a lower cost, loosely regulated supply may be used.

An additional advantage of CMOS is that its circuitry is fully static. CMOS microcomputers can be operated at any clock rate less than the guaranteed maximum thus conserving power since power consumption increases with higher clock frequencies. Static operation is also advantageous during product development.

Table 13–2 lists the common trade-offs between the MC6805 in CMOS and HMOS (NMOS). Remember that HMOS is the "shrinking" of NMOS.

Hardware

Functional blocks. Figure 13–18 details the hardware functional blocks common to all M6805 family versions.

Table 13–2 NMOS vs. CMOS Trade-Offs

THE NMOS VS CMOS TRADE-OFFS

	MC6805 IN NMOS	MC146805 IN CMOS
PRICE	LOWER	LOW
POWER DISSIPATION	200–300 mW	.5–20 mW
STANDBY POWER	NO STANDBY MODE	.15–15 mW
VOLTAGE RANGE	4.75–5.75 Vdc	3.0–8.0 Vdc
CYCLE RANGE	100 KHz–1 MHz	0 Hz–1 MHz
CYCLES/INST	5.36, Avg	4.02, Avg
EXPANSION BUS	NOT PLANNED	YES
NOISE IMMUNITY	GOOD	BETTER

(Courtesy Motorola Inc.)

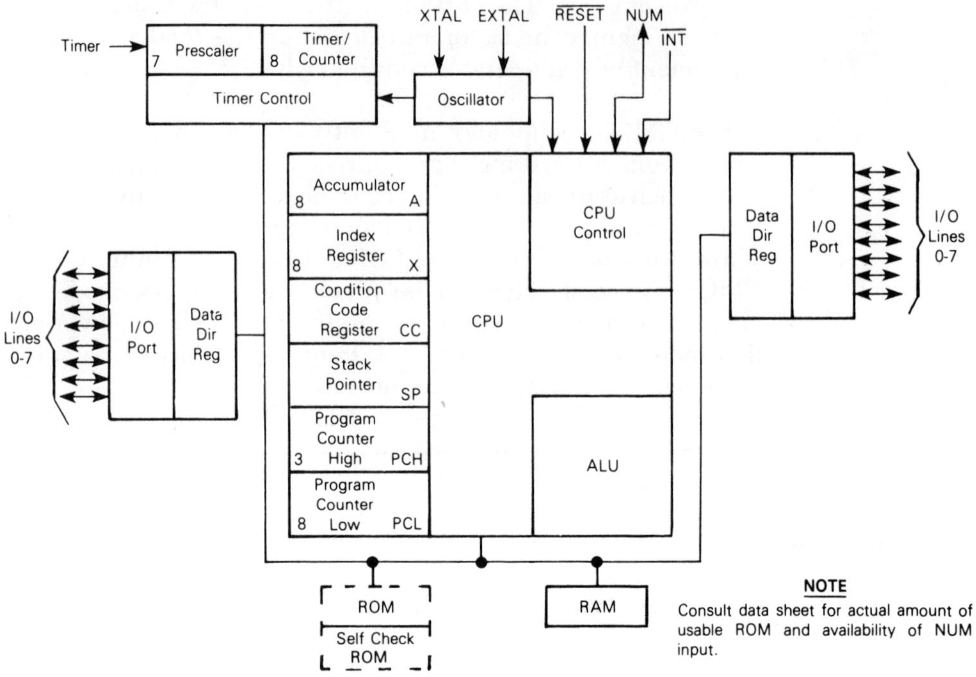

Fig. 13–18. MC6805 family basic microcomputer block diagram. (*Courtesy Motorola Inc.*)

The central processor unit (CPU) contains the 8-bit arithmetic logic unit, accumulator, program counter, index register, stack pointer, condition code register, instruction decoder and timing and control logic. These elements resemble the M6800 family reflecting the M6805 family heritage.

The on-chip RAM permits the microcomputer versions to operate without external memory. The addressing modes and register-like memory operations use this RAM to the fullest extent possible.

Parallel I/0 capability, with each pin programmable as an input or as an output, is built into every unit.

The external interrupt input and the capability for multiple nesting of subroutines and interrupts are features usually found on much more powerful architectures. They permit an M6805 family MCU to be used in projects usually considered too complex for microcomputers.

An on-chip time/counter greatly simplifies software development and extends the microcomputer capability. This 8-bit counter and its prescaler can be programmed for innumerable functions:

1. Generating an interrupt at software selected intervals
2. An event counter generating an interrupt after some software selected number of external events
3. Timekeeping
4. Measuring and generating pulses
5. Counting external events
6. "Waking up" the processor from the power-saving WAIT mode (CMOS versions).

The external interrupt and timer/counter interrupt are vectored to different service routine addresses. This greatly simplifies interrupt programming. It also speeds execution of interrupt routines by eliminating software interrupt polling for determining the source of the interrupt.

The first sixteen address spaces are reserved for memory mapped I/0 registers. The programmer can take full advantage of the versatile addressing modes and register-like RAM operations.

Family options. In addition to the common hardware described previously, users can make selections from among devices having a combination of hardware options.

1. *Choice of technology:* HMOS units are generally selected unless the application specifically requires one of the unique characteristics of CMOS.

2. *ROM:* User ROM sizes range from none (for the microprocessor) to 2K and larger. When self-check ROM is part of the device, the ROM area used in the self-check operation is not included in published ROM sizes. The user gets the entire ROM space for his program. A small portion of the ROM is located in page zero (the direct page) to facilitate more efficient access to lookup tables using all available addressing modes. This ROM can be used for program storage as well as lookup tables.

3. *RAM:* The initial M6805 family versions contain either 64 or 112 bytes of on-chip RAM which is located in page zero. Future versions will accommodate additional or differing amounts of RAM.

4. *I/0 ports:* Package size options permit as many as four, full 8-bit bidirectional I/0 ports. Each pin is defined under software control as an input or output by loading a data direction register.

5. *Electrical options:* TTL compatibility, CMOS compatibility and high-current outputs designed to drive darlington transistors and LEDs.

6. *Complex I/O functions:* Available in selected versions. For example, one family member has an on-chip, high-speed, successive approximation type, 8-bit analog-to-digital converter.

7. *Expandable CMOS microprocessor version:* With a multiplexed address-then-data bus, it is used with related peripheral and memory ICs to implement larger systems. It is also used for prototyping ROM-based microcomputers.

8. *Zero-crossing detection circuitry:* Internally connected to the external interrupt-input pin of some versions, it can be interfaced with a power line or other source of periodic input for timekeeping functions. It can also be used by the program to synchronize outputs to the zero-crossing of the power line voltage.[7]

Programming Model

The M6805 family processor contains five registers. The accumulator (A) and index register (X) are 8-bit registers while the condition code (CC) register contains five bits. The program counter (PC) and stack pointer (S) vary in length depending upon the version of the family. The PC of initial version is 11, 12, or 13 bits long depending on memory size. Regarding accessing memory, S is the same length as PC. However, the high order bits are fixed. The initial versions have either five or six register bits in S, depending upon the size of on-chip RAM.

The M6805 family register architecture is shown in Fig. 13–19.

Accumulator (A). The A register is a general purpose accumulator used by the program for arithmetic calculations and data manipulations.

Index register (X). The X register is used during the indexed modes of addressing and also functions as an auxiliary accumulator. In indexed instructions, the X register provides an 8-bit value that is added to an optional instruction-provided value to create an effective address. It is also used for limited calculations and data manipulation. The full set of read/modify/write instructions operate on both the X register and the accumulator. Code sequences that do not employ the index register for indexed addressing can use X as a temporary storage cell or accumulator.

Program counter (PC). The program counter points to the next instruction to be executed by the processor. The family architecture supports a PC of up to sixteen bits.

[7] *M6805, M146805 Family Microcomputer/Microprocessor Users Manual* (Austin, Texas: Motorola Inc., 1980), pp. 1-1–1-6, B-1–B-2.

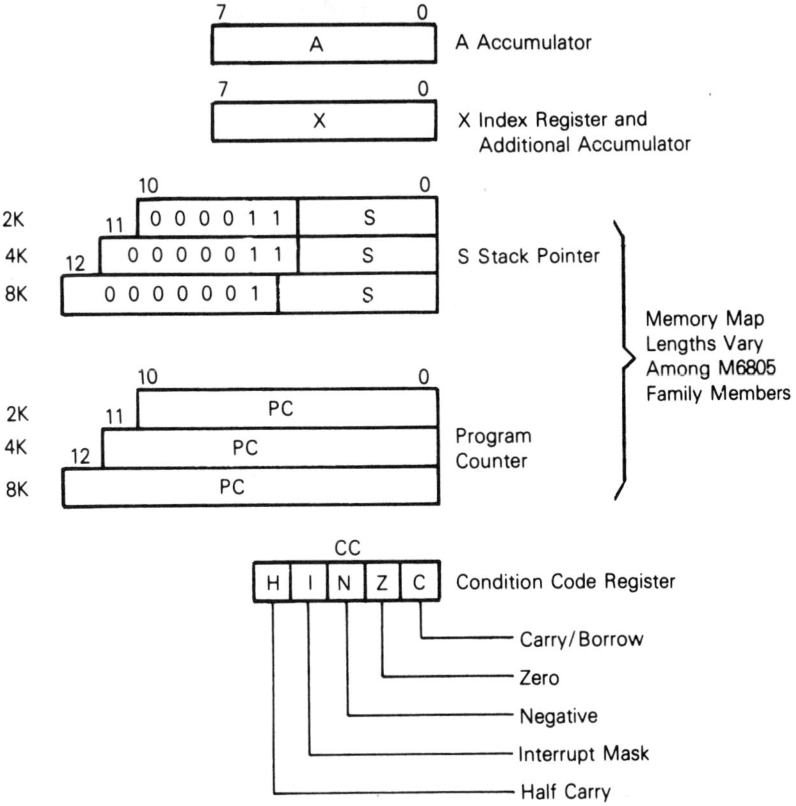

Fig. 13–19. MC6805 family register architecture. (*Courtesy Motorola Inc.*)

Stack pointer (SP). The stack pointer contains the address of the top of a push-down/pull-up stack located in RAM. It is used under hardware control, to automatically store return addresses (two bytes) on subroutine calls as well as all registers (five bytes) during interrupts. The saved registers may be interleaved on the stack permitting nesting of subroutines and interrupts, subroutine interrupts, interrupts calling subroutines.

Since the M6805 family is a family of parts, the actual size of the stack pointer varies with RAM size. But from the programmer's perspective, the stack pointers all appear similar on different versions. Both the hardware $\overline{\text{RESET}}$ pin and the reset stack pointer (RSP) instruction reset the stack pointer to its maximum value. The stack pointer always points to the next free location on the stack. Each "push" decrements while each "pull" increments it. ("Push" and "pull" are not available as user instructions in the M6805 family.)

The allowed stack length is typically traded off against needed data RAM space when handling nested subroutine calls and interrupts.

Condition code register (CC). This register contains various flag bits that reflect the current state of the processor. Most CC bits reflect the results of the last executed data reference instruction. These CC bits are:

1. *Half Carry* (H) is set when a carry occurs between bits 3 and 4 during an ADD or ADC instruction. The half carry flag can be used in BCD addition subroutines.
2. *Interrupt Mask* (I) disables or masks the external interrupt and timer interrupt when it is set. Clearing the I-bit allows interrupts to be enabled. If an interrupt occurs while the I-bit is set, the interrupt is latched and causes the interrupt vector to be fetched when the I-bit is next cleared.
3. *Negative Bit* (N) is set when bit 7 of the result of the last data manipulation, arithmetic or logical operation is set. This indicates that the result of the operation was negative.
4. *Zero Bit* (Z) is set if the result of the last data manipulation, arithmetic or logical operation was zero.
5. *Carry Bit* (C) is set if a carry or borrow out of the 8-bit ALU occurred during the last arithmetic operation. The C-bit is also set during shift, rotate and bit test instructions.[8]

The MC6805R2 HMOS Microcomputer

As noted earlier, there are a number of members in the M6805 microcomputer/microprocessor family. This section provides a close, detailed look at one of its most powerful members—the MC6805R2.

Features. The MC6805R2 microcomputer unit (MCU) is an 8-bit machine that contains a CPU, on-chip clock, ROM, RAM, I/0, 4-channel 8-bit A/D and timer. Its hardware and software highlights are given in Table 13–3.

The footprint of the MC6805R2 MCU appears in Fig. 13–20.

In Fig. 13–18, the M6805 family basic microcomputer block diagram indicates the hardware that is common to all M6805 family members. Figure 13–21 is the block diagram for the MC6805R2 HMOS MCU.

[8] *M6805 Family Users Manual,* pp. 3-1–3-4.

Table 13–3 MC6805R2 Hardware/Software Features

HARDWARE FEATURES	SOFTWARE FEATURES
8-Bit Architecture	Similar to M6800
64 Bytes of RAM	Byte Efficient Instruction Set
Memory Mapped I/O	Easy to Program
2048 Bytes of User ROM	True Bit Manipulation
Internal 8-Bit Timer with 7-Bit Prescaler	Bit Test and Branch Instructions
4 Vectored Interrupts; Timer, Software and Two External	Versatile Interrupt Handling
24 TTL/CMOS Compatible I/O Lines with 8 of these LED Compatible	Versatile Index Register
8 Input Lines	Powerful Indexed Addressing for Tables
A/D Converter	Full Set of Conditional Branches
8-Bit Conversion	Memory Usable as Registers/Flags
4 Multiplexed Analog Inputs	Single Instruction Memory Examine/Change
± 1/2 LSB Quantizing Error	10 Powerful Addressing Modes
± 1/2 LSB All Other Errors	All Addressing Modes Apply to ROM, RAM, and I/O
± 1 LSB Total Error (max)	User Callable Self-Check Subroutines
Ratiometric Conversion	
Zero-Crossing Detection	
On-Chip Clock Generator	
Self-Check Mode	
Master Reset	
Low Voltage Inhibit	
Complete Development System Support on EXORciser	
5 Vdc Single Supply	

(Courtesy Motorola Inc.)

One very obvious enhancement of the MC6805R2 in Fig. 13–21 is the A/D (analog-to-digital converter) section.

Memory map. The MCU is capable of addressing 4096 bytes of memory and I/0 registers with its program counter. It has implemented 2316 of these bytes consisting of: 2048 user ROM bytes, 192 self test ROM bytes, 64 user RAM bytes and 12 I/0 bytes. See Fig. 13–22 for the memory map.

The user ROM has been split into three areas. The first area is memory locations $080 to $0FF. The user can access these ROM locations utilizing the direct addressing mode. The main user ROM area is from $7C0 to $F37. The last eight ROM memory locations at the top of memory are for the interrupt vectors.

The MCU reserves the first sixteen memory locations for I/0 features. Twelve of them have been implemented. These locations are

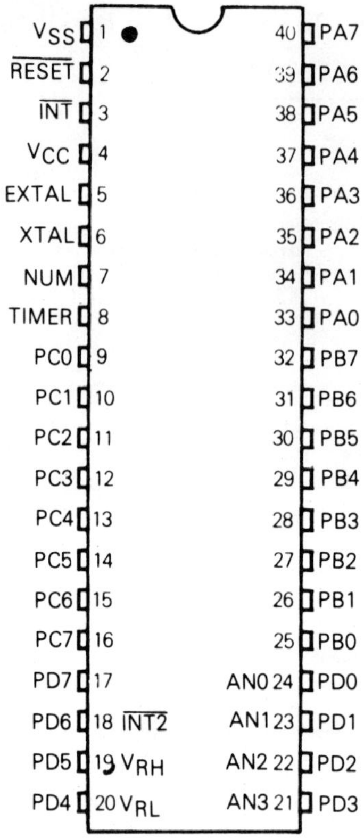

Fig. 13–20. MC6805R2 MCU footprint. (*Courtesy Motorola Inc.*)

used for ports, the port DDRs, the timer, the $\overline{\text{INT2}}$ miscellaneous register and the A/D. Refer to Table 13–4 for the register configuration of these locations.

Sixty-four bytes of user RAM are provided. The last thirty-one bytes of user RAM \$061 to \$07F are shared with the stack area. The stack area must be used with care if data is stored there.[9]

Enhanced Microcomputer Test Capability

As the complexity of VLSI (very large scale integration) rises, increasingly complex and costly test hardware is required. This is especially true of ROM-based microcomputers. Implementation of the user's program in ROM essentially creates a custom part for every cus-

[9] *MC6805R2 Advance Information ADI-845* (Austin, Texas: Motorola Inc., 1980), pp. 1–14.

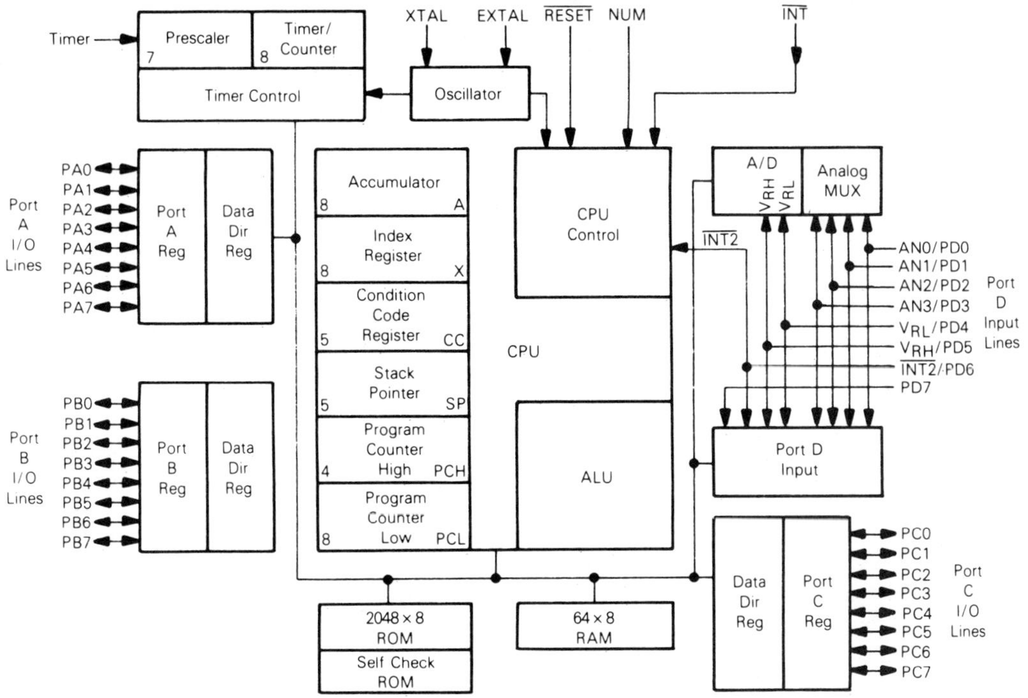

Fig. 13–21. MC6805R2 HMOS microcomputer block diagram. (*Courtesy Motorola Inc.*)

tomer program. Incoming inspection testing is an added cost for the user.

M6805 family microcomputers have a sophisticated on-chip self-check capability. A ROM area separate from the user's ROM contains a program designed to exercise the majority of on-chip hardware. The self-check ROM is accessed only when the microcomputer is placed in the self-check mode.

The self-check program is designed to exercise the on-chip circuitry to ensure that it is operable. The test program includes software for checking the RAM, ROM, I/0 ports, external interrupt and the timer. Although it cannot check execution of every possible instruction, it is designed to exercise the vast majority of on-chip logic.

The self-check program requires user assembly of only a socket and a few inexpensive components. The assembled tester is contrasted to the most advanced and expensive integrated circuit testers used by Motorola for final factory test. Figure 13–23 is a schematic diagram of the typical connections required to test the MC6805R2 MCU.

Table 13–4 MC6805R2 MCU Register Configuration.

PORT DATA DIRECTION REGISTER (DDR)

7							0

(1) Write Only; reads as all 1's
(2) 1 = Output, 0 = Input
(3) Port A ADDR = $004
Port B ADDR = $005
Port C ADDR = $006
Port D ADDR = None; Port D is Input only

PORT DATA REGISTER

7							0

Port A ADDR = $000
Port B ADDR = $001
Port C ADDR = $002
Port D ADDR = $003

TIMER CONTROL/STATUS REGISTER (TCSR)

$009	7	6			3			0
			1	1		1	1	1

Bit 7 – Timer Interrupt Request Status Bit Set when TDR goes to zero; must be cleared by software
Bit 6 – Timer Interrupt Mask Bit; 1 = timer masked (disabled)
Bit 3 – Always reads as a 0; clears prescaler when written to a logic 1
Bits 5, 4, 2, 1, 0 read 1's – unused bits

TIMER DATA REGISTER (TDR)

$008	7							0
	MSB							LSB

MISCELLANEOUS REGISTER (MR)

$00A	7	6						0
			1	1	1	1	1	1

Bit 7 – INT2 Interrupt Request Bit Set when falling edge detected on INT2 pin must be cleared by software
Bit 6 – INT2 Interrupt Mask Bit 1 = INT2 Interrupt masked (disabled)
Bit 5 – 0 Read as 1's – unused bits

A/D CONTROL/STATUS REGISTER (ACSR)

$00E	7					2	1	0
		1	1	1	1			

Bit 7 – Conversion complete status FLAG Set when conversion is complete; Cleared ONLY ON A WRITE TO ACSR READABLE, NOT WRITABLE
Bits 2, 1, 0 – A/D input Mux Selection (see Table 2)
Bits 6, 5, 4, 3 read as 1's – unused bits

A/D RESULT REGISTER (ARR)

$00F	7							0
	MSB							LSB

(Courtesy Motorola Inc.)

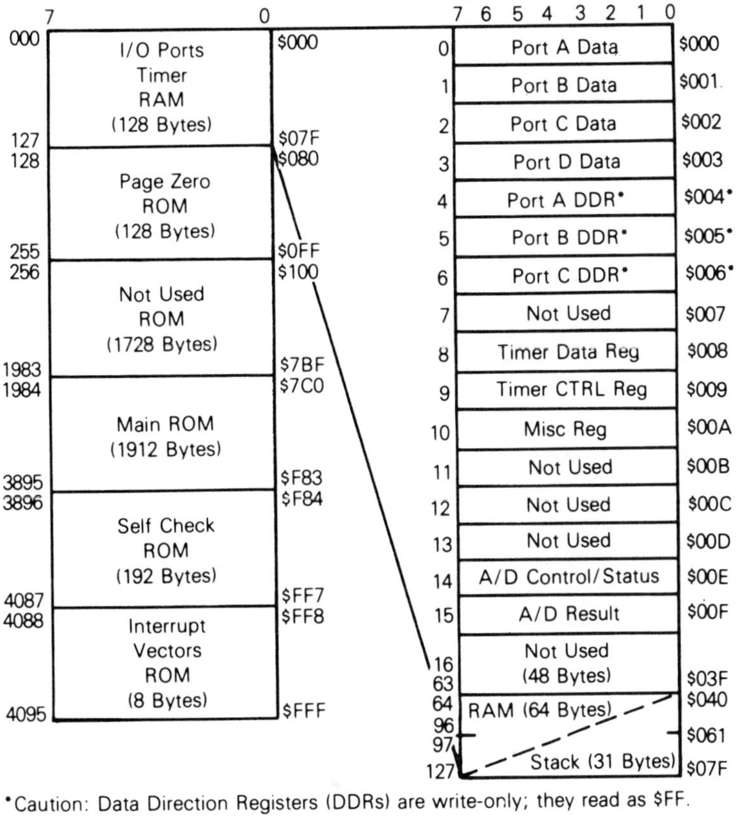

Fig. 13–22. MC6805R2 MCU memory map. (*Courtesy Motorola Inc.*)

During the test, all four LED indicators will flash. If the LED indicators do not flash, the unit is defective. A complete list of LED definitions appears in Table 13–5. Other members of the family require similar connections to match their specific I/0 configurations.

The MC146805E2 CMOS Microprocessor

The MC146805E2 MPU is designed as a general purpose CMOS microprocessor for applications requiring a multi-chip CMOS system. It also serves as a development tool for ROM based microcomputer versions. It is supported by a line of CMOS memories, peripherals and high speed logic to simplify system design.

The 40-pin microprocessor contains the processor, 112 bytes of RAM, an expansion bus and sixteen I/0 lines. The eight low order ad-

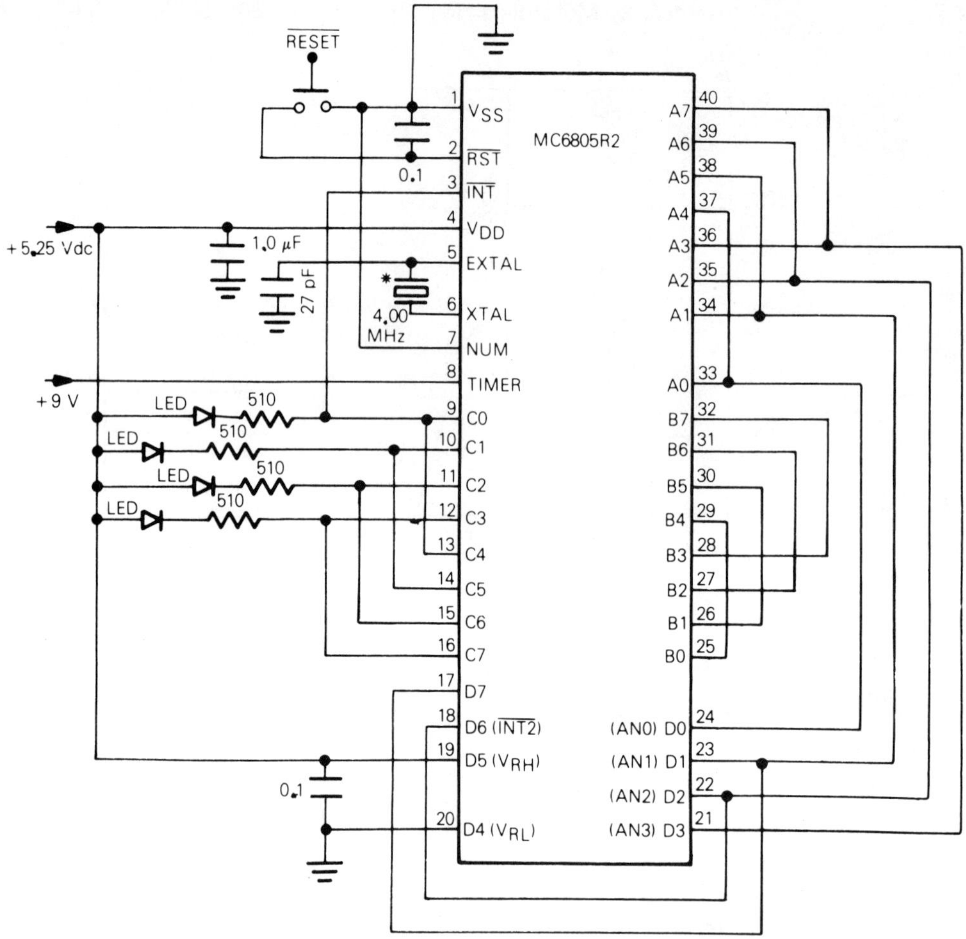

*Use jumper if RC mask option is selected. This connection depends on clock oscillator mask option.

Fig. 13–23. Example of self-check schematic diagram for MC6805R2. (*Courtesy Motorola Inc.*)

Table 13–5 MC6805R2 Self Test LED Definitions

C0	C1	C2	C3	Remarks [1:LED ON; 0:LED OFF]
1	0	1	0	Bad I/O
0	0	1	0	Bad Timer
1	1	0	0	Bad RAM
0	1	0	0	Bad ROM
1	0	0	0	Bad A/D
0	0	0	0	Bad Interrupts or Request Flag
All Flashing				Good Part

Anything else bad Part, Bad Port 3, Bad ISP, etc.

(*Courtesy Motorola Inc.*)

Table 13–6 MC146805E2 CMOS Microprocessor Hardware/Software Features

HARDWARE FEATURES	SOFTWARE FEATURES
Full Speed Operating Power of 20 mW	Similar to the MC6800
Standby Power Less than 1 mW	Efficient Use of Program Space
8-Bit Architecture	Versatile Interrupt Handling
112 Bytes of On-Chip RAM	True Bit Manipulation
16 Bidirectional I/O Lines	Addressing Modes With Indexed Addressing for Tables
Internal 8-Bit Timer with Software Programmable 7-Bit Prescaler	Efficient Instruction Set
External Timer Input	Memory Mapped I/O
Full External and Timer Interrupts	Two Power Saving Standby Modes
Multiplexed Address/Data Bus	
Master Reset and Power-On Reset	
Multiplexed Address/Data Bus	
Master Reset and Power-On Reset	
Capable of Addressing Up to 8k Bytes of External Memory	
Single 3 to 6 Volt Supply, Higher Voltage Version Soon	
On-Chip Oscillator	
40-Pin Dual-In-Line Package	
Chip Carrier Also Available	

(Courtesy Motorola Inc.)

dress bits and eight data bits are time multiplexed on the bus pins. Multiplexing of the bus is controlled by three bus control lines. Five additional nonmultiplexed address lines permit a total address of 8K bytes. Bank switching techniques could be used to extend this address space as required. System interface problems are reduced by including bus driver outputs on all bus pins.[10]

A summary of the MC146805E2 CMOS microprocessor hardware and software features are given in Table 13–6.

The MC68705P3 EPROM Microcomputer

The MC68705P3 MCU is an EPROM member of the M6805 family. The user programmable EPROM replaces the usual factory programmed ROM, thereby reducing the development costs and turn around time for prototype evaluation. This 8-bit microcomputer contains a CPU, on-chip clock, EPROM, bootstrap ROM, RAM, I/0 and a

[10] *M6805 Family Users Manual*, pp. 1-7–1-8.

Table 13–7 MC6805/MC146805 Instruction Set Op Code Map.

	Bit Manipulation		Branch	Read/Modify/Write					Control		Register/Memory						
	BTB	BSC	REL	DIR	INH(A)	INH(X)	IX1	IX	INH	INH	IMM	DIR	EXT	IX2	IX1	IX	
Low \ Hi	0 0000	1 0001	2 0010	3 0011	4 0100	5 0101	6 0110	7 0111	8 1000	9 1001	A 1010	B 1011	C 1100	D 1101	E 1110	F 1111	Hi \ Low
0 0000	10 5 BRSET0 3 BTB	7 5 BSET0 2 BSC	4 3 BRA 2 REL	6 5 NEG 2 DIR	4 3 NEGA 1 INH	4 3 NEGX 1 INH	7 6 NEG 2 IX1	6 5 NEG 1 IX	9 9 RTI 1 INH		2 2 SUB 2 IMM	4 3 SUB 2 DIR	5 4 SUB 3 EXT	6 5 SUB 3 IX2	5 4 SUB 2 IX1	4 3 SUB 1 IX	0 0000
1 0001	10 5 BRCLR0 3 BTB	7 5 BCLR0 2 BSC	4 3 BRN 2 REL						6 6 RTS 1 INH		2 2 CMP 2 IMM	4 3 CMP 2 DIR	5 4 CMP 3 EXT	6 5 CMP 3 IX2	5 4 CMP 2 IX1	4 3 CMP 1 IX	1 0001
2 0010	10 5 BRSET1 3 BTB	7 5 BSET1 2 BSC	4 3 BHI 2 REL								2 2 SBC 2 IMM	4 3 SBC 2 DIR	5 4 SBC 3 EXT	6 5 SBC 3 IX2	5 4 SBC 2 IX1	4 3 SBC 1 IX	2 0010
3 0011	10 5 BRCLR1 3 BTB	7 5 BCLR1 2 BSC	4 3 BLS 2 REL	6 5 COM 2 DIR	4 3 COMA 1 INH	4 3 COMX 1 INH	7 6 COM 2 IX1	6 5 COM 1 IX	11 10 SWI 1 INH		2 2 CPX 2 IMM	4 3 CPX 2 DIR	5 4 CPX 3 EXT	6 5 CPX 3 IX2	5 4 CPX 2 IX1	4 3 CPX 1 IX	3 0011
4 0100	10 5 BRSET2 3 BTB	7 5 BSET2 2 BSC	4 3 BCC 2 REL	6 5 LSR 2 DIR	4 3 LSRA 1 INH	4 3 LSRX 1 INH	7 6 LSR 2 IX1	6 5 LSR 1 IX			2 2 AND 2 IMM	4 3 AND 2 DIR	5 4 AND 3 EXT	6 5 AND 3 IX2	5 4 AND 2 IX1	4 3 AND 1 IX	4 0100
5 0101	10 5 BRCLR2 3 BTB	7 5 BCLR2 2 BSC	4 3 BCS 2 REL								2 2 BIT 2 IMM	4 3 BIT 2 DIR	5 4 BIT 3 EXT	6 5 BIT 3 IX2	5 4 BIT 2 IX1	4 3 BIT 1 IX	5 0101
6 0110	10 5 BRSET3 3 BTB	7 5 BSET3 2 BSC	4 3 BNE 2 REL	6 5 ROR 2 DIR	4 3 RORA 1 INH	4 3 RORX 1 INH	7 6 ROR 2 IX1	6 5 ROR 1 IX			2 2 LDA 2 IMM	4 3 LDA 2 DIR	5 4 LDA 3 EXT	6 5 LDA 3 IX2	5 4 LDA 2 IX1	4 3 LDA 1 IX	6 0110
7 0111	10 5 BRCLR3 3 BTB	7 5 BCLR3 2 BSC	4 3 BEQ 2 REL	6 5 ASR 2 DIR	4 3 ASRA 1 INH	4 3 ASRX 1 INH	7 6 ASR 2 IX1	6 5 ASR 1 IX		2 2 TAX 1 INH		5 4 STA 2 DIR	6 5 STA 3 EXT	7 6 STA 3 IX2	6 5 STA 2 IX1	5 4 STA 1 IX	7 0111
8 1000	10 5 BRSET4 3 BTB	7 5 BSET4 2 BSC	4 3 BHCC 2 REL	6 5 LSL 2 DIR	4 3 LSLA 1 INH	4 3 LSLX 1 INH	7 6 LSL 2 IX1	6 5 LSL 1 IX		2 2 CLC 1 INH	2 2 EOR 2 IMM	4 3 EOR 2 DIR	5 4 EOR 3 EXT	6 5 EOR 3 IX2	5 4 EOR 2 IX1	4 3 EOR 1 IX	8 1000
9 1001	10 5 BRCLR4 3 BTB	7 5 BCLR4 2 BSC	4 3 BHCS 2 REL	6 5 ROL 2 DIR	4 3 ROLA 1 INH	4 3 ROLX 1 INH	7 6 ROL 2 IX1	6 5 ROL 1 IX		2 2 SEC 1 INH	2 2 ADC 2 IMM	4 3 ADC 2 DIR	5 4 ADC 3 EXT	6 5 ADC 3 IX2	5 4 ADC 2 IX1	4 3 ADC 1 IX	9 1001
A 1010	10 5 BRSET5 3 BTB	7 5 BSET5 2 BSC	4 3 BPL 2 REL	6 5 DEC 2 DIR	4 3 DECA 1 INH	4 3 DECX 1 INH	7 6 DEC 2 IX1	6 5 DEC 1 IX		2 2 CLI 1 INH	2 2 ORA 2 IMM	4 3 ORA 2 DIR	5 4 ORA 3 EXT	6 5 ORA 3 IX2	5 4 ORA 2 IX1	4 3 ORA 1 IX	A 1010
B 1011	10 5 BRCLR5 3 BTB	7 5 BCLR5 2 BSC	4 3 BMI 2 REL							2 2 SEI 1 INH	2 2 ADD 2 IMM	4 3 ADD 2 DIR	5 4 ADD 3 EXT	6 5 ADD 3 IX2	5 4 ADD 2 IX1	4 3 ADD 1 IX	B 1011
C 1100	10 5 BRSET6 3 BTB	7 5 BSET6 2 BSC	4 3 BMC 2 REL	6 5 INC 2 DIR	4 3 INCA 1 INH	4 3 INCX 1 INH	7 6 INC 2 IX1	6 5 INC 1 IX		2 2 RSP 1 INH		3 2 JMP 2 DIR	4 3 JMP 3 EXT	5 4 JMP 3 IX2	4 3 JMP 2 IX1	3 2 JMP 1 IX	C 1100
D 1101	10 5 BRCLR6 3 BTB	7 5 BCLR6 2 BSC	4 3 BMS 2 REL	6 4 TST 2 DIR	4 3 TSTA 1 INH	4 3 TSTX 1 INH	7 5 TST 2 IX1	6 4 TST 1 IX		2 2 NOP 1 INH	8 6 BSR 2 REL	7 5 JSR 2 DIR	8 6 JSR 3 EXT	9 7 JSR 3 IX2	8 6 JSR 2 IX1	7 5 JSR 1 IX	D 1101
E 1110	10 5 BRSET7 3 BTB	7 5 BSET7 2 BSC	4 3 BIL 2 REL						* 2 STOP 1 INH		2 2 LDX 2 IMM	4 3 LDX 2 DIR	5 4 LDX 3 EXT	6 5 LDX 3 IX2	5 4 LDX 2 IX1	4 3 LDX 1 IX	E 1110
F 1111	10 5 BRCLR7 3 BTB	7 5 BCLR7 2 BSC	4 3 BIH 2 REL	6 5 CLR 2 DIR	4 3 CLRA 1 INH	4 3 CLRX 1 INH	7 6 CLR 2 IX1	6 5 CLR 1 IX	* 2 WAIT 1 INH	2 2 TXA 1 INH		5 4 STX 2 DIR	6 5 STX 3 EXT	7 6 STX 3 IX2	6 5 STX 2 IX1	5 4 STX 1 IX	F 1111

*CMOS only

Abbreviations for Address Modes

INH	Inherent
IMM	Immediate
DIR	Direct
EXT	Extended
REL	Relative
BSC	Bit Set/Clear
BTB	Bit Test and Branch
IX	Indexed (No Offset)
IX1	Indexed, 1 Byte (8-Bit) Offset
IX2	Indexed, 2 Byte (16-Bit) Offset

LEGEND

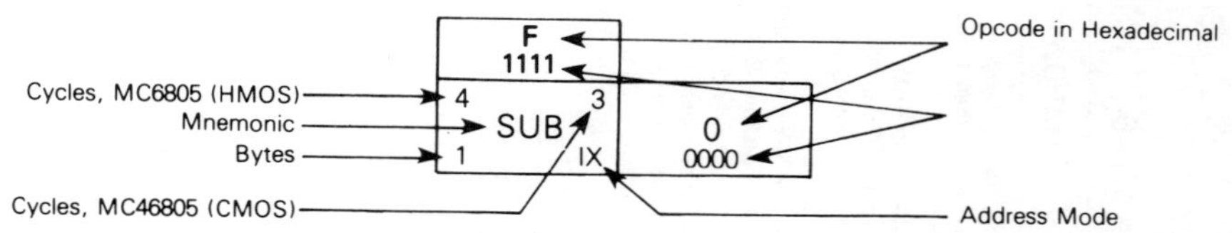

(Courtesy Motorola Inc.)

programmable timer. Because of these features, the MC68705P3 offers the user a means of designing an M6805 family MCU into his system as a prototype evaluation, a low volume production run or a pilot production run.

The key features of this MCU are: 112 bytes of RAM, 1804 bytes of EPROM, internal 8-bit timer with 7-bit prescaler, zero-cross detection on $\overline{\text{INT}}$ input, 20 TTL/CMOS I/0 lines, on-chip clock and direct emulation of the MC6805P2 masked ROM version.

The Motorola M6805 MCU family instruction set op code map in Table 13–7 concludes this section.

THE MC6809

Today, there is a lot of controversy about where a microcomputer turns into a "mini." While a number of benchmarks have been suggested, it is generally conceded that 16-bit processing capability constitutes a minimum "mini" requirement.

The MC6809 microprocessor at least borders on minicomputer capabilities. A model of the MC6809 internal structure and expanded block diagram appear in Fig. 13–24.

The MC6809 has 16-bit capability with 50% more throughput than the MC6800. It operates at 2 MHz, adds sixteen new addressing modes, utilizes an expanded instruction set with high-level language capability while maintaining compatibility with the MC6800 microprocessor components family.[11]

Description

This section contains a general description of the Motorola MC6809 and MC6809E MPUs. The terms MPU, processor and M6809 are used throughout this section to refer to both the MC6809 and MC6809E processors. When a topic relates to only one of the processors, that specific designator (MC6809 or MC6809E) is used.

The MC6809 and MC6809E microprocessors are greatly enhanced, upward compatible, computationally faster extensions of the MC6800 microprocessor. Enhancements such as additional registers (a Y index register, a U stack pointer and a direct page register) and instructions (such as MUL) simplify software design. Improved addressing modes have also been implemented. Upward compatibility is guaranteed since MC6800 assembly language programs can be assembled using

[11] *Microcomputer Components*, p. 7.

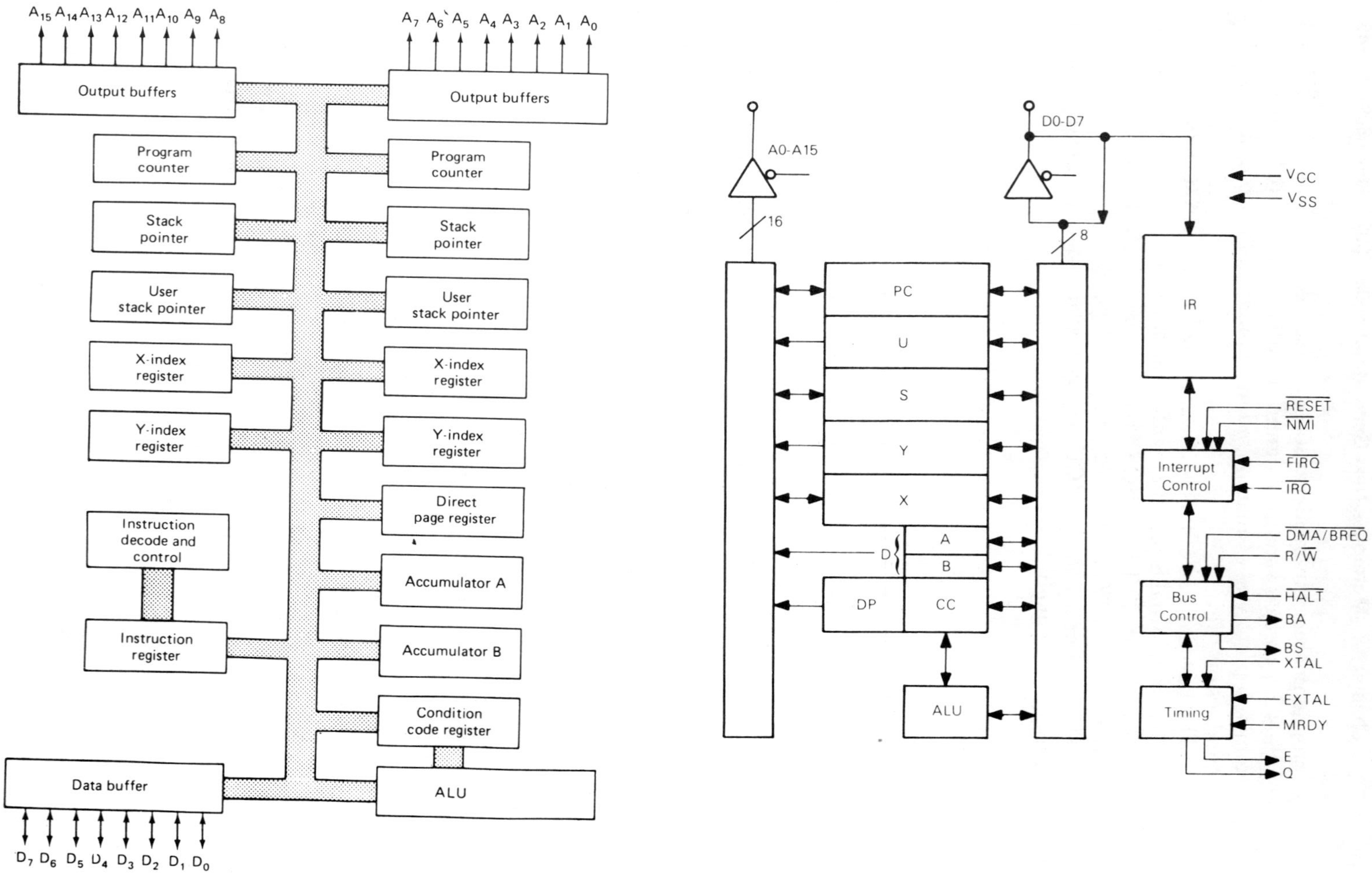

Fig. 13–24. MC6809 internal structure (a) and expanded block diagram (b). (*Courtesy Motorola Inc.*)

the Motorola MC6809 macro assembler. This code, while not as compact as native M6809 code, is, in most cases, 100% functional.

Both address and data are available from the processor earlier in an instruction cycle than from the MC6800 which simplifies hardware design. Two clock signals, E (the MC6800 $\phi 2$) and a new **quadrature** clock Q (which leads E by one-quarter cycle) also simplify hardware design.

A memory ready (MRDY) input is provided on the MC6809 for working with slow memories. This input stretches both the processor internal cycle and direct memory access bus cycle times but allows internal operations to continue at full speed. A direct memory access request ($\overline{\text{DMA/BREQ}}$) input provides immediate memory access or dynamic memory refresh operations; this input halts the internal MC6809 clocks. Because the processor's registers are dynamic, an internal counter periodically recovers the bus from direct memory access operations and performs a true processor refresh cycle to allow unlimited length direct memory access operation. An interrupt acknowledge signal is available to allow development of vectoring by interrupt device hardware or detection of operating system calls.

Three prioritized, vectored, hardware interrupt levels are available: nonmaskable, fast and normal. The highest and lowest priority interrupts (nonmaskable and interrupt request) are the normal interrupts used in the M6800 family. A new interrupt on this processor is the fast interrupt request which provides faster service to its interrupt input by only stacking the program counter and condition code register and then servicing the interrupt.

Modern programming techniques such as **position independent,** system independent and **reentrant** programming are readily supported by these processors.

Programming Model

By referring to Fig. 13–25, note that this third generation addition to the M6800 family has major architectural improvements including:

- Two 16-bit index registers
- Two 16-bit indexable stack pointers: U is controlled exclusively by the programmer and S is used automatically by the processor during subroutine calls and interrupts but can also be used by the programmer.
- Two 8-bit accumulators that can be **concatenated** to form one 16-bit accumulator (D).
- Direct page register allows direct addressing throughout memory. The contents of this 8-bit register are concatenated with the byte

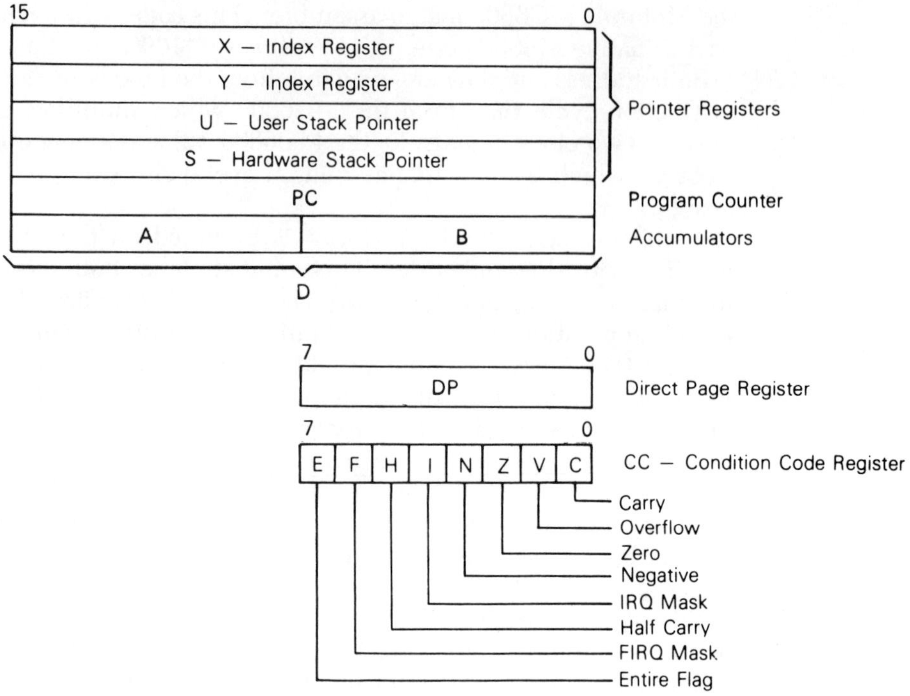

Fig. 13–25. M6809 programming model. (*Courtesy Motorola Inc.*)

following the direct addressing mode operation code to form a 16-bit effective address.

Hardware Features

The processor pin assignments appear in Fig. 13–26. Several of the key hardware features are:

- On-chip oscillator (4 × f_0 XTAL)
- $\overline{\text{DMA}}/\overline{\text{BREQ}}$, (direct memory access/bus request) suspends program execution and makes buses available for DMA operation or memory refresh
- $\overline{\textbf{FIRQ}}$ (Fast interrupt request) input stacks only the condition code register and the program counter
- MRDY (memory read) input extends data access time for use with slow memory
- Interrupt acknowledge output allows vectoring by devices

- Sync acknowledge output allows for synchronization to external event
- Single bus cycle reset
- NMI blocked after reset until after first load of stack pointer
- Early address valid allows use with slower memories
- Early write-data for dynamic memories

Several new features merit special attention.

MC6809 clocks. The MC6809 has four pins committed to developing the clock signals needed for internal and system operation. They are: the oscillator pins EXTAL and XTAL; the standard M6800 enable (E) clock; and a new quadrature (Q) clock.

The oscillator (EXTAL, XTAL) pins are used to connect the processor's internal oscillator to an external, parallel-resonant crystal. They can also be used for input of an external TTL timing signal by grounding the XTAL pin and applying the input to the EXTAL pin. The crystal or the external timing source is four times the resulting bus frequency.

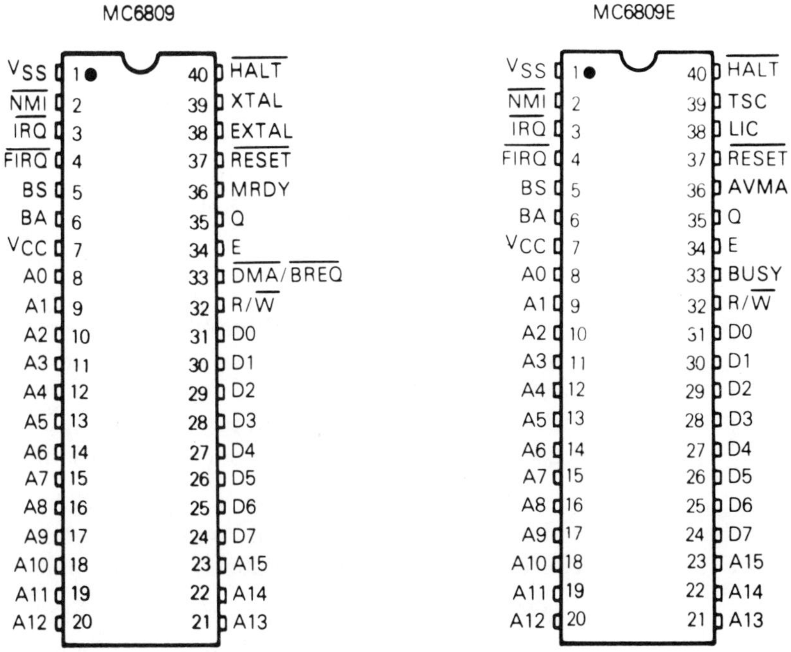

Fig. 13–26. Processor pin assignments. (*Courtesy Motorola Inc.*)

The enable (E) clock is similar to the phase 2 ($\phi 2$) MC6800 bus timing clock. The leading edge indicates to memory and peripherals that the data is stable and to begin writing operations. Data movement occurs after the Q clock is high and is latched on the trailing edge of E. Data is valid from the processor during a write operation by the rising edge of E.

The quadrature (Q) clock leads the E clock by approximately one-half of the E clock time. Address information from the processor is valid with the leading edge of the Q clock. The Q clock is a new signal in these processors and does not have an equivalent clock within the MC6800 bus timing.

MC6809E clocks (E and Q). The MC6809E has two pins provided for the TTL clock signal inputs required for internal operation. They are the standard M6800 enable (E) clock and the quadrature (Q) clock. The Q input must lead the E input. Addresses will be valid from the processor (on address delay time after the falling edge of E) and data will be latched from the bus by the falling edge of E. The Q input is fully TTL compatible. The E input is used to drive the internal MOS circuitry directly and therefore requires input levels above the normal TTL levels.

Last instruction cycle (LIC) (MC6809E). This output goes high during the last cycle of every instruction and its high-to-low transition indicates that the first byte of an op cycle will be latched at the end of the present bus cycle.

Processor state indicators (BA, BS). The processor uses these two output lines to indicate the present processor state. These pins are valid with the leading edge of the Q clock.

The bus available (BA) output indicates that the address and data buses and the read/write output are in the high impedance state. This signal can be used to indicate to bus-sharing or direct memory access systems that the buses are available. When BA goes low, an additional dead cycle elapses before the processor regains control of the buses.

The bus status (BS) output is used in conjunction with the BA output to indicate the present state of the processor. Table 13–8 lists the BA and BS outputs and the processor states they indicate.

Advanced valid memory address (AVMA) (MC6809E). This output signal indicates that the MC6809E will use the bus in the following bus cycle. It is low when the MC6809E is in a halt or sync state.

Busy (MC6809E). This output indicates that bus rearbitration should be deferred and provides the indivisible memory operation required for a test-and-set primitive. It is high for the first two cycles of any read/modify/write instruction, high during the first byte of a dou-

Table 13–8 BA/BS Signal Coding

BA	BS	PROCESSOR STATE
0	0	Normal (Running)
0	1	Interrupt or Reset Acknowledge
1	0	Sync Acknowledge
1	1	Halt/Bus Grant Acknowledged

(Courtesy Motorola Inc.)

ble-byte access, and high during the first byte of any indirect access or vector fetch operation.

Software Features

Programs developed for the MC6800 can be easily converted for use with the MC6809 or MC6809E by running the source code through an M6809 macro assembler or a cross assembler.

The addressing modes of any microprocessor provide it with the capability to efficiently address memory to obtain data and instructions. The MC6809 and MC6809E have a versatile set of addressing modes that allow them to function using modern programming techniques. While the software features have been expanded, note that the addressing modes and instructions of these processors are upward compatible with the MC6800. The old addressing modes have been retained and many new ones have been added.[12]

Some of the major software features of the M6809 are:

- MC6800 upward compatible addressing modes
- Direct addressing anywhere in memory map
- Long relative branches
- Program counter relative
- True indirect addressing
- Expanded indexed addressing
  0, 5, 8 or 16-bit constant offsets
  8 or 16-bit accumulator offsets
  Auto-increment/decrement by 1 or 2
- 1464 instructions with unique addressing modes
- 8 × 8 unsigned multiply
- 16-bit arithmetic
- Transfer/exchange all registers
- Push/pull AND registers or any set of registers
- Load effective address

[12] *MC6809-MC6809E Microprocessor Programming Manual* (Austin, Texas: Motorola Inc., 1981), pp. 1-1–1-12.

Instruction Set

The complete instruction set for the M6809 is given in Table 13–9. The instruction set can be functionally divided into five categories. They are:

1. 8-bit accumulator and memory instructions
2. 16-bit accumulator and memory instructions
3. Index register/stack pointer instructions
4. Branch instructions
5. Miscellaneous instructions

The M6809 instructions and their variations grouped in the five categories are listed in the appendix.

Table 13–9 M6809 Instruction Set.

Instruction	Description	Instruction	Description
ABX	Add Accumulator B into Index Register X	DAA	Decimal Addition Adjust
ADC	Add with Carry into Register	DEC	Decrement
ADD	Add Memory into Register	EOR	Exclusive OR
AND	Logical AND Memory into Register	EXG	Exchange Registers
ASL	Arithmetic Shift Left	INC	Increment
ASR	Arithmetic Shift Right	JMP	Jump
BCC	Branch on Carry Clear	JSR	Jump to Subroutine
BCS	Branch on Carry Set	LD	Load Register from Memory
BEQ	Branch on Equal	LEA	Load Effective Address
BGE	Branch on Greater Than or Equal to Zero	LSL	Logical Shift Left
BGT	Branch on Greater	LSR	Logical Shift Right
BHI	Branch if Higher	MUL	Multiply
BHS	Branch if Higher or Same	NEG	Negate
BIT	Bit Test	NOP	No Operation
BLE	Branch if Less than or Equal to Zero	OR	Inclusive OR Memory into Register
BLO	Branch on Lower	PSH	Push Registers
BLS	Branch on Lower or Same	PUL	Pull Registers
BLT	Branch on Less than Zero	ROL	Rotate Left
BMI	Branch on Minus	ROR	Rotate Right
BNE	Branch Not Equal	RTI	Return from Interrupt
BPL	Branch on Plus	RTS	Return from Subroutine
BRA	Branch Always	SBC	Subtract with Borrow
BRN	Branch Never	SEX	Sign Extend
BSR	Branch to Subroutine	ST	Store Register into Memory
BVC	Branch on Overflow Clear	SUB	Subtract Memory from Register
BVS	Branch on Overflow Set	SWI	Software Interrupt
CLR	Clear	SYNC	Synchronize to External Event
CMP	Compare Memory from a Register	TFR	Transfer Register to Register
COM	Complement	TST	Test
CWAI	Clear CC bits and Wait for Interrupt		

(Courtesy Motorola Inc.)

Op Code Map

Table 13–10 (a) is the op code map for M6809 processors. The number(s) by each instruction indicates the number of machine cycles required to execute that instruction. When the number contains a "1" (e.g., 4 + 1), it indicates that the indexed addressing mode is being used and that an additional number of machine cycles may be required. Refer to Table 13–10 (b) to determine the additional machine cycles to be added.

Some instructions in the op code map have two numbers, the second one in parenthesis, indicating that the instruction involves a branch. The parenthetical number applies if the branch is taken.

The "page 2, page 3" notation in column one means that all page 2 instructions are preceded by a hexadecimal 10 op code and all page 3 instructions are preceded by a hexadecimal 11 op code.

Special M6809 Support Chips

MC6829 MMU. The MC6829 memory management unit (**MMU**) allows an M6809-based system to address a 2 megabyte memory space. Its principal function is to expand the address space of the MC6809 from 64K bytes to a maximum of 2 megabytes. Each MMU can handle four different concurrent tasks including DMA. The MMU also protects the address space of one task from modification by another task.

Memory address space expansion is accomplished by applying the upper five address lines of the processor (A11–A15) along with the contents of a 5-bit task register to an internal high speed mapping RAM. The MMU output consists of ten physical address lines (PA11–PA20) which, when combined with the eleven lower address lines of the processor (A0–A10), form a physical address space of 2 megabytes.

Each task is assigned memory in increments of 2K bytes up to a total of 64K bytes. In this manner, the address spaces of different tasks can be kept separate from one another. The resulting simplification of the address space programming model increases the software reliability of a complex multiprocess system.[13]

A block diagram of the MC6829 MMU appears in Fig. 13–27.

Building an MMU system. Up to eight chips may be connected in parallel to create a maximum of thirty-two tasks. All MMU pins except one ($\overline{KVA}$) may be wired in parallel. Each MMU chip contains 1280 bits of fast on-chip lookup RAM which is accessible ten bits at a time

[13] *MC6829 HMOS Memory Management Unit Advance Information ADI-846-R1* (Austin, Texas: Motorola Inc., 1981), p. 1.

Table 13–10(a) Op Code Map.

Least Significant Four Bits	Most-Significant Four Bits: DIR		REL		ACCA	ACCB	IND	EXT	IMM	DIR	IND	EXT	IMM	DIR	IND	EXT	
	0000	0001	0010	0011	0100	0101	0110	0111	1000	1001	1010	1011	1100	1101	1110	1111	
	0	1	2	3	4	5	6	7	8	9	A	B	C	D	E	F	
	6		3 BRA	4+1	2	2	6+1	7	2	4	4+1	5	2	4	4+1	5	
0000 0	NEG	PAGE2		LEAX		NEG				SUBA				SUBB			0
			3 BRN/	4+1					2	4	4+1	5	2	4	4+1	5	
0001 1	—	PAGE3	5 LBRN	LEAY	—					CMPA				CMPB			1
		2	3 BHI/	4+1					2	4	4+1	5	2	4	4+1	5	
0010 2	—	NOP	5(6) LBHI	LEAS	—					SBCA				SBCB			2
	6	2	3 BLS/	4+1	2	2	6+1	7	4,6,6+1,7	5,7,7+1,8		5,7,7+1,8	4	6	6+1	7	
0011 3	COM	SYNC	5(6) LBLS	LEAU		COM			SUBD /	CMPD /		CMPU		ADDD			3
	6		3 BHS	5+1/by	2	2	6+1	7	2	4	4+1	5	2	4	4+1	5	
0100 4	LSR	—	5(6) (BCC)	PSHS		LSR				ANDA				ANDB			4
			3 BLO	5+1/by					2	4	4+1	5	2	4	4+1	5	
0101 5	—	—	5(6) (BCS)	PULS	—					BITA				BITB			5
	6	5	3 BNE/	5+1/by	2	2	6+1	7	2	4	4+1	5	2	4	4+1	5	
0110 6	ROR	LBRA	5(6) LBNE	PSHU		ROR				LDA				LDB			6
	6	9	3 BEQ/	5+1/by	2	2	6+1	7	—	4	4+1	5	—	4	4+1	5	
0111 7	ASR	LBSR	5(6) LBEQ	PULU		ASR					STA				STB		7
	6 ASL		3 BVC/		2	2	6+1	7	2	4	4+1	5	2	4	4+1	5	
1000 8	(LSL)	—	5(6) LBVC	—		ASL (LSL)				EORA				EORB			8
	6	2	3 BVS/	5	2	2	6+1	7	2	4	4+1	5	2	4	4+1	5	
1001 9	ROL	DAA	5(6) LBVS	RTS		ROL				ADCA				ADCB			9
	6	3	3 BPL/	3	2	2	6+1	7	2	4	4+1	5	2	4	4+1	5	
1010 A	DEC	ORCC	5(6) LBPL	ABX		DEC				ORA				ORB			A
			3 BMI/	6/15					2	4	4+1	5	2	4	4+1	5	
1011 B	—	—	5(6) LBMI	RTI	—					ADDA				ADDB			B
	6	3	3 BGE/	20	2	2	6+1	7	4,6,6+1,7	5,7,7+1,8		5,7,7+1,8	3	5	5+1	6	
1100 C	INC	ANDCC	5(6) LBGE	CWAI		INC			CMPX /	CMPY /		CMPS		LDD			C
	6	2	3 BLT/	11	2	2	6+1	7	7	7	7+1	8	—	5	5+1	6	
1101 D	TST	SEX	5(6) LBLT	MUL		TST			BSR		JSR				STD		D
	3	8	3 BGT/				3+1	4	3,5,5+1,6		4,6,6+1,7		3,5,5+1,6		4,6,6+1,7		
1110 E	JMP	EXG	5(6) LBGT	—	—			JMP	LDX /		LDY		LDU /		LDS		E
	6	7	3 BLE/	19/20/20	2	2	6+1	7	—	5,5+1,6		6,6+1,7	—	5,5+1,6		6,6+1,7	
1111 F	CLR	TFR	5(6) LBLE	SWI/2/3		CLR				STX /		STY		STU /		STS	F

Table 13–10(b) Indexed Addressing Mode Data.

Type	Forms	Non Indirect				Indirect			
		Assembler Form	Postbyte OP Code	~	#	Assembler Form	Postbyte OP Code	~	#
Constant Offset From R (twos complement offset)	No Offset	,R	1RR00100	0	0	[,R]	1RR10100	3	0
	5 Bit Offset	n, R	0RRnnnnn	1	0	defaults to 8-bit			
	8 Bit Offset	n, R	1RR01000	1	1	[n, R]	1RR11000	4	1
	16 Bit Offset	n, R	1RR01001	4	2	[n, R]	1RR11001	7	2
Accumulator Offset From R (twos complement offset)	A — Register Offset	A, R	1RR00110	1	0	[A, R]	1RR10110	4	0
	B — Register Offset	B, R	1RR00101	1	0	[B, R]	1RR10101	4	0
	D — Register Offset	D, R	1RR01011	4	0	[D, R]	1RR11011	7	0
Auto Increment/Decrement R	Increment By 1	,R+	1RR00000	2	0	not allowed			
	Increment By 2	,R++	1RR00001	3	0	[,R++]	1RR10001	6	0
	Decrement By 1	,-R	1RR00010	2	0	not allowed			
	Decrement By 2	,--R	1RR00011	3	0	[,--R]	1RR10011	6	0
Constant Offset From PC (twos complement offset)	8 Bit Offset	n, PCR	1XX01100	1	1	[n, PCR]	1XX11100	4	1
	16 Bit Offset	n, PCR	1XX01101	5	2	[n, PCR]	1XX11101	8	2
Extended Indirect	16 Bit Address	—	—	—	—	[n]	10011111	5	2

R = X, Y, U or S   X = 00   Y = 01
X = Don't Care   U = 10   S = 11

~ and # Indicate the number of additional cycles and bytes for the particular variation

(Courtesy Motorola Inc.)

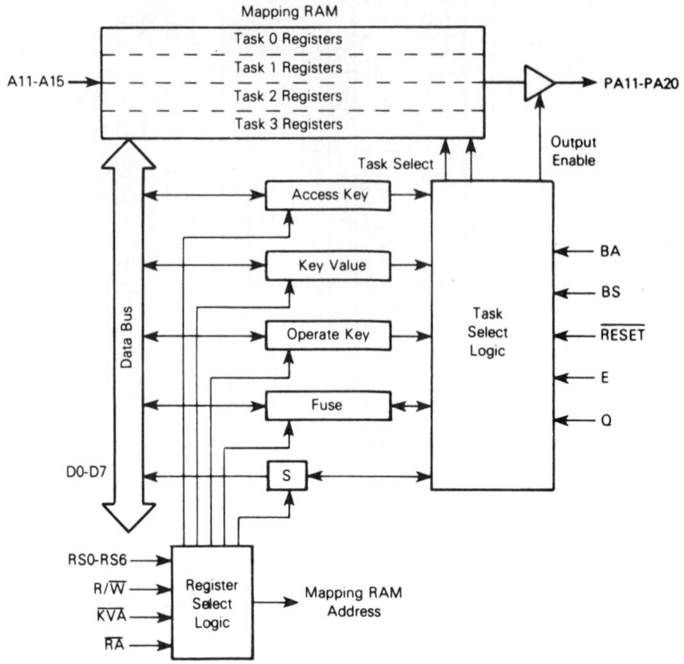

Fig. 13–27. MC6829 MMU block diagram. (*Courtesy Motorola Inc.*)

for mapping purposes and at two and eight bits at a time when the O/S (operating system) is changing the contents of RAM.

In addition to the lookup RAM, each MMU contains a separate copy of the access key, operate key, fuse register, key value register and S-bit. A CPU write to access, operate or fuse register causes all registers on all MMUs to be updated. In contrast, the lookup RAM for each chip is updated only when the top three bits of the access key match the key value register for that chip.

During mapping operations, each MMU compares the value in its operate key (top three bits) with its key value register and responds only if a match is found. Similarly, when the processor reads the RAM, each MMU compares its key value with the access key.

Figure 13–28 is a block diagram exemplifying a typical MMU system.

MC6839 floating-point ROM. The MC6839 standard product ROM provides floating point capability for the MC6809 and MC6809E MPUs. The MC6839 implements the entire *IEEE Proposed Standard for Binary Floating Point Arithmetic Draft 8.0.* It provides a simple,

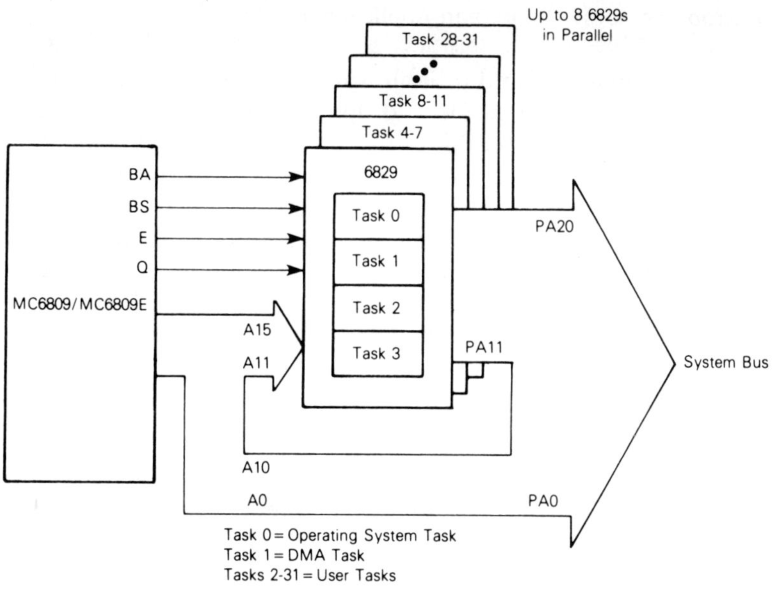

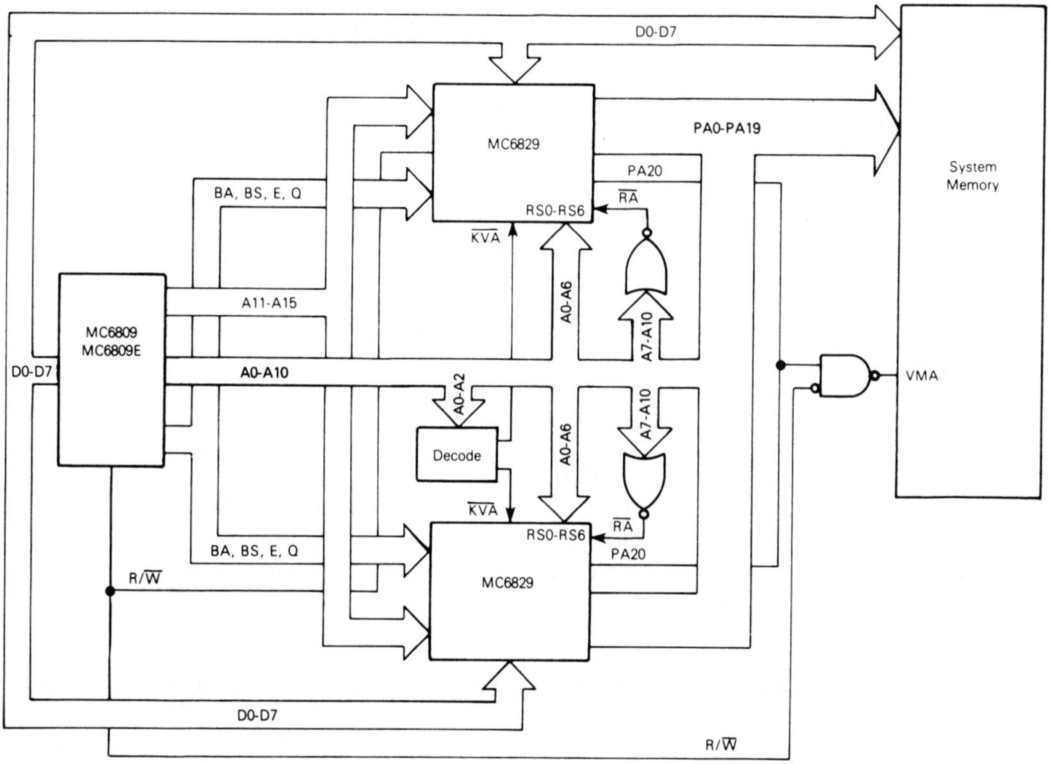

Fig. 13–28. MC6809/MC6829 MMU system configuration. (*Courtesy Motorola Inc.*)

economical and reliable solution to a wide variety of numerical applications. The single and double precision formats provide results bit-for-bit reproducible across all Draft 6.0 implementations while the extended format provides the extra precision needed for the intermediate results of long calculations, particularly the implementation of transcendental functions and interest calculations. All applications benefit from extensive error checking and well defined responses to exceptions, which are strengths of the IEEE proposed standard.

The MC6839 takes full advantage of the advance architectural features of the M6809. It is position independent and totally reentrant, facilitating its use in real time, multi-tasking systems.

The key features of the MC6839 are:

- Totally position independent: operates in any contiguous 8K blocks of memory
- Reentrant
  No use of absolute RAM
  All memory references made relative to stack pointer
- Flexible user interface. Operands are passed to the package by two methods:
  (1) Machine registers are used as pointers to operands
  (2) Operands are pushed onto the hardware stack (facilitates use of the MC6839 in high level language implementations)
- Easy to use two/three address architecture: the user specifies addresses of operands and result and need not be concerned with any internal registers or intermediate results.
- Complete implementation of the Proposed IEEE Standard Draft 6.0
  Includes all precisions, modes and operations required or suggested by the Standard
  Single, double and extended formats
  Includes the following operations: add, subtract, multiply, divide, remainder, square root, integer part, absolute value, negate, predicate compares, condition code compares, convert integer ⟷ floating point, convert binary floating point ⟷ decimal string.[14]

Table 13–11 lists the MC6839 calling sequences and op codes.

[14] *MC68A39/MC68B39 Floating-Point Read-Only Memory Advance Information ADI-857* (Austin, Texas: Motorola Inc., 1981), p. 1.

Table 13–11 MC6839 Calling Sequences and Op Codes.

Function	Opcode	Register Calling Sequence	Stack Calling Sequence[1]
FADD FSUB FMUL FDIV	\$00 \$02 \$04 \$06	U ← Addr. of Argument #1 Y ← Addr. of Argument #2 D ← Addr. of FPCB X ← Addr. of Result LBSR FPREQ FCB <opcode>	Push Argument #1 Push Argument #2 Push Addr. of FPCB LBSR FPSTAK FCB <opcode> Pull Result
FREM FSQRT FINT FFIXS FFIXD FAB FNEG FFLTS FFLTD	\$08 \$12 \$14 \$16 \$18 \$1E \$20 \$24 \$26	Y ← Addr. of Argument D ← Addr. of FPCB X ← Addr. of Result LBSR FPREG FCB <opcode>	Push Argument Push Addr. of FPCB LBSR FPSTAK FCB <opcode> Pull Result
FCMP FTCMP FPCMP FTPCMP	\$8A \$CC \$8E \$D0	U ← Addr. of Argument #1 Y ← Addr. of Argument #2 D ← Addr. of FPCB X ← Parameter Word LBSR FPREG FCB <opcode> NOTE: Result returned in the CC register. For predicate compares the Z-Bit is set if predicate is affirmed cleared if disaffirmed.	Push Argument #1 Push Argument #2 Push Parameter Word Push Addr. of FPCB LBSR FPSTAK FCB <opcode> Pull Result (if predicate compare) NOTE: Result returned in the CC register for regular compares. For predicate compares a one byte result is returned on the top of the stack. The result is zero if affirmed and – 1(\$FF) if disaffirmed.
FMOV	\$9A	U ← Precision Parameter Word Y ← Addr. of Argument D ← Addr. of FPCB X ← Addr. of Result LBSR FPREG FCB <opcode>	Push Argument Push Precision Parameter Word Push Addr. of FPCB LBSR FPSTAK FCB <opcode> Pull Result
BINDEC	\$1C	U ← k (# of digits in result) Y ← Addr. of Argument D ← Addr. of FPCB X ← Addr. of Decimal Result LBSR FPREG FCB <opcode>	Push Argument Push k Push Addr. of FPCB LBSR FPSTAK FCB <opcode> Pull BCD String
DECBIN	\$22	U ← Addr. of BCD Input String D ← Addr. of FPCB X ← Addr. of Binary Result LBSR FPREG FCB <opcode>	Push Addr. of BCD Input String Push Addr. of FPCB LBSR FPSTAK FCB <opcode> Pull Binary Result

[1] All arguments are pushed on the stack least-significant bytes first so that the high-order byte is always pushed last and resides in the lowest address.

Entry points to the MC6839 are defined as follows:
FPREG = ROM start + \$3D
FPSTAK = ROM start + \$3F

(Courtesy Motorola Inc.)

M6800 FAMILY HARDWARE COMPATIBILITY

The advanced family of microprocessors/microcomputers described in this chapter is compatible with all M6800 peripheral parts. The M6800 family contains a number of compatible LSI components that make the development of communications interface equipment quick, easy and relatively inexpensive.

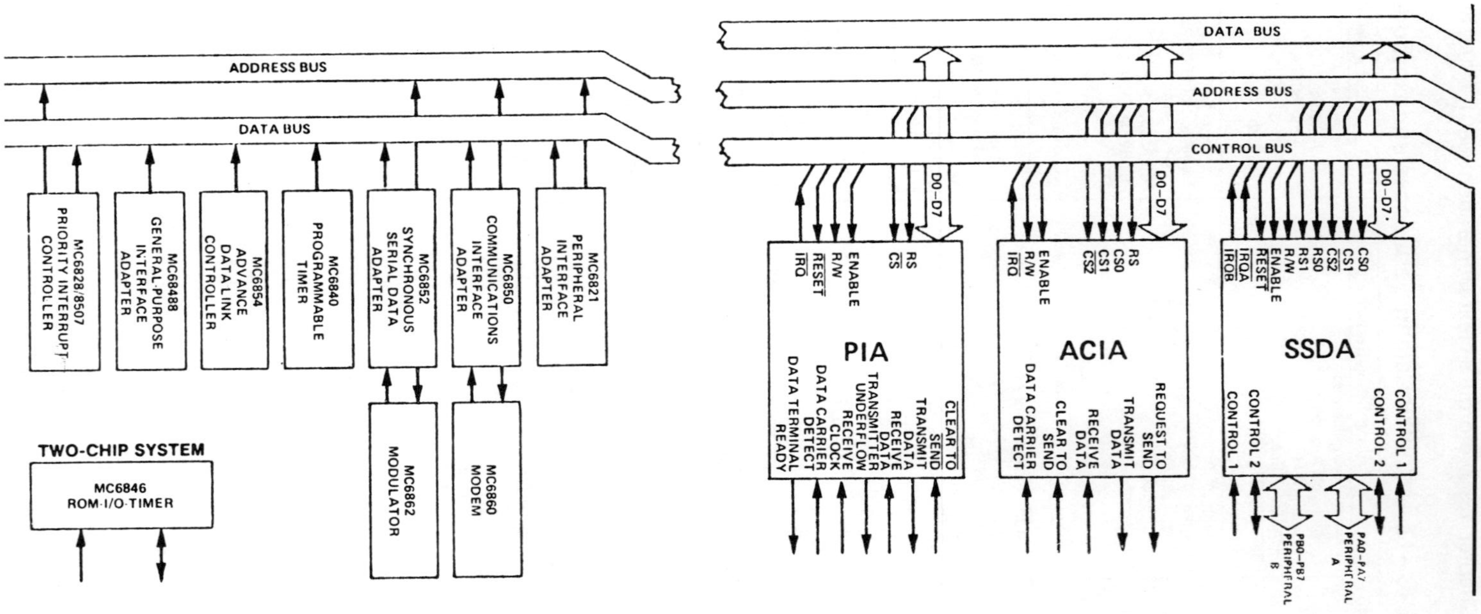

Fig. 13–29. M6800 peripheral family block diagram. (*Courtesy Motorola Inc.*)

Figure 13–29 shows an M6800 peripheral family block diagram.

Following is a brief description of the interface integrated circuits which appear in Fig. 13–29. They are included here to demonstrate the versatility and scope of possible applications that will center around the M6800 microprocessor/microcomputer family.

1. *MC6846 ROM I/0 Timer.* Highly efficient interface chip contains 2048 bytes of ROM together with a 16-bit programmable timer-counter and an 8-bit bidirectional data port for peripheral interface. In conjunction with MC6802 MPU, it constitutes a versatile 2-chip microcomputer system. Compatibility with other M6800 interface and peripheral circuits permits system expansion to any required additional complexity at low cost.

The built-in ROM provides read-only storage for a minimum microcomputer system and is mask-programmable to the user's specifications. The timer may be programmed to count events, measure frequencies and time intervals, generate square waves, etc. The I/O port is under software control and includes two handshake control lines for asynchronous interface with peripherals.

2. *MC6821 Peripheral Interface Adapter (PIA).* This parallel-oriented peripheral interface circuit is one of the most important interface circuits available. It contains two I/O circuit blocks, each capable of controlling an independent 8-bit peripheral data bus. Multiple PIAs can be used with a single system and selectively addressed by means of chip-select inputs. Each peripheral data line can be programmed to act as an input or output and each of four control/interrupt lines can operate in one of several control modes.

3. *MC6828/8507 Priority Interrupt Controller (PIC).* This bipolar device is used to add prioritized responses to inputs of microprocessor systems. The performance has been optimized for the MC6800 system but will serve to eliminate input polling routines from any processor system.

With the PIC, each interrupting device is assigned a unique ROM location which contains the starting address of the appropriate service routine. After the MPU detects and responds to an interrupt, the PIC directs the MPU to the proper memory location.

4. *MC6840 Programmable Timer.* This component is designed to provide variable system time intervals. It has three 16-bit binary counters, three corresponding control registers and a status register. The counters are under software control and may be used to cause system interrupts and/or generate output signals. The MC6840 may be utilized for frequency measurements, event counting, interval measuring and similar tasks.

5. *MC68488 General Purpose Interface Adapter.* The MC68488 GPIA interfaces between the IEEE 488 standard instrument bus and the MC6800 system. With it, many instruments may be interconnected and remotely and automatically controlled or programmed. Data may be taken from, sent to or transferred between instruments.

The MC68488 will automatically handle all handshake protocol needed on the instrument bus.

6. *MC6860 0-600 bps Digital Modem.* The MC6860 is a MOS subsystem designed to be integrated into a wide range of equipment utilizing serial data communications, including stand-alone modems, data-storage devices, remote-data communications terminals and I/O interfaces for minicomputers.

The modem provides the necessary modulation, demodulation and supervisory control functions to implement a serial data communications line, over a voice grade channel, utilizing frequency shift keying (FSK) at bit rates up to 600 bps.

The modem is compatible with the M6800 microcomputer family, interfacing directly with the asynchronous communications interface adapter to provide low-speed data communications capability.

7. *MC6850 Asynchronous Communications Interface Adapter (ACIA).* This circuit provides the data formatting and control to interface serial asynchronous data communications information to bus organized systems.

The parallel data of the bus system is serially transmitted and received by the asynchronous data interface with proper formatting and error checking. The functional configuration of the ACIA is programmed via the data bus during system initialization. A programmable control register provides variable word lengths, clock division ratios, transmit control, receive control and interrupt control. Three control lines allow the ACIA to interface directly with the MC6860 digital modem.

8. *MC6854 Advanced Data Link Controller (ADLC).* The MC6854 ADLC performs the complex MPU/data communication link function for the Advanced Data Communication Control Procedure (ADCCP), High Level Data Link Control (HLDC) and Synchronous Data Link Control (SDLC) standards.

In a bit-oriented data communication system the data is transmitted and received in a synchronous serial form.

The serial data stream must be converted into parallel, analyzed and stored (for use by the MPU) in order for data link management to be accomplished. Similarly, parallel data from the MPU system must be serialized with the appropriate frame control information in order to conform to the bit-oriented protocol standards. The Advanced Data Link Controller (ADLC) provides these functions.

9. *MC6852 Synchronous Serial Data Adapter (SSDA).* Provides interface between the MC6800 MPU System and synchronous data terminals such as floppy disk equipment, cassette or cartridge tape controllers, numerical control systems and other systems requiring movement of data blocks. Operates at speeds up to 600 kbps.

10. *MC6862 Digital Modulator.* Offers the necessary modulation and control functions to implement a serial data communications link over voice-grade channels at bit rates of 1200 and 2400 bps.[15]

11. *MC6859 Data Security Device (DSD).* The MC6859 is a monolithic MOS integrated circuit designed to be integrated into a wide range of equipment requiring protection of data by the use of cryptographic measures. The cryptographic algorithm utilized by the device is the Data Encryption Standard (DES). Through the use of flexible on-chip control and status circuitry and external control lines, the DSD provides direct capability of adapting the functional implementation of the DES algorithm for various specific system requirements for data protection.[16]

SUMMARY

The M6800 microprocessor/microcomputer family, including Motorola's next generation is summarized in Fig. 13–30. The MC6800 16-bit microcomputer is included and will be discussed in Chapter 15, "Looking Ahead. . . ."

QUESTIONS

1. What are the major differences between the MC6800 and MC6802 MPUs?
2. What makes the MC6801 an MCU rather than an MPU?
3. What is the major difference between the MC6801 and the MC6803?
4. How does the MC6802 compare with the MC6808 microprocessor?
5. List at least five features of the MC6805R2 MCU.
6. In general, which processor would be considered more powerful: the MC6801 or the MC6808? Why?

[15] *Microcomputer Components,* pp. 10–11.

[16] *MC6859 MOS Data Security Device Advance Information ADI-827* (Austin, Texas: Motorola, Inc., 1980), p. 1.

MC	# PINS/PACKAGE	# ADDRESS LINES	# DATA LINES	ADDRESS SPACE	MAXIMUM EXTERNAL CLOCK FREQ. (MHz)	MAXIMUM INTERNAL CLOCK FREQ. (MHz)	# INSTRUCTIONS	# ADDRESSING MODES	MINIMUM INSTRUCTION TIME (ns)	#INTERRUPT VECTORS	RAM ON CHIP (# BYTES)	ROM ON CHIP (# BYTES)	UART ON CHIP	TIMER ON CHIP
6800 68A00 68B00	40	16	8	64K	1.0 1.5 2.0	1.0 1.5 2.0	72	6	2.0 1.3 1.0	4	NO	NO	NO	NO
6801*	40	0 8 16	8	0 .25K 64K	4.0	1.0	83	6	2.0	8	128	2048	YES	YES
6802	40	16	8	64K	4.0	1.0	72	6	2.0	4	128	NO	NO	NO
6803	40	16	8	64K	4.0	1.0	83	6	2.0	8	128	NO	YES	YES
6805	28	I/O PORTS	I/O PORTS	N/A	4.0	1.0	60	12	2.0	4	64	1100	NO	YES
146805	28/40	I/O PORTS	I/O PORTS	N/A	4.0	1.0	62	12	2.0	4	112	2304	NO	YES
6808	40	16	8	64K	1.0	1.0	72	6	2.0	4	NO	NO	NO	NO
6809 68A09 68B09	40	16	8	64K	4.0 6.0 8.0	1.0 1.5 2.0	59	10	2.0 1.3 1.0	7	NO	NO	NO	NO
68,000	64	23	16	16M	8.0	8.0	59	14	0.5	192	NO	NO	NO	NO

*** EROM VERSION IS 68701**

Fig. 13–30. Summary of Motorola's microprocessors/microcomputers. (*Courtesy Motorola Inc.*)

7. Explain the main differences between CMOS and HMOS technology.
8. Which of the following processors have onboard multiply?

MC6802	MC6805R2	MC6808
MC6801	MC6803	MC6809

9. List the internal registers of the MC6809.
10. Describe the characteristics of the MC6829 and the MC6839 peripheral parts.

Chapter 14

Motorola 6800 Family Applications

GLOSSARY

A/D Analog-to-digital converter. A device or subsystem that changes real-world analog data to a form compatible with binary processing.

Device-dependent messages Messages used by the devices interconnected via the interface system that are carried by, but not used or processed by, the interface system directly.

GP-IB A standardization of bus levels, number of lines and line characteristics to allow easy interconnection of instruments into microcomputer controlled systems regardless of the equipment manufacturer.

Interface messages Messages used to manage the interface system itself and sent to cause a state transition within another interface function.

Listener A device that can be addressed by an interface message to receive device-dependent messages from another device connected to the interface system.

Programmable That characteristic of a device that makes it capable of accepting data to alter the state of its internal circuitry to perform two or more specific tasks.

Programmable measuring apparatus A measuring apparatus that performs specified operations on command from the system. If it is a measuring apparatus proper, it transmits the results of the measurement(s) to the system.

PTM Programmable timer module. The Motorola MC6840 is a programmable subsystem component of the M6800 family designed to provide variable system time intervals. The counters are under software control and may be used to cause system interrupts and/or generate output signals.

Talker A device that can be addressed by an interface message to send device-dependent messages to another device connected to the interface system.

Transducer A device that converts something measureable, often a physical property such as pressure, temperature, or flow, into another form such as an electrical signal.

VDG Video display generator. A device that provides a means of interfacing a microprocessor to a commercial color or black and white television receiver for display purposes in the form of alphanumerics and/or graphics.

Upon reaching this point in the text, the reader should, hopefully, feel rather comfortable with this very new and exciting area of electronics technology. While holding the conviction that the microprocessor is the "greatest thing on earth," the question may be asked, "What in the world can a microprocessor be used for—other than to completely confuse and/or impress the electronics novice?" That is certainly a valid question and it is the main objective of this chapter to present several very real and practical applications which have their entire functions centered around the microprocessor.

The application examples are presented at a fundamental level to insure that the circuit interaction with the microprocessor and final end results are clear rather than tangled up in the intricate circuit considerations which are beyond the scope of this text.

When designing a microprocessor system, one of the recurring problems is that of getting signals into and out of the microprocessor. As was discussed in earlier chapters, the microprocessor manufacturers have designed a number of support integrated circuits to help remedy this I/O problem. However, interfacing a sophisticated piece of test equipment along with a number of electronic instruments has caused a multifaceted problem involving the lack of a standard for all the different types of devices and equipment or the absence of capability for the manufacturers of microprocessors and instruments as well as for the users of both the microprocessor systems and instrument systems.

Examples of the many details and complexity of a typical interface system would involve discussion of a large number of integrated circuits covering their electrical characteristics including logic levels, timing, handshaking and partitioning. Furthermore, keep in mind that, more often than not, confusion exists relating to connector terminals, identification, definitions and standard conventions, which is certain to cause all kinds of ambiguity.

THE IEEE 488 GENERAL PURPOSE INTERFACE BUS

A solution to the above problems is found in the IEEE 488 General Purpose Interface Bus, or, as it is often referred to, the GP-IB. This latter designation, GP-IB, will be used throughout this chapter.

Description

According to Motorola Inc. literature, the GP-IB is a byte-serial, bit-parallel interface system primarily defined for programmable measurement instrument systems. The general system defines all circuits, cables, connectors, control protocol and message repertoire to ensure unambiguous data transfer between devices.

The system has the following defined constraints:

1. No more than fifteen devices can be interconnected by a single contiguous bus.
2. Total transmission length is not to exceed twenty meters, or two meters times the number of devices, whichever is less.
3. Data rate through any signal line must be less than, or equal to one Megabit/second.
4. All data exchange is to be digital (as opposed to analog).

The GP-IB system is structured with sixteen transmission lines. They consist of:

1. Eight data bus lines, permitting transmission of ASCII characters. Data is asynchronous and generally bidirectional.
2. Three data byte transfer control lines (handshake).
3. Five general interface management signal lines.

These lines may employ either open-collector (not open-collector in an absolute sense due to the termination networks on the bus) or 3-state drive elements with certain constraints on the SRQ, MRFD, DI01-8 and NDAC lines.[1]

[1] *Getting Aboard the 488-1975 Bus* (Phoenix, Arizona: Motorola Inc., 1977), p. 1.

Implementation—The Motorola MC68488 GPIA

In order to create a complete system, an interface must be achieved between the GP-IB and the Motorola MC6800 microprocessor. The means for this interface is provided by the MC68488 general purpose interface adapter which offers the advantage of overall reduction in external components as well as the simplicity of interfacing circuitry.

General description. A visual concept of a possible bus structure appears in Fig. 14–1.

The important points in Fig. 14–1 concern the signal flow to or from the MPU (MC6800 or MC6802 which were discussed in Chapters 12 and 13), to or from the MC68488 GPIA and to or from the MC3448A bidirectional transceivers. The MC3448A bidirectional transceivers are connected to a bus which handles the functions of data bus, data byte transfer control (handshake) and the general interface management. These signals will be sent to and/or from such instruments that have the intelligence to react as a device controller, device **talker** and a device **listener.**

The GP-IB instrument bus provides a means for controlling and moving data from complex systems of multiple instruments. A final point that must not be overlooked is that the MC68488 GPIA automatically handles all handshake protocol needed on the instrument bus.[2]

Specific characteristics. The following is a summary of the specific characteristics of the MC68488 GPIA. They will become more understandable in the application of the GPIA which will conclude this first MC6800 microprocessor application.

1. Single or dual primary address recognition
2. Secondary address capability
3. Complete source acceptor handshakes
4. Programmable interrupts
5. RFD holdoff to prevent data overrun
6. Operates with DMA controller
7. Serial and parallel polling capability
8. Talk-only or listen-only capability
9. Selectable automatic features to minimize software
10. Synchronization trigger output
11. MC6800 bus compatible.[3]

Advantages. The Motorola MC6800/MC68488/MC3448A is a cost-effective and highly flexible solution to the implementation of the GP-

[2] *General Purpose Interface Adapter MC68488 Advance Information ADI-462* (Austin, Texas: Motorola Inc., 1977), p. 1.

[3] *GPIA MC68488 Advance Information,* p. 1.

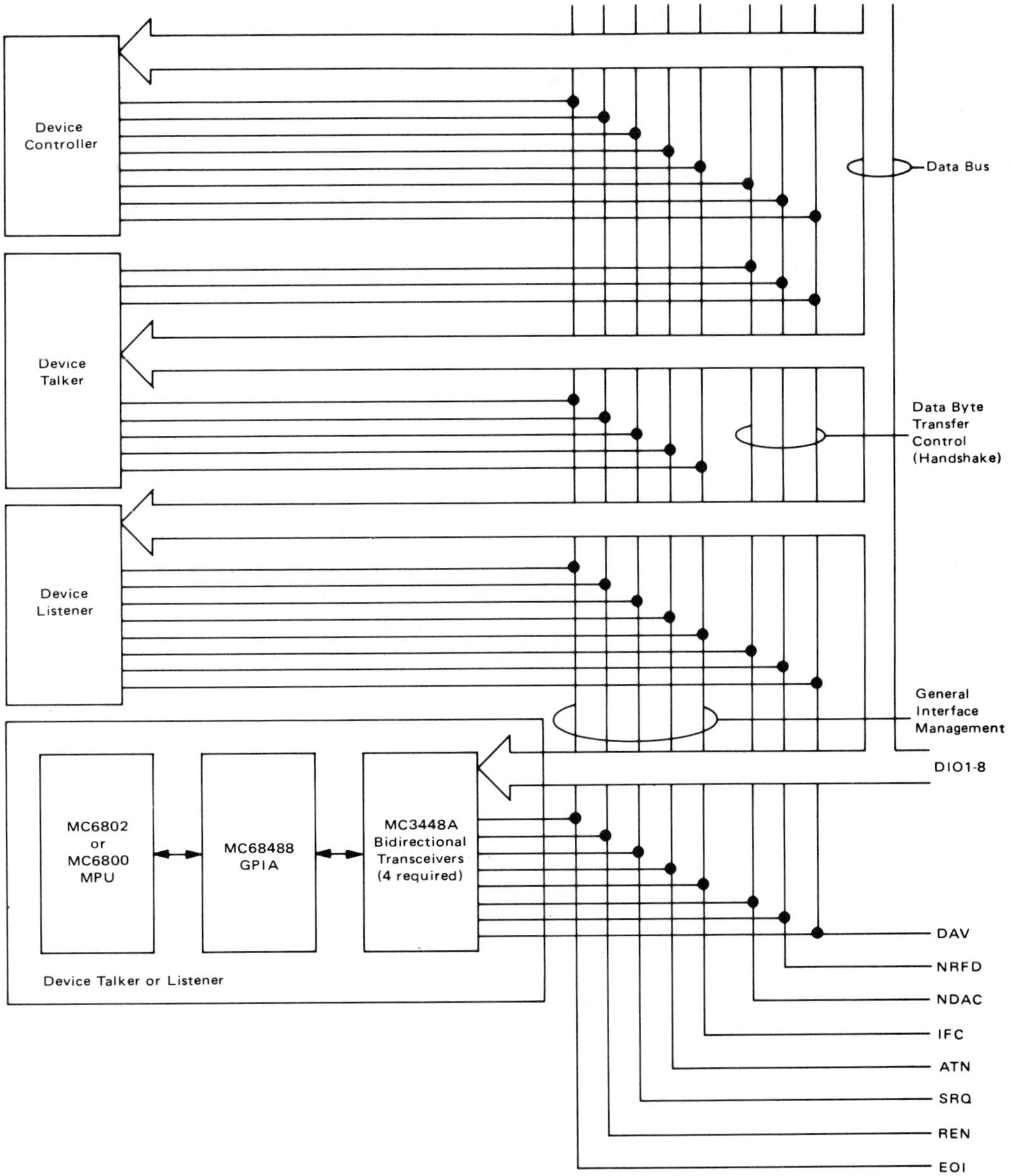

Fig. 14–1. Possible bus structure. (*Courtesy Motorola Inc.*)

IB instrumentation standard. This chip complement provides complete talker/listener capabilities. Controller function may also be generated with these ICs and some supportive logic and memory/software.

In addition to the two dedicated GP-IB devices, the entire M6800 family is available to configure more extensive measurement system designs. ROMs, RAMs, EPROMs, PIAs, ACIAs, clocks, **programmable** timers, bus extenders and modems are also offered in the M6800 family of devices.[4]

An example of an expanded GPIA/MPU system appears in Fig. 14–2.

When studying Fig. 14–2, note the additional use of ROMs, RAMs, address decode logic, data bus, address bus, the system clock and the like. All of these concepts have been stressed throughout the book as necessary support items to make "the microprocessor" a viable system.

Complete System Example

HP-IB 59309A digital clock description. The 59309A shown in Fig. 14–3 provides a front panel display of the date and time on a 24-hour basis. When used in a system, the 59309A is fully programmable and outputs the date and time onto the HP-IB (which is Hewlett-Packard's name for the GP-IB application) for printout or other systems use. The display is a row of digits indicating the following information:

MONTH	DAY OF MONTH	HOUR	MINUTE	SECOND
MM	DD	HH	MM	SS

For example:

01	25	09	54	26[5]

The major point of interest here is that the HP-IB 59309A complies with the standards set by the GP-IB (IEEE 488) instrumentation bus and therefore is fully compatible and can be interfaced via the GP-IB with any instruments or computer system following the standard.

Digital clock applications. These typical applications as well as the basic description of the HP-IB are taken from the *Hewlett-Packard Operating and Service Manual* for this instrument.

The HP-IB 59309A can be used as a system time-of-day source remotely via the HP-IB instrument bus. Examples of specific applications are:

[4] *Getting Aboard the 488-1975 Bus*, p. 33.

[5] *Operating and Service Manual 59309A HP-IB Digital Clock* (Santa Clara, California: Hewlett-Packard Company, 1976), p. 1–1.

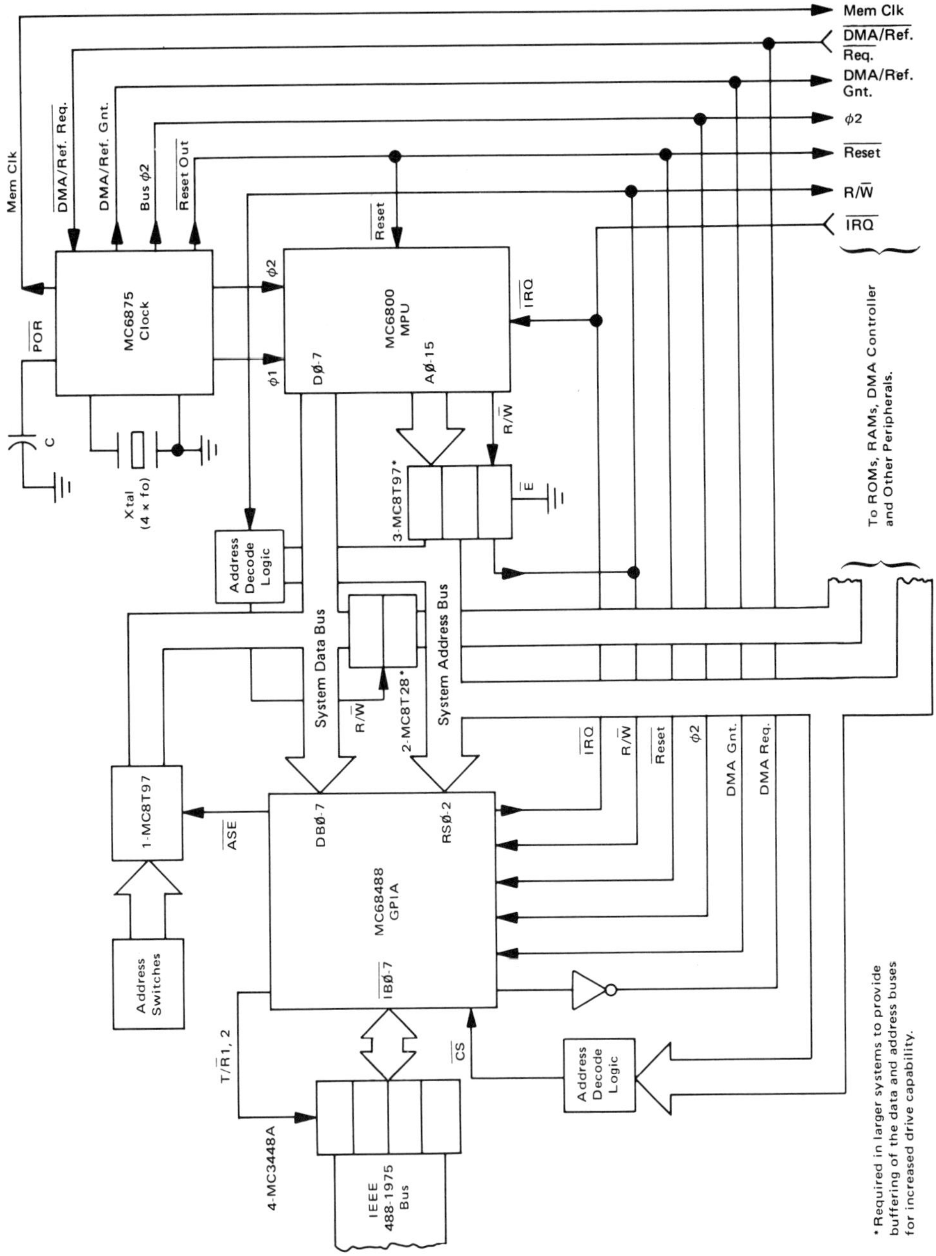

Fig. 14–2. Expanded GPIA/MPU system. *(Courtesy Motorola Inc.)*

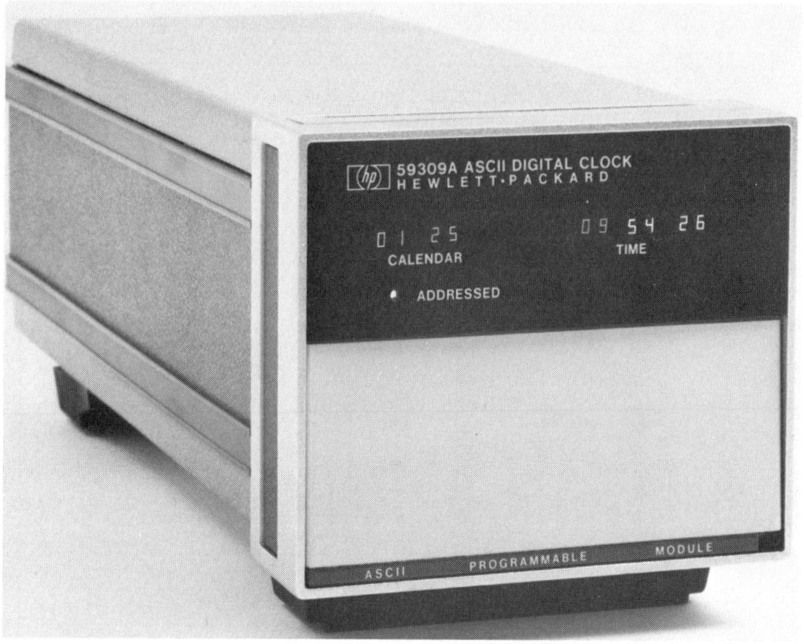

Fig. 14–3. HP59309A. (*Courtesy Hewlett-Packard Company*)

1. A data source for the HP-IB to provide calendar and time-of day data for use by a system. For example, the 59309A can be used to start and stop measurements by having the controller run in a software loop looking for correct time or it can be used to supply information to data logging devices to record time of events.

2. A master clock to control remote readout devices.

3. Data logging complete with time information. The time at which data points are taken, or a printout made, is a vital part of a data record. With the 59309A in a system, time and data can be recorded simultaneously.[6]

Digital clock theory of operation. The general instrument theory of operation discussed in this section is presented as a block diagram in Fig. 14–4.

1 MHz Oscillator Clock operation of the HP 59309A is controlled by the 1 MHz oscillator on A3 calendar oscillator assembly. This oscil-

[6] *59309A HP-IB Manual*, p. 1–2.

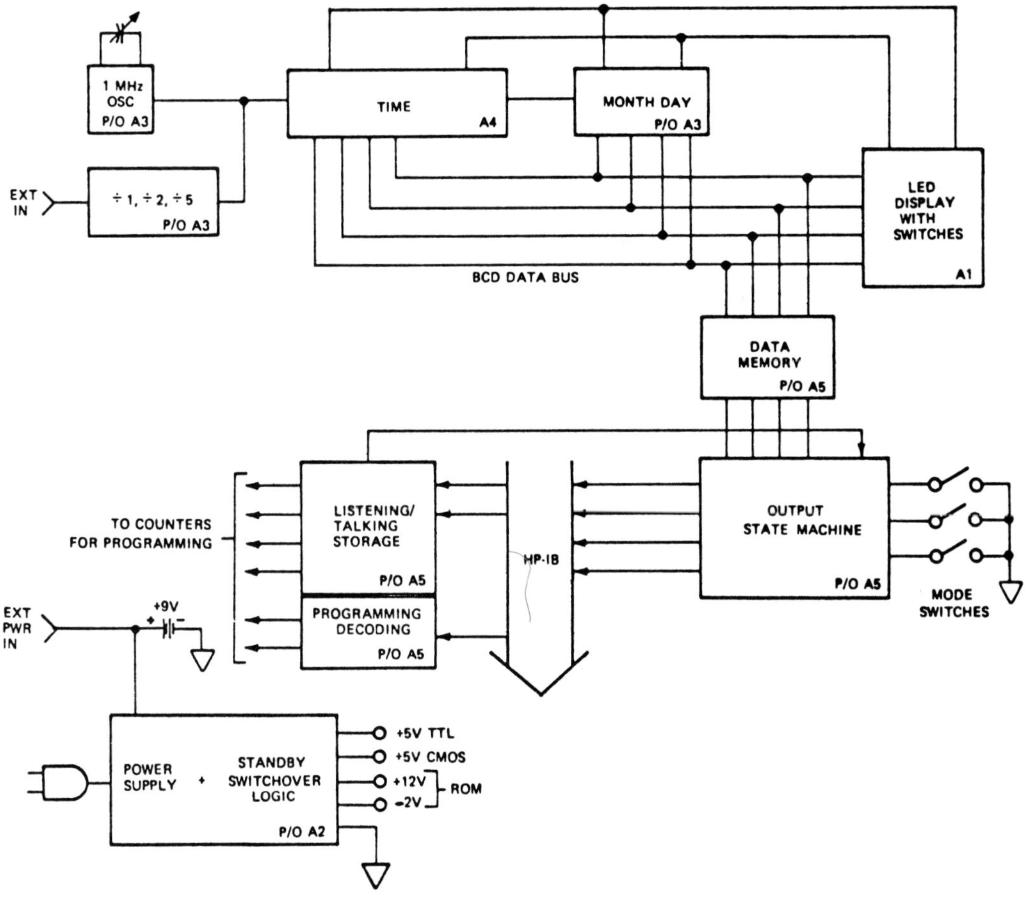

Fig. 14–4. HP59309A block diagram. (*Courtesy Hewlett-Packard Company*)

lator is an ambient temperature, crystal-controlled time base. The 1 MHz output is supplied to the time-base divider on A4 time assembly.

Time-Base Divider The A4 time-base divider receives the 1 MHz signal and divides it down to the one-pulse-per-second signal which is sent to the seconds counter. The A4 time-base divider also supplies 4-bit digit position information to the digit position encoder. In addition, the C line signal is generated as a master clock to synchronize operation of the circuits in the A5 bus I/O assembly.

Seconds, Minutes and Hours Counters The seconds counter divides the 1-second signal by 60 and sends the resulting 1-minute signal to the minutes counter. The minutes counter divides the 1-minute signal by 60 and sends the resulting 1-hour signal to the hours counter. The hours counter divides the 1-hour signal by 24 and sends the 1-day signal to the A3 calendar oscillator assembly. Each counter outputs a BCD code to indicate the number of minutes, hours, seconds, etc. that have been counted. These codes are combined with the appropriate digit position bits (1 and 2 for seconds, 3 and 4 for minutes, etc.) to synchronize strobing of the seconds, minutes, and hours information on the data bus for use in the display.

Digit Position Decoder The digit position decoder receives the 4-bit BCD code from the time-base divider and decodes it to a 10-bit output that is sent to the front panel display to strobe the digit position one after the other. The 10-bit output is supplied, through the digit position bus drivers to synchronize the outputs of the counters on the A3 and A4 boards on the data bus with the strobing of the display.

Days and Months Counters The days counter receives the 1-day signal from the hours counter and counts the days of the month (28, 29, 30 or 31 days, depending on the month being counted and whether it is leap-year or not). The months counter is clocked by the days counter at the end of a month and counts the months of the year. Each counter outputs a BCD code to indicate the number of days and months that have been accumulated. These codes are combined with the appropriate digit position bits to synchronize the strobing of the days and months information on the data bus for use in the display.

Input Processing The input circuits on the A5 bus I/O assembly process software instructions for the remote programming mode of the 59309A. The run and hold signals are sent to the time-base divider and the update and reset signals are sent to the counter circuits. The input processing circuits supply the store, DAC and RFD qualifiers to the output state machine.

Output State Machine The output state machine controls the operation of the talk output of the 59309A. The 4-bit codes from the data bus and the 4-digit position bits from the time-base divider are processed by the output state machine to develop the talk output to the bus.[7]

The material presented on the theory operation of the 59309A is a good example of instrumentation using integrated circuit technology. However, the block diagram was included primarily to demonstrate an actual electronic instrument which utilizes the GP-IB interface bus.

Digital clock pin connections. Referring to Fig. 14–4, note the HP-IB which is compatible with the GP-IB. A closer look at the actual dig-

[7] *59309A HP-IB Manual*, pp. 4–1 & 4–3.

ital bus connector pin designations and digital bus pin summary appear in Fig. 14–5.

Now that the instrument to be interfaced to the microprocessor system has been described in general, the interconnecting of the instrument to the microprocessor system, for which the MC68488 general-purpose interface adapter is designed, can be discussed.

Interfacing the HP-IB via the MC68488 GPIA. At the beginning of this chapter, it was mentioned that the task of connecting **programmable measuring apparatus** that are GP-IB compatible to a microprocessor system was a complex operation. This is precisely where the microprocessor system user can really appreciate the main advantages of using the Motorola MC68488 GPIA to handle this intricate interfacing with relative ease. In order to understand the point in question, refer to Fig. 14–5 and pay particular attention to the connector terminals pins that are labeled DI01, DI02, DI03, DI04, DI05, DI06, DI07, DI08, E01, DAV, NRFD, NDAC, IFC, SRQ, ATN and REN.

These sixteen lines are the lines that need to be connected to the microprocessor system via the MC68488 GPIA.

Refer to Fig. 14–6 and notice that these same sixteen lines are connected to the MC68488 GPIA through four MC3448A bidirectional transceivers. These MC3448A integrated circuits are quad bidirectional transceivers for mating MOS or bipolar logic systems to the GP-IB bus. Each channel provides back-to-back driver and receiver elements plus the required bus terminations. Direction of data flow is controlled by 3-state disabling of the undesired direction element (driver or receiver).[8]

In completing the interface, all that is needed is to electrically connect the line from the HP-IB connector labeled DI01 to the line labeled DI01 on the MC68488/MC3448A GPIA system and then connect the line labeled DI02 on the HP-IB connector to the line labeled DI02 on the MC68488/MC3448A GPIA and so on. The major point here is that the previous task of complex logic levels, timing, handshaking and other important details have already been taken into account and are being handled by the MC68488 GPIA.

In summarizing this first application, the authors' hope is that the reader understands the extremely important role that dedicated support integrated circuits perform in a complete microprocessor system which then becomes more properly referred to as a microcomputer system.

Summary of IEEE GP-IB. Referring to the example system configuration shown in Fig. 14–6, consider the three groups of interface

[8] *Getting Aboard the 488-1975 Bus,* p. 29.

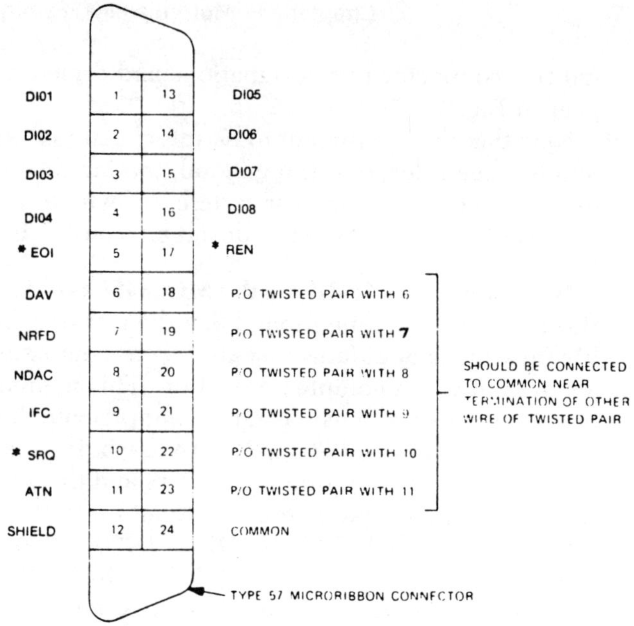

* THESE PINS ARE TERMINATED WITH RESISTIVE NETWORKS (SEE SCHEMATIC) AND NORMALLY FLOAT AT APPROXIMATELY 3V.

NOTE 1: PINS 18 THROUGH 23 SHOULD BE CONNECTED TO COMMON NEAR THE TERMINATION OF THE OTHER WIRE OF ITS TWISTED PAIR.

NOTE 2: PIN 12 IS CONNECTED TO COMMON THROUGH THE TALK ONLY SWITCH WHEN IN TALK ONLY MODE. OTHERWISE PIN 12 IS NOT CONNECTED.

DIGITAL BUS PIN SUMMARY

Pin No.	Line Name	Use
1–4, 13–15	DIO1–7	Carries character to 59309A for clock updating or for processing as Bus commands.
16	DIO8	Not monitored or driven; terminated by resistive network.
6 7 8	DAV NRFD NDAC	These three lines make up the "handshake" system on the HP-IB. DAV is monitored and driven and NRFD and NDAC are driven by 59309A to control rate of data transferred on DIO lines.
9	IFC	Unconditionally clears Listen and Talk FF's, halting remote operation.
11	ATN	Indicates to 59309A whether character on DIO lines is Bus Command or for clock updating.
5	EOI	Not monitored or driven; terminated by resistive network.
10	SRQ	Not monitored or driven; terminated by resistive network.
12	Shield	Connected to common through TALK ONLY switch on rear panel.
18–24	Common	Connected to chassis common.

Fig. 14–5. Digital bus pin summary and digital bus connector pin designs. (*Courtesy Hewlett-Packard Company*)

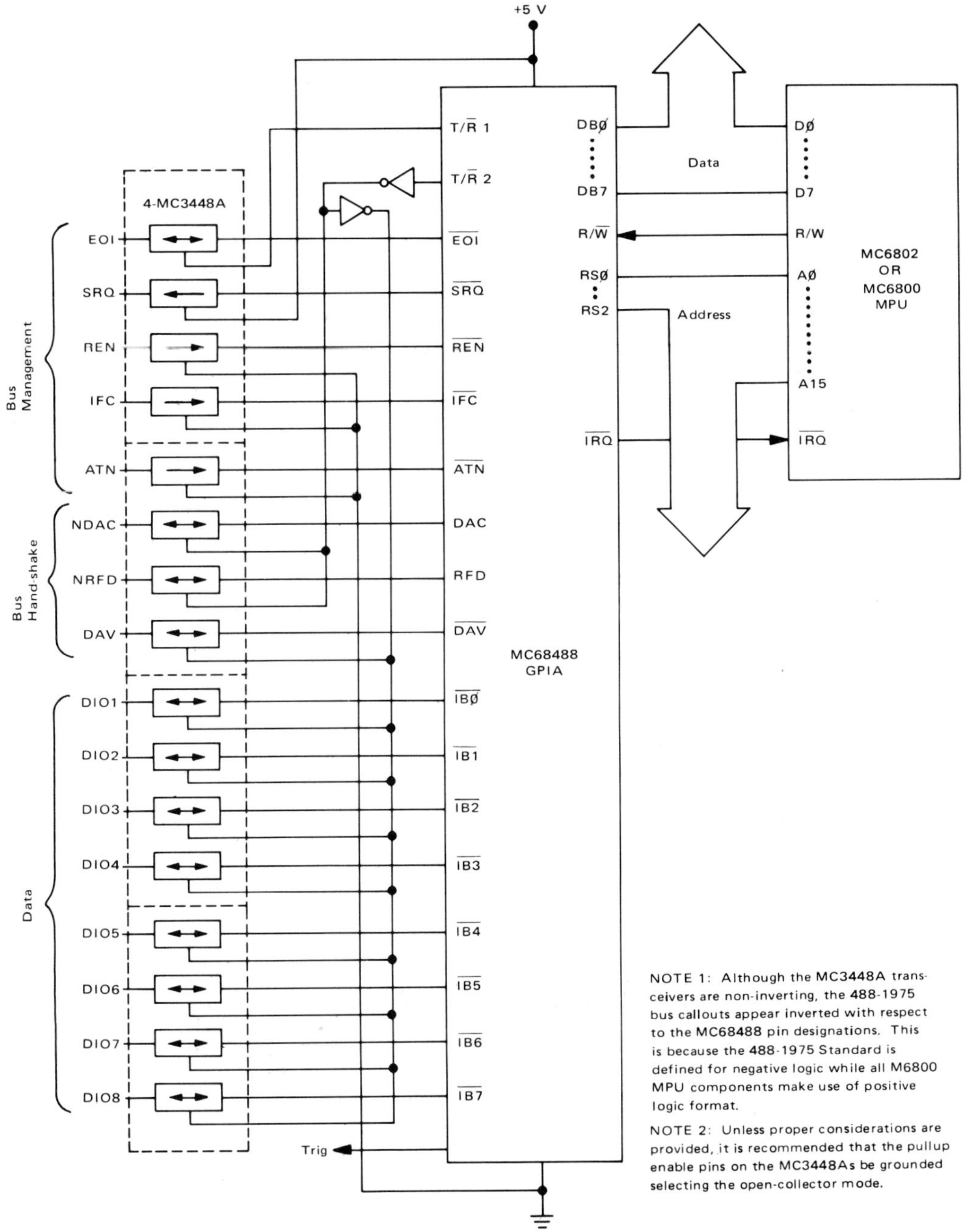

NOTE 1: Although the MC3448A transceivers are non-inverting, the 488-1975 bus callouts appear inverted with respect to the MC68488 pin designations. This is because the 488-1975 Standard is defined for negative logic while all M6800 MPU components make use of positive logic format.

NOTE 2: Unless proper considerations are provided, it is recommended that the pullup enable pins on the MC3448As be grounded selecting the open-collector mode.

Fig. 14–6. System configuration. (*Courtesy Motorola Inc.*)

lines that comprise the GP-IB bus: the bus management lines, the bus handshake (transfer) lines and the data (signal) lines.

Bus management lines (E01, SRQ, REN, IFC, ANT): These lines are used to manage an orderly flow of information across the interface lines.

Bus handshake (transfer) lines (NDAC, NRFD, DAV): These lines allow for proper transfer of each data byte on the bus between sources and acceptors.

Data (signal) lines: These bidirectional lines allow for the flow of 7-bit ASCII **interface messages** and **device-dependent messages.** Data appears on these lines in a bit-parallel byte-serial form. These lines are buffered by the MC3448A transceivers and applied to the 488 GP-IB (DI01-DI08).[9]

This completes the rather general explanation of an MC6800/6802 application using the IEEE GP-IB which, because of its versatility, adaptability and universality, is beginning to appear in the up-to-date electronic laboratories throughout the industry.

VIDEO DISPLAY GENERATOR (VDG)

This section is intended to give another typical example of application, by demonstrating how microprocessors can be the focal point of a video display generator or **VDG** which is a very essential part of a complete microcomputer system. First, the Motorola MC6847 VDG will be used and second, a similar VDG, the S68047, manufactured by American Microsystems, Inc. will be utilized.

The purpose of presenting these somewhat similar devices manufactured by two different companies is twofold. First, the authors wish to show two different application examples using the same MC6800/6802 microprocessor. Second, this points out the little known fact that it is not uncommon for more than one company to manufacture and market either the same device or one with almost the same capabilities.

Motorola MC6847 VDG

The description, features and the typical application that follow are courtesy of Motorola Inc.

[9] *Getting Aboard the 488-1975 Bus,* p. 22.

Description. The Motorola MC6847 Video Display Generator (VDG) provides a means of interfacing the Motorola M6800 microprocessor family (or similar products) to a commercially available color or black and white television receiver. Applications of the VDG include video games, bioengineering displays, education, communications and any place graphics are required.

The VDG reads data from memory and produces a composite video signal which will allow the generation of alphanumeric or graphic displays. The generated composite video may be up modulated to either Channel 3 or 4 by using the compatible MC1372 (TV Chroma and Video modulator). The up modulated signal is suitable for application to the antenna of a color TV.

Features. The MC6847 VDG has the following features:

- Generates four different alphanumeric display modes and eight graphic display modes
- Compatible with the M6800 family
- Compatible with the MC1372 modulator
- The alphanumeric modes display 32 characters per line by 16 lines
- An internal multiplexer allows the use of either the internal ROM or an external character generator
- An external character generator can be used to extend the internal character set for "limited graphics" shapes
- A mask-programmable internal character generator ROM is available on special order
- One display mode offers 8-color 64-by-32 density graphics in an alphanumeric display mode
- One display mode offers 4-color 64-by-48 density graphics in an alphanumeric display mode
- All alphanumeric modes have a selectable video inverse
- Generates full composite video signal
- Generates R-Y and B-Y signals for external color modulator
- Full graphic modes offer 64-by-64, 128-by-64, 128-by-96, 128-by-192, or 256-by-192 densities
- Full graphic modes allow 2-color or 4-color data structures
- Full graphic modes use one of two 4-color sets or one of two 2-color sets
- Available in either an interlace mode (NTSC Standard) or noninterlace mode[10]

[10] *MC6847 Advance Information Sheet ADI-492* (Phoenix, Arizona: Motorola Inc., 1978), p. 1.

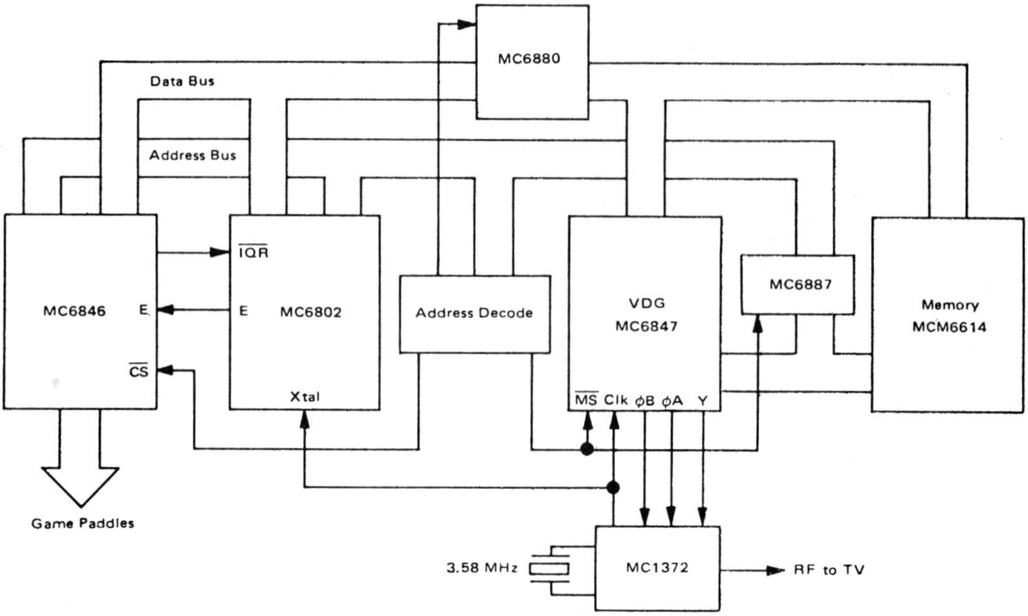

Mnemonic	Pin Numbers	Function
V_{CC}	17	+5V
V_{SS}	1	Ground
CLK	33	Color burst clock 3.58 MHz (input)
DA0-DA12	22, 23, 24, 25, 26 13, 14, 15, 16, 18, 19, 20, 21	Address lines to display memory, high impedance during memory select ($\overline{MS}$)
DD0-DD5	3, 4, 5, 6, 7, 8	Data from display memory RAM or ROM
DD6, DD7	2, 40	Data from display memory in graphic mode; data also in alpha external mode; color data in alpha semigraphic 4 or 6
ϕA, ϕB, Y	11, 10, 28	Chrominance and luminance analog (R-Y, B-Y, Y) output to RF modulator (MC1372)
CHB	9	Chroma bias; reference ϕA and ϕB levels
$\overline{RP}$	36	Row preset — Output to provide timing for external character generator.
$\overline{HS}$	38	Horizontal Sync — Output to provide timing for external character generator.
INV	32	Inverts video in all alpha modes
$\overline{INT}$/EXT	31	Switches to external ROM in alpha mode and between SEMIG-4 and SEMIG-6 in semigraphics
$\overline{A}$/S	34	Alpha/Semigraphics; selects between alpha and semigraphics in alpha mode
$\overline{MS}$	12	Memory select forces VDG address buffers to high-impedance state
$\overline{A}$/G	35	Switches between alpha and graphic modes
$\overline{FS}$	37	Field Synchronization goes low at bottom of active display area.
CSS	39	Color set select; selects between two alpha display colors or between two color sets in semigraphics 6 and full graphics
GM0-GM2	30, 29, 27	Graphic mode select; select one of eight graphic modes.

Fig. 14–7. Block diagram of use of the VDG in a TV game. (*Courtesy Motorola Inc.*)

A typical application. A typical TV game is indicated in Fig. 14–7 complete with mnemonics, pin numbers and a brief function description.

The American Microsystems, Inc. S68047 VDG

The description, features and typical application of the AMI S68047 are courtesy of American Microsystems, Inc. A microphoto of the S68047 chip is shown in Fig. 14–8.

Description. The video display generator (VDG) is designed to produce composite video suitable for display on a consumer black and white or color television receiver. The VDG will produce 1-color alphanumeric or graphic display with black background or color graphic displays applicable to video games or small computers. A VDG block diagram is shown in Fig. 14–9.

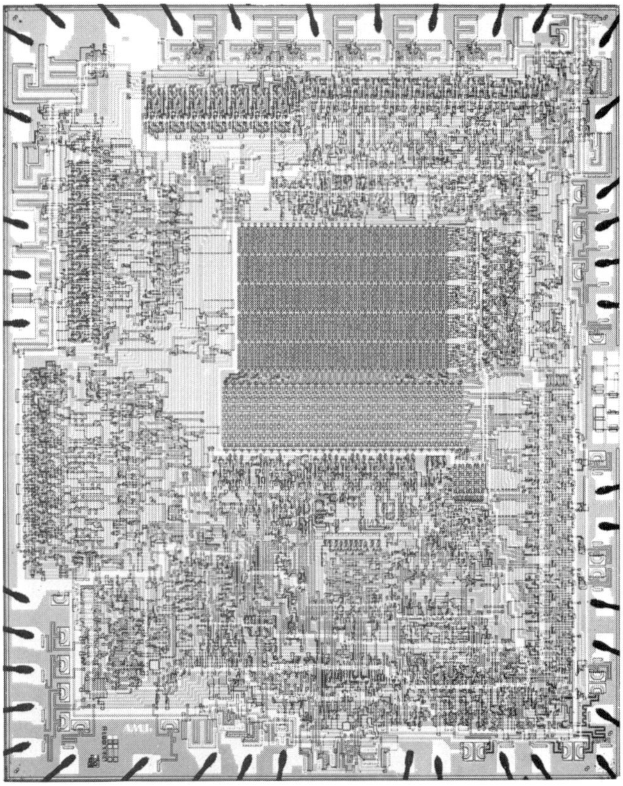

Fig. 14–8. Microphoto of S68047 VDG. (*Courtesy American Microsystems, Inc.*)

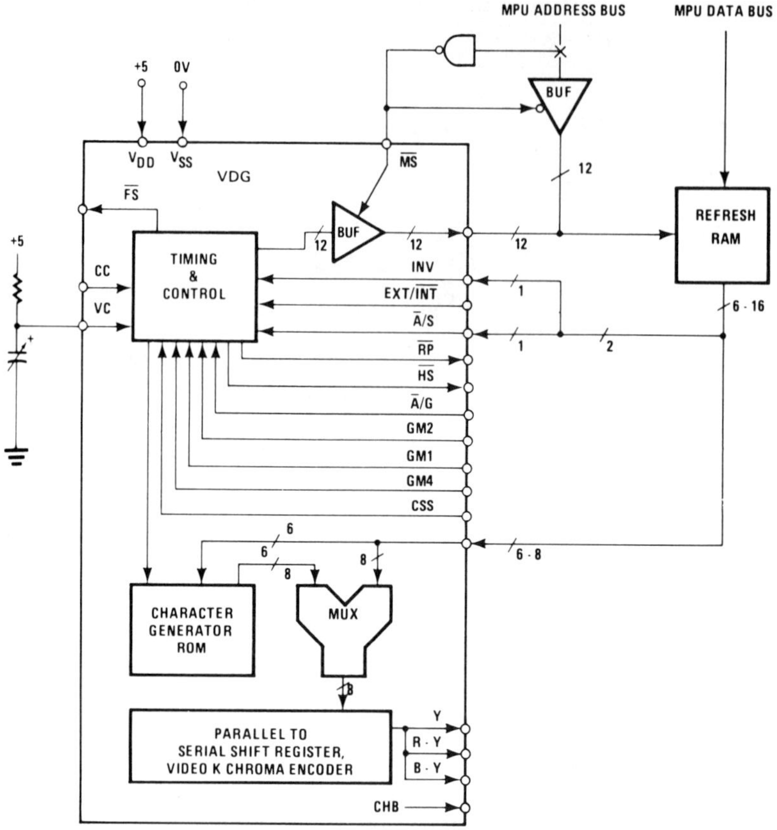

Fig. 14–9. VDG block diagram. (*Courtesy American Microsystems, Inc.*)

Features. The features of the VDG include:

- Compatible with 8-bit computer/processor
- External display memory multiplexer allows direct access by MPU
- Generates full composite video signal
- Controls external color modulator
- Generates four alphanumeric and eight graphic and two semigraphic display modes
- All four alphanumeric modes display thirty-two characters on sixteen lines
- All alphanumeric modes have video inverse
- Alphanumeric external mode has external ROM to extend internal character set for "limited graphics" shapes
- Semigraphic 4-display mode offers nine color 64-by-32 density graphics in an alphanumeric display

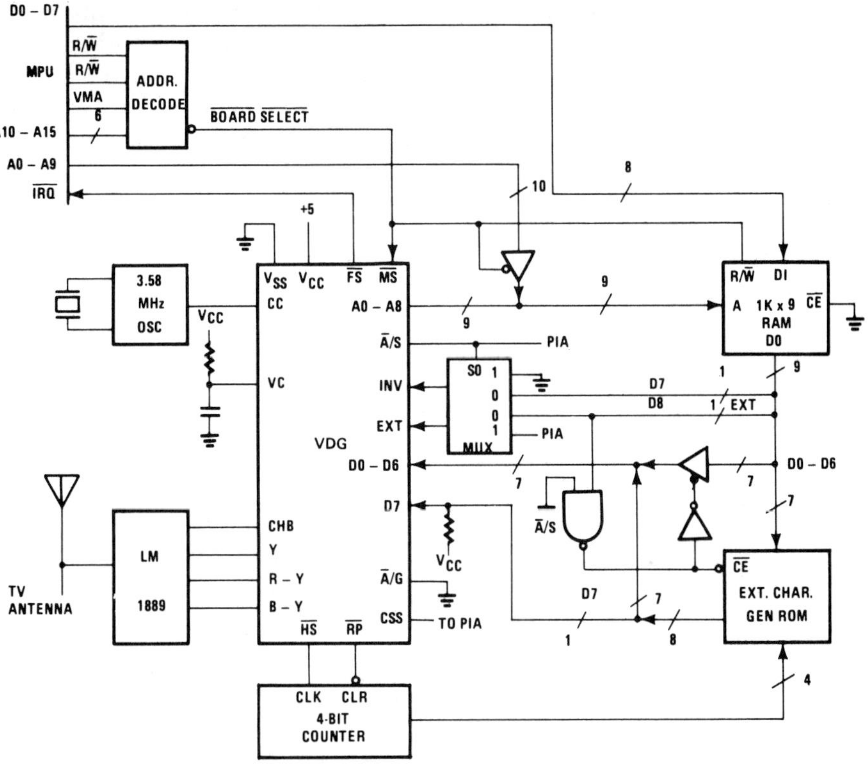

Fig. 14–10. Typical system. (*Courtesy American Microsystems, Inc.*)

- Semigraphic 6-display mode offers five color 64-by-48 density graphics in an alphanumeric display
- Full graphic modes offer 64-by-64, 128-by-64, 128-by-96, 256-by-96, 128-by-192, or 256-by-192 densities
- Full graphic modes allow 2-color and 4-color data structures
- Full graphic modes use one of two 4-color sets or one of two 2-color sets
- Alphanumeric internal mode has internal 5-by-7 character set[11]

Typical application. The S68047 VDG makes new MPU applications practical wherever there is a television: in education, resource planning, bookkeeping, communications and games. The VDG in conjunction with a TV set makes the home computer viable. It is designed to require minimum support components and allows users to select unique configurations geared to their needs.

A typical system is shown in Fig. 14–10.

[11] *Video Display Generator (VDG) S68047 Advanced Product Description* (Santa Clara, California: American Microsystems, Inc., 1978), p. 1.

The system shown in Fig. 14–10 has the ability to display normal and/or inverted 5-by-7 ASCII characters and color semigraphics simultaneously on one raster scan. If two S4016 type RAMs are used, the VDG displays the upper half of display RAM (512 words). The lower half is made available for scratch use by a program. Ten 3-state buffers allow data to be manipulated in the refresh RAM by the MPU. The eight control inputs may be generated through a PIA (S6820) where the processor is flagged by $\overline{\text{HS}}$ or $\overline{\text{FS}}$ VDG outputs.[12]

MC6850 ACIA/MC6860 MODEM

As mentioned in Chapter 7, "Input/Output," the ACIA provides an effective approach for adding asynchronous data communications links to a microcomputer system. The ACIA/modem interface is ideal when microcomputer systems need to communicate in an efficient mode with peripheral equipment, such as teletypewriters, CRT terminals, keyboards, and printers over a long distance.

Recall that the microprocessor manipulates parallel data-byte information at very high speeds compared to the relatively slow speed asynchronous data format needed to communicate with most peripherals. This is the precise task that the MC6850 ACIA performs. One side of the ACIA is directly bus compatible with Motorola's M6800 family of microprocessors while the "outer side" is compatible with asynchronous data format peripherals.

At times it is advantageous to have a microprocessor system transmit and receive data with other computers or computer related equipment that is some distance away. One application that implements the ACIA/modem circuitry to answer this need appears in Fig. 14–11.

Note that the ACIA provides a means to control the modem for the transmission of data to and from a remote terminal such as a teletypewriter, over the standard telephone lines. The modem function can be implemented with a low speed modem such as the MC6860. The MC6860 uses a frequency shift keying (FSK) technique for the transmission of data up to a maximum data rate of 600 bps.

A typical system consists of a local modem and a similar modem at the remote terminal. The local modem converts the digital data from the ACIA to analog form for transmission over the telephone lines. Likewise, analog data received from the remote modem is converted

[12] *VDG S68047 Description*, p. 11.

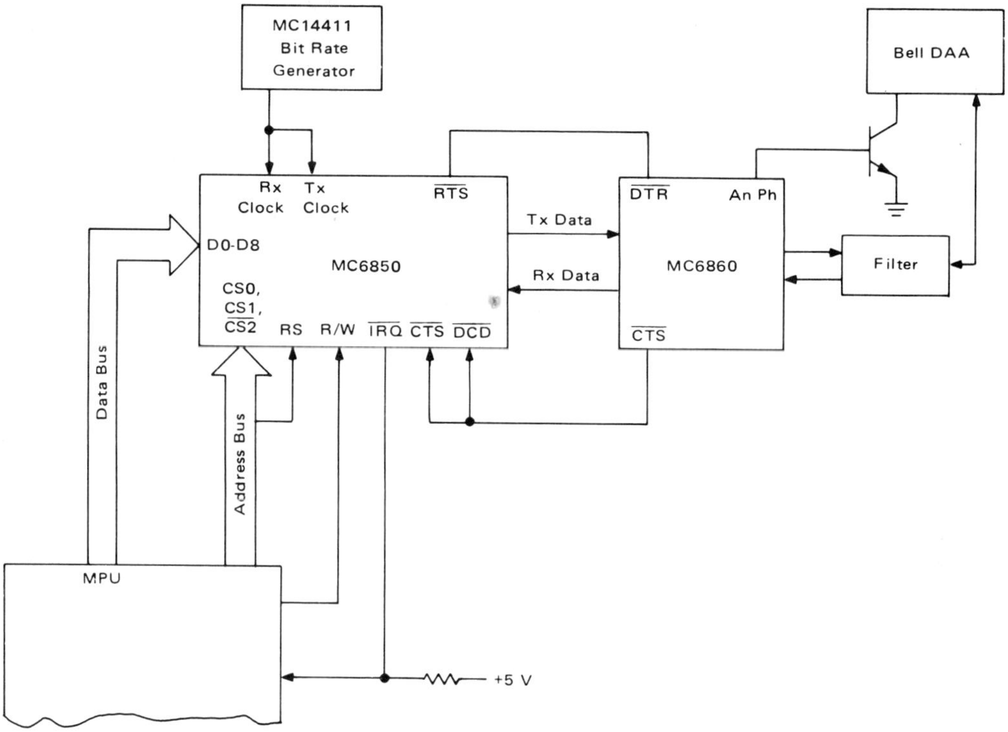

Fig. 14–11. ACIA/modem interface application. (*Courtesy Motorola Inc.*)

back to digital form by the local modem for use by the microcomputer system via the ACIA.[13]

MC6840 PROGRAMMABLE TIMER MODULE (PTM)

The MC6840 PTM frees the MPU and its associated RAM from the timing function task. The three 16-bit wide timers in the PTM will not "bother" the MPU until they have a result of their preprogrammed task. This is especially valuable when long time outs are involved.

The basic block diagram of the MC6840 PTM is shown in Fig. 14–12.

[13] *Device Operation and System Implementation of the Asynchronous Communications Interface Adapter (MC6850) Application Note AN-754* (Phoenix, Arizona: Motorola Inc., 1975), pp. 1, 9.

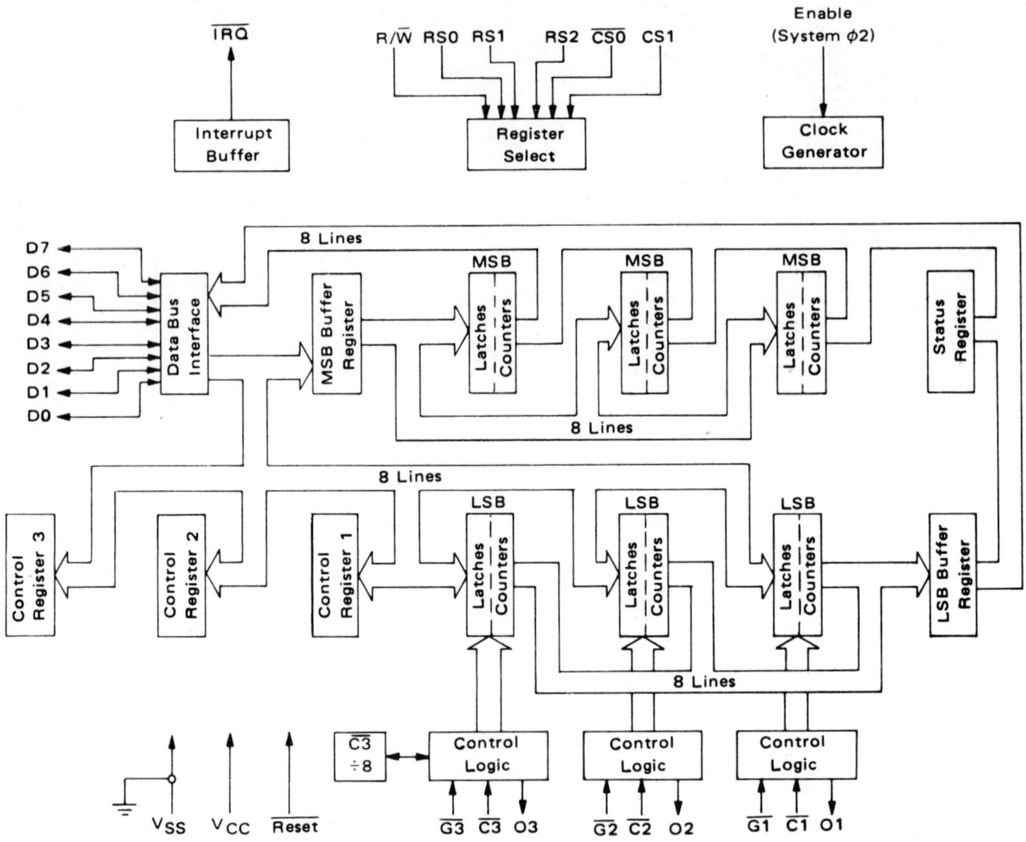

Fig. 14–12. MC6840 PTM basic block diagram. (*Courtesy Motorola Inc.*)

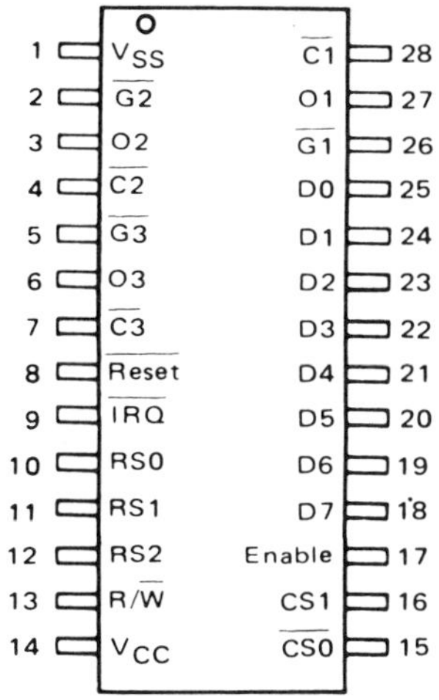

Fig. 14–13. MC6840 PTM pin assignment. (*Courtesy Motorola Inc.*)

The MC6840 pin assignments are given in Fig. 14–13.

Theory of Operation

The MC6840 is a totally compatible member of the M6800 family of peripheral parts. The eight write only and seven read only registers of the PTM appear as eight memory locations to the MPU. The PTM consists of three 16-bit independent timers each capable of four basic modes of operation. Each mode, in turn, has several programmable variations that may be used to suit an individual application.

Figure 14–14 illustrates the straightforward interfacing used to interconnect the PTM with the MC6800 or MC6802 MPU.

Referring to Fig. 14–14, note that the base PTM address has been completely decoded for hexadecimal address $5000. The dollar sign ($) is the Motorola assembler notation to indicate a hexadecimal-based number. A further look at Fig. 14–14 indicates that the two hex inverters and a 13-input NAND gate LS device decode the address and minimize the loading effect on the address bus. If complete address decoding is not necessary, as in a minimum parts count system, two ICs may be eliminated. However, this must be done with care to avoid addressing conflicts. The three least significant bits of the 16-bit address lines are connected directly to the three register select inputs. These three least significant bits, in conjunction with the state of the read/write control line, select the seven read only and the eight write only registers accessible to the MPU.

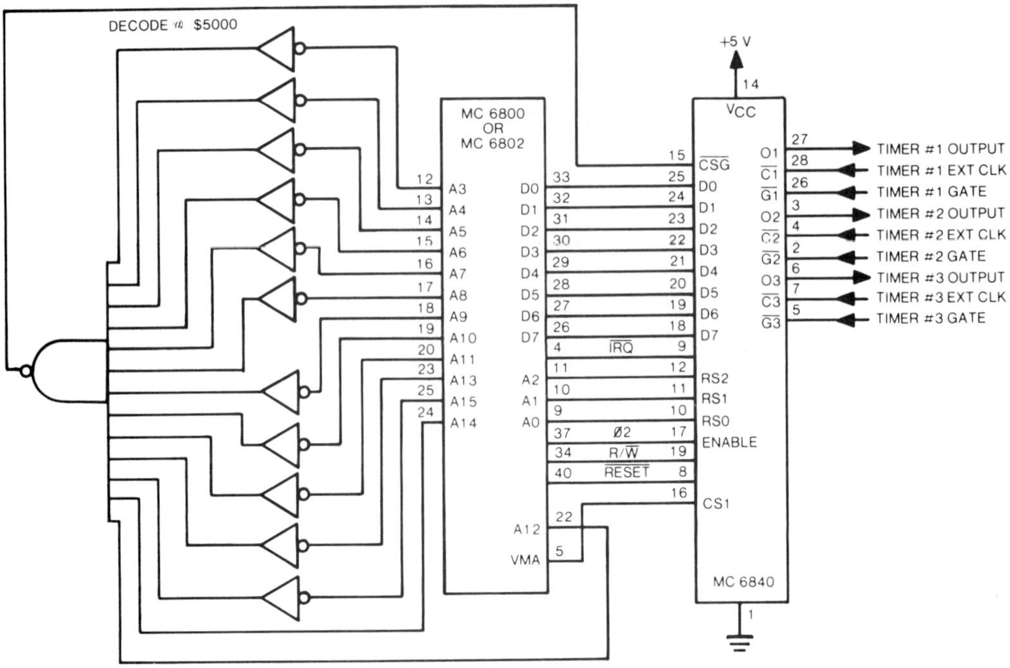

Fig. 14–14. MC6840 PTM interfaced to MPU. (*Courtesy Motorola Inc.*)

Because timing plays a very important function in all micro-based systems, the applications of a programming timer module like the MC6840 are virtually endless.

Basic Modes of Operation

The MC6840 PTM has four basic modes of operation: continuous mode, single-shot mode, period measurement mode, and pulse width measurement mode.

Continuous mode. In this mode, the timer counts down its initial programmed timer data word (sixteen bits) to zero. This is called a time out (TO) and may generate an interrupt if it is so programmed. The continuous output is shown in Fig. 14–15.

Note that the output is low for the first time out period and then changes state for each subsequent time out period. This produces a 50% duty cycle square wave twice the duration of the time out.

Single-shot mode. The single-shot mode is similar to the continuous mode except that the output produces only one high pulse for the time out period. In this mode, the timer operates as a programmable,

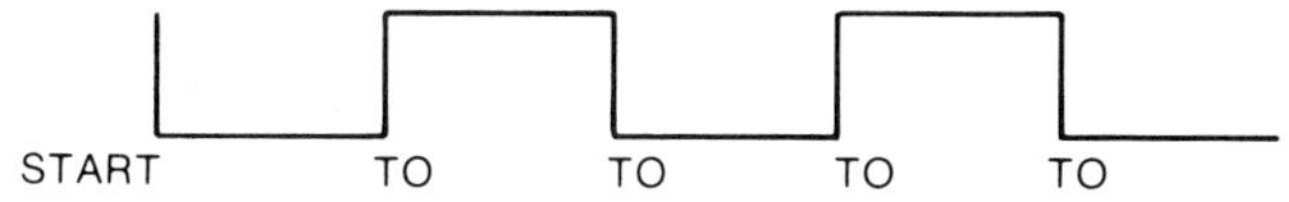

Fig. 14–15. MC6840 PTM continuous mode output. (*Courtesy Motorola Inc.*)

Fig. 14–16. MC6840 PTM single-shot mode. (*Courtesy Motorola Inc.*)

retriggerable one-shot. The output waveform for this single-shot mode is given in Fig. 14–16.

Period measurement mode. The third mode of operation possible with the MC6840 PTM is called the period measurement mode. One operation performed in this mode is measuring the period (reciprocal of the frequency) of a given digital signal. An example of this waveform appears in Fig. 14–17.

When the pulse goes low the first time, the timer starts counting down from its programmed number. When the signal goes low again, the timer stops counting down and generates an interrupt. The MPU can then easily determine the frequency $\left(\frac{1}{p} = f\right)$.

Pulse width measurement mode. The PWMM or pulse width measurement mode can determine the width of a given pulse. It measures down time of a digital signal in the same manner as the period measurement mode. The timer starts decrementing when the input pulse goes low and stops decrementing and generates an interrupt when the input pulse returns to high as shown in Fig. 14–18.

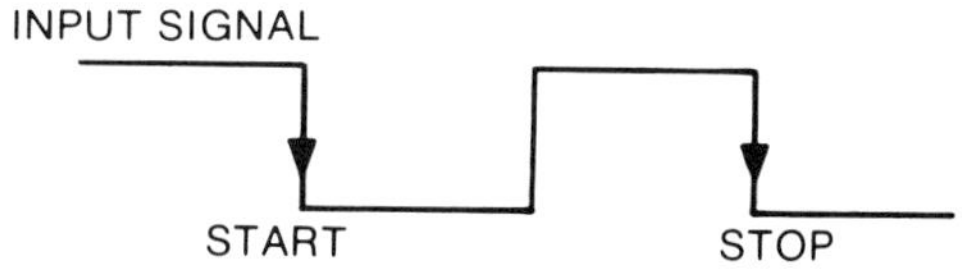

Fig. 14–17. MC6840 PTM period measurement mode. (*Courtesy Motorola Inc.*)

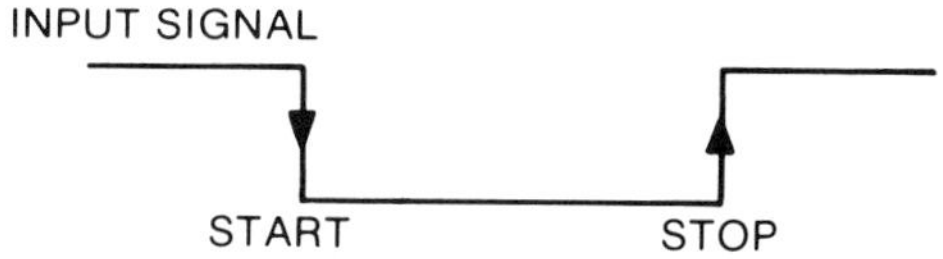

Fig. 14–18. MC6840 PTM pulse width measurement mode. (*Courtesy Motorola Inc.*)

There are many variations of operation using the four modes just described. The three timers are independent and each may be:

1. Cascaded with another timer
2. Operated in any of three basic modes
3. Programmed to use the internal clock or an external clock.[14]

ANALOG-TO-DIGITAL CONVERSION

The actual signals that are available from most sensing devices such as photo cells, flow meters, and temperature sensing units, all function as transducers. They convert some form of energy to an electrical signal that changes in an analog fashion. The change is usually slow and has many different levels between being fully on and completely off. This is a typical characteristic of most natural energy sources like light, water flow, and heat.

A frequently encountered problem is converting these analog electrical signals into precise digital equivalents. This problem is most often solved by using an analog-to-digital converter.

The digital equivalent process is necessary before a microprocessor or microcomputer can use analog information. Recall that the microprocessor, like all digital machines, can only work with or understand 1s and 0s. Analog signals, on the other hand, can be divided into many levels between the fully on (1) and completely off (0) such as 0.1, 0.3, 0.5, 0.8, 0.9.

One of the latest members of the M6800 family that addresses this need is the MC6805R2L1/P1 which has an A/D converter onboard with the following characteristics:

- 8-bit conversion
- 4 multiplexed analog inputs
- ± 1/2 LSB quantizing error
- ± 1 LSB total erros (maximum)
- Ratiometric conversion

When the MC6805R2L1/P1 microcomputer is connected as shown in Fig. 14–19, the user can implement the A/D section without requiring any additional circuitry.

A brief explanation of the analog select operation is in order.

The analog input is selected by setting the three switches con-

[14] *Programmable Timer Fundamentals and Applications* (Austin, Texas: Motorola Inc., 1979), pp. 1–1, 1–2, 2–1.

Table 14–1 A/D input MUX selection.

Control Status Register			Input Selected
CSR2	CSR1	CSR0	
0	0	0	AN0
0	0	1	AN1
0	1	0	AN2
0	1	1	AN3
1	0	0	V_{RH}*
1	0	1	V_{RL}*
1	1	0	$V_{RH}/4$*
1	1	1	$V_{RH}/2$*

*Internal (Calibration) levels
(*Courtesy Motorola Inc.*)

nected to A0, A1, and A2 in various open-close combinations. Refer to Table 14–1.

The components required in Fig. 14–19 are standard parts except for the 7-segment display and the 10-turn potentiometer. The two 7-segment displays (with decoders) are Texas Instruments TIL-311 displays. They are connected to display the result in hexadecimal. The 10-turn potentiometer is connected across the voltage reference input. It allows for the application of a controlled voltage to one of the analog inputs. This connection can be made using pin-and-jack jumpering from the 10-turn potentiometer to one of the AN0-AN3 inputs.

An inside look at the analog-to-digital and analog select multiplex (MUX) block diagram appears in Fig. 14–20.[15]

SUMMARY

In this chapter, the reader has been exposed to several applications that are directly centered around the M6800 microprocessor/microcomputer family. The first example indicated the necessary interfacing, specifically the IEEE GP-IB, that is used to make communication possible between the microprocessor and instruments and related electronic equipment that is IEEE GP-IB compatible.

The video display generator application, like the IEEE GP-IB, is very dependent on the microprocessor for successful operation.

The ACIA/modem application illustrates a typical microprocessor long distance communications technique.

[15] *MC6805R2 Advance Information Sheet ADI-845* (Austin, Texas: Motorola Inc., 1980), p. 23.

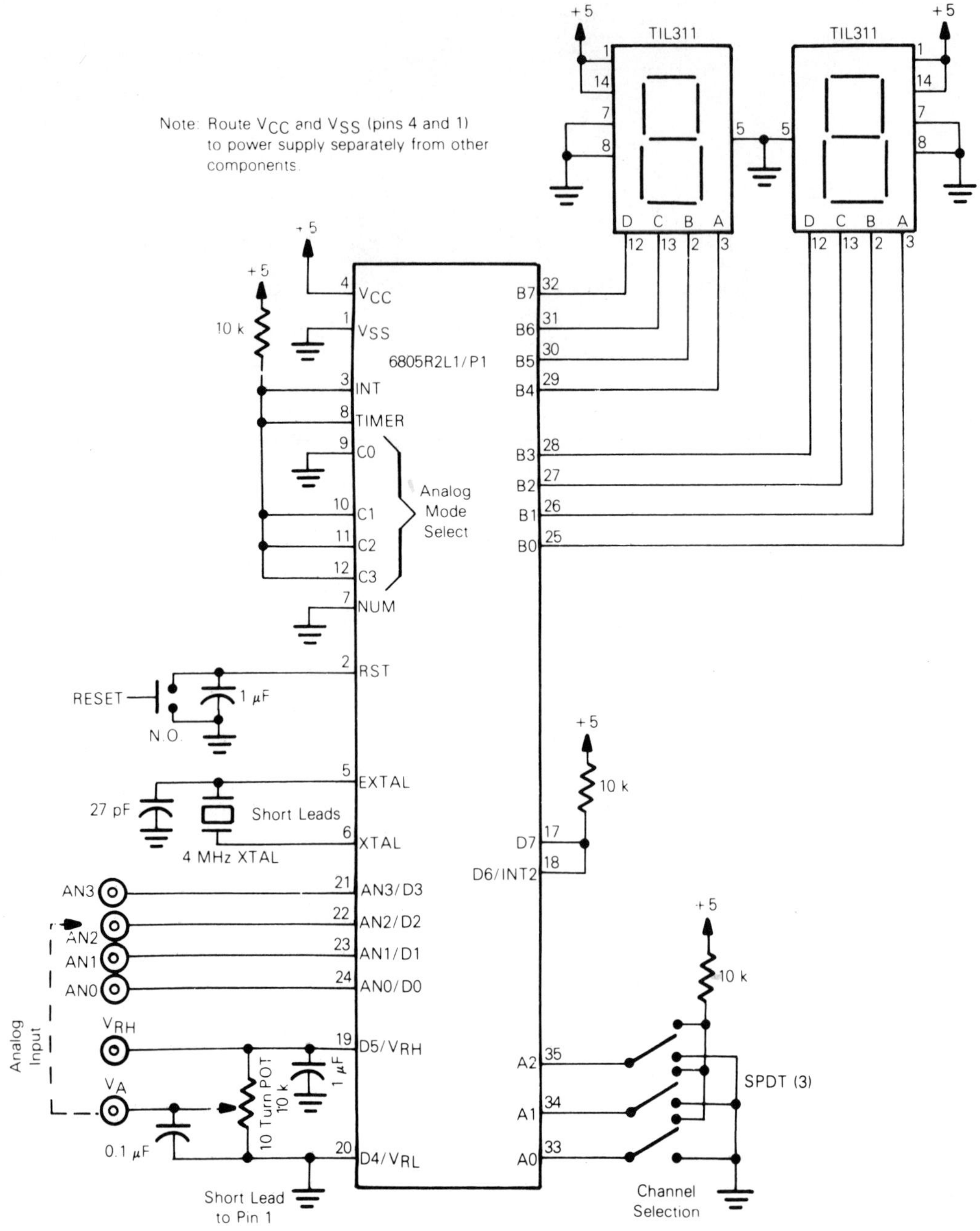

Fig. 14–19. MC6805R2L1/P1 A/D conversion. (*Courtesy Motorola Inc.*)

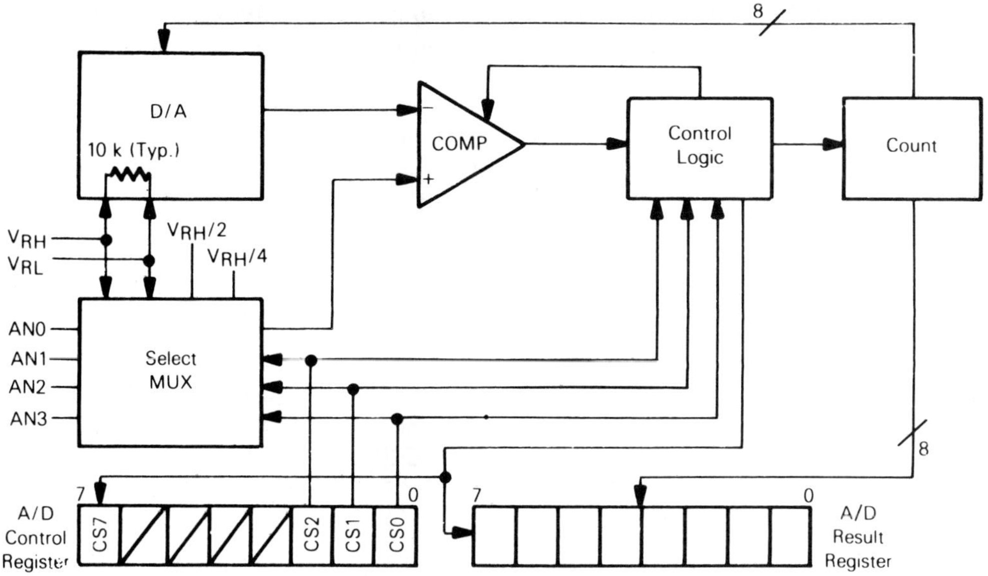

Fig. 14–20. MC6805R2L1/P1 A/D block diagram. (*Courtesy Motorola Inc.*)

The PTM demonstrates a microsupport device that frees the MPU from the time consuming task of precise timing pulses. It also eliminates the usual heavy software overhead involved when the MPU is required to perform these timing functions.

The final application using the MC6805 microcomputer-based A/D conversion exemplifies the state-of-the-art in single chip applications.

These are only a few of literally thousands of applications which depend on and will continue to depend on microprocessor technology.

QUESTIONS

1. Explain in your own words what the IEEE GP-IB is.
2. List at least three types of test equipment that could be interfaced to a microprocessor.
3. Can you think of a system that could make use of The Hewlett-Packard model 59309A digital clock? Explain.
4. What functions does the MC3448A IC perform in the overall IEEE GP-IB system?
5. List several application examples for the AMI S68047 VDG.
6. List several application examples for the Motorola MC6847 VDG.

7. Can a modem be used in a microprocessor circuit without a serial-to-parallel/parallel-to-serial device such as the ACIA? Why or why not?
8. List the four modes of operation of the MC6840 PTM.
9. What is the basic difference between the PTM's period measurement mode and the pulse width measurement mode?
10. List the logic level (0/1) for the MC6805R2L1/P1 A/D input MUX selection of:

INPUT SELECTED	CONTROL STATUS REGISTER		
AN0	CSR0 =	CSR1 =	CSR2 =
AN1	CSR0 =	CSR1 =	CSR2 =
AN2	CSR0 =	CSR1 =	CSR2 =
AN3	CSR0 =	CSR1 =	CSR2 =

Chapter 15

Looking Ahead . . .

This chapter is designed to look at two things: first, the kind of approach you may wish to adopt in continuing to learn about microprocessors and second, some of the more recent advances in microprocessors that are going to become common in the near future.

This book has been written using the Intel 8080 and the Motorola MC6800 microprocessors because their software and hardware are typical examples of today's microprocessors.

Whether this book has been used as a text in an introductory microprocessor class or as a self-study book for gaining background, by reading the previous chapter, you have reached the point where basic terminology connected with microprocessors is familiar. The basic concepts and understanding of how microprocessors operate has been achieved. You are therefore ready to continue learning in more detail how to deal with specific problems and devices. This can be done by several methods. If you are in a formal classroom environment, obviously you can take the next course. If you are studying on your own, however, the procedure may not be simple. So some suggestions may be helpful.

FURTHER STUDY SUGGESTIONS

The microprocessor manufacturers have provided for the study of microprocessors by developing relatively inexpensive prestructured systems. These training modules provide all the fundamental hardware necessary for a basic system. They usually provide the main processing unit, a method of code input (usually a hexadecimal keypad), some form of output (usually a segmented 7 LED display), a resident monitor for the system in ROM, a limited amount of RAM memory (usually 1/4 to 1 K byte), space for expansion (usually wire-wrap area or empty socket positions) and access to the bus structures through standard jacks or edge connectors.

Of course, spending more money would buy more sophisticated capabilities but, for the person wishing to learn both hardware and software at the machine level, these training modules are ideal. In most cases, the buyer will have to provide the power supply which meets the voltage and current requirements of the system.

It is also sound judgment to be in contact with other people interested in discussing and learning microprocessors. Therefore, the forming of or joining a microprocessor group or computer club is a good idea. The meetings, discussion and informational exchanges that go on in these groups can be of immeasurable value to both the beginner and the "Old Pro."

Be prepared to spend a reasonable amount of money. Computers are not any longer the expensive devices they once were but they also are not down to the price of a transistor radio. And do not expect to have a complete system with CRT, teletype and floppy disk set up in a matter of a few weeks unless a larger cash outlay is made. A better procedure is to buy a basic capability first and then build it up as the learning process goes on.

It is not absolutely essential that the person studying microprocessors have a system to work with but experience has proven that the learning period is dramatically shortened by means of "hands on" experience. And eventually one does have to put into practice what one has learned or it is of not lasting value.

So much for the advice and suggestions to the independent learner. In this last chapter, some of the devices which have developed out of the M6800 and 8080 families will also be discussed.

A LOOK AT INTEL

Over the past several years Intel has developed several new systems and devices that are 8080 upward compatible. That is, the language set used by the 8080 is either enhanced or is a proper subset of the more advanced chip so that programs written for the basic 8080 device will also be functional on the new product. This section will concentrate on two of the new devices: the 8085 and 8086. The 8085 became more or less the standard about 1978. The 8086 was recently released by Intel and is making strong inroads in the 16-bit market.

The 8085

The 8085 is essentially an 8080 with added speed, efficiency, and two new instructions. The 8085 is capable of running at 320 nano-seconds as opposed to the 8080's 180-nanosecond rate. The 8085's more efficient structuring method is multiplexing. The 8085 is still housed in a 40-pin package, but several new lines have been added because the address data bus of the 8080 has been combined into a single set of eight bits, AD0 through AD7. The data and addresses of the lower eight bits of the 15-bit address are multiplexed on the 8-bit bus. Also, the clock, the system controller, and the bus buffering and latching which were external to the 8080 have been moved on-board the 8085. Two new lines added to the 8085 are direct serial data input and output lines: serial input data (SID) and serial output data (SOD). Because of the multiplexing, the 8085 requires one additional line called the address latching enable (ALE). Its voltage level and edge indicate when the address is valid.

Additionally, four new vectored interrupt lines have been added to the 8085: a nonmaskable interrupt called the TRAP line, and the 5.5, 6.5, and 7.5 interrupt connections.

Further, two status bits have been put into the 8085 structure to indicate the type of data bus operation that will occur in the next machine cycle. These play a similar role to the status bits of the 8080 data bus, but are already latched within the 8085 structure and simply indicate memory or I/O read or write status.

Two new 8085 instructions, read interrupt mask (RIM) and set interrupt mask (SIM), relate to the SID and SOD lines and the masking and handling of vectored interrupt systems. These new instructions deal with the control and manipulation of the internal bit structures that control the vectored interrupt mask. They allow prioritizing, holding interrupts, masking of interrupts, the unmasking of specific vectors, and the setting and resetting of serial data bits that enter and exit through the SID and SOD lines. As with most internal registers in programmable devices, these bits must obey the proper coding and control operations as specified by the manufacturer's user's manual.

The configuration of the 8085 provides for an efficient, low package count for a complete system. A minimum system requires a three package count.

Intel compares the 8080 and the 8085 systems in the following way:

1. The access times from address leaving the processor to returning data are almost identical, even though the 8085 is operating 50% faster than the 8080.

2. With the addition of an 8212 latch to the 8085, the basic timings of the two systems are very similar.

3. The 8085 has more time for address setup to $\overline{RD}$ than the 8080.

4. The MCS-80 has a wider $\overline{RD}$ signal, but a narrower $\overline{WR}$ signal than the 8085.

5. The MCS-80 provides stable data setup to the leading and trailing edges of $\overline{WR}$, while the 8085 provides stable data setup to only the trailing edge of $\overline{WR}$.

6. The MCS-80 control signals have different widths and occur at different points in the machine cycle, while the 8085 control signals have identical timing.

7. The MCS-80 data and address hold times are adversely affected by the processor preparing to enter the hold state. The 8085 has identical timing regardless of entering hold.

8. All output signals of the 8085 have -400 μa of source current and 2.0 ma of sink current. The 8085 also has input voltage levels of $V_{IL} = 0.8$ V and $V_{IH} = 2.0$ V.

The MCS-85 bus is compatible because it requires only an 8212 latch to generate an MCS-80 type bus. If the four control signals, $\overline{MEMR}$, $\overline{MEMW}$, $\overline{IOR}$ and $\overline{IOW}$ are desired, they can be generated from $\overline{RD}$, $\overline{WR}$ and $\overline{IO/M}$ with a decoder or a few gates. The MCS-85 bus is also fast. While running at 3 MHz, the 8085 generates better timing signals than the MCS-80 does at 2 MHz. Furthermore, the multiplexed bus structure does not slow the 8085 down because it is using the internal states to overlap the fetch and execution portions of different machine cycles. Finally, the MCS-85 can be slowed down or sped up considerably while still providing reasonable timing.

The MCS-85 system bus also meets the goal of being easy to use. The $\overline{RD}$, $\overline{WR}$ and $\overline{INTA}$ control signals all have identical timing which is not affected by the CPU preparing to enter the hold state. Furthermore, the address and data bus have good setup and hold times relative to the control signals. The voltage and current levels for the interface signals will all drive buses of up to 40 MOS devices or 1 schottky TTL device.

The MCS-85 system bus is also efficient. Efficiency is the reason that the lower eight address lines are multiplexed with the data bus. Every chip that needs to use both $A_0 - A_7$ and $D_0 - D_7$ saves seven pins (the eighth pin is used for ALE) on the interface to the processor. That means that seven more pins per part are available to either add features to the part or to use a smaller package in some cases. In the 3-chip system the use of the MCS-85 bus saves $3 \times 7 = 21$ pins which are used for extra I/O and interrupt lines. The reduced number of pins and the fact that compatible pinouts were used provides for an extremely compact, simple and efficient printed circuit. Great care was taken when the pinouts were assigned to ensure that the signals would flow easily from chip to chip to chip.

The 8086

It would seem that the world is never satisfied with the speed and power of existing data processing systems. The express desire of every data process design is to process an infinite amount of data in zero time which, of course, is impossible. The real world limit to processing speed is the speed of light. Even as a processor could process data at picosecond rates it is futile to do so when it takes from two to three nanoseconds for the data to travel from its source to its destination.

The answer to the need for speed and power is quite simple in concept, but quite complex in accomplishment. The answer is to create a very simple system that can process a greater number of bits at one time while allowing several processors to work together simultaneously. The future of data processing at the microprocessor level lies in the ability to provide multiprocessing network capability. Intel has responded to this need with the 8086 microprocessor.

The 8086 microprocessor is a true 16-bit processor capable of operating at clock frequencies from 5 to 8 MHz. The 8086 assembly language instruction set is not upward compatible with the 8080 base language. However, it can be assembled upward from the 8080 language. That is, any programs written in 8080 or 8085 code may be assembled into 8086 sequences using the 8086 assembler.

The 8086 central processing unit achieves its speed by having the internal workings divided into two separate units: an execution unit (EU) and a bus interface unit (BIU). These halves of the CPU operate on an asynchronous basis. The bus interface unit handles all of the interfaces and data handling with the external bus. It generates the external memory and I/O addresses and has a six-byte queue. Whenever the execution unit needs to access memory or I/O device, it makes an access request to the interface unit. If the bus interface is not currently busy, it acknowledges the bus access from the EU and performs the instructional fetch machine cycles to fill the six-byte instructional object code queue. The CPU takes its instruction codes from the queue. Therefore, the instruction fetch time is essentially zero.

The 8086 also has built-in logic to handle bus access priorities for multiple CPU configurations. In this configuration each CPU has its own local memory and simultaneously shares a common memory with other CPUs or multiprocessors on the same bus arrangement. The 8086 cannot operate by itself. It requires an 8284 clock generator driver and an 8288 bus controller in the system. This is similar to the 8080 device which required an 8224 chip to operate.

The 8086 system is operated in basically two different modes. The minimum mode is essentially a stand-alone mode with a one- or two-board single CPU system in operation. The maximum mode is used in multiprocessor and/or co-processor configuration. The programming model of the 8086 in Fig. 15–1 illustrates that the 8086 has many more registers available than the 8080 did. The familiar accumulator B, C, and D registers are present but in the 8086 they are 16-bit registers.

The 8086 base pointer, source index register, and destination index are new to the 8080 user. The names of the registers will seem slightly uncomfortable to the 8080 user at the beginning. Although the stack is used in the general register, the addressing modes in the 8086 provide for a different instruction of the address to be accessed in memory. A set of four segment registers, CS or code segment, DS or data segment, ES or extra segment, SS or stack segment, are contained within the BIU, and all instructional fetches are made from the address CS. IP means that the segment register and the offset register are merged into a single address which is then latched and put out as a 20-bit code allowing for one megabyte of direct addressing. (See Fig. 15–1.)

Figure 15–1 also illustrates an offset technique used in the address. The segment registers consisting of 16 bits are added to the 16 bits of offset address with the lower four bits left at 0000. Therefore, the instructions must be fetched from an even-numbered hexidecimal code.

There are four basic addressing modes that can be used: register-to-register addressing, immediate-to-register addressing, register to and from memory, and immediate to and from memory. Whenever a memory reference is used, one of the four segment registers is also used with the offset to access the location.

The addressing scheme of the 8086 takes time to master. It is relatively complex because of allowances for multiple access and multiple CPU systems where more than one CPU shares a common memory while each CPU must also keep track of its own program locations.

Since the addressing modes of the 8086 are quite complex they take a good deal of time to master. Let us then move on quickly to a summary of the instruction set categories.

The 8086 instruction set consists of roughly 70 instructions and up to 30 addressing modes. The basic categories of instructions are the data transfer instructions including move, push, pop, exchange, in, out, and a variety of load instructions for the various registers. Arithmetic instructions include add, add with carry, increment, subtract, subtract with borrow, decrement, compare, ASCII adjust, decimal adjust, multiple-unsigned, multiple-signed, ASCII adjust for multiplication, divide, integer division-signed, ASCII adjust for divide, convert

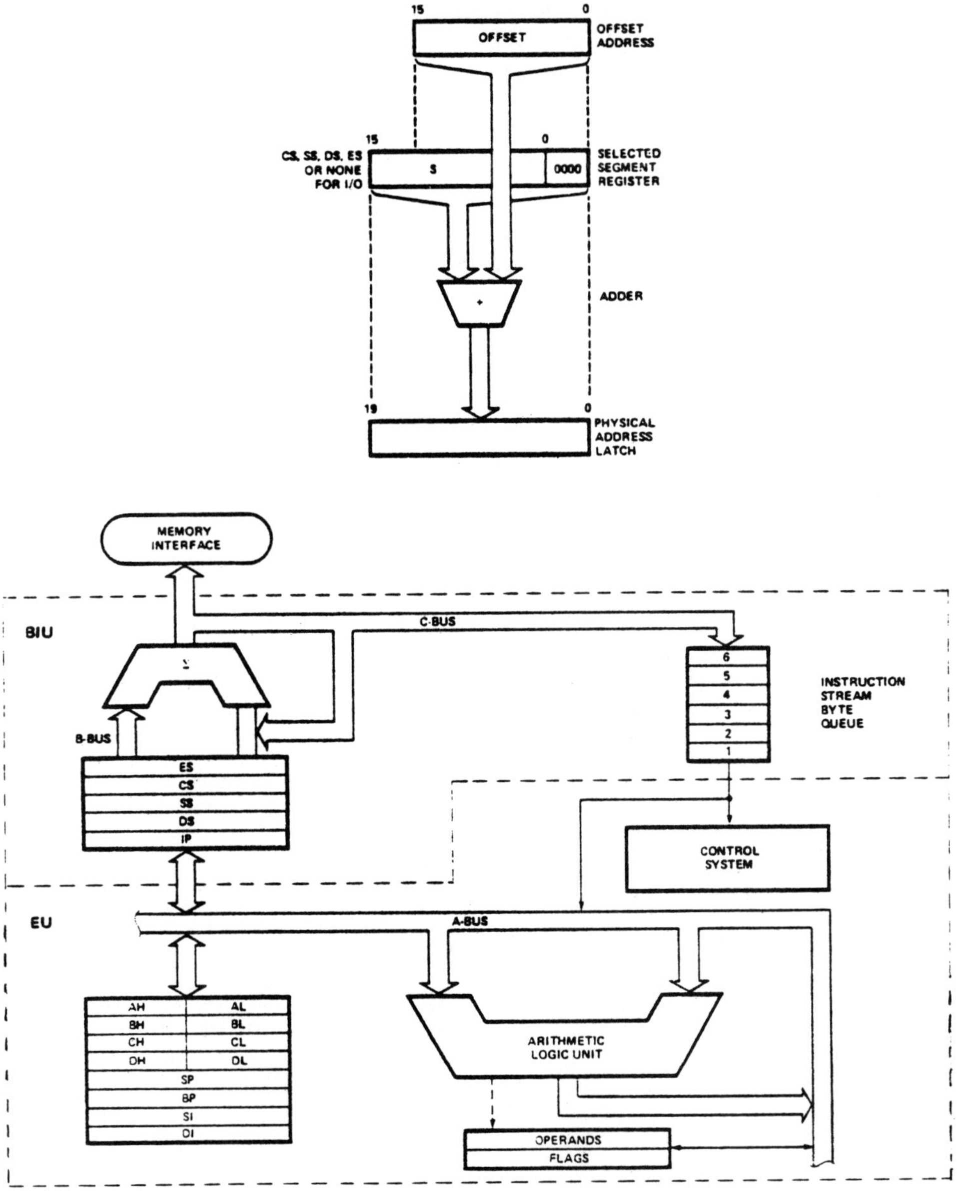

Fig. 15–1. 8086 programming model and offset technique.

bytes to words, convert word to doubleword. A logical set uses the standard NOT, shift logically left (arithmetic left), shift logically right (an arithmetic right), rotate right and left, rotate through carry (flags left), rotate through carry (flags right), AND instruction, test, OR, and EXCLUSIVE OR functions.

Control categories are call, jump, and return, and an extensive group of jump conditional. There is another category of processor control functions having to do with setting the flag structures of the 8086 with halt, wait, and escape functions.

Finally, the string manipulations operations allow the use of ASCII strings and strings of operation including repeat, move bytes or words, compare bytes or words, scan for bytes or words, load bytes or words to the AL and AX, and store bytes and words from AL and AX. The list of instructions just briefly summarized is almost infinitely expandable by 30 addressing modes.

A LOOK AT MOTOROLA

The Motorola MC68000

Because of advances in semiconductor technology, a single silicon chip can contain a microprocessor at least an order of magnitude higher in performance and circuit complexity than has been previously available. The MC68000 is the first of a family of such VLSI microprocessors from Motorola. It combines state-of-the-art technology and advanced circuit design techniques with computer sciences to achieve an architecturally advanced 16-bit microprocessor. Advances such as dry plasma etching, projection printing, and HMOS circuit design techniques (shown in Fig. 15–2) have provided a sound technological base for a large degree of innovative freedom resulting in microprocessors that are easy to use, more reliable and more flexible for applications while maximizing performance.

The resources available to the MC68000 user consist of the following:

- 32-bit data and address registers
- 16-megabyte direct addressing range
- 56 powerful instruction types
- Operations on five main data types
- Memory mapped I/O
- 14 addressing modes

Particular emphasis has been given to making the architecture regular with respect to the registers, instructions (including all addressing

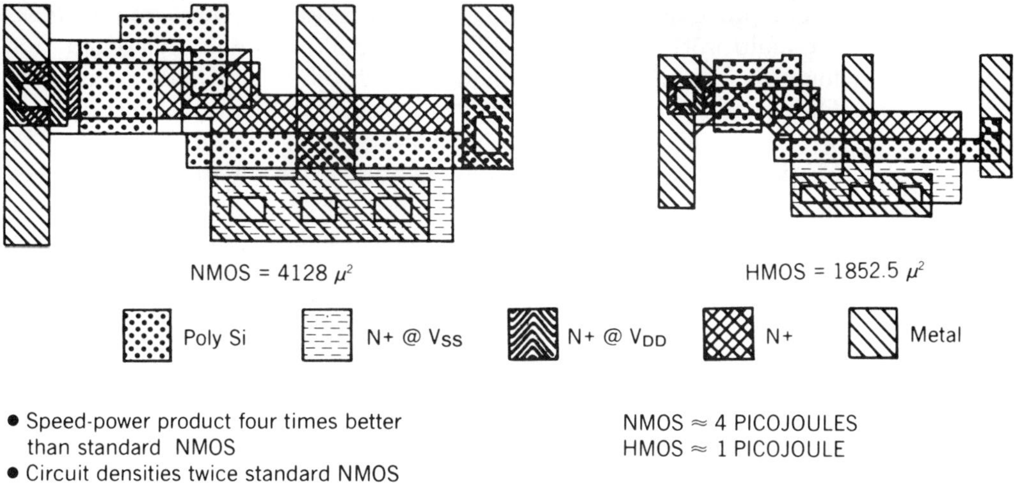

Fig. 15–2. HMOS circuit design techniques. (*Courtesy Motorola Inc.*)

modes), and data types. A consistent structure makes the architecture easy to learn and program, and, in the process, reduces both the time required to write programs and the space required to store programs. The net result is a great reduction in the cost and risk of developing software.

High systems throughput (up to an aggregate of two million instruction and data word transfers per second) is achieved even with readily available standard product memories with comparatively slow access times. The design flexibility of the data bus allows the mixing of slow and fast memories or peripherals with the processor, automatically optimizing the transfer rate on every access to keep the system operating at peak efficiency.

The hardware design of the CPU was heavily influenced by advances made in software technology. High level language compilers as well as code produced from high level languages must run efficiently on the new generation 16-bit and 32-bit microprocessors. The MC68000 supports high level languages with its consistent architecture, multiple registers and stacks, large addressing range, and high level language oriented instructions such as LINK, UNLK, CHK. Also, operating systems for controlling the software operating environment of the MC68000 are supported by privileged instructions, memory management, a powerful vectored multilevel interrupt and trap structure, and specific instructions including MOVEP, MOVEM, TRAP.

The processor also provides both hardware and software interlocks for multiprocessor systems. The MC68000 contains bus arbitration logic for sharing bus and memory with other MC68000 processors, DMA, and similar devices. Multiprocessor systems are also supported with software instructions (TAS—test and set operand). The MC68000 offers the maximum flexibility for microprocessor-based multiprocessor systems.

Advanced architecture processors must not only offer efficient solutions to large, complex problems but must also be able to handle the small, simple problems with proportional efficiency. The MC68000 has been designed to offer the maximum in performance and versatility to solve simple and complex problems efficiently.

As shown in the programming model in Fig. 15–3, the MC68000 has seventeen 32-bit registers in addition to the 32-bit program

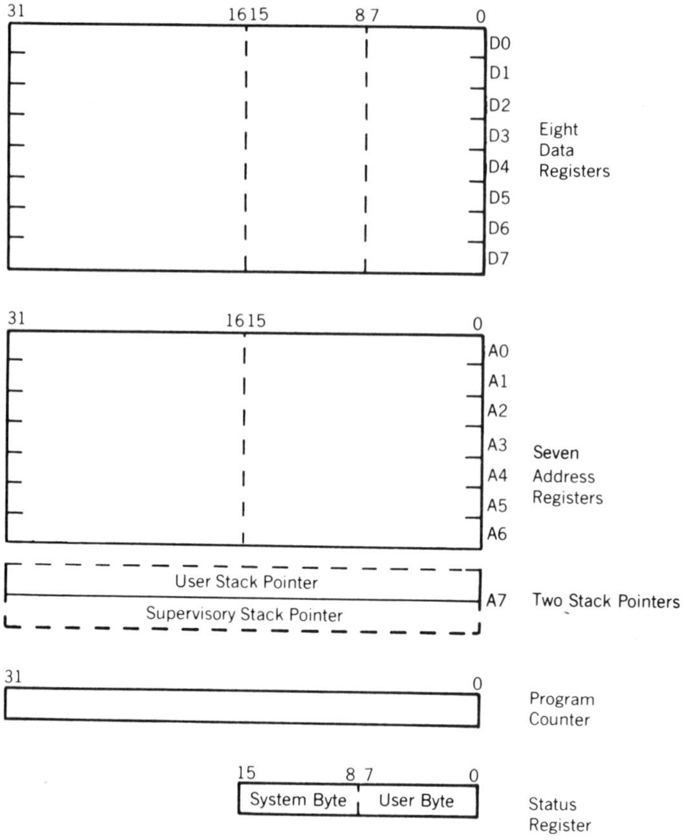

Fig. 15–3. MC68000 programming model. (*Courtesy Motorola Inc.*)

counter and 16-bit status register. The first eight registers (D0–D7) are used as data registers for byte (8-bit), word (16-bit), and long word (32-bit) data operations. The second set of seven registers (A0–A6) and the system stack pointer (A7) may be used as software stack pointers and base address registers. In addition, these registers may be used for word and long word address operations. All of the seventeen registers may be used as index registers.

The 24-bit address bus provides a memory addressing range of more than 16 megabytes (actually 16,777,216 bytes). This large range of addressing capability, coupled with a memory management unit, allows large, modular programs to be developed and operated without resorting to cumbersome and time consuming software bookkeeping and paging techniques.

The status register, shown in Fig. 15–4, contains the interrupt mask (eight levels available) as well as the condition codes, overflow (V), zero (Z) negative (N), carry (C), and extend (X). Additional status bits indicate that the processor is in a trace (T) mode and/or in a supervisor (S) state. Ample space remains in the status register for future extensions of the MC68000 family.

Five basic data types are supported:

- Bits
- BCD digits (4-bits)
- Bytes (8-bits)
- Words (16 bits)
- Long words (32-bits)

In addition, operations on other data types such as memory addresses and status word data are provided in the instruction set.

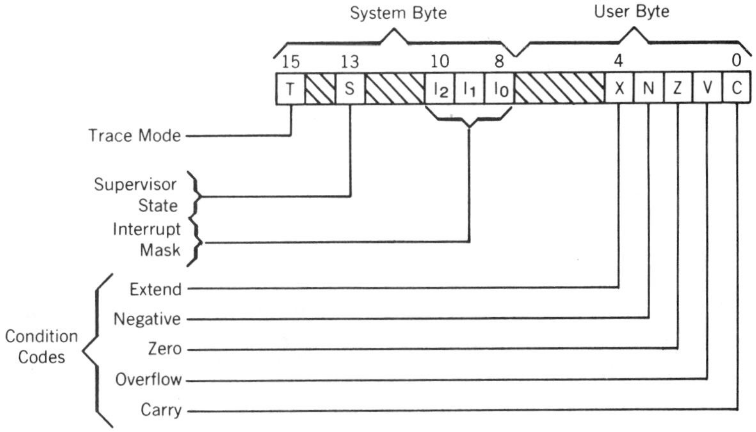

Fig. 15–4. MC68000 status register. (*Courtesy Motorola Inc.*)

Table 15–1 MC68000 Data Addressing Modes

Mode	Generation
Register Direct Addressing	
Data Register Direct	EA = Dn
Address Register Direct	EA = An
Absolute Data Addressing	
Absolute Short	EA = (Next Word)
Absolute Long	EA = (Next Two Words)
Program Counter Relative Addressing	
Relative with Offset	EA = (PC) + d_{16}
Relative with Index and Offset	EA = (PC) + (Xn) + d_8
Register Indirect Addressing	
Register Indirect	EA = (An)
Postincrement Register Indirect	EA = (An), An ← An + N
Predecrement Register Indirect	An ← An − N, EA = (An)
Register Indirect With Offset	EA = (An) + d_{16}
Indexed Register Indirect With Offset	EA = (An) + (Xn) + d_8
Immediate Data Addressing	
Immediate	DATA = Next Word(s)
Quick Immediate	Inherent Data
Implied Addressing	
Implied Register	EA = SR, USP, SP, PC

NOTES:

EA = Effective Address
An = Address Register
Dn = Data Register
Xn = Address or Data Register used as Index Register
SR = Status Register
PC = Program Counter
d_8 = Eight-bit Offset (displacement)
d_{16} = Sixteen-bit Offset (displacement)
N = 1 for Byte, 2 for Words and 4 for Long Words
( ) = Contents of
← = Replaces

(Courtesy Motorola Inc.)

The fourteen flexible modes shown in Table 15–1 include six basic types:

- Register direct
- Register indirect
- Absolute
- Immediate
- Program counter relative
- Implied

Included in the register indirect addressing modes is the capability to do postincrementing, predecrementing, offsetting, and indexing. Program counter relative mode can also be modified via indexing and offsetting.

The MC68000 instruction set is shown in Table 15–2. Some additional instructions, appearing in Table 15–3, are variations or subsets of these.

Table 15–2 MC68000 Instruction Set

Mnemonic	Description
ABCD	Add Decimal with Extend
ADD	Add
AND	Logical And
ASL	Arithmetic Shift Left
ASR	Arithmetic Shift Right
B_{cc}	Branch Conditionally
BCHG	Bit Test and Change
BCLR	Bit Test and Clear
BRA	Branch Always
BSET	Bit Test and Set
BSR	Branch to Subroutine
BTST	Bit Test
CHK	Check Register Against Bounds
CLR	Clear Operand
CMP	Compare
DB_{cc}	Test Cond., Decrement and Branch
DIVS	Signed Divide
DIVU	Unsigned Divide
EOR	Exclusive Or
EXG	Exchange Registers
EXT	Sign Extend
JMP	Jump
JSR	Jump to Subroutine
LEA	Load Effective Address
LINK	Link Stack
LSL	Logical Shift Left
LSR	Logical Shift Right
MOVE	Move
MOVEM	Move Multiple Registers
MOVEP	Move Peripheral Data
MULS	Signed Multiply
MULU	Unsigned Multiply
NBCD	Negate Decimal with Extend
NEG	Negate
NOP	No Operation
NOT	One's Complement
OR	Logical Or
PEA	Push Effective Address
RESET	Reset External Devices
ROL	Rotate Left without Extend
ROR	Rotate Right without Extend
ROXL	Rotate Left with Extend
ROXR	Rotate Right with Extend
RTE	Return from Exception
RTR	Return and Restore
RTS	Return from Subroutine

(*Courtesy Motorola Inc.*)

Table 15–2 MC68000 Instruction Set (continued)

Mnemonic	Description
SBCD	Subtract Decimal with Extend
Scc	Set Conditional
STOP	Stop
SUB	Subtract
SWAP	Swap Data Register Halves
TAS	Test and Set Operand
TRAP	Trap
TRAPV	Trap on Overflow
TST	Test
UNLK	Unlink

(Courtesy Motorola Inc.)

Table 15–3 MC6800 Variations of Instruction Types

Instruction Type	Variation	Description
ADD	**ADD**	Add
	ADDA	Add Address
	ADDQ	Add Quick
	ADDI	Add Immediate
	ADDX	Add with Extend
AND	**AND**	Logical And
	ANDI	And Immediate
CMP	**CMP**	Compare
	CMPA	Compare Address
	CMPM	Compare Memory
	CMPI	Compare Immediate
EOR	**EOR**	Exclusive Or
	EORI	Exclusive Or Immediate
MOVE	**MOVE**	Move
	MOVEA	Move Address
	MOVEQ	Move Quick
	MOVE from SR	Move from Status Register
	MOVE to SR	Move to Status Register
	MOVE to CCR	Move to Condition Codes
	MOVE to USP	Move to User Stack Pointer
NEG	**NEG**	Negate
	NEGX	Negate with Extend
OR	**OR**	Logical Or
	ORI	Or Immediate
SUB	**SUB**	Subtract
	SUBA	Subtract Address
	SUBI	Subtract Immediate
	SUBQ	Subtract Quick
	SUBX	Subtract with Extend

(Courtesy Motorola Inc.)

Special emphasis has been given to the instruction set's support of structured high level languages to facilitate ease of programming. Each instruction, with few exceptions, operates on bytes, words, and long words. Most instructions can use any of the fourteen addressing modes. Combining instruction types, data types, and addressing modes, over 1000 useful instructions are provided. These instructions include signed and unsigned multiply and divide, "quick" arithmetic operations, BCD arithmetic, and expanded operations (through traps). Additionally, the MC68000's highly symmetric, proprietary microcoded structure provides a sound, flexible base for the future.[1]

Figure 15–5 is a microphoto of the MC68000.

Note that the M68000 family is a not-so-distant relative of the MC6800. All M6800 family peripherals (refer to Chapter 13) interface directly with the MC68000, so upward compatibility is built in.

State-of-the-Art M68000 Peripheral Devices

Figure 15–6 indicates a number of new peripheral parts that have been designed specifically for the MC68000 MPU.

The MC68120 Intelligent Peripheral Controller (IPC) is a general purpose, user programmable, peripheral controller. It contains a system interface, an 8-bit CPU, a serial communications interface, twenty-one parallel I/O lines, a 16-bit timer, 2048 bytes of ROM and eight operating modes. In addition, the MC68120 features 128 bytes of dual-ported RAM and six semaphore registers that are accessable to both the internal CPU and an external processor or device through the system interface. The MC68120 provides all the control signals necessary to interface with the asynchronous bus of the MC68000.

The MC68122 Cluster Terminal Controller (CTC) relieves the host processor of the tast of coordinating the communications between one or more terminals. Messages containing either text or control commands are passed between the host processor and the controller according to the requirements of the application program being run. Standard terminal devices and protocols are supported. Output-only or input-only devices such as line printers may also be attached. The CTC supports its own local bus for message buffering and interface to communications devices or, operating in a single device mode, supports a single serial port.

The MC68230 Parallel Interface/Timer (PI/T) is a general purpose programmable parallel interface device that meets most system parallel I/O and timing needs. The parallel interfaces of the PI/T may be

[1] *MC68000 16-Bit Microprocessor User's Manual* (Austin, Texas: Motorola Inc., 1980), pp. 1-1–1-5.

Fig. 15–5. The MC68000 microprocessing unit. (*Courtesy Motorola Inc.*)

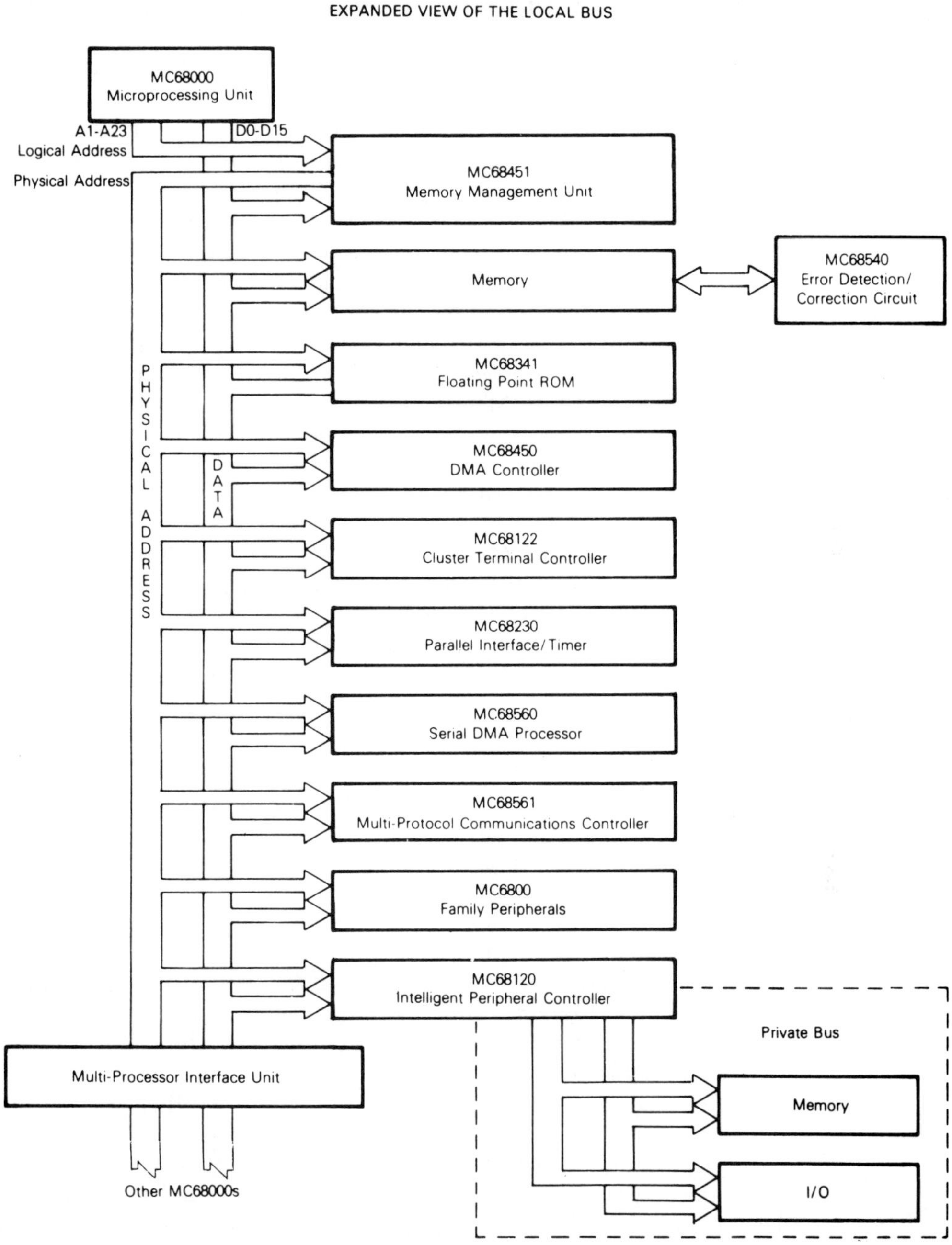

Fig. 15–6. M68000 peripheral devices. (*Courtesy Motorola Inc.*)

used to connect a wide variety of peripheral devices to the MC68000 bus. The PI/T can be programmed to generate interrupt requests to the MC68000 or DMA requests to the MC68450 Direct Memory Access Controller, on demand of the peripheral. No external logic is needed to connect the PI/T to the DMAC or to the MC68000. The PI/T also provides complete port and timer status information.

The MC68230 contains two multi-mode, double buffered I/O ports (Port A and Port B), a third 8-bit I/O port, and a 24-bit programmable timer. The PI/T also contains flexible prioritization logic for generating unique interrupt vectors. Autovectored interrupts are also supported. Port C pins provide either another port pin or special functions consisting of interrupt, timer, or DMA control lines.

The MC68341 Floating-Point ROM is a position independent/reentrant floating point ROM programmed for the MC68000 instruction set. It uses the unimplemented instruction TRAP to simulate hardware floating point and has single, double, and extended formats. All operations are done to extended precision. The two-device set has an upper byte and a lower byte.

The MC68450 Direct Memory Access Controller (*DMAC*) offers the system designer unparalleled performance where both speed and flexibility in data transfer are required. Sophisticated chaining techniques, memory-to-memory block transfers, and variable bus bandwidth utilization result in optimum data transfers. Internal 32-bit address registers provide upward software compatibility with future M68000 family processors.

The MC68451 Memory Management Unit (*MMU*) provides address translation and protection of the 16-megabyte addressing space of the MC68000. The MMU can be accessed by any potential bus master such as instruction set processors or DMA controllers. Each bus master (or processor) in the MC68000 family provides a function code and an address during each bus cycle. The function code specifies an address space while the address specifies a location within that address space. The function codes are provided by the MC68000 to distinguish between program and data spaces as well as supervisor and user spaces. This separation of address space provides the basis of protection in an operating system. By simplifying the programming model of the address space, the MMU also increase the reliability of a complex multiprocess system.

The MC68540 Error Detection and Correction Circuit (*EDAC*) performs the error check/correct function in both 8-bit and 16-bit data bus systems and is directly expandable to 32-bit operation. The EDAC contains an internal diagnostic register and a set of flexible diagnostic operating modes to facilitate system diagnostic testing and error logging. All required bus buffering is handled within the device to reduce the need for support circuitry.

The MC68560 Serial Direct Memory Access (*SDMA*) Processor provides a high speed serial link between microprocessors or intelligent controllers in distributed processing systems. Using IBM's Synchronous Data Link Control (SDLC) protocol, the MC68560 is capable of handling multidrop, point-to-point, or loop configuration in full or half duplex environments.

The serial link is configured with a primary SDMA connected to one or more secondary SDMAs. The primary station (SDMA and its associated processor) has the responsibility for the data link control such as polling the secondary SDMAs. The secondary SDMAs have the ability to respond to most link level commands received over the serial bus and also handle some error recovery without intervention from the local processor. Both the primary and secondary SDMAs have the responsibility for data integrity and validation.

The MC68561 Multi-Protocol Communications Controller (*MPCC*) is a serial data communications interface for the M68000 family. This device meets the basic interface requirements of asynchronous, bit- and byte-oriented synchronous communication protocol. To keep device count low, the MPCC also contains an internal crystal oscillator and baud rate generator.

Motorola's Microcomputer Evaluation/Training Modules

MEK6800D2 Evaluation Module is a fully functional microcomputer system based on the MC6800 microprocessing unit and its family of associated memory and I/O devices.

The MEK6800D2 is designed to provide a completely self-contained method for evaluating the characteristics of the MC6800 family and is quite popular for classroom use. The standard unit includes the following devices:

1 MC6800 MPU

1 MCM6830 ROM (with JBUG monitor 1024-by-8)

3 MCM6810 RAMs (128-by-8)

2 MC6820 peripheral interface adapters (PIA)

1 MC6850 asynchronous communications interface adapter (ACIA)

1 MC6871B clock generator

An assembled unit is shown in Fig. 15–7.

The microcomputer module printed circuit board is preengineered to accept the following additional components for expanding its capability:

2 MCM6810 RAMs (128-by-8)

2 MCM68708 EPROMs (1024-by-8)

3 MC8T97 buffers

2 MC8T26 bidirectional buffers

The expansion capability provides for a variety of user operations modes.

A block diagram of the MEK6800D2 appears in Fig. 15–8.

The integral keyboard-display module can be used in conjunction with the JBUG monitor program for entering and debugging user programs. Programs can also be loaded and dumped via the audio cassette interface. The keyboard, display and audio cassette circuitry are on a separate printed circuit board so that the ACIA and a second PIA are available if the user has access to an RS-232 or TTY terminal. Wire-wrap space for up to twenty 16-pin DIP packages is available for user designed circuitry on the microcomputer module. A user generated terminal control program designed to interface with either the PIA or the ACIA can be entered via the integral keyboard. Alternatively, the kit will accept (in place of the JBUG) the Motorola MINIbug II monitor program. MINIbug II has monitor and diagnostic capabilities similar to JBUG but is intended for use with RS-232 and TTY type terminals.

The module also permits several different memory configurations. The two MCM6810 128-by-8 RAMs provided with the standard kit will accommodate programs of up to 256 bytes in length (the third MCM6810 is reversed for use by the monitor program). Addition of the two optional RAMs expands the capability to 512 bytes. Strapping options for the additional ROM sockets permits any of the following combinations.

1024 bytes in 512-by-8-bit PROMs (MCM7641)

2048 bytes in 1024-by-8-bit EPROMs (MCM68708)

2048 bytes in 1024-by-8-bit mask-programmed ROMs (MCM68308 —same pin-out as MCM68708)

4096 bytes in 2048-by-8-bit mask-programmed ROMs (MCM68316 —same pin-out as MCM68708 except EPROM programming pin is used as additional addressing pin)

The general memory organization of the MEK6800D2 is shown in Fig. 15–9.

Finally, by adding the optional buffers in the spaces provided upgrades the module to EXORciser-compatible status; hence, all the EXORciser I/O and memory modules can be used with the module. (The EXORciser development system will be discussed later in this section.) For example, addition of MINIbug II, an 8 K memory board and the EXORciser's resident editor/assembler to the microcomputer

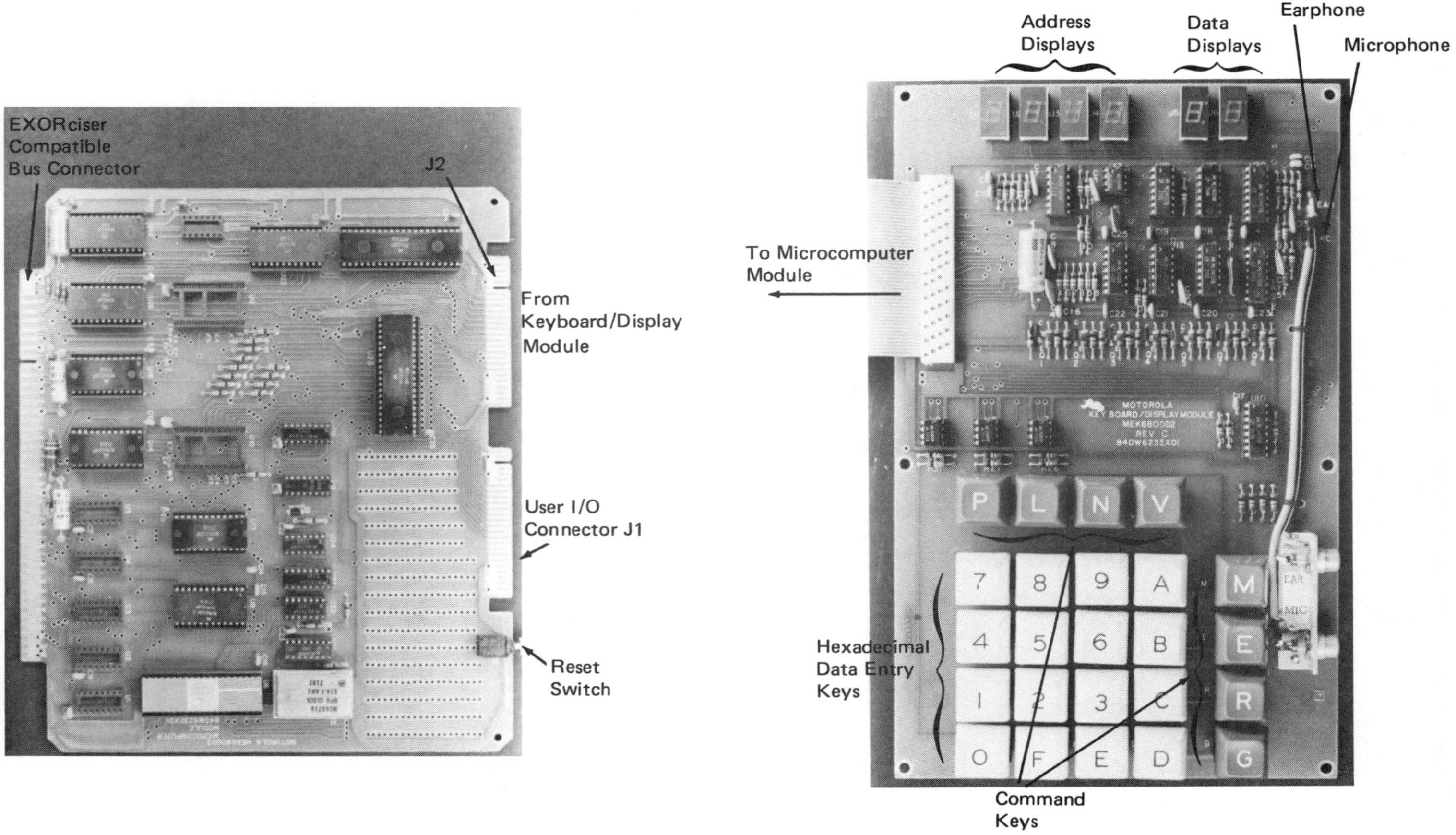

Fig. 15–7. MEK6800D2 evaluation module. (*Photo by Skutans*)

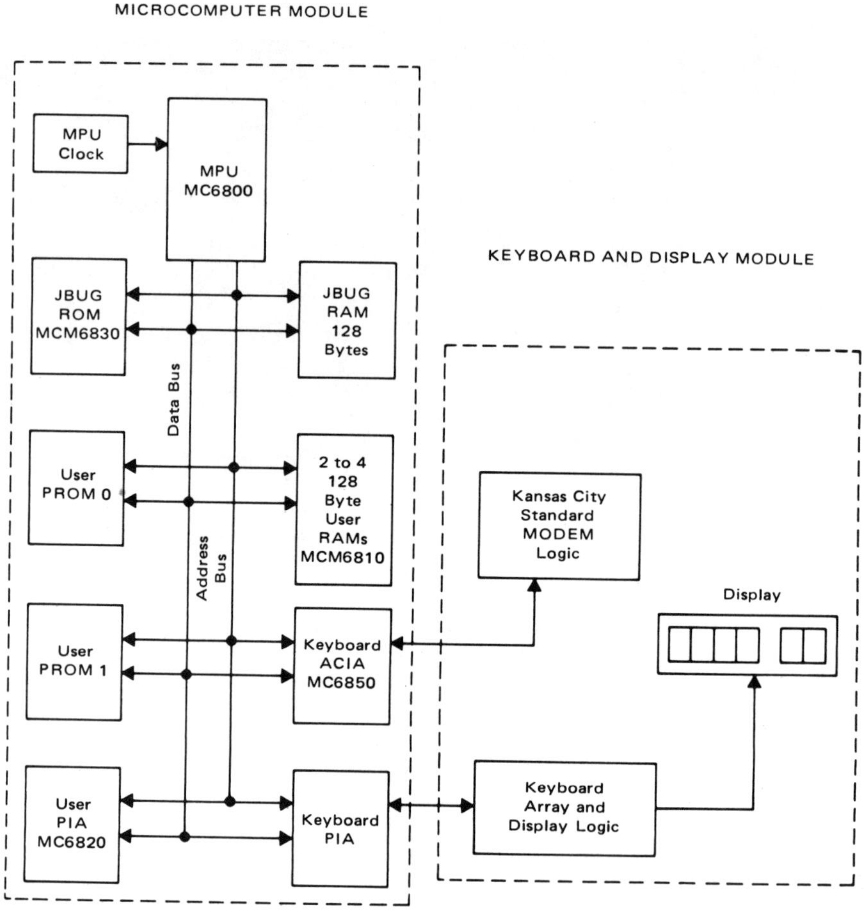

Fig. 15–8. MEK6800D2 block diagram. (*Courtesy Motorola Inc.*)

module creates a complete development/prototyping tool.[2]

The MEK6802D5 Microcomputer Evaluation Board is a basic, low cost system that can be used to evaluate the M6800 microcomputer family of components. It is a useful tool for learning programming techniques and developing custom microprocessor applications.

The system consists of an MC6802 microprocessor, D5BUG firmware in an MC68A316E ROM, six 7-segment multiplexed displays, a 25-key scanned keypad, 300 baud K.C. standard cassette interface, and an onboard power supply capable of driving the minimum system.

[2] *Motorola MEK6800D2 Manual* (Phoenix, Arizona: Motorola Inc., 1977), pp. 1.1–1.3.

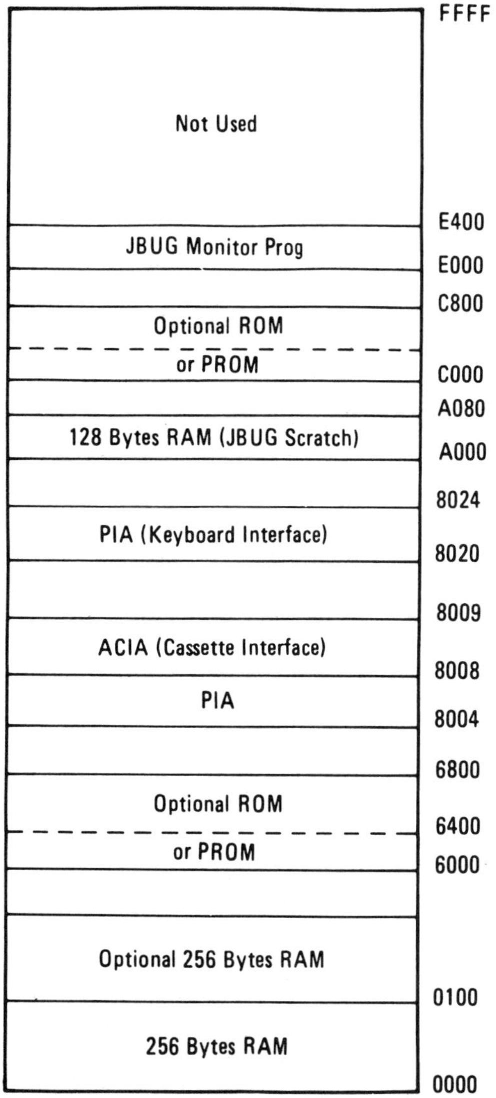

Fig. 15–9. Memory map for MEK6800D2. (*Courtesy Motorola Inc.*)

A wire wrap area and an uncommitted user PIA are provided for the creation of desired options. Provisions are also made to add two MCM2114 1K × 4 RAMs, a 24-pin ROM or EPROM, and bus buffers to an 86-pin connector.

All components, including the AC transformer required for the minimum system, are supplied with the MEK6802D5. The system compo-

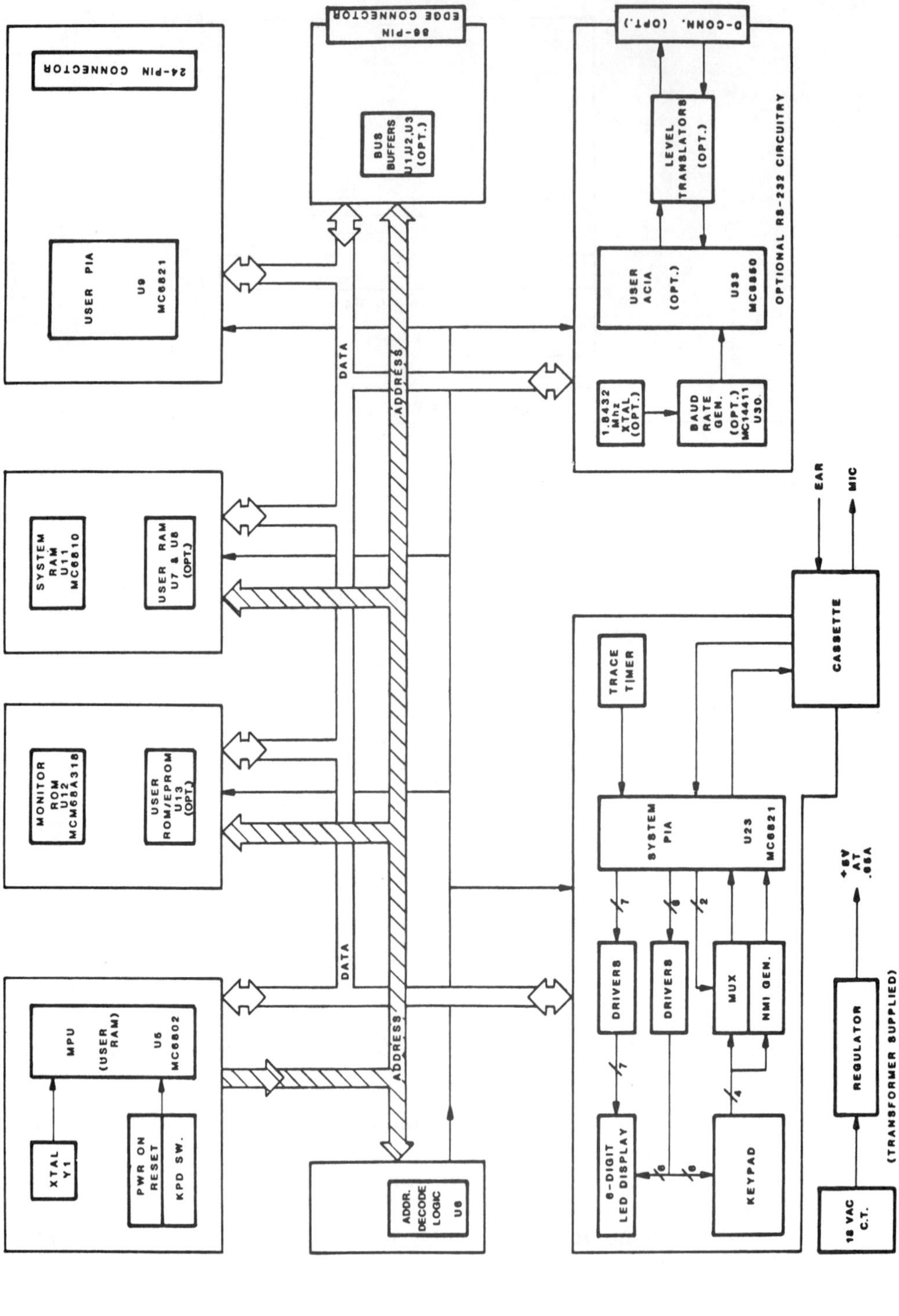

Fig. 15–10. MEK6802D5 evaluation board block diagram. *(Courtesy Motorola Inc.)*

nents illustrated in the Fig. 15–10 block diagram are described in the following paragraphs.

The MC6802 MPU (U5) generates the system clock and executes the programs residing in D5BUG as well as user programs. There are 128 bytes of RAM reserved for the user included in the MC6802 located in addresses 0000 to 007F.

The MC68A316E D5BUG (U12) is a factory programmed ROM, also known as a monitor, which contains the operating system firmware programs that control the D5 system.

Two peripheral interface adapters (PIAs) are onboard. The MC6821 PIA (U23) interfaces the keypad and display to the MPU (U5). This device transmits data in parallel form in either direction and provides a flow path for data in and out of the system. This PIA also interfaces the cassette interface circuitry and the trace-one instruction time to the MPU (U5). The user PIA (U9) interfaces the D5 to external devices or systems for the user production of custom designs. It provides two 8-bit bidirectional data ports and four control lines connected to a 24-pin DIP socket located adjacent to U9.

The MC6810 static RAM (U11) is used as a scratchpad for the MPU (U5). It provides 128 bytes of flag, data, and stack area for the D5BUG operating system. Twenty-four bytes constitute the user's stack area.

The LED display system consists of six LEDS (U15, U16, U17, U18, U20, U21), anode drivers Q1 through Q7 and cathode drivers U24 through U26. The system PIA (U23) uses seven lines to drive the anode drivers and six lines to drive the cathode drivers.

The keyboard generates an interrupt to the processor when a key is pressed. The system firmware causes the processor to search for the key closure and act upon it.

The MCM2124 RAMs (U7, U8) are optional devices. There are two 18-pin sockets for installing these 1K × 4-bit static RAMs.

The bus drivers (U1, U2, U3) are optional devices used to interface the processor and the 86-pin connector to expand the MEK6802D5 system.

Figure 15–11 illustrates the component arrangement and functions.

The MEK6802D5 can be supplied to interface to the widely used RS-232 bus.

An ACIA converts the parallel data on the data bus to a serial form suitable for transmission over a communications system. The ACIA transmits and receives data and allows the D5 to be used as a remotely controlled processor. An MC14411 bit-rate generator supplies the special frequency that the ACIA requires in making the conversion from parallel to serial data. An installed jumper determines the frequency of data formatted in serial form. A socket allows cabling to the RS-232 line.

Fig. 15–11. MEK6802D5 component function location diagram. (*Courtesy Motorola Inc.*)

The optional bus buffers (U1, U2, U3) are for expanding the D5 through an 86-pin edge connector. This is accomplished by plugging in an IC in the supplied sockets. Note that U10, also a bus driver, is part of the basic D5 since the processor's R/W output cannot drive all the inputs in the basic system or the bus. All the control signals, data, and addresses are available on this bus for system expansion.

The MEK6809D4 Advanced Microcomputer Evaluation Board shown in Fig. 15–12 and the MEK68KPD Keypad/Display Unit provide the necessary hardware and firmware for a computer system based on the Motorola MC6809 high performance microprocessor. The system forms an evaluation tool to facilitate the application of Motorola microprocessors and associated components.

The MEK6809D4A is used with an MEK68KPD and is complete with a power supply. The MEK6809D4B requires an external power supply and is used with an RS-232 terminal or an MEK68R2D CRT interface plus a CRT and an ASCII keyboard.

The user can prototype dedicated systems plus write and evaluate software programs in machine language using a cassette recorder/player for data storage. Provisions are made for extensive system expansion.

A block diagram of the system is shown in Fig. 15–13.

The CPU consists of an MC6809 high performance microprocessor, a 2.579 MHz crystal and buffers that interface the MC6809 to other circuit blocks on the D4 board. The MC6809 supports programming

Fig. 15–12. MEK6809D4 advanced microcomputer evaluation board. (*Courtesy Motorola Inc.*)

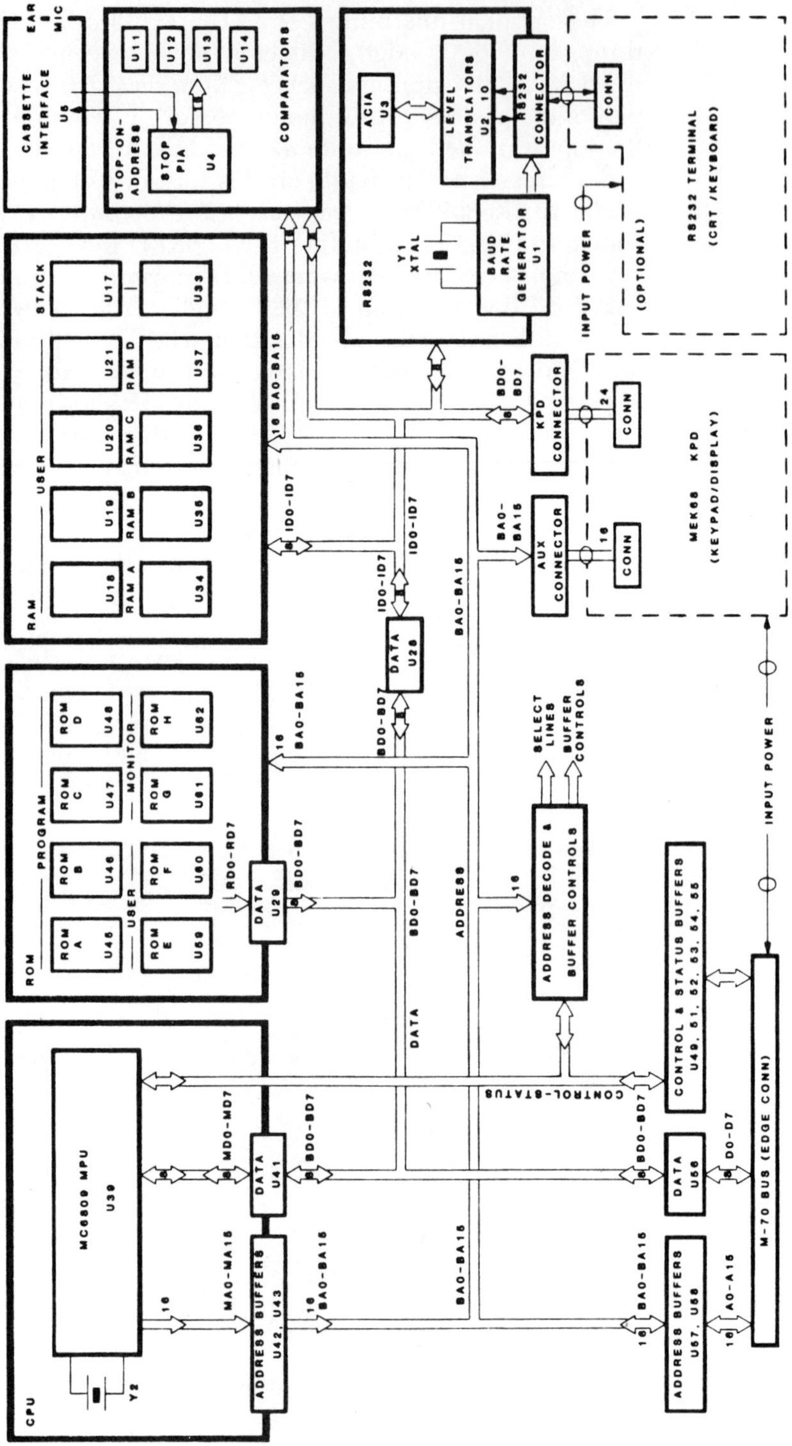

Fig. 15–13. MEK6809D4 block diagram. *(Courtesy Motorola Inc.)*

techniques such as position independence, reentrancy and modular programming. Its hardware and software features make it suitable for higher level language execution or standard controller application.

The ROM system consists of eight ROM sockets that can be configured to accept various combinations of ROM types. These configurations are controlled by mini-jumpers that may be easily moved without the need for tools. Mapping of the eight ROMs in memory space is accomplished by a mapping ROM that is used as a programmed logic array. A paging technique allows up to 192K bytes of ROM to be used in the D4 system.

There are two groups of 1K × 4 RAMs: stack RAM and user RAM. The stack RAM is mainly used for the D4 operating system stack and scratchpad RAM. Also, 512 bytes at memory location $E400 through $E7FF are available for user RAM application. The user RAM is a 4K × 8 block that can be positioned anywhere in the D4 memory map using jumper connections.

In some microprocessor systems, the address flow is from the microprocessor through buffers and to the mother board bus. The D4 uses a more complex arrangement that permits disabling the microprocessor. This allows addresses to be fed to the D4 from an external source and to access board components, and permits DMA for some applications.

There are four bidirectional data bus buffers used in the D4: a ROM buffer, a RAM I/O buffer, an edge buffer, and an MPU buffer. Each buffer has an enable and a direction input. Control logic configures these buffers to route data between sections of the D4 board.

The stop-on-address circuit enables a user program to be executed until a certain address is reached. The address to be stopped on is stored and, when the board address bus bits coincide, an output results. This causes a nonmaskable interrupt to occur that switches the microprocessor to a service routine.

The RS-232 specification defines a standard for interconnecting computer terminals of different makes. The ACIA converts the parallel data on the buses to serial data which is then translated into RS-232 levels.

The D4 uses very few components to interface a tape recorder to its operating system. Most of the cassette operation occurs in software to create tapes and recover data from tapes. The tape information consists of a stream of 1200 and 2400 Hz serial audio data.

The *MEK68KPD* shown in Fig. 15–14 includes a 25-key keypad, eight 7-segment LED displays, an onboard +5 volt power supply, and an uncommitted MC6821 PIA. Provisions are made for disconnection of the onboard regulators when an external +5 volt supply is used. A wire-wrap area is provided for custom circuitry and a 16-pin socket

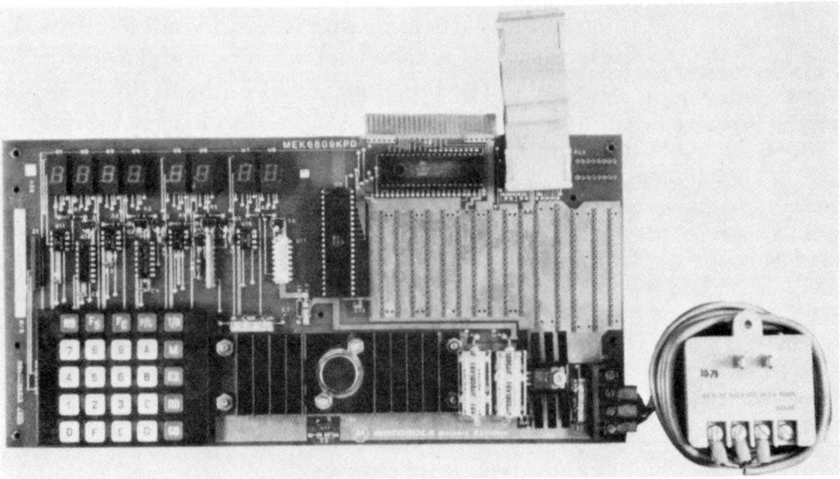

Fig. 15–14. MEK68KPD module. (*Courtesy Motorola Inc.*)

allows for additional signals to be brought to or from this wire-wrap area.

Figure 15–15 is a block diagram of the MEK68KPD. Refer to Fig. 15–13 to see how it interfaces into the MEK6809D4 system.[3]

The MEX68KDM MC68000 Design Module provides an easy and convenient means of designing with and evaluating the MC68000 processor. Figure 15–16 is a photo of this design module.

As shown in Fig. 15–17, this module provides the necessary RAM, ROM, timer, and I/O for initial system emulation or system prototyping. Two serial RS-232 ports are provided for communications between the MEX68KDM module and a terminal or host computer. The terminal operator may download a machine file previously edited and assembled on a host computer such as an IBM 370, PDP-11, or M6809 EXORciser into the onboard 32K byte memory.

Once a memory file is resident in RAM, the user may begin his program debug phase using the extensive MACSBUG command structure provided in ROM. The MACSBUG command summary provided in ROM is listed in Table 15–4. Some key new debug commands beyond the usual trace and breakpoint modes should be noted.

MACSBUG provides symbol referencing and printing, offset ad-

[3] *MEK6809D4 Advanced Microcomputer Evaluation Board, ADI-544* (Austin, Texas: Motorola Inc., 1980), pp. 1,7,8.

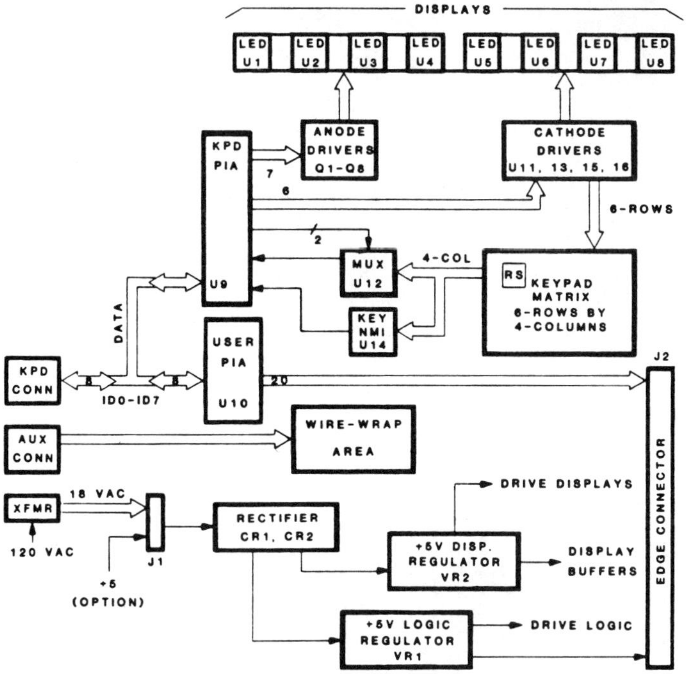

Fig. 15–15. MEK68KPD block diagram. (*Courtesy Motorola Inc.*)

dressing, memory move, calls to utility routines, host computer communications, effective address windows to memory data, a memory test routine, I/O port assignment at the command level, and trace display selection.

The memory map for the MEX68KDM allows the system designer to use any of the on-card I/O as well as additional external memory or I/O. An M6800 bus interface card is provided to allow the MEX68KDM to read or write data to an external M6800 memory or I/O card in either the upper or lower data byte positions.

The MEX68KDM Design Module can be used in three different configurations. First, it can stand alone with the user providing his own power supply and RS-232 terminal. Second, it can be used in an existing EXORciser development system in the nonexpanded bus mode. Third it can be used in a card cage with other M6800 memory or I/O boards in the expanded mode.[4]

[4] *MEX68KDM* (Phoenix, Arizona: Motorola Inc., 1979), pp. 1–3.

Fig. 15–16. MC68000 design module. (*Courtesy Motorola Inc.*)

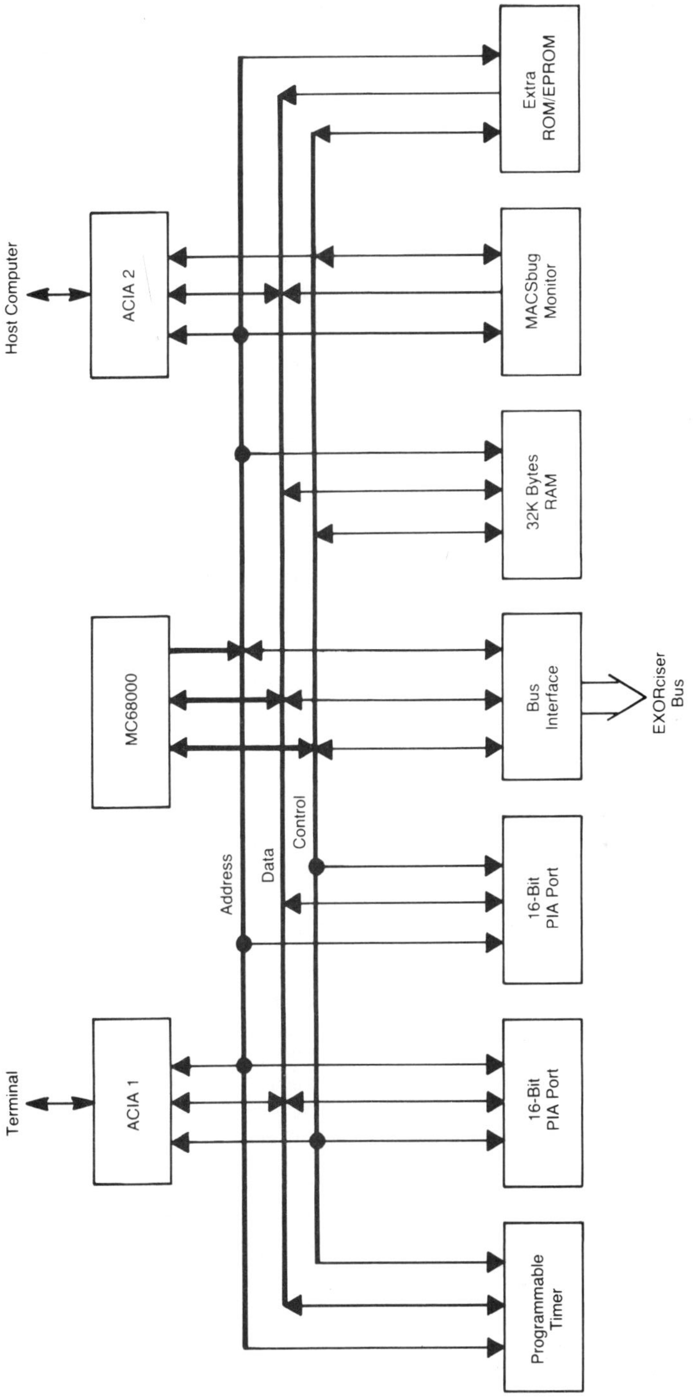

Fig. 15–17. MEX68KDM functonal block diagram. *(Courtesy Motorola Inc.)*

Table 15–4 MACSBUG Command Summary.

reg#	print a register#
reg# hexdata	put a hex value in the register #
reg# 'ASCII'	put hex — equivalent characters in register #
reg#/	print the old value and request new value
class	print all registers of a class (A or D)
class/	sequence through — print old value request new
R	print the trace display
R reg#. len	put a register in the display
R ALl	set all registers to appear in the display
R Clear	take all registers out of the display
T count	turn the trace mode on, trace count instructions (default 1)
T TILL Address	trace until this address
T OFF	turn trace display off — print only when stopping
LOop low high	suppress trace display when tracing through range
(CR)	carriage return — trace one instruction, trace must be on
hex number	trace this many instructions, trace mode must be on
Breakpoint	print all breakpoint addresses
B add/count	set a new breakpoint and optional count
B -address	clear a breakpoint
B CLear	clear all breakpoints
Go	start running from address in program counter
Go address	start running from this address
Go TILL add.	set temporary breakpoint
W#	print the effective address of the window
W#. len EA	define the length and addressing mode (address) of a window
M#	memory through a window (same syntax as register)
FOrmat hex	program/initialize an ACIA
NUll hex	set character null pads
CR hex	set carriage return null pads
SPeed baud	set null pads to default values
#decimal	convert decimal number to hex
#$hex	convert hex to decimal
P2	enter transparent mode, host and console linked
(CTL Q)	control 'Q' ends transparent mode
*..data..	transmit command to host
CAll address	JSR to user utility routine
COpy start end start2	copy memory from one location to another
PRint[S] start end	hex — ASCII memory dump
PUnch start end	print 'S' records (tape image)
REad	expect to receive 'S' records
VErify	check memory against 'S' records
SM address data	set memory with data
Offset address	define an offset
SYmbol NAME value	define and print symbols

(*Courtesy Motorola Inc.*)

Development Systems

The M68ADS1A Development System. The M68ADS1A shown in Fig. 15–18, as its name implies, is a complete development system used in the design of M6800 microcomputer applications. It is built around the two basic modules: the M68ACI and M68DIM1A. The M68ACI is a complete computer on a single printed circuit board and will operate with either dynamic or static memories and will interface directly with a 20 ma current loop, TTL or RS-232C terminal. The M68DIM1A display interface module is a complete alphanumeric interface to the CRT monitor. The M68DIM1 includes a 1-page memory, an ASCII character generator and a video signal generator.

When combined together, the two modules make up a system which allows the user not only to check out and execute his target program (debugging capability) but also to efficiently carry on dialog with the machine (terminal capability).

The debugging capability is derived from the MINIbug II monitor functions, while the terminal capability is centered around an input/output supervising firmware (IOS) which monitors the data ex-

Fig. 15–18. M68ADS1A development system. (*Courtesy Motorola Inc.*)

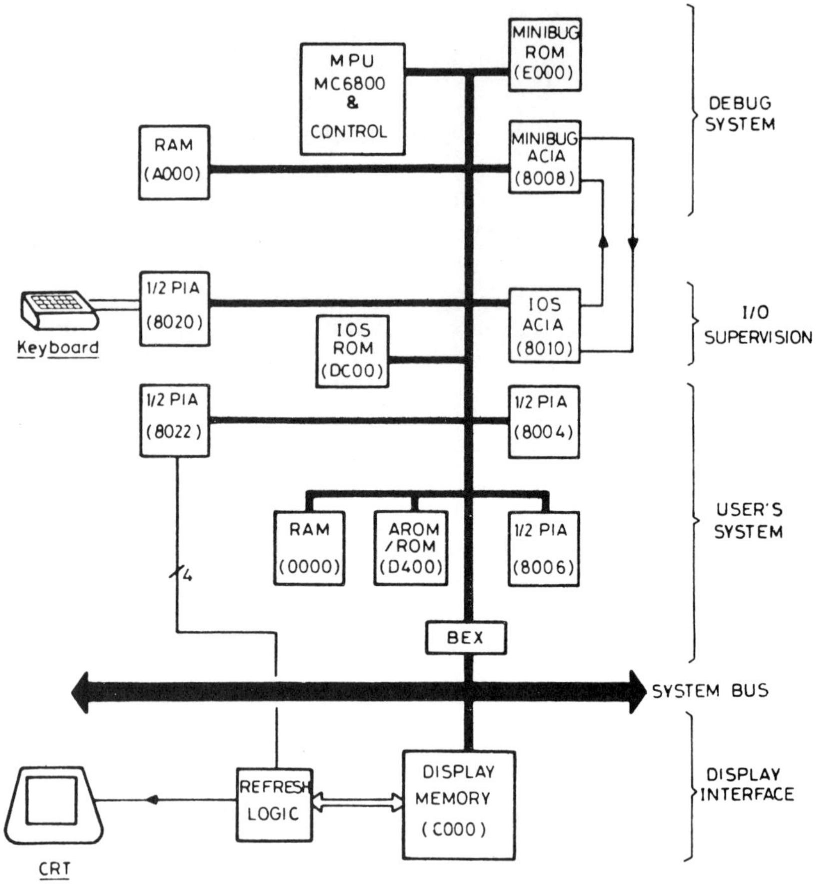

Fig. 15–19. M68ADS1A block diagram. (*Courtesy Motorola Inc.*)

changed between the user's or MINIbug II program and the system peripherals such as CRT, keyboard and audio recorder.[5]

1. **Block diagram description.** As illustrated in Fig. 15–19, the M68ADS1A system appears as split into four subsystems:

• A debug section consisting of the MC6800 microprocessor, the MINIbug II monitor stored in a 1 K byte ROM (MCM44506L); 128 bytes of RAM used for temporary storage (MCM6810) and an MC6850 ACIA (hereafter referred to as "MINIbug ACIA") through which data is transferred to or from the monitor

[5] *Motorola M68ADS1A Development System User's Manual* (Phoenix, Arizona: Motorola Inc., 1978), p. 2.1.

• An I/O supervision section based on the IOS firmware (MCM44615 ROM) which monitors the data exchanged between the MINIbug ACIA and the system peripherals through another ACIA identified as the "IOS ACIA." As shown, half of a PIA interfaces this section to an ASCII keyboard and the other PIA side conveys signals mainly used for controlling the DMA logic on the M68DIM1A module

• A user's section consisting of 256 bytes of RAM (MCM6810), 2048 bytes of AROM (two MCM68708s) and one-half of a PIA

• A display interface section provided by the M68DIM1A module which takes care of displaying the ASCII characters stored in its 512 bytes RAM (four MCM6810s)

Therefore, the development system integrates two key facilities (debugging and communication) required to start the development of small programs that can be executed in the RAM area of the M68AC1 board. Should the user need additional memory or I/O adapters, he may easily expand the system capacity by adding bus compatible plus-in modules (EXORciser or micromodule families).

The following discusses the basic M68ADS1A system and the optional peripherals or modules which may be added to ease and speed up the application design cycle.

2. **Basic development system.** The M68ADS1A system includes:

(a) Two peripheral devices:
M68KBD1 full ASCII keyboard
M68MDM1 5-inch display monitor
(b) Interconnection elements
M68BSC1 bus system card: this bus board includes three slots, two of them being equipped with eighty-six pin connectors to plug in the M68SAC1 and M68DIM1A modules.
M68UCC1 cable set to connect the modules to their associated peripherals.
(c) M68SAC1 and M68DIM1A Modules
The various components on these cards occupy the memory areas listed below and illustrated in the memory map shown in Fig. 15–20.

0000–00FF: Two MCM6810 RAMs, individually selectable

8000–8023: M68ADS1A interface adapters and user's I/O port

• One-half of an MC6821 PIA (8006–8007) provides the user with the capability to drive his own I/O peripheral logic

• MINIbug ACIA (MC6850) located at base address 8008

• IOS ACIA located at base address 8010

• One-half of an MC6820 PIA (8020–8021) interfacing to the M68-KBD 1 keyboard

• One-half of an MC6820 PIA (8022–8023) which controls part of the display DMA logic

A000–A07F: One MCM6810 RAM used for temporary storage by IOS and MINIbug II.

C000–C1FF: display memory consisting of four MCM6810 RAMs.

D400–DBFF: two sockets to plug in two 1 K byte MCM68708 AROMs or two 1 K byte MCM68308 ROMs.

DC00–DFFF: IOS ROM (MCM44615)

E000–E3FF: MINIbug II ROM (MCM44506).

The field D400–DBFF, which is normally occupied by two AROMs on the M68AC1 module, can be disabled and duplicated on another

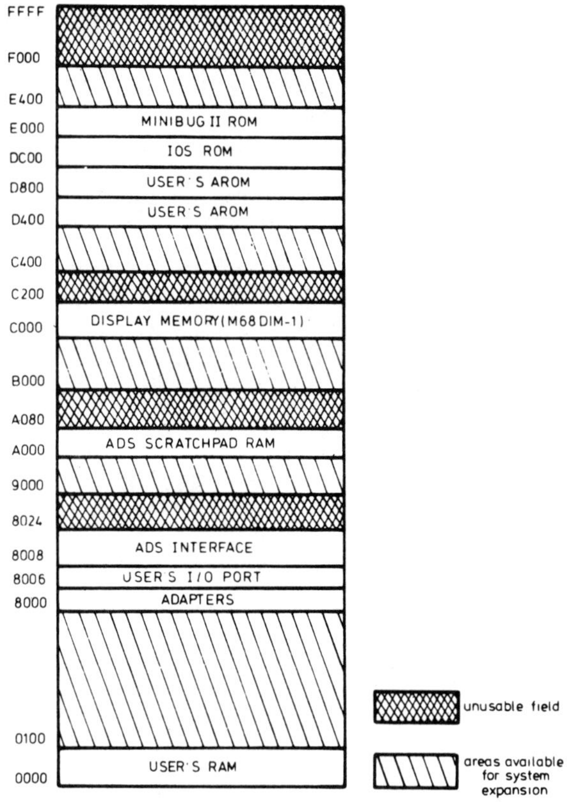

Fig. 15–20. M68ADS1A memory map. (*Courtesy Motorola Inc.*)

RAM module on the system bus. This allows the user to write and debug an application program in RAM in the same area as the one the program will execute once burnt into AROMs or ROMs.[6]

In summary, the M68ADS1A development system provides a low-cost keyboard-to-CRT data input and display capability and offers options for easy expansion into an economical development system. Any terminal with an RS-232C or 20 ma loop port can be interfaced to the M68ADS1A.[7]

The EXORciser—Model M68SDT. The Motorola MC6800 development system, considered the "Cadillac" in the Motorola 8-bit line, is the EXORciser.

1. **An Overview.** The EXORciser is a modularized, expandable instrument that permits "instant breadboarding" and evaluation of any MC6800-based microcomputer system. It consists of a prewired, bus-oriented chassis and power supply together with three basis modules —an MPU module, a debug module and a baud rate module. These provide the basic control and interface functions of a microcomputer and house the system development and diagnostic programs. A number of separately available, optional memory modules and additional interface modules (up to twelve) may be added simply by plugging them into existing prewired sockets. They convert the basic system into an exact prototype of a desired end system. Then the EXORciser, with its built-in EXbug firmware, enables the designer to configure, evaluate and debug his final system hardware and software using actual MC6800 components.[8]

2. **Description of Operation.** The basic EXORciser contains the common ingredients of a microcomputer and offers the system designer a low cost, versatile means of achieving unique final-system performance through the selective addition of separately available, optional modules. These separate assemblies plug directly into the EXORciser's bus so the system expansion becomes quick, easy and essentially error-proof. With provisions for up to twelve add-on assemblies, a system of almost any complexity can rapidly be assembled.

The illustration in Fig. 15–21 shows the major components of the basic EXORciser as well as those of several optional EXORciser modules.

[6] *M68ADS1A User's Manual*, p. 2.2.

[7] *The M68ADS1 Development System, Issue* A (Phoenix, Arizona: Motorola Inc., 1977), p. 1.

[8] *M68SDT EXORciser Emulator for M6800 Based Systems, Issue* A (Phoenix, Arizona: Motorola Inc., 1976), p. 2.

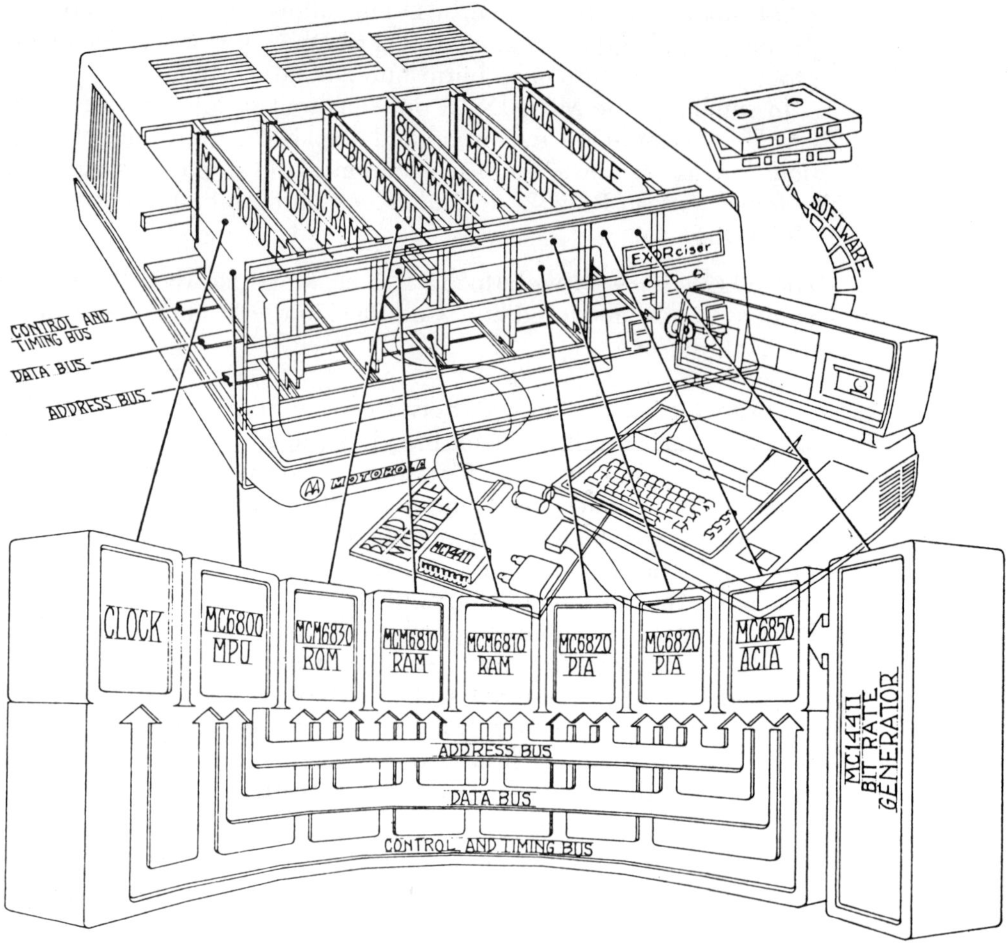

Fig. 15–21. "Inside look" at the EXORciser. (*Courtesy Motorola Inc.*)

Supplied with the basic EXORciser are the MPU module, the debug module and the baud rate module. The baud rate module contains, primarily, an MC14411 bit rate generator that determines the data transfer rate between an external terminal and the EXORciser. The module supplies eight switch selectable baud rates. The baud rate module, as shown, also provides the terminal connections and serves as a feed-through between the terminal and the EXbug firmware or the debug module.

The MPU module includes a built-in, crystal controlled 1 MHz clock that provides the timing for the microprocessor system under development, as well as for the rest of the EXORciser. In addition, this module houses the MC6800 microprocessing unit which imparts to the EXORciser its computation and control capabilities.

The debug module, through its EXbug firmware stored in the module's three MCM6830 ROMs, enables the user to evaluate and debug a system under development. The module's two MC6810 RAMs provide a 256-byte scratchpad memory for the EXbug routines.

The functional subsystems of the basic EXORciser are supplemented by a power supply and a bus-oriented distribution system. This bus system transfers the power supply voltage as well as the data, address and control signals to the optional modules.

Conspicuous by their absence from the basic EXORciser are the memory and input/output modules needed to turn this tool into a functional system. These memory and input/output modules are available as separate, optional modules and give the systems designer the flexibility to configure any desired system. Overall, the EXORciser can address up to 65 K bytes of memory and addresses the input/output modules (as well as the memory modules) as memory.[9]

The EXORciser II. The latest model in the EXORciser line is the MC6809-based Model II shown in Fig. 15–22.

With optional accessories, the EXORciser II design and diagnostic functions can be extended to other members of the M6800 family as well as to other Motorola families including the HMOS MC68000, MC3870, and CMOS MC146805 microcomputers.

[9] *M68SDT EXORciser Emulator*, p. 4.

Fig. 15–22. EXORciser II. (*Courtesy Motorola Inc.*)

The EXORset 30A. This desk top system provides a means of efficient and fast software development. The EXORset 30A shown in Fig. 15–23 fills the gap between low cost evaluation modules and high end development. The major features of the EXORset 30A are:

- MC6809 microprocessor based
- Full ASCII keyboard with sixteen user-assigned function keys
- Dual/double-sided mini floppy disk drives
- Nine-inch CRT display. Twenty-two lines of 80 characters or sixteen lines of 40 characters. Simultaneously displays a full 320 × 256 dot high density graphic image.
- 48K RAM and twelve sockets for 24K of EPROM/ROM
- Software development package

  EXORbug system monitor firmware
  XDOS operating system
  M6809 assembler
  CRT editor
  Hardware/software diagnostics
  BASIC-M interactive compiler[10]

The MC68000 EXORmacs development system. The EXORmacs is a state-of-the-art development system for advanced 16/32 bit systems. The delivered system includes chassis, six resident modules, terminal, disk, and development software.

Designed for flexibility and ease of use, EXORmacs takes advantage of the power and features of the MC68000 microprocessor. EXORmacs supports 16-bit and future 32-bit microprocessor designs and provides high level language through Pascal.

Support products may be added to the basic EXORmacs system to achieve a full multi-user, multi-tasking development station.

The basic configuration of EXORmacs consists of six resident modules (MPU, DEbug, Universal Disk Controller, and 256K bytes of RAM) and development software package. A set of peripherals supports the system software. The EXORterm 155 intelligent terminal provides efficient user input/output. EXORdisk III provides one megabyte of file storage with expansion via EXORdisk IIIE to a full two megabytes. A high-speed printer with a full 132 character line of print is optionally available. These units are shown in Fig. 15–24.

The 15-card EXORmacs chassis houses six cards for the basic development system, a switching power supply and cooling fans. The front

[10] *Motorola Microcomputer Development Systems* (Phoenix, Arizona: Motorola Inc., 1980), pp. 7–8.

Fig. 15–23. EXORset 30A. (*Courtesy Motorola Inc.*)

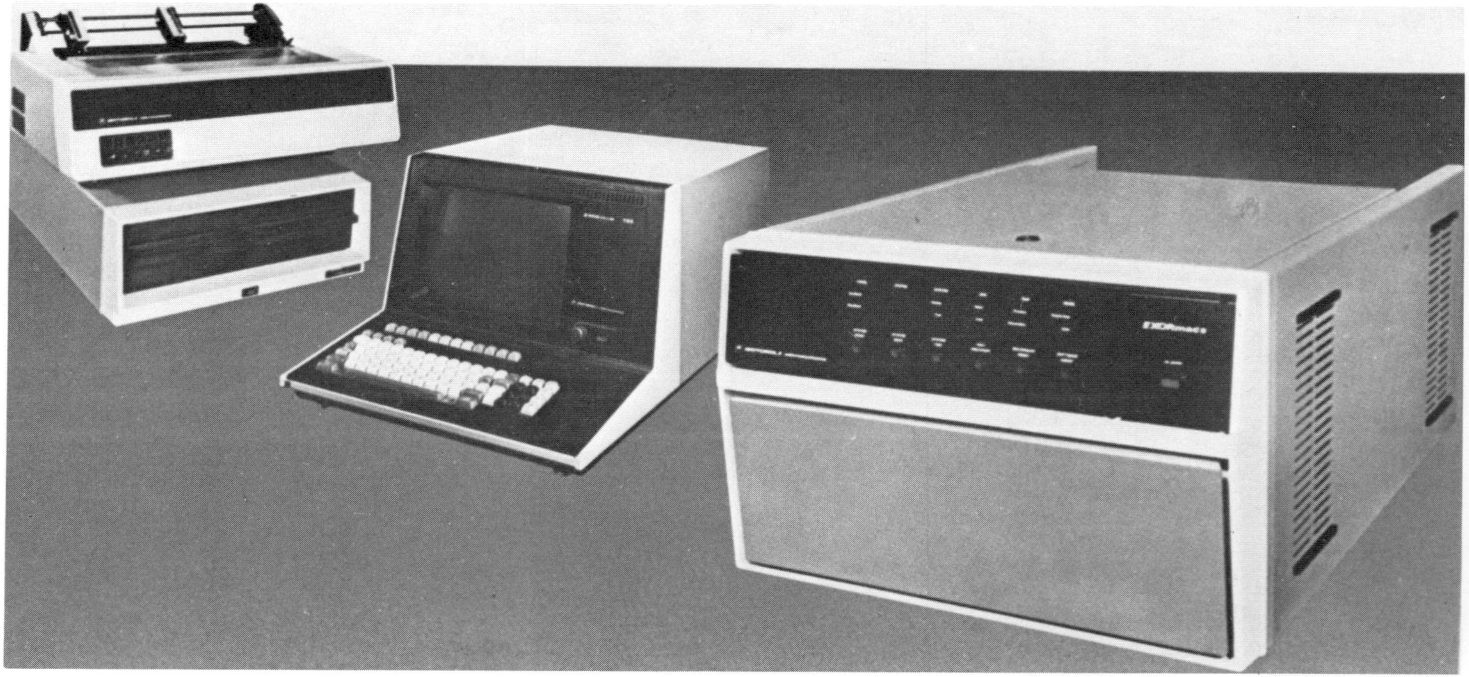

Fig. 15–24. Basic EXORmacs development system. (*Courtesy Motorola Inc.*)

control panel provides manual control input capability as well as visual indication of current system status and existing error conditions.

EXORmacs software package. The M68000 software development package provides designers with cost effective tools for application design and implementation. A versatile CRT-oriented Text Editor aids in program preparation and modification. Pascal, FORTRAN, and Structured Macro Assembler permit the designer to choose the language or languages that best fit his requirements.

A flexible Linkage Editor permits development to proceed in a modular top down process by combining separately written modules, written in different languages, into an executable unit. Finally, a powerful symbolic debugger aids the designer during program checkout, permitting debugging at the source level even for those programs written in multiple languages.

EXORmacs multi-user configuration. The EXORmacs design system allows more than one software and/or hardware designer to work simultaneously by the addition of a hard disk subsystem for mass file storage and one or more Multi-Channel Communication Modules as shown in Fig. 15–25.

The EXORmacs Hard Disk subsystem consists of a VERSAbus interface module that utilizes an Intelligent Peripheral Controller interconnected to a Disk Interface Module. The Disk Interface Module interconnects to the Hard Disk Drives. The Disk Interface Module provides an industry-standard Storage Module Drive (SMD) interface to two drives, thus allowing interconnection of fixed and removable cartridge-type drive.

To provide the I/O interface between multiple users of EXORmacs, an intelligent communications controller is required. The Multi-Channel Communications Module (MCCM) provides this interface for four users through individual serial RS-232 ports. The MCCM also provides a printer port for these four users to share. Within the module are individual baud rate generators so that each user may program his transfer rate to suit his terminal.

Each Communications Module will support four EXORterm 155s which provide editing and debug capabilities for EXORmacs. Additional MCCM and memory modules can be selected to meet the expanded capacity of multi-user development.[11]

As was stated at the beginning of this text, the field of microprocessors is a fast paced and dynamic area. While this book is being produced, the manufacturers of microprocessor systems are competitively researching and producing new devices and systems to place on

[11] *Development Systems*, pp. 3,6,7,16.

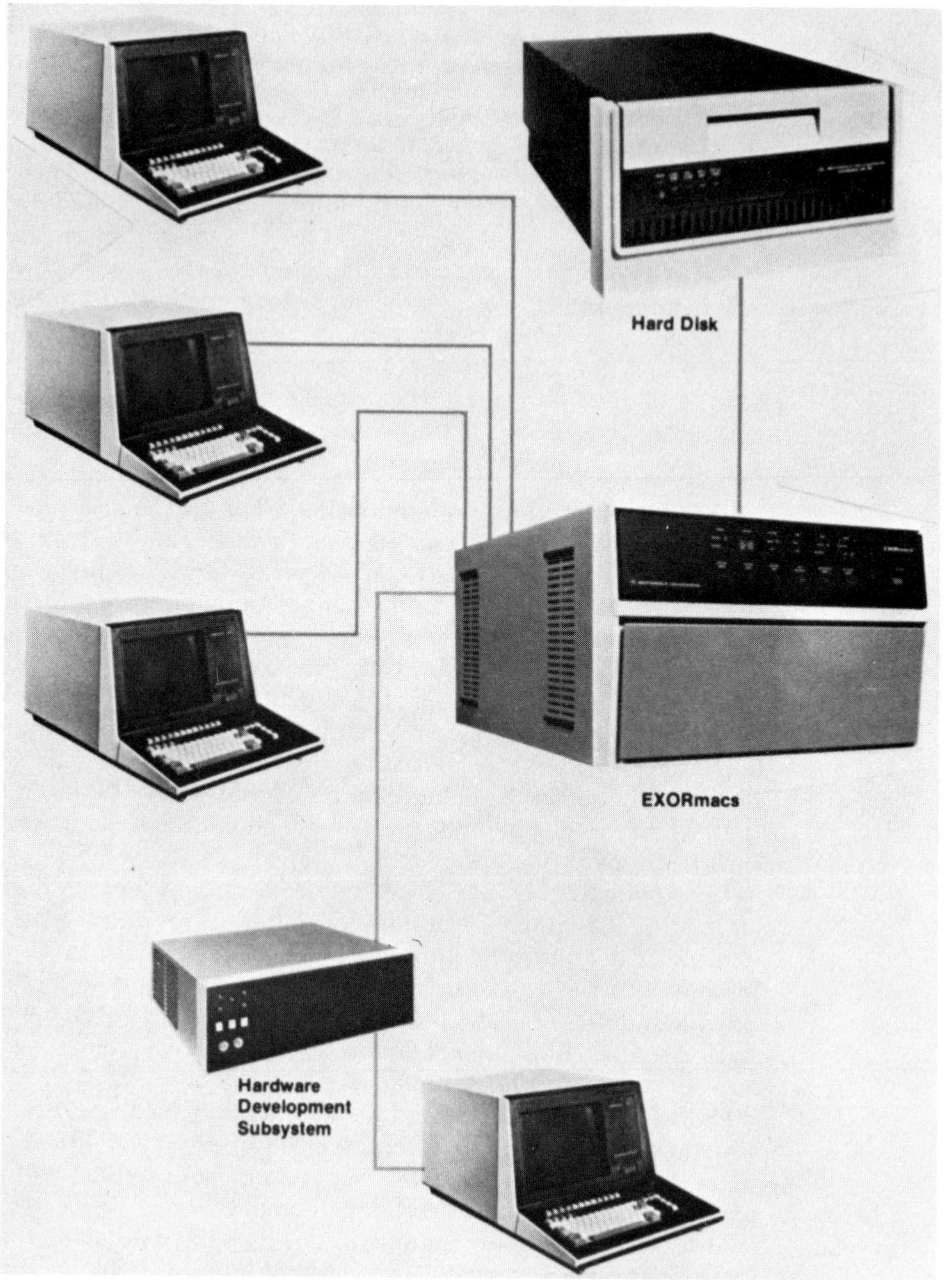

Fig. 15–25. EXORmacs multi-user configuration. (*Courtesy Motorola Inc.*)

the market. It is the authors' hope that, by means of this text, the reader has gained the fundamental insights necessary to understanding and learning these new devices and system as they are introduced. The text should be the beginning and the framework for the reader's continued study.

Appendix 1

Numbering Systems

Powers of Two

2^n	n	2^{-n}
1	0	1.0
2	1	0.5
4	2	0.25
8	3	0.125
16	4	0.062 5
32	5	0.031 25
64	6	0.015 625
128	7	0.007 812 5
256	8	0.003 906 25
512	9	0.001 953 125
1 024	10	0.000 976 562 5
2 048	11	0.000 488 281 25
4 096	12	0.000 244 140 625
8 192	13	0.000 122 070 312 5
16 384	14	0.000 061 035 156 25
32 768	15	0.000 030 517 578 125
65 536	16	0.000 015 258 789 062 5

(Reprinted by Permission of Intel Corporation, © 1977)

POWERS OF 16 (IN BASE 10)

16^n	n	16^{-n}				
1	0	0.10000	00000	00000	00000	$\times 10$
16	1	0.62500	00000	00000	00000	$\times 10^{-1}$
256	2	0.39062	50000	00000	00000	$\times 10^{-2}$
4 096	3	0.24414	06250	00000	00000	$\times 10^{-3}$
65 536	4	0.15258	78906	25000	00000	$\times 10^{-4}$
1 048 576	5	0.95367	43164	06250	00000	$\times 10^{-6}$
16 777 216	6	0.59604	64477	53906	25000	$\times 10^{-7}$
268 435 456	7	0.37252	90298	46191	40625	$\times 10^{-8}$
4 294 967 296	8	0.23283	06436	53869	62891	$\times 10^{-9}$
68 719 476 736	9	0.14551	91522	83668	51807	$\times 10^{-10}$
1 099 511 627 776	10	0.90949	47017	72928	23792	$\times 10^{-12}$
17 592 186 044 416	11	0.56843	41886	08080	14870	$\times 10^{-13}$
281 474 976 710 656	12	0.35527	13678	80050	09294	$\times 10^{-14}$
4 503 599 627 370 496	13	0.22204	46049	25031	30808	$\times 10^{-15}$
72 057 594 037 927 936	14	0.13877	78780	78144	56755	$\times 10^{-16}$
1 152 921 504 606 846 976	15	0.86736	17379	88403	54721	$\times 10^{-18}$

POWERS OF 10 (IN BASE 16)

10^n	n	10^{-n}				
1	0	1.0000	0000	0000	0000	
A	1	0.1999	9999	9999	999A	
64	2	0.28F5	C28F	5C28	F5C3	$\times 16^{-1}$
3E8	3	0.4189	374B	C6A7	EF9E	$\times 16^{-2}$
2710	4	0.68DB	8BAC	710C	B296	$\times 16^{-3}$
1 86A0	5	0.A7C5	AC47	1B47	8423	$\times 16^{-4}$
F 4240	6	0.10C6	F7A0	B5ED	8D37	$\times 16^{-4}$
98 9680	7	0.1AD7	F29A	BCAF	4858	$\times 16^{-5}$
5F5 E100	8	0.2AF3	1DC4	6118	73BF	$\times 16^{-6}$
3B9A CA00	9	0.44B8	2FA0	9B5A	52CC	$\times 16^{-7}$
2 540B E400	10	0.6DF3	7F67	SEF6	EADF	$\times 16^{-8}$
17 4876 E800	11	0.AFEB	FF0B	CB24	AAFF	$\times 16^{-9}$
E8 D4A5 1000	12	0.1197	9981	2DEA	1119	$\times 16^{-9}$
918 4E72 A000	13	0.1C25	C268	4976	81C2	$\times 16^{-10}$
5AF3 107A 4000	14	0.2D09	370D	4257	3604	$\times 16^{-11}$
3 8D7E A4C6 8000	15	0.480E	BE7B	9D58	566D	$\times 16^{-12}$
23 8652 6FC1 0000	16	0.734A	CA5F	6226	F0AE	$\times 16^{-13}$
163 4578 5D8A 0000	17	0.B877	AA32	36A4	B449	$\times 16^{-14}$
DE0 B6B3 A764 0000	18	0.1272	5DD1	D243	ABA1	$\times 16^{-14}$
8AC7 2304 89E8 0000	19	0.1D83	C94F	B6D2	AC35	$\times 16^{-15}$

(Reprinted by permission of Intel Corporation, © 1977)

HEXADECIMAL AND DECIMAL CONVERSION

From hex: locate each hex digit in its corresponding column position and note the decimal equivalents. Add these to obtain the decimal value.

From decimal: (1) locate the largest decimal value in the table that will fit into the decimal number to be converted, and (2) note its hex equivalent and hex column position. (3) Find the decimal remainder. Repeat the process on this and subsequent remainders.

HEXADECIMAL COLUMNS											
6		5		4		3		2		1	
HEX	= DEC	HEX	= DEC	HEX	= DEC	HEX	= DEC	HEX	= DEC	HEX	= DEC
0	0	0	0	0	0	0	0	0	0	0	0
1	1,048,576	1	65,536	1	4,096	1	256	1	16	1	1
2	2,097,152	2	131,072	2	8,192	2	512	2	32	2	2
3	3,145,728	3	196,608	3	12,288	3	768	3	48	3	3
4	4,194,304	4	262,144	4	16,384	4	1,024	4	64	4	4
5	5,242,880	5	327,680	5	20,480	5	1,280	5	80	5	5
6	6,291,456	6	393,216	6	24,576	6	1,536	6	96	6	6
7	7,340,032	7	458,752	7	28,672	7	1,792	7	112	7	7
8	8,388,608	8	524,288	8	32,768	8	2,048	8	128	8	8
9	9,437,184	9	589,824	9	36,864	9	2,304	9	144	9	9
A	10,485,760	A	655,360	A	40,960	A	2,560	A	160	A	10
B	11,534,336	B	720,896	B	45,056	B	2,816	B	176	B	11
C	12,582,912	C	786,432	C	49,152	C	3,072	C	192	C	12
D	13,631,488	D	851,968	D	53,248	D	3,328	D	208	D	13
E	14,680,064	E	917,504	E	54,344	E	3,584	E	224	E	14
F	15,728,640	F	983,040	F	61,440	F	3,840	F	240	F	15
0 1 2 3		4 5 6 7		0 1 2 3		4 5 6 7		0 1 2 3		4 5 6 7	
BYTE				BYTE				BYTE			

(*Courtesy Motorola Inc.*)

Number Coding Schemes

DECIMAL	BINARY	OCTAL	HEXADECIMAL	BINARY CODED DECIMAL
0	00000	00	0 0	0000 0000
1	00001	01	0 1	0000 0001
2	00010	02	0 2	0000 0010
3	00011	03	0 3	0000 0011
4	00100	04	0 4	0000 0100
5	00101	05	0 5	0000 0101
6	00110	06	0 6	0000 0110
7	00111	07	0 7	0000 0111
8	01000	10	0 8	0000 1000
9	01001	11	0 9	0000 1001
10	01010	12	0 A	0001 0000
11	01011	13	0 B	0001 0001
12	01100	14	0 C	0001 0010
13	01101	15	0 D	0001 0011
14	01110	16	0 E	0001 0100
15	01111	17	0 F	0001 0101
16	10000	20	1 0	0001 0110

Appendix 2

ASCII Code Conversion Table

BITS 4 thru 6	—	0	1	2	3	4	5	6	7
	0	NUL	DLE	SP	0	@	P		p
	1	SOH	DC1	!	1	A	Q	a	q
	2	STX	DC2	"	2	B	R	b	r
	3	ETX	DC3	#	3	C	S	c	s
	4	EOT	DC4	$	4	D	T	d	t
	5	ENQ	NAK	%	5	E	U	e	u
BITS 0 thru 3	6	ACK	SYN	&	6	F	V	f	v
	7	BEL	ETB	'	7	G	W	g	w
	8	BS	CAN	(	8	H	X	h	x
	9	HT	EM	)	9	I	Y	i	y
	A	LF	SUB	*	:	J	Z	j	z
	B	VT	ESC	+	;	K	[	k	{
	C	FF	FS	,	<	L	/	l	/
	D	CR	GS	-	=	M	]	m	}
	E	SO	RS	.	>	N	^	n	≈
	F	SI	US	/	?	O	—	o	DEL

Appendix 3

Integrated Circuits

STANDARD INTEGRATED CIRCUITS

7400 Series TTL

PART NUMBER	DEVICE DESCRIPTION
7400	Quad 2-In NAND Gate
7401	Quad 2-In NAND Gate (O.C.)
7402	Quad 2-In NOR Gate
7403	Quad 2-In NAND Gate (O.C.)
7404	Hex Inverter
7405	Hex Inverter (O.C.)
7406	Hex Inverter (O.C.)
7407	Hex Buffer (O.C.)
7408	Quad 2-In AND Gate
7409	Quad 2-In AND Gate (O.C.)
7410	Triple 3-In NAND Gate
7411	Triple 3-In AND Gate
7412	Triple 3-In NAND Gate (O.C.)
7413	Dual 4-In Schmitt Trigger
7414	Hex Schmitt Trigger Inverter
7416	Hex Inverter (O.C.)
7417	Hex Buffer (O.C.)
7420	Dual 4-In NAND Gate
7421	Dual 4-In AND Gate
7423	Expandable Dual 4-In NOR Gate
7425	Dual 4-In NOR Gate w/Strobe
7426	Quad 2-In NAND Gate (O.C.)
7427	Triple 3-In NOR Gate

PART NUMBER	DEVICE DESCRIPTION
7428	Quad 2-In NOR Buffer
7430	8-In NAND Gate
7432	Quad 2-In OR Gate
7433	Quad 2-In NOR Buffer (O.C.)
7437	Quad 2-In NAND Buffer
7438	Quad 2-In NAND Buffer (O.C.)
7439	Quad 2-In NAND Buffer (O.C.)
7440	Dual 4-In NAND Buffer
7442	BCD-to-Decimal Decoder
7445	BCD-to-Decimal Decoder/Driver
7446	BCD-to-7 Seg. Decoder/Driver
7447	BCD-to-7 Seg. Decoder/Driver
7448	BCD-to-7 Seg. Decoder/Driver
7450	Dual 2-Wide 2-In AND-OR-INV Gate
7451	Dual 2-Wide 2-In AND-OR-INV Gate
7453	Expandable 4-Wide AND-OR-INV Gate
7454	4-Wide AND-OR-INVERT Gate
7460	Dual 4-In Expander
7470	JK Flip-Flop
7472	JK M/S Flip-Flop
7473	Dual JK M/S Flip-Flop
7474	Dual D Flip-Flop
7475	Quad Latch
7476	Dual JK M/S Flip-Flop
7480	Gated Full Adder
7483	4-Bit Binary Full Adder
7485	4-Bit Comparator
7486	Quad 2-In Exclusive OR Gate
7489	64-Bit RAM
7490	Decade Counter
7491	8-Bit Shift Register
7492	Divide-by-Twelve Counter
7493	4-Bit Binary Counter
7494	4-Bit Shift Register
7495	4-Bit RS LS Register
7496	5-Bit Shift Register
74100	Quad Latch
74107	Dual JK Flip-Flop
74109	Dual JK Flip-Flop
74116	Dual 4-Bit Latch with Clear
74121	Monostable Multivibrator
74122	Monostable Multivibrator

PART NUMBER	DEVICE DESCRIPTION
74123	Dual Monostable Multivibrator
74125	Tri-State Quad 2-In Buffer
74126	Tri-State Quad 2-In Buffer
74128	Quad 2-In NOR Buffer
74132	Quad Schmitt Trigger
74141	NIXIE Driver
74145	BCD-to-Decimal Decoder/Driver
74147	10-to-4 Priority Encoder
74148	8-to-4 Priority Encoder
74150	16-to-1 Multiplexer
74151	8-to-1 Multiplexer
74153	Dual 4-to-1 Multiplexer
74154	4-to-16 Decoder/Demultiplexer
74155	Dual 2-to-4 Decoder/Demultiplexer
74156	Dual 2-to-4 Decoder/Demultiplexer
74157	Quad 2-to-1 Multiplexer
74160	Presettable Decade Counter
74161	Presettable Binary Counter
74162	Presettable Decade Counter
74163	Presettable Binary Counter
74164	8-Bit SI PO Shift Register
74165	8-Bit SI PO Shift Register
74166	8-Bit SI PO Shift Register
74170	4-by-4 Register File
74173	Tri-State Quad D Flip-Flop
74174	Hex D Flip-Flop
74175	Quad D Flip-Flop
74176	Presettable Decade Counter
74177	Presettable Binary Counter
74180	9-Bit Parity Generator/Checker
74181	Arithmetic Logic Unit
74182	Look-Ahead Carry Generator
74184	BCD-to-Binary Converter
74185	Binary-to-BCD Converter
74189	Tri-State 64-Bit RAM
74190	Up/Down Decade Counter
74191	Up/Down Binary Counter
74192	Up/Down Decade Counter
74193	Up/Down Binary Counter
74194	4-Bit Bidirectional Shift Register
74195	4-Bit Parallel Access Shift Register
74196	Presettable Decade Counter

PART NUMBER	DEVICE DESCRIPTION
74197	Presettable Binary Counter
74198	PI PO 8-Bit Shift Register
74199	PI PO 8-Bit Shift Register
74221	Dual Monostable w/Schmitt Trigger Input
74251	Tri-State 8-to-1 Multiplexer
74279	Quad SR Latch
74298	Quad 2-In Multiplexer with Storage
74365	Tri-State Hex Buffer
74366	Tri-State Hex Inverter
74367	Tri-State Hex Buffer
74368	Tri-State Hex Inverter

4000 Series CMOS

PART NUMBER	DEVICE DESCRIPTION
4000	Dual 3-In NOR Plus Inverter
4001	Quad 2-In NOR Gate
4002	Dual 4-In NOR Gate
4006	18-Stage Shift Register
4007	Dual Complementary Pair Plus Inverter
4008	4-Bit Full Adder
4009	Hex Inverter Buffer
4010	Hex Buffer
4011	Quad 2-In NAND Gate
4012	Dual 4-In NAND Gate
4013	Dual D Flip-Flop
4014	8-Stage Shift Register
4015	Dual 4-State Shift Register
4016	Quad Bilateral Switch
4017	Decade Counter/Driver
4018	Presettable Divide-by-N Counter
4019	Quad AND-OR Select Gate
4020	14-Stage Binary Counter
4021	8-Stage Shift Register
4022	Divide-by-8 Counter/Decoder
4023	Triple 3-In NAND Gate
4024	7-Stage Binary Counter
4025	Triple 3-In NOR Gate

PART NUMBER	DEVICE DESCRIPTION
4026	Decade Counter w/Decoded 7 Seg. Output
4027	Dual JK M/S Flip-Flop
4028	BCD-to-Decimal Decoder
4029	Presettable Up/Down BCD/Binary Counter
4030	Quad Exclusive OR Gate
4033	Decade Counter w/Decoded 7 Seg. Output
4034	8-Stage Bidirectional Register
4035	4-Stage Shift Register
4040	12-Stage Binary Counter
4041	Quad Buffer
4042	Quad D Latch
4043	Quad NOR R/S Latch
4044	Quad NAND R/S Latch
4046	Micropower Phase Locked Loop
4049	Hex Inverting Buffer
4050	Hex Buffer
4051	8-Channel Analog Mux/Demux
4052	Differential 4-Channel Analog Mux/Demux
4053	Triple 2-Channel Analog Mux/Demux
4060	14-Stage Binary Counter/Oscillator
4066	Quad Bilateral Switch
4071	Quad 2-In OR Gate
4072	Dual 4-In OR Gate
4073	Triple 3-In AND Gate
4075	Triple 3-In OR Gate
4081	Quad 2-In AND Gate
4082	Dual 4-In AND Gate
4502	Strobed Hex Inverter
4510	BCD Up/Down Counter
4511	BCD-to-7 Seg. Latch/Decoder/Driver
4514	4-Bit Latch/4-to-16 Line Decoder
4515	4-Bit Latch/4-to-16 Line Decoder
4516	Binary Up/Down Counter
4518	Dual BCD Up Counter
4520	Dual Binary Up Counter
4527	BCD Rate Multiplier
4528	Dual Monostable Multivibrator
4585	4-Bit Magnitude Comparator

INTEL MICROPROCESSOR—INTEGRATED CIRCUITS

FUNCTION	PART NUMBER	DESCRIPTION
Memory and I/O Expanders	8155	RAM I/O
	8355	ROM I/O
	8755	EPROM I/O
RAMS (Static)	8101A-4	256-by-4
	8102A-4	1 K-by-1
	8111A-4	256-by-4
	5101	256-by-4 CMOS
	2114	1 K-by-4
RAMS (Dynamic)	2104A-4	4 K-by-1
	2107B-4	4 K-by-1
	2116-4	16 K-by-1
RAM Support Circuits	3222	Refresh Controller
	3232	Refresh Counter/Multiplexer
	3242	Refresh Counter/Multiplexer
ROMs	8308	1 K-by-8
	8316A	2 K-by-8
	2316E	2 K-by-8
EPROMS	1702A-2	256-by-8
	8708	1 K-by-8
	2708	1 K-by-8
	2716	2 K-by-8
Peripherals	8205	1-8 Decoder
	8212	8-bit Latch
	8214	Priority Unit
	8216	4-bit Bus Driver
	8224	Clock Generator
	8226	4-bit Bus Driver
	8228	System Controller
	8238	System Controller
	8251	USART
	8253	Interval Timer
	8255A	PPI Programmable Peripheral Interface
	8257	DMA Direct Memory Access
	8259	Interrupt Controller
	8271	Floppy Disk Controller
	8273	SDLC Synchronous Data Link Control
	8275	CRT Controller
	8279	KYBD/Display Interface

MOTOROLA MICROPROCESSOR—INTEGRATED CIRCUITS

FUNCTION	PART NUMBER	DESCRIPTION
RAMs (MOS dynamic)	MCM4027	4096-by-1
	MCM4116	16384-by-1
	MCM4517	16384-by-1
	MCM6632	32768-by-1
	MCM6633	32768-by-1
	MCM6664	65536-by-1
	MCM6665	65536-by-1
RAMs (MOS static)	MCM6810	128-by-8
	MCM2114	1024-by-4
	MCM2115	1024-by-1
	MCM2125	1024-by-1
	MCM6641	4096-by-1
	MCM2147	4096-by-1
RAMs (CMOS static)	MCM5101	256-by-4
	MCM65147	4096-by-1
ROMs (MOS static)	MCM6670	128-by-(7-by-5)
	MCM66700	128-by-(9-by-7)
ROMs (Binary)	MCM68308	1024-by-8
	MCM68A316	2048-by-8
	MCM68A332	4096-by-8
	MCM68364	8192-by-8
	MCM68365	8192-by-8
	MCM68366	8192-by-8
ROMs (CMOS)	MCM14524	256-by-4
	MCM65516	2048-by-8
EPROMs (MOS)	MCM2708	1024-by-8
	MCM2716	2048-by-8
	MCM2532	4096-by-8
	MCM68764	8192-by-8
	MCM68766	8192-by-8
EEPROMs (MOS)	MCM2801	16-by-16
	MCM2802	32-by-32
	MCM2816	2048-by-8
Microprocessor ICs and peripherals	MC1372	Color Television Modulator
	MC3446A	Quad Bidirectional Bus Transceiver

Motorola Microprocessor—Integrated Circuits (*continued*)

FUNCTION	PART NUMBER	DESCRIPTION
Microprocessor ICs and peripherals	MC3447	Octal Bidirectional Instrumentation Bus (GPIB) Transceiver
	MC3448A	Quad Bidirectional Instrumentation Bus (GPIB) Transceiver
	MC3482/MC6882	Quad Buffer/Latch
	MC3870	8-Bit Single-Chip Microcontroller
	MC6800	8-Bit Microprocessor Unit (MPU)
	MC6801/03/03NR	8-Bit Microcomputer/Microprocessor Unit (MCU/MPU)
	MC6802/02NS/08	8-Bit Microprocessor with Clock and Optional RAM
	MC6805P2	8-Bit HMOS 1K Single-Chip Microcomputer
	MC6805P4	8-Bit HMOS 2K Microcomputer
	MC6805R2	8-Bit HMOS 2K Single-Chip Microcomputer with A/D
	MC6805T2	8-Bit HMOS 2K Single-Chip Microcomputer with PLL
	MC6805U2	8-Bit HMOS 2K Single-Chip Microcomputer
	MC6809/MC6809E	8-/16-Bit HMOS Microprocessor
	MC6821	Peripheral Interface Adapter (PIA)
	MC6822	Industrial Interface Adapter (IA)
	MC6828	Priority Interrupt Controller (PIC)
	MC6829	Memory Management Unit (MMU)
	MC6835	CRT Controller (CRTC)
	MC6839	Floating-Point ROM
	MC6840	Programmable Timer (PTM)
	MC6843	Floppy Disk Controller (FDC)
	MC6844	Direct Memory Access Controller (DMAC)
	MC6845	CRT Controller (CRTC)
	MC6846	ROM-I/O-Timer
	MC6847	Video Display Generator (VDG)
	MC6850	Asynchronous Interface Adapter (ACIA)
	MC6852	Synchronous Serial Data Adapter (SSDA)
	MC6854	Advanced Data Link Controller (ADLC)
	MC6855	Serial Direct Memory Access Processor
	MC6859	Data Security Device (DSD)
	MC6860	0-66 BPS Digital Modem
	MC6862	2400 BPS Digital Modulator

Motorola Microprocessor—Integrated Circuits (*continued*)

FUNCTION	PART NUMBER	DESCRIPTION
Microprocessor ICs and peripherals	MC6870A/71A	Two-Phase Microprocessor Clock
	MC6875	Two-Phase Clock Generator
	MC6880A/8T26	Quad Bus Transceiver
	MC6883	Synchronous Address Multiplexer
	MC6889/MC8T28	Quad Bus Transceiver
	MC68000	16-Bit HMOS Microprocessor
	MC68120/121	Intelligent Peripheral Controller (IPC)
	MC68122	Cluster Terminal Controller (CTC)
	MC68230	Parallel Interface/Timer (PI/T)
	MC68450	Direct Memory Access Controller (DMAC)
	MC68451	Memory Management Unit (MMU)
	MC68488	General Purpose Interface Adapter (GPIA)
	MC68701	EPROM Microcomputer/Microprocessor
	MC68705P3	8-Bit HMOS 1.8K EPROM Single-Chip Microcomputer
	MC68705R3	8-Bit HMOS 3.7K EPROM Single-Chip Microcomputer with A/D
	MC68705U3	8-Bit HMOS 3.7K EPROM Single-Chip Microcomputer
	MC141000	4-Bit CMOS 1K Microcomputer
	MC141099	4-Bit CMOS 1K Microcomputer (External ROM)
	MC141200	4-Bit CMOS 1K Microcomputer
	MC146805E2	8-Bit CMOS Microprocessor with RAM and I/O
	MC146805F2	8-Bit CMOS 1K Single-Chip Microcomputer
	MC146805G2	8-Bit CMOS 2K Single-Chip Microcomputer
	MC146818	CMOS Real-Time Clock plus RAM
	MC146823	CMOS Parallel Interface

Appendix 4

Standard Logic Symbols

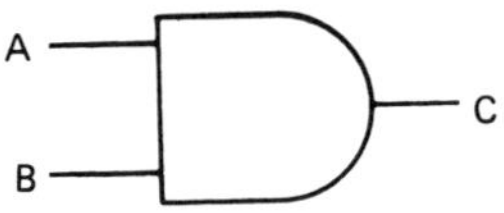

A	B	C
0	0	0
0	1	0
1	0	0
1	1	1

AND

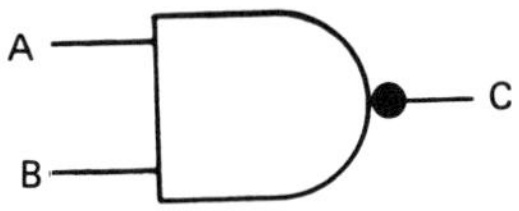

A	B	C
0	0	1
0	1	1
1	0	1
1	1	0

NAND

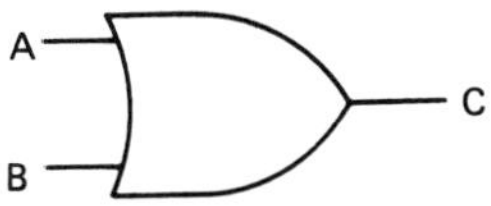

A	B	C
0	0	0
0	1	1
1	0	1
1	1	1

OR

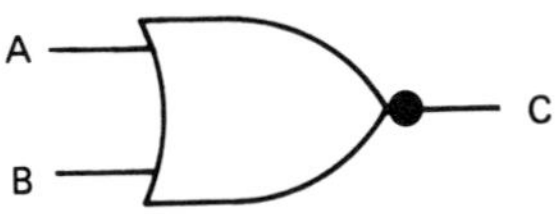

A	B	C
0	0	1
0	1	0
1	0	0
1	1	0

NOR

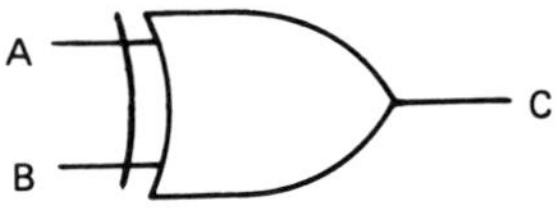

A	B	C
0	0	0
0	1	1
1	0	1
1	1	0

EXCLUSIVE OR

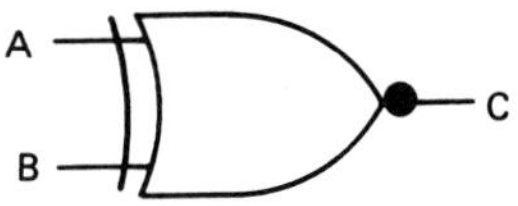

A	B	C
0	0	1
0	1	0
1	0	0
1	1	1

EXCLUSIVE NOR

A	B
0	1
1	0

NOT

Appendix 5

Instruction Sets

MOTOROLA MC6800 INSTRUCTION SET

TABLE 1 – MEMORY MAP FOR INTERRUPT VECTORS

Vector MS	Vector LS	Description
FFFE	FFFF	Restart
FFFC	FFFD	Non-maskable Interrupt
FFFA	FFFB	Software Interrupt
FFF8	FFF9	Interrupt Request

TABLE 2 – MICROPROCESSOR INSTRUCTION SET – ALPHABETIC SEQUENCE

ABA	Add Accumulators
ADC	Add with Carry
ADD	Add
AND	Logical And
ASL	Arithmetic Shift Left
ASR	Arithmetic Shift Right
BCC	Branch if Carry Clear
BCS	Branch if Carry Set
BEQ	Branch if Equal to Zero
BGE	Branch if Greater or Equal Zero
BGT	Branch if Greater than Zero
BHI	Branch if Higher
BIT	Bit Test
BLE	Branch if Less or Equal
BLS	Branch if Lower or Same
BLT	Branch if Less than Zero
BMI	Branch if Minus
BNE	Branch if Not Equal to Zero
BPL	Branch if Plus
BRA	Branch Always
BSR	Branch to Subroutine
BVC	Branch if Overflow Clear
BVS	Branch if Overflow Set
CBA	Compare Accumulators
CLC	Clear Carry
CLI	Clear Interrupt Mask
CLR	Clear
CLV	Clear Overflow
CMP	Compare
COM	Complement
CPX	Compare Index Register
DAA	Decimal Adjust
DEC	Decrement
DES	Decrement Stack Pointer
DEX	Decrement Index Register
EOR	Exclusive OR
INC	Increment
INS	Increment Stack Pointer
INX	Increment Index Register
JMP	Jump
JSR	Jump to Subroutine
LDA	Load Accumulator
LDS	Load Stack Pointer
LDX	Load Index Register
LSR	Logical Shift Right
NEG	Negate
NOP	No Operation
ORA	Inclusive OR Accumulator
PSH	Push Data
PUL	Pull Data
ROL	Rotate Left
ROR	Rotate Right
RTI	Return from Interrupt
RTS	Return from Subroutine
SBA	Subtract Accumulators
SBC	Subtract with Carry
SEC	Set Carry
SEI	Set Interrupt Mask
SEV	Set Overflow
STA	Store Accumulator
STS	Store Stack Register
STX	Store Index Register
SUB	Subtract
SWI	Software Interrupt
TAB	Transfer Accumulators
TAP	Transfer Accumulators to Condition Code Reg.
TBA	Transfer Accumulators
TPA	Transfer Condition Code Reg. to Accumulator
TST	Test
TSX	Transfer Stack Pointer to Index Register
TXS	Transfer Index Register to Stack Pointer
WAI	Wait for Interrupt

TABLE 3 – ACCUMULATOR AND MEMORY INSTRUCTIONS

		ADDRESSING MODES															BOOLEAN/ARITHMETIC OPERATION	COND. CODE REG.					
		IMMED			DIRECT			INDEX			EXTND			IMPLIED			(All register labels refer to contents)	5	4	3	2	1	0
OPERATIONS	MNEMONIC	OP	~	#	OP	~	#	OP	~	#	OP	~	#	OP	~	#		H	I	N	Z	V	C
Add	ADDA	8B	2	2	9B	3	2	AB	5	2	BB	4	3				A + M → A	↕	●	↕	↕	↕	↕
	ADDB	CB	2	2	DB	3	2	EB	5	2	FB	4	3				B + M → B	↕	●	↕	↕	↕	↕
Add Acmltrs	ABA													1B	2	1	A + B → A	↕	●	↕	↕	↕	↕
Add with Carry	ADCA	89	2	2	99	3	2	A9	5	2	B9	4	3				A + M + C → A	↕	●	↕	↕	↕	↕
	ADCB	C9	2	2	D9	3	2	E9	5	2	F9	4	3				B + M + C → B	↕	●	↕	↕	↕	↕
And	ANDA	84	2	2	94	3	2	A4	5	2	B4	4	3				A · M → A	●	●	↕	↕	R	●
	ANDB	C4	2	2	D4	3	2	E4	5	2	F4	4	3				B · M → B	●	●	↕	↕	R	●
Bit Test	BITA	85	2	2	95	3	2	A5	5	2	B5	4	3				A · M	●	●	↕	↕	R	●
	BITB	C5	2	2	D5	3	2	E5	5	2	F5	4	3				B · M	●	●	↕	↕	R	●
Clear	CLR							6F	7	2	7F	6	3				00 → M	●	●	R	S	R	R
	CLRA													4F	2	1	00 → A	●	●	R	S	R	R
	CLRB													5F	2	1	00 → B	●	●	R	S	R	R
Compare	CMPA	81	2	2	91	3	2	A1	5	2	B1	4	3				A – M	●	●	↕	↕	↕	↕
	CMPB	C1	2	2	D1	3	2	E1	5	2	F1	4	3				B – M	●	●	↕	↕	↕	↕
Compare Acmltrs	CBA													11	2	1	A – B	●	●	↕	↕	↕	↕
Complement, 1's	COM							63	7	2	73	6	3				$\overline{M}$ → M	●	●	↕	↕	R	S
	COMA													43	2	1	$\overline{A}$ → A	●	●	↕	↕	R	S
	COMB													53	2	1	$\overline{B}$ → B	●	●	↕	↕	R	S
Complement, 2's	NEG							60	7	2	70	6	3				00 – M → M	●	●	↕	↕	①	②
(Negate)	NEGA													40	2	1	00 – A → A	●	●	↕	↕	①	②
	NEGB													50	2	1	00 – B → B	●	●	↕	↕	①	②
Decimal Adjust, A	DAA													19	2	1	Converts Binary Add. of BCD Characters into BCD Format	●	●	↕	↕	↕	③
Decrement	DEC							6A	7	2	7A	6	3				M – 1 → M	●	●	↕	↕	4	●
	DECA													4A	2	1	A – 1 → A	●	●	↕	↕	4	●
	DECB													5A	2	1	B – 1 → B	●	●	↕	↕	4	●
Exclusive OR	EORA	88	2	2	98	3	2	A8	5	2	B8	4	3				A⊕M → A	●	●	↕	↕	R	●
	EORB	C8	2	2	D8	3	2	E8	5	2	F8	4	3				B⊕M → B	●	●	↕	↕	R	●
Increment	INC							6C	7	2	7C	6	3				M + 1 → M	●	●	↕	↕	⑤	●
	INCA													4C	2	1	A + 1 → A	●	●	↕	↕	⑤	●
	INCB													5C	2	1	B + 1 → B	●	●	↕	↕	⑤	●
Load Acmltr	LDAA	86	2	2	96	3	2	A6	5	2	B6	4	3				M → A	●	●	↕	↕	R	●
	LDAB	C6	2	2	D6	3	2	E6	5	2	F6	4	3				M → B	●	●	↕	↕	R	●
Or, Inclusive	ORAA	8A	2	2	9A	3	2	AA	5	2	BA	4	3				A + M → A	●	●	↕	↕	R	●
	ORAB	CA	2	2	DA	3	2	EA	5	2	FA	4	3				B + M → B	●	●	↕	↕	R	●

Push Data	PSHA													36	4	1	A → M_{SP}, SP − 1 → SP	●	●	●	●	●	●
	PSHB													37	4	1	B → M_{SP}, SP − 1 → SP	●	●	●	●	●	●
Pull Data	PULA													32	4	1	SP + 1 → SP, M_{SP} → A	●	●	●	●	●	●
	PULB													33	4	1	SP + 1 → SP, M_{SP} → B	●	●	●	●	●	●
Rotate Left	ROL							69	7	2	79	6	3				M	●	●	↕	↕	(6)	↕
	ROLA													49	2	1	A	●	●	↕	↕	(6)	↕
	ROLB													59	2	1	B C b7 ← b0	●	●	↕	↕	(6)	↕
Rotate Right	ROR							66	7	2	76	6	3				M	●	●	↕	↕	(6)	↕
	RORA													46	2	1	A	●	●	↕	↕	(6)	↕
	RORB													56	2	1	B C b7 → b0	●	●	↕	↕	(6)	↕
Shift Left, Arithmetic	ASL							68	7	2	78	6	3				M	●	●	↕	↕	(6)	↕
	ASLA													48	2	1	A ← 0	●	●	↕	↕	(6)	↕
	ASLB													58	2	1	B C b7 b0	●	●	↕	↕	(6)	↕
Shift Right, Arithmetic	ASR							67	7	2	77	6	3				M	●	●	↕	↕	(6)	↕
	ASRA													47	2	1	A	●	●	↕	↕	(6)	↕
	ASRB													57	2	1	B b7 b0 C	●	●	↕	↕	(6)	↕
Shift Right, Logic	LSR							64	7	2	74	6	3				M	●	●	R	↕	(6)	↕
	LSRA													44	2	1	A 0 →	●	●	R	↕	(6)	↕
	LSRB													54	2	1	B b7 b0 C	●	●	R	↕	(6)	↕
Store Acmltr.	STAA				97	4	2	A7	6	2	B7	5	3				A → M	●	●	↕	↕	R	●
	STAB				D7	4	2	E7	6	2	F7	5	3				B → M	●	●	↕	↕	R	●
Subtract	SUBA	80	2	2	90	3	2	A0	5	2	B0	4	3				A − M → A	●	●	↕	↕	↕	↕
	SUBB	C0	2	2	D0	3	2	E0	5	2	F0	4	3				B − M → B	●	●	↕	↕	↕	↕
Subtract Acmltrs.	SBA													10	2	1	A − B → A	●	●	↕	↕	↕	↕
Subtr. with Carry	SBCA	82	2	2	92	3	2	A2	5	2	B2	4	3				A − M − C → A	●	●	↕	↕	↕	↕
	SBCB	C2	2	2	D2	3	2	E2	5	2	F2	4	3				B − M − C → B	●	●	↕	↕	↕	↕
Transfer Acmltrs	TAB													16	2	1	A → B	●	●	↕	↕	R	●
	TBA													17	2	1	B → A	●	●	↕	↕	R	●
Test, Zero or Minus	TST							6D	7	2	7D	6	3				M − 00	●	●	↕	↕	R	R
	TSTA													4D	2	1	A − 00	●	●	↕	↕	R	R
	TSTB													5D	2	1	B − 00	●	●	↕	↕	R	R
																		H	I	N	Z	V	C

LEGEND:

OP Operation Code (Hexadecimal);
~ Number of MPU Cycles;
= Number of Program Bytes;
+ Arithmetic Plus;
− Arithmetic Minus;
· Boolean AND;
M_{SP} Contents of memory location pointed to be Stack Pointer;

+ Boolean Inclusive OR;
⊕ Boolean Exclusive OR;
$\overline{M}$ Complement of M;
→ Transfer Into;
0 Bit = Zero;
00 Byte = Zero;

Note – Accumulator addressing mode instructions are included in the column for IMPLIED addressing

CONDITION CODE SYMBOLS:

H Half-carry from bit 3;
I Interrupt mask
N Negative (sign bit)
Z Zero (byte)
V Overflow, 2's complement
C Carry from bit 7
R Reset Always
S Set Always
↕ Test and set if true, cleared otherwise
● Not Affected

TABLE 4 – INDEX REGISTER AND STACK MANIPULATION INSTRUCTIONS

		IMMED			DIRECT			INDEX			EXTND			IMPLIED				COND. CODE REG.					
																		5	4	3	2	1	0
POINTER OPERATIONS	MNEMONIC	OP	~	#	OP	~	#	OP	~	#	OP	~	#	OP	~	#	BOOLEAN/ARITHMETIC OPERATION	H	I	N	Z	V	C
Compare Index Reg	CPX	8C	3	3	9C	4	2	AC	6	2	BC	5	3				$X_H - M, X_L - (M+1)$	•	•	⑦	↕	⑧	•
Decrement Index Reg	DEX													09	4	1	$X - 1 \to X$	•	•	•	↕	•	•
Decrement Stack Pntr	DES													34	4	1	$SP - 1 \to SP$	•	•	•	•	•	•
Increment Index Reg	INX													08	4	1	$X + 1 \to X$	•	•	•	↕	•	•
Increment Stack Pntr	INS													31	4	1	$SP + 1 \to SP$	•	•	•	•	•	•
Load Index Reg	LDX	CE	3	3	DE	4	2	EE	6	2	FE	5	3				$M \to X_H, (M+1) \to X_L$	•	•	⑨	↕	R	•
Load Stack Pntr	LDS	8E	3	3	9E	4	2	AE	6	2	BE	5	3				$M \to SP_H, (M+1) \to SP_L$	•	•	⑨	↕	R	•
Store Index Reg	STX				DF	5	2	EF	7	2	FF	6	3				$X_H \to M, X_L \to (M+1)$	•	•	⑨	↕	R	•
Store Stack Pntr	STS				9F	5	2	AF	7	2	BF	6	3				$SP_H \to M, SP_L \to (M+1)$	•	•	⑨	↕	R	•
Indx Reg → Stack Pntr	TXS													35	4	1	$X - 1 \to SP$	•	•	•	•	•	•
Stack Pntr → Indx Reg	TSX													30	4	1	$SP + 1 \to X$	•	•	•	•	•	•

TABLE 5 – JUMP AND BRANCH INSTRUCTIONS

OPERATIONS	MNEMONIC	RELATIVE			INDEX			EXTND			IMPLIED			BRANCH TEST	COND. CODE REG.					
															5	4	3	2	1	0
		OP	~	#	OP	~	#	OP	~	#	OP	~	#		H	I	N	Z	V	C
Branch Always	BRA	20	4	2										None	•	•	•	•	•	•
Branch If Carry Clear	BCC	24	4	2										C = 0	•	•	•	•	•	•
Branch If Carry Set	BCS	25	4	2										C = 1	•	•	•	•	•	•
Branch If = Zero	BEQ	27	4	2										Z = 1	•	•	•	•	•	•
Branch If ⩾ Zero	BGE	2C	4	2										N ⊕ V = 0	•	•	•	•	•	•
Branch If > Zero	BGT	2E	4	2										Z + (N ⊕ V) = 0	•	•	•	•	•	•
Branch If Higher	BHI	22	4	2										C + Z = 0	•	•	•	•	•	•
Branch If ⩽ Zero	BLE	2F	4	2										Z + (N ⊕ V) = 1	•	•	•	•	•	•
Branch If Lower Or Same	BLS	23	4	2										C + Z = 1	•	•	•	•	•	•
Branch If < Zero	BLT	2D	4	2										N ⊕ V = 1	•	•	•	•	•	•
Branch If Minus	BMI	2B	4	2										N = 1	•	•	•	•	•	•
Branch If Not Equal Zero	BNE	26	4	2										Z = 0	•	•	•	•	•	•
Branch If Overflow Clear	BVC	28	4	2										V = 0	•	•	•	•	•	•
Branch If Overflow Set	BVS	29	4	2										V = 1	•	•	•	•	•	•
Branch If Plus	BPL	2A	4	2										N = 0	•	•	•	•	•	•
Branch To Subroutine	BSR	8D	8	2										} See Special Operations	•	•	•	•	•	•
Jump	JMP				6E	4	2	7E	3	3				} See Special Operations	•	•	•	•	•	•
Jump To Subroutine	JSR				AD	8	2	BD	9	3				} See Special Operations	•	•	•	•	•	•
No Operation	NOP										01	2	1	Advances Prog. Cntr. Only	•	•	•	•	•	•
Return From Interrupt	RTI										3B	10	1		(10)					
Return From Subroutine	RTS										39	5	1	} See Special Operations	•	•	•	•	•	•
Software Interrupt	SWI										3F	12	1	} See Special Operations	•	•	•	•	•	•
Wait for Interrupt*	WAI										3E	9	1	} See Special Operations	•	(11)	•	•	•	•

*WAI puts Address Bus, R/W, and Data Bus in the three-state mode while VMA is held low.

(*Courtesy Motorola Inc.*)

TABLE 6 – CONDITION CODE REGISTER MANIPULATION INSTRUCTIONS

		IMPLIED				COND. CODE REG. 5	4	3	2	1	0
OPERATIONS	MNEMONIC	OP	~	=	BOOLEAN OPERATION	H	I	N	Z	V	C
Clear Carry	CLC	0C	2	1	0 → C	•	•	•	•	•	R
Clear Interrupt Mask	CLI	0E	2	1	0 → I	•	R	•	•	•	•
Clear Overflow	CLV	0A	2	1	0 → V	•	•	•	•	R	•
Set Carry	SEC	0D	2	1	1 → C	•	•	•	•	•	S
Set Interrupt Mask	SEI	0F	2	1	1 → I	•	S	•	•	•	•
Set Overflow	SEV	0B	2	1	1 → V	•	•	•	•	S	•
Acmltr A → CCR	TAP	06	2	1	A → CCR	(12)					
CCR → Acmltr A	TPA	07	2	1	CCR → A	•	•	•	•	•	•

CONDITION CODE REGISTER NOTES: (Bit set if test is true and cleared otherwise)

1	(Bit V)	Test: Result = 10000000?
2	(Bit C)	Test: Result = 00000000?
3	(Bit C)	Test: Decimal value of most significant BCD Character greater than nine? (Not cleared if previously set.)
4	(Bit V)	Test: Operand = 10000000 prior to execution?
5	(Bit V)	Test: Operand = 01111111 prior to execution?
6	(Bit V)	Test: Set equal to result of N⊕C after shift has occurred.
7	(Bit N)	Test: Sign bit of most significant (MS) byte = 1?
8	(Bit V)	Test: 2's complement overflow from subtraction of MS bytes?
9	(Bit N)	Test: Result less than zero? (Bit 15 = 1)
10	(All)	Load Condition Code Register from Stack. (See Special Operations)
11	(Bit I)	Set when interrupt occurs. If previously set, a Non-Maskable Interrupt is required to exit the wait state.
12	(All)	Set according to the contents of Accumulator A.

TABLE 7 – INSTRUCTION ADDRESSING MODES AND ASSOCIATED EXECUTION TIMES
(Times in Machine Cycles)

	(Dual Operand)	ACCX	Immediate	Direct	Extended	Indexed	Implied	Relative
ABA		•	•	•	•	•	2	•
ADC	x	•	2	3	4	5	•	•
ADD	x	•	2	3	4	5	•	•
AND	x	•	2	3	4	5	•	•
ASL		2	•	•	6	7	•	•
ASR		2	•	•	6	7	•	•
BCC		•	•	•	•	•	•	4
BCS		•	•	•	•	•	•	4
BEA		•	•	•	•	•	•	4
BGE		•	•	•	•	•	•	4
BGT		•	•	•	•	•	•	4
BHI		•	•	•	•	•	•	4
BIT	x	•	2	3	4	5	•	•
BLE		•	•	•	•	•	•	4
BLS		•	•	•	•	•	•	4
BLT		•	•	•	•	•	•	4
BMI		•	•	•	•	•	•	4
BNE		•	•	•	•	•	•	4
BPL		•	•	•	•	•	•	4
BRA		•	•	•	•	•	•	4
BSR		•	•	•	•	•	•	8
BVC		•	•	•	•	•	•	4
BVS		•	•	•	•	•	•	4
CBA		•	•	•	•	•	2	•
CLC		•	•	•	•	•	2	•
CLI		•	•	•	•	•	2	•
CLR		2	•	•	6	7	•	•
CLV		•	•	•	•	•	2	•
CMP	x	•	2	3	4	5	•	•
COM		2	•	•	6	7	•	•
CPX		•	3	4	5	6	•	•
DAA		•	•	•	•	•	2	•
DEC		2	•	•	6	7	•	•
DES		•	•	•	•	•	4	•
DEX		•	•	•	•	•	4	•
EOR	x	•	2	3	4	5	•	•

	(Dual Operand)	ACCX	Immediate	Direct	Extended	Indexed	Implied
INC		2	•	•	6	7	•
INS		•	•	•	•	•	4
INX		•	•	•	•	•	4
JMP		•	•	•	3	4	•
JSR		•	•	•	9	8	•
LDA	x	•	2	3	4	5	•
LDS		•	3	4	5	6	•
LDX		•	3	4	5	6	•
LSR		2	•	•	6	7	•
NEG		2	•	•	6	7	•
NOP		•	•	•	•	•	2
ORA	x	•	2	3	4	5	•
PSH		•	•	•	•	•	4
PUL		•	•	•	•	•	4
ROL		2	•	•	6	7	•
ROR		2	•	•	6	7	•
RTI		•	•	•	•	•	10
RTS		•	•	•	•	•	5
SBA		•	•	•	•	•	2
SBC	x	•	2	3	4	5	•
SEC		•	•	•	•	•	2
SEI		•	•	•	•	•	2
SEV		•	•	•	•	•	2
STA	x	•	•	4	5	6	•
STS		•	•	5	6	7	•
STX		•	•	5	6	7	•
SUB	x	•	2	3	4	5	•
SWI		•	•	•	•	•	12
TAB		•	•	•	•	•	2
TAP		•	•	•	•	•	2
TBA		•	•	•	•	•	2
TPA		•	•	•	•	•	2
TST		2	•	•	6	7	•
TSX		•	•	•	•	•	4
TSX		•	•	•	•	•	4
WAI		•	•	•	•	•	9

NOTE: Interrupt time is 12 cycles from the end of the instruction being executed, except following a WAI instruction. Then it is 4 cycles.

SUMMARY OF CYCLE BY CYCLE OPERATION

Table 8 provides a detailed description of the information present on the Address Bus, Data Bus, Valid Memory Address line (VMA), and the Read/Write line (R/W) during each cycle for each instruction.

This information is useful in comparing actual with expected results during debug of both software and hardware as the control program is executed. The information is categorized in groups according to Addressing Mode and Number of Cycles per instruction. (In general, instructions with the same Addressing Mode and Number of Cycles execute in the same manner; exceptions are indicated in the table.)

TABLE 8 – OPERATION SUMMARY

Address Mode and Instructions	Cycles	Cycle #	VMA Line	Address Bus	R/W Line	Data Bus
IMMEDIATE						
ADC EOR ADD LDA AND ORA BIT SBC CMP SUB	2	1	1	Op Code Address	1	Op Code
		2	1	Op Code Address + 1	1	Operand Data
CPX LDS LDX	3	1	1	Op Code Address	1	Op Code
		2	1	Op Code Address + 1	1	Operand Data (High Order Byte)
		3	1	Op Code Address + 2	1	Operand Data (Low Order Byte)
DIRECT						
ADC EOR ADD LDA AND ORA BIT SBC CMP SUB	3	1	1	Op Code Address	1	Op Code
		2	1	Op Code Address + 1	1	Address of Operand
		3	1	Address of Operand	1	Operand Data
CPX LDS LDX	4	1	1	Op Code Address	1	Op Code
		2	1	Op Code Address + 1	1	Address of Operand
		3	1	Address of Operand	1	Operand Data (High Order Byte)
		4	1	Operand Address + 1	1	Operand Data (Low Order Byte)

STA	4	1	1	Op Code Address	1	Op Code
		2	1	Op Code Address + 1	1	Destination Address
		3	0	Destination Address	1	Irrelevant Data (Note 1)
		4	1	Destination Address	0	Data from Accumulator
STS STX	5	1	1	Op Code Address	1	Op Code
		2	1	Op Code Address + 1	1	Address of Operand
		3	0	Address of Operand	1	Irrelevant Data (Note 1)
		4	1	Address of Operand	0	Register Data (High Order Byte)
		5	1	Address of Operand + 1	0	Register Data (Low Order Byte)

INDEXED

JMP	4	1	1	Op Code Address	1	Op Code
		2	1	Op Code Address + 1	1	Offset
		3	0	Index Register	1	Irrelevant Data (Note 1)
		4	0	Index Register Plus Offset (w/o Carry)	1	Irrelevant Data (Note 1)
ADC EOR ADD LDA AND ORA BIT SBC CMP SUB	5	1	1	Op Code Address	1	Op Code
		2	1	Op Code Address + 1	1	Offset
		3	0	Index Register	1	Irrelevant Data (Note 1)
		4	0	Index Register Plus Offset (w/o Carry)	1	Irrelevant Data (Note 1)
		5	1	Index Register Plus Offset	1	Operand Data
CPX LDS LDX	6	1	1	Op Code Address	1	Op Code
		2	1	Op Code Address + 1	1	Offset
		3	0	Index Register	1	Irrelevant Data (Note 1)
		4	0	Index Register Plus Offset (w/o Carry)	1	Irrelevant Data (Note 1)
		5	1	Index Register Plus Offset	1	Operand Data (High Order Byte)
		6	1	Index Register Plus Offset + 1	1	Operand Data (Low Order Byte)

TABLE 8 – OPERATION SUMMARY (Continued)

Address Mode and Instructions	Cycles	Cycle #	VMA Line	Address Bus	R/W Line	Data Bus
INDEXED (Continued)						
STA	6	1	1	Op Code Address	1	Op Code
		2	1	Op Code Address + 1	1	Offset
		3	0	Index Register	1	Irrelevant Data (Note 1)
		4	0	Index Register Plus Offset (w/o Carry)	1	Irrelevant Data (Note 1)
		5	0	Index Register Plus Offset	1	Irrelevant Data (Note 1)
		6	1	Index Register Plus Offset	0	Operand Data
ASL LSR ASR NEG CLR ROL COM ROR DEC TST INC	7	1	1	Op Code Address	1	Op Code
		2	1	Op Code Address + 1	1	Offset
		3	0	Index Register	1	Irrelevant Data (Note 1)
		4	0	Index Register Plus Offset (w/o Carry)	1	Irrelevant Data (Note 1)
		5	1	Index Register Plus Offset	1	Current Operand Data
		6	0	Index Register Plus Offset	1	Irrelevant Data (Note 1)
		7	1/0 (Note 3)	Index Register Plus Offset	0	New Operand Data (Note 3)
STS STX	7	1	1	Op Code Address	1	Op Code
		2	1	Op Code Address + 1	1	Offset
		3	0	Index Register	1	Irrelevant Data (Note 1)
		4	0	Index Register Plus Offset (w/o Carry)	1	Irrelevant Data (Note 1)
		5	0	Index Register Plus Offset	1	Irrelevant Data (Note 1)
		6	1	Index Register Plus Offset	0	Operand Data (High Order Byte)
		7	1	Index Register Plus Offset + 1	0	Operand Data (Low Order Byte)
JSR	8	1	1	Op Code Address	1	Op Code
		2	1	Op Code Address + 1	1	Offset
		3	0	Index Register	1	Irrelevant Data (Note 1)
		4	1	Stack Pointer	0	Return Address (Low Order Byte)
		5	1	Stack Pointer – 1	0	Return Address (High Order Byte)
		6	0	Stack Pointer – 2	1	Irrelevant Data (Note 1)
		7	0	Index Register	1	Irrelevant Data (Note 1)
		8	0	Index Register Plus Offset (w/o Carry)	1	Irrelevant Data (Note 1)

EXTENDED

JMP	3	1	1	Op Code Address	1	Op Code
		2	1	Op Code Address + 1	1	Jump Address (High Order Byte)
		3	1	Op Code Address + 2	1	Jump Address (Low Order Byte)
ADC EOR ADD LDA AND ORA BIT SBC CMP SUB	4	1	1	Op Code Address	1	Op Code
		2	1	Op Code Address + 1	1	Address of Operand (High Order Byte)
		3	1	Op Code Address + 2	1	Address of Operand (Low Order Byte)
		4	1	Address of Operand	1	Operand Data
CPX LDS LDX	5	1	1	Op Code Address	1	Op Code
		2	1	Op Code Address + 1	1	Address of Operand (High Order Byte)
		3	1	Op Code Address + 2	1	Address of Operand (Low Order Byte)
		4	1	Address of Operand	1	Operand Data (High Order Byte)
		5	1	Address of Operand + 1	1	Operand Data (Low Order Byte)
STA A STA B	5	1	1	Op Code Address	1	Op Code
		2	1	Op Code Address + 1	1	Destination Address (High Order Byte)
		3	1	Op Code Address + 2	1	Destination Address (Low Order Byte)
		4	0	Operand Destination Address	1	Irrelevant Data (Note 1)
		5	1	Operand Destination Address	0	Data from Accumulator
ASL LSR ASR NEG CLR ROL COM ROR DEC TST INC	6	1	1	Op Code Address	1	Op Code
		2	1	Op Code Address + 1	1	Address of Operand (High Order Byte)
		3	1	Op Code Address + 2	1	Address of Operand (Low Order Byte)
		4	1	Address of Operand	1	Current Operand Data
		5	0	Address of Operand	1	Irrelevant Data (Note 1)
		6	1/0 (Note 3)	Address of Operand	0	New Operand Data (Note 3)

(*Courtesy Motorola Inc.*)

TABLE 8 – OPERATION SUMMARY (Continued)

Address Mode and Instructions	Cycles	Cycle #	VMA Line	Address Bus	R/W Line	Data Bus
EXTENDED (Continued)						
STS STX	6	1	1	Op Code Address	1	Op Code
		2	1	Op Code Address + 1	1	Address of Operand (High Order Byte)
		3	1	Op Code Address + 2	1	Address of Operand (Low Order Byte)
		4	0	Address of Operand	1	Irrelevant Data (Note 1)
		5	1	Address of Operand	0	Operand Data (High Order Byte)
		6	1	Address of Operand + 1	0	Operand Data (Low Order Byte)
JSR	9	1	1	Op Code Address	1	Op Code
		2	1	Op Code Address + 1	1	Address of Subroutine (High Order Byte)
		3	1	Op Code Address + 2	1	Address of Subroutine (Low Order Byte)
		4	1	Subroutine Starting Address	1	Op Code of Next Instruction
		5	1	Stack Pointer	0	Return Address (Low Order Byte)
		6	1	Stack Pointer – 1	0	Return Address (High Order Byte)
		7	0	Stack Pointer – 2	1	Irrelevant Data (Note 1)
		8	0	Op Code Address + 2	1	Irrelevant Data (Note 1)
		9	1	Op Code Address + 2	1	Address of Subroutine (Low Order Byte)
INHERENT						
ABA DAA SEC ASL DEC SEI ASR INC SEV CBA LSR TAB CLC NEG TAP CLI NOP TBA CLR ROL TPA CLV ROR TST COM SBA	2	1	1	Op Code Address	1	Op Code
		2	1	Op Code Address + 1	1	Op Code of Next Instruction

DES DEX INS INX	4	1	1	Op Code Address	1	Op Code
		2	1	Op Code Address + 1	1	Op Code of Next Instruction
		3	0	Previous Register Contents	1	Irrelevant Data (Note 1)
		4	0	New Register Contents	1	Irrelevant Data (Note 1)
PSH	4	1	1	Op Code Address	1	Op Code
		2	1	Op Code Address + 1	1	Op Code of Next Instruction
		3	1	Stack Pointer	0	Accumulator Data
		4	0	Stack Pointer − 1	1	Accumulator Data
PUL	4	1	1	Op Code Address	1	Op Code
		2	1	Op Code Address + 1	1	Op Code of Next Instruction
		3	0	Stack Pointer	1	Irrelevant Data (Note 1)
		4	1	Stack Pointer + 1	1	Operand Data from Stack
TSX	4	1	1	Op Code Address	1	Op Code
		2	1	Op Code Address + 1	1	Op Code of Next Instruction
		3	0	Stack Pointer	1	Irrelevant Data (Note 1)
		4	0	New Index Register	1	Irrelevant Data (Note 1)
TXS	4	1	1	Op Code Address	1	Op Code
		2	1	Op Code Address + 1	1	Op Code of Next Instruction
		3	0	Index Register	1	Irrelevant Data
		4	0	New Stack Pointer	1	Irrelevant Data
RTS	5	1	1	Op Code Address	1	Op Code
		2	1	Op Code Address + 1	1	Irrelevant Data (Note 2)
		3	0	Stack Pointer	1	Irrelevant Data (Note 1)
		4	1	Stack Pointer + 1	1	Address of Next Instruction (High Order Byte)
		5	1	Stack Pointer + 2	1	Address of Next Instruction (Low Order Byte)

(*Courtesy Motorola Inc.*)

TABLE 8 – OPERATION SUMMARY (Continued)

Address Mode and Instructions	Cycles	Cycle #	VMA Line	Address Bus	R/W Line	Data Bus
INHERENT (Continued)						
WAI	9	1	1	Op Code Address	1	Op Code
		2	1	Op Code Address + 1	1	Op Code of Next Instruction
		3	1	Stack Pointer	0	Return Address (Low Order Byte)
		4	1	Stack Pointer – 1	0	Return Address (High Order Byte)
		5	1	Stack Pointer – 2	0	Index Register (Low Order Byte)
		6	1	Stack Pointer – 3	0	Index Register (High Order Byte)
		7	1	Stack Pointer – 4	0	Contents of Accumulator A
		8	1	Stack Pointer – 5	0	Contents of Accumulator B
		9	1	Stack Pointer – 6 (Note 4)	1	Contents of Cond. Code Register
RTI	10	1	1	Op Code Address	1	Op Code
		2	1	Op Code Address + 1	1	Irrelevant Data (Note 2)
		3	0	Stack Pointer	1	Irrelevant Data (Note 1)
		4	1	Stack Pointer + 1	1	Contents of Cond. Code Register from Stack
		5	1	Stack Pointer + 2	1	Contents of Accumulator B from Stack
		6	1	Stack Pointer + 3	1	Contents of Accumulator A from Stack
		7	1	Stack Pointer + 4	1	Index Register from Stack (High Order Byte)
		8	1	Stack Pointer + 5	1	Index Register from Stack (Low Order Byte)
		9	1	Stack Pointer + 6	1	Next Instruction Address from Stack (High Order Byte)
		10	1	Stack Pointer + 7	1	Next Instruction Address from Stack (Low Order Byte)

SWI	12	1	1	Op Code Address	1	Op Code
		2	1	Op Code Address + 1	1	Irrelevant Data (Note 1)
		3	1	Stack Pointer	0	Return Address (Low Order Byte)
		4	1	Stack Pointer – 1	0	Return Address (High Order Byte)
		5	1	Stack Pointer – 2	0	Index Register (Low Order Byte)
		6	1	Stack Pointer – 3	0	Index Register (High Order Byte)
		7	1	Stack Pointer – 4	0	Contents of Accumulator A
		8	1	Stack Pointer – 5	0	Contents of Accumulator B
		9	1	Stack Pointer – 6	0	Contents of Cond. Code Register
		10	0	Stack Pointer – 7	1	Irrelevant Data (Note 1)
		11	1	Vector Address FFFA (Hex)	1	Address of Subroutine (High Order Byte)
		12	1	Vector Address FFFB (Hex)	1	Address of Subroutine (Low Order Byte)
RELATIVE						
BCC BHI BNE BCS BLE BPL BEQ BLS BRA BGE BLT BVC BGT BMI BVS	4	1	1	Op Code Address	1	Op Code
		2	1	Op Code Address + 1	1	Branch Offset
		3	0	Op Code Address + 2	1	Irrelevant Data (Note 1)
		4	0	Branch Address	1	Irrelevant Data (Note 1)
BSR	8	1	1	Op Code Address	1	Op Code
		2	1	Op Code Address + 1	1	Branch Offset
		3	0	Return Address of Main Program	1	Irrelevant Data (Note 1)
		4	1	Stack Pointer	0	Return Address (Low Order Byte)
		5	1	Stack Pointer – 1	0	Return Address (High Order Byte)
		6	0	Stack Pointer – 2	1	Irrelevant Data (Note 1)
		7	0	Return Address of Main Program	1	Irrelevant Data (Note 1)
		8	0	Subroutine Address	1	Irrelevant Data (Note 1)

Note 1. If device which is addressed during this cycle uses VMA, then the Data Bus will go to the high impedance three-state condition. Depending on bus capacitance, data from the previous cycle may be retained on the Data Bus.
Note 2. Data is ignored by the MPU.
Note 3. For TST, VMA = 0 and Operand data does not change.
Note 4. While the MPU is waiting for the interrupt, Bus Available will go high indicating the following states of the control lines: VMA is low; Address Bus, R/W, and Data Bus are all in the high impedance state.

(*Courtesy Motorola Inc.*)

TABLE 9 – SPECIAL OPERATIONS

SPECIAL OPERATIONS

JSR, JUMP TO SUBROUTINE:

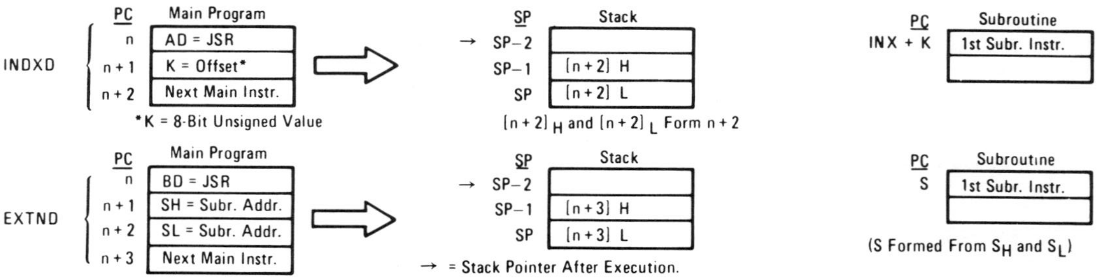

BSR, BRANCH TO SUBROUTINE:

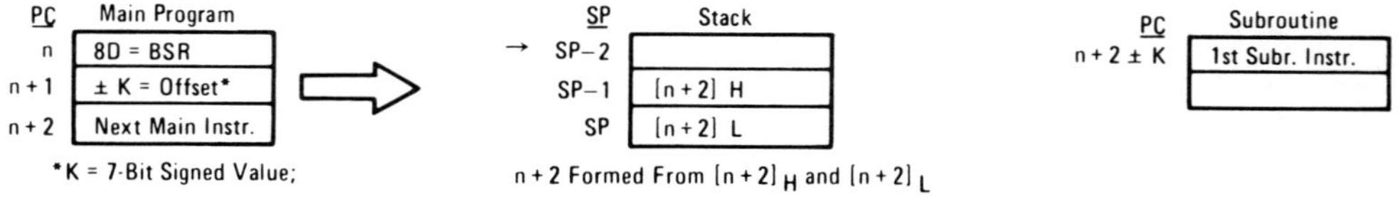

JMP, JUMP:

RTS, RETURN FROM SUBROUTINE:

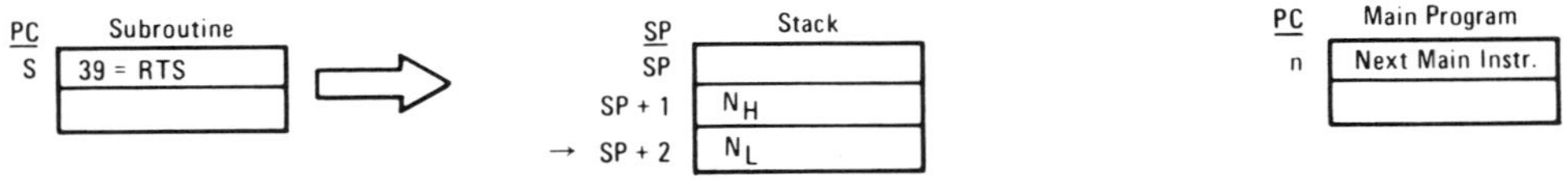

RTI, RETURN FROM INTERRUPT:

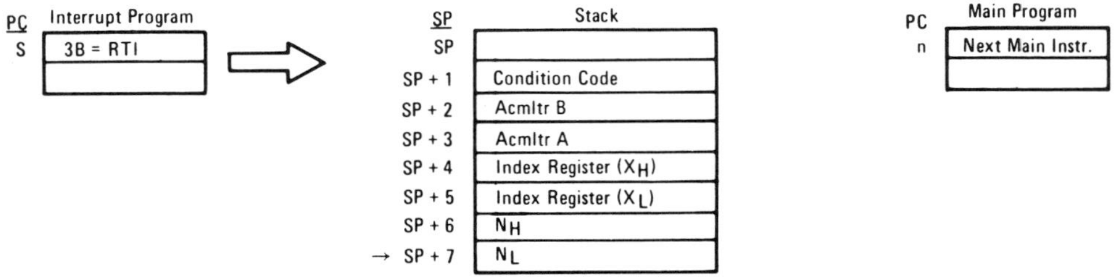

(Courtesy Motorola Inc.)

TABLE 10—HEXADECIMAL VALUES OF MACHINE CODES

00	*			40	NEG	A		80	SUB	A	IMM	C0	SUB	B	IMM
01	NOP			41	*			81	CMP	A	IMM	C1	CMP	B	IMM
02	*			42	*			82	SBC	A	IMM	C2	SBC	B	IMM
03	*			43	COM	A		83	*			C3	*		
04	*			44	LSR	A		84	AND	A	IMM	C4	AND	B	IMM
05	*			45	*			85	BIT	A	IMM	C5	BIT	B	IMM
06	TAP			46	ROR	A		86	LDA	A	IMM	C6	LDA	B	IMM
07	TPA			47	ASR	A		87	*			C7	*		
08	INX			48	ASL	A		88	EOR	A	IMM	C8	EOR	B	IMM
09	DEX			49	ROL	A		89	ADC	A	IMM	C9	ADC	B	IMM
0A	CLV			4A	DEC	A		8A	ORA	A	IMM	CA	ORA	B	IMM
0B	SEV			4B	*			8B	ADD	A	IMM	CB	ADD	B	IMM
0C	CLC			4C	INC	A		8C	CPX	A	IMM	CC	*		
0D	SEC			4D	TST	A		8D	BSR		REL	CD	*		
0E	CLI			4E	*			8E	LDS		IMM	CE	LDX		IMM
0F	SEI			4F	CLR	A		8F	*			CF	*		
10	SBA			50	NEG	B		90	SUB	A	DIR	D0	SUB	B	DIR
11	CBA			51	*			91	CMP	A	DIR	D1	CMP	B	DIR
12	*			52	*			92	SBC	A	DIR	D2	SBC	B	DIR
13	*			53	COM	B		93	*			D3	*		
14	*			54	LSR	B		94	AND	A	DIR	D4	AND	B	DIR
15	*			55	*			95	BIT	A	DIR	D5	BIT	B	DIR
16	TAB			56	ROR	B		96	LDA	A	DIR	D6	LDA	B	DIR
17	TBA			57	ASR	B		97	STA	A	DIR	D7	STA	B	DIR
18	*			58	ASL	B		98	EOR	A	DIR	D8	EOR	B	DIR
19	DAA			59	ROL	B		99	ADC	A	DIR	D9	ADC	B	DIR
1A	*			5A	DEC	B		9A	ORA	A	DIR	DA	ORA	B	DIR
1B	ABA			5B	*			9B	ADD	A	DIR	DB	ADD	B	DIR
1C	*			5C	INC	B		9C	CPX		DIR	DC	*		
1D	*			5D	TST	B		9D	*			DD	*		
1E	*			5E	*			9E	LDS		DIR	DE	LDX		DIR
1F	*			5F	CLR	B		9F	STS		DIR	DF	STX		DIR
20	BRA		REL	60	NEG		IND	A0	SUB	A	IND	E0	SUB	B	IND
21	*			61	*			A1	CMP	A	IND	E1	CMP	B	IND

22	BHI		REL	62	*			A2	SBC	A	IND	E2	SBC	B	IND
23	BLS		REL	63	COM		IND	A3	*			E3	*		
24	BCC		REL	64	LSR		IND	A4	AND	A	IND	E4	AND	B	IND
25	BCS		REL	65	*			A5	BIT	A	IND	E5	BIT	B	IND
26	BNE		REL	66	ROR		IND	A6	LDA	A	IND	E6	LDA	B	IND
27	BEQ		REL	67	ASR		IND	A7	STA	A	IND	E7	STA	B	IND
28	BVC		REL	68	ASL		IND	A8	EOR	A	IND	E8	EOR	B	IND
29	BVS		REL	69	ROL		IND	A9	ADC	A	IND	E9	ADC	B	IND
2A	BPL		REL	6A	DEC		IND	AA	ORA	A	IND	EA	ORA	B	IND
2B	BMI		REL	6B	*			AB	ADD	A	IND	EB	ADD	B	IND
2C	BGE		REL	6C	INC		IND	AC	CPX		IND	EC	*		
2D	BLT		REL	6D	TST		IND	AD	JSR		IND	ED	*		
2E	BGT		REL	6E	JMP		IND	AE	LDS		IND	EE	LDX		IND
2F	BLE		REL	6F	CLR		IND	AF	STS		IND	EF	STX		IND
30	TSX			70	NEG		EXT	B0	SUB	A	EXT	F0	SUB	B	EXT
31	INS			71	*			B1	CMP	A	EXT	F1	CMP	B	EXT
32	PUL	A		72	*			B2	SBC	A	EXT	F2	SBC	B	EXT
33	PUL	B		73	COM		EXT	B3	*			F3	*		
34	DES			74	LSR		EXT	B4	AND	A	EXT	F4	AND	B	EXT
35	TXS			75	*			B5	BIT	A	EXT	F5	BIT	B	EXT
36	PSH	A		76	ROR		EXT	B6	LDA	A	EXT	F6	LDA	B	EXT
37	PSH	B		77	ASR		EXT	B7	STA	A	EXT	F7	STA	B	EXT
38	*			78	ASL		EXT	B8	EOR	A	EXT	F8	ADC	B	EXT
39	RTS			79	ROL		EXT	B9	ADC	A	EXT	F9	ADC	B	EXT
3A	*			7A	DEC		EXT	BA	ORA	A	EXT	FA	ORA	B	EXT
3B	RTI			7B	*			BB	ADD	A	EXT	FB	ADD	B	EXT
3C	*			7C	INC		EXT	BC	CPX		EXT	FC	*		
3D	*			7D	TST		EXT	BD	JSR		EXT	FD	*		
3E	WAI			7E	JMP		EXT	BE	LDS		EXT	FE	LDX		EXT
3F	SWI			7F	CLR		EXT	BF	STS		EXT	FF	STX		EXT

Notes: 1. Addressing Modes:

A = Accumulator A
B = Accumulator B
REL = Relative
IND = Indexed
IMM = Immediate
DIR = Direct

2. Unassigned code indicated by "*".

(*Courtesy Motorola Inc.*)

M6800 PROGRAM

72 INSTRUCTIONS
6 ADDRESSING MODES

DATA HANDLING INSTRUCTIONS
(Data Movement)

FUNCTION	MNEMONIC	OPERATION
LOAD ACMLTR	LDAA	M → A
	LDAB	M → B
PUSH DATA	PSHA	A → M_{SP}, SP − 1 → SP
	PSHB	B → M_{SP}, SP − 1 → SP
PULL DATA	PULA	SP + 1 → SP, M_{SP} → A
	PULB	SP + 1 → SP, M_{SP} → B
STORE ACMLTR	STAA	A → M
	STAB	B → M
TRANSFER ACMLTRS	TAB	A → B
	TBA	B → A

(*Courtesy Motorola Inc.*)

DATA HANDLING INSTRUCTIONS (ALTER DATA)

FUNCTION	MNEMONIC	OPERATION
CLEAR	CLR CLRA CLRB	00 → M 00 → A 00 → B
DECREMENT	DEC DECA DECB	M − 1 → M A − 1 → A B − 1 → B
INCREMENT	INC INCA INCB	M + 1 → M A + 1 → A B + 1 → B
COMPLEMENT, 2'S (NEGATE)	NEG NEGA NEGB	00 − M → M 00 − A → A 00 − B → B
COMPLEMENT, 1'S	COM COMA COMB	$\overline{M}$ → M $\overline{A}$ → A $\overline{B}$ → B

TR1076

DATA HANDLING INSTRUCTIONS (SHIFT AND ROTATE)

FUNCTION	MNEMONIC		OPERATION
ROTATE LEFT	ROL ROLA ROLB	M A B	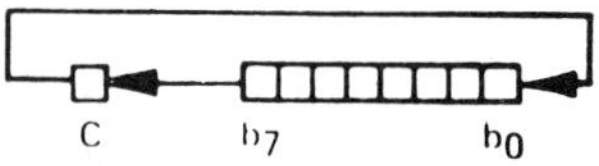
ROTATE RIGHT	ROR RORA RORB	M A B	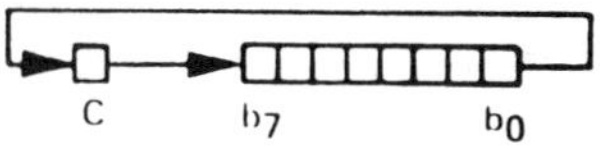
SHIFT LEFT, ARITHMETIC	ASL ASLA ASLB	M A B	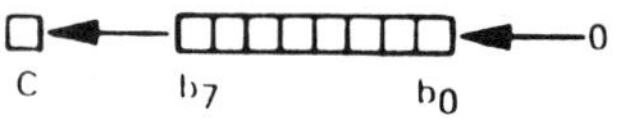
SHIFT RIGHT, ARITHMETIC	ASR ASRA ASRB	M A B	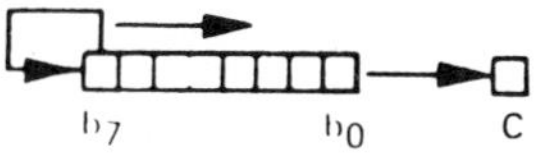
SHIFT RIGHT, LOGIC	LSR LSRA LSRB	M A B	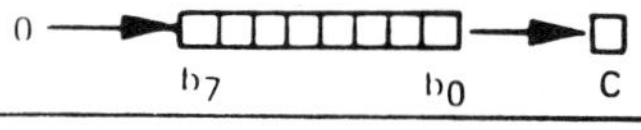

ARITHMETIC INSTRUCTIONS

FUNCTION	MNEMONIC	OPERATION
ADD	ADDA ADDB	A + M → A B + M → B
ADD ACCUMULATORS	ABA	A + B → A
ADD WITH CARRY	ADCA ADCB	A + M + C → A B + M + C → B
COMPLEMENT, 2'S (NEGATE)	NEG NEGA NEGB	00 − M → M 00 − A → A 00 − B → B
DECIMAL ADJUST, A	DAA	CONVERTS BINARY ADD. OF BCD CHARACTERS INTO BCD FORMAT
SUBTRACT	SUBA SUBB	A − M → A B − M → B
SUBTRACT ACCUMULATORS	SBA	A − B → A
SUBTRACT WITH CARRY	SBCA SBCB	A − M − C → A B − M − C → B

LOGIC INSTRUCTIONS

FUNCTION	MNEMONIC	OPERATION
AND	ANDA ANDB	A • M → A B • M → B
COMPLEMENT, 1'S	COM COMA COMB	$\overline{M}$ → M $\overline{A}$ → A $\overline{B}$ → B
EXCLUSIVE OR	EORA EORB	A ⊕ M → A B ⊕ M → B
OR, INCLUSIVE	ORA A ORA B	A + M → A B + M → B

JUMP AND BRANCH INSTRUCTIONS

FUNCTION	MNEMONIC	BRANCH TEST
BRANCH ALWAYS	BRA	NONE
BRANCH IF CARRY CLEAR	BCC	$C = 0$
BRANCH IF CARRY SET	BCS	$C = 1$
BRANCH IF = ZERO	BEQ	$Z = 1$
BRANCH IF ≥ ZERO	BGE	$N \oplus V = 0$
BRANCH IF > ZERO	BGT	$Z + (N \oplus V) = 0$
BRANCH IF HIGHER	BHI	$C + Z = 0$
BRANCH IF ≤ ZERO	BLE	$Z + (N \oplus V) = 1$
BRANCH IF LOWER OR SAME	BLS	$C + Z = 1$
BRANCH IF < ZERO	BLT	$N \oplus V = 1$
BRANCH IF MINUS	BMI	$N = 1$
BRANCH IF NOT EQUAL ZERO	BNE	$Z = 0$
BRANCH IF PLUS	BPL	$N = 0$

JUMP AND BRANCH INSTRUCTIONS

FUNCTION	MNEMONIC	BRANCH TEST
BRANCH IF OVERFLOW CLEAR	BVC	$V = 0$
BRANCH IF OVERFLOW SET	BVS	$V = 1$
BRANCH TO SUBROUTINE	BSR	
JUMP	JMP	
JUMP TO SUBROUTINE	JSR	
NO OPERATION	NOP	ADVANCES PROG. CNTR. ONLY
RETURN FROM SUBROUTINE	RTS	

DATA TEST INSTRUCTIONS

FUNCTION	MNEMONIC	TEST
BIT TEST	BITA	A • M
	BIT B	B • M
COMPARE	CMPA	A – M
	CMPB	B – M
	CBA	A – B
TEST, ZERO OR MINUS	TST	M – 00
	TSTA	A – 00
	TSTB	B – 00

CONDITION CODE REGISTER INSTRUCTIONS

FUNCTION	MNEMONIC	OPERATION
CLEAR CARRY	CLC	0 → C
CLEAR INTERRUPT MASK	CLI	0 → I
CLEAR OVERFLOW	CLV	0 → V
SET CARRY	SEC	1 → C
SET INTERRUPT MASK	SEI	1 → I
SET OVERFLOW	SEV	1 → V
ACMLTR A → CCR	TAP	A → CCR
CCR → ACMLTR A	TPA	CCR → A

INDEX REGISTER AND STACK POINTER INSTRUCTIONS

FUNCTION	MNEMONIC	OPERATION
COMPARE INDEX REG	CPX	$X_H - M, X_L - (M + 1)$
DECREMENT INDEX REG	DEX	$X - 1 \rightarrow X$
DECREMENT STACK PNTR	DES	$SP - 1 \rightarrow SP$
INCREMENT INDEX REG	INX	$X + 1 \rightarrow X$
INCREMENT STACK PNTR	INS	$SP + 1 \rightarrow SP$
LOAD INDEX REG	LDX	$M \rightarrow X_H, (M + 1) \rightarrow X_L$
LOAD STACK PNTR	LDS	$M \rightarrow SP_H, (M + 1) \rightarrow SP_L$
STORE INDEX REG	STX	$X_H \rightarrow M, X_L \rightarrow (M + 1)$
STORE STACK PNTR	STS	$SP_H \rightarrow M, SP_L \rightarrow (M + 1)$
INDX REG → STACK PNTR	TXS	$X - 1 \rightarrow SP$
STACK PNTR → INDX REG	TSX	$SP + 1 \rightarrow X$

INTERRUPT HANDLING INSTRUCTIONS

FUNCTION	MNEMONIC	OPERATION
SOFTWARE INTERRUPT	SWI	$REGS \rightarrow M_{SP}$ $SP-7 \rightarrow SP$ $M_{FFFA} \rightarrow PCH$ $M_{FFFB} \rightarrow PCL$ $1 \rightarrow I$
RETURN FROM INTERRUPT	RTI	$M_{SP} \rightarrow REGS$ $SP+7 \rightarrow SP$
WAIT FOR INTERRUPT	WAI	$REGS \rightarrow M_{SP}$ $SP-7 \rightarrow SP$

ACCUMULATOR/INHERENT ADDRESSING

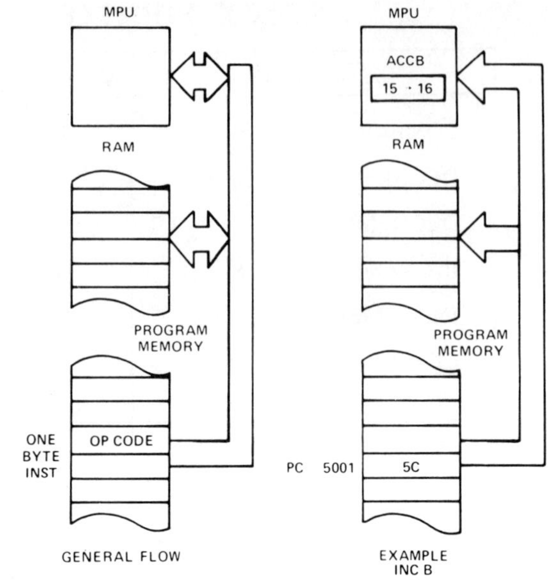

IMMEDIATE ADDRESSING

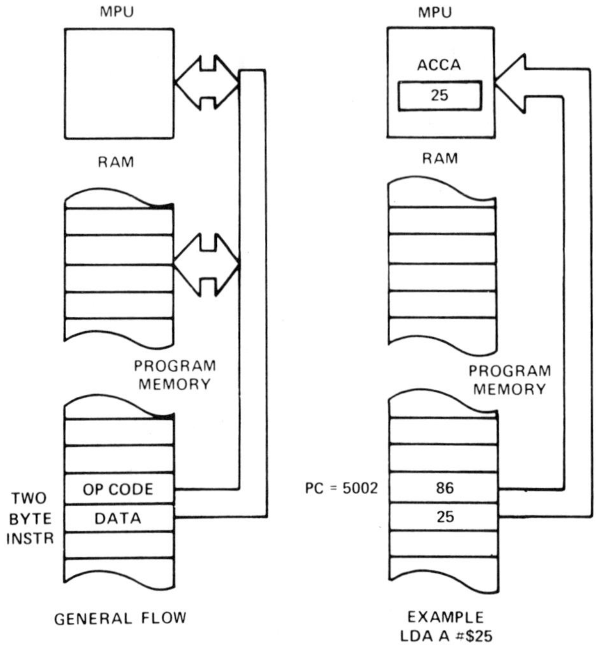

DIRECT ADDRESSING

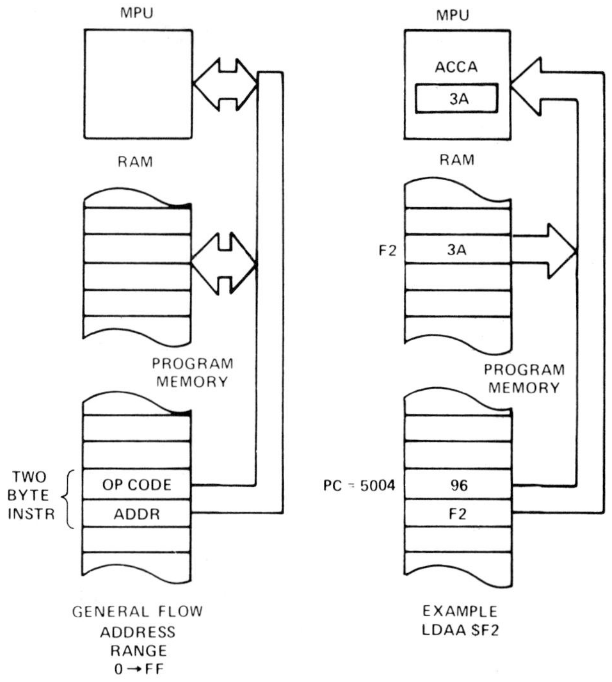

EXTENDED ADDRESSING

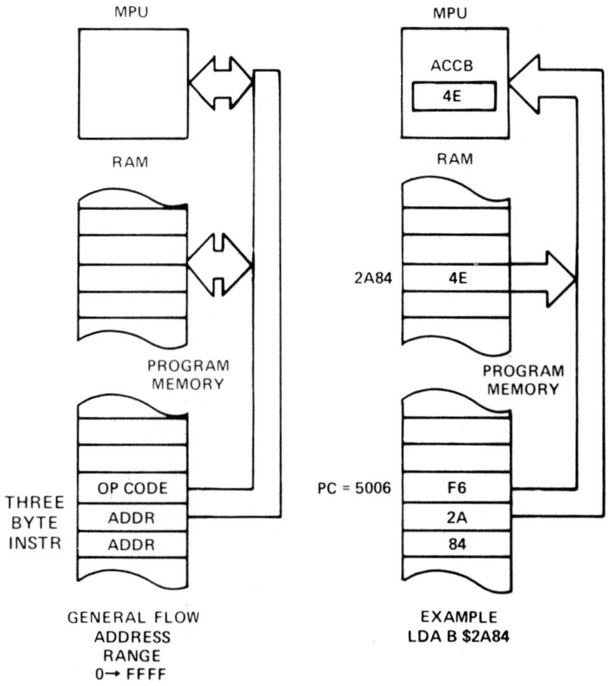

INDEXED ADDRESSING

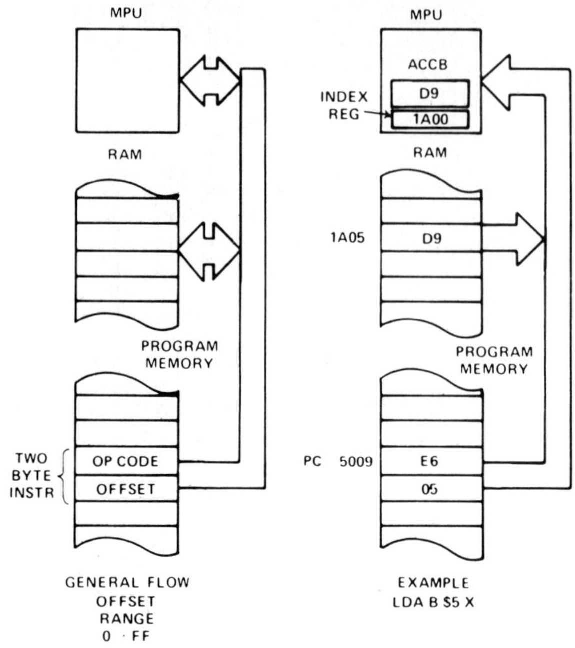

RELATIVE ADDRESSING

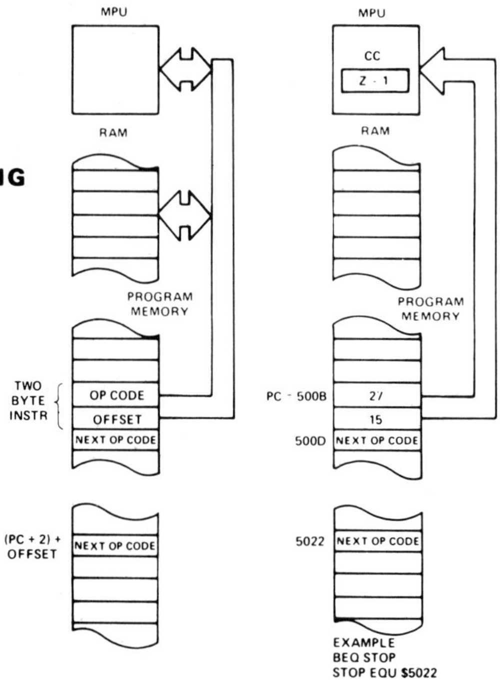

Definition of the Executable Instructions

A.1 Nomenclature

The following nomenclature is used in the subsequent definitions.

(a) *Operators*

( )	=	contents of
←	=	is transferred to
↑	=	"is pulled from stack"
↓	=	"is pushed into stack"
·	=	Boolean AND
⊙	=	Boolean (Inclusive) OR
⊕	=	Exclusive OR
≈	=	Boolean NOT

(b) *Registers in the MPU*

ACCA	=	Accumulator A
ACCB	=	Accumulator B
ACCX	=	Accumulator ACCA or ACCB
CC	=	Condition codes register
IX	=	Index register, 16 bits
IXH	=	Index register, higher order 8 bits
IXL	=	Index register, lower order 8 bits
PC	=	Program counter, 16 bits
PCH	=	Program counter, higher order 8 bits
PCL	=	Program counter, lower order 8 bits
SP	=	Stack pointer
SPH	=	Stack pointer high
SPL	=	Stack pointer low

(c) *Memory and Addressing*

M	=	A memory location (one byte)
M +1	=	The byte of memory at 0001 plus the address of the memory location indicated by "M."
Rel	=	Relative address (i.e. the two's complement number stored in the second byte of machine code corresponding to a branch instruction).

(d) *Bits 0 thru 5 of the Condition Codes Register*

C	=	Carry — borrow	bit — 0
V	=	Two's complement overflow indicator	bit — 1
Z	=	Zero indicator	bit — 2
N	=	Negative indicator	bit — 3
I	=	Interrupt mask	bit — 4
H	=	Half carry	bit — 5

(e) *Status of Individual Bits BEFORE Execution of an Instruction*

An	=	Bit n of ACCA (n=7,6,5,...,0)
Bn	=	Bit n of ACCB (n=7,6,5,...,0)
IXHn	=	Bit n of IXH (n=7,6,5,...,0)

(Courtesy Motorola Inc.)

IXLn = Bit n of IXL (n=7,6,5,...,0)
Mn = Bit n of M (n=7,6,5,...,0)
SPHn = Bit n of SPH (n=7,6,5,...,0)
SPLn = Bit n of SPL (n=7,6,5,...,0)
Xn = Bit n of ACCX (n=7,6,5,...,0)

(f) *Status of Individual Bits of the RESULT of Execution of an Instruction*

(i) For 8-bit Results

Rn = Bit n of the result (n =7,6,5,...,0)

This applies to instructions which provide a result contained in a single byte of memory or in an 8-bit register.

(ii) For 16-bit Results

RHn = Bit n of the more significant byte of the result (n =7,6,5,...,0)

RLn = Bit n of the less significant byte of the result (n =7,6,5,...,0)

This applies to instructions which provide a result contained in two consecutive bytes of memory or in a 16-bit register.

A.2 Executable Instructions (definition of)

Detailed definitions of the 72 executable instructions of the source language are provided on the following pages.

Add Accumulator B to Accumulator A **ABA**

Operation: ACCA ← (ACCA) + (ACCB)

Description: Adds the contents of ACCB to the contents of ACCA and places the result in ACCA.

Condition Codes:
- H: Set if there was a carry from bit 3; cleared otherwise.
- I: Not affected.
- N: Set if most significant bit of the result is set; cleared otherwise.
- Z: Set if all bits of the result are cleared; cleared otherwise.
- V: Set if there was two's complement overflow as a result of the operation; cleared otherwise.
- C: Set if there was a carry from the most significant bit of the result; cleared otherwise.

Boolean Formulae for Condition Codes:

$$H = A_3 \cdot B_3 + B_3 \cdot \overline{R}_3 + \overline{R}_3 \cdot A_3$$
$$N = R_7$$
$$Z = \overline{R}_7 \cdot \overline{R}_6 \cdot \overline{R}_5 \cdot \overline{R}_4 \cdot \overline{R}_3 \cdot \overline{R}_2 \cdot \overline{R}_1 \cdot \overline{R}_0$$
$$V = A_7 \cdot B_7 \cdot \overline{R}_7 + \overline{A}_7 \cdot \overline{B}_7 \cdot R_7$$
$$C = A_7 \cdot B_7 + B_7 \cdot \overline{R}_7 + \overline{R}_7 \cdot A_7$$

Addressing Modes, Execution Time, and Machine Code (hexadecimal/octal/decimal):

Addressing Modes	Execution Time (No. of cycles)	Number of bytes of machine code	Coding of First (or only) byte of machine code		
			HEX.	OCT.	DEC.
Inherent	2	1	1B	033	027

ADC

Add with Carry

Operation: ACCX ← (ACCX) + (M) + (C)

Description: Adds the contents of the C bit to the sum of the contents of ACCX and M, and places the result in ACCX.

Condition Codes:
- H Set if there was a carry from bit 3; cleared otherwise.
- I: Not affected.
- N: Set if most significant bit of the result is set; cleared otherwise.
- Z: Set if all bits of the result are cleared; cleared otherwise.
- V: Set if there was two's complement overflow as a result of the operation; cleared otherwise.
- C: Set if there was a carry from the most significant bit of the result; cleared otherwise.

Boolean Formulae for Condition Codes:

$$H = X_3 \cdot M_3 + M_3 \cdot \overline{R}_3 + \overline{R}_3 \cdot X_3$$
$$N = R_7$$
$$Z = \overline{R}_7 \cdot \overline{R}_6 \cdot \overline{R}_5 \cdot \overline{R}_4 \cdot \overline{R}_3 \cdot \overline{R}_2 \cdot \overline{R}_1 \cdot \overline{R}_0$$
$$V = X_7 \cdot M_7 \cdot \overline{R}_7 + \overline{X}_7 \cdot \overline{M}_7 \cdot R_7$$
$$C = X_7 \cdot M_7 + M_7 \cdot \overline{R}_7 + \overline{R}_7 \cdot X_7$$

Addressing Formats:

See Table A-1

Addressing Modes, Execution Time, and Machine Code (hexadecimal/ octal/ decimal):

(DUAL OPERAND)

Addressing Modes	Execution Time (No. of cycles)	Number of bytes of machine code	Coding of First (or only) byte of machine code		
			HEX.	OCT.	DEC.
A IMM	2	2	89	211	137
A DIR	3	2	99	231	153
A EXT	4	3	B9	271	185
A IND	5	2	A9	251	169
B IMM	2	2	C9	311	201
B DIR	3	2	D9	331	217
B EXT	4	3	F9	371	249
B IND	5	2	E9	351	233

Add Without Carry **ADD**

Operation: ACCX ← (ACCX) + (M)

Description: Adds the contents of ACCX and the contents of M and places the result in ACCX.

Condition Codes:
- H: Set if there was a carry from bit 3; cleared otherwise.
- I: Not affected.
- N: Set if most significant bit of the result is set; cleared otherwise.
- Z: Set if all bits of the result are cleared; cleared otherwise.
- V: Set if there was two's complement overflow as a result of the operation; cleared otherwise.
- C: Set if there was a carry from the most significant bit of the result; cleared otherwise.

Boolean Formulae for Condition Codes:

$$H = X_3 \cdot M_3 + M_3 \cdot \overline{R}_3 + \overline{R}_3 \cdot X_3$$
$$N = R_7$$
$$Z = \overline{R}_7 \cdot \overline{R}_6 \cdot \overline{R}_5 \cdot \overline{R}_4 \cdot \overline{R}_3 \cdot \overline{R}_2 \cdot \overline{R}_1 \cdot \overline{R}_0$$
$$V = X_7 \cdot M_7 \cdot \overline{R}_7 + \overline{X}_7 \cdot \overline{M}_7 \cdot R_7$$
$$C = X_7 \cdot M_7 + M_7 \cdot \overline{R}_7 + \overline{R}_7 \cdot X_7$$

Addressing Formats:

See Table A-1

Addressing Modes, Execution Time, and Machine Code (hexadecimal/ octal/ decimal):

(DUAL OPERAND)

Addressing Modes	Execution Time (No. of cycles)	Number of bytes of machine code	Coding of First (or only) byte of machine code		
			HEX.	OCT.	DEC.
A IMM	2	2	8B	213	139
A DIR	3	2	9B	233	155
A EXT	4	3	BB	273	187
A IND	5	2	AB	253	171
B IMM	2	2	CB	313	203
B DIR	3	2	DB	333	219
B EXT	4	3	FB	373	251
B IND	5	2	EB	353	235

AND

Logical AND

Operation: ACCX ← (ACCX) · (M)

Description: Performs logical "AND" between the contents of ACCX and the contents of M and places the result in ACCX. (Each bit of ACCX after the operation will be the logical "AND" of the corresponding bits of M and of ACCX before the operation.)

Condition Codes:
- H: Not affected.
- I: Not affected.
- N: Set if most significant bit of the result is set; cleared otherwise.
- Z: Set if all bits of the result are cleared; cleared otherwise.
- V: Cleared.
- C: Not affected.

Boolean Formulae for Condition Codes:

$N = R_7$

$Z = \overline{R}_7 \cdot \overline{R}_6 \cdot \overline{R}_5 \cdot \overline{R}_4 \cdot \overline{R}_3 \cdot \overline{R}_2 \cdot \overline{R}_1 \cdot \overline{R}_0$

$V = 0$

Addressing Formats:

See Table A-1

Addressing Modes, Execution Time, and Machine Code (hexadecimal/ octal/ decimal):

Addressing Modes	Execution Time (No. of cycles)	Number of bytes of machine code	Coding of First (or only) byte of machine code		
			HEX.	OCT.	DEC.
A IMM	2	2	84	204	132
A DIR	3	2	94	224	148
A EXT	4	3	B4	264	180
A IND	5	2	A4	244	164
B IMM	2	2	C4	304	196
B DIR	3	2	D4	324	212
B EXT	4	3	F4	364	244
B IND	5	2	E4	344	228

Arithmetic Shift Left **ASL**

Operation:

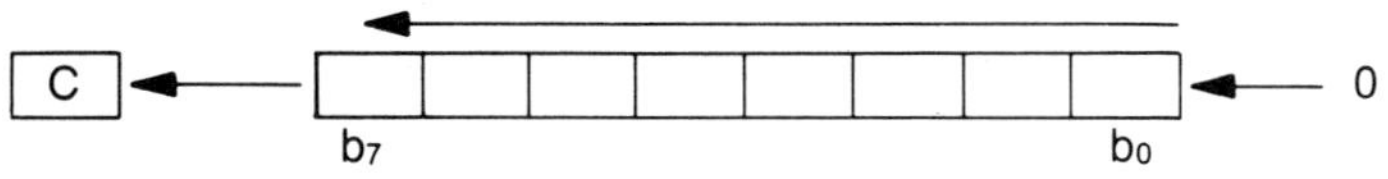

Description: Shifts all bits of the ACCX or M one place to the left. Bit 0 is loaded with a zero. The C bit is loaded from the most significant bit of ACCX or M.

Condition Codes:
- H: Not affected.
- I: Not affected.
- N: Set if most significant bit of the result is set; cleared otherwise.
- Z: Set if all bits of the result are cleared; cleared otherwise.
- V: Set if, after the completion of the shift operation, EITHER (N is set and C is cleared) OR (N is cleared and C is set); cleared otherwise.
- C: Set if, before the operation, the most significant bit of the ACCX or M was set; cleared otherwise.

Boolean Formulae for Condition Codes:

$N = R_7$

$Z = \overline{R}_7 \cdot \overline{R}_6 \cdot \overline{R}_5 \cdot \overline{R}_4 \cdot \overline{R}_3 \cdot \overline{R}_2 \cdot \overline{R}_1 \cdot \overline{R}_0$

$V = N \oplus C = [N \cdot \overline{C}] \odot [\overline{N} \cdot C]$

(the foregoing formula assumes values of N and C after the shift operation)

$C = M_7$

Addressing Formats

See Table A-3

Addressing Modes, Execution Time, and Machine Code (hexadecimal/octal/decimal):

Addressing Modes	Execution Time (No. of cycles)	Number of bytes of machine code	Coding of First (or only) byte of machine code		
			HEX.	OCT.	DEC.
A	2	1	48	110	072
B	2	1	58	130	088
EXT	6	3	78	170	120
IND	7	2	68	150	104

ASR

Arithmetic Shift Right

Operation:

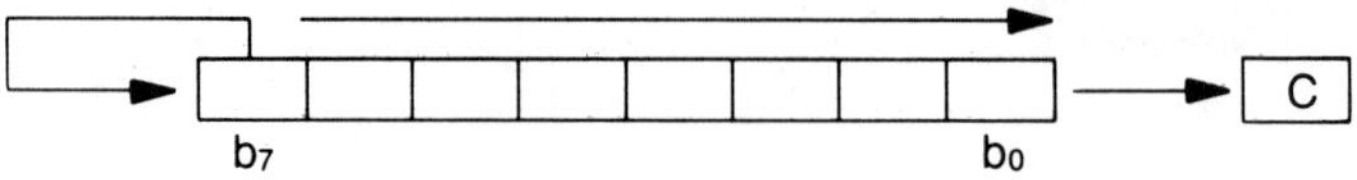

Description: Shifts all bits of ACCX or M one place to the right. Bit 7 is held constant. Bit 0 is loaded into the C bit.

Condition Codes:
- H: Not affected.
- I: Not affected.
- N: Set if the most significant bit of the result is set; cleared otherwise.
- Z: Set if all bits of the result are cleared; cleared otherwise.
- V: Set if, after the completion of the shift operation, EITHER (N is set and C is cleared) OR (N is cleared and C is set); cleared otherwise.
- C:. Set if, before the operation, the least significant bit of the ACCX or M was set; cleared otherwise.

Boolean Formulae for Condition Codes:

$N = R_7$

$Z = \overline{R}_7 \cdot \overline{R}_6 \cdot \overline{R}_5 \cdot \overline{R}_4 \cdot \overline{R}_3 \cdot \overline{R}_2 \cdot \overline{R}_1 \cdot \overline{R}_0$

$V = N \oplus C = [N \cdot \overline{C}] \odot [\overline{N} \cdot C]$

(the foregoing formula assumes values of N and C after the shift operation)

$C = M_0$

Addressing Formats:

See Table A-3

Addressing Modes, Execution Time, and Machine Code (hexadecimal/ octal/ decimal):

Addressing Modes	Execution Time (No. of cycles)	Number of bytes of machine code	Coding of First (or only) byte of machine code		
			HEX.	OCT.	DEC.
A	2	1	47	107	071
B	2	1	57	127	087
EXT	6	3	77	167	119
IND	7	2	67	147	103

Branch if Carry Clear **BCC**

Operation: PC ← (PC) + 0002 + Rel if (C)=0

Description: Tests the state of the C bit and causes a branch if C is clear.

See BRA instruction for further details of the execution of the branch.

Condition Codes: Not affected.

Addressing Formats:

See Table A-8.

Addressing Modes, Execution Time, and Machine Code (hexadecimal/octal/decimal):

Addressing Modes	Execution Time (No. of cycles)	Number of bytes of machine code	Coding of First (or only) byte of machine code		
			HEX.	OCT.	DEC.
REL	4	2	24	044	036

Branch if Carry Set **BCS**

Operation: PC ← (PC) + 0002 + Rel if (C)=1

Description: Tests the state of the C bit and causes a branch if C is set.

See BRA instruction for further details of the execution of the branch.

Condition Codes: Not affected.

Addressing Formats:

See Table A-8.

Addressing Modes, Execution Time, and Machine Code (hexadecimal/octal/decimal):

Addressing Modes	Execution Time (No. of cycles)	Number of bytes of machine code	Coding of First (or only) byte of machine code		
			HEX.	OCT.	DEC.
REL	4	2	25	045	037

BEQ

Branch if Equal

Operation: $PC \leftarrow (PC) + 0002 + Rel$ if $(Z)=1$

Description: Tests the state of the Z bit and causes a branch if the Z bit is set.

See BRA instruction for further details of the execution of the branch.

Condition Codes: Not affected.

Addressing Formats:

See Table A-8.

Addressing Modes, Execution Time, and Machine Code (hexadecimal/ octal/ decimal):

Addressing Modes	Execution Time (No. of cycles)	Number of bytes of machine code	Coding of First (or only) byte of machine code		
			HEX.	OCT.	DEC.
REL	4	2	27	047	039

BGE

Branch if Greater than or Equal to Zero

Operation: $PC \leftarrow (PC) + 0002 + Rel$ if $(N) \oplus (V) = 0$

i.e. if $(ACCX) \geq (M)$

(Two's complement numbers)

Description: Causes a branch if (N is set and V is set) OR (N is clear and V is clear).

If the BGE instruction is executed immediately after execution of any of the instructions CBA, CMP, SBA, or SUB, the branch will occur if and only if the two's complement number represented by the minuend (i.e. ACCX) was greater than or equal to the two's complement number represented by the subtrahend (i.e. M).

See BRA instruction for details of the branch.

Condition Codes: Not affected.

Addressing Formats:

See Table A-8.

Addressing Modes, Execution Time, and Machine Code (hexadecimal/ octal/ decimal):

Addressing Modes	Execution Time (No. of cycles)	Number of bytes of machine code	Coding of First (or only) byte of machine code		
			HEX.	OCT.	DEC.
REL	4	2	2C	054	044

Branch if Greater than Zero

BGT

Operation: PC ← (PC) + 0002 + Rel if (Z) ⊙ [(N) ⊕ (V)] = 0

i.e. if (ACCX) > (M)

(two's complement numbers)

Description: Causes a branch if [Z is clear] AND [(N is set and V is set) OR (N is clear and V is clear)].

If the BGT instruction is executed immediately after execution of any of the instructions CBA, CMP, SBA, or SUB, the branch will occur if and only if the two's complement number represented by the minuend (i.e. ACCX) was greater than the two's complement number represented by the subtrahend (i.e. M).

See BRA instruction for details of the branch.

Condition Codes: Not affected.

Addressing Formats:

See Table A-8.

Addressing Modes, Execution Time, and Machine Code (hexadecimal/octal/decimal):

Addressing Modes	Execution Time (No. of cycles)	Number of bytes of machine code	Coding of First (or only) byte of machine code		
			HEX.	OCT.	DEC.
REL	4	2	2E	056	046

Branch if Higher

BHI

Operation: PC ← (PC) + 0002 + Rel if (C) · (Z)=0

i.e. if (ACCX) > (M)

(unsigned binary numbers)

Description: Causes a branch if (C is clear) AND (Z is clear).

If the BHI instruction is executed immediately after execution of any of the instructions CBA, CMP, SBA, or SUB, the branch will occur if and only if the unsigned binary number represented by the minuend (i.e. ACCX) was greater than the unsigned binary number represented by the subtrahend (i.e. M).

See BRA instruction for details of the execution of the branch.

Condition Codes: Not affected.

Addressing Formats:

See Table A-8.

Addressing Modes, Execution Time, and Machine Code (hexadecimal/octal/decimal):

Addressing Modes	Execution Time (No. of cycles)	Number of bytes of machine code	Coding of First (or only) byte of machine code		
			HEX.	OCT.	DEC.
REL	4	2	22	042	034

BIT

Bit Test

Operation: (ACCX) (M)

Description: Performs the logical "AND" comparison of the contents of ACCX and the contents of M and modifies condition codes accordingly. Neither the contents of ACCX or M operands are affected. (Each bit of the result of the "AND" would be the logical "AND" of the corresponding bits of M and ACCX.)

Condition Codes:
- H: Not affected.
- I: Not affected.
- N: Set if the most significant bit of the result of the "AND" would be set; cleared otherwise.
- Z: Set if all bits of the result of the "AND" would be cleared; cleared otherwise.
- V: Cleared.
- C: Not affected.

Boolean Formulae for Condition Codes:

$N = R_7$

$Z = \overline{R_7} \cdot \overline{R_6} \cdot \overline{R_5} \cdot \overline{R_4} \cdot \overline{R_3} \cdot \overline{R_2} \cdot \overline{R_1} \cdot \overline{R_0}$

$V = 0$

Addressing Formats:

See Table A-1.

Addressing Modes, Execution Time, and Machine Code (hexadecimal/ octal/ decimal):

Addressing Modes	Execution Time (No. of cycles)	Number of bytes of machine code	Coding of First (or only) byte of machine code		
			HEX.	OCT.	DEC.
A IMM	2	2	85	205	133
A DIR	3	2	95	225	149
A EXT	4	3	B5	265	181
A IND	5	2	A5	245	165
B IMM	2	2	C5	305	197
B DIR	3	2	D5	325	213
B EXT	4	3	F5	365	245
B IND	5	2	E5	345	229

Branch if Less than or Equal to Zero

BLE

Operation: PC ← (PC) + 0002 + Rel if $(Z) \odot [(N) \oplus (V)] = 1$

i.e. if (ACCX) ≤ (M)

(two's complement numbers)

Description: Causes a branch if [Z is set] OR [(N is set and V is clear) OR (N is clear and V is set)].

If the BLE instruction is executed immediately after execution of any of the instructions CBA, CMP, SBA, or SUB, the branch will occur if and only if the two's complement number represented by the minuend (i.e. ACCX) was less then or equal to the two's complement number represented by the subtrahend (i.e. M).

See BRA instruction for details of the branch.

Condition Codes: Not affected.

Addressing Formats:

See Table A-8.

Addressing Modes, Execution Time, and Machine Code (hexadecimal/octal/decimal):

Addressing Modes	Execution Time (No. of cycles)	Number of bytes of machine code	Coding of First (or only) byte of machine code		
			HEX.	OCT.	DEC.
REL	4	2	2F	057	047

BLS

Branch if Lower or Same

Operation: PC ← (PC) + 0002 + Rel if (C)⨀(Z) = 1

i.e. if (ACCX) ≤ (M)

(unsigned binary numbers)

Description: Causes a branch if (C is set) OR (Z is set).

If the BLS instruction is executed immediately after execution of any of the instructions CBA, CMP, SBA, or SUB, the branch will occur if and only if the unsigned binary number represented by the minuend (i.e. ACCX) was less than or equal to the unsigned binary number represented by the subtrahend (i.e. M).

See BRA instruction for details of the execution of the branch.

Condition Codes: Not affected.

Addressing Formats:

See Table A-8.

Addressing Modes, Execution Time, and Machine Code (hexadecimal/octal/decimal):

Addressing Modes	Execution Time (No. of cycles)	Number of bytes of machine code	Coding of First (or only) byte of machine code		
			HEX.	**OCT.**	**DEC.**
REL	4	2	23	043	035

Branch if Less than Zero **BLT**

Operation: PC ← (PC) + 0002 + Rel if (N) ⊕ (V) = 1
i.e. if (ACCX) < (M)
(two's complement numbers)

Description: Causes a branch if (N is set and V is clear) OR (N is clear and V is set).

If the BLT instruction is executed immediately after execution of any of the instructions CBA, CMP, SBA, or SUB, the branch will occur if and only if the two's complement number represented by the minuend (i.e. ACCX) was less than the two's complement number represented by the subtrahend (i.e. M).

See BRA instruction for details of the branch.

Condition Codes: Not affected.

Addressing Formats:

See Table A-8.

Addressing Modes, Execution Time, and Machine Code (hexadecimal/octal/decimal):

Addressing Modes	Execution Time (No. of cycles)	Number of bytes of machine code	Coding of First (or only) byte of machine code		
			HEX.	OCT.	DEC.
REL	4	2	2D	055	045

Branch if Minus **BMI**

Operation: PC← (PC) + 0002 + Rel if (N) =1

Description: Tests the state of the N bit and causes a branch if N is set.

See BRA instruction for details of the execution of the branch.

Condition Codes: Not affected.

Addressing Formats:

See Table A-8.

Addressing Modes, Execution Time, and Machine Code (hexadecimal/octal/decimal):

Addressing Modes	Execution Time (No. of cycles)	Number of bytes of machine code	Coding of First (or only) byte of machine code		
			HEX.	OCT.	DEC.
REL	4	2	2B	053	043

BNE

Branch if Not Equal

Operation: PC ← (PC) + 0002 + Rel if (Z) = 0

Description: Tests the state of the Z bit and causes a branch if the Z bit is clear. See BRA instruction for details of the execution of the branch.

Condition Codes: Not affected.

Addressing Formats:

See Table A-8.

Addressing Modes, Execution Time, and Machine Code (hexadecimal/ octal/ decimal):

Addressing Modes	Execution Time (No. of cycles)	Number of bytes of machine code	Coding of First (or only) byte of machine code		
			HEX.	OCT.	DEC.
REL	4	2	26	046	038

BPL

Branch if Plus

Operation: PC ← (PC) + 0002 + Rel if (N) =0

Description: Tests the state of the N bit and causes a branch if N is clear. See BRA instruction for details of the execution of the branch.

Condition Codes: Not affected.

Addressing Formats:

See Table A-8.

Addressing Modes, Execution Time, and Machine Code (hexadecimal/ octal/ decimal):

Addressing Modes	Execution Time (No. of cycles)	Number of bytes of machine code	Coding of First (or only) byte of machine code		
			HEX.	OCT.	DEC.
REL	4	2	2A	052	042

Branch Always **BRA**

Operation: PC ← (PC) + 0002 + Rel

Description: Unconditional branch to the address given by the foregoing formula, in which R is the relative address stored as a two's complement number in the second byte of machine code corresponding to the branch instruction.

Note: The source program specifies the destination of any branch instruction by its absolute address, either as a numerical value or as a symbol or expression which can be numerically evaluated by the assembler. The assembler obtains the relative address R from the absolute address and the current value of the program counter PC.

Condition Codes: Not affected.

Addressing Formats:

See Table A-8.

Addressing Modes, Execution Time, and Machine Code (hexadecimal/ octal/ decimal):

Addressing Modes	Execution Time (No. of cycles)	Number of bytes of machine code	Coding of First (or only) byte of machine code		
			HEX.	OCT.	DEC.
REL	4	2	20	040	032

BSR

Branch to Subroutine

Operation: PC ← (PC) + 0002

↓ (PCL)

SP ← (SP) − 0001

↓ (PCH)

SP ← (SP) − 0001

PC ← (PC) + Rel

Description: The program counter is incremented by 2. The less significant byte of the contents of the program counter is pushed into the stack. The stack pointer is then decremented (by 1). The more significant byte of the contents of the program counter is then pushed into the stack. The stack pointer is again decremented (by 1). A branch then occurs to the location specified by the program.

See BRA instruction for details of the execution of the branch.

Condition Codes: Not affected.

Addressing Formats:

See Table A-8.

Addressing Modes, Execution Time, and Machine Code (hexadecimal/ octal/ decimal):

Addressing Modes	Execution Time (No. of cycles)	Number of bytes of machine code	Coding of First (or only) byte of machine code		
			HEX.	OCT.	DEC.
REL	8	2	8D	215	141

BRANCH TO SUBROUTINE EXAMPLE

			Memory Location	Machine Code (Hex)	Label	Operator	Operand
A.	*Before*						
	PC	←	$1000	8D		BSR	CHARLI
			$1001	50			
	SP	←	$EFFF				
B.	*After*						
	PC	←	$1052	**	CHARLI	***	*****
	SP	←	$EFFD				
			$EFFE	10			
			$EFFF	02			

Branch if Overflow Clear **BVC**

Operation: $PC \leftarrow (PC) + 0002 + Rel$ if $(V) = 0$

Description: Tests the state of the V bit and causes a branch if the V bit is clear.

See BRA instruction for details of the execution of the branch.

Condition Codes: Not affected.

Addressing Formats:

See Table A-8.

Addressing Modes, Execution Time, and Machine Code (hexadecimal/octal/decimal):

Addressing Modes	Execution Time (No. of cycles)	Number of bytes of machine code	Coding of First (or only) byte of machine code		
			HEX.	OCT.	DEC.
REL	4	2	28	050	040

Branch if Overflow Set **BVS**

Operation: $PC \leftarrow (PC) + 0002 + Rel$ if $(V) = 1$

Description: Tests the state of the V bit and causes a branch if the V bit is set.

See BRA instruction for details of the execution of the branch.

Condition Codes: Not affected.

Addressing Formats:

See Table A-8.

Addressing Modes, Execution Time, and Machine Code (hexadecimal/octal/decimal):

Addressing Modes	Execution Time (No. of cycles)	Number of bytes of machine code	Coding of First (or only) byte of machine code		
			HEX.	OCT.	DEC.
REL	4	2	29	051	041

CBA

Compare Accumulators

Operation: (ACCA) − (ACCB)

Description: Compares the contents of ACCA and the contents of ACCB and sets the condition codes, which may be used for arithmetic and logical conditional branches. Both operands are unaffected.

Condition Codes:
- H: Not affected.
- I: Not affected.
- N: Set if the most significant bit of the result of the subtraction would be set; cleared otherwise.
- Z: Set if all bits of the result of the subtraction would be cleared; cleared otherwise.
- V: Set if the subtraction would cause two's complement overflow; cleared otherwise.
- C: Set if the subtraction would require a borrow into the most significant bit of the result; clear otherwise.

Boolean Formulae for Condition Codes:

$$N = R_7$$
$$Z = \overline{R}_7 \cdot \overline{R}_6 \cdot \overline{R}_5 \cdot \overline{R}_4 \cdot \overline{R}_3 \cdot \overline{R}_2 \cdot \overline{R}_1 \cdot \overline{R}_0$$
$$V = A_7 \cdot \overline{B}_7 \cdot \overline{R}_7 + \overline{A}_7 \cdot B_7 \cdot R_7$$
$$C = \overline{A}_7 \cdot B_7 + B_7 \cdot R_7 + R_7 \cdot \overline{A}_7$$

Addressing Modes, Execution Time, and Machine Code (hexadecimal/ octal/ decimal):

Addressing Modes	Execution Time (No. of cycles)	Number of bytes of machine code	Coding of First (or only) byte of machine code		
			HEX.	OCT.	DEC.
INHERENT	2	1	11	021	017

Clear Carry **CLC**

Operation: C bit ← 0

Description: Clears the carry bit in the processor condition codes register.

Condition Codes:
H: Not affected.
I: Not affected.
N: Not affected.
Z: Not affected.
V: Not affected.
C: Cleared

Boolean Formulae for Condition Codes:
C = 0

Addressing Modes, Execution Time, and Machine Code (hexadecimal/octal/decimal):

Addressing Modes	Execution Time (No. of cycles)	Number of bytes of machine code	Coding of First (or only) byte of machine code		
			HEX.	OCT.	DEC.
INHERENT	2	1	0C	014	012

Clear Interrupt Mask **CLI**

Operation: I bit ← 0

Description: Clears the interrupt mask bit in the processor condition codes register. This enables the microprocessor to service an interrupt from a peripheral device if signalled by a high state of the "Interrupt Request" control input.

Condition Codes:
H: Not affected.
I: Cleared.
N: Not affected.
Z: Not affected.
V: Not affected.
C: Not affected.

Boolean Formulae for Condition Codes:
I = 0

Addressing Modes, Execution Time, and Machine Code (hexadecimal/octal/decimal):

Addressing Modes	Execution Time (No. of cycles)	Number of bytes of machine code	Coding of First (or only) byte of machine code		
			HEX.	OCT.	DEC.
INHERENT	2	1	0E	016	014

CLR

Clear

Operation: ACCX ← 00
or: M ← 00

Description: The contents of ACCX or M are replaced with zeros.

Condition Codes:
H: Not affected.
I: Not affected.
N: Cleared
Z: Set
V: Cleared
C: Cleared

Boolean Formulae for Condition Codes:
N = 0
Z = 1
V = 0
C = 0

Addressing Formats:

See Table A-3.

Addressing Modes, Execution Time, and Machine Code (hexadecimal/octal/decimal):

Addressing Modes	Execution Time (No. of cycles)	Number of bytes of machine code	Coding of First (or only) byte of machine code		
			HEX.	OCT.	DEC.
A	2	1	4F	117	079
B	2	1	5F	137	095
EXT	6	3	7F	177	127
IND	7	2	6F	157	111

Clear Two's Complement Overflow Bit

CLV

Operation: V bit ← 0

Description: Clears the two's complement overflow bit in the processor condition codes register.

Condition Codes:
H: Not affected.
I: Not affected.
N: Not affected.
Z: Not affected.
V: Cleared.
C: Not affected.

Boolean Formulae for Condition Codes:
$V = 0$

Addressing Modes, Execution Time, and Machine Code (hexadecimal/ octal/ decimal):

Addressing Modes	Execution Time (No. of cycles)	Number of bytes of machine code	Coding of First (or only) byte of machine code		
			HEX.	OCT.	DEC.
INHERENT	2	1	0A	012	010

CMP

Compare

Operation: (ACCX) − (M)

Description: Compares the contents of ACCX and the contents of M and determines the condition codes, which may be used subsequently for controlling conditional branching. Both operands are unaffected.

Condition Codes:
- H: Not affected.
- I: Not affected.
- N: Set if the most significant bit of the result of the subtraction would be set; cleared otherwise.
- Z: Set if all bits of the result of the subtraction would be cleared; cleared otherwise.
- V: Set if the subtraction would cause two's complement overflow; cleared otherwise.
- C: Carry is set if the absolute value of the contents of memory is larger than the absolute value of the accumulator; reset otherwise.

Boolean Formulae for Condition Codes:

$N = R_7$

$Z = \overline{R_7} \cdot \overline{R_6} \cdot \overline{R_5} \cdot \overline{R_4} \cdot \overline{R_3} \cdot \overline{R_2} \cdot \overline{R_1} \cdot \overline{R_0}$

$V = X_7 \cdot \overline{M_7} \cdot \overline{R_7} + \overline{X_7} \cdot M_7 \cdot R_7$

$C = \overline{X_7} \cdot M_7 + M_7 \cdot R_7 + R_7 \cdot \overline{X_7}$

Addressing Formats:

See Table A-1.

Addressing Modes, Execution Time, and Machine Code (hexadecimal/ octal/ decimal):

(DUAL OPERAND)

Addressing Modes	Execution Time (No. of cycles)	Number of bytes of machine code	Coding of First (or only) byte of machine code		
			HEX.	OCT.	DEC.
A IMM	2	2	81	201	129
A DIR	3	2	91	221	145
A EXT	4	3	B1	261	177
A IND	5	2	A1	241	161
B IMM	2	2	C1	301	193
B DIR	3	2	D1	321	209
B EXT	4	3	F1	361	241
B IND	5	2	E1	341	225

Complement **COM**

Operation: $ACCX \leftarrow \approx (ACCX) = FF - (ACCX)$
or: $M \leftarrow \approx (M) = FF - (M)$

Description: Replaces the contents of ACCX or M with its one's complement. (Each bit of the contents of ACCX or M is replaced with the complement of that bit.)

Condition Codes:
- H: Not affected.
- I: Not affected.
- N: Set if most significant bit of the result is set; cleared otherwise.
- Z: Set if all bits of the result are cleared; cleared otherwise.
- V: Cleared.
- C: Set.

Boolean Formulae for Condition Codes:

$N = R_7$

$Z = \overline{R_7} \cdot \overline{R_6} \cdot \overline{R_5} \cdot \overline{R_4} \cdot \overline{R_3} \cdot \overline{R_2} \cdot \overline{R_1} \cdot \overline{R_0}$

$V = 0$

$C = 1$

Addressing Formats:

See Table A-3.

Addressing Modes, Execution Time, and Machine Code (hexadecimal/octal/decimal):

Addressing Modes	Execution Time (No. of cycles)	Number of bytes of machine code	Coding of First (or only) byte of machine code		
			HEX.	OCT.	DEC.
A	2	1	43	103	067
B	2	1	53	123	083
EXT	6	3	73	163	115
IND	7	2	63	143	099

CPX

Compare Index Register

Operation: (IXL) − (M+1)
(IXH) − (M)

Description: The more significant byte of the contents of the index register is compared with the contents of the byte of memory at the address specified by the program. The less significant byte of the contents of the index register is compared with the contents of the next byte of memory, at one plus the address specified by the program. The Z bit is set or reset according to the results of these comparisons, and may be used subsequently for conditional branching.

The N and V bits, though determined by this operation, are not intended for conditional branching.

The C bit is not affected by this operation.

Condition Codes:
- H: Not affected.
- I: Not affected.
- N: Set if the most significant bit of the result of the subtraction from the more significant byte of the index register would be set; cleared otherwise.
- Z: Set if all bits of the results of both subtractions would be cleared; cleared otherwise.
- V: Set if the subtraction from the more significant byte of the index register would cause two's complement overflow; cleared otherwise.
- C: Not affected.

Boolean Formulae for Condition Codes:

$$N = RH_7$$

$$Z = (\overline{RH_7} \cdot \overline{RH_6} \cdot \overline{RH_5} \cdot \overline{RH_4} \cdot \overline{RH_3} \cdot \overline{RH_2} \cdot \overline{RH_1} \cdot \overline{RH_0}) \cdot (\overline{RL_7} \cdot \overline{RL_6} \cdot \overline{RL_5} \cdot \overline{RL_4} \cdot \overline{RL_3} \cdot \overline{RL_2} \cdot \overline{RL_1} \cdot \overline{RL_0})$$

$$V = IXH_7 \cdot \overline{M_7} \cdot \overline{RH_7} + \overline{IXH_7} \cdot M_7 \cdot RH_7$$

Addressing Formats:

See Table A-5.

Addressing Modes, Execution Time, and Machine Code (hexadecimal/octal/decimal):

Addressing Modes	Execution Time (No. of cycles)	Number of bytes of machine code	Coding of First (or only) byte of machine code		
			HEX.	OCT.	DEC.
IMM	3	3	8C	214	140
DIR	4	2	9C	234	156
EXT	5	3	BC	274	188
IND	6	2	AC	254	172

Operation: Adds hexadecimal numbers 00, 06, 60, or 66 to ACCA, and may also set the carry bit, as indicated in the following table:

State of C-bit before DAA (Col. 1)	Upper Half-byte (bits 4-7) (Col. 2)	Initial Half-carry H-bit (Col.3)	Lower to ACCA (bits 0-3) (Col. 4)	Number Added after by DAA (Col. 5)	State of C-bit DAA (Col. 6)
0	0-9	0	0-9	00	0
0	0-8	0	A-F	06	0
0	0-9	1	0-3	06	0
0	A-F	0	0-9	60	1
0	9-F	0	A-F	66	1
0	A-F	1	0-3	66	1
1	0-2	0	0-9	60	1
1	0-2	0	A-F	66	1
1	0-3	1	0-3	66	1

Note: Columns (1) through (4) of the above table represent all possible cases which can result from any of the operations ABA, ADD, or ADC, with initial carry either set or clear, applied to two binary-coded-decimal operands. The table shows hexadecimal values.

Description: If the contents of ACCA and the state of the carry-borrow bit C and the half-carry bit H are all the result of applying any of the operations ABA, ADD, or ADC to binary-coded-decimal operands, with or without an initial carry, the DAA operation will function as follows.

Subject to the above condition, the DAA operation will adjust the contents of ACCA and the C bit to represent the correct binary-coded-decimal sum and the correct state of the carry.

Condition Codes:
- H: Not affected.
- I: Not affected.
- N: Set if most significant bit of the result is set; cleared otherwise.
- Z: Set if all bits of the result are cleared; cleared otherwise.
- V: Not defined.
- C: Set or reset according to the same rule as if the DAA and an immediately preceding ABA, ADD, or ADC were replaced by a hypothetical binary-coded-decimal addition.

Boolean Formulae for Condition Codes:

$N = R_7$

$Z = \overline{R}_7 \cdot \overline{R}_6 \cdot \overline{R}_5 \cdot \overline{R}_4 \cdot \overline{R}_3 \cdot \overline{R}_2 \cdot \overline{R}_1 \cdot \overline{R}_0$

C = See table above.

Addressing Modes, Execution Time, and Machine Code (hexadecimal/ octal/ decimal):

Addressing Modes	Execution Time (No. of cycles)	Number of bytes of machine code	Coding of First (or only) byte of machine code		
			HEX.	OCT.	DEC.
INHERENT	2	1	19	031	025

DEC

Decrement

Operation: ACCX ← (ACCX) − 01
or: M ← (M) − 01

Description: Subtract one from the contents of ACCX or M.

The N, Z, and V condition codes are set or reset according to the results of this operation.

The C bit is not affected by the operation.

Condition Codes:
- H: Not affected.
- I: Not affected.
- N: Set if most significant bit of the result is set; cleared otherwise.
- Z: Set if all bits of the result are cleared; cleared otherwise.
- V: Set if there was two's complement overflow as a result of the operation; cleared otherwise. Two's complement overflow occurs if and only if (ACCX) or (M) was 80 before the operation.
- C: Not affected.

Boolean Formulae for Condition Codes:

$$N = R_7$$

$$Z = \overline{R}_7 \cdot \overline{R}_6 \cdot \overline{R}_5 \cdot \overline{R}_5 \cdot \overline{R}_4 \cdot \overline{R}_3 \cdot \overline{R}_2 \cdot \overline{R}_1 \cdot \overline{R}_0$$

$$V = X_7 \cdot \overline{X}_6 \cdot \overline{X}_5 \cdot \overline{X}_4 \cdot \overline{X}_3 \cdot \overline{X}_2 \cdot \overline{X}_0 = \overline{R}_7 \cdot R_6 \cdot R_5 \cdot R_4 \cdot R_3 \cdot R_2 \cdot R_1 \cdot R_0$$

Addressing Formats:

See Table A-3.

Addressing Modes, Execution Time, and Machine Code (hexadecimal/ octal/ decimal):

Addressing Modes	Execution Time (No. of cycles)	Number of bytes of machine code	Coding of First (or only) byte of machine code		
			HEX.	OCT.	DEC.
A	2	1	4A	112	074
B	2	1	5A	132	090
EXT	6	3	7A	172	122
IND	7	2	6A	152	106

Decrement Stack Pointer

DES

Operation: SP ← (SP) − 0001

Description: Subtract one from the stack pointer.

Condition Codes: Not affected.

Addressing Modes, Execution Time, and Machine Code (hexadecimal/octal/decimal):

Addressing Modes	Execution Time (No. of cycles)	Number of bytes of machine code	Coding of First (or only) byte of machine code		
			HEX.	OCT.	DEC.
INHERENT	4	1	34	064	052

Decrement Index Register

DEX

Operation: IX ← (IX) − 0001

Description: Subtract one from the index register.

Only the Z bit is set or reset according to the result of this operation.

Condition Codes:
- H: Not affected.
- I: Not affected.
- N: Not affected.
- Z: Set if all bits of the result are cleared; cleared otherwise.
- V: Not affected.
- C: Not affected.

Boolean Formulae for Condition Codes:

$$Z = (\overline{RH_7} \cdot \overline{RH_6} \cdot \overline{RH_5} \cdot \overline{RH_4} \cdot \overline{RH_3} \cdot \overline{RH_2} \cdot \overline{RH_1} \cdot \overline{RH_0}) \cdot (\overline{RL_7} \cdot \overline{RL_6} \cdot \overline{RL_5} \cdot \overline{RL_4} \cdot \overline{RL_3} \cdot \overline{RL_2} \cdot \overline{RL_1} \cdot \overline{RL_0})$$

Addressing Modes, Execution Time, and Machine Code (hexadecimal/octal/decimal):

Addressing Modes	Execution Time (No. of cycles)	Number of bytes of machine code	Coding of First (or only) byte of machine code		
			HEX.	OCT.	DEC.
INHERENT	4	1	09	011	009

EOR

Exclusive OR

Operation: ACCX ← (ACCX) ⊕ (M)

Description: Perform logical "EXCLUSIVE OR" between the contents of ACCX and the contents of M, and place the result in ACCX. (Each bit of ACCX after the operation will be the logical "EXCLUSIVE OR" of the corresponding bit of M and ACCX before the operation.)

Condition Codes:
- H: Not affected.
- I: Not affected.
- N: Set if most significant bit of the result is set; cleared otherwise.
- Z: Set if all bits of the result are cleared; cleared otherwise.
- V: Cleared
- C: Not affected.

Boolean Formulae for Condition Codes:

$N = R_7$

$Z = \overline{R_7} \cdot \overline{R_6} \cdot \overline{R_5} \cdot \overline{R_4} \cdot \overline{R_3} \cdot \overline{R_2} \cdot \overline{R_1} \cdot \overline{R_0}$

$V = 0$

Addressing Formats:

See Table A-1.

Addressing Modes, Execution Time, and Machine Code (hexadecimal/ octal/ decimal):

Addressing Modes	Execution Time (No. of cycles)	Number of bytes of machine code	Coding of First (or only) byte of machine code		
			HEX.	OCT.	DEC.
A IMM	2	2	88	210	136
A DIR	3	2	98	230	152
A EXT	4	3	B8	270	184
A IND	5	2	A8	250	168
B IMM	2	2	C8	310	200
B DIR	3	2	D8	330	216
B EXT	4	3	F8	370	248
B IND	5	2	E8	350	232

Increment **INC**

Operation: ACCX ← (ACCX) + 01
or: M ← (M) + 01

Description: Add one to the contents of ACCX or M.

The N, Z, and V condition codes are set or reset according to the results of this operation.

The C bit is not affected by the operation.

Condition Codes:
- H: Not affected.
- I: Not affected.
- N: Set if most significant bit of the result is set; cleared otherwise.
- Z: Set if all bits of the result are cleared; cleared otherwise.
- V: Set if there was two's complement overflow as a result of the operation; cleared otherwise. Two's complement overflow will occur if and only if (ACCX) or (M) was 7F before the operation.
- C: Not affected.

Boolean Formulae for Condition Codes:

$$N = R_7$$
$$Z = \overline{R}_7 \cdot \overline{R}_6 \cdot \overline{R}_5 \cdot \overline{R}_4 \cdot \overline{R}_3 \cdot \overline{R}_2 \cdot \overline{R}_1 \cdot \overline{R}_0$$
$$V = \overline{X}_7 \cdot X_6 \cdot X_5 \cdot X_4 \cdot X_3 \cdot X_2 \cdot X_1 \cdot X_0$$
$$C = \overline{R}_7 \cdot \overline{R}_6 \cdot \overline{R}_5 \cdot \overline{R}_4 \cdot \overline{R}_3 \cdot \overline{R}_2 \cdot \overline{R}_1 \cdot \overline{R}_0$$

Addressing Formats:

See Table A-3.

Addressing Modes, Execution Time, and Machine Code (hexadecimal/octal/decimal):

Addressing Modes	Execution Time (No. of cycles)	Number of bytes of machine code	Coding of First (or only) byte of machine code		
			HEX.	OCT.	DEC.
A	2	1	4C	114	076
B	2	1	5C	134	092
EXT	6	3	7C	174	124
IND	7	2	6C	154	108

INS

Increment Stack Pointer

Operation: SP ← (SP) + 0001

Description: Add one to the stack pointer.

Condition Codes: Not affected.

Addressing Modes, Execution Time, and Machine Code (hexadecimal/ octal/ decimal):

Addressing Modes	Execution Time (No. of cycles)	Number of bytes of machine code	Coding of First (or only) byte of machine code		
			HEX.	OCT.	DEC.
INHERENT	4	1	31	061	049

INX

Increment Index Register

Operation: IX ← (IX) + 0001

Description: Add one to the index register.

Only the Z bit is set or reset according to the result of this operation.

Condition Codes:
- H: Not affected.
- I: Not affected.
- N: Not affected.
- Z: Set if all 16 bits of the result are cleared; cleared otherwise.
- V: Not affected.
- C: Not affected.

Boolean Formulae for Condition Codes:

$$Z = (\overline{RH_7}\cdot\overline{RH_6}\cdot\overline{RH_5}\cdot\overline{RH_4}\cdot\overline{RH_3}\cdot\overline{RH_2}\cdot\overline{RH_1}\cdot\overline{RH_0})\cdot(\overline{RL_7}\cdot\overline{RL_6}\cdot\overline{RL_5}\cdot\overline{RL_4}\cdot\overline{RL_3}\cdot\overline{RL_2}\cdot\overline{RL_1}\cdot\overline{RL_0})$$

Addressing Modes, Execution Time, and Machine Code (hexadecimal/ octal/ decimal):

Addressing Modes	Execution Time (No. of cycles)	Number of bytes of machine code	Coding of First (or only) byte of machine code		
			HEX.	OCT.	DEC.
INHERENT	4	1	08	010	008

Jump **JMP**

Operation: PC ← numerical address

Description: A jump occurs to the instruction stored at the numerical address. The numerical address is obtained according to the rules for EXTended or INDexed addressing.

Condition Codes: Not affected.

Addressing Formats:

See Table A-7.

Addressing Modes, Execution Time, and Machine Code (hexadecimal/ octal/ decimal):

Addressing Modes	Execution Time (No. of cycles)	Number of bytes of machine code	Coding of First (or only) byte of machine code		
			HEX.	OCT.	DEC.
EXT	3	3	7E	176	126
IND	4	2	6E	156	110

JSR

Jump to Subroutine

Operation:

Either: PC ← (PC) + 0003 (for EXTended addressing)

or: PC ← (PC) + 0002 (for INDexed addressing)

Then: ↓ (PCL)

SP ← (SP) − 0001

↓ (PCH)

SP ← (SP) − 0001

PC ← numerical address

Description: The program counter is incremented by 3 or by 2, depending on the addressing mode, and is then pushed onto the stack, eight bits at a time. The stack pointer points to the next empty location in the stack. A jump occurs to the instruction stored at the numerical address. The numerical address is obtained according to the rules for EXTended or INDexed addressing.

Condition Codes: Not affected.

Addressing Formats:

See Table A-7.

Addressing Modes, Execution Time, and Machine Code (hexadecimal/ octal/ decimal):

Addressing Modes	Execution Time (No. of cycles)	Number of bytes of machine code	Coding of First (or only) byte of machine code		
			HEX.	OCT.	DEC.
EXT	9	3	BD	275	189
IND	8	2	AD	255	173

JUMP TO SUBROUTINE EXAMPLE (extended mode)

			Memory Location	Machine Code (Hex)	Assembler Language Label	Assembler Language Operator	Assembler Language Operand
A.	*Before:*						
	PC	→	$0FFF	BD		JSR	CHARLI
			$1000	20			
			$1001	77			
	SP	←	$EFFF				
B.	*After:*						
	PC	→	$2077	**	CHARLI	***	*****
	SP	→	$EFFD				
			$EFFE	10			
			$EFFF	02			

Load Accumulator **LDA**

Operation: ACCX ← (M)

Description: Loads the contents of memory into the accumulator. The condition codes are set according to the data.

Condition Codes:
H: Not affected.
I: Not affected.
N: Set if most significant bit of the result is set; cleared otherwise.
Z: Set if all bits of the result are cleared; cleared otherwise.
V: Cleared.
C: Not affected.

Boolean Formulae for Condition Codes:

$$N = R_7$$
$$Z = \overline{R}_7 \cdot \overline{R}_6 \cdot \overline{R}_5 \cdot \overline{R}_4 \cdot \overline{R}_3 \cdot \overline{R}_2 \cdot \overline{R}_1 \cdot \overline{R}_0$$
$$V = 0$$

Addressing Formats:

See Table A-1.

Addressing Modes, Execution Time, and Machine Code (hexadecimal/octal/decimal):
(DUAL OPERAND)

Addressing Modes	Execution Time (No. of cycles)	Number of bytes of machine code	Coding of First (or only) byte of machine code		
			HEX.	OCT.	DEC.
A IMM	2	2	86	206	134
A DIR	3	2	96	226	150
A EXT	4	3	B6	266	182
A IND	5	2	A6	246	166
B IMM	2	2	C6	306	198
B DIR	3	2	D6	326	214
B EXT	4	3	F6	366	246
B IND	5	2	E6	346	230

LDS

Load Stack Pointer

Operation: SPH ← (M)
SPL ← (M+1)

Description: Loads the more significant byte of the stack pointer from the byte of memory at the address specified by the program, and loads the less significant byte of the stack pointer from the next byte of memory, at one plus the address specified by the program.

Condition Codes:
- H: Not affected.
- I: Not affected.
- N: Set if the most significant bit of the stack pointer is set by the operation; cleared otherwise.
- Z: Set if all bits of the stack pointer are cleared by the operation; cleared otherwise.
- V: Cleared.
- C: Not affected.

Boolean Formulae for Condition Codes:

$$N = RH_7$$

$$Z = (\overline{RH_7} \cdot \overline{RH_6} \cdot \overline{RH_5} \cdot \overline{RH_4} \cdot \overline{RH_3} \cdot \overline{RH_2} \cdot \overline{RH_1} \cdot \overline{RH_0}) \cdot (\overline{RL_7} \cdot \overline{RL_6} \cdot \overline{RL_5} \cdot \overline{RL_4} \cdot \overline{RL_3} \cdot \overline{RL_2} \cdot \overline{RL_1} \cdot \overline{RL_0})$$

$$V = 0$$

Addressing Formats:

See Table A-5.

Addressing Modes, Execution Time, and Machine Code (hexadecimal/ octal/ decimal):

Addressing Modes	Execution Time (No. of cycles)	Number of bytes of machine code	Coding of First (or only) byte of machine code		
			HEX.	OCT.	DEC.
IMM	3	3	8E	216	142
DIR	4	2	9E	236	158
EXT	5	3	BE	276	190
IND	6	2	AE	256	174

Load Index Register **LDX**

Operation: IXH ← (M)
IXL ← (M+1)

Description: Loads the more significant byte of the index register from the byte of memory at the address specified by the program, and loads the less significant byte of the index register from the next byte of memory, at one plus the address specified by the program.

Condition Codes:
- H: Not affected.
- I: Not affected.
- N: Set if the most significant bit of the index register is set by the operation; cleared otherwise.
- Z: Set if all bits of the index register are cleared by the operation; cleared otherwise.
- V: Cleared.
- C: Not affected.

Boolean Formulae for Condition Codes:

$$N = RH_7$$
$$Z = (\overline{RH_7} \cdot \overline{RH_6} \cdot \overline{RH_5} \cdot \overline{RH_4} \cdot \overline{RH_3} \cdot \overline{RH_2} \cdot \overline{RH_1} \cdot \overline{RH_0}) \cdot (\overline{RL_7} \cdot \overline{RL_6} \cdot \overline{RL_5} \cdot \overline{RL_4} \cdot \overline{RL_3} \cdot \overline{RL_2} \cdot \overline{RL_1} \cdot \overline{RL_0})$$
$$V = 0$$

Addressing Formats:

See Table A-5.

Addressing Modes, Execution Time, and Machine Code (hexadecimal/octal/decimal):

Addressing Modes	Execution Time (No. of cycles)	Number of bytes of machine code	Coding of First (or only) byte of machine code		
			HEX.	OCT.	DEC.
IMM	3	3	CE	316	206
DIR	4	2	DE	336	222
EXT	5	3	FE	376	254
IND	6	2	EE	356	238

LSR

Logical Shift Right

Operation:

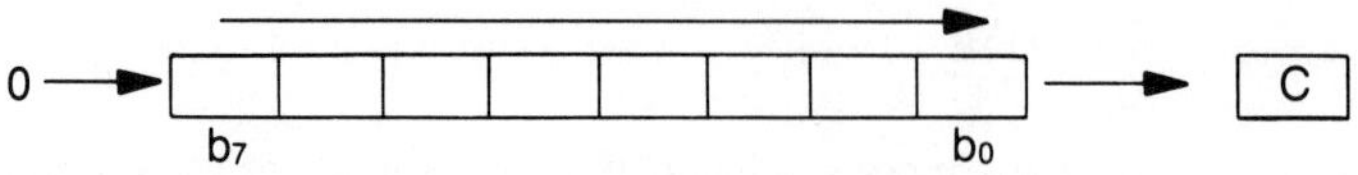

Description: Shifts all bits of ACCX or M one place to the right. Bit 7 is loaded with a zero. The C bit is loaded from the least significant bit of ACCX or M.

Condition Codes:
- H: Not affected.
- I: Not affected.
- N: Cleared.
- Z: Set if all bits of the result are cleared; cleared otherwise.
- V: Set if, after the completion of the shift operation, EITHER (N is set and C is cleared) OR (N is cleared and C is set); cleared otherwise.
- C: Set if, before the operation, the least significant bit of the ACCX or M was set; cleared otherwise.

Boolean Formulae for Condition Codes:

$N = 0$

$Z = \overline{R_7} \cdot \overline{R_6} \cdot \overline{R_5} \cdot \overline{R_4} \cdot \overline{R_3} \cdot \overline{R_2} \cdot \overline{R_1} \cdot \overline{R_0}$

$V = N \oplus C = [N \cdot \overline{C}] \odot [\overline{N} \cdot C]$

(the foregoing formula assumes values of N and C after the shift operation).

$C = M_0$

Addressing Formats:

See Table A-3.

Addressing Modes, Execution Time, and Machine Code (hexadecimal/ octal/ decimal):

Addressing Modes	Execution Time (No. of cycles)	Number of bytes of machine code	Coding of First (or only) byte of machine code		
			HEX.	OCT.	DEC.
A	2	1	44	104	068
B	2	1	54	124	084
EXT	6	3	74	164	116
IND	7	2	64	144	100

Negate **NEG**

Operation: ACCX ← − (ACCX) = 00 − (ACCX)
or: M ← − (M) = 00 − (M)

Description: Replaces the contents of ACCX or M with its two's complement. Note that 80 is left unchanged.

Condition Codes:
- H: Not affected.
- I: Not affected.
- N: Set if most significant bit of the result is set; cleared otherwise.
- Z: Set if all bits of the result are cleared; cleared otherwise.
- V: Set if there would be two's complement overflow as a result of the implied subtraction from zero; this will occur if and only if the contents of ACCX or M is 80.
- C: Set if there would be a borrow in the implied subtraction from zero; the C bit will be set in all cases except when the contents of ACCX or M is 00.

Boolean Formulae for Condition Codes:

$$N = R_7$$
$$Z = \overline{R}_7 \cdot \overline{R}_6 \cdot \overline{R}_5 \cdot \overline{R}_4 \cdot \overline{R}_3 \cdot \overline{R}_2 \cdot \overline{R}_1 \cdot \overline{R}_0$$
$$V = R_7 \cdot \overline{R}_6 \cdot \overline{R}_5 \cdot \overline{R}_4 \cdot \overline{R}_3 \cdot \overline{R}_2 \cdot \overline{R}_1 \cdot \overline{R}_0$$
$$C = R_7 + R_6 + R_5 + R_4 + R_3 + R_2 + R_1 + R_0$$

Addressing Formats:

See Table A-3.

Addressing Modes, Execution Time, and Machine Code (hexadecimal/ octal/ decimal):

Addressing Modes	Execution Time (No. of cycles)	Number of bytes of machine code	Coding of First (or only) byte of machine code		
			HEX.	OCT.	DEC.
A	2	1	40	100	064
B	2	1	50	120	080
EXT	6	3	70	160	112
IND	7	2	60	140	096

NOP

No Operation

Description: This is a single-word instruction which causes only the program counter to be incremented. No other registers are affected.

Condition Codes: Not affected.

Addressing Modes, Execution Time, and Machine Code (hexadecimal/octal/decimal):

Addressing Modes	Execution Time (No. of cycles)	Number of bytes of machine code	Coding of First (or only) byte of machine code		
			HEX.	OCT.	DEC.
INHERENT	2	1	01	001	001

ORA

Inclusive OR

Operation: ACCX ← (ACCX)⊙(M)

Description: Perform logical "OR" between the contents of ACCX and the contents of M and places the result in ACCX. (Each bit of ACCX after the operation will be the logical "OR" of the corresponding bits of M and of ACCX before the operation).

Condition Codes:
- H: Not affected.
- I: Not affected.
- N: Set if most significant bit of the result is set; cleared otherwise.
- Z: Set if all bits of the result are cleared; cleared otherwise.
- V: Cleared.
- C: Not affected.

Boolean Formulae for Condition Codes:

$N = R_7$

$Z = \overline{R_7} \cdot \overline{R_6} \cdot \overline{R_5} \cdot \overline{R_4} \cdot \overline{R_3} \cdot \overline{R_2} \cdot \overline{R_1} \cdot \overline{R_0}$

$V = 0$

Addressing Formats:

See Table A-1.

Addressing Modes, Execution Time, and Machine Code (hexadecimal/octal/decimal):

(DUAL OPERAND)

Addressing Modes	Execution Time (No. of cycles)	Number of bytes of machine code	Coding of First (or only) byte of machine code		
			HEX.	OCT.	DEC.
A IMM	2	2	8A	212	138
A DIR	3	2	9A	232	154
A EXT	4	3	BA	272	186
A IND	5	2	AA	252	170
B IMM	2	2	CA	312	202
B DIR	3	2	DA	332	218
B EXT	4	3	FA	372	250
B IND	5	2	EA	352	234

Push Data Onto Stack

PSH

Operation: ↓ (ACCX)
SP ← (SP) − 0001

Description: The contents of ACCX is stored in the stack at the address contained in the stack pointer. The stack pointer is then decremented.

Condition Codes: Not affected.

Addressing Formats:

See Table A-4.

Addressing Modes, Execution Time, and Machine Code (hexadecimal/ octal/ decimal):

Addressing Modes	Execution Time (No. of cycles)	Number of bytes of machine code	Coding of First (or only) byte of machine code		
			HEX.	OCT.	DEC.
A	4	1	36	066	054
B	4	1	37	067	055

Pull Data from Stack

PUL

Operation: SP ← (SP) + 0001
↑ ACCX

Description: The stack pointer is incremented. The ACCX is then loaded from the stack, from the address which is contained in the stack pointer.

Condition Codes: Not affected.

Addressing Formats:

See Table A-4.

Addressing Modes, Execution Time, and Machine Code (hexadecimal/ octal/ decimal):

Addressing Modes	Execution Time (No. of cycles)	Number of bytes of machine code	Coding of First (or only) byte of machine code		
			HEX.	OCT.	DEC.
A	4	1	32	062	050
B	4	1	33	063	051

ROL

Rotate Left

Operation:

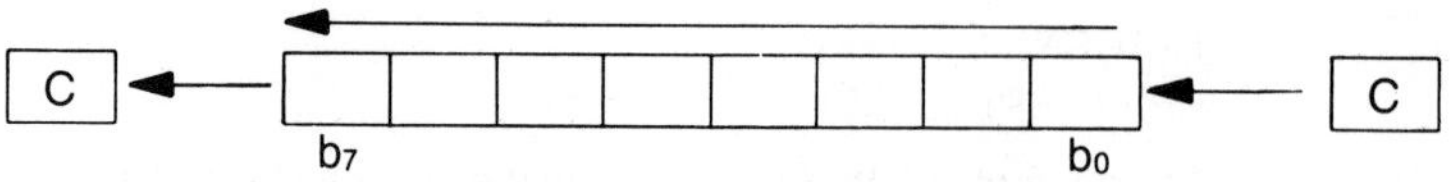

Description: Shifts all bits of ACCX or M one place to the left. Bit 0 is loaded from the C bit. The C bit is loaded from the most significant bit of ACCX or M.

Condition Codes:
- H: Not affected.
- I: Not affected.
- N: Set if most significant bit of the result is set; cleared otherwise.
- Z: Set if all bits of the result are cleared; cleared otherwise.
- V: Set if, after the completion of the operation, EITHER (N is set and C is cleared) OR (N is cleared and C is set); cleared otherwise.
- C: Set if, before the operation, the most significant bit of the ACCX or M was set; cleared otherwise.

Boolean Formulae for Condition Codes:

$N = R_7$

$Z = \overline{R_7} \cdot \overline{R_6} \cdot \overline{R_5} \cdot \overline{R_4} \cdot \overline{R_3} \cdot \overline{R_2} \cdot \overline{R_1} \cdot \overline{R_0}$

$V = N \oplus C = [N \cdot \overline{C}] \odot [\overline{N} \cdot C]$

(the foregoing formula assumes values of N and C after the rotation)

$C = M_7$

Addressing Formats:

See Table A-3

Addressing Modes, Execution Time, and Machine Code (hexadecimal/octal/decimal):

Addressing Modes	Execution Time (No. of cycles)	Number of bytes of machine code	Coding of First (or only) byte of machine code		
			HEX.	OCT.	DEC.
A	2	1	49	111	073
B	2	1	59	131	089
EXT	6	3	79	171	121
IND	7	2	69	151	105

Rotate Right **ROR**

Operation:

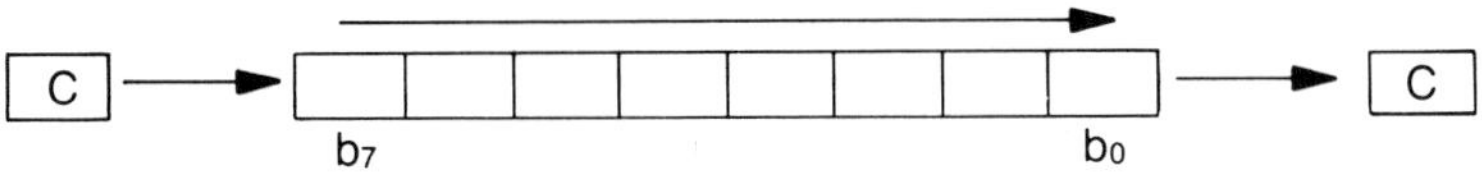

Description: Shifts all bits of ACCX or M one place to the right. Bit 7 is loaded from the C bit. The C bit is loaded from the least significant bit of ACCX or M.

Condition Codes:
H: Not affected.
I: Not affected.
N: Set if most significant bit of the result is set; cleared otherwise.
Z: Set if all bits of the result are cleared; cleared otherwise.
V: Set if, after the completion of the operation, EITHER (N is set and C is cleared) OR (N is cleared and C is set); cleared otherwise.
C: Set if, before the operation, the least significant bit of the ACCX or M was set; cleared otherwise.

Boolean Formulae for Condition Codes:

$N = R_7$

$Z = \overline{R}_7 \cdot \overline{R}_6 \cdot \overline{R}_5 \cdot \overline{R}_4 \cdot \overline{R}_3 \cdot \overline{R}_2 \cdot \overline{R}_1 \cdot \overline{R}_0$

$V = N \oplus C = [N \cdot \overline{C}] \odot [\overline{N} \cdot C]$

(the foregoing formula assumes values of N and C after the rotation)

$C = M_0$

Addressing Formats:

See Table A-3

Addressing Modes, Execution Time, and Machine Code (hexadecimal/ octal/ decimal):

Addressing Modes	Execution Time (No. of cycles)	Number of bytes of machine code	Coding of First (or only) byte of machine code		
			HEX.	OCT.	DEC.
A	2	1	46	106	070
B	2	1	56	126	086
EXT	6	3	76	166	118
IND	7	2	66	146	102

RTI

Operation:

SP ← (SP) + 0001 , ↑CC
SP ← (SP) + 0001 , ↑ACCB
SP ← (SP) + 0001 , ↑ACCA
SP ← (SP) + 0001 , ↑IXH
SP ← (SP) + 0001 , ↑IXL
SP ← (SP) + 0001 , ↑PCH
SP ← (SP) + 0001 , ↑PCL

Description: The condition codes, accumulators B and A, the index register, and the program counter, will be restored to a state pulled from the stack. Note that the interrupt mask bit will be reset if and only if the corresponding bit stored in the stack is zero.

Condition Codes: Restored to the states pulled from the stack.

Addressing Modes, Execution Time, and Machine Code (hexadecimal/ octal/ decimal):

Addressing Modes	Execution Time (No. of cycles)	Number of bytes of machine code	Coding of First (or only) byte of machine code		
			HEX.	OCT.	DEC.
INHERENT	10	1	3B	073	059

Return from Interrupt

Example

		Memory Location	Machine Code (Hex)	Label	Assembler Language Operator	Operand
A.	*Before*					
PC	→	$D066	3B		RTI	
SP	→	$EFF8				
		$EFF9	11HINZVC	(binary)		
		$EFFA	12			
		$EFFB	34			
		$EFFC	56			
		$EFFD	78			
		$EFFE	55			
		$EFFF	67			
B.	*After*					
PC	→	$5567	**		***	*****
		$EFF8				
		$EFF9	11HINZVC	(binary)		
		$EFFA	12			
		$EFFB	34			
		$EFFC	56			
		$EFFD	78			
		$EFFE	55			
SP	→	$EFFF	67			

CC = HINZVC (binary)
ACCB = 12 (Hex)   IXH = 56 (Hex)
ACCA = 34 (Hex)   IXL = 78 (Hex)

RTS

Return from Subroutine

Operation: SP ← (SP) + 0001
↑ PCH
SP ← (SP) + 0001
↑ PCL

Description: The stack pointer is incremented (by 1). The contents of the byte of memory, at the address now contained in the stack pointer, are loaded into the 8 bits of highest significance in the program counter. The stack pointer is again incremented (by 1). The contents of the byte of memory, at the address now contained in the stack pointer, are loaded into the 8 bits of lowest significiance in the program counter.

Condition Codes: Not affected.

Addressing Modes, Execution Time, and Machine Code (hexadecimal/ octal/ decimal):

Addressing Modes	Execution Time (No. of cycles)	Number of bytes of machine code	Coding of First (or only) byte of machine code		
			HEX.	OCT.	DEC.
INHERENT	5	1	39	071	057

Return from Subroutine

EXAMPLE

		Memory Location	Machine Code (Hex)	Label	Assembler Language Operator	Operand
A.	*Before*					
	PC	$30A2	39		RTS	
	SP	$EFFD				
		$EFFE	10			
		$EFFF	02			
B.	*After*					
	PC	$1002	**		***	*****
		$EFFD				
		$EFFE	10			
	SP	$EFFF	02			

SBA

Subtract Accumulators

Operation: ACCA ← (ACCA) − (ACCB)

Description: Subtracts the contents of ACCB from the contents of ACCA and places the result in ACCA. The contents of ACCB are not affected.

Condition Codes:
- H: Not affected.
- I: Not affected.
- N: Set if most significant bit of the result is set; cleared otherwise.
- Z: Set if all bits of the result are cleared; cleared otherwise.
- V: Set if there was two's complement overflow as a result of the operation.
- C: Carry is set if the absolute value of accumulator B plus previous carry is larger than the absolute value of accumulator A; reset otherwise.

Boolean Formulae for Condition Codes:

$N = R_7$

$Z = \overline{R_7} \cdot \overline{R_6} \cdot \overline{R_5} \cdot \overline{R_4} \cdot \overline{R_3} \cdot \overline{R_2} \cdot \overline{R_1} \cdot \overline{R_0}$

$V = A_7 \cdot \overline{B_7} \cdot \overline{R_7} + \overline{A_7} \cdot B_7 \cdot R_7$

$C = \overline{A_7} \cdot B_7 + B_7 \cdot R_7 + R_7 \cdot \overline{A_7}$

Addressing Modes, Execution Time, and Machine Code (hexadecimal/ octal/ decimal):

Addressing Modes	Execution Time (No. of cycles)	Number of bytes of machine code	Coding of First (or only) byte of machine code		
			HEX.	OCT.	DEC.
INHERENT	2	1	10	020	016

SBC

Subtract with Carry

Operation: ACCX ← (ACCX) − (M) − (C)

Description: Subtracts the contents of M and C from the contents of ACCX and places the result in ACCX.

Condition Codes:
- H: Not affected.
- I: Not affected.
- N: Set if most significant bit of the result is set; cleared otherwise.
- Z: Set if all bits of the result are cleared; cleared otherwise.
- V: Set if there was two's complement overflow as a result of the operation; cleared otherwise.
- C: Carry is set if the absolute value of the contents of memory plus previous carry is larger than the absolute value of the accumulator; reset otherwise.

Boolean Formulae for Condition Codes:

$$N = R_7$$
$$Z = \overline{R_7} \cdot \overline{R_6} \cdot \overline{R_5} \cdot \overline{R_4} \cdot \overline{R_3} \cdot \overline{R_2} \cdot \overline{R_1} \cdot \overline{R_0}$$
$$V = X_7 \cdot \overline{M_7} \cdot \overline{R_7} + \overline{X_7} \cdot M_7 \cdot R_7$$
$$C = \overline{X_7} \cdot M_7 + M_7 \cdot R_7 + R_7 \cdot \overline{X_7}$$

Addressing Formats:

See Table A-1.

Addressing Modes, Execution Time, and Machine Code (hexadecimal/octal/decimal):

(DUAL OPERAND)

Addressing Modes	Execution Time (No. of cycles)	Number of bytes of machine code	Coding of First (or only) byte of machine code		
			HEX.	OCT.	DEC.
A IMM	2	2	82	202	130
A DIR	3	2	92	222	146
A EXT	4	3	B2	262	178
A IND	5	2	A2	242	162
B IMM	2	2	C2	302	194
B DIR	3	2	D2	322	210
B EXT	4	3	F2	362	242
B IND	5	2	E2	342	226

SEC

Set Carry

Operation: C bit ← 1

Description: Sets the carry bit in the processor condition codes register.

Condition Codes:
H: Not affected.
I: Not affected.
N: Not affected.
Z: Not affected.
V: Not affected.
C: Set.

Boolean Formulae for Condition Codes:
C = 1

Addressing Modes, Execution Time, and Machine Code (hexadecimal/ octal/ decimal):

Addressing Modes	Execution Time (No. of cycles)	Number of bytes of machine code	Coding of First (or only) byte of machine code		
			HEX.	OCT.	DEC.
INHERENT	2	1	0D	015	013

SEI

Set Interrupt Mask

Operation: I bit ← 1

Description: Sets the interrupt mask bit in the processor condition codes register. The microprocessor is inhibited from servicing an interrupt from a peripheral device, and will continue with execution of the instructions of the program, until the interrupt mask bit has been cleared.

Condition Codes:
H: Not affected.
I: Set.
N: Not affected.
Z: Not affected.
V: Not affected.
C: Not affected.

Boolean Formulae for Condition Codes:
I = 1

Addressing Modes, Execution Time, and Machine Code (hexadecimal/ octal/ decimal):

Addressing Modes	Execution Time (No. of cycles)	Number of bytes of machine code	Coding of First (or only) byte of machine code		
			HEX.	OCT.	DEC.
INHERENT	2	1	0F	017	015

Set Two's Complement Overflow Bit **SEV**

Operation: V bit ← 1

Description: Sets the two's complement overflow bit in the processor condition codes register.

Condition Codes:
H: Not affected.
I: Not affected.
N: Not affected.
Z: Not affected.
V: Set.
C: Not affected.

Boolean Formulae for Condition Codes:
$V = 1$

Addressing Modes, Execution Time, and Machine Code (hexadecimal/octal/decimal):

Addressing Modes	Execution Time (No. of cycles)	Number of bytes of machine code	Coding of First (or only) byte of machine code		
			HEX.	OCT.	DEC.
INHERENT	2	1	0B	013	011

STA

Store Accumulator

Operation: M ← (ACCX)

Description: Stores the contents of ACCX in memory. The contents of ACCX remains unchanged.

Condition Codes:
- H: Not affected.
- I: Not affected.
- N: Set if the most significant bit of the contents of ACCX is set; cleared otherwise.
- Z: Set if all bits of the contents of ACCX are cleared; cleared otherwise.
- V: Cleared.
- C: Not affected.

Boolean Formulae for Condition Codes:

$$N = X_7$$
$$Z = \overline{X_7}\cdot\overline{X_6}\cdot\overline{X_5}\cdot\overline{X_4}\cdot\overline{X_3}\cdot\overline{X_2}\cdot\overline{X_1}\cdot\overline{X_0}$$
$$V = 0$$

Addressing Formats:

See Table A-2.

Addressing Modes, Execution Time, and Machine Code (hexadecimal/ octal/ decimal):

Addressing Modes	Execution Time (No. of cycles)	Number of bytes of machine code	Coding of First (or only) byte of machine code		
			HEX.	OCT.	DEC.
A DIR	4	2	97	227	151
A EXT	5	3	B7	267	183
A IND	6	2	A7	247	167
B DIR	4	2	D7	327	215
B EXT	5	3	F7	367	247
B IND	6	2	E7	347	231

Store Stack Pointer **STS**

Operation: $M \leftarrow (SPH)$
$M + 1 \leftarrow (SPL)$

Description: Stores the more significant byte of the stack pointer in memory at the address specified by the program, and stores the less significant byte of the stack pointer at the next location in memory, at one plus the address specified by the program.

Condition Codes:
- H: Not affected.
- I: Not affected.
- N: Set if the most significant bit of the stack pointer is set; cleared otherwise.
- Z: Set if all bits of the stack pointer are cleared; cleared otherwise.
- V: Cleared.
- C: Not affected.

Boolean Formulae for Condition Codes:

$$N = SPH_7$$

$$Z = (\overline{SPH_7} \cdot \overline{SPH_6} \cdot \overline{SPH_5} \cdot \overline{SPH_4} \cdot \overline{SPH_3} \cdot \overline{SPH_2} \cdot \overline{SPH_1} \cdot \overline{SPH_0}) \cdot (\overline{SPL_7} \cdot \overline{SPL_6} \cdot \overline{SPL_5} \cdot \overline{SPL_4} \cdot \overline{SPL_3} \cdot \overline{SPL_2} \cdot \overline{SPL_1} \cdot \overline{SPL_0})$$

$$V = 0$$

Addressing Formats:

See Table A-6.

Addressing Modes, Execution Time, and Machine Code (hexadecimal/ octal/ decimal):

Addressing Modes	Execution Time (No. of cycles)	Number of bytes of machine code	Coding of First (or only) byte of machine code		
			HEX.	OCT.	DEC.
DIR	5	2	9F	237	159
EXT	6	3	BF	277	191
IND	7	2	AF	257	175

STX

Store Index Register

Operation: $M \leftarrow (IXH)$
$M + 1 \leftarrow (IXL)$

Description: Stores the more significant byte of the index register in memory at the address specified by the program, and stores the less significant byte of the index register at the next location in memory, at one plus the address specified by the program.

Condition Codes:
- H: Not affected.
- I: Not affected.
- N: Set if the most significant bite of the index register is set; cleared otherwise.
- Z: Set if all bits of the index register are cleared; cleared otherwise.
- V: Cleared.
- C: Not affected.

Boolean Formulae for Condition Codes:

$$N = IXH_7$$
$$Z = (\overline{IXH_7} \cdot \overline{IXH_6} \cdot \overline{IXH_5} \cdot \overline{IXH_4} \cdot \overline{IXH_3} \cdot \overline{IXH_2} \cdot \overline{IXH_1} \cdot \overline{IXH_0}) \cdot (\overline{IXL_7} \cdot \overline{IXL_6} \cdot \overline{IXL_5} \cdot \overline{IXL_4} \cdot \overline{IXL_3} \cdot \overline{IXL_2} \cdot \overline{IXL_1} \cdot \overline{IXL_0})$$
$$V = 0$$

Addressing Formats:

See Table A-6.

Addressing Modes, Execution Time, and Machine Code (hexadecimal/ octal/ decimal):

Addressing Modes	Execution Time (No. of cycles)	Number of bytes of machine code	Coding of First (or only) byte of machine code		
			HEX.	OCT.	DEC.
DIR	5	2	DF	337	223
EXT	6	3	FF	377	255
IND	7	2	EF	357	239

Subtract **SUB**

Operation: ACCX ← (ACCX) − (M)

Description: Subtracts the contents of M from the contents of ACCX and places the result in ACCX.

Condition Codes:
- H: Not affected.
- I: Not affected.
- N: Set if most significant bit of the result is set; cleared otherwise.
- Z: Set if all bits of the result are cleared; cleared otherwise.
- V: Set if there was two's complement overflow as a result of the operation; cleared otherwise.
- C: Set if the absolute value of the contents of memory are larger than the absolute value of the accumulator; reset otherwise.

Boolean Formulae for Condition Codes:

$N = R_7$

$Z = \overline{R}_7 \cdot \overline{R}_6 \cdot \overline{R}_5 \cdot \overline{R}_4 \cdot \overline{R}_3 \cdot \overline{R}_2 \cdot \overline{R}_1 \cdot \overline{R}_0$

$V = X_7 \cdot \overline{M}_7 \cdot \overline{R}_7 \cdot \overline{X}_7 \cdot M_7 \cdot R_7$

$C = \overline{X}_7 \cdot M_7 + M_7 \cdot R_7 + R_7 \cdot \overline{X}_7$

Addressing Formats:

See Table A-1.

Addressing Modes, Execution Time, and Machine Code (hexadecimal/octal/decimal):

(DUAL OPERAND)

Addressing Modes	Execution Time (No. of cycles)	Number of bytes of machine code	Coding of First (or only) byte of machine code		
			HEX.	OCT.	DEC.
A IMM	2	2	80	200	128
A DIR	3	2	90	220	144
A EXT	4	3	B0	260	176
A IND	5	2	A0	240	160
B IMM	2	2	C0	300	192
B DIR	3	2	D0	320	208
B EXT	4	3	F0	360	240
B IND	5	2	E0	340	224

SWI

Software Interrupt

Operation:

PC ← (PC) + 0001
↓ (PCL) , SP ← (SP)-0001
↓ (PCH) , SP ← (SP)-0001
↓ (IXL) , SP ← (SP)-0001
↓ (IXH) , SP ← (SP)-0001
↓ (ACCA) , SP ← (SP)-0001
↓ (ACCB) , SP ← (SP)-0001
↓ (CC) , SP ← (SP)-0001
I ← 1
PCH ← (n-0005)
PCL ← (n-0004)

Description: The program counter is incremented (by 1). The program counter, index register, and accumulator A and B, are pushed into the stack. The condition codes register is then pushed into the stack, with condition codes H, I, N, Z, V, C going respectively into bit positions 5 thru 0, and the top two bits (in bit positions 7 and 6) are set (to the 1 state). The stack pointer is decremented (by 1) after each byte of data is stored in the stack.

The interrupt mask bit is then set. The program counter is then loaded with the address stored in the software interrupt pointer at memory locations (n-5) and (n-4), where n is the address corresponding to a high state on all lines of the address bus.

Condition Codes:

H: Not affected.
I: Set.
N: Not affected.
Z: Not affected.
V: Not affected.
C: Not affected.

Boolean Formula for Condition Codes:

I = 1

Addressing Modes, Execution Time, and Machine Code (hexadecimal/ octal/ decimal):

Addressing Modes	Execution Time (No. of cycles)	Number of bytes of machine code	Coding of First (or only) byte of machine code		
			HEX.	OCT.	DEC.
INHERENT	12	1	3F	077	063

Software Interrupt

EXAMPLE

A. *Before:*

CC = HINZVC (binary)

ACCB = 12 (Hex) IXH = 56 (Hex)

ACCA = 34 (Hex) IXL = 78 (Hex)

		Memory Location	Machine Code (Hex)	Label	Assembler Language Operator	Operand
PC	→	$5566	3F		SWI	
SP	→	$EFFF				
		$FFFA	D0			
		$FFFB	55			

B. *After:*

PC	→	$D055		
SP	→	$EFF8		
		$EFF9	11HINZVC	(binary)
		$EFFA	12	
		$EFFB	34	
		$EFFC	56	
		$EFFD	78	
		$EFFE	55	
		$EFFF	67	

Note: This example assumes that FFFF is the memory location addressed when all lines of the address bus go to the high state.

TAB

Transfer from Accumulator A to Accumulator B

Operation: ACCB ← (ACCA)

Description: Moves the contents of ACCA to ACCB. The former contents of ACCB are lost. The contents of ACCA are not affected.

Condition Codes:
- H: Not affected.
- I: Not affected.
- N: Set if the most significant bit of the contents of the accumulator is set; cleared otherwise.
- Z: Set if all bits of the contents of the accumulator are cleared; cleared otherwise.
- V: Cleared.
- C: Not affected.

Boolean Formulae for Condition Codes:

$N = R_7$

$Z = \overline{R_7} \cdot \overline{R_6} \cdot \overline{R_5} \cdot \overline{R_4} \cdot \overline{R_3} \cdot \overline{R_2} \cdot \overline{R_1} \cdot \overline{R_0}$

$V = 0$

Addressing Modes, Execution Time, and Machine Code (hexadecimal/ octal/ decimal):

Addressing Modes	Execution Time (No. of cycles)	Number of bytes of machine code	Coding of First (or only) byte of machine code		
			HEX.	OCT.	DEC.
INHERENT	2	1	16	026	022

Transfer from Accumulator A to Processor Condition Codes Register **TAP**

Operation: CC ← (ACCA)

Bit Positions

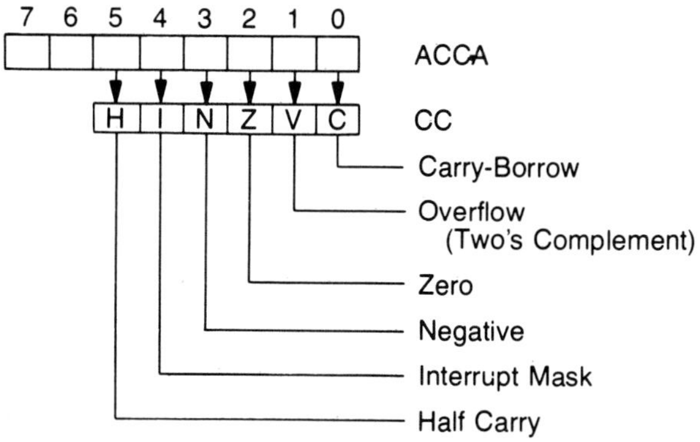

Description: Transfers the contents of bit positions 0 thru 5 of accumulator A to the corresponding bit positions of the processor condition codes register. The contents of accumulator A remain unchanged.

Condition Codes: Set or reset according to the contents of the respective bits 0 thru 5 of accumulator A.

Addressing Modes, Execution Time, and Machine Code (hexadecimal/ octal/ decimal):

Addressing Modes	Execution Time (No. of cycles)	Number of bytes of machine code	Coding of First (or only) byte of machine code		
			HEX.	OCT.	DEC.
INHERENT	2	1	06	006	006

TBA

Transfer from Accumulator B to Accumulator A

Operation: ACCA ← (ACCB)

Description: Moves the contents of ACCB to ACCA. The former contents of ACCA are lost. The contents of ACCB are not affected.

Condition Codes:
- H: Not affected.
- I: Not affected.
- N: Set if the most significant accumulator bit is set; cleared otherwise.
- Z: Set if all accumulator bits are cleared; cleared otherwise.
- V: Cleared.
- C: Not affected.

Boolean Formulae for Condition Codes:

$N = R_7$

$Z = \overline{R_7} \cdot \overline{R_6} \cdot \overline{R_5} \cdot \overline{R_4} \cdot \overline{R_3} \cdot \overline{R_2} \cdot \overline{R_1} \cdot \overline{R_0}$

$V = 0$

Addressing Modes, Execution Time, and Machine Code (hexadecimal/octal/decimal):

Addressing Modes	Execution Time (No. of cycles)	Number of bytes of machine code	Coding of First (or only) byte of machine code		
			HEX.	OCT.	DEC.
INHERENT	2	1	17	027	023

Transfer from Processor Condition Codes Register to Accumulator A

TPA

Operation: ACCA ← (CC)

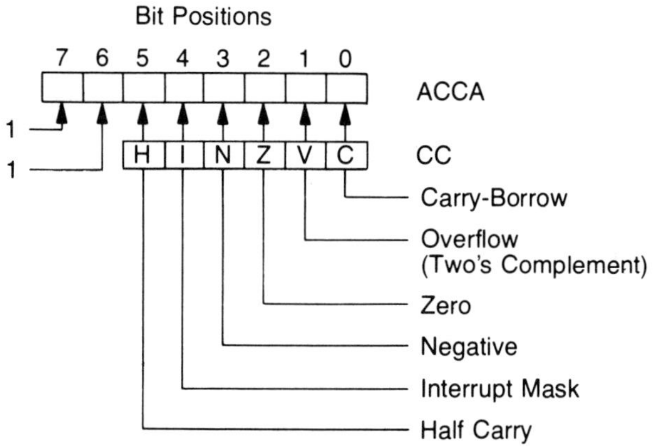

Description: Transfers the contents of the processor condition codes register to corresponding bit positions 0 thru 5 of accumulator A. Bit positions 6 and 7 of accumulator A are set (i.e. go to the "1" state). The processor condition codes register remains unchanged.

Condition Codes: Not affected.

Addressing Modes, Execution Time, and Machine Code (hexadecimal/ octal/ decimal):

Addressing Modes	Execution Time (No. of cycles)	Number of bytes of machine code	Coding of First (or only) byte of machine code		
			HEX.	OCT.	DEC.
INHERENT	2	1	07	007	007

TST

Test

Operation: (ACCX) − 00
(M) − 00

Description: Set condition codes N and Z according to the contents of ACCX or M.

Condition Codes:
H: Not affected.
I: Not affected.
N: Set if most significant bit of the contents of ACCX or M is set; cleared otherwise.
Z: Set if all bits of the contents of ACCX or M are cleared; cleared otherwise.
V: Cleared.
C: Cleared.

Boolean Formulae for Condition Codes:

$N = M_7$

$Z = \overline{M_7} \cdot \overline{M_6} \cdot \overline{M_5} \cdot \overline{M_4} \cdot \overline{M_3} \cdot \overline{M_2} \cdot \overline{M_1} \cdot \overline{M_0}$

$V = 0$

$C = 0$

Addressing Formats:

See Table A-3.

Addressing Modes, Execution Time, and Machine Code (hexadecimal/ octal/ decimal):

Addressing Modes	Execution Time (No. of cycles)	Number of bytes of machine code	Coding of First (or only) byte of machine code		
			HEX.	OCT.	DEC.
A	2	1	4D	115	077
B	2	1	5D	135	093
EXT	6	3	7D	175	125
IND	7	2	6D	155	109

Transfer from Stack Pointer to Index Register **TSX**

Operation: IX ← (SP) + 0001

Description: Loads the index register with one plus the contents of the stack pointer. The contents of the stack pointer remain unchanged.

Condition Codes: Not affected.

Addressing Modes, Execution Time, and Machine Code (hexadecimal/octal/decimal):

Addressing Modes	Execution Time (No. of cycles)	Number of bytes of machine code	Coding of First (or only) byte of machine code		
			HEX.	OCT.	DEC.
INHERENT	4	1	30	060	048

Transfer From Index Register to Stack Pointer **TXS**

Operation: SP ← (IX) − 0001

Description: Loads the stack pointer with the contents of the index register, minus one. The contents of the index register remain unchanged.

Condition Codes: Not affected.

Addressing Modes, Execution Time, and Machine Code (hexadecimal/octal/decimal):

Addressing Modes	Execution Time (No. of cycles)	Number of bytes of machine code	Coding of First (or only) byte of machine code		
			HEX.	OCT.	DEC.
INHERENT	4	1	35	.065	053

WAI

Wait for Interrupt

Operation: PC ← (PC) + 0001
↓ (PCL) , SP ← (SP)-0001
↓ (PCH) , SP ← (SP)-0001
↓ (IXL) , SP ← (SP)-0001
↓ (IXH) , SP ← (SP)-0001
↓ (ACCA) , SP ← (SP)-0001
↓ (ACCB) , SP ← (SP)-0001
↓ (CC) , SP ← (SP)-0001

Condition Codes: Not affected.

Description: The program counter is incremented (by 1). The program counter, index register, and accumulators A and B, are pushed into the stack. The condition codes register is then pushed into the stack, with condition codes H, I, N, Z, V, C going respectively into bit positions 5 thru 0, and the top two bits (in bit positions 7 and 6) are set (to the 1 state). The stack pointer is decremented (by 1) after each byte of data is stored in the stack.

Execution of the program is then suspended until an interrupt from a peripheral device is signalled, by the interrupt request control input going to a low state.

When an interrupt is signalled on the interrupt request line, and provided the I bit is clear, execution proceeds as follows. The interrupt mask bit is set. The program counter is then loaded with the address stored in the internal interrupt pointer at memory locations (n-7) and (n-6), where n is the address corresponding to a high state on all lines of the address bus.

Condition Codes:
H: Not affected.
I: Not affected until an interrupt request signal is detected on the interrupt request control line. When the interrupt request is received the I bit is set and further execution takes place, provided the I bit was initially clear.
N: Not affected.
Z: Not affected.
V: Not affected.
C: Not affected.

Addressing Modes, Execution Time, and Machine Code (hexadecimal/ octal/ decimal):

Addressing Modes	Execution Time (No. of cycles)	Number of bytes of machine code	Coding of First (or only) byte of machine code		
			HEX.	OCT.	DEC.
INHERENT	9	1	3E	076	062

Addressing Mode of Second Operand	First Operand	
	Accumulator A	Accumulator B
IMMediate	CCC A #number CCC A #symbol CCC A #expression CCC A #'C	CCC B #number CCC B #symbol CCC B #expression CCC B #'C
DIRect or EXTended	CCC A number CCC A symbol CCC A expression	CCC B number CCC B symbol CCC B expression
INDexed	CCC A X CCC Z ,X CCC A number,X CCC A symbol,X CCC A expression,X	CCC B X CCC B ,X CCC B number,X CCC B symbol,X CCC B expression,X

Notes: 1. CCC = mnemonic operator of source instruction.
2. "symbol" may be the special symbol "*".
3. "expression" may contain the special symbol "*".
4. space may be omitted before A or B.

Applicable to the following source instructions:

ADC ADD AND BIT CMP
EOR LDA ORA SBC SUB

*Special symbol indicating program-counter.

TABLE A-1. Addressing Formats (1)

Addressing Mode of Second Operand	First Operand	
	Accumulator A	Accumulator B
DIRect or EXTended	STA A number STA A symbol STA A expression	STA B number STA B symbol STA B expression
INDexed	STA A X STA A ,X STA A number,X STA A symbol,X STA A expression,X	STA B X STA B ,X STA B number,X STA B symbol,X STA B expression,X

Notes: 1. "symbol" may be the special symbol "*".
2. "expression" may contain the special symbol "*".
3. Space may be omitted before A or B.

Applicable to the source instruction:

STA

*Special symbol indicating program-counter.

TABLE A-2. Addressing Formats (2)

Operand or Addressing Mode	Formats
Accumulator A	CCC A
Accumulator B	CCC B
EXTended	CCC number CCC symbol CCC expression
INDexed	CCC X CCC ,X CCC number,X CCC symbol,X CCC expression,X

Notes: 1. CCC = mnemonic operator of source instruction.
2. "symbol" may be the special symbol "*".
3. "expression" may contain the special symbol "*".
4. Space may be omitted before A or B.

Applicable to the following source instructions:

ASL ASR CLR COM DEC INC
LSR NEG ROL ROR TST

*Special symbol indicating program-counter.

TABLE A-3. Addressing Formats (3)

Operand	Formats
Accumulator A	CCC A
Accumulator B	CCC B

Notes: 1. CCC = mnemonic operator of source instruction.
2. Space may be omitted before A or B.

Applicable to the following source instructions:

PSH PUL

TABLE A-4. Addressing Formats (4)

Addressing Mode	Formats
IMMediate	CCC #number CCC #symbol CCC #expression CCC #'C
DIRect or EXTended	CCC number CCC symbol CCC expression
INDexed	CCC X CCC ,X CCC number,X CCC symbol,X CCC expression,X

Notes: 1. CCC = mnemonic operator of source instruction.
2. "symbol" may be the special symbol "*".
3. "expression" may contain the special symbol "*".

Applicable to the following source instructions:

CPX LDS LDX

*Special symbol indicating program-counter.

TABLE A-5. Addressing Formats (5)

Addressing Mode	Formats
DIRect or EXTended	CCC number CCC symbol CCC expression
INDexed	CCC X CCC ,X CCC number,X CCC symbol,X CCC expression,X

Notes: 1. CCC = mnemonic operator of source instruction.
2. "symbol" may be the special symbol "*".
3. "expression" may contain the special symbol "*".

Applicable to the following source instructions:

STS STX

*Special symbol indicating program-counter.

TABLE A-6. Addressing Formats (6)

Addressing Mode	Formats
EXTended	CCC number CCC symbol CCC expression
INDexed	CCC X CCC ,X CCC number,X CCC symbol,X CCC expression,X

Notes: 1. CCC = mnemonic operator of source instruction.
2. "symbol" may be the special symbol "*".
3. "expression" may contain the special symbol "*".

Applicable to the following source instructions:

JMP JSR

*Special symbol indicating program-counter.

TABLE A-7. Addressing Formats (7)

Addressing Mode	Formats
RELative	CCC number CCC symbol CCC expression

Notes: 1. CCC = mnemonic operator of source instruction.
2. "symbol" may be the special symbol "*".
3. "expression" may contain the special symbol "*".

Applicable to the following source instructions:

BCC BCS BEQ BGE BGT BHI BLE BLS
BLT BMI BNE BPL BRA BSR BVC BVS

*Special symbol indicating program-counter.

TABLE A-8. Addressing Formats (8)

MOTOROLA M6809 INSTRUCTION SET

8-Bit Accumulator and Memory Instructions

Instruction	Description
ADCA, ADCB	Add memory to accumulator with carry
ADDA, ADDB	Add memory to accumulator
ANDA, ANDB	And memory with accumulator
ASL, ASLA, ASLB	Arithmetic shift of accumulator or memory left
ASR, ASRA, ASRB	Arithmetic shift of accumulator or memory right
BITA, BITB	Bit test memory with accumulator
CLR, CLRA, CLRB	Clear accumulator or memory location
CMPA, CMPB	Compare memory from accumulator
COM, COMA, COMB	Complement accumulator or memory location
DAA	Decimal adjust A accumulator
DEC, DECA, DECB	Decrement accumulator or memory location
EORA, EORB	Exclusive or memory with accumulator
EXG R1, R2	Exchange R1 with R2 (R1, R2 = A, B, CC, DP)
INC, INCA, INCB	Increment accumulator or memory location
LDA, LDB	Load accumulator from memory
LSL, LSLA, LSLB	Logical shift left accumulator or memory location
LSR, LSRA, LSRB	Logical shift right accumulator or memory location
MUL	Unsigned multiply ($A \times B \rightarrow D$)
NEG, NEGA, NEGB	Negate accumulator or memory
ORA, ORB	Or memory with accumulator
ROL, ROLA, ROLB	Rotate accumulator or memory left
ROR, RORA, RORB	Rotate accumulator or memory right
SBCA, SBCB	Subtract memory from accumulator with borrow
STA, STB	Store accumulator to memroy
SUBA, SUBB	Subtract memory from accumulator
TST, TSTA, TSTB	Test accumulator or memory location
TFR R1, R2	Transfer R1 to R2 (R1, R2 = A, B, CC, DP)

NOTE: A, B, CC, or DP may be pushed to (pulled from) either stack with PSHS, PSHU (PULS, PULU) instructions.

16-Bit Accumulator and Memory Instructions

Instruction	Description
ADDD	Add memory to D accumulator
CMPD	Compare memory from D accumulator
EXG D, R	Exchange D with X, Y, S, U, or PC
LDD	Load D accumulator from memory
SEX	Sign Extend B accumulator into A accumulator
STD	Store D accumulator to memory
SUBD	Subtract memory from D accumulator
TFR D, R	Transfer D to X, Y, S, U, or PC
TFR R, D	Transfer X, Y, S, U, or PC to D

NOTE: D may be pushed (pulled) to either stack with PSHS, PSHU (PULS, PULU) instructions.

Index/Stack Pointer Instructions

Instruction	Description
CMPS, CMPU	Compare memory from stack pointer
CMPX, CMPY	Compare memory from index register
EXG R1, R2	Exchange D, X, Y, S, U or PC with D, X, Y, S, U or PC
LEAS, LEAU	Load effective address into stack pointer
LEAX, LEAY	Load effective address into index register
LDS, LDU	Load stack pointer from memory
LDX, LDY	Load index register from memory
PSHS	Push A, B, CC, DP, D, X, Y, U, or PC onto hardware stack
PSHU	Push A, B, CC, DP, D, X, Y, X, or PC onto user stack
PULS	Pull A, B, CC, DP, D, X, Y, U, or PC from hardware stack
PULU	Pull A, B, CC, DP, D, X, Y, S, or PC from hardware stack
STS, STU	Store stack pointer to memory
STX, STY	Store index register to memory
TFR R1, R2	Transfer D, X, Y, S, U, or PC to D, X, Y, S, U, or PC
ABX	Add B accumulator to X (unsigned)

Branch Instructions

Instruction	Description
	SIMPLE BRANCHES
BEQ, LBEQ	Branch if equal
BNE, LBNE	Branch if not equal
BMI, LBMI	Branch if minus
BPL, LBPL	Branch if plus
BCS, LBCS	Branch if carry set
BCC, LBCC	Branch if carry clear
BVS, LBVS	Branch if overflow set
BVC, LBVC	Branch if overflow clear
	SIGNED BRANCHES
BGT, LBGT	Branch if greater (signed)
BVS, LBVS	Branch if invalid twos complement result
BGE, LBGE	Branch if greater than or equal (signed)
BEQ, LBEQ	Branch if equal
BNE, LBNE	Branch if not equal
BLE, LBLE	Branch if less than or equal (signed)
BVC, LBVC	Branch if valid twos complement result
BLT, LBLT	Branch if less than (signed)
	UNSIGNED BRANCHES
BHI, LBHI	Branch if higher (unsigned)
BCC, LBCC	Branch if higher or same (unsigned)
BHS, LBHS	Branch if higher or same (unsigned)
BEQ, LBEQ	Branch if equal
BNE, LBNE	Branch if not equal
BLS, LBLS	Branch if lower or same (unsigned)
BCS, LBCS	Branch if lower (unsigned)
BLO, LBLO	Branch if lower (unsigned)
	OTHER BRANCHES
BSR, LBSR	Branch to subroutine
BRA, LBRA	Branch always
BRN, LBRN	Branch never

Miscellaneous Instructions

Instruction	Description
ANDCC	AND condition code register
CWAI	AND condition code register, then wait for interrupt
NOP	No operation
ORCC	OR condition code register
JMP	Jump
JSR	Jump to subroutine
RTI	Return from interrupt
RTS	Return from subroutine
SWI, SWI2, SWI3	Software interrupt (absolute indirect)
SYNC	Synchronize with interrupt line

THE 8080 INSTRUCTION SET

The 8080 instruction set includes five different types of instructions:

- **Data Transfer Group**—move data between registers or between memory and registers
- **Arithmetic Group** – add, subtract, increment or decrement data in registers or in memory
- **Logical Group** – AND, OR, EXCLUSIVE-OR, compare, rotate or complement data in registers or in memory
- **Branch Group** – conditional and unconditional jump instructions, subroutine call instructions and return instructions
- **Stack, I/O and Machine Control Group** – includes I/O instructions, as well as instructions for maintaining the stack and internal control flags.

Instruction and Data Formats:

Memory for the 8080 is organized into 8-bit quantities, called Bytes. Each byte has a unique 16-bit binary address corresponding to its sequential position in memory.

The 8080 can directly address up to 65,536 bytes of memory, which may consist of both read-only memory (ROM) elements and random-access memory (RAM) elements (read/write memory).

Data in the 8080 is stored in the form of 8-bit binary integers:

DATA WORD

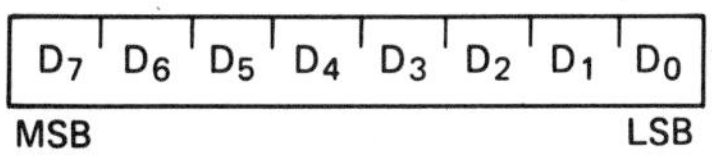

When a register or data word contains a binary number, it is necessary to establish the order in which the bits of the number are written. In the Intel 8080, BIT 0 is referred to as the **Least Significant Bit (LSB)**, and BIT 7 (of an 8 bit number) is referred to as the **Most Significant Bit (MSB)**.

The 8080 program instructions may be one, two or three bytes in length. Multiple byte instructions must be stored in successive memory locations; the address of the first byte is always used as the address of the instructions. The exact instruction format will depend on the particular operation to be executed.

Single Byte Instructions

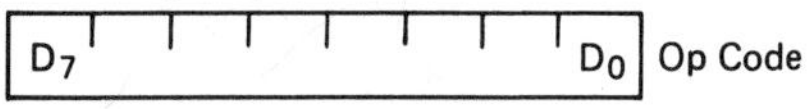

Two-Byte Instructions

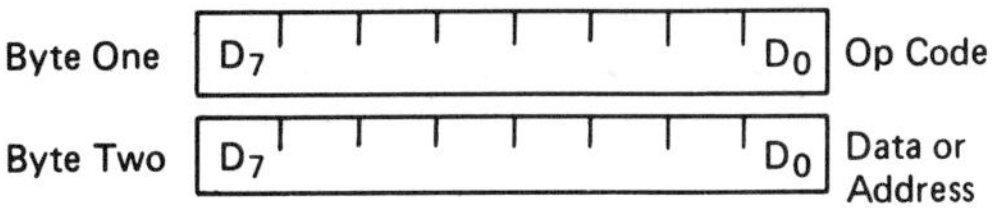

Three-Byte Instructions

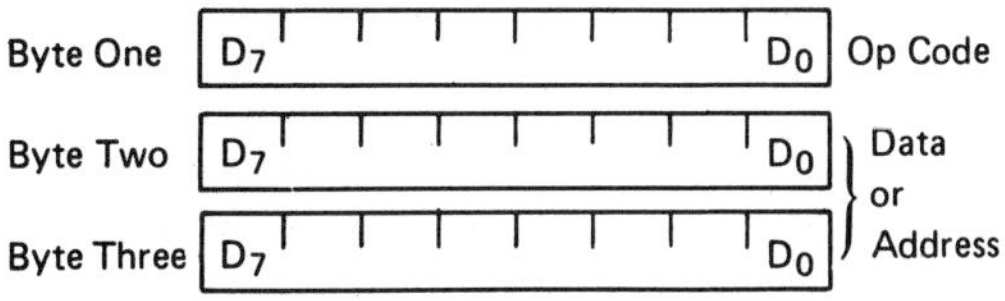

Addressing Modes:

Often the data that is to be operated on is stored in memory. When multi-byte numeric data is used, the data, like instructions, is stored in successive memory locations, with the least significant byte first, followed by increasingly significant bytes. The 8080 has four different modes for addressing data stored in memory or in registers:

- Direct – Bytes 2 and 3 of the instruction contain the exact memory address of the data item (the low-order bits of the address are in byte 2, the high-order bits in byte 3).
- Register – The instruction specifies the register or register-pair in which the data is located.
- Register Indirect – The instruction specifies a register-pair which contains the memory address where the data is located (the high-order bits of the address are in the first register of the pair, the low-order bits in the second).
- Immediate – The instruction contains the data itself. This is either an 8-bit quantity or a 16-bit quantity (least significant byte first, most significant byte second).

Unless directed by an interrupt or branch instruction, the execution of instructions proceeds through consecutively increasing memory locations. A branch instruction can specify the address of the next instruction to be executed in one of two ways:

- Direct – The branch instruction contains the address of the next instruction to be executed. (Except for the 'RST' instruction, byte 2 contains the low-order address and byte 3 the high-order address.)
- Register indirect – The branch instruction indicates a register-pair which contains the address of the next instruction to be executed. (The high-order bits of the address are in the first register of the pair, the low-order bits in the second.)

The RST instruction is a special one-byte call instruction (usually used during interrupt sequences). RST includes a three-bit field; program control is transferred to the instruction whose address is eight times the contents of this three-bit field.

Condition Flags:

There are five condition flags associated with the execution of instructions on the 8080. They are Zero, Sign, Parity, Carry, and Auxiliary Carry, and are each represented by a 1-bit register in the CPU. A flag is "set" by forcing the bit to 1; "reset" by forcing the bit to 0.

Unless indicated otherwise, when an instruction affects a flag, it affects it in the following manner:

Zero: If the result of an instruction has the value 0, this flag is set; otherwise it is reset.

Sign: If the most significant bit of the result of the operation has the value 1, this flag is set; otherwise it is reset.

Parity: If the modulo 2 sum of the bits of the result of the operation is 0, (i.e., if the result has even parity), this flag is set; otherwise it is reset (i.e., if the result has odd parity).

Carry: If the instruction resulted in a carry (from addition), or a borrow (from subtraction or a comparison) out of the high-order bit, this flag is set; otherwise it is reset.

Auxiliary Carry: If the instruction caused a carry out of bit 3 and into bit 4 of the resulting value, the auxiliary carry is set; otherwise it is reset. This flag is affected by single precision additions, subtractions, increments, decrements, comparisons, and logical operations, but is principally used with additions and increments preceding a DAA (Decimal Adjust Accumulator) instruction.

Symbols and Abbreviations:

The following symbols and abbreviations are used in the subsequent description of the 8080 instructions:

SYMBOLS	MEANING
accumulator	Register A
addr	16-bit address quantity
data	8-bit data quantity
data 16	16-bit data quantity
byte 2	The second byte of the instruction
byte 3	The third byte of the instruction
port	8-bit address of an I/O device
r,r1,r2	One of the registers A,B,C,D,E,H,L
DDD,SSS	The bit pattern designating one of the registers A,B,C,D,E,H,L (DDD=destination, SSS=source):

DDD or SSS	REGISTER NAME
111	A
000	B
001	C
010	D
011	E
100	H
101	L

rp — One of the register pairs:

B represents the B,C pair with B as the high-order register and C as the low-order register;

D represents the D,E pair with D as the high-order register and E as the low-order register;

H represents the H,L pair with H as the high-order register and L as the low-order register;

SP represents the 16-bit stack pointer register.

RP — The bit pattern designating one of the register pairs B,D,H,SP:

RP	REGISTER PAIR
00	B-C
01	D-E
10	H-L
11	SP

rh	The first (high-order) register of a designated register pair.
rl	The second (low-order) register of a designated register pair.
PC	16-bit program counter register (PCH and PCL are used to refer to the high-order and low-order 8 bits respectively).
SP	16-bit stack pointer register (SPH and SPL are used to refer to the high-order and low-order 8 bits respectively).
r_m	Bit m of the register r (bits are number 7 through 0 from left to right).
Z,S,P,CY,AC	The condition flags: Zero, Sign, Parity, Carry, and Auxiliary Carry, respectively.

( )	The contents of the memory location or registers enclosed in the parentheses.
$\leftarrow$	"Is transferred to"
$\wedge$	Logical AND
$\forall$	Exclusive OR
$\vee$	Inclusive OR
+	Addition
−	Two's complement subtraction
*	Multiplication
$\leftrightarrow$	"Is exchanged with"
—	The one's complement (e.g., $(\overline{A})$)
n	The restart number 0 through 7
NNN	The binary representation 000 through 111 for restart number 0 through 7 respectively.

Description Format:

The following pages provide a detailed description of the instruction set of the 8080. Each instruction is described in the following manner:

1. The MAC 80 assembler format, consisting of the instruction mnemonic and operand fields, is printed in **BOLDFACE** on the left side of the first line.
2. The name of the instruction is enclosed in parenthesis on the right side of the first line.
3. The next line(s) contain a symbolic description of the operation of the instruction.
4. This is followed by a narative description of the operation of the instruction.
5. The following line(s) contain the binary fields and patterns that comprise the machine instruction.
6. The last four lines contain incidental information about the execution of the instruction. The number of machine cycles and states required to execute the instruction are listed first. If the instruction has two possible execution times, as in a Conditional Jump, both times will be listed, separated by a slash. Next, any significant data addressing modes (see Page 4-2) are listed. The last line lists any of the five Flags that are affected by the execution of the instruction.

Data Transfer Group:

This group of instructions transfers data to and from registers and memory. **Condition flags are not affected** by any instruction in this group.

MOV r1, r2 (Move Register)

(r1) $\leftarrow$ (r2)

The content of register r2 is moved to register r1.

0	1	D	D	D	S	S	S

Cycles: 1
States: 5
Addressing: register
Flags: none

MOV r, M (Move from memory)

(r) $\leftarrow$ ((H) (L))

The content of the memory location, whose address is in registers H and L, is moved to register r.

0	1	D	D	D	1	1	0

Cycles: 2
States: 7
Addressing: reg. indirect
Flags: none

MOV M, r (Move to memory)

((H) (L)) $\leftarrow$ (r)

The content of register r is moved to the memory location whose address is in registers H and L.

0	1	1	1	0	S	S	S

Cycles: 2
States: 7
Addressing: reg. indirect
Flags: none

MVI r, data (Move Immediate)

(r) $\leftarrow$ (byte 2)

The content of byte 2 of the instruction is moved to register r.

0	0	D	D	D	1	1	0
data							

Cycles: 2
States: 7
Addressing: immediate
Flags: none

MVI M, data (Move to memory immediate)

((H) (L)) ← (byte 2)

The content of byte 2 of the instruction is moved to the memory location whose address is in registers H and L.

0	0	1	1	0	1	1	0
data							

Cycles: 3
States: 10
Addressing: immed./reg. indirect
Flags: none

STA addr (Store Accumulator direct)

((byte 3)(byte 2)) ← (A)

The content of the accumulator is moved to the memory location whose address is specified in byte 2 and byte 3 of the instruction.

0	0	1	1	0	0	1	0
low-order addr							
high-order addr							

Cycles: 4
States: 13
Addressing: direct
Flags: none

LXI rp, data 16 (Load register pair immediate)

(rh) ← (byte 3),
(rl) ← (byte 2)

Byte 3 of the instruction is moved into the high-order register (rh) of the register pair rp. Byte 2 of the instruction is moved into the low-order register (rl) of the register pair rp.

0	0	R	P	0	0	0	1
low-order data							
high-order data							

Cycles: 3
States: 10
Addressing: immediate
Flags: none

LHLD addr (Load H and L direct)

(L) ← ((byte 3)(byte 2))
(H) ← ((byte 3)(byte 2) + 1)

The content of the memory location, whose address is specified in byte 2 and byte 3 of the instruction, is moved to register L. The content of the memory location at the succeeding address is moved to register H.

0	0	1	0	1	0	1	0
low-order addr							
high-order addr							

Cycles: 5
States: 16
Addressing: direct
Flags: none

LDA addr (Load Accumulator direct)

(A) ← ((byte 3)(byte 2))

The content of the memory location, whose address is specified in byte 2 and byte 3 of the instruction, is moved to register A.

0	0	1	1	1	0	1	0
low-order addr							
high-order addr							

Cycles: 4
States: 13
Addressing: direct
Flags: none

SHLD addr (Store H and L direct)

((byte 3)(byte 2)) ← (L)
((byte 3)(byte 2) + 1) ← (H)

The content of register L is moved to the memory location whose address is specified in byte 2 and byte 3. The content of register H is moved to the succeeding memory location.

0	0	1	0	0	0	1	0
low-order addr							
high-order addr							

Cycles: 5
States: 16
Addressing: direct
Flags: none

LDAX rp (Load accumulator indirect)

(A) ← ((rp))

The content of the memory location, whose address is in the register pair rp, is moved to register A. Note: only register pairs rp=B (registers B and C) or rp=D (registers D and E) may be specified.

0	0	R	P	1	0	1	0

Cycles: 2
States: 7
Addressing: reg. indirect
Flags: none

STAX rp (Store accumulator indirect)

((rp)) ← (A)

The content of register A is moved to the memory location whose address is in the register pair rp. Note: only register pairs rp=B (registers B and C) or rp=D (registers D and E) may be specified.

0	0	R	P	0	0	1	0

Cycles: 2
States: 7
Addressing: reg. indirect
Flags: none

XCHG (Exchange H and L with D and E)

(H) ↔ (D)
(L) ↔ (E)

The contents of registers H and L are exchanged with the contents of registers D and E.

1	1	1	0	1	0	1	1

Cycles: 1
States: 4
Addressing: register
Flags: none

Arithmetic Group:

This group of instructions performs arithmetic operations on data in registers and memory.

Unless indicated otherwise, all instructions in this group affect the Zero, Sign, Parity, Carry, and Auxiliary Carry flags according to the standard rules.

All subtraction operations are performed via two's complement arithmetic and set the carry flag to one to indicate a borrow and clear it to indicate no borrow.

ADD r (Add Register)

(A) ← (A) + (r)

The content of register r is added to the content of the accumulator. The result is placed in the accumulator.

1	0	0	0	0	S	S	S

Cycles: 1
States: 4
Addressing: register
Flags: Z,S,P,CY,AC

ADD M (Add memory)

(A) ← (A) + ((H) (L))

The content of the memory location whose address is contained in the H and L registers is added to the content of the accumulator. The result is placed in the accumulator.

1	0	0	0	0	1	1	0

Cycles: 2
States: 7
Addressing: reg. indirect
Flags: Z,S,P,CY,AC

ADI data (Add immediate)

(A) ← (A) + (byte 2)

The content of the second byte of the instruction is added to the content of the accumulator. The result is placed in the accumulator.

1	1	0	0	0	1	1	0
data							

Cycles: 2
States: 7
Addressing: immediate
Flags: Z,S,P,CY,AC

ADC r (Add Register with carry)

(A) ← (A) + (r) + (CY)

The content of register r and the content of the carry bit are added to the content of the accumulator. The result is placed in the accumulator.

1	0	0	0	1	S	S	S

Cycles: 1
States: 4
Addressing: register
Flags: Z,S,P,CY,AC

ADC M (Add memory with carry)

(A) ← (A) + ((H) (L)) + (CY)

The content of the memory location whose address is contained in the H and L registers and the content of the CY flag are added to the accumulator. The result is placed in the accumulator.

1	0	0	0	1	1	1	0

Cycles: 2
States: 7
Addressing: reg. indirect
Flags: Z,S,P,CY,AC

SUB M (Subtract memory)

(A) ← (A) – ((H) (L))

The content of the memory location whose address is contained in the H and L registers is subtracted from the content of the accumulator. The result is placed in the accumulator.

1	0	0	1	0	1	1	0

Cycles: 2
States: 7
Addressing: reg. indirect
Flags: Z,S,P,CY,AC

ACI data (Add immediate with carry)

(A) ← (A) + (byte 2) + (CY)

The content of the second byte of the instruction and the content of the CY flag are added to the contents of the accumulator. The result is placed in the accumulator.

1	1	0	0	1	1	1	0
data							

Cycles: 2
States: 7
Addressing: immediate
Flags: Z,S,P,CY,AC

SUI data (Subtract immediate)

(A) ← (A) – (byte 2)

The content of the second byte of the instruction is subtracted from the content of the accumulator. The result is placed in the accumulator.

1	1	0	1	0	1	1	0
data							

Cycles: 2
States: 7
Addressing: immediate
Flags: Z,S,P,CY,AC

SUB r (Subtract Register)

(A) ← (A) – (r)

The content of register r is subtracted from the content of the accumulator. The result is placed in the accumulator.

1	0	0	1	0	S	S	S

Cycles: 1
States: 4
Addressing: register
Flags: Z,S,P,CY,AC

SBB r (Subtract Register with borrow)

(A) ← (A) – (r) – (CY)

The content of register r and the content of the CY flag are both subtracted from the accumulator. The result is placed in the accumulator.

1	0	0	1	1	S	S	S

Cycles: 1
States: 4
Addressing: register
Flags: Z,S,P,CY,AC

SBB M (Subtract memory with borrow)

(A) ← (A) – ((H) (L)) – (CY)

The content of the memory location whose address is contained in the H and L registers and the content of the CY flag are both subtracted from the accumulator. The result is placed in the accumulator.

1	0	0	1	1	1	1	0

Cycles: 2
States: 7
Addressing: reg. indirect
Flags: Z,S,P,CY,AC

SBI data (Subtract immediate with borrow)

(A) ← (A) – (byte 2) – (CY)

The contents of the second byte of the instruction and the contents of the CY flag are both subtracted from the accumulator. The result is placed in the accumulator.

1	1	0	1	1	1	1	0
data							

Cycles: 2
States: 7
Addressing: immediate
Flags: Z,S,P,CY,AC

INR r (Increment Register)

(r) ← (r) + 1

The content of register r is incremented by one. Note: All condition flags **except CY** are affected.

0	0	D	D	D	1	0	0

Cycles: 1
States: 5
Addressing: register
Flags: Z,S,P,AC

INR M (Increment memory)

((H) (L)) ← ((H) (L)) + 1

The content of the memory location whose address is contained in the H and L registers is incremented by one. Note: All condition flags **except CY** are affected.

0	0	1	1	0	1	0	0

Cycles: 3
States: 10
Addressing: reg. indirect
Flags: Z,S,P,AC

DCR r (Decrement Register)

(r) ← (r) – 1

The content of register r is decremented by one. Note: All condition flags **except CY** are affected.

0	0	D	D	D	1	0	1

Cycles: 1
States: 5
Addressing: register
Flags: Z,S,P,AC

DCR M (Decrement memory)

((H) (L)) ← ((H) (L)) – 1

The content of the memory location whose address is contained in the H and L registers is decremented by one. Note: All condition flags **except CY** are affected.

0	0	1	1	0	1	0	1

Cycles: 3
States: 10
Addressing: reg. indirect
Flags: Z,S,P,AC

INX rp (Increment register pair)

(rh) (rl) ← (rh) (rl) + 1

The content of the register pair rp is incremented by one. Note: **No condition flags are affected.**

0	0	R	P	0	0	1	1

Cycles: 1
States: 5
Addressing: register
Flags: none

DCX rp (Decrement register pair)

(rh) (rl) ← (rh) (rl) – 1

The content of the register pair rp is decremented by one. Note: **No condition flags are affected.**

0	0	R	P	1	0	1	1

Cycles: 1
States: 5
Addressing: register
Flags: none

DAD rp (Add register pair to H and L)

(H) (L) ← (H) (L) + (rh) (rl)

The content of the register pair rp is added to the content of the register pair H and L. The result is placed in the register pair H and L. Note: **Only the CY flag is affected.** It is set if there is a carry out of the double precision add; otherwise it is reset.

0	0	R	P	1	0	0	1

Cycles: 3
States: 10
Addressing: register
Flags: CY

DAA (Decimal Adjust Accumulator)

The eight-bit number in the accumulator is adjusted to form two four-bit Binary-Coded-Decimal digits by the following process:

1. If the value of the least significant 4 bits of the accumulator is greater than 9 **or** if the AC flag is set, 6 is added to the accumulator.
2. If the value of the most significant 4 bits of the accumulator is now greater than 9, **or** if the CY flag is set, 6 is added to the most significant 4 bits of the accumulator.

NOTE: All flags are affected.

0	0	1	0	0	1	1	1

Cycles: 1
States: 4
Flags: Z,S,P,CY,AC

Logical Group:

This group of instructions performs logical (Boolean) operations on data in registers and memory and on condition flags.

Unless indicated otherwise, all instructions in this group affect the Zero, Sign, Parity, Auxiliary Carry, and Carry flags according to the standard rules.

ANA r (AND Register)

(A) ← (A) $\wedge$ (r)

The content of register r is logically anded with the content of the accumulator. The result is placed in the accumulator. **The CY flag is cleared.**

1	0	1	0	0	S	S	S

Cycles: 1
States: 4
Addressing: register
Flags: Z,S,P,CY,AC

ANA M (AND memory)

(A) ← (A) $\wedge$ ((H) (L))

The contents of the memory location whose address is contained in the H and L registers is logically anded with the content of the accumulator. The result is placed in the accumulator. **The CY flag is cleared.**

1	0	1	0	0	1	1	0

Cycles: 2
States: 7
Addressing: reg. indirect
Flags: Z,S,P,CY,AC

ANI data (AND immediate)

(A) ← (A) $\wedge$ (byte 2)

The content of the second byte of the instruction is logically anded with the contents of the accumulator. The result is placed in the accumulator. **The CY and AC flags are cleared.**

1	1	1	0	0	1	1	0
data							

Cycles: 2
States: 7
Addressing: immediate
Flags: Z,S,P,CY,AC

XRA r (Exclusive OR Register)

(A) ← (A) $\forall$ (r)

The content of register r is exclusive-or'd with the content of the accumulator. The result is placed in the accumulator. **The CY and AC flags are cleared.**

1	0	1	0	1	S	S	S

Cycles: 1
States: 4
Addressing: register
Flags: Z,S,P,CY,AC

XRA M (Exclusive OR Memory)

$(A) \leftarrow (A) \forall ((H)\ (L))$

The content of the memory location whose address is contained in the H and L registers is exclusive-OR'd with the content of the accumulator. The result is placed in the accumulator. **The CY and AC flags are cleared.**

1	0	1	0	1	1	1	0

Cycles: 2
States: 7
Addressing: reg. indirect
Flags: Z,S,P,CY,AC

XRI data (Exclusive OR immediate)

$(A) \leftarrow (A) \forall (\text{byte } 2)$

The content of the second byte of the instruction is exclusive-OR'd with the content of the accumulator. The result is placed in the accumulator. **The CY and AC flags are cleared.**

1	1	1	0	1	1	1	0
data							

Cycles: 2
States: 7
Addressing: immediate
Flags: Z,S,P,CY,AC

ORA r (OR Register)

$(A) \leftarrow (A)\ V\ (r)$

The content of register r is inclusive-OR'd with the content of the accumulator. The result is placed in the accumulator. **The CY and AC flags are cleared.**

1	0	1	1	0	S	S	S

Cycles: 1
States: 4
Addressing: register
Flags: Z,S,P,CY,AC

ORA M (OR memory)

$(A) \leftarrow (A)\ V\ ((H)\ (L))$

The content of the memory location whose address is contained in the H and L registers is inclusive-OR'd with the content of the accumulator. The result is placed in the accumulator. **The CY and AC flags are cleared.**

1	0	1	1	0	1	1	0

Cycles: 2
States: 7
Addressing: reg. indirect
Flags: Z,S,P,CY,AC

ORI data (OR Immediate)

$(A) \leftarrow (A)\ V\ (\text{byte } 2)$

The content of the second byte of the instruction is inclusive-OR'd with the content of the accumulator. The result is placed in the accumulator. **The CY and AC flags are cleared.**

1	1	1	1	0	1	1	0
data							

Cycles: 2
States: 7
Addressing: immediate
Flags: Z,S,P,CY,AC

CMP r (Compare Register)

$(A) - (r)$

The content of register r is subtracted from the accumulator. The accumulator remains unchanged. The condition flags are set as a result of the subtraction. **The Z flag is set to 1 if $(A) = (r)$. The CY flag is set to 1 if $(A) < (r)$.**

1	0	1	1	1	S	S	S

Cycles: 1
States: 4
Addressing: register
Flags: Z,S,P,CY,AC

CMP M (Compare memory)

(A) – ((H) (L))

The content of the memory location whose address is contained in the H and L registers is subtracted from the accumulator. The accumulator remains unchanged. The condition flags are set as a result of the subtraction. The Z flag is set to 1 if (A) = ((H) (L)). The CY flag is set to 1 if (A) < ((H) (L)).

1	0	1	1	1	1	1	0

Cycles: 2
States: 7
Addressing: reg. indirect
Flags: Z,S,P,CY,AC

CPI data (Compare immediate)

(A) – (byte 2)

The content of the second byte of the instruction is subtracted from the accumulator. The condition flags are set by the result of the subtraction. The Z flag is set to 1 if (A) = (byte 2). The CY flag is set to 1 if (A) < (byte 2).

1	1	1	1	1	1	1	0
data							

Cycles: 2
States: 7
Addressing: immediate
Flags: Z,S,P,CY,AC

RLC (Rotate left)

$(A_{n+1}) \leftarrow (A_n)$; $(A_0) \leftarrow (A_7)$
$(CY) \leftarrow (A_7)$

The content of the accumulator is rotated left one position. The low order bit and the CY flag are both set to the value shifted out of the high order bit position. **Only the CY flag is affected.**

0	0	0	0	0	1	1	1

Cycles: 1
States: 4
Flags: CY

RRC (Rotate right)

$(A_n) \leftarrow (A_{n-1})$; $(A_7) \leftarrow (A_0)$
$(CY) \leftarrow (A_0)$

The content of the accumulator is rotated right one position. The high order bit and the CY flag are both set to the value shifted out of the low order bit position. **Only the CY flag is affected.**

0	0	0	0	1	1	1	1

Cycles: 1
States: 4
Flags: CY

RAL (Rotate left through carry)

$(A_{n+1}) \leftarrow (A_n)$; $(CY) \leftarrow (A_7)$
$(A_0) \leftarrow (CY)$

The content of the accumulator is rotated left one position through the CY flag. The low order bit is set equal to the CY flag and the CY flag is set to the value shifted out of the high order bit. **Only the CY flag is affected.**

0	0	0	1	0	1	1	1

Cycles: 1
States: 4
Flags: CY

RAR (Rotate right through carry)

$(A_n) \leftarrow (A_{n+1})$; $(CY) \leftarrow (A_0)$
$(A_7) \leftarrow (CY)$

The content of the accumulator is rotated right one position through the CY flag. The high order bit is set to the CY flag and the CY flag is set to the value shifted out of the low order bit. **Only the CY flag is affected.**

0	0	0	1	1	1	1	1

Cycles: 1
States: 4
Flags: CY

CMA (Complement accumulator)

$(A) \leftarrow (\overline{A})$

The contents of the accumulator are complemented (zero bits become 1, one bits become 0). **No flags are affected.**

0	0	1	0	1	1	1	1

Cycles: 1
States: 4
Flags: none

CMC (Complement carry)

(CY) ← $(\overline{CY})$

The CY flag is complemented. **No other flags are affected.**

0	0	1	1	1	1	1	1

Cycles: 1
States: 4
Flags: CY

STC (Set carry)

(CY) ← 1

The CY flag is set to 1. **No other flags are affected.**

0	0	1	1	0	1	1	1

Cycles: 1
States: 4
Flags: CY

Branch Group:

This group of instructions alter normal sequential program flow.

Condition flags are not affected by any instruction in this group.

The two types of branch instructions are unconditional and conditional. Unconditional transfers simply perform the specified operation on register PC (the program counter). Conditional transfers examine the status of one of the four processor flags to determine if the specified branch is to be executed. The conditions that may be specified are as follows:

CONDITION		CCC
NZ	– not zero (Z = 0)	000
Z	– zero (Z = 1)	001
NC	– no carry (CY = 0)	010
C	– carry (CY = 1)	011
PO	– parity odd (P = 0)	100
PE	– parity even (P = 1)	101
P	– plus (S = 0)	110
M	– minus (S = 1)	111

JMP addr (Jump)

(PC) ← (byte 3) (byte 2)

Control is transferred to the instruction whose address is specified in byte 3 and byte 2 of the current instruction.

1	1	0	0	0	0	1	1
low-order addr							
high-order addr							

Cycles: 3
States: 10
Addressing: immediate
Flags: none

Jcondition addr (Conditional jump)

If (CCC),

(PC) ← (byte 3) (byte 2)

If the specified condition is true, control is transferred to the instruction whose address is specified in byte 3 and byte 2 of the current instruction; otherwise, control continues sequentially.

1	1	C	C	C	0	1	0
low-order addr							
high-order addr							

Cycles: 3
States: 10
Addressing: immediate
Flags: none

CALL addr (Call)

((SP) – 1) ← (PCH)

((SP) – 2) ← (PCL)

(SP) ← (SP) – 2

(PC) ← (byte 3) (byte 2)

The high-order eight bits of the next instruction address are moved to the memory location whose address is one less than the content of register SP. The low-order eight bits of the next instruction address are moved to the memory location whose address is two less than the content of register SP. The content of register SP is decremented by 2. Control is transferred to the instruction whose address is specified in byte 3 and byte 2 of the current instruction.

1	1	0	0	1	1	0	1
low-order addr							
high-order addr							

Cycles: 5
States: 17
Addressing: immediate/reg. indirect
Flags: none

Ccondition addr (Condition call)

If (CCC),

((SP) − 1) ← (PCH)

((SP) − 2) ← (PCL)

(SP) ← (SP) − 2

(PC) ← (byte 3) (byte 2)

If the specified condition is true, the actions specified in the CALL instruction (see above) are performed; otherwise, control continues sequentially.

1	1	C	C	C	1	0	0
low-order addr							
high-order addr							

Cycles: 3/5
States: 11/17
Addressing: immediate/reg. indirect
Flags: none

RET (Return)

(PCL) ← ((SP));

(PCH) ← ((SP) + 1);

(SP) ← (SP) + 2;

The content of the memory location whose address is specified in register SP is moved to the low-order eight bits of register PC. The content of the memory location whose address is one more than the content of register SP is moved to the high-order eight bits of register PC. The content of register SP is incremented by 2.

1	1	0	0	1	0	0	1

Cycles: 3
States: 10
Addressing: reg. indirect
Flags: none

Rcondition (Conditional return)

If (CCC),

(PCL) ← ((SP))

(PCH) ← ((SP) + 1)

(SP) ← (SP) + 2

If the specified condition is true, the actions specified in the RET instruction (see above) are performed; otherwise, control continues sequentially.

1	1	C	C	C	0	0	0

Cycles: 1/3
States: 5/11
Addressing: reg. indirect
Flags: none

RST n (Restart)

((SP) − 1) ← (PCH)

((SP) − 2) ← (PCL)

(SP) ← (SP) − 2

(PC) ← 8 * (NNN)

The high-order eight bits of the next instruction address are moved to the memory location whose address is one less than the content of register SP. The low-order eight bits of the next instruction address are moved to the memory location whose address is two less than the content of register SP. The content of register SP is decremented by two. Control is transferred to the instruction whose address is eight times the content of NNN.

1	1	N	N	N	1	1	1

Cycles: 3
States: 11
Addressing: reg. indirect
Flags: none

15	14	13	12	11	10	9	8	7	6	5	4	3	2	1	0
0	0	0	0	0	0	0	0	0	0	N	N	N	0	0	0

Program Counter After Restart

PCHL (Jump H and L indirect – move H and L to PC)

(PCH) ← (H)

(PCL) ← (L)

The content of register H is moved to the high-order eight bits of register PC. The content of register L is moved to the low-order eight bits of register PC.

1	1	1	0	1	0	0	1

Cycles: 1
States: 5
Addressing: register
Flags: none

Stack, I/O, and Machine Control Group:

This group of instructions performs I/O, manipulates the Stack, and alters internal control flags.

Unless otherwise specified, **condition flags are not affected by any instructions in this group.**

FLAG WORD

D_7	D_6	D_5	D_4	D_3	D_2	D_1	D_0
S	Z	0	AC	0	P	1	CY

PUSH rp (Push)

((SP) – 1) ← (rh)
((SP) – 2) ← (rl)
(SP) ← (SP) – 2

The content of the high-order register of register pair rp is moved to the memory location whose address is one less than the content of register SP. The content of the low-order register of register pair rp is moved to the memory location whose address is two less than the content of register SP. The content of register SP is decremented by 2. **Note: Register pair rp = SP may not be specified.**

1	1	R	P	0	1	0	1

Cycles: 3
States: 11
Addressing: reg. indirect
Flags: none

POP rp (Pop)

(rl) ← ((SP))
(rh) ← ((SP) + 1)
(SP) ← (SP) + 2

The content of the memory location, whose address is specified by the content of register SP, is moved to the low-order register of register pair rp. The content of the memory location, whose address is one more than the content of register SP, is moved to the high-order register of register pair rp. The content of register SP is incremented by 2. **Note: Register pair rp = SP may not be specified.**

1	1	R	P	0	0	0	1

Cycles: 3
States: 10
Addressing: reg. indirect
Flags: none

PUSH PSW (Push processor status word)

((SP) – 1) ← (A)
$((SP) - 2)_0$ ← (CY), $((SP) - 2)_1$ ← 1
$((SP) - 2)_2$ ← (P), $((SP) - 2)_3$ ← 0
$((SP) - 2)_4$ ← (AC), $((SP) - 2)_5$ ← 0
$((SP) - 2)_6$ ← (Z), $((SP) - 2)_7$ ← (S)
(SP) ← (SP) – 2

The content of register A is moved to the memory location whose address is one less than register SP. The contents of the condition flags are assembled into a processor status word and the word is moved to the memory location whose address is two less than the content of register SP. The content of register SP is decremented by two.

1	1	1	1	0	1	0	1

Cycles: 3
States: 11
Addressing: reg. indirect
Flags: none

POP PSW (Pop processor status word)

(CY) ← $((SP))_0$
(P) ← $((SP))_2$
(AC) ← $((SP))_4$
(Z) ← $((SP))_6$
(S) ← $((SP))_7$
(A) ← ((SP) + 1)
(SP) ← (SP) + 2

The content of the memory location whose address is specified by the content of register SP is used to restore the condition flags. The content of the memory location whose address is one more than the content of register SP is moved to register A. The content of register SP is incremented by 2.

1	1	1	1	0	0	0	1

Cycles: 3
States: 10
Addressing: reg. indirect
Flags: Z,S,P,CY,AC

XTHL (Exchange stack top with H and L)

(L) ↔ ((SP))

(H) ↔ ((SP) + 1)

The content of the L register is exchanged with the content of the memory location whose address is specified by the content of register SP. The content of the H register is exchanged with the content of the memory location whose address is one more than the content of register SP.

1	1	1	0	0	0	1	1

Cycles: 5
States: 18
Addressing: reg. indirect
Flags: none

SPHL (Move HL to SP)

(SP) ← (H) (L)

The contents of registers H and L (16 bits) are moved to register SP.

1	1	1	1	1	0	0	1

Cycles: 1
States: 5
Addressing: register
Flags: none

IN port (Input)

(A) ← (data)

The data placed on the eight bit bi-directional data bus by the specified port is moved to register A.

1	1	0	1	1	0	1	1
port							

Cycles: 3
States: 10
Addressing: direct
Flags: none

OUT port (Output)

(data) ← (A)

The content of register A is placed on the eight bit bi-directional data bus for transmission to the specified port.

1	1	0	1	0	0	1	1
port							

Cycles: 3
States: 10
Addressing: direct
Flags: none

EI (Enable interrupts)

The interrupt system is enabled **following the execution of the next instruction.**

1	1	1	1	1	0	1	1

Cycles: 1
States: 4
Flags: none

DI (Disable interrupts)

The interrupt system is disabled **immediately following the execution of the DI instruction.**

1	1	1	1	0	0	1	1

Cycles: 1
States: 4
Flags: none

HLT (Halt)

The processor is stopped. The registers and flags are unaffected.

0	1	1	1	0	1	1	0

Cycles: 1
States: 7
Flags: none

NOP (No op)

No operation is performed. The registers and flags are unaffected.

0	0	0	0	0	0	0	0

Cycles: 1
States: 4
Flags: none

INSTRUCTION SET

Summary of Processor Instructions

Mnemonic	Description	D_7	D_6	D_5	D_4	D_3	D_2	D_1	D_0	Clock[2] Cycles
		Instruction Code[1]								
MOV r_1, r_2	Move register to register	0	1	D	D	D	S	S	S	5
MOV M, r	Move register to memory	0	1	1	1	0	S	S	S	7
MOV r, M	Move memory to register	0	1	D	D	D	1	1	0	7
HLT	Halt	0	1	1	1	0	1	1	0	7
MVI r	Move immediate register	0	0	D	D	D	1	1	0	7
MVI M	Move immediate memory	0	0	1	1	0	1	1	0	10
INR r	Increment register	0	0	D	D	D	1	0	0	5
DCR r	Decrement register	0	0	D	D	D	1	0	1	5
INR M	Increment memory	0	0	1	1	0	1	0	0	10
DCR M	Decrement memory	0	0	1	1	0	1	0	1	10
ADD r	Add register to A	1	0	0	0	0	S	S	S	4
ADC r	Add register to A with carry	1	0	0	0	1	S	S	S	4
SUB r	Subtract register from A	1	0	0	1	0	S	S	S	4
SBB r	Subtract register from A with borrow	1	0	0	1	1	S	S	S	4
ANA r	And register with A	1	0	1	0	0	S	S	S	4
XRA r	Exclusive Or register with A	1	0	1	0	1	S	S	S	4
ORA r	Or register with A	1	0	1	1	0	S	S	S	4
CMP r	Compare register with A	1	0	1	1	1	S	S	S	4
ADD M	Add memory to A	1	0	0	0	0	1	1	0	7
ADC M	Add memory to A with carry	1	0	0	0	1	1	1	0	7
SUB M	Subtract memory from A	1	0	0	1	0	1	1	0	7
SBB M	Subtract memory from A with borrow	1	0	0	1	1	1	1	0	7
ANA M	And memory with A	1	0	1	0	0	1	1	0	7
XRA M	Exclusive Or memory with A	1	0	1	0	1	1	1	0	7
ORA M	Or memory with A	1	0	1	1	0	1	1	0	7
CMP M	Compare memory with A	1	0	1	1	1	1	1	0	7
ADI	Add immediate to A	1	1	0	0	0	1	1	0	7
ACI	Add immediate to A with carry	1	1	0	0	1	1	1	0	7
SUI	Subtract immediate from A	1	1	0	1	0	1	1	0	7
SBI	Subtract immediate from A with borrow	1	1	0	1	1	1	1	0	7
ANI	And immediate with A	1	1	1	0	0	1	1	0	7
XRI	Exclusive Or immediate with A	1	1	1	0	1	1	1	0	7
ORI	Or immediate with A	1	1	1	1	0	1	1	0	7
CPI	Compare immediate with A	1	1	1	1	1	1	1	0	7
RLC	Rotate A left	0	0	0	0	0	1	1	1	4
RRC	Rotate A right	0	0	0	0	1	1	1	1	4
RAL	Rotate A left through carry	0	0	0	1	0	1	1	1	4
RAR	Rotate A right through carry	0	0	0	1	1	1	1	1	4
JMP	Jump unconditional	1	1	0	0	0	0	1	1	10
JC	Jump on carry	1	1	0	1	1	0	1	0	10
JNC	Jump on no carry	1	1	0	1	0	0	1	0	10
JZ	Jump on zero	1	1	0	0	1	0	1	0	10
JNZ	Jump on no zero	1	1	0	0	0	0	1	0	10
JP	Jump on positive	1	1	1	1	0	0	1	0	10
JM	Jump on minus	1	1	1	1	1	0	1	0	10
JPE	Jump on parity even	1	1	1	0	1	0	1	0	10
JPO	Jump on parity odd	1	1	1	0	0	0	1	0	10
CALL	Call unconditional	1	1	0	0	1	1	0	1	17
CC	Call on carry	1	1	0	1	1	1	0	0	11/17
CNC	Call on no carry	1	1	0	1	0	1	0	0	11/17
CZ	Call on zero	1	1	0	0	1	1	0	0	11/17
CNZ	Call on no zero	1	1	0	0	0	1	0	0	11/17
CP	Call on positive	1	1	1	1	0	1	0	0	11/17
CM	Call on minus	1	1	1	1	1	1	0	0	11/17
CPE	Call on parity even	1	1	1	0	1	1	0	0	11/17
CPO	Call on parity odd	1	1	1	0	0	1	0	0	11/17
RET	Return	1	1	0	0	1	0	0	1	10
RC	Return on carry	1	1	0	1	1	0	0	0	5/11
RNC	Return on no carry	1	1	0	1	0	0	0	0	5/11
RZ	Return on zero	1	1	0	0	1	0	0	0	5/11
RNZ	Return on no zero	1	1	0	0	0	0	0	0	5/11
RP	Return on positive	1	1	1	1	0	0	0	0	5/11
RM	Return on minus	1	1	1	1	1	0	0	0	5/11
RPE	Return on parity even	1	1	1	0	1	0	0	0	5/11
RPO	Return on parity odd	1	1	1	0	0	0	0	0	5/11
RST	Restart	1	1	A	A	A	1	1	1	11
IN	Input	1	1	0	1	1	0	1	1	10
OUT	Output	1	1	0	1	0	0	1	1	10
LXI B	Load immediate register Pair B & C	0	0	0	0	0	0	0	1	10
LXI D	Load immediate register Pair D & E	0	0	0	1	0	0	0	1	10
LXI H	Load immediate register Pair H & L	0	0	1	0	0	0	0	1	10
LXI SP	Load immediate stack pointer	0	0	1	1	0	0	0	1	10
PUSH B	Push register Pair B & C on stack	1	1	0	0	0	1	0	1	11
PUSH D	Push register Pair D & E on stack	1	1	0	1	0	1	0	1	11
PUSH H	Push register Pair H & L on stack	1	1	1	0	0	1	0	1	11
PUSH PSW	Push A and Flags on stack	1	1	1	1	0	1	0	1	11
POP B	Pop register pair B & C off stack	1	1	0	0	0	0	0	1	10
POP D	Pop register pair D & E off stack	1	1	0	1	0	0	0	1	10
POP H	Pop register pair H & L off stack	1	1	1	0	0	0	0	1	10
POP PSW	Pop A and Flags off stack	1	1	1	1	0	0	0	1	10
STA	Store A direct	0	0	1	1	0	0	1	0	13
LDA	Load A direct	0	0	1	1	1	0	1	0	13
XCHG	Exchange D & E, H & L Registers	1	1	1	0	1	0	1	1	4
XTHL	Exchange top of stack, H & L	1	1	1	0	0	0	1	1	18
SPHL	H & L to stack pointer	1	1	1	1	1	0	0	1	5
PCHL	H & L to program counter	1	1	1	0	1	0	0	1	5
DAD B	Add B & C to H & L	0	0	0	0	1	0	0	1	10
DAD D	Add D & E to H & L	0	0	0	1	1	0	0	1	10
DAD H	Add H & L to H & L	0	0	1	0	1	0	0	1	10
DAD SP	Add stack pointer to H & L	0	0	1	1	1	0	0	1	10
STAX B	Store A indirect	0	0	0	0	0	0	1	0	7
STAX D	Store A indirect	0	0	0	1	0	0	1	0	7
LDAX B	Load A indirect	0	0	0	0	1	0	1	0	7
LDAX D	Load A indirect	0	0	0	1	1	0	1	0	7
INX B	Increment B & C registers	0	0	0	0	0	0	1	1	5
INX D	Increment D & E registers	0	0	0	1	0	0	1	1	5
INX H	Increment H & L registers	0	0	1	0	0	0	1	1	5
INX SP	Increment stack pointer	0	0	1	1	0	0	1	1	5
DCX B	Decrement B & C	0	0	0	0	1	0	1	1	5
DCX D	Decrement D & E	0	0	0	1	1	0	1	1	5
DCX H	Decrement H & L	0	0	1	0	1	0	1	1	5
DCX SP	Decrement stack pointer	0	0	1	1	1	0	1	1	5
CMA	Complement A	0	0	1	0	1	1	1	1	4
STC	Set carry	0	0	1	1	0	1	1	1	4
CMC	Complement carry	0	0	1	1	1	1	1	1	4
DAA	Decimal adjust A	0	0	1	0	0	1	1	1	4
SHLD	Store H & L direct	0	0	1	0	0	0	1	0	16
LHLD	Load H & L direct	0	0	1	0	1	0	1	0	16
EI	Enable Interrupts	1	1	1	1	1	0	1	1	4
DI	Disable interrupt	1	1	1	1	0	0	1	1	4
NOP	No-operation	0	0	0	0	0	0	0	0	4

NOTES: 1. DDD or SSS – 000 B – 001 C – 010 D – 011 E – 100 H – 101 L – 110 Memory – 111 A.

2. Two possible cycle times, (5/11) indicate instruction cycles dependent on condition flags.

MNEMONIC	OP CODE		M1[1]					M2		
	$D_7 D_6 D_5 D_4$	$D_3 D_2 D_1 D_0$	T1	T2[2]	T3	T4	T5	T1	T2[2]	T3
MOV r1, r2	0 1 D D	D S S S	PC OUT STATUS	PC = PC +1	INST→TMP/IR	(SSS)→TMP	(TMP)→DDD			
MOV r, M	0 1 D D	D 1 1 0				X[3]		HL OUT STATUS[6]	DATA →	DDD
MOV M, r	0 1 1 1	0 S S S				(SSS)→TMP		HL OUT STATUS[7]	(TMP) →	DATA BUS
SPHL	1 1 1 1	1 0 0 1				(HL) →	SP			
MVI r, data	0 0 D D	D 1 1 0				X		PC OUT STATUS[6]	B2 →	DDDD
MVI M, data	0 0 1 1	0 1 1 0				X			B2 →	TMP
LXI rp, data	0 0 R P	0 0 0 1				X			PC = PC + 1 B2 →	r1
LDA addr	0 0 1 1	1 0 1 0				X			PC = PC + 1 B2 →	Z
STA addr	0 0 1 1	0 0 1 0				X			PC = PC + 1 B2 →	Z
LHLD addr	0 0 1 0	1 0 1 0				X			PC = PC + 1 B2 →	Z
SHLD addr	0 0 1 0	0 0 1 0				X		PC OUT STATUS[6]	PC = PC + 1 B2 →	Z
LDAX rp[4]	0 0 R P	1 0 1 0				X		rp OUT STATUS[6]	DATA →	A
STAX rp[4]	0 0 R P	0 0 1 0				X		rp OUT STATUS[7]	(A) →	DATA BUS
XCHG	1 1 1 0	1 0 1 1				(HL)←→(DE)				
ADD r	1 0 0 0	0 S S S				(SSS)→TMP (A)→ACT		[9]	(ACT)+(TMP)→A	
ADD M	1 0 0 0	0 1 1 0				(A)→ACT		HL OUT STATUS[6]	DATA →	TMP
ADI data	1 1 0 0	0 1 1 0				(A)→ACT		PC OUT STATUS[6]	PC = PC + 1 B2 →	TMP
ADC r	1 0 0 0	1 S S S				(SSS)→TMP (A)→ACT		[9]	(ACT)+(TMP)+CY→A	
ADC M	1 0 0 0	1 1 1 0				(A)→ACT		HL OUT STATUS[6]	DATA →	TMP
ACI data	1 1 0 0	1 1 1 0				(A)→ACT		PC OUT STATUS[6]	PC = PC + 1 B2 →	TMP
SUB r	1 0 0 1	0 S S S				(SSS)→TMP (A)→ACT		[9]	(ACT)-(TMP)→A	
SUB M	1 0 0 1	0 1 1 0				(A)→ACT		HL OUT STATUS[6]	DATA →	TMP
SUI data	1 1 0 1	0 1 1 0				(A)→ACT		PC OUT STATUS[6]	PC = PC + 1 B2 →	TMP
SBB r	1 0 0 1	1 S S S				(SSS)→TMP (A)→ACT		[9]	(ACT)-(TMP)-CY→A	
SBB M	1 0 0 1	1 1 1 0				(A)→ACT		HL OUT STATUS[6]	DATA →	TMP
SBI data	1 1 0 1	1 1 1 0				(A)→ACT		PC OUT STATUS[6]	PC = PC + 1 B2 →	TMP
INR r	0 0 D D	D 1 0 0				(DDD)→TMP (TMP) + 1→ALU	ALU→DDD			
INR M	0 0 1 1	0 1 0 0				X		HL OUT STATUS[6]	DATA → (TMP)+1 →	TMP ALU
DCR r	0 0 D D	D 1 0 1				(DDD)→TMP (TMP)+1→ALU	ALU→DDD			
DCR M	0 0 1 1	0 1 0 1				X		HL OUT STATUS[6]	DATA → (TMP)-1 →	TMP ALU
INX rp	0 0 R P	0 0 1 1				(RP) + 1 →	RP			
DCX rp	0 0 R P	1 0 1 1				(RP) - 1 →	RP			
DAD rp[8]	0 0 R P	1 0 0 1				X		(ri)→ACT	(L)→TMP, (ACT)+(TMP)→ALU	ALU→L, CY
DAA	0 0 1 0	0 1 1 1				DAA→A, FLAGS[10]				
ANA r	1 0 1 0	0 S S S				(SSS)→TMP (A)→ACT		[9]	(ACT)+(TMP)→A	
ANA M	1 0 1 0	0 1 1 0	PC OUT STATUS	PC = PC + 1	INST→TMP/IR	(A)→ACT		HL OUT STATUS[6]	DATA →	TMP

M3			M4			M5				
T1	T2[2]	T3	T1	T2[2]	T3	T1	T2[2]	T3	T4	T5
HL OUT STATUS[7]	(TMP) →	DATA BUS								
PC OUT STATUS[6]	PC = PC + 1 B3 →	rh								
↑	PC = PC + 1 B3 →	W	WZ OUT STATUS[6]	DATA →	A					
↕	PC = PC + 1 B3 →	W	WZ OUT STATUS[7]	(A) →	DATA BUS					
↓	PC = PC + 1 B3 →	W	WZ OUT STATUS[6]	DATA → WZ = WZ + 1	L	WZ OUT STATUS[6]	DATA →	H		
PC OUT STATUS[6]	PC = PC + 1 B3 →	W	WZ OUT STATUS[7]	(L) → WZ = WZ + 1	DATA BUS	WZ OUT STATUS[7]	(H) →	DATA BUS		
[9]	(ACT)+(TMP)→A									
[9]	(ACT)+(TMP)→A									
[9]	(ACT)+(TMP)+CY→A									
[9]	(ACT)+(TMP)+CY→A									
[9]	(ACT)-(TMP)→A									
[9]	(ACT)-(TMP)→A									
[9]	(ACT)-(TMP)-CY→A									
[9]	(ACT)-(TMP)-CY→A									
HL OUT STATUS[7]	ALU →	DATA BUS								
HL OUT STATUS[7]	ALU →	DATA BUS								
(rh)→ACT	(H)→TMP (ACT)+(TMP)+CY→ALU	ALU→H, CY								
[9]	(ACT)+(TMP)→A									

MNEMONIC	OP CODE		M1[1]					M2		
	$D_7D_6D_5D_4$	$D_3D_2D_1D_0$	T1	T2[2]	T3	T4	T5	T1	T2[2]	T3
ANI data	1 1 1 0	0 1 1 0	PC OUT STATUS	PC = PC + 1	INST→TMP/IR	(A)→ACT		PC OUT STATUS[6]	PC = PC + 1 B2 →	TMP
XRA r	1 0 1 0	1 S S S				(A)→ACT (SSS)→TMP		[9]	(ACT)+(TPM)→A	
XRA M	1 0 1 0	1 1 1 0				(A)→ACT		HL OUT STATUS[6]	DATA →	TMP
XRI data	1 1 1 0	1 1 1 0				(A)→ACT		PC OUT STATUS[6]	PC = PC + 1 B2 →	TMP
ORA r	1 0 1 1	0 S S S				(A)→ACT (SSS)→TMP		[9]	(ACT)+(TMP)→A	
ORA M	1 0 1 1	0 1 1 0				(A)→ACT		HL OUT STATUS[6]	DATA →	TMP
ORI data	1 1 1 1	0 1 1 0				(A)→ACT		PC OUT STATUS[6]	PC = PC + 1 B2 →	TMP
CMP r	1 0 1 1	1 S S S				(A)→ACT (SSS)→TMP		[9]	(ACT)-(TMP), FLAGS	
CMP M	1 0 1 1	1 1 1 0				(A)→ACT		HL OUT STATUS[6]	DATA →	TMP
CPI data	1 1 1 1	1 1 1 0				(A)→ACT		PC OUT STATUS[6]	PC = PC + 1 B2 →	TMP
RLC	0 0 0 0	0 1 1 1				(A)→ALU ROTATE		[9]	ALU→A, CY	
RRC	0 0 0 0	1 1 1 1				(A)→ALU ROTATE		[9]	ALU→A, CY	
RAL	0 0 0 1	0 1 1 1				(A), CY→ALU ROTATE		[9]	ALU→A, CY	
RAR	0 0 0 1	1 1 1 1				(A), CY→ALU ROTATE		[9]	ALU→A, CY	
CMA	0 0 1 0	1 1 1 1				$(\bar{A})$→A				
CMC	0 0 1 1	1 1 1 1				$\overline{CY}$→CY				
STC	0 0 1 1	0 1 1 1				1→CY				
JMP addr	1 1 0 0	0 0 1 1				X		PC OUT STATUS[6]	PC = PC + 1 B2 →	Z
J cond addr[17]	1 1 C C	C 0 1 0				JUDGE CONDITION		PC OUT STATUS[6]	PC = PC + 1 B2 →	Z
CALL addr	1 1 0 0	1 1 0 1				SP = SP - 1		PC OUT STATUS[6]	PC = PC + 1 B2 →	Z
C cond addr[17]	1 1 C C	C 1 0 0				JUDGE CONDITION IF TRUE, SP = SP - 1		PC OUT STATUS[6]	PC = PC + 1 B2 →	Z
RET	1 1 0 0	1 0 0 1				X		SP OUT STATUS[15]	SP = SP + 1 DATA →	Z
R cond addr[17]	1 1 C C	C 0 0 0			INST→TMP/IR	JUDGE CONDITION[14]		SP OUT STATUS[15]	SP = SP + 1 DATA →	Z
RST n	1 1 N N	N 1 1 1			φ→W INST→TMP/IR	SP = SP - 1		SP OUT STATUS[16]	SP = SP - 1 (PCH) →	DATA BUS
PCHL	1 1 1 0	1 0 0 1			INST→TMP/IR	(HL) → PC				
PUSH rp	1 1 R P	0 1 0 1				SP = SP - 1		SP OUT STATUS[16]	SP = SP - 1 (rh) →	DATA BUS
PUSH PSW	1 1 1 1	0 1 0 1				SP = SP - 1		SP OUT STATUS[16]	SP = SP - 1 (A) →	DATA BUS
POP rp	1 1 R P	0 0 0 1				X		SP OUT STATUS[15]	SP = SP + 1 DATA →	r1
POP PSW	1 1 1 1	0 0 0 1				X		SP OUT STATUS[15]	SP = SP + 1 DATA →	FLAGS
XTHL	1 1 1 0	0 0 1 1				X		SP OUT STATUS[15]	SP = SP + 1 DATA →	Z
IN port	1 1 0 1	1 0 1 1				X		PC OUT STATUS[6]	PC = PC + 1 B2 →	Z, W
OUT port	1 1 0 1	0 0 1 1				X		PC OUT STATUS[6]	PC = PC + 1 B2 →	Z, W
EI	1 1 1 1	1 0 1 1				SET INTE F/F				
DI	1 1 1 1	0 0 1 1				RESET INTE F/F				
HLT	0 1 1 1	0 1 1 0				X		PC OUT STATUS	HALT MODE[20]	
NOP	0 0 0 0	0 0 0 0	PC OUT STATUS	PC = PC + 1	INST→TMP/IR	X				

M3			M4			M5						
T1	T2[2]	T3	T1	T2[2]	T3	T1	T2[2]	T3	T4	T5		
9]	(ACT)+(TMP)→A											
9]	(ACT)+(TMP)→A											
9]	(ACT)+(TMP)→A											
9]	(ACT)+(TMP)→A											
9]	(ACT)+(TMP)→A											
9]	(ACT)-(TMP); FLAGS											
9]	(ACT)-(TMP); FLAGS											
C OUT TATUS[6]	PC = PC + 1 B3 →	W									WZ OUT STATUS[11]	(WZ) + 1 → PC
C OUT TATUS[6]	PC = PC + 1 B3 →	W									WZ OUT STATUS[11,12]	(WZ) + 1 → PC
C OUT TATUS[6]	PC = PC + 1 B3 →	W	SP OUT STATUS[16]	(PCH) → SP = SP - 1	DATA BUS	SP OUT STATUS[16]	(PCL) →	DATA BUS			WZ OUT STATUS[11]	(WZ) + 1 → PC
C OUT TATUS[6]	PC = PC + 1 B3 →	W[13]	SP OUT STATUS[16]	(PCH) → SP = SP - 1	DATA BUS	SP OUT STATUS[16]	(PCL) →	DATA BUS			WZ OUT STATUS[11,12]	(WZ) + 1 → PC
P OUT TATUS[15]	SP = SP + 1 DATA →	W									WZ OUT STATUS[11]	(WZ) + 1 → PC
P OUT TATUS[15]	SP = SP + 1 DATA →	W									WZ OUT STATUS[11,12]	(WZ) + 1 → PC
P OUT TATUS[16]	(TMP = 00NNN000) → (PCL) →	Z DATA BUS									WZ OUT STATUS[11]	(WZ) + 1 → PC
P OUT TATUS[16]	(rl) →	DATA BUS										
P OUT TATUS[16]	FLAGS →	DATA BUS										
P OUT TATUS[15]	SP = SP + 1 DATA →	rh										
OUT TATUS[15]	SP = SP + 1 DATA →	A										
P OUT TATUS[15]	DATA →	W	SP OUT STATUS[16]	(H) →	DATA BUS	SP OUT STATUS[16]	(L) →	DATA BUS	(WZ) →	HL		
Z OUT TATUS[18]	DATA →	A										
Z OUT TATUS[18]	(A) →	DATA BUS										

NOTES:

1. The first memory cycle (M1) is always an instruction fetch; the first (or only) byte, containing the op code, is fetched during this cycle.

2. If the READY input from memory is not high during T2 of each memory cycle, the processor will enter a wait state (TW) until READY is sampled as high.

3. States T4 and T5 are present, as required, for operations which are completely internal to the CPU. The contents of the internal bus during T4 and T5 are available at the data bus; this is designed for testing purposes only. An "X" denotes that the state is present, but is only used for such internal operations as instruction decoding.

4. Only register pairs rp = B (registers B and C) or rp = D (registers D and E) may be specified.

5. These states are skipped.

6. Memory read sub-cycles; an instruction or data word will be read.

7. Memory write sub-cycle.

8. The READY signal is not required during the second and third sub-cycles (M2 and M3). The HOLD signal is accepted during M2 and M3. The SYNC signal is not generated during M2 and M3. During the execution of DAD, M2 and M3 are required for an internal register-pair add; memory is not referenced.

9. The results of these arithmetic, logical or rotate instructions are not moved into the accumulator (A) until state T2 of the next instruction cycle. That is, A is loaded while the next instruction is being fetched; this overlapping of operations allows for faster processing.

10. If the value of the least significant 4-bits of the accumulator is greater than 9 <u>or</u> if the auxiliary carry bit is set, 6 is added to the accumulator. If the value of the most significant 4-bits of the accumulator is now greater than 9, <u>or</u> if the carry bit is set, 6 is added to the most significant 4-bits of the accumulator.

11. This represents the first sub-cycle (the instruction fetch) of the next instruction cycle.

12. If the condition was met, the contents of the register pair WZ are output on the address lines ($A_{0\text{-}15}$) instead of the contents of the program counter (PC).

13. If the condition was not met, sub-cycles M4 and M5 are skipped; the processor instead proceeds immediately to the instruction fetch (M1) of the next instruction cycle.

14. If the condition was not met, sub-cycles M2 and M3 are skipped; the processor instead proceeds immediately to the instruction fetch (M1) of the next instruction cycle.

15. Stack read sub-cycle.

16. Stack write sub-cycle.

17. CONDITION

CONDITION	CCC
NZ – not zero (Z = 0)	000
Z – zero (Z = 1)	001
NC – no carry (CY = 0)	010
C – carry (CY = 1)	011
PO – parity odd (P = 0)	100
PE – parity even (P = 1)	101
P – plus (S = 0)	110
M – minus (S = 1)	111

18. I/O sub-cycle: the I/O port's 8-bit select code is duplicated on address lines 0-7 ($A_{0\text{-}7}$) and 8-15 ($A_{8\text{-}15}$).

19. Output sub-cycle.

20. The processor will remain idle in the halt state until an interrupt, a reset or a hold is accepted. When a hold request is accepted, the CPU enters the hold mode; after the hold mode is terminated, the processor returns to the halt state. After a reset is accepted, the processor begins execution at memory location zero. After an interrupt is accepted, the processor executes the instruction forced onto the data bus (usually a restart instruction).

SSS or DDD	Value	rp	Value
A	111	B	00
B	000	D	01
C	001	H	10
D	010	SP	11
E	011		
H	100		
L	101		

Glossary

ACIA Asynchronous Communications Interface Adapter. The MC6850 provides the data formatting and control to interface serial asynchronous data communications information to parallel bus-organized systems. It functions either as a serial-to-parallel converter or as a parallel-to-serial converter.

Active high/low A statement referring to the signal requirement to cause the device to become active. "Active" refers to the state or condition of operation. Computer components are active when they are directed or excited by a control signal.

A/D Analog-to-digital converter. A device or subsystem that changes real-world analog data to a form compatible with binary processing.

Address A character or group of characters that identify a register. A particular part of storage, or some other data source or destination.

Addressing mode The method that selected registers use when locating the source or the destination operands.

Addressing, symbolic A fundamental procedure or method of addressing, using an address (symbolic address) chosen for convenience in programming or by the programmer, in which translation of the symbolic address into an absolute address is required before it can be used in the computer.

Charles Sippl and David A. Kidd. *Microcomputer Dictionary and Guide* (Portland, Ore.: Matrix Publishers, Inc., 1975) from which approximately 160 definitions in this glossary were excerpted.

Algorithm A fixed step-by-step procedure for finding a solution to a problem.

ANSI (American National Standards Institute) Formerly ASA and USASI, an organization that develops and publishes industry standards.

Application package A set of computer programs and/or subroutines used to solve problems in a particular application such as business, science or finance.

Architecture The functional capabilities provided by the manufacturer in the design of the device including such specifications as word length, voltage, and other logical and electrical requirements.

Arithmetic logic unit (ALU) The central processing unit chip logic which actually executes the operations requested by an input command. The ALU is the heart and one of the essential components of a microprocessor. It is the operative base between the registers and the control block. The ALU performs various forms of addition and subtraction, and the extension of these to multiplication, division, exponentiation. The logic mode relates to the operations of gating, masking, and other manipulations of the contents of the registers.

ASCII American Standard Code for Information Interchange. A widely used code in which alphanumerics, punctuation marks, and certain special machine characters are represented by unique 7-bit binary numbers.

ASCII code A code that relates 96 displayed characters (64 without lower case) and 32 nondisplayed control characters to a sequence of 7 on or off choices.

Assembler A software program that translates symbolically represented instructions into their binary equivalents.

Assembler error message An error in source statements detected by an assembler.

Assembler language A source language that includes symbolic machine language statements in which there is a one-to-one correspondence with the instruction formats and data formats of the computer.

Assembler, macro A two-pass assembly on some computers which is available with subprogram literal and power macrofacilities.

Assembler pseudo operation An assembler instruction that does not assemble into microcomputer instructions directly, but controls the assembly of instructions that do. Common pseudo ops are origin, comments, equal.

Assembly A process by which instructions written in symbolic form by the programmer are changed to machine language.

Assembly language In microprocessor programs, a series of source statements using mnemonic symbols that assist in the definition of the instruction and are then translated into machine-understandable object codes such as binary Os and 1s.

Assembly program A program that translates a program written in pseudo language (symbolic language) to a corresponding program in machine language. Principally designed to relieve the programmer of the task of assigning actual storage locations to instructions and data when coding a program and to permit use of mnemonic operation codes rather than numeric operation codes.

Asynchronous Operation of a switching network by a free running signal that triggers successive instructions; the completion of one instruction triggers the next.

Asynchronous operation A system in which the speed (or frequency) of operation is not related to the frequency of the system to which it is connected.

Auto loader A program that allows program loading to be initiated automatically, remotely or from a front panel switch. The signal operation provides loading from teletypewriter paper tape, cassette, magnetic tape, and/or disk.

AVMA Advanced valid memory address. An output signal indicating that the MC6809E will use the bus in the following bus cycle.

Backplane, microcomputer A typical bus-oriented backplane is used as a data highway between logic memory and process input/output modules.

Base (Base number) The radix of a number system; 10 is the radix for the decimal system, 2 is the radix for the binary system (base 2).

Base complement A number derived from the finite positional notation of another by one of the following rules: true complement—subtract each digit from 1 less than the base, then add 1 to the least significant digit and execute all required carries; base minus 1's complement—subtract each digit from 1 less than the base.

BASIC Beginner's All-purpose Instruction Code. A high level programming language commonly used in small personal computers. A time-sharing computer programming language similar to FORTRAN II.

Baud A unit of data transmission speed, sometimes variable, but usually bits per second.

Baud rate Measurement of data flow in which the number of signal elements per second is based on the duration of the shortest element. When each element carries one bit, the baud rate is numerically equal to bits per second (bps).

BCD (binary coded decimal) A positional value code in which each decimal digit is binary coded into 4-bit "words."

Bidirectional An interface port or bus line that can be used to transfer data in either direction; for example, to or from the microprocessor.

Bidirectional bus driver Circuitry that provides for both electrical isolation and increased current load capability in both signal flow directions. When an arrangement provides for multiple line handling, it becomes a bus driver.

Binary A number system using 2 as its base and only the digits 0 and 1.

Bit A single binary digit consisting of either a 0 or a 1 symbol.

Bit string A string of binary digits in which the position of each binary digit is considered as an independent unit.

Boolean algebra A mathematical system of logic that deals with classes, propositions, and on-off circuit elements associated by operators as AND, OR, NOT, EXCEPT, IF-THEN, which permits computations and demonstrations in any other mathematical system.

Bootstrap A technique or device designed to bring itself into a desired state by means of its own action. A machine routine whose first few instructions are sufficient to bring the rest of itself into the computer from an input device.

Branch A departure from the normal sequence of executing instructions in a computer; *synonymous with* jump.

Branch conditional A point at which alternate paths of accomplishment can be caused to occur depending on conditions.

Branching A method of selecting, on the basis of the computer results, the next operation to execute while a program is in progress.

Branch unconditional To always continue operation at some other point.

Breadboard An experimental or rough construction model of a process, device, or construction.

Breakpoint An operator-installed branch point that causes a break in the processor activity, allowing for analysis of existing conditions.

Buffer A device designed to be inserted between devices or program elements to match impedances or peripheral equipment speeds, prevent mixed interactions, supply additional drive or relay capability, or simply delay the rate of information flow; classified as inverting or noninverting.

Bug A program defect or error. Any circuit fault due to improper design or construction. A mistake or malfunction.

Bus One or more conductors used as a path over which information is transmitted.

Bus driver A specifically designed integrated circuit that is added to the data bus system to facilitate proper drive to the CPU when several devices are tied to the bus lines. Such circuits are required because of capacitive loading that slows down the data rate and prevents proper time sequencing of microprocessor operation.

Byte A group of adjacent binary digits processed as a unit. Usually an 8-bit parallel grouping.

Carry A digit or equivalent signal resulting from an arithmetic operation that causes a positional digit to equal or exceed the base of the numbering system. A binary bit or flag indicating that a previous computer operation has resulted in an overflow of register capacity.

Cell The storage for one unit of information, usually one character or one word. A location specified by whole or part of the address with the capability to store.

Central processing unit (CPU) The brain of a computing machine. Performs control, input/output, arithmetic, and logical operations by executing instructions obtained from memory sources.

Chaining A system of storing records in which each record belongs to a list or group of records and has a linking field for tracing the chain.

Character One of a set of elements which may be arranged in ordered groups to express information. Each character has two forms: a man-intelligible form and a computer-intelligible form.

Chip A single substrate on which all the active and passive elements of an electronic circuit have been fabricated by various semiconductor technologies.

Clear To place one or more storage locations into a prescribed state, usually 0 the space character; opposite of set.

Clock A pulse generator that controls the timing of the switching circuits and memory states, thus determining the speed at which the major portion of the computer or timing circuits operate.

Clock pulse In instrument or device designed to generate pulses that control the timing of the switching circuits in microprocessor operation.

CMOS Complementary metal-oxide-semiconductor. A technology that uses both P- and N-channel devices on the same silicon substrate.

Code A system of characters and rules for representing information. Digital codes may represent numbers, letters of the alphabet, control signals and the like as a group of discrete bits rather than as a continuous signal.

Code conversion A process for changing the bit grouping for a character in one code into the corresponding bit grouping for a character in a second code.

Compiler An automatic computer coding system that generates and assembles a program from instructions written by a programmer or prepared by equipment manufacturers or software companies.

Concatenated Linked together in a series or chain. For example, two 8-bit bytes can be concatenated to form one 16-bit word.

Conditional jump A specific instruction that depends on the result of some arithmetical or logical operation or the state of some switch or indicator and will or will not cause a jump or skip to another preset instruction.

Console A computer unit where the control keys and certain special devices are located; may contain the start key, stop key, power key, sense switches, as well as lights that display the information located in certain registers.

Control To exert influence or cause change. Devices that carry out instructions in proper sequence and apply signals to other devices.

Control bus A group of bidirectional lines originating either at the CPU or the peripheral equipment used to control transfer or reception of signals to or from the CPU.

Control register A register that stores the current instruction governing the operation of the computer for a cycle; *also called* instruction register.

Control unit That section which directs the sequence of operations, interrupts coded instructions and sends the proper signals to other circuits to carry out instructions.

Control word (data) One or more items of data whose 0 and 1 arrangement determines the mode of operation, direction or selection of a particular device, port or program flow.

Conversational language A language that utilizes a near-English character set which facilitates communication between the computer and the user.

CPU Central processing unit.

Cross assembler A program run on one computer for the purpose of translating instructions for a different computer.

CS Abbreviation for chip select.

Cursor A position indicator frequently employed in a display on a video terminal to indicate a character to be corrected or a position in which data is to be entered.

Daisy chain Bus lines that are interconnected with units so that the signal passes from one unit to the next in serial fashion.

Data Facts, numbers or other information that can be processed or produced by a computer.

Data bus Eight bidirectional lines capable of transferring data to and from the CPU, storage and peripheral devices.

Data format Rules and procedures describing the way data are held in a file or record, whether in character or binary form.

Debouncing Eliminating unwanted pulse variations caused by mechanically generated pulses when contacts repeatedly make and break in a bouncing manner.

Debug Using an instruction, program or action designed in microprocessor software to search for, correct or eliminate sources of errors in programs.

Decimal system Base-ten number system.

Decoding assignment The use of hardware circuit configurations to determine the function that a particular line performs when used for addressing.

Delimiter A computer character that limits a string of characters and therefore cannot be a member of the string.

Development system A piece of equipment used to design and test prototype operations utilizing both hardware and software techniques.

Device-dependent messages Messages used by the devices interconnected via the interface system that are carried by, but not used or processed by, the interface system directly.

D flip-flop A delay flip-flop whose output is a function of the input that appeared one pulse earlier.

Diagnostic A program that utilizes specific functions and capabilities of a system to test or exercise those functions, giving indications of their correctness.

Direction control The process of diverting or altering the flow of data between various devices and systems. Usually accomplished by enabling buffers with decoded control signals.

Discrete circuit An electronic circuit built of separate, individually manufactured, tested and assembled diodes, resistors, transistors, capacitors and other electronic components.

DMA A mechanism for the high-speed direct transfer of information between memory and peripherals without CPU intervention.

Dynamic random access memory A memory device that stores data as charge on a capacitive component and therefore needs refreshing regularly in order to retain its contents.

Edge triggered Circuit action initiated at the rising and falling edge of the control pulse.

Editor A general purpose text editing program used to prepare source program tapes; original text entered via the teletypewriter and held in memory may be changed or corrected.

EEPROM Electrically erasable programmable read only memory.

Enable A signal condition that permits some specific event to proceed whenever it is ready.

Entry point A specific location in a program segment that other segments can reference; the point or points at which a program can be activated by an operator or an operating system.

EPROM Erasable programmable read-only memory; ideally suited for uses where fast turnaround and pattern experimentation are important.

Execute To perform a specified operational sequence in a program. A command in the program register is performed upon the address indicated.

Executive routine A routine designed to control the loading, relocation, execution and possibly the scheduling of other routines; part of the basic operating system that maintains ultimate control of the computer at all times. Control always returns to the executive routine when any controlled routine finishes its functions or when an unexpected stop or trap occurs. *Also called* supervisory routine, monitor.

Fan-in The number of inputs available to a specific logic stage or function.

Fan-out The number of circuits that can be supplied with input signals from an output terminal of a circuit or unit.

Fetch The portion of a computer cycle during which the location of the next instruction is determined. The instruction is taken from memory, modified if necessary, and then entered into the register.

Firmware Microprogramming and specific software instructions that have been burned into a ROM control block.

$\overline{\text{FIRQ}}$ Fast interrupt request. An interrupt request that stacks only the contents of the condition code register and the program counter.

Fixed point arithmetic A method of calculation in which operations take place in an invariant manner and in which the computer does not consider the location of the radix point.

Flag A bit or bits stored for later use, indicating the existence of a previous or present condition.

Flip-flop A circuit having two stable states and two input terminals (or signals) corresponding to each of the two states. The circuit remains in either state until the corresponding signal is applied.

Floating point arithmetic Arithmetic used in a computer where the computer keeps track of the decimal point (contrasted with fixed point arithmetic)

Flow chart A programmer's tool for determining a sequence of operations as charted using sets of symbols, directional marks and other representations to indicate stepped procedures of computer operation; a chart containing all the logical steps in a particular computer program; *also called* flow diagram.

Gate A circuit having two or more inputs and one output. The output depends on the combination of logic signals at the inputs. The five basic gates are: AND, OR, NAND, NOR, EXCLUSIVE OR.

GP-IB A standardization of bus levels, number of lines and line characteristics to allow easy interconnection of instruments into microcomputer controlled systems regardless of the equipment manufacturer.

Half duplex A system that permits electrical communications in one direction between stations; S/O for send only; R/O for receive only; S/R for send or receive.

Handshaking Electrical provision for verification that a proper data transfer has occurred. A data-ready/data-received signal scheme that assures orderly data transfer.

Hangup A condition in which the central processor is attempting to perform an illegal or forbidden operation or in which it is continually repeating the same routine.

Hardware The physical parts or electronic circuitry of a computer system in contrast to the "soft" or programming and firmware components; the components of circuits may be active, passive or both.

Hexadecimal Base-sixteen number system.

High level language A language in which each instruction or statement corresponds to several machine code instructions.

High Z A condition of high-impedance characteristics causing a low current load effect.

HMOS High density, short channel MOS.

Housekeeping Computer operations, such as setting up constants and variables for use in the program, that contribute directly to the proper operation of the computer but not to the solution of the problem.

ICE An In-Circuit Emulator that is plugged directly into the user's system in a real time environment. It is used to control, interrogate, revise and completely debug a user's system in its own environment.

IEEE Institute of Electrical and Electronics Engineers.

Index register A register designed to modify the operand address in an instruction or base address by addition or subtraction, yielding a new effective address.

Inhibiting input A computer gate input that can prevent any output which might otherwise occur.

Input/output device Computer hardware capable of entering data into a computer or transferring data from a computer; abbreviated I/O.

Instruction Information that, when properly coded and introduced as a unit into a digital computer, causes the computer to perform one or more of its operations; commonly includes one or more addresses.

Instruction cycle The process of fetching an instruction from memory and executing it.

Instruction set The total structured group of characters to be transferred to the computer as operations are executed.

Integrated circuit An interconnected array of conventional components fabricated on and in a single crystal of semiconductor material by etching, doping, and diffusion, and capable of performing a complete circuit function.

Interface messages Messages used to manage the interface system itself and sent to cause a state transition within another interface function.

Interfacing The process of developing an electrical circuit that enables a device to yield or acquire information from another device.

Interpreter A program that operates directly on a source program in memory, translates the instructions of the source program one by one and executes them immediately.

Interrupt A signal that halts the operation of a running program to perform a special, high-priority routine.

I/O Input/output.

Iterating Repeating an operation or program loop several times in a progressive manner, each repetition or iteration accomplishing a fractional portion of the final result.

Label A set of symbols used to identify or describe an item, record, message or file. Used in place of absolute memory address in microcomputer programming.

Large-scale integration (LSI) The accumulation and design of a large number of circuits (1000 or more) on a single semiconductor chip.

Latch A circuit that can be locked into a particular condition and will remain stable until changed; also, to hold a particular condition of output.

Leading edge The rising or falling edge of a pulse that occurs first in time.

Level triggered Circuit action is initiated by the presence of the control signal voltage.

Library A collection of standard and proven routines and subroutines by which problems and parts of problems can be solved.

Light pen A high speed, photosensitive device that can cause a computer to change or modify the display on the cathode-ray tube.

Listener A device that can be addressed by an interface message to receive device-dependent messages from another device connected to the interface system.

Loading An indication that current is being drawn. Connecting a device that draws current from the line creates loading.

Logic A mathematical approach to the solution of complex situations by the use of symbols to define basic concepts. The three basic logic symbols are AND, OR, and NOT.

Logic analyzer A device used in the first steps of troubleshooting —locating the problem by examining the sequence of events leading up to a failure.

Lookup table A collection of data in a form suitable for ready reference.

Loop A sequence of instructions that is written only once but executed many times (iterated) until some predefined condition is met.

Low level language A language close to the machine code of a computer whose instructions usually bear a one-to-one relationship with the machine code.

Machine cycle The basic microprocessor cycle, the shortest complete process or action that is repeated as well as the minimum length of time in which it can be performed.

Machine language The basic binary code used by all computers. It can be written in either hexadecimal or octal.

Machine level In binary form. Used to indicate language sophistication or capability as contrasted to a high level language.

Macro code A coding system that assembles groups of computer instructions into single code words and therefore requires interpretation or translation so that an automatic computer can follow it.

Macroinstruction An instruction consisting of a sequence of micro instructions which are inserted into an object routine for performing a specific operation.

Mask A device made of a thin sheet of metal that contains an open pattern used to shield selected portions of a base during a deposition process.

Masking A technique for sensing specific binary conditions and ignoring others typically accomplished by placing 0s in bit positions of no interest and 1s in bit positions to be sensed.

Memory A storage device into which information can be inserted and held for use at a later time.

Memory-mapped I/O The process of connecting memory address lines to I/O decoding systems so that I/O devices are handled and treated as memory locations.

Microcomputer A complete computing system, consisting of hardware and software, whose main processing blocks are made of semiconductor integrated circuits.

Microinstruction A bit pattern stored in a microprogram memory word that specifies the operation of the individual LSI computing elements and related subunits such as main memory and input/output interfaces.

Microprocessor The semiconductor central processing unit (CPU) and one of the principal components of the microcomputer.

MMU Memory management unit.

Mnemonics A programming short-hand using letters, numbers, and symbols adopted by each manufacturer to represent the instruction in his instruction set.

Modem A MOdulator/DEModulator device that converts signals in one form to another kind of equipment. In particular, the device that changes digital data to a form suitable for computers and terminals to communicate over telephone lines.

Monitor The software or hardware that observes, supervises, controls or verifies the operations of a system.

Monitor programs The part of an operating system that contains routines and is needed for continuous system operation.

MPU Microprocessor unit.

Multilevel interrupt The possibility of more than one direct interrupt connection to the device provided by the manufacturer; may be vectored or nonvectored.

Multiplexing A process of transmitting more than one signal at a time over a single link, route or channel in a communications system.

Multiprocessor (multiprocessing) Various computer configurations consisting of more than one independently initiable processor, each having access to a common, jointly-addressable memory.

Nest A subroutine or block of data embedded into a larger routine or block of data.

NMOS N-channel metal oxide on silicon technology.

Nonvolatile A memory type that holds data even if power has been disconnected.

Numbering system A system of abstract symbols used to express quantity.

Object code The result of a compilation or assembly in the form of executable machine code or code suitable for processing to produce executable machine code.

Octal Base-eight numbering system.

On-line Equipment, devices or systems in direct interactive communication with the central processing unit.

Operand The fundamental quantity which specifies where the mathematical or logical operation is to be performed.

Operating Code (op code) The specific code containing source statements that generates machine codes after assembly.

Page A set of 4096 consecutive bytes, the first byte of which is located at a storage address that is a multiple of 4096 (an address whose 12 low-order bits are 0)

Parity A binary digit appended to an array of bits to make the sum of all the bits always odd or always even. A method for checking the accuracy of transmitted or transferred binary data.

Partitioning The isolation, identification, or separation of functions or job blocks. The defining of submodules or routines necessary to a program solution.

Peripheral equipment Units that work in conjunction with a computer but are not a part of it, for example, a tape reader, analog-to-digital converter, typewriter.

Polling An important multiprocessing method used to identify the source of interrupt requests. When several interrupts occur simultaneously, the control program makes the decision as to which one will be serviced first.

Port An electrical logic circuit configuration that is a signal input or output access point the the microprocessor bus system.

Position independent A program that will run correctly when the same machine code is positioned arbitrarily in memory.

Precision Exact, careful, strict. Pertaining to clarity and care in procedural accomplishment.

Port An electrical logic circuit configuration which provides access to the microprocessor system from a peripheral location or provides the microprocessor access to the peripheral location.

Primitive A basic or fundamental unit; often the lowest level of a machine instruction or lowest unit of language translation.

Priority The relative weight of importance assigned.

Program A set of instructions arranged in a proper sequence for directing a digital computer in performing a desired operation or operations.

Program counter (PC) A register in the CPU that holds addresses necessary to step the machine through the various programs. It specifies the address of the next instruction byte to be fetched from memory and is automatically incremented after each fetch cycle.

Programmable That characteristic of a device that makes it capable of accepting data to alter the state of its internal circuitry to perform two or more specific tasks.

Programmable interface A general purpose I/O device, a typical TTL-compatible interface.

Programmable measuring apparatus A measuring apparatus that performs specified operations on command from the system. If it is a measuring apparatus proper, it transmits the results of the measurement(s) to the system.

Programmed I/O The control of data flow in and out of the microprocessor completely under software direction. It implies a lack of independent port activity.

Programming model Pictorial representation of the functional elements and architectural features that can be manipulated by the instruction set.

PROM Programmable read only memory. A semiconductor diode array that is manufactured with a pattern of either all 1s or all 0s and is user programmed by fusing or burning out diode junctions.

Pseudo op (pseudo code) A code that expresses programs in source language. An arbitrary code independent of the hardware of a computer and designed for convenience in programming.

PTM Programmable timer module. The Motorola MC6840 is a programmable subsystem component of the M6800 family designed to provide variable system timer intervals. The counters are under software control and may be used to cause system interrupts and/or generate output signals.

Quadrature clock The Q (quadrature) clock leads the E clock by approximately one-half the E clock time. Address information from the processor is valid with the leading edge of the Q clock.

RAM Random access memory. Provides immediate access to any storage location point in the memory by means of vertical and horizontal coordinates. Information may be written in or read out in the same very fast procedure.

Read The process of accessing data from external storage. The transfer of information between devices.

Real time The performance of a computation during the actual time that the related physical process transpires so that results of the computation can be used in guiding the physical process.

Recursion A routine that calls itself.

Reentrant A routine that allocates different local variable storage upon each entry. Thus, a later entry does not destroy the processing associated with an earlier entry.

Register A memory device capable of containing one or more computer bits or words. It has zero memory latency time and negligible memory access time.

Robot An independently operating system that simulates manlike activities and cognitive interaction with the environment in which it resides.

ROM Read-only memory. A nonvolatile memory device programmed by a mask pattern as part of the final manufacturing stage. Information is stored permanently or semi-permanently and is read out but not altered in operation.

Routine A set of computer instructions arranged in a correct sequence and used to direct a computer in performing one or more desired operations.

RS flip-flop A flip-flop consisting of two cross-coupled NAND gates having two inputs designated R and S. A 1 on the S input and a 1 on the R input resets (clears) the flip-flop to the 0 state. A 1 on the R input and 0 on the S input sets it to the 1 state.

RST flip-flop A flip-flop having three inputs: R, S and T. This unit works like the RS flip-flop except that the T input is used to cause the flip-flop to change states.

Scanning The process of polling the interrupting devices to determine the origin of the interrupt signal. Differentiation between polled I/O and polled interrupts.

Scratchpad A nickname for CPU memory that pertains to information the CPU holds temporarily. RAM or registers that are used to store temporary, intermediate results (data) or memory addresses (pointers).

Single-line interrupt Indication that the manufacturer has provided only one direct interrupt connection to the device; may be vectored or, more commonly, nonvectored.

Single step An operation in which each step is performed by manual control.

Solderless breadboards A plug-in breadboard for 14-pin and 16-pin DIPs and other packages that employ plug-in socket pins instead of the usual wire-wrap or solder connections.

Software Programs, languages and procedures of a computer system.

Source program A program that can be translated automatically into machine language.

Source statement A program statement not written in machine language. It is usually written in mnemonics or three character symbols.

Stack A block of successive memory locations that are accessible from one end on a last-in-first-out (LIFO) basis.

Stack pointer Coordinated with the storing and retrieval of information in the stack.

Static operation Data stored in a conventional bistable flip-flop that need not be refreshed.

Status word A binary arrangement providing indication of present condition.

Straight-line coding Any computer program that can be completed by carrying out sequentially each program instruction, for example, one without branch points or loop instructions.

Subroutine A subordinate program that can be used repeatedly throughout a major program. A minor series of program operations.

Symbol complement (base minus 1's complement) Complementing procedure of subtracting a digit from the highest symbolic value in the number system.

Synchronous A switching network that operates at the same frequency and phase. A constant time interval between successive bits, characters and events.

Syntax The rules governing the structure of a language.

Talker A device that can be addressed by an interface message to send device-dependent messages to another device connected to the interface system.

3-state device Any integrated circuit device in which the two of the states are conventional binary (0,1) and the third state is high-impedance. The high-impedance state on the device's output reduces power drain and allows other devices to access the common bus.

Throughput The speed with which problems, programs or segments are performed.

Time-sharing A computing technique allowing more than one terminal device to use the input, processing and output facilities of a central computer simultaneously.

Timing diagram A pictorial diagram showing the various time relationships among a variety of interdependent pulses or signals.

Top-down approach A method or technique of programming which advocates proceeding from the general to the specific with constant quality assurance checks within the structure.

Trailing edge The rising or falling edge of a pulse that occurs last in a related pair of edges.

Transducer A device that converts something measureable, often a physical property such as pressure, temperature, or flow, into another form such as an electrical signal.

Trap An unprogrammed conditional jump to a known location.

Trigger A pulse that starts an action which then functions for a certain length of time under its own control.

Truth table A mathematical table showing the Boolean algebra relationships of variables.

TTL Transistor-transistor logic. A kind of bipolar circuit arrangement that takes its name from the way the basic transistor components are interconnected.

UART Universal asynchronous receiver/transmitter. In a UART, the transmitter converts parallel data bits into serial form for transmission; the receive section does the reverse operation.

Ultraviolet The electromagnetic radiation at frequencies higher than those of visible light and with wavelengths of about 200 to 4000 angstrom units.

USART Universal synchronous/asynchronous transmitter/receiver chip.

USRT Universal synchronous receiver/transmitter.

Utility programs A collection of problem-state programs designed for use by a systems programmer in performing such functions as changing or extending the indexing structure of the catalog.

VDG Video display generator. A device that provides a means of interfacing a microprocessor to a commercial color or black and white television receiver for display purposes in the form of alphanumerics and/or graphics.

Vector A location finder (address) usually indicating the starting point of a particular operation or routine. An automatic prestored address used in the interrupt process.

Vectored interrupt Term indicating an automatic branch operation to a predetermined start point when an interrupt occurs.

VLSI Very large scale integration.

Volatile Storage medium continuous power dissipation in order to retain information.

Wire wrap An alternative to soldering, consisting of winding a number of turns of wire around a metal post that has at least two sharp edges.

Word A group of characters occupying one storage location in a computer and treated by the computer circuits as an entity, by the control unit as an instruction and by the arithmetic unit as a quantity.

Write The process of sending data to an external storage device or system. To record information in a register, location or other storage device or medium.

Zero page addressing In some systems the zero page instructions allow for shorter code and execution times by fetching only the second byte of the instruction and assuming a zero high address byte. Careful use of the zero page can result in significant increase in code efficiency.

Bibliography

Altman, Laurence and Stephen E. Scrupski, Editors. *Applying Microprocessors.* Electronics Magazine Book Series. New York: McGraw-Hill Publications Co., 1976.

Barden, William Jr. *How to Program Micro Computers* (1st ed.). Indianapolis, Ind.: Howard W. Sams & Co., Inc., 1977.

Bishop, Ron. *Basic Microprocessors and the 6800.* Rochelle Park, N.J.: Hayden Book Company, Inc., 1978.

Boylestad, Robert L. and Louis Nashelsky. *Electronic Devices and Circuit Theory* (2nd ed.). Englewood Cliffs, N.J.: Prentice-Hall, Inc., 1978.

Camenzind, Hans R. *Electronic Integrated Systems Design.* Microelectronics Series. New York: Van Nostrand Reinhold Company, 1972.

Coughlin, Robert F. and Frederick F. Driscoll. *Operational Amplifiers and Linear Integrated Circuits.* Englewood Cliffs, N.J.: Prentice-Hall, Inc., 1977.

Deem, Bill; Kenneth Muchow; and Anthony Zeppa. *Digital Computer Circuits and Concepts* (2nd ed.). Reston, Va.: Reston Publishing Company, Inc., 1977.

Fairchild Camera & Instrument Co. *Semiconductor Processing.* Reston, Va.: Reston Publishing Company, Inc., 1978.

Fiore, Vito; James J. Farrell III; and Vicki Fiore. *Microprocessor Applications: The Motorola M6800 Family.* Reston, Va.: Reston Publishing Company, Inc., 1983.

Gardner, Hershal. *Handbook of Solid-State Troubleshooting.* Reston, Va.: Reston Publishing Company, Inc., 1976.

Gothmann, William H. *Digital Electronics: An Introduction to Theory and Practice.* Englewood Cliffs, N.J.: Prentice-Hall, Inc., 1977.

Hewlett-Packard 59309A HP-IB Digital Clock Operating and Service Manual. Santa Clara, Cal.: Hewlett-Packard Company, 1976.

Iliardi, Frank A. *Computer Circuit Analysis: Theory and Applications.* Englewood Cliffs, N.J.: Prentice-Hall, Inc., 1976.

Intel Data Catalog. Santa Clara, Calif.: Intel Corporation, 1978.

Intel 8080 Microcomputer Systems User's Manual. Santa Clara, Calif.: Intel Corporation, 1975.

Intel MCS 8085 User's Manual. Santa Clara, Calif.: Intel Corporation, 1977.

Intel Memory Design Handbook. Santa Clara, Calif.: Intel Corporation, 1977.

Intel SDK-85 User's Manual (preliminary). Santa Clara, Calif.: Intel Corporation, 1977.

Jacobowitz, Henry. *Computer Arithmetic* (1st ed.). New York: John F. Rider Publisher Inc., 1962.

Klingman, Edwin E. *Microprocessor System Design.* Englewood Cliffs, N.J.: Prentice-Hall, Inc., 1977.

Lancaster, Don. *TTL CookBook.* Indianapolis, Ind.: Howard W. Sams & Co., Inc., 1974.

Larsen, David G. and Peter R. Rony. *The Bugbooks I & II.* Derby, Conn.: E & L Instruments, Inc., 1974.

——. *The Bugbook IIA.* Derby, Conn.: E & L Instruments, Inc., 1975.

Larsen, David G.; Peter R. Rony; and Jonathan A. Titus. *The Bugbook III.* Derby, Conn.: E & L Instruments, Inc., 1975.

——. *The Bugbook V, Module One.* Derby, Conn.: E & L Instruments, Inc., 1976.

Ledgard, Henry F. *Programming Proverbs.* Rochelle Park, N.J.: Hayden Book Co., Inc., 1975.

Lenk, John D. *Handbook of Simplified Solid-State Circuit Design, Revised and Enlarged.* Englewood Cliffs, N.J.: Prentice-Hall, Inc., 1978.

——. *Logic Designer's Manual.* Reston, Va.: Reston Publishing Company, Inc., 1977.

Leventhal, Lance A. *6800 Assembly Language Programming.* Berkeley, Calif.: Osborne & Associates, Inc., 1978.

——. *The 6800 Microprocessor.* Rochelle Park, N.J.: Hayden Book Company, Inc., 1978.

——. *8080A/8085 Assembly Language Programming.* Berkeley, Calif.: Osborne & Associates, Inc., 1978.

Levine, Morris E. *Digital Theory and Practice Using Integrated Circuits.* Englewood Cliffs, N.J.: Prentice-Hall, Inc., 1978.

Lytel, Allan. *Fundamentals of Computer Math.* Edited by A.A. Wicks. Indianapolis, Ind.: Howard W. Sams & Co., Inc. 1964.

Mandl, Matthew. *Solid-State Circuit Design Users' Manual.* Reston, Va.: Reston Publishing Company, Inc., 1977.

McKay, Charles W. *Digital Circuits: A Preparation for Microprocessors.* Englewood Cliffs, N.J.: Prentice-Hall, Inc., 1978.

Microprocessors: Individual Learning Program. Benton Harbor, Mich.: Heath Company, 1977.

Miller, Richard W. *Servomechanisms: Devices and Fundamentals.* Reston, Va.: Reston Publishing Company, Inc., 1977.

Motorola MC6809-MC6809E Microprocessor Programming Manual. Austin, Texas: Motorola Inc., 1981.

Motorola MC68000 16-Bit Microprocessor User's Manual. Austin, Texas: Motorola Inc., 1980.

Motorola MEK6800D2 Manual (2nd ed.). Austin, Texas: Motorola Inc., 1977.

Motorola Microcomputer Components—System on Silicon. Phoenix, Ariz.: Motorola Inc., 1978.

Motorola Microcomputer Development Systems. Phoenix, Ariz.: Motorola Inc., 1980.

Motorola M6800 Microcomputer System Design Data. Phoenix, Ariz.: Motorola Inc., 1976.

Motorola M6805, M146805 Family Microcomputer/Microprocessor User's Manual. Austin, Texas: Motorola Inc., 1980.

Motorola M6800 Microprocessor Applications Manual (1st ed.). Phoenix, Ariz.: Motorola Inc., 1975.

Motorola M6800 Microprocessor Course. Phoenix, Ariz.: Motorola Inc., 1977.

Motorola M6800 Programming Reference Manual (1st ed.). Phoenix, Ariz.: Motorola Inc., 1976.

Motorola M68ADS1A Development System User's Manual. Phoenix, Ariz.: Motorola Inc., 1978.

Motorola Programmable Timer Fundamentals and Applications. Austin, Texas: Motorola Inc., 1979.

Murphy, John S. *Basics of Digital Computers.* Vol. 1. New York: John F. Rider Publishers, Inc., 1958.

Nashelsky, Louis. *Digital Computer Theory.* New York: John Wiley & Sons, Inc., 1966.

Osborne, Adam. *An Introduction to Microcomputers.* Vols. 1 and 2. Berkeley, Calif.: Adam Osborne and Associates, Incorporated, 1976.

——. *6800 Programming for Logic Design.* Berkeley, Calif.: Adam Osborne and Associates, Incorporated, 1977.

Poe, Elmer. *Using the 6800 Microprocessor.* Indianapolis, Ind.: Howard W. Sams & Co., Inc., 1978.

Queyssac, Daniel, General Editor. *Understanding Microprocessors.* Phoenix, Ariz.: Motorola Inc.

Ritter-Sanders, Miles Jr. *Handbook of Advanced Solid-State Troubleshooting.* Reston, Va.: Reston Publishing Company, Inc., 1977.

Robinson, Vester. *Manual of Solid State Circuit Design and Troubleshooting.* Reston, Va.: Reston Publishing Company, Inc., 1977.

Rutkowski, George B. and Jerome E. Oleksy. *Fundamentals of Digital Electronics—A Laboratory Text.* Englewood Cliffs, N.J.: Prentice-Hall, Inc., 1978.

Shacklette, L.W. and H.A. Ashworth. *Using Digital and Analog Integrated Circuits.* Englewood Cliffs, N.J.: Prentice-Hall, Inc., 1978.

Sippl, Charles J. and David A. Kidd. *Microcomputer Dictionary and Guide.* Portland, Ore.: Matrix Publishers, Inc., 1975.

Tocci, Ronald J. *Digital Systems: Principles and Applications.* Englewood Cliffs, N.J.: Prentice-Hall, Inc., 1977.

Weller, Walter J. *Assembly Level Programming for Small Computers.* Lexington, Mass.: D.C. Heath and Co., 1975.

Wester, John G. and William D. Simpson. *Software Design for Microprocessors.* Dallas, Texas: Texas Instruments Incorporated, 1976.

Wojslaw, Charles. *Integrated Circuits: Theory and Applications.* Reston, Va.: Reston Publishing Company, Inc., 1978.

Index